JERUSALEM

Jerusalem

The Holy City in the Eyes
of Chroniclers, Visitors, Pilgrims, and
Prophets from the Days of Abraham
to the Beginnings of
Modern Times

F. E. Peters

PRINCETON UNIVERSITY PRESS

PRINCETON, NEW JERSEY

Contents

Preface *ix*

Acknowledgments *xiii*

1. Holy Land, Holy City *3*

2. Jews and Greeks in Jerusalem *42*

3. Not a Stone Upon a Stone: The Destruction of the Holy City *88*

4. Mother of All the Churches *131*

5. The Holy House: The Muslims Come to Jerusalem *176*

6. The Uncertain Glory: Jerusalem Under the Abbasids and Fatimids, A.D. 750-1000 *215*

7. The Coming of the Crusade *251*

8. Jerusalem Under the Latin Cross *283*

9. The Holy War of Islam *333*

10. The Face of Medieval Jerusalem *379*

11. Piety and Polemic: The Crusader Legacy in the Holy City *427*

12. The End of the Middle Ages *479*

13. Jerusalem Observed: The Medieval City Through Modern Eyes *535*

Notes *587*

Works Cited *623*

Index *637*

Preface

THE WORLD'S three great monotheistic religions, Judaism, Christianity, and Islam, all claim Abraham as their father and Jerusalem as their Holy City. Their claim upon Abraham's paternity has made them, somewhat unhappily to each other, members of the same family; but their claim upon that same city has rendered all three of them something more perilous, neighbors in a narrow space. And in that place they continue to debate their family ties and fight their sad and bitter fight over their father's property in Jerusalem.

There is no other city like it, so solemn yet modest, so attractive and so intelligible; so earthly, even provincial, and yet somehow spiritual and universal. It does not seem like a provocative place, Jerusalem, though hundreds of thousands have fought and died to possess it, or perhaps simply to possess the idea that it represents. Jerusalem appears at times almost indifferent to this attention, busy with its own commerce in the way of holy cities. Why here, one wonders? Then one turns onto a road coming down and east from the Jewish quarter, or westward over the summit of the Mount of Olives, and suddenly, before one's eyes stands the enormous and unearthly golden dome, floating suspended in that extraordinary place the Muslims call, with good reason, the *Haram al-Sharif*, "the Noble Sanctuary." It is a Muslim shrine, a piece of only one group's claim to Jerusalem, and yet the Dome of the Rock somehow explains and reveals all the other Jerusalems, particularly the one that gave birth to the idea. Here indeed is the House of God.

This is a book about that city and about that house, told to a great extent in the words of the people who best knew it and most cared about it, for good or ill: the generations of rulers, priests, pilgrims, chroniclers, soldiers, merchants, and tourists who passed through its gates. Some stayed and some left, but all who are represented in the chapters that follow had something to say about the city. Some of what they wrote are prayers and songs and benedictions; other accounts read like curses, filled with sadness, rage, or frustration. Tears stain many of the pages. Only a few visitors were unmoved by the Holy City that each had struggled so hard to reach. Some came to rule or destroy the city; others to pray there or scold, or simply to observe. They were invaders or exiles or prisoners; on crusade or pilgrimage or assignment; old or young, most of them weary, and all with expectations. Most had fed, as we might expect, upon the accounts and fantasies of their predecessors before coming to Jerusalem and writing their own.

This book has been made, not from the words of one group or one set of partisans, but from as wide and diverse a selection as I could manage, so that the reader might see the city whole, as it appeared at every stage of its history in the eyes of Jews, Christians, and Muslims, true-believers, skeptics, and all. And one other. I too have been to Jerusalem, whether as pilgrim or as researcher, I confess I cannot always say. And I have felt the pleasures and rages and tears and awe the city usually provokes in its visitors. But unlike my predecessors cited in the pages that follow, I have tried to still my own tongue and confine myself to merely putting their voices into some kind of historical context that makes their reflections more intelligible at this long remove. While I have favorites among those reporters, and some I would rather not have met, I have attempted not to take sides in the ongoing disputes or make a case concerning this city whose very walls shake with special pleading and exclusive claims. I have supplied the connective tissue between the selections and explained where I have thought necessary; but I have left, I hope, the arguments to others more eager and better equipped to make them.

Despite all intent, it may be that I have over-explained, and the reader who judges it so is invited to ignore the notes that are added at the end of the book, which explain still further. Or if he or she requires or prefers others' explanations, I have supplied guidance to those too, in a bibliography of works cited, where the choices of instructor are, as the reader might suspect, plentiful.

Some translations of the texts cited in this book have been done by others, all acknowledged, some by myself. In using others' translations, I have made cuts, but otherwise only changed spellings, chiefly in names, for the sake of uniformity; added emphases; translated technical terms that had been simply transcribed; and converted Hebrew and Muslim dates into those of the more familiar Christian era.

I have had help in producing this book, and not only from the long-dead pilgrims and chroniclers who supplied the texts upon which I have drawn. Many of the helping hands are still quick: Michael Burgoyne and John Wilkinson at the British School, whose contributions are often and gratefully signalled on these pages; Archie Walls, who once introduced me to the delights of Jerusalem; Miryam and David Ayalon, Meir Ben-Dov, Père Benoit, Moshe Gil, and Yoram Tsafrir, all of whom gave graciously of their time and considerable learning; Dan Urman of Ben Gurion University, and Meti and Leah as well, whose kindnesses have been many; Jacob Neusner, who read parts of the manuscript and made valuable suggestions, and Jack Finegan, who went over it in painstaking detail and contributed to making it better, though neither of course bears any responsibility for what I have chosen to say or not to say; Doris Miller, who had mostly to put up with the bad parts of both manuscript and author, as usual, and emerged radiant, again as usual; John R. Hayes of the Mobil Oil Corporation, who happily started me on Jerusalem in another context and provoked this work as well; Jill Claster of Washington Square College and Leslie Berlowitz of the Humanities Council of New York University, who voted "yes" on this; and finally Ralph Minasian and the Hagop Kevorkian Fund who have been so generous in their support of my work and that of my students over what are by now more than a few years. To all of them I am grateful, and more.

The reader will perhaps allow a small note of personal pride mixed with gratitude in my acknowledgment of my own students' able and plenteous help with this project. They not only did or revised some of the translations I use here, where their names are duly recorded, but they have also provided comments, suggestions, interest, and encouragement. I thank Rami Arav, Raymond Harari, Elisabeth Koehldorfer, David Nelson, Karl Schaefer, Lauren Strober, Michael Swartz, Mary Tahan, Elizabeth Waller, and most particularly Sandra Levy, who gave to this book as if it were her own, which in a sense it is. She will have her very own one day, I do not doubt, and better.

My thanks as always to my colleagues at New York University: the contemporary sages R. Ross Brann, R. Baruch Levine, and R. Lawrence Schiffman, who always help where it is most needed; and Vivian Brawer, for keeping the book and me and an entire university department together, which is always desperately needed and which she always does elegantly and graciously. And to Mary Battistessa Peters, who sustains me and has the time and energy and intelligence to maintain the rest of the world and her friends and herself in excellent running order as well. It is still impressive.

Secret Harbour, V.I.   F. E. Peters
August 1984

Acknowledgments

TRANSLATIONS done by others, published or unpublished, are noted either in the text itself or in the final section entitled "Works Cited," where all particulars regarding authors, publishers, and dates and places of publication are provided.

Nevertheless, the author wishes to make special acknowledgment to the following for their kind cooperation in the use of previously published and copyrighted material: Ernest Benn, B'nai B'rith International Commission on Adult Jewish Education, E. J. Brill, *Byzantion*, Cambridge University Press, *Church History*, Columbia University Press, The Hakluyt Society, Franciscan Printing Press, Institut français d'études arabes de Damas, London University, *Bulletin of the School of African and Oriental Studies*, The Islamic Cultural Centre (London), The Israel Ministry of Defense Publishing Company, The Jewish Publication Society of America, *Journal of Jewish Studies*, Keter Publishing Company, Khayat Book and Publishing Company, Longman Group, Thomas Nelson and Sons, Oxford University Press, Pantheon Books, Princeton University Press, Sepher-Hermon Press, State University of New York Press, University of California Press, University of Tennessee Press, and Yale University Press.

The selections from Josephus are reprinted by permission of the publishers and the Loeb Classical Library. Quotations are drawn from *The Antiquities*, translated by H. St. J. Thackeray (books I-VII), R. Marcus (books VIII-XIV), A. Wikgren (books XV-XVII), and L. Feldman (books XVIII-XX), and *The Jewish War*, translated by H. St. J. Thackeray (Cambridge, Massachusetts: Harvard University Press, 1926-1965).

Selections from *The New English Bible*: Copyright © The Delegates of the Oxford University Press and the Syndics of the Cambridge University Press, 1961, 1970. Reprinted by permission.

Selections from *Roads to Zion: Four Centuries of Travelers' Reports* by K. Wilhelm, translated by I. M. Lask, copyright renewed 1948 by Schocken Books Inc., are reprinted by permission from Schocken Books Inc.

The maps reproduced here were first published in Dan Bahat, *Carta's Historical Atlas of Jerusalem* (Jerusalem: Carta, the Israel Map and Publishing Company, 1983), pp. 13, 21, 35, 41, 55, 63, and appear here through the kind permission of the publisher.

ACKNOWLEDGMENTS

Many of the splendid aerial photographs in this book are published here for the first time and have been selected from the unique collection of Pictorial Archive, Jerusalem. Pictorial Archive has made a special study of the biblical landscape in general and of Jerusalem in particular and offers a variety of important teaching aids on the subject, including sets of aerial colour slides, audio-visual presentations and large format map-posters covering the First Temple, Second Temple, Byzantine, Crusader, and Islamic periods. Teachers of these subjects and leaders of tours to the Holy Land are recommended to apply for additional information to: Pictorial Archive, The Old School, P.O. Box 19823, Jerusalem.

JERUSALEM

── 1 ──

Holy Land, Holy City

God is in its midst; it will not be toppled.
—*Psalm 46*

Eretz Israel / A Land for Israel

FIRST the land, then the city. It could hardly have been otherwise with the nomadic Hebrews, a tiny cluster of tribes that possessed as yet only a name. Those obscure wanderers, or at least the peoples they later claimed as their fathers, lived in a time and a land that was only beginning to experiment with cities, but there was no place even in those as yet rude settlements for the Hebrews or their tribal progenitor Abram. So when his God approached Abram, as the collective tribal memory of the people later recalled, the talk was not of cities but of a different kind of dream: the richness of descendants and the almost unimaginable boon of a land of their own for that innumerable progeny:

The word of the Lord came to Abram in a vision, saying:
　　　　"Fear not, Abram
　　　　I am a shield to you;
　　　　Your reward shall be very great."

Abram, the tribal chieftain, thought immediately of family and heirs. Now an old man, he was still childless; others would inherit whatever the Lord chose to grant him.

The Lord took him outside and said, "Look toward heaven and count the stars, if you are able to count them." And He added, "So shall your off-spring be." And because he put his trust in the Lord, He reckoned it to his merit. (Genesis 15:1-6[1])

The faith of Abram, "which was reckoned to him as righteousness," as the Christian Apostle Paul later put it, was both touching and impressive, but what followed must have seemed absurd on the face of it: the shaykh of this insignificant clan called the Hebrews was promised for his offspring all the lands between the borders of Egypt and the great Euphrates, the domains of other more powerful and numerous peoples. But there was no mistake. In the richly layered texts that make up the book of Genesis the promise of progeny and land returns, now more concrete, more specific, and more urgent:

3

When Abram was ninety-nine years old, the Lord appeared to Abram and said to him: "I am El-Shaddai. Walk in My ways and be blameless, so that I may set My covenant between Me and you, and multiply your descendants." Abram threw himself on his face; and God spoke to him further, "As for Me, this is My covenant with you: You shall be the father of a multitude of nations. And you shall no longer be called Abram, but your name shall be Abraham, for I make you father of a multitude of nations. I will make you exceedingly fertile, make nations of you; and kings shall come forth from you. I will maintain My covenant between Me and you, and your offspring to come, as an everlasting covenant throughout the ages, to be God to you and to your offspring to come. I give the land you sojourn in to you and your offspring to come, all the land of Canaan, as an everlasting possession. I will be their God." (Genesis 17:1-8)

Blessed with the hindsight of history, we can savor the full irony of the promise and its fulfillment. Abraham did indeed sire a tribe, those later Beni Israel or Children of Israel; they were a small people, surely, lost in the masses of Egypt or Mesopotamia, negligible when measured by the Hittites or the peoples of Akkad. But the rhetoric of Abraham's God, or its enthusiastic understanding by the patriarch's descendants, was far outstripped by the reality, since Abraham fathered not only the Children of Israel but the hundreds of millions of Christians and Muslims, who, like the Jews, claim Abraham as their father. "Look toward heaven and count the stars," God had said. Abraham could not even have imagined the galaxies that lay beyond his upraised eyes. [2]

The "Friend of God" at Hebron

So Abraham submitted himself to circumcision, the sign of God's covenant. Then he did the same with Ishmael, his son by the Egyptian slave concubine Hagar, and finally with all members of his household. But it was not Ishmael through whom God's promise to Abraham would be fulfilled. That was revealed in the following year when Abraham once again found himself in the presence of his God, now in a village that made up part of the settlement called Hebron:

The Lord appeared to him [Abraham] by the terebinths of Mamre; he was sitting at the entrance of his tent as the day grew hot. Looking up, he saw three men standing near him. As soon as he saw them, he ran from the entrance of his tent to greet them and, bowing to the ground, he said, "My lords, if it please you, do not go on past your servant. Let a little water be brought; bathe your feet and recline under a tree. And let me fetch a morsel of bread that you may refresh yourselves; then go on—seeing that you come your servant's way." They replied, "Do as you have said." (Genesis 18:1-5)

This unaffected hospitality of an old man sitting beneath the trees in one of the villages of Hebron elicited a remarkable reward. Abraham and his wife Sarah, both long past the time for such things, would have a son of their own:

The Lord took note of Sarah as He had promised, and the Lord did for Sarah as He had spoken. Sarah conceived and bore a son to Abraham for his old age, at the set time of which God had spoken. Abraham gave his newborn son, whom Sarah had borne him, the name of Isaac. And when his son Isaac was eight days old, Abraham circumcised him, as God had commanded him. . . . The boy grew up and was weaned, and Abraham held a great feast on the the day that Isaac was weaned.

Sarah saw the son, whom Hagar the Egyptian had borne to Abraham, playing. She said to Abraham, "Cast out that slave girl and her son, for the son of that slave shall not share in the inheritance with my son Isaac." The matter distressed Abraham greatly, for it concerned a son of his. But God said to Abraham, "Do not be distressed over the boy or your slave; whatever Sarah tells you, do as she says, for it is through Isaac that off-spring shall be continued for you. As for the son of the slave-woman, I will make an nation of him too, for he is your seed." (Genesis 21:1-13)

We cannot know what the latter promise meant at that time and place, but much later generations of Jews, Christians, and eventually Muslims read it as the charter of Arab greatness, and the "Ishmaelites" or "Hagarenes" became inextricably linked with that "land for Israel" which was still in the future of Abraham's descendants. [3]

Jerusalem Before Israel

History and the uncertain swirl of Near Eastern politics carried the still modest descendants of the patriarch Abraham to a cruel bondage in Egypt, then to release and wandering through Sinai, where, upon a mountain deep in that wilderness, God's earlier promise to Abraham was renewed, and the terms of God's decree were spelled out. Through Moses, the leader of God's people, the Law was given to the Children of Israel.

Moses, the prophet and lawgiver who guided the tribal descendants of Abraham and Isaac and Jacob through their most crucial time of trial, would never see the land promised by the Covenant; the conquest and occupation of the land of Canaan fell to others. But before that occurred, we are given a brief and tantalizing glimpse of that land and one of its cities in the first half of the fourteenth century B.C. The correspondence between the pharaoh of Egypt and the governors of his provinces abroad has been preserved at the ancient Egyptian site known as Tell el-Amarneh, and a number of the letters discovered there are from a certain Abdi-Hiba, a troubled fief-holder in one of the Egyptian king's distant holdings in Palestine:

This is what your servant Abdi-Hiba states: Know that this of Jerusalem was given me neither by my father nor by my mother but by the mighty arm of the king. . . . Let the king, my master know that I am not able to send a caravan to the king, my master—that you may know. I attest: the king has set his name in the land of Jerusalem forever, so that he cannot abandon the lands of Jerusalem. (Tell el-Amarnah: letter no. 287: ll. 25-60)

The Conquest of Canaan

How and with what difficulty the conquest of Canaan was accomplished, whether by the intervention of God or by the human hand of the Israelites, does not concern us here. It is enough to cite the summary provided in retrospect by Joshua, with the moral strictures and conditions that the God of Israel imposed upon His people:

Much later, after the Lord had given Israel rest from all the enemies around them, and when Joshua was old and well advanced in years, Joshua summoned all Israel, their elders and commanders, their magistrates and officials, and said to them. "I have grown old and am advanced in years. You have seen all that the Lord your God has done to all those nations on your account, for it was the Lord your God who fought for you. See, I have allotted to you, by your tribes, [the territory of] those nations that still remain, and that of all the nations that I have destroyed, from the Jordan to the Mediterranean Sea in the west. The Lord your God himself will thrust them out on your account and drive them out to make way for you, and you shall occupy their land as the Lord your God promised you.

"Be most resolute to observe faithfully all that is written in the book of the Teaching of Moses, without ever deviating from it to the right or to the left, and without intermingling with those nations which are left among you. Do not utter the names of their gods or swear by them; do not serve them or bow down to them. But hold fast to the Lord your God as you have done this day. The Lord has driven out great, powerful nations on your account, and not a man has withstood you to this day. A single man of you would put a thousand to flight, for the Lord your God

has been fighting for you, as He promised you. For your own sakes, there-fore, be most mindful to love the Lord your God. For should you turn away and attach yourselves to the remnant of those nations—to those that are left among you—and intermarry with them, you joining them and they joining you, know for certain that the Lord will not continue to drive those nations out before you; they shall become a snare and a trap for you, a scourge to your sides and thorns in your eyes, until you perish from this good land which the Lord your God has given you." (Joshua 23:1-13)

David and Jerusalem

The newly installed tribes were scattered across the hill country of Canaan, but in this difficult time of transition from a nomadic to a settled people, different needs arose to confront the newcomers: the need for greater coherence and, in the end, for a king of Israel. With God's guidance, the choice fell upon the youthful shepherd-warrior David, and it is with David that Jerusalem enters the history of the Children of Israel:

All the elders of Israel came to David at Hebron, and King David made a pact with them in Hebron before the Lord. And they anointed David king over Israel. David was thirty years old when he became king, and he reigned forty years. In Hebron he reigned over Judah seven years and six months, and in Jerusalem he reigned over all Israel and Judah thirty-three years.

The king and his men set out for Jerusalem against the Jebusites who inhabited the region. David was told, "You shall never get in here. Even the blind and the lame will turn you back"—they meant: David will never enter here—but David captured the stronghold of Sion; it is now the City of David. On that occasion David said: "Those who attack the Jebusites shall reach the water channel and [strike down] the lame and the blind, who are hateful to David." That is why they say: "No one who is blind or lame may enter the House." (2 Samuel 5:3-8)

There is little enlightenment in this account. Without counsel or ado the Israelites attacked and took a city called by the alien cult name of Jerusalem, "the Foundation of the God Shalem." It was the same city, it appears, from which there once came out, in Abraham's day, without introduction and without sequel, the mysterious figure of the priest-king Melchizedek, with whose "God Most High" Abraham had a special relationship:

And Melchizedek, king of Salem, brought out bread and wine. He was a priest of God Most High. He blessed him, saying,

"Blessed be Abram of God Most High,
Creator of heaven and earth.
And blessed be God Most High,
Who has delivered your foes into your hand"
And [Abram] gave him a tenth of everything. (Genesis 14:18-20)

Jerusalem was now, however, a Jebusite settlement, as it had been in Abdi-Hiba's day, and earlier in the biblical account itself (Judg. 19:10). It possessed a citadel called Sion and was firmly held, it appears, since the city's conquest was postponed to near the end of the Israelite occupation of the land of Canaan. And Jerusalem was a strong and good place since David chose it, over Hebron and all the other cult stations in that land, Israelite and others, to be his capital.

David occupied the stronghold and renamed it the City of David; David also fortified the surrounding area, from the Millo inwards. David kept growing stronger, for the Lord, the God of Hosts, was with him.

King Hiram of Tyre sent envoys with cedar logs, carpenters, and stonemasons; and they built a palace for David. Thus David knew that the Lord had established him as king over Israel and had exalted his kingship for the sake of His people Israel.

After he left Hebron, David took more concubines and wives in Jerusalem; and more sons and daughters were born to David. These are the names of the children born to him in Jerusalem: Shammua, Shohab, Nathan, and Solomon, Ibhar, Elishua, Nepheg, and Japhia, Elishama, Eliada, and Eliphelet. (2 Samuel 5:9-16)

The City of David—now called after its Israelite king whose property it was, instead of by the perhaps still too pagan name of "Jerusalem"—was located on a ridge that extended southward from the higher Mount Moriah to the north. East and west of Moriah and its southern spur lay two valleys, Kedron on the east and what was later known as the Tyropean Valley on the west. They both drained southward and merged at the southern tip of the City of David to wind their way south then east into the Judean wilderness.

The southern spur, already called Sion and later, if not in David's own time, Ophel or the Hump, first offered the advantage of easy defense, particularly after David reenforced the terrace walls—the Millo of the text[4]—that ran along its side, and more, it possessed a perennial source of water, the Gihon spring, low on its eastern slope.[5]

The Ark Installed

David settled in and began to fit himself and his new capital with the trappings of tenth-century royalty: first a palace, materials, and craftsmen

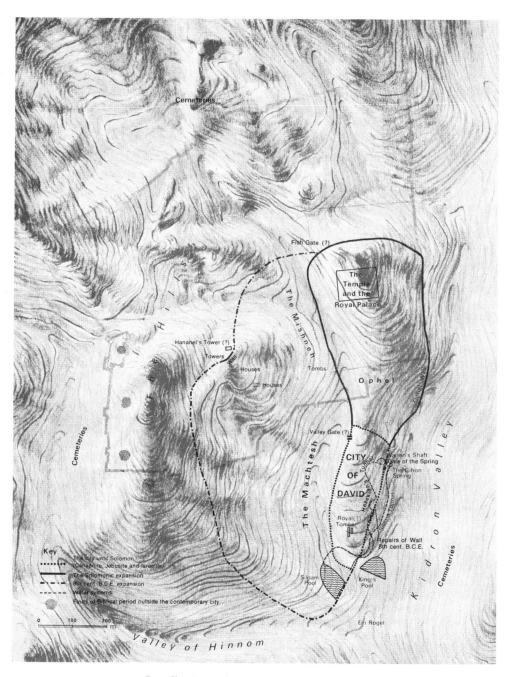

Israelite Jerusalem (ca. 1000-586 B.C.).
Permission Carta, Jerusalem

9

supplied by the king of Phoenician Tyre; [6] and then housing for a more properly Israelite token of power and legitimacy, the Ark of the Covenant. This portable shrine-throne had accompanied the Israelites throughout their wanderings between Egypt and Canaan and in the opening years of David's reign was still being lodged in one or another of the Israelite cult stations in the conquered lands. This pledge of God's promise, and so of religious legitimacy, was now ceremoniously carried to within the City of David and installed, by a conservative reflex, in exactly the kind of tent that had sheltered it in the desert wilderness:

David again assembled all the picked men of Israel, 30,000 strong. Then David and all the troops that were with him set out for Baalim of Judah to bring up from there the Ark of God to which the Name was attached, the name Lord of Hosts Enthroned on the Cherubim.

They loaded the Ark of God onto a new cart and conveyed it from the house of Abinadab which was on the hill; and Abinadab's son, Uzza and Ahio, guided the new cart. They conveyed it from Abinadab's house on the hill, [Uzza walking] alongside the Ark of God and Ahio walking in front of the Ark. Meanwhile David and all the House of Israel danced before the Lord to [the sound of] all kinds of cypress wood [instruments], with lyres, harps, timbrels, sistrums and cymbals. (2 Samuel 6:1-5)

There was an accident, however, and the transfer of the Ark to the City of David was delayed for three months. The Ark rested in the house of Obed-edom, a man of Gath in Philistia.

It was reported to King David: "The Lord has blessed Obed-edom's house and all that belongs to him because of the Ark of God." Thereupon David went and brought up the Ark of God from the house of Obed-edom to the City of David, amid rejoicing. When the bearers of the Ark of the Lord had moved forward six paces, he sacrificed an ox and a fatling. David, whirled with all his might before the Lord; David was girt with a linen ephod. Thus David and all the House of Israel brought up the Ark of the Lord with shouts and with blasts of the horn. . . .

They brought in the Ark of the Lord and set it up in its place inside the tent which David had pitched for it, and David sacrificed burnt offerings and the offerings of well-being before the Lord. When David finished sacrificing the burnt offerings and the offerings of well-being, he blessed the people in the name of the Lord of Hosts. (2 Samuel 6:12-18)

When the king was settled in his palace and the Lord had granted him safety from all the enemies around him, the king said to the prophet Nathan, "Here I am dwelling in a house of cedar, while the Ark of God abides in a tent!" Nathan said to the king, "Go and do whatever you have in mind, for the Lord is with you." But that same night the word of the Lord came to Nathan: "Go and say to My servant David: Thus said the Lord: Are you the one to build a house for Me to dwell in? From the day that I brought the people of Israel out of Egypt to this day I have not dwelt in a house, but moved about in Tent and Tabernacle. As I moved about Wherever the Israelites went, did I ever reproach any of the tribal leaders whom I appointed to care for My people Israel: Why have you not built me a house of cedar? . . ."

"The Lord declares to you that He, the Lord, will establish a house for you. When your days are done and you lie with your fathers, I will raise up your offspring after you, one of your own issue, and I will establish his kingship. He shall build a house for My name, and I will establish his royal throne forever. . . ." (2 Samuel 7:1-13)

Thus on a note of celebration, and of some doubt and hesitation as well, the Ark of the Covenant—the sign of God's compact with the Children of Israel first made through Abraham then renewed through Moses on Sinai—was installed in David's new urban capital in Judea. The two-century tradition of a portable shrine still clung to the Ark, and we are not very surprised to find it lodged in what was perhaps a more permanent replica of the tent that was its housing thoughout the wanderings in the wilderness and then in various towns and cities of Israel. But the Israelites were no longer nomads; they had settled into Israel, whose cities were now their cities, and there in the newly named City of David, the once Jebusite Jerusalem, there was already talk of a "House of the Lord" on the model of what the Israelites could observe all about them.

The Threshing-Floor on Mount Moriah

Within the walled settlement of David's city—some of the wall was the Israelites' work; other parts were earlier built by the Jebusites they had partially displaced—lived perhaps 2,500 people, including the royal court, the garrison, priests and Levites of the Israelite cult, craftsmen, traders, and whatever Jebusites chose to remain there after the conquest. [7] That much is history and can be verified out by the texts found in the excavations carried on by Kenyon, Shiloh, and others on the site of David's settlement. But the Bible is not merely the record of wars and buildings; it is a sacred history as well, and it is in the latter mode that the narrative in the second book of Samuel proceeds. David, now filled with pride and assurance, determines to take a census of his people, an act which, once done, begins to bother the conscience of the king:

11

Afterwards David reproached himself for having numbered the people. And David said to the Lord, "I have sinned grievously in what I have done. Please, O Lord, remit the guilt of Your servant, for I have acted foolishly. [The Lord sends a pestilence upon Israel as a punishment for David's folly. Seventy thousand people die.] But when the angel extended his hand against Jerusalem to destroy it, the Lord renounced further punishment and said to the angel who was destroying the people, "Enough! Stay your hand!" The angel of the Lord was then by the threshing floor of Araunah the Jebusite.

When David saw the angel who was striking down the people, he said to the Lord, "I alone am guilty, I alone have done wrong, but these poor sheep, what have they done? Let Your hand fall upon me and my father's house!"

Gad [the seer of the king] came to David the same day and said to him, "Go and set up an altar to the Lord on the threshing floor of Araunah the Jebusite." David went up, following Gad's instruction, as the Lord had commanded. Araunah looked out and saw the king and his courtiers approaching him. So Araunah went out and bowed low to the king, with his face to the ground. And Araunah asked, "Why has my lord the king come to his servant?" David replied "To buy the threshing floor from you, that I may build an altar to the Lord and that the plague against the people may be checked." And Araunah said to David, "Let my lord the king take it and offer up whatever he sees fit. Here are oxen for a burnt offering, and the threshing floor and the gear of the oxen for wood. All this, O king, Araunah gives to Your Majesty. And may the Lord," Araunah added, "respond to you with favor."

But the king replied to Araunah, "No, I will buy them from you at a price. I cannot sacrifice to the Lord my God burnt offerings that have cost me nothing." So David bought the threshing floor and the oxen for fifty shekels of silver. And David built there an altar to the Lord and sacrificed burnt offerings and offerings of well-being. The Lord responded to the plea for the land; and the plague against Israel was checked. (2 Samuel 24:10-25)

There is nothing in this account to suggest that we are dealing with anything more than a simple threshing ground that was rendered holy by a secondary act of divine providence, secondary in the sense that God did not manifest Himself here but rather stayed the sword of His avenging angel. David built an altar in this place. But as we shall see, this otherwise unnoteworthy Jebusite threshing floor, at the highest point of Mount Moriah, would later become the site and center of the principal and then the unique Jewish sanctuary in the land of Israel. One cannot but wonder if it was merely grain that was of concern in that high place, or had David expropriated, "bought," as the biblical narrative insists, a Jebusite holy place and converted it into an Israelite one. [8]

Solomon and the Temple

Apparently David had more royal and elaborate plans for Araunah's threshing floor than the erection of a mere altar. The narrative in 2 Samuel suggests a Davidic temple and then turns aside to other matters, but the parallel account in Chronicles, where Araunah is called Ornan, is both specific and detailed:

At that time, when David saw that the Lord answered him at the thresh-ing floor of Ornan the Jebusite, then he sacrificed there—for the taber-nacle of the Lord, which Moses had made in the wilderness, and the altar of burnt offerings, were at that time at Gibeon, and David was unable to go to it to worship the Lord because he was terrified by the sword of the angel of the Lord. David said, "Here will be the House of the Lord and here the altar of burnt offerings for Israel."

David gave orders to assemble the aliens living in the land of Israel, and assigned them to be hewers, to quarry and dress stones for building the House of God. Much iron for nails for the doors of the gates and for clasps did David lay aside, and so much copper it could not be weighed, and cedar logs without number—for the Sidonians and Tyrians brought many cedar logs to David.

For David thought, "My son Solomon is an untried youth, and the House to be built for the Lord is to be made exceedingly great to win fame and glory throughout all the lands; let me then lay aside material for him." So David laid aside much material before he died. (1 Chronicles 21:28–22:5)

David gave his son Solomon the plan of the porch [of the Temple] and its houses, its storerooms, and upper chambers and inner chambers; and the place of the Ark-cover; and the plan of all that he had by the spirit: of the courts of the House of the Lord and all its surrounding cham-bers. . . . "All this that the Lord made me understand by His hand on me," David said, "I give you in writing—the plan of all the works." (1 Chronicles 28:11-19)

By this account, then, it was David himself who, under the guidance of the Lord, drew up the plans for the temple that was to rise on the summit of the eastern hill of Jerusalem. But as with Moses, detained from entering the Land of Promise, it was reserved for another to build the House of the Lord: David's son Solomon, again with the aid of both craftsmen and materials supplied by the more advanced society of Sidon and Tyre in Phoenicia, since as Solomon himself confessed to Hiram of Tyre, "we have none so skilled at felling timber as your Sidonians" (1 Kgs. 5:6).

In the four hundred and eightieth year after the Israelites left the land of Egypt, in the month of Ziv—that is, the second month—in the fourth year of his reign over Israel [ca. 967 B.C.], Solomon began to build the House of the Lord. The House which King Solomon built for the Lord was sixty cubits [90 ft.] long, twenty cubits [30 ft.] wide, and thirty cubits [45 ft.] high. The portico in front of the Great Hall of the House was twenty cubits long—along the width of the House—and ten cubits deep to the front of the House. He made windows for the House, recessed and latticed. Against the outside wall of the House—the outside walls of the House enclosing the Great Hall and the Shrine [or Holy of Holies]—he built a storied structure; and he made side chambers all around. The lowest story was five cubits wide, the middle one six cubits wide and the third seven cubits wide; for he provided recesses round the outside of the House so as not to penetrate the walls of the House. When the House was built, only finished stones cut at the quarry were used; so that no hammer or ax or any iron tool was heard in the House while it was being built. [9] *(1 Kings 6:1-7)*

Thus the House of the Lord was built on the mount from which the City of David extended as a southern spur. It is not made clear in the text, but we assume that Solomon built the Temple atop the threshing floor that his father had purchased from Araunah the Jebusite, though it must surely have extended far beyond it. We are merely guessing, however, and, perhaps somewhat more dangerously, envisioning backward from the platform that sits atop that hill today, the Muslims' Haram al-Sharif. We imagine it as Herod's first-century platform, which was built in turn on the site of Zerubbabel's earlier sixth-century platform, just as the latter was built atop Solomon's. The material evidence is entirely lacking, however, for even the site of Solomon's House of the Lord. [10]

At the center of the Temple complex, shielded from the profanity without, was an inner sanctuary, and inside it, the sacred Ark of the Covenant: [11]

When Solomon had completed the construction of the House, he paneled the walls of the House on the inside with planks of cedar. . . . Twenty cubits from the rear of the House, he built [a partition] of cedar planks from the floor to the walls [or rafters]; he furnished its interior to serve as a shrine, as the Holy of Holies. . . . In the innermost part of the House, he fixed a Shrine in which to place the Ark of the Lord's Covenant. The interior of the Shrine was twenty cubits long, twenty cubits wide, and twenty cubits high. He overlaid it with solid gold; he similarly overlaid [its] cedar altar. Solomon overlaid the interior of the House with solid gold, and he inserted golden chains into the door of the Shrine. . . .

In the Shrine he made two cherubim of olive wood, each ten cubits high. [One] had a wing measuring five cubits and another wing measuring five cubits, so that the spread from wing tip to wing tip was ten cubits; and the wingspread of the other cherub was also ten cubits. . . . He placed the cherubim inside the inner chamber. . . . (1 Kings 6:14-27)

The Royal Palace and Quarter

The work on the Temple proper took seven years; but for another thirteen Solomon was engaged on a project that must have been equally dear to the imperially minded king and was at least as impressive as the Temple, though somewhat scanted in the biblical narrative: his palace complex with its residences, throne room, hall of justice, and perhaps an arsenal: [12]

It took Solomon thirteen years to build his palace, until his whole palace was completed. He built the Lebanon Forest House with four rows of cedar columns, and with hewn cedar beams above the columns. Its length was one hundred cubits, its breadth fifty cubits, and its height thirty cubits. It was paneled above with cedar, with the planks that were above on the forty-five columns—fifteen in each row. . . . He made the portico of columns fifty cubits long and thirty cubits wide; the portico was in front [of the columns], and there were columns with a canopy in front of them. He made the throne portico, where he was to pronounce judgments—the Hall of Judgment. It was paneled with cedar from floor to floor.

The house that he used as a residence, in the rear courtyard, back of the portico, was of the same construction. Solomon also constructed a palace like that portico for the daughter of Pharaoh, whom he had married. [13] All of these buildings, from foundation to coping and all the way out to the great courtyard, were of choice stones, hewn according to measure, smoothed on all sides. The foundations were huge blocks of choice stone, stones of ten cubits and stones of eight cubits; and above were choice stones, hewn according to measure. The large surrounding courtyard had three tiers of hewn stone and a row of cedar beams, the same as for the inner court of the House of the Lord and for the portico of the house. (1 Kings 7:1-12)

Temple and palace sat cheek to jowl, the first on the summit of Moriah, the latter immediately to the south, though probably still above the City of David extending southward on the Ophel and perhaps constituting an entire "royal quarter." [14] This proximity of royal house and divine house, probably natural to Solomon and his generation, was decidedly less acceptable to a later one. Hundreds of years later, when the prophet Ezekiel was contemplating, across the ruins of Solomon's Temple, a new and finer House of the Lord, it had no place in or near it for the profanity of kings and their corpses:

The Presence of the Lord entered the Temple by the gate that faced east-ward. A spirit carried me into the inner court, and lo, the Presence of the Lord filled the Temple; and I heard speech addressed to me from the Temple, though the man [guiding me] was standing beside me. It said to me: "O mortal, this is the place of My throne and the place for the soles of My feet, where I will dwell in the midst of the people of Israel forever. The House of Israel and their kings must not again defile My holy name by their apostasy and by the corpses of their kings at their death. When they placed their threshold next to My threshold and their doorposts next to My doorposts with only a wall between Me and them, they would defile My holy name by the abominations that they committed, and I consumed them in My anger. Therefore, let them put their apostasy and the corpses of their kings far from Me, and I will dwell among them forever. (Ezekiel 43:4-9)

The House of the Lord

But to return to the completion of Solomon's House of the Lord, there followed a ceremony similar to the one that had occurred in David's day, the installation of the Ark of the Covenant in its holy and inviolable housing within Solomon's sanctuary:

Then Solomon convoked the elders of Israel—all the heads of the tribes and the ancestral chieftains of the Israelites—before King Solomon in Je-rusalem, to bring up the Ark of the Covenant of the Lord from the City of David, that is, Sion. All the men of Israel gathered before King Solomon at the Feast [of Tabernacles] in the month of Ethanim—that is, the seventh month. When all the elders of Israel had come, the priests lifted the Ark and carried up the Ark of the Lord. Then the priests and the Levites brought the Tent of Meeting and all the holy vessels that were in the Tent. Meanwhile King Solomon and the whole community of Israel, who were assembled with him before the Ark, were sacrificing sheep and oxen in such abundance that they could not be numbered or counted.

The priests brought in the Ark of the Lord's Covenant to its place underneath the wings of the cherubim, in the Shrine of the House, in the Holy of Holies; for the cherubim had their wings spread over the place of the Ark, so that the cherubim shielded the Ark and its poles from above. The poles projected so that the ends of the poles were visible in the Sanctuary in front of the Shrine, but they could not be seen outside; and there they remain to this day. There was nothing inside the Ark but the two tablets of stone which Moses placed there at Horeb, when the Lord made [a covenant] with the Israelites after their departure from the land of Egypt. (1 Kings 8:1-9)

Finally, Solomon's work is validated by a miracle that signals God's possession of His own House:

When Solomon finished praying, fire descended from heaven and consumed the burnt offering and the sacrifices, and the glory of the Lord filled the House. (2 Chronicles 7:1)

The narrative in Kings passes directly to another passage quite different in tone from the one just cited. It is a meditation by Solomon himself in the form of an interior dialogue on the propriety of God's possessing a house, and it almost certainly reflects the sensibility of a later, post-Exilic age, which had lost the Temple and for whom the God of Israel dwelled nowhere if not in the universal heaven:

[And Solomon continued] "But will God really dwell on earth? Even the heavens to their uttermost reaches cannot contain You, how much less this House which I have built! Yet turn, O Lord my God, to the prayer and supplication of Your servant, and hear the cry and prayer which Your servant offers before you this day. May Your eyes be open day and night toward this House, toward the place of which You have said, 'My name shall abide there.' May You heed the prayers which Your servant will offer toward this place. And when You hear the supplications which Your servant and Your people Israel offer toward this place, give heed in Your heavenly abode—give heed and pardon. . . .

"When they sin against You—for there is no man who does not sin—and You are angry with them and deliver them to the enemy, and their captors carry them off to an enemy land, near or far; and then they take it to heart in the land to which they have been carried off, and they repent and make supplication to You in the land of their captors, saying 'We have sinned, we have acted perversely, we have acted wickedly,' and they turn back to You with their heart and soul, in the land of the enemies who

17

have carried them off, and they pray to You in the direction of their land which You gave to their fathers, and of the city which You have chosen and of the House which I have built for Your name—oh, give heed in your heavenly abode to their prayer and supplication. . . ." (1 Kings 8:27-49)

There are new motifs here, the notion of God's choice not merely of a people and a land for them, but of the city itself. When that passage was set down Jerusalem was already sanctified and Jews everywhere were called upon to turn toward it in their prayers: as a later Muslim would put it, Jerusalem had become the *qibla*, or "prayer-direction," of Israel.

David may not have written them, as the tradition asserts, but the "Songs of Sion" that are scattered through the collection called the Book of Psalms capture the mood of confidence and exaltation of the new Israel with the Presence of the Lord now enthroned in the city that was its heart:

> I rejoiced when they said to me,
>   "We are going to the House of the Lord."
> Our feet stand inside your gates, O Jerusalem:
> Jerusalem built up, a city knit together,
>   to which tribes would make pilgrimage,
>   the tribes of the Lord,
>   —as was enjoined upon Israel—
>   to praise the name of the Lord.
> There the thrones of judgment stood,
>   thrones of the house of David.
> Pray for the well-being of Jerusalem:
>   "May those who love you be at peace;
>   peace in your citadels."
> For the sake of my kin and friends,
>   I pray for your well-being;
> For the sake of the House of the Lord our God
>   I seek your good. (Psalm 122)

Jerusalem and the Kingdom of Judah

Solomon put down the foundations of empire, but many years were to pass before the organic machinery of polity and rule grew to maturity in Jerusalem and the rest of the kingdom. Most of the process is lost to our sight since it was not of great concern to the anonymous transmitters who stand behind the books called Kings and Chronicles. There are only glimpses, like that of King Jehoshaphat (872-848 B.C.) setting up a judicial machinery, with competence in matters of both religious and royal statute law, as well as what appears to be a policing body involving the Levites:

He appointed judges in the land in all the fortified cities of Judah, in each and every town. He charged the judges: "Consider what you are doing; for you judge not on behalf of men, but on behalf of the Lord, and He is with you when you pass judgment." . . . Jehoshaphat also appointed in Jerusalem some Levites and priests and heads of the clans of Israelites for rendering judgment in matters of the Lord, and for disputes. Then they returned to Jerusalem. He charged them, "This is how you shall act in the fear of the Law, with fidelity, and with whole heart. When a dispute comes before you from your living in their towns, whether about homicide, or about ritual, or laws, or rules, you must instruct them so that they do not incur guilt before the Lord and wrath be upon you and your brothers. Act so and you will not incur guilt. See, Amariah the chief priest is over you in all cases concerning the Lord, and Zebadiah son of Ishmael is the commander of the house of Judah in all cases concerning the king; the Levites are at your disposal; act with resolve and the Lord will be with the good. (2 Chronicles 19:5-11)

Here we see the priests and Levites in their role as judges, arbitrators, and peace officers, but their chief function in Jerusalem was as ministers of the liturgical services required on both a daily basis and across an annual cycle by the Mosaic law. Priests and Levites were not new officials in Israel; their origins go back to the time of the Israelites' release from Egypt. And the law delivered to Moses on Sinai made elaborate provision for the support of both priests and Levites dedicated to the service of the Lord. What had changed, however, was the architectural institutionalization of that service in the Temple in Jerusalem, which, with its altar, courts, and outbuildings, constituted an immense liturgical and commercial "industry." The Mosaic law never envisioned such a permanent complex and so made no provisions for its upkeep or expenses, thus it fell to a later generation of Israelites to address themselves to the problem. Solomon himself may have done so, but our first detailed account comes a century and a half later, from the reign of Jehoash, who was king of Judah from 835 to 796 B.C.:

Jehoash said to the priests, "All the money, current money, brought into the House of the Lord as sacred donations—any money a man may pay as the money equivalent of persons, or any other money that a man may be minded to bring to the House of the Lord—let the priests receive it, each from his benefactor; they, in turn, shall make repairs on the House, wherever damage may be found."

19

But in the twenty-third year of King Jehoash [it was found that] the priests had not made repairs on the House. So King Jehoash summoned the priest Jehoiada and the other priests and said to them, "Why have you not kept the House in repair? Now do not accept money from your benefactors any more, but have it donated [directly] for the repair of the house." The priests agreed that they would neither accept money from the people nor make repairs on the House. . . .

And the priest Jehoiada took a chest and bored a hole in its lid. He placed it at the right side of the altar as one entered the House of the Lord, and the priestly guards of the threshold deposited there all the money that was brought into the House of the Lord. Whenever they saw that there was much money in the chest, the royal scribe and the high priest would come up and put the money accumulated in the House of the Lord into bags, and they would count it. Then they would deliver the money that was weighed out to overseers of the work, who were in charge of the House of the Lord. These in turn used to pay the carpenters and the laborers who worked in the House of the Lord, and the masons and stonecutters. They also paid for wood and for quarried stone with which to make repairs on the House of the Lord, and for every other expenditure that had to be made in repairing the House. However, no silver bowls and no snuffers, basins, or trumpets—no vessels of gold or silver—were made at the House of the Lord from the money brought into the House of the Lord; this was given only to the overseers of the work for the repair of the House of the Lord. No check was kept on the men to whom the money was delivered to pay the workers; for they dealt honestly. Money brought as a guilt offering or a sin offering was not deposited in the House of the Lord; it went to the priests. (2 Kings 12:5-16)

The Claims of Empire

The internal concerns betrayed in this text were almost a luxury in that and the following century. Immediately upon the death of Solomon the kingdom he had fashioned began to come apart, and his successors in Jerusalem ruled only over a kingdom of Judah, not over the entire Children of Israel. And more dangerously to both Jewish kingdoms, Israel in the north and Judah in the south, and in the end most fatally for Jerusalem, the immense military and commercial empires that were forming in Mesopotamia had a grasp long enough to reach into Palestine. The final effect was their political and military domination of the Jewish states, but even before that occurred, the world around the Israelites was pressing its claims in other equally disturbing ways.

When Ahaz was ruler in Jerusalem in about 732 B.C., he, like many another king in that city, was constrained to use both Temple and palace treasures to buy off the powerful Assyrian Tiglath-pileser, then already in Damascus. Then he resorted to another tactic, perhaps to win sympathy in Damascus, perhaps simply out of emulation or even a desire to modernize the religious cult of the Israelites, and at its very heart and center:

When King Ahaz went to Damascus to greet King Tiglath-pileser of Assyria, he saw the altar in Damascus. King Ahaz sent the priest Uriah a sketch of the altar and a detailed plan of its construction. The priest Uriah did just as King Ahaz had instructed him from Damascus; the priest Uriah built the altar before King Ahaz returned from Damascus. When the king returned from Damascus, and when the king saw the altar, the king drew near the altar, ascended it, and offered his burnt offering and meal offering; he poured his libation, and he dashed the blood of his offering of well-being against the altar. As for the bronze altar which had been before the Lord [cf. 1 Kgs. 8:64], he moved it from its place in front of the Temple, between the [new] altar and the House of the Lord, and placed it on the north side of the [new] altar. And King Ahaz commanded the priest Uriah: "On the great [new] altar you shall offer the morning burnt offering and the evening meal offering and the king's burnt offering and his meal offering, and the burnt offerings of all the people of the land, their meal offerings and their libations. And against it you shall dash the blood of all the burnt offerings and all the blood of the sacrifices. And I will decide about the bronze altar." Uriah did just as King Ahaz commanded.

King Ahaz cut off the insets—the laver stands—and removed the lavers from them. He also removed the tank from the bronze oxen that supported it and set it on a stone pavement—on account of the king of Assyria. He also extended to the House of the Lord the sabbath passage that had been built in the palace and the king's outer entrance. (2 Kings 16:10-18)

Hezekiah and Sennacherib

Ahaz or events may have saved Judah on this occasion, but nothing could save the northern kingdom of Israel, which fell to the Assyrians in 723 B.C. The reverberations of that conquest were assuredly felt in Jerusalem, though we reconstruct what was happening to the city not so much from the texts as from the archeological evidence. [15] Solomon's Jerusalem was still narrowly confined to the City of David on the Ophel and the Temple and palace quarter on the summit of Moriah directly adjoining it to the north. By the eighth century, however, the city's population had spread, without benefit of royal investment as far as we can see, down into the Tyropean Valley to the west of the Temple mount and even up onto the slopes of the western hill of Jerusalem, the later "Upper City." By 700 B.C. Jerusalem was three or four times the size of what it had been under Solomon, with a population growth from perhaps 6,000 or 8,000 in the earlier era to about 24,000 in the late eighth century, an explosion in area and numbers that appears to be directly connected to the flight of Jews southward to the Holy City before the advance of the Assyrians into Samaria. [16]

The Assyrians arrived before Jerusalem when Hezekiah was king in 701 B.C., and that ruler's first response was much the same as Ahaz's had been, to strip off some of the Temple and palace treasures in the hope of buying off the attackers:

In the fourteenth year of King Hezekiah, King Sennecharib of Assyria marched against all the fortified towns of Judah and seized them. King Hezekiah sent this message to the king of Assyria at Lachish: "I have done wrong; withdraw from me; and I shall bear whatever you impose upon me." So the king of Assyria imposed upon King Hezekiah of Judah a payment of three hundred talents of silver and thirty talents of gold. Hezekiah gave him all the silver that was on hand in the House of the Lord and in the treasuries of the palace. At that time Hezekiah cut down the doors and the doorposts of the Temple of the Lord, which King Hezekiah had overlaid [with gold] and gave them to the king of Assyria. (2 Kings 18:13-16)

Gihon and Siloam

Tribute was only a temporary expedient, however. When it became clear that the Assyrians would return and attack not only Judah but Jerusalem itself, Hezekiah took other measures:

King Sennacherib of Assyria invaded Judah and encamped against its fortified towns with the aim of taking them over. When Hezekiah saw that Sennacherib had come, intent on making war against Jerusalem, he consulted with his officers and warriors about stopping the flow of the springs outside the city; and they supported him. A large force was assembled to stop up all the springs and the wadi that flowed through the land, for otherwise, they thought, the king of Assyria would come and find water in abundance. (2 Chronicles 32:1-4)

The second book of Kings puts it more succinctly:

. . . he made the pool and the conduit and brought the water into the city. . . . (2 Kings 20:20)

Hezekiah brought the water into Jerusalem from the city's perennial source, the spring Gihon low down on the eastern slope of the City of David, by cutting a tunnel or conduit through some 1,700 feet of bedrock under the city to emerge on the southwest side, where the water ran forth into a pool called Siloam. [17] The tunnel was rediscovered in the nineteenth century, and in 1880 a construction inscription came to light about twenty feet into the tunnel on the Siloam end. The workers, it was now clear, had begun at either end and worked toward each other. The inscription commemorates their breakthrough:

(the completion of) the boring work. And this is the story of the boring through. While [the cutters were working with their] axes, each toward his fellow, and while there were still three cubits to be cut through, the voice of a man [was heard] calling to his fellow, for there was a crevice on the right. . . . And on the day of the boring through, the cutters broke through each to meet his fellow, axe opposite axe. Then the water ran from the spring to the pool for twelve hundred cubits, and the height of the rock above the stone-cutters was one hundred cubits.

Thus water was insured *within* the city's defenses, since Jerusalem now extended much farther west than it once had; that extension is likewise reflected in Hezekiah's preparations for the assault:

Then the king acted with vigor; rebuilding the whole breached wall, raising towers on it; and building another wall outside it. He fortified the Millo of the City of David;[18] and made a great quantity of arms and shields. He appointed battle officers over the people; then, gathering them to him in the square of the city gate, he rallied them, saying, "Be strong and of good courage; do not be frightened or dismayed by the king of Assyria or by the horde that he has with him. With him is an arm of flesh, but with us is the Lord our God, to help us and fight our battles." The people were encouraged by the speech of King Hezekiah of Judah. (2 Chronicles 32:5-8)

Isaiah: Jerusalem's Prophet
of Doom and Hope

Jerusalem has never lacked for interpreters of its own misfortunes: prophets filled and moved by the awesome spirit of God, historians instructed by the lessons of the past, philosophers and theologians in search of God's or nature's meaning amidst the ruins. Many of them were outsiders, but Hezekiah's contemporary Isaiah, the first of the line of the Holy City's prophetic visionaries was, as far as we can make out, a native son speaking with dread and hope of the Assyrian threat to his own city:

> *Your land is a waste, your cities burnt down;*
> *Before your eyes, the yield of your soil*
>   *is consumed by strangers—*
> *A wasteland as overthrown by strangers!*
> *Fair Sion is left,*
>   *like a booth in a vineyard,*
>   *like a hut in a cucumber field*
>   *like a city beleaguered*
> *Had not the Lord of Hosts left us some survivors,*
>   *we should be like Sodom,*
>   *another Gomorrah. (Isaiah 1:7-9)*

There was, nonetheless, hope for a better future. Even if it were postponed to the remote "end of days," Jerusalem would stand at the heart of Isaiah's, and so all of Israel's, vision of universal peace:

> *In the days to come*
> *the Mount of the Lord's House*
> *shall stand firm above the mountains,*
>   *and tower above the hills.*
> *All the nations shall gaze on it with joy,*
> *and the many peoples shall go and shall say:*
> *"Come, let us go up to the Mount of the Lord,*
>   *to the House of the God of Jacob,*
>   *that He may instruct us in His ways,*
>   *and that we may walk in His paths."*
> *For instruction shall come forth from Sion,*
>   *the word of the Lord from Jerusalem;*
> *Thus He will judge among the nations,*
>   *and arbitrate for the many peoples.*
> *And they shall beat their swords into plowshares*
>   *and their spears into pruning hooks;*
> *nation shall not take up sword against nation;*
>   *they shall never again know war. (Isaiah 2:2-4)*

The Assyrians Attack

The fulfillment of this noble vision was not to be known in Isaiah's day, but the doom he foresaw was fast approaching the gates of the Holy City.

We have two accounts of the final Assyrian assault on Jerusalem in 701, the first from a royal inscription of Sennacherib; the second, more laconic and theological, from the second book of Kings:

As for Hezekiah the Jew, who did not bow in submission to my yoke, I besieged and conquered forty-six of his strong walled towns and a great number of smaller villages in their neighborhood by building earth-ramps and then bringing up battering rams, as well as by the attack of foot-soldiers, by breaching the wall, tunnelling and sapper operations. From among their number I brought out 200,150 people, young and old, male and female, a great many horses, mules, donkeys, camels, large and small cattle, and accounted them the spoils of war. The king himself I shut up like a caged bird within Jerusalem, his royal city. I put observation-posts tightly around it and turned back to his doom anyone who came out of its city gates. . . . As for Hezekiah, the terrible splendor of my lordship overwhelmed both him and the irregular and regular troops which he had conscripted to strengthen his royal city of Jerusalem and had gotten for his protection, together with thirty talents of gold, three hundred talents of silver, precious stones, antimony, large blocks of red stone, ivory inlaid couches, ivory arm-chairs, elephant hides . . . all kinds of valuable treasures as well as his daughters, concubines, male and female musicians he later sent to me at Nineveh, my majestic city. He sent a personal messenger to deliver the tribute and make a slave's act of obedience. (The Taylor Prism)

That night the angel of the Lord went out and struck down a hundred and eighty-five thousand men in the Assyrian camp, and the following morning they were all dead corpses. So King Sennacherib of Assyria broke camp, and retreated, and stayed in Nineveh. (2 Kings 19:35-36)

Profanation and Reform

If not destroyed, Jerusalem was deeply shaken by this event and by those of a more religious character that followed. The royal annals of the books of Kings are not always generous on such matters, but from as far back as the reign of Solomon there were non-Israelite cult places that continued to be frequented not only in the vicinity of Jerusalem (1 Kgs. 11:5-8) [19] but even in the city itself; during the reigns of Jehoram, Athaliah, and Ahaz there was a priesthood and temple to Baal within the Holy City (2 Kgs. 11:18). But the most serious intrusion of paganism took place during the long reign of Hezekiah's son Manasseh:

Manasseh was twelve years old when he became king, and he reigned fifty-five years in Jerusalem. . . . He did what was displeasing to the Lord,

25

following the abhorrent practices of the nations which the Lord had dispossessed before the Israelites. He rebuilt the shrines which his father Hezekiah had destroyed, he erected altars for Baal and made a sacred post, as King Ahab of Israel had done. He bowed down before all the host of heaven and worshiped them, and he built altars for them in the House of the Lord, of which the Lord had said "I will establish My name in Jerusalem." He built altars for all the host of heaven in the two courts of the House of the Lord. . . . The sculptured image of Asherah which he made, he placed in the House, 20 *concerning which the Lord had said to David and to his son Solomon, "In this House and in Jerusalem, which I chose out of all the tribes of Israel, I will establish My name forever. . . ."* (2 Kings 21:1-7)

Reaction and reform came in the reign of Josiah (640-609 B.C.), who "did right in the eyes of the Lord; he followed closely in the footsteps of his forefather David, swerving neither right nor left." (2 Kgs. 22:1-2). Well established in the eighteenth year of his rule, in 622 B.C. the king put his hand to the task. To all appearances it began simply as necessary repairs on the Temple, which Josiah delegated to his adjutant-general Shaphan, but the work turned out to be something more than structural:

The high priest Hilkiah said to the scribe Shaphan, "I have found a scroll of the Teaching in the House of the Lord." And Hilkiah gave the scroll to Shaphan, who read it. . . . The scribe Shaphan then went to the king and reported to the king . . . "The high priest Hilkiah has given me a scroll"; and Shaphan read it to the king. When the king heard the contents of the scroll of the Teaching, he rent his clothes. And the king gave orders to the priest Hilkiah, and to Ahikam son of Shaphan, Achbor son of Michaiah, the scribe Shaphan, and Asaiah the king's minister. "Go, inquire of the Lord on my behalf, and on behalf of the people, and on behalf of all Judah, concerning the words of this scroll that had been found. For great indeed must be the wrath of the Lord that has been kindled against us because our fathers did not obey the words of the scroll to do all that has been prescribed for us." (2 Kings 22:8-13)

The "scroll of the Teaching" may have been the core of the book included in the Bible as Deuteronomy, or "The Second Book of Law," and the discovery was read as a divine signal for reform. 21 This conclusion was confirmed when king and minister consulted Huldah the prophetess "at her home in the Mishneh quarter of Jerusalem" (2 Kgs. 22:14) and were admonished that unless the terms of the Covenant were restored, God's wrath would descend upon the nation:

At the king's summons, all the elders of Judah and Jerusalem assembled before him. The king went up to the House of the Lord, together with all the men of Judah and the inhabitants of Jerusalem, and the priests and the prophets—all the people, young and old. And he read to them the entire text of the covenant scroll which had been found in the House of the Lord. The king stood by the pillar and solemnized the covenant before the Lord: that they would follow the Lord and observe His commandments, His injunctions, and His laws with all their heart and soul, so that they would fulfill all the terms of this covenant as inscribed upon the scroll. And all the people entered into the covenant.

Then the king ordered the high priest Hilkiah, the priests of the second rank, and the guards on the threshold to bring out of the Temple of the Lord all the objects made for Baal and Asherah and all the host of heaven. He burned them outside Jerusalem in the fields of Kedron, and he removed the ashes to Bethel. He suppressed the idolatrous priests whom the kings of Judah had appointed to make offerings at the shrines in the towns of Judah and in the environs of Jerusalem, and those who made offerings to Baal, to the sun and moon and the constellations—all the host of heaven. He brought out [the image of] Asherah from the House of the Lord to the Kedron Valley outside Jerusalem, and burned it in the Kedron Valley; he beat it to dust and scattered the dust over the burial ground of the common people. He tore down the cubicles of the male prostitutes in the House of the Lord, at the place where the women wove coverings for Asherah. (2 Kings 23:1-7)

Then, as a final step in a process of cultic centralization that had begun with David's choice of Jerusalem as his capital and his placing of the Ark on Mount Moriah, Josiah decreed that the Temple of Jerusalem should be the sole place where the Israelites might offer sacrifice to their God:

He brought all the priests from the towns of Judah [to Jerusalem] and defiled the shrines where the priests had been making offerings—from Geba to Beer-sheba. He also demolished the shrines of the gates, which were at the entrance of the gate of Joshua, the city prefect—which were on a person's left [as he entered] the city gate. The priests of the shrines, however, did not ascend the altar of the Lord in Jerusalem, but they ate unleavened bread along with their kinsmen. . . . The king commanded all the people, "Offer the passover sacrifice to the Lord your God as prescribed in this scroll of the covenant." Now the passover sacrifice had been offered in that manner in the days of the chieftains [that is, the Judges] who ruled Israel, or during the days of the kings of Israel and the kings of Judah. Only in the eighteenth year of King Josiah was such a passover sacrifice offered in that manner to the Lord in Jerusalem. (2 Kings 23:8-9, 21-23[22])

The Temple and the Ark

In distant Mesopotamia, meantime, the Assyrians were replaced by the rising power of a new Semitic dynasty, the Babylonians, and once again the long imperial arm reached out of the east toward Syria, Palestine, and Egypt. The Babylonians arrived before Jerusalem in 597 B.C.:

Jehoiachin was eighteen years old when he became king, and he reigned three months in Jerusalem; his mother's name was Nehushta, daughter of Elnathan of Jerusalem. He did what was displeasing to the Lord, just as his father [Jehoahaz] had done. At that time the troops of Nebuchadnezzar king of Babylon marched against Jerusalem, and the city came under siege. King Nebuchadnezzar of Babylon advanced the city while his troops were besieging it. Thereupon King Jehoiachin of Judah, along with his mother and his courtiers, commanders, and officers, surrendered to the king of Babylon. The king of Babylon took him captive in the eighth year of his reign. He carried off from Jerusalem all the treasures of the House of the Lord and the treasures of the royal palace; he stripped off all the golden decorations in the Temple of the Lord—which King Solomon of Israel had made—as the Lord had warned. (2 Kings 24:8-13)

By this account Jerusalem was taken but not destroyed, though the Temple was stripped of its remaining treasures. Oddly, there is no mention of the Ark in this connection, though it was assuredly not to be found in any of the later versions of the Temple. Indeed, Jeremiah during the exile that followed the Babylonian assaults was already instructing the Children of Israel that the Ark would play no part in their future restoration:

Turn back, rebellious children—declares the Lord. Though I have rejected you, I will take you, one from a town and two from a clan, and bring you to Sion. I will give you shepherds after My own heart, who will pasture you with knowledge and skill. And when you increase and are fertile in the land, in those days—declares the Lord, men shall no longer speak of the Ark of the Covenant of the Lord, nor shall it come to mind. They shall not mention it, or miss it, or make another. At that time they shall call Jerusalem "Throne of the Lord." . . . (Jeremiah 3:14-17)

This was not the last word on the subject, however. Many centuries later the second book of Maccabees returns knowingly to the fate of the Ark of the Covenant:

The records show that it was the prophet Jeremiah who ordered the exiles to hide the fire [of the Temple altar before being taken off into exile], as has been mentioned; also that, having given them the law, he charged them not to neglect the ordinances of the Lord, or to be led astray [in Babylonia] by the sight of images of gold and silver with all their finery. In similar words he appealed to them not to abandon the law. Further, this document records that, prompted by a divine message, the prophet gave orders that the Tent of the Meeting and the ark should go with him. Then he went away to the mountain [Nebo] from the top of which Moses saw God's promised land. When he reached the mountain, Jeremiah found a cave-dwelling; he carried the tent, the ark and the incense-altar into it, then blocked up the entrance. Some of his companions came to mark out the way, but were unable to find it. When Jeremiah learnt of this he reprimanded them. "The place shall remain unknown," he said, "until God finally gathers his people together and shows mercy to them. Then the Lord will bring these things to light again, and the glory of the Lord will appear with the cloud, as it was seen both in the time of Moses and when Solomon prayed that the shrine might be worthily consecrated." (2 Maccabees 2:1-8)

By the second century A.D., when the Mishna was edited, this recollection was reduced to a faint and distant echo:

There were thirteen Shofar-chests, thirteen tables, and thirteen prostrations in the Temple. They of the House of Gamaliel and of R. Hanina the Prefect of the Priests used to make fourteen prostrations. And where was the added one? Opposite the wood-store, for thus was the tradition among them from their forefathers that there the Ark lay hidden.

Once when a priest was occupied [therein] he saw a block of pavement that was different from the rest. He went in and told his fellow, but before he could make an end of the matter his life departed. So they knew assuredly that there the Ark lay hidden. (Danby 1933: 158)

A second Mishnaic text, this from the tractate Yoma, adds an interesting new detail, which developed a long and complex history. There was, it seems, a stone somehow connected with the Ark, and so the Holy of Holies; it was called the "Stone of Foundation": [23]

. . . He [the high priest] went through the Sanctuary until he came to the space between the two curtains separating the Sanctuary from the Holy of Holies. . . . He went along between them until he reached the north side; when he reached the north he turned round to the south and went on with the curtain on his left hand until he reached the Ark. When he reached the Ark he put the fire-pan between the two bars. He heaped up the incense on the coals and the whole place became filled with smoke. He came out the way he went in, and in the outer space he prayed a short prayer. He did not prolong his prayer lest he put Israel in terror.

After the Ark was taken away a stone remained there from the time of the early prophets [i.e., David and Solomon] and it was called "Shetiyah" (Foundation). On this he used to put [the fire-pan]. (Danby 1933: 167)

Destruction and Exile

To return to Nebuchadnezzar, in 597 the Babylonians did not content themselves with stripping the Temple and departing; following what was by then a common practice, they carried off the most useful members of the community for resettlement in their kingdom in Babylonia:

He [Nebuchadnezzar] exiled all of Jerusalem: all the commanders and all the warriors—ten thousand exiles—as well as all the craftsmen and smiths; only the poorest people of the land were left. He deported Jehoiachin to Babylon; and the king's wives and officers and notables of the land were brought as exiles from Jerusalem to Babylon. All the able men, to the number of seven thousand—all of them warriors trained for battle—and a thousand craftsmen and smiths were brought to Babylon as exiles by the king of Babylon. And the king of Babylon appointed Mattaniah, Jehoiachin's uncle, king in his place, changing his name to Zedekiah. (2 Kings 24:14-17)

The vassal Zedekiah was intended to serve his Babylonian master on the latter's own terms, but such must not have been the case since Nebuchadnezzar returned and in 586 B.C. once again stood before the walls of Jerusalem. There was resistance on the part of the decimated Israelites, but the city fell, as inevitably it had to, and on this occasion the punishment was not looting or the exaction of tribute but the wholesale destruction of the city and another draft of exiles for Babylon:

In the ninth year of his reign, on the tenth day of the tenth month, Nebuchadnezzar moved against Jerusalem with his whole army. He besieged it and built towers against it all around. The city continued in a state of siege until the eleventh year of King Zedekiah. By the ninth day [of the fourth month] the famine had become acute in the city; there was no food left for the common people. Then [the wall of] the city was breached. All the soldiers [left the city] by night through the gate between the double walls, which is near the king's garden—the Chaldeans were all around the city; and [the king] set out for the Arabah.

The attempt to flee was unsuccessful. Zedekiah was captured near Jericho, brought back to Jerusalem and blinded.

On the seventh day of the fifth month—that was the nineteenth year of

King Nebuchadnezzar of Babylon—Nebuzaradan, the chief of the guards, an officer of the king of Babylon, came to Jerusalem. He burned the House of the Lord, the king's palace, and all the houses of Jerusalem; he burned down the house of every notable person. The entire Chaldean force that was with the chief of the guard tore down the walls of Jerusalem on every side. The remnant of the people that was left in the city, the defectors who had gone over to the king of Babylon—and the remnants of the population—were taken into exile by Nebuzaradan, the chief of the guards. But some of the poorest in the land were left by the chief of the guards, to be vinedressers and field hands. (2 Kings 25:1-12)

In 586 Jerusalem stood bare, its walls torn down, its Temple, homes, and public buildings burned, much of its population carried off into exile in Babylonia. The effects of this on the future evolution of the life and cult practices of the Children of Israel were enormous and far-reaching, but to confine ourselves to the city of Jerusalem, the most permanent consequence of the Babylonian assault was the destruction of the City of David and its effective elimination from the future development of the larger city of Jerusalem. Since the Millo so carefully tended by David from the very outset of the Israelite occupation had been torn down, the southeastern spur of the Jerusalem mountain complex could no longer be easily defended, so later generations of Jews, Christians, and Muslims in Jerusalem extended themselves west and north of the Temple mount and left the Ophel to go its own way as an undeveloped suburb, sometimes inside and sometimes outside the city wall, but never again a very important or prosperous part of the city's life. [24]

A Lament for Jerusalem

More than a mere collection of homes and buildings had been affected by the Babylonian assault on the City of David. God's Holy City, this Jerusalem "once called Perfect in beauty, Joy of the whole earth" (Lam. 2:15), had been destroyed, His Temple razed. The theological and spiritual echoes of it, and the sadness too, run deeply through the book of Lamentations:

> *The Lord acted like a foe; he laid waste Israel,*
> *Laid waste all her citadels,*
> *Destroyed her strongholds.*
> *He has increased within Fair Judah,*
> *Mourning and moaning.*

He has stripped His Booth like a garden,
He has destroyed His Tabernacle.
The Lord has ended in Sion
Festival and sabbath;
In His raging anger He has spurned
King and priest.
The Lord has rejected His altar,
Disdained His Sanctuary.
He has handed over to the foe
The walls of its citadels;
and laid a curse upon his sanctuary.
They raised a shout in the House of the Lord
As on a festival day.
The Lord resolved to destroy
The wall of Fair Sion.
He measured with a line, refrained not
From bringing destruction.
He has made wall and rampart to mourn,
Together they languish.
Her gates have sunk into the ground,
He has smashed her bars to bits;
her kings and her leaders are in exile,
Instruction is no more. . . . (Lamentations 2:5-9)

And that other voice of the exile, buried deep in the Book of Psalms, more terrible and unforgiving, but which nonetheless gave the Children of Israel their chief anthem of hope for a city lost and, if they could but keep the memory alive, inevitably to be regained:

By the rivers of Babylon,
  there we sat,
  sat and wept,
  as we thought of Sion.
There on the poplars
  we hung up our lyres,
  for our captors asked us there for songs,
  our tormentors for amusement,
  "Sing us one of the songs of Sion."
How could we sing a song of the Lord on alien soil?

If I forget you, O Jerusalem,
  let my right hand wither;
  let my tongue stick to my palate

32

if I cease to think of you,
if I do not keep Jerusalem in memory
even at my happiest hour.

Remember, O Lord, against the Edomites
the day of Jerusalem's fall;
how they cried "Strip her, strip her
to her very foundations!"
Fair Babylon, you predator,
a blessing on him who repays you in kind
what you have inflicted on us;
a blessing on him who seizes your babies
and dashes them against the rocks! (Psalm 137)

A Vision of the New Jerusalem

Both city and Temple would be rebuilt, as we shall see, but before, during, and even after that occurred, a new vision of Jerusalem and the House of the Lord was being fashioned by the spiritual leaders of the people in exile. It appears, for example, in the perfervid oracles of the prophet Ezekiel, who lived through the Babylonian calamity into a Babylonian exile, and foresaw a new Temple in a new, utopian Jerusalem:

In the twenty-fifth year of our exile, the fourteenth year after the city had fallen, at the beginning of the year, the tenth day of the month—on that very day [probably April 28, 573 B.C.]—the hand of the Lord came upon me and he brought me there. He brought me, in visions of God, to the Land of Israel, and He set me on a very high mountain on which there seemed to be the outline of a city on the south. He brought me over to it, and there, standing at the gate, was a man who shone like copper. In his hand were a cord of linen and a measuring rod. The man spoke to me: "Mortal, look closely and listen attentively and note well everything I am going to show you—for you have been brought here in order to be shown—and report everything you see to the House of Israel." (Ezekiel 40:1-4)

Then he led me to a gate, a gate that faced east. And there, coming from the east with a roar like the roar of mighty waters, was the Presence of the God of Israel, and the earth was lit up by His Presence. The vision was like the vision I had seen when He came to destroy the city, the very same vision that I had seen by the Chebar Canal. Forthwith, I fell on my face.

The Presence of the Lord entered the Temple by the gate that faced eastward.

33

A spirit carried me into the inner court, and lo, the Presence of the Lord filled the Temple; and I heard speech addressed to me from the Temple, though the man was standing beside me. It said to me:

"O mortal, this is the place of My throne and the place for the soles of My feet, where I will dwell in the midst of the people of Israel forever. . . . You, O mortal, describe the Temple to the House of Israel, and let them measure its design. But let them be ashamed of their iniquities. . . . Such are the instructions for the Temple on the top of the mountain: the entire area of its enclosure shall be most holy. . . ." (Ezekiel: 43:1-12)

He led me back to the outer gate of the Sanctuary that faced east; it was shut. And the Lord said to me: This gate is to be kept shut, and is not be opened! No one shall enter by it because the Lord, the God of Israel, has entered by it; therefore it shall remain shut. Only the prince may sit in it and eat bread before the Lord, since he is a prince; he shall enter by way of the vestibule of the gate, and shall depart by the same way. (Ezekiel: 44:1-3)

Whatever his intent, Ezekiel's words had in fact a permanent effect on the topography of Jerusalem. The eastern side of the Temple area, and the gate that was and is called Golden and still stands sealed there today, acquired a profound Messianic significance. It was there, by tradition, that Jesus entered the city, and it is still there that, faces turned toward the east, Jews, Christians, and Muslims await the coming of Ezekiel's prince as Mahdi or Messiah.

The Return to the Holy City

The restoration of Jerusalem and its Temple took place by means and on a scale somewhat less dramatic than envisioned by Ezekiel. With a change of regime in Mesopotamia, where the more relaxed and tolerant Achemenians of Iran replaced the lords of Babylon, the Jewish exiles who wished to return to Judea were permitted to do so. What followed is told in the biblical books of Ezra and Nehemiah, and though we cannot sort out the relationship and chronology of the two with perfect assurance, the overall portrait is clear enough, from the very opening of the book of Ezra:

In the first year of King Cyrus of Persia [538 B.C.], when the word of the Lord spoken by Jeremiah was fulfilled, the Lord roused the spirit of King Cyrus Persia to issue a proclamation throughout his realm by word of mouth and in writing as follows:

"Thus said King Cyrus of Persia: The Lord of Heaven has given me all the kingdoms of the earth and has charged me with building Him a house

in Jerusalem, which is in Judah. Anyone of you of all His people—may his God be with him, and let him go up to Jerusalem that is in Judah and build the House of the Lord the God of Israel, the God that is in Jerusalem; and who stay behind, wherever he may be living, let the people of his place assist him [that is, the returnee] with silver, gold, goods, and livestock, beside the freewill offerings to the House of God in Jerusalem. (Ezra 1:1-4)

The statement is calm and matter of fact, but the reaction among the exiles must have been one of relief and jubilation, and we catch an echo of it in the words of "Second Isaiah," the anonymous prophet of the exile whose utterances have been attached to the book called after the visionary of Hezekiah's time:

> *Comfort, oh comfort My people,*
> *Says your God*
> *Speak tenderly to Jerusalem*
> *and declare to her*
> *That her term of service is over,*
> *that her iniquity is expiated;*
> *For she has received at the hand of the Lord*
> *double for all her sins.* (Isaiah 40:1-2)
>
> *Awake, awake, O Sion!*
> *Clothe yourself in splendor;*
> *Put on your robes of majesty,*
> *Jerusalem, holy city!*
> *For the uncircumcised and the unclean*
> *Shall never enter you again.*
>
> *Arise, shake off the dust,*
> *Sit [on your throne], Jerusalem!*
> *Loose the bonds from your neck,*
> *O captive one, Fair Sion!* (Isaiah: 52:1)

The Cult of the Lord Restored

Among the first of the projects undertaken by the returnees was the restoration of the sacrificial worship of the God of Israel in the only place where that was now possible, on the Temple mount in Jerusalem:

When the seventh month arrived—the Israelites being settled in their towns—the entire people assembled as one man in Jerusalem. Then Jeshua son of Jozadak and his fellow priests, and Zerubbabel son of Shealtiel and his brothers set to and built the altar of the God of Israel to offer burnt offerings upon it as is written in the Teaching of Moses. They set up the altar on its site because they were in fear of the peoples of the land, and they offered burnt offerings on it to the Lord, burnt offerings each morning and evening. Then they celebrated festival of Tabernacles as is written, with its daily burnt offerings in the proper quantities, on each day as is prescribed for it, followed by the regular burnt offerings and the offerings for the new moons and for all the sacred fixed times of the Lord, and whatever freewill offerings were made to the Lord. From the first day of the seventh month they began to make burnt offerings to the Lord, though the foundation of the Temple of the Lord had not been laid. . . . In the second year after their arrival at the House of God at Jerusalem, in the second month, Zerubbabel son of Shealtiel and Jeshua son of Jozadak, and the rest of their brother priests and Levites, and all who had come from captivity to Jerusalem, as their first step appointed Levites from the age of twenty and upward to supervise the work of the House of the Lord. . . .

When the builders had laid the foundations of the Temple of the Lord, priests in their vestments with trumpets, Levites sons of Asaph with cymbals were stationed to give praise the Lord, as King David of Israel had prescribed. . . . All the people raised a great shout extolling the Lord because the foundation of the House of the Lord had been laid. Many of the priests and Levites and the chiefs of clans, the old men who had seen the first house, wept loudly at the sight of the founding of this house. Many others shouted joyously at the top of their voices. The people could not distinguish the shouts of joy from the people's weeping, for the people raised a great shout, the sound of which could be heard from afar. (Ezra 3:1-13)

Nehemiah in Jerusalem

The exiles' fears concerning the local population were well-founded. The Samaritans in particular, the Israelites' relatives and rivals from the old northern kingdom, violently opposed the reopening of the Judean Temple. The argument was inevitably carried to the shah, where it dragged on for years. Sometime during that interval, in 445 B.C. perhaps, a new figure enters upon the scene. Ezra was a member of the religious community, a scribe, and a priest; but Nehemiah the Jew, on the other hand, was a high secular official at the shah's court, the "cup-bearer of the king."

In the month of Kislev of the twentieth year, when I was in the fortress of Shushan [that is, Susa], Hanani, one of my brothers, together with some men of Judah, arrived, and I asked them about the Jews, the remnant who had survived the captivity, and about Jerusalem. They replied, "The survivors who have survived the captivity there in the province are in dire trouble and disgrace; Jerusalem's wall is full of breaches, and its gates had been destroyed by fire." When I heard that, I sat and wept. . . . (Nehemiah 1:1-4)

The highly placed Nehemiah requested permission of the shah to return to "the city where my forefathers are buried" and to rebuild its walls and citadel. Permission was granted.

When Sanballat the Horonite and Tobiah the Ammonite servant heard, it displeased them greatly that someone had come, intent on improving the condition of the Israelites. I arrived in Jerusalem. After I was there three days I got up at night, I and a few men with me, and telling no one what my God had put into my mind to do for Jerusalem, and taking no other beast than the one on which I was riding, I went out by the Valley Gate, at night, towards the Jackals' Spring and the Dung Gate; and I surveyed the walls of Jerusalem that were breached, and its gates, consumed by fire. I proceeded to the Fountain Gate and to the King's Pool, where there was no room for the beast under me to continue. So I went up the wadi by night, surveying the wall, and, entering again by the Valley Gate, I returned. The prefects knew nothing of where I had gone or what I had done, since I had not yet divulged it to the Jews—the priests, the nobles, the prefects, or the rest of the officials. (Nehemiah: 2:10-16)

Setting up an altar in Jerusalem was a religious affront to the Samaritans, who worshipped Yahweh exclusively on Mount Gerizim, but the reconstruction of the walls of Jerusalem was another matter entirely, a piece of political daring that challenged the local Samaritan, Ammonite, and Arab dynasts who regarded Judea as either innocuous or their own possession (Neh. 2:19). Nehemiah went ahead with the work nonetheless, often under armed protection, and we are given a detailed account of it in the third chapter of the book transmitted under his name, which thus provides the most complete and specific information we possess on the topography of Israelite Jerusalem. From it and the admittedly scanty archeological evidence from this period it is possible to fashion some idea of the shape and extent of Jerusalem during its time of recovery from the disaster visited upon it by the Babylonians. [25]

The city had been grievously depopulated, as Nehemiah himself confesses (11:1-2)—one modern estimate puts the population at 10,000 [26]—and the absence on the western hill of the remains of any buildings from Nehemiah's day strongly suggests that Jerusalem had contracted back to its earlier configuration of a city more or less around the Ophel spur. [27] There were some houses in the city when the exiles returned since the Babylonians had not burned all the private dwellings (2 Kgs. 25:9), and there were frequent complaints that the new arrivals spent more time with their own homes than in attempting to rebuild the Temple (Haggai 1:4, 9). More, in the account in Nehemiah 3 it is often individuals' houses that are used as reference points in allocating responsibility for rebuilding sectors of the wall. Even the wall itself, with its elaborate nomenclature of gates, indicates that enough of at least the old city survived to enable the new builders to attempt to restore it and not build it afresh.

Nehemiah seems to have assigned the reconstruction of each segment of the wall to the groups that lived near it. On that basis it appears that the specialized bazaars, like those of the goldsmiths and spice dealers were ranged along the western side of the city, while the priests and Temple servants lived, as we might expect, at its eastern side, close to the Temple. On the north the prospect was more military, with two towers—the Tower of Hananel and the Tower of the Hundred—ranged across the northern stretch of the Temple area, perhaps in its northwest corner; this may have constituted the citadel that Nehemiah had received permission to reconstruct (Neh. 2:8). [28] And it is this same place that figures in Nehemiah's arrangements for the civil administration of the city:

When the wall was rebuilt, and I had set up the doors, tasks were assigned to the gate-keepers, the singers, and the Levites. I put Hanani my brother and Hananiah, the captain of the fortress, in charge of Jerusalem, for he was a more trustworthy and God-fearing than most. I said to them, "The gates of Jerusalem are not to be opened until the heat of the day, and before you leave your posts let the gates be closed and barred. And assign the inhabitants of Jerusalem to watches, each man to his watch, and each in front of his own house."

The city was broad and large, the people in it were few, and houses were not yet built. My God put it into my mind to assemble the nobles, the prefects, and the people, in order to register them by families. I found the genealogical register of those who were the first to come back. . . . (Nehemiah 7:1-5)

The officers of the people settled in Jerusalem; the rest of the people cast lots for one out of ten to come and settle in the holy city of Jerusalem, and the other nine-tenths to stay in the towns. The people gave their blessing to all the men who willingly settled in Jerusalem. (Nehemiah: 11:1-2)

When all was finally in order, there took place a formal dedication of the walls and, incidentally, another tour of the terrain of the new Jerusalem:

At the dedication of the wall of Jerusalem, the Levites, wherever they lived were sought out and brought to Jerusalem to celebrate a joyful dedication with thanksgiving and with song, accompanied by cymbals, harps, and lyres. . . . The priests and Levites purified themselves; then they purified the people, and the gates, and the wall. I had the officers of Judah go up onto the wall, and I appointed two large thanksgiving [choirs] and processions. [One marched] south on the wall, to the Dung Gate. . . . From there to Fountain Gate, where they ascended the steps of the City of David directly before them, by the ascent on the wall, above the house of David, [and onward] to the Water Gate on the east. The other thanksgiving [choir] marched on the wall in the opposite direction, with me and half the people behind it, above the Tower of Ovens to the Broad Wall; and above the Gate of Ephraim, the Jeshanah Gate, the Fish Gate, the Tower of Hananel, the Tower of the Hundred, to the Sheep Gate; and they halted at the Gate of the Prison Compound, both thanksgiving choirs halted at the House of God. . . . (Nehemiah 12:27-40)

The Second Temple

There was still no formal Temple structure in Jerusalem, however, and the task of rebuilding it figures nowhere in the plans of Nehemiah, whose post was a purely civil one. The initiative came from quite another source, the prophets Haggai and Zechariah, and with explicit permission of the Shah Darius:

"Now you, Tattenai, [the decree ran] governor of the province of Beyond the River [Euphrates], Shethar-bozenai, and colleagues, the officials of the province of Beyond the River, stay away from the place. Allow the work of this House of God to go on; let the governor of the Jews and the elders of the Jews rebuild this House of God on its [original] site. And I hereby issue an order concerning what you must do to help these elders of the Jews rebuild this House of God: the expenses are to be paid to these men with dispatch out of the resources of the king, derived from the taxes of the province of Beyond the River, so that the work not be stopped. They are to be given daily, without fail, whatever they need of young bulls, rams, or lambs as burnt offerings for the God of Heaven, and wheat, salt, wine, and oil, at the order of the priests in Jerusalem, so that they may offer pleasing sacrifices to the God of Heaven and pray for the life of the king and his sons."

Then Tattenai, [Achaemenian] governor of the province of Beyond the River, Shethar-bozenai, and their colleagues carried out with dispatch what King Darius had written. So the elders of the Jews progressed in the *building, urged on by the prophesying of Haggai the prophet and Zechariah son of Iddo, and they brought the building to completion under the aegis of the God of Israel and by the order of Cyrus and Darius and King Artaxerxes of Persia. The house was completed on the third of the month of Adar in the sixth year of the reign of King Darius. (Ezra 6:6-15)*

Thus we are given to believe that Zerubbabel's Temple stood where Solomon's had before it. [29] We have no reason to think otherwise as regards the site. But even though we are assured through Haggai that people old enough to remember Solomon's building found the new Temple not unlike the old (Haggai 2:3), it is difficult to think of this as anything but a validation of authenticity. Solomon's resources and ambitions in the tenth century B.C. were substantially greater than those of Zerubbabel in the fifth, and the Second Temple, like the rebuilt Jerusalem, must have reflected the straitened circumstances of the people who lived there, as those priests and Levites and elders whom we saw weeping in disappointment at the sight of the new Temple's foundations poignantly attests.

But a fresh start had been made in Jerusalem, and the hopes earlier expressed by Isaiah seemed to Zechariah, the prophet of this age who was present at the momentous beginnings, now at last close to fulfillment:

Thus said the Lord of Hosts: Take courage, you who now hear these words which the prophets spoke when the foundations were laid for the rebuilding of the Temple, the House of the Lord of Hosts.

Thus said the Lord, I have returned to Sion, and I will dwell in Jerusalem. Jerusalem will be called the City of Faithfulness and the mountain of the Lord of Hosts the Holy Mountain.

Thus said the Lord of Hosts: Once again there shall be old men and old women in the squares of Jerusalem, each with staff in hand because of their great age. And the squares of the city shall be crowded with boys and girls playing in the squares. . . . I will rescue my people from the lands of the east and lands of the west, I will bring them back home to dwell in Jerusalem. They shall be my people and I shall be their God—in truth and sincerity. (Zechariah 8:9, 3-8)

Finally, the Mosaic constitution of the restored Jewish theocracy had once again to be promulgated, and it is here perhaps that Ezra enters the story of Jerusalem:

After these events, during the reign of King Artaxerxes of Persia . . . Ezra came up from Babylon. He was a scribe expert in the Teaching of Moses which the Lord the God of Israel had given, whose request the king had granted in its entirety, thanks to the benevolence of the Lord toward him. . . . For Ezra had dedicated himself to study the Teaching of the Lord so as to observe it, and to teach laws and rules to Israel. (Ezra 7:1-10)

When the seventh month arrived—the Israelites being [settled] in their towns—the entire people assembled as one man in the square before the Water Gate, and they asked Ezra the scribe to bring the scroll of the Teaching of Moses, with which the Lord had charged Israel. On the first day of the seventh month, Ezra the priest brought the Teaching before the congregation, men and women and all who could listen with understanding. He read from it, facing the square before the Water Gate, from the first light until midday, to the men and women and those who could understand; the ears of all the people were given to the scroll of the Teaching.

Ezra the scribe stood on a wooden tower made for the purpose. . . . Ezra opened the scroll in the sight of all the people, for he was above all the people; as he opened it, all the people stood up. Ezra blessed the Lord, the great God, and all the people answered "Amen, Amen" with hands upraised. Then they bowed their heads and prostrated themselves before the Lord with the faces to the ground. Jeshua, Bani, Sherebiah, Jamin, Akkub, Shabbethai, Hodiah, Maaseiah, Kelita, Azariah, Jozabad, Hanan, Pelaiah, the Levites explained the Teaching to the people, while the people stood in their places. They read from the scroll of the Teaching of God, translating it [into Aramaic] and giving the sense, so they understood the reading. (Nehemiah 8:1-8)

By 400 B.C., then, Jerusalem was the slowly reviving center of a modest Jewish temple-state in Judea. There were subsidies from the shah to ease what must have been difficult economic circumstances in a city that had few resources in the best of times. The book of Ezra notes that aid. But its chief concerns lay elsewhere. The closing chapters of that work are given over to Ezra's strenuous efforts to reestablish the tribal and religious purity of the people of Israel, even to the point of dissolving long-standing marriages. It is not a new motif—the religious leaders of the Jews had struggled since Sinai against contamination and assimilation—but at this point it seems somewhat outstripped by circumstances: within less than a century Judea, and indeed all of the Jewish communities that were beginning to take root outside of Palestine as well, would be faced by a challenge far more alluring and dangerous than foreign brides.

Jews and Greeks in Jerusalem

*So Hellenism reached a high point with the introduction of foreign
customs. . . . As a result, the priests no longer had any enthusiasm
for their duties at the altar, but despised the Temple and neglected
the sacrifices. . . . They cared nothing for their hereditary dignities,
but cared above everything for Hellenic honors.*
—2 Maccabees

ACCORDING to a tale first told by Josephus in his *Jewish Antiquities*, Alexander the Great turned aside from his conquest of Gaza in the summer of 332 B.C. and went up to Jerusalem to settle a dispute between the Jews and the Samaritans. There is little truth in the story, as its own details betray; Alexander actually went directly from Gaza to Egypt. But it was inconceivable to a later generation of Jews that one of the great legendary figures of Near Eastern history should not acknowledge, at least by his presence, the Holy City and the religious community that had its center there. Later rabbis, too, however fierce they might have been in their condemnation of the Hellenism, whose chief herald Alexander was, took the romance of the great conqueror into their embrace. [1]

Alexander did not introduce Hellenism to Palestine; the material remains of Greek culture appear at Palestinian sites well before his arrival and hasty departure. There is no such evidence at Jerusalem, however; for all its Jewish celebrity, the city was too remote from the commercial and strategic considerations of the eastern Mediterranean world over which the values, the style, and the ideas of the Greeks were slowly spreading in the fourth pre-Christian century. Even after Greek influence yielded to Greek sovereignty over Palestine in the generations after Alexander, Jerusalem continues to show almost no archeological trace of the Hellenic artifacts and style that everywhere begin to mark the presence of the new Greek rulers. [2]

Jerusalem in 300 B.C.

Hellenic curiosity far outstripped Greek sovereignty, however, and the generation of Greeks who succeeded Alexander developed an appetite for the manners and customs of the once despised *barbaroi* who lived beyond the pale of Hellenism. One of these Greeks was Hecateus of Abdera, who in about 300 B.C. knew a good deal about Jerusalem. The source is Josephus, who is quoting an otherwise lost work by Hecateus:

Again, here is his description of Jerusalem itself, the city which we have inhabited from remote ages, of its great beauty and extent, its numerous population, and the Temple buildings: "The Jews have many fortresses and villages in different parts of the country, but only one fortified city, which has a circumference of fifty stades [about 10 miles] and some 120,000 inhabitants; they call it Jerusalem. Nearly in the center of the city stands a stone wall, enclosing an area about five plethra [500 ft.] long and a hundred cubits [about 150 ft.] broad, approached by a pair of gates. Within this enclosure is a square altar, built of heaped up stones, unhewn and unwrought; each side is twenty cubits [30 ft.] long and the height is ten cubits [15 ft.]. Beside it is a great edifice, containing an altar and a lampstand, both made of gold and weighing two talents; upon these is a light which is never extinguished by night or day. There is not a single statue or votive offering, no trace of a plant, in the form of a sacred grove or the like. Here priests pass their nights and days performing certain rites of purification, and abstaining altogether from wine while in the temple." (Josephus, Against Apion: 196-199)

So the city appeared to a Greek not too long after Alexander had come and gone from the Near East. Somewhat later the city entertained a Jewish visitor, a certain Aristeas, who was supposedly part of an embassy to Palestine but whose account of Jerusalem reads more like the visit of a pilgrim to the Holy City. The time is uncertain, perhaps as early as 270 B.C. or as late as 130 B.C.:

When we reached the area we saw the city situated in the center of all Judea atop a mountain which rises up to a great height. The Temple stood on its top in great splendor; and there were three encompassing walls, about seventy cubits [about 105 ft.] in height and of a breadth and length in proportion to the construction of the building. The whole of it was built with a lavishness and a richness beyond all comparison. From the construction of the doorway and its fastenings to the door-posts and the solidity of the lintel it was clear that no expense had been spared in it. . . .

The building faces toward the east and its back is to the west. The whole floor is paved with stones and slopes downward in such as way as to permit its being flushed with water so as to wash away the blood of the sacrifices; for many myriads of animals are offered there on the feast days. The water supply is inexhaustible since there is an abundant natural spring that gushes out from inside the Temple area, and in addition there are remarkable underground reservoirs which cannot be described. These ex-

tend, as was said, to a distance of five stades around the foundations of the Temple. Each of these reservoirs have many pipes, so that the various channels converge at the several reservoirs. The floors and sides of these reservoirs, it was explained, were overlaid with lead, and then thickly plastered, so that everything was rendered secure. There were many outlets, they said, at the foot of the altar, visible only to those who were engaged in the services, so that the vast accumulation of sacrificial blood is cleansed away almost instantly. . . .

So that we might understand everything, we went up on the city's citadel which is situated nearby [the Temple] and we looked around us. The citadel is located on a very high point and is fortified with a number of towers which are built out of large blocks of stone to the very top, as a protection, so we were told, for the Temple precincts. Thus, in the event of any attack or revolution or enemy invasion, no one could make his way onto the walls which surround the Temple. On the towers of the citadel there are set ballistae and various other engines of war, and their great height commands the previously mentioned. More, the towers are guarded by the most trustworthy men. . . . They were extremely careful even when they had received an order from their commander to admit certain visitors as sightseers, as happened in our case, and even though we were unarmed and there were only two of us, they would barely admit us to study the arrangements for the sacrifices. They told us they were bound to such behavior by oaths: they had all sworn, and of necessity and from religious scruple they fulfilled the terms of their oath, so that even though they were five hundred in number, they would not admit more than five persons at the same time; the citadel was, in fact, the entire defense of the Temple, and the one who built it had thus secured its protection.[3]

And the following passage suggests that we are already looking upon the patterned, right-angle layout of a Hellenistic city imposed on the familiar undulating topography of Jerusalem:

The extent of the city is middling [or symmetrical], its extent being about forty stades, as far as one can guess. In the location of its towers and of its thoroughfares, some of which appear above and some below, with cross-streets cutting across them, it has the familiar appearance of a theater, for, since the city is built atop a mountain, its parts rise one above another, and there are stairs to the thorough streets. Some people make their way to the higher level and some come down to the lower, and they are careful to keep apart from each other as they walk, so that those who are in a state of purification may not touch anything impure. (Letter of Aristeas)

Jerusalem under the Greek Monarchies

After Alexander, the Ptolemies ruled Palestine from Egypt for a spell; then in 200 B.C. they were replaced by the Seleucids, another dynasty founded by one of Alexander's generals, who eventually held sway over most of Western Asia from their capital at Antioch. We learn little from either the archeological or the literary sources about Ptolemaic hegemony over Jerusalem. Rather, record of the Jewish experience of Greek rule in their homeland begins with the Seleucids:

When Antiochus the Great [223-187 B.C.] reigned over Asia it was the lot of the Jews, as also of the inhabitants of Coele-Syria, to undergo great hardships through the devastation of their land. For while Antiochus was at war with Ptolemy Philopator and with his son Ptolemy, surnamed Epiphanes, and whether he was victorious or defeated, they experienced the same fate. . . . But not long afterward Antiochus defeated [the Egyptian general] Scopas in a battle near the sources of the Jordan [200 B.C.], and destroyed a greater part of his army. And later, when Antiochus took possession of the cities in Coele-Syria which Scopas had held, and Samaria, the Jews of their own will went over to him and admitted him to their city and made abundant provision for his entire army and his elephants; and they readily joined his forces in besieging the garrison which had been left by Scopas in the citadel of Jerusalem. Accordingly, Antiochus, considering it just to requite the zeal and exertions of the Jews on his behalf, wrote to his governors and Friends (of the King), bearing witness to the Jews concerning the good treatment he had received at their hands and announcing the rewards which he had decided to give them on that account. . . . (Josephus, Ant. XII 3, 3⁴)

Jewish Privileges, 200 B.C.

Josephus then reproduces the document Antiochus wrote, which carries us right into the heart of the complex and often tortured relations between the Jerusalem Jews and their Greco-Macedonian sovereigns in Antioch:

King Antiochus to Ptolemy, greetings. Since the Jews, beginning from the time that we entered their territory, have testified to their zeal in our regard, and since, from our arrival in their city they have received us in a magnificent manner and came out to meet us with their senate [gerousia, literally "Council of Elders"], have contributed generously to the upkeep of our soldiers and our elephants, and have assisted us in capturing the Egyptian garrison in the citadel [akra], we have judged it proper that

*we too should respond to those good offices by restoring their city de-
stroyed by the misfortunes of war and repopulating it by bringing back
all those people dispersed from it.*

*First we have decided by reasons of piety to furnish for the sacrifices a
contribution of sacrificial offerings and wine and oil and incense to the
value of 20,000 [drachmas] of silver, and of flour of grain in sacred artabas
according to the measure of the country, 1,460 mediamni of wheat and
375 mediamni of salt. I wish all these contributions be furnished them as
I have commanded and that the work on the Temple be achieved, the
stoas and whatever else needs be built. Let wood be provided from both
Judea itself and from among the other peoples and from the Lebanon,
without being taxed. Likewise for the other things required to make the
restoration of the Temple outstanding.*

*All of that people will be governed according to their ancestral laws,
and their Council of Elders and priests and scribes of the Temple and the
sacred chanters will be exempt from the capitation tax, the crown tax, and
that on salt. And so that the city might more quickly be repopulated, I
grant to those who now live in it and those who will return until the
month of Hyperberetaios to be exempt from tax for a period of three
years. Further we exempt them in the future from one third of the taxes
in order to compensate them for their losses. As for those who have been
taken from the city and reduced to slavery, to them and their offspring we
grant their freedom and bid their goods be restored to them. (Josephus,
Ant. XII, 3, 3)*

This is in many ways a unique document, the oldest Greek decree pertaining to Jerusalem and establishing the rights and privileges of the Jews
under the Seleucid monarchy.[5] It is contracted between the king and the
"Council of Elders," the ruling body of the Jews, called the "Sanhedrin"
in Roman times, though what their powers and functions were at this
period is unknown. In gratitude for their support against the Egyptians,
Antiochus proposes to rebuild the city, which was on more than one occasion the scene of fighting between the Ptolemies and the Seleucids in
202-200 B.C. Antiochus had good reason to reward his supporters in Jerusalem; as it turned out, the Ptolemies had their faction in the city as
well.

Antiochus did more than rebuild the city of Jerusalem, however; he
guaranteed that "all of that people [*ethnos*] will be governed by their ancestral laws." These ancestral laws were of course the Mosaic Law, the
founding charter of the Jews and the principle that constituted them in
Antiochus' eyes a single people, the "*ethnos* of the Jews," as other texts call
them. The guarantee was not new. Josephus says that the Ptolemies and

even Alexander himself had given such a promise earlier, and we have already seen (Chapter One) that the Persian shah had issued a similar guarantee to the exiles returned from Babylonia.

The Finances of the Temple

In this same passage Antiochus undertook to underwrite the cost of sacrifices in the Temple. Jewish law provided tithe income for the priests and Levites who served in the Temple [6] but said nothing about the expenses of the prescribed sacrifices. Ezekiel, writing during the Exile and dreaming of restoration, proposed that the future and idealized prince of Israel bear the costs of all the expensive sacrifices made on behalf of the people:

The burnt offerings, the meal offerings, and the libations on [pilgrimage] festivals, new moons, sabbaths—all fixed occasions—of the House of Israel shall be the obligation of the prince; he shall provide the sin offering, the meal offerings, the burnt offerings, and the offerings of well-being, to make expiation for the House of Israel. (Ezekiel 45:17[7])

No such prince arrived, of course, and the Temple, without endowed lands or estates, had to make shift as it could. One resource was a new tax voluntarily undertaken by the people at the time of Nehemiah and specifically earmarked for the Temple sacrifices:

We have laid upon ourselves obligations: To charge ourselves one third of a shekel yearly for the service of the House of our God—for the rows of bread, for the regular meal offering and the regular burnt offering, [for those of the] sabbaths, new moons, festivals, for consecrations, for sin offerings to atone for Israel, and for all the work in the House of our God. (Nehemiah 10:32-33)

We hear no more of this voluntary tax, however, until the second century B.C., when it is apparently revived as a half-shekel Temple tax and justified as a religious obligation, possibly for the benefit of Diaspora Jews, by reference back to the Mosaic legislation in Exodus 30:12-16. [8] But this tax was levied under the Jewish sovereigns called Hasmoneans and Herodians. In the third century B.C. it was the pagan Antiochus who ruled Judea, and *he* bore the expense, and the ruler's privilege, of underwriting the sacrifices; this practice was resumed when the Romans took formal possession of Judea in A.D. 6. [9]

The custom of supporting the Temple sacrifices continued under later Seleucid sovereigns, as this passage from the Book of Maccabees attests, even as it reveals some of the temptations and mischief associated with the Temple's finances:

During the rule of High Priest Onias, the Holy City enjoyed complete peace and prosperity, and the laws were still observed most scrupulously, because he was a pious man and hated wickedness. The [Seleucid] kings themselves held the sanctuary in honor and used to embellish the Temple with the most splendid gifts; even Seleucus [Seleucus IV Philopator, 187-175 B.C.], king of Asia, bore all the expenses of the sacrificial worship from his own revenues.

But a certain Simon, of the clan Bilgah, who had been appointed administrator of the Temple, quarrelled with the high priest about the regulation of the city market. Unable to get the better of Onias, he went to Apollonius, son of Thraseus, then governor of Coele-Syria and Phoenicia, and alleged that the treasury at Jerusalem was filled with untold riches—indeed the total of the accumulated balances was incalculable and did not correspond with the account for the sacrifices; he suggested that their balances might be brought under the control of the king. When Apollonius met the king, he reported what he had been told about the riches. The king selected Heliodorus, his chief minister, with orders to remove these treasures.

When he [Heliodorus] arrived in Jerusalem and had been courteously received by the high priest and the citizens, he explained why he had come: he told them about the allegations and asked if they were in fact true. The high priest intimated that the deposits were held in trust for widows and orphans, apart from what belonged to Hyrcanus, the son of Tobias, a man of very high standing; the matter was being misrepresented by the impious Simon. In all there were four hundred talents of silver and two hundred of gold. It was unthinkable, he said, that wrong should be done to those who had relied on the sanctity of the place, on the dignity and inviolability of the world-famous Temple. But Heliodorus, in virtue of the king's orders, replied that these deposits without question be handed over to the royal treasury. [10] *(2 Maccabees 3:1-13)*

Josephus later tells us that Antiochus III (the Great) also intervened directly in the religious matters of the Temple in Jerusalem, announcing by public proclamation that the force of royal command now stood behind the Jews' own prescriptions of ritual purity. [11]

Now these were the contents of the letter. And out of reverence for the Temple he also published throughout the kingdom a grave and holy public notice with these terms. "It is prohibited for any foreigner to go into the sanctuary forbidden to the Jews themselves, except for those who have been purified and are so permitted according to the ancestral law. It is prohibited to bring into the city either horsemeat or the flesh of a mule or a wild or domesticated ass, of the panther, the fox, or the hare, or in general of any of the animals forbidden to the Jews. It is prohibited bringing in their skins. Nor can they be raised in the city. It is prohibited using any but traditionally butchered animals, from among which it is also prescribed that the sacrifices for God be chosen. Whoever shall transgress any one of these [prohibitions] shall pay to the priests a fine of 3,000 silver drachmas."[12] (Josephus, Ant. XII, 3, 4)

The Hellenization of Jerusalem

Onto this apparently placid scene in 175 B.C. came "that wicked man" Antiochus IV, surnamed, in the ordinary grandiose style of the times, "Epiphanes," the "God-Made-Manifest":[13]

Alexander [the Great] had reigned twelve years when he died [323 B.C.]. His generals took over the government, each in his own province. On his death they were all crowned as kings, and their descendants succeeded them for many years. They brought untold miseries upon the world.
   A scion of this stock was that wicked man Antiochus Epiphanes, son of King Antiochus [III]. He had been a hostage in Rome before he succeeded to the throne in the year 137 of the Greek era [175 B.C.]. At that time there appeared in Israel a group of renegade Jews who incited the people. "Let us enter into a covenant with the Gentiles round about," they said, "because disaster after disaster has overtaken us since we segregated ourselves from them." The people thought this a good argument, and some of them in their enthusiasm went to the king and received authority to introduce non-Jewish laws and customs. They built a sports stadium in Gentile style in Jerusalem. They removed the marks of their circumcision and they repudiated the holy covenant. They intermarried with Gentiles and abandoned themselves to evil ways. (1 Maccabees 1:7-16)

The author of the first book of Maccabees had the advantage of considerable hindsight on the matter of Antiochus IV, but as the text readily admits, the Greek king had neither planted the enthusiasm for things Greek among the Jews of Jerusalem nor even encouraged them to pursue that enthusiasm by introducing some of the hallmarks of urban Hellenism into the city. The initiative came from within, from the "Hellenizers" among the Jews in what was by then a large and populous and prosperous city, as both Hecateus and Aristeas bore witness. Jews were spreading all over the eastern Mediterranean, and their prosperity was shared by Jerusalem, or at least by the upper class constituted by the higher priesthoods and those most intimately connected with the Holy City's chief and almost unique business, the Temple. And with prosperity came the attraction to the life and the mores of the people who had brought it, the Hellenes. Not their gods, certainly, which every Jew despised, but the easily identified style that manifested itself in the art and the architecture that was beginning to fill up the Near Eastern landscape and in the manner of life that was on prominent and attractive display in Alexandria, where many Jews now lived. Hellenism had no need of Antiochus Epiphanes to make its case: the Jews themselves reached out for it, and the Seleucid sovereign was happy to oblige. [14]

Antioch-at-Jerusalem

But when Seleucus was dead [175 B.C.] and had been succeeded by Antiochus, known as Epiphanes, Jason, Onias' brother, obtained the high priesthood by corrupt means. He petitioned the king and promised him 360 talents in silver coin immediately and 80 talents from future revenues. In addition he undertook to pay another 150 talents for the authority to institute a sports stadium, to arrange for the education of young men there, and to enroll in Jerusalem a group to be known as "Antiochenes." The king agreed, and as soon as he had seized the high priesthood, Jason made the Jews conform to the Greek way of life.

He set aside the royal privileges established for the Jews through the agency of John, the father of that Eupolemus who negotiated a treaty of friendship and alliance with the Romans. He abolished the lawful way of life and introduced practices which were against the law. He lost no time in establishing a sports stadium at the foot of the citadel itself, and he made the most outstanding of the young men assume the Greek athlete's hat. So Hellenism reached a high point with the introduction of foreign customs through the boundless wickedness of the impious Jason, no true high priest. As a result, the priests no longer had any enthusiasm for their duties at the altar, but despised the Temple and neglected the sacrifices; and in defiance of the law they eagerly contributed to the expenses of the wrestling school whenever the opening gong called them. They placed no honor on their hereditary dignities, but cared above everything for Hellenic honors. . . . (2 Maccabees 4:7-16)

Josephus has his own, somewhat more political version of the same events:

About this same time High Priest Onias also died, and Antiochus gave

The Madaba map of Jerusalem (ca. A.D. 570). The view is from the west and above. Two colonnaded Roman-era *cardos*, or market streets, running north-south across the city are clearly visible, as are the Damascus Gate on the north (left) and the Church of the Holy Sepulcher in the center.

The Chapel of the Ascension, on the site of the ancient Imbomon, with flanking minaret. The present structure is post-Crusader.

Facing page. The eastern hill of Jerusalem from the south. The ridge of the hill in the foreground is the site of the "City of David," the earliest Israelite settlement at Jerusalem.

PICTORIAL ARCHIVE (Near Eastern History) Est., The Old School, P.O. Box 19823, Jerusalem.

Aerial view from the north of the Church of the Holy Sepulcher as it looks today. The large dome right of center sits atop Jesus' tomb. On the left is the line of the chief Roman cardo of Jerusalem, and above, to the south of the church, the criss-crossed area that was once the site of Hadrian's forum, later that of the Crusader Hospital, and is now called the Muristan.

Facing page. The entry to the Greek architect Comnenus' edicule beneath the dome of the Church of the Holy Sepulcher (1808).

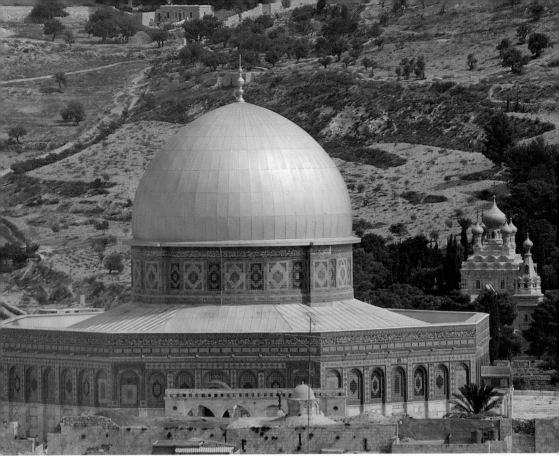

The Muslims' Dome of the Rock on the Haram al-Sharif (A.D. 692), from the west.

Facing page. The ambulatories of the Dome of the Rock.

The Jews pray at the Western Wall of the platform of Herod's first-century Temple. Atop that same platform, Muslims venerate the site of both Solomon's Temple and Muhammad's Night Journey at the Dome of the Rock.

the high priesthood to his brother, for the son whom Onias had left was still an infant. . . . Jesus, however—this was the brother of Onias—was deprived of the high priesthood when the king became angry with him and gave it to his youngest brother, named Onias. . . . Now Jesus changed his name to Jason while Onias was called Menelaus. And when the former high priest Jesus rose up against Menelaus, who was appointed after him, the populace was divided between the two, the [pro-Seleucid] Tobiads being on the side of Menelaus, while the majority of the people supported Jason; and being hard pressed by him, Menelaus and the Tobiads withdrew, and going to Antiochus informed him that they wished to abandon their country's laws and the way of life prescribed by these and to follow the king's laws and adopt the Greek way of life. . . . (Josephus, Ant. XII, 5, 1)

The Maccabees passage must be read carefully. Buried in it is an important phrase "and to enroll in Jerusalem a group to be known as 'Antiochenes' " What Jason petitioned and received was permission to juridically constitute Jerusalem a *polis*, a Greek city-state, with all the rights, privileges, and prestige thereof. He then proceeded to introduce into "Antioch," as it was now called in honor of its patron, the institutions that characterized such a urban form: the citizens, those who qualified in terms of property and standing, possibly no more that 3,000 adult males, [15] were formally enrolled as citizens of the new *polis*, and since Hellenism was not a matter of blood but of acculturation, their offspring were committed to an education in the *gymnasion*, the secondary, almost a finishing school for aspiring Hellenes and now located next to the citadel in the northwest corner of the Temple.[16] Since there already was a Council of Elders who ruled Jerusalem under the high priest, it was probably composed of precisely the wealthiest and the most Hellenized members of the community, it seems likely that that same body was simply converted into the senate or *boulê* that every Hellenized city possessed.

The Abomination of Desolation

The actions of Jason, now openly assisted by Antiochus, who had no reason to do otherwise, must surely have scandalized many, but there is no suggestion of any formal repression: the law of the land was still the Law of Moses, however that was understood in that time and place. But there was more, and worse, to follow. Jason held office for three years—174-171 B.C.—until, as Josephus tells us, Menelaus promised even larger sums to Antiochus and thus had Jason deposed and himself named high priest. There may have been more than money involved, however; Menelaus, described in 2 Maccabees as having "the temper of a cruel tyrant and the fury of a savage beast," was also a patent supporter of the crown, and in 170 B.C. Antiochus had need of such:

About this time [170-169 B.C.] Antiochus undertook his second invasion of Egypt. . . . Upon a false report of Antiochus' death, Jason collected no less than a thousand men and made a surprise attack upon Jerusalem. The defenders on the wall were driven back and the city was finally taken; Menelaus took refuge in the citadel, and Jason continued to massacre his fellow citizens without pity. . . . He did not, however, gain control of the government; he gained only dishonor as the result of his plot, and returned again as a fugitive to Ammonite territory. . . .

When news of this reached the king [Antiochus], it became clear to him that Judea was in a state of rebellion. So he set out from Egypt in a savage mood, took Jerusalem by storm, and ordered his troops to cut down without mercy everyone they met and to slaughter those who took refuge in the houses. Young and old were massacred, girls and infants butchered. By the end of three days their losses had amounted to 80,000, and as many sold into slavery.

Not satisfied with this, the king had the audacity to enter the holiest Temple on earth, guided by Menelaus, who had turned traitor both to his religion and his country. He laid impious hands on the sacred vessels; his desecrating hands swept together the votive offerings which other kings had set up to enhance the splendor and fame of the shrine. (2 Maccabees 5:1-16)

1 Maccabees adds a few details on the spoliation of the Temple:

In his arrogance he entered the Temple and carried off the golden altar, the lamp stand with all its equipment, the table for the Bread of the Presence, the sacred cups and bowls, the golden censers, the curtain and the crowns. He stripped off all the gold plating from the Temple front. He seized the silver, gold, and precious vessels, and whatever secret treasures he found, he took them all with him when he left for his own country. (1 Maccabees 1:21-24)

Sometime about 174 B.C. Antiochus had elevated Jerusalem to the high status of *polis*; now in his anger at what seemed like a transparent act of treason committed while he was at war with Egypt, and after another disastrous foray into Egypt in 168, in the following year he degraded the city to the lowest and most humiliating rank of all, that of a military colony, and then banned the very practice of Judaism:

Two years later the king sent to the towns of Judea a high revenue official, who arrived at Jerusalem with a powerful force. His language was friendly, but full of guile. For, once he had gained the city's confidence, he suddenly attacked it. He dealt it a heavy blow and killed many Israelites, plundering the city and setting it ablaze. He pulled down houses and walls on every side; women and children were made prisoners, and the cattle seized.

The City of David was turned into a citadel [*akra*], enclosed by a high, stout wall with strong towers, and garrisoned by impious foreigners and renegades. Having made themselves secure, they accumulated arms and provisions, and deposited there the massed plunder of Jerusalem. There they lay in ambush, a lurking threat to the Temple and a perpetual menace to Israel. (*1 Maccabees 1:29-36*)

Moreover, the king forbade them to offer the daily sacrifices which they used to offer to God in accordance with their law, and after plundering the entire city, he killed some of the people and some he took captive together with their women and children, so that the number of those taken alive came to 10,000. And he burnt the finest parts of the city and pulling down the walls, built the citadel [*akra*] in the Lower City; for it was high enough to overlook the Temple and it was for this reason that he fortified it with high walls and towers and stationed a Macedonian garrison there. Nonetheless, there remained in the Akra those of the people who were impious and of bad character, and at their hands the citizens were destined to suffer terrible things. (*Josephus, Ant. XII, 5, 4*)

The king then issued a decree throughout his empire: his subjects were all to become one people and abandon their own laws and religion. The nations everywhere complied with the royal command, and many in Israel accepted the foreign worship, sacrificing to idols and profaning the sabbath. Moreover, the king sent agents with written orders to Jerusalem and the towns of Judea. Ways and customs foreign to the country were to be introduced. Burnt-offerings, sacrifices and libations in the Temple were forbidden. . . .

Such was the decree which the king issued to all his subjects. He appointed superintendents over all of the people and instructed the towns of Judea to offer sacrifice, town by town. People thronged to their side in large numbers, every one of them a traitor to the law. . . . (*1 Maccabees 1:41-64*)

This was a full-scale pogrom, indeed, an attempt to exterminate the Jewish religion, quite unlike anything Jerusalem had experienced before. And though there are trails of political clues across the acts of Antiochus, there can be no certainty that they lead to either the full or the true story of the events of 167 B.C. [17] This is how one Jew read them, however, the prophetic author of the Book of Daniel:

At the appointed time he [Antiochus] will again invade the south [Egypt], but the second time will not be like the first. Ships from Kittim [Rome] will come against him. He will be checked, and will turn back, raging against the Holy Covenant. Having done his pleasure, he will then attend to those who forsake the Holy Covenant. Forces will be levied by him; they will desecrate the Temple, the fortress [the citadel]; they will abolish the regular offering and set up an appalling abomination. (Daniel 11:29-31)

And so in fact it happened:

. . . King Antiochus sent an elderly Athenian to force the Jews to abandon their ancestral customs and no longer regulate their lives according to the laws of God. He was also commissioned to pollute the Temple at Jerusalem and dedicate it to Olympian Zeus, and to dedicate the sanctuary on Mount Gerizim to Zeus, God of Hospitality, following the practice of the local inhabitants.

This evil hit them hard and was a severe trial. The Gentiles filled the Temple with licentious revelry; they took their pleasure with prostitutes and had intercourse with women in the sacred precincts. They brought forbidden things inside, and heaped the altar with impure offerings prohibited by the law. It was forbidden either to observe the sabbath or keep the traditional festivals, or to admit being a Jew at all. On the monthly celebration of the king's birthday, the Jews were driven by brute force to eat the entrails of the sacrificial victims; and on the feast of Dionysus they were forced to wear ivy wreaths and join the procession in his honor. (2 Maccabees 6:1-7)

On the fifteenth day of the month of Kislev in the year 145 [December 7, 167 B.C.] the "Appalling Abomination" was set up on the altar. Pagan altars were built throughout the towns of Judea; incense was offered at the doors of houses and in the streets. All scrolls of the Law which were found were torn up and burnt. Anyone discovered in possession of a Book of the Covenant, or conforming to the law, was put to death by the king's sentence. . . .

On the twenty-fifth day of the month they offered sacrifice on the pagan altar which was on top of the altar of the Lord. . . . (1 Maccabees 1:54-60)

The later Fathers of the Christian Church imagined that the "appalling abomination" was an idol brought into the very Sanctuary of the Temple, but a reading of the two texts cited above point to something different: the setting up of an idol, perhaps an amorphous sacred stone of the type commonly worshipped in the East, on the Altar of Sacrifice outside the

Holy of Holies.[18] More than that, Antiochus made a direct assault on the Jews' carefully calibrated definition of the holiness of the place by breaking down the gates and walls that separated the sacred precinct from the profane world outside and so let the miasma of impurity seep within that place (1 Macc. 4:38).

The Akra

As the texts themselves stress, this was not intended to be a temporary or a transient operation. Jerusalem was rendered defenseless by being stripped of her walls, and a part of the city identified by Maccabees as the City of David and by Josephus as the "Lower City" was heavily fortified and garrisoned by Syrian troops. How strong a place it was is shown by the fact that it held out in the heart of Jerusalem through and after the Maccabean war of independence and was not dismantled until the time of the Hasmonean Simon in 142 B.C. Dismantled then too well, it seems, for today there is no trace and little conviction as to where this important structure in Jerusalem's history was located.[19] We know that it dominated the Temple, indeed was higher than that building, and that it was large enough to lodge within its protective walls "those of the people who were impious and of bad character," in short, the Jewish Hellenizers of Jerusalem.

By Josephus' day Sion and the City of David had been transferred from their original place on the spur emerging southward from the Temple mount to the western hill of the city. When we add to this the fact that for Josephus the Lower City also included the eastern face of the western hill, it appears that for Josephus at least, who never saw the site, the Akra had been somewhere on the western hill of Jerusalem, facing the Temple *across* the Tyropean Valley. There are many modern scholars who agree, Kathleen Kenyon and Michael Avi-Yonah among them. But the problem remains of how a fortification could control the Temple from across the Tyropean Valley, which was certainly far deeper then than it is today. It is still tempting, then, to put the Akra where the texts seem to point, namely to the immediate south of the Temple.[20]

The Maccabean Restoration

The origins and early unfolding of the Maccabean rebellion against Seleucid oppression do not directly concern us here since most of events connected with them took place outside Jerusalem, which continued to be held by a Syrian garrison and their Jewish sympathizers in the Akra. There was an early and brief Maccabean occupation of the Holy City but its permanent reappropriation awaited more convincing military triumphs over the Syrian forces, as occurred at Bethsura in 164 B.C. It was only then that Jerusalem could be entered and the Temple restored:

But Judas and his brothers said: "Now that our enemies have been crushed, let us go up to Jerusalem to cleanse the Temple and rededicate it." So the whole army was assembled and went up to Mount Sion. There they found the Temple laid waste, the altar profaned, the gates burnt down, the courts overgrown like a thicket or wooded hill-side, and the priests' rooms in ruin. . . .

Then Judas detailed troops to engage the garrison of the citadel while he cleansed the Temple. He selected priests without blemish, devoted to the law, and they purified the Temple, removing to an unclean place the stones which defiled it. They discussed what to do with the altar of burnt offering, which was profaned, and rightly decided to demolish it, for fear it might become a standing reproach to them because it had been defiled by the Gentiles. They therefore pulled down the altar and stored away the stones in a fitting place on the Temple hill, until a prophet should arise who could be consulted about them. They took unhewn stones, as the law commands, and built a new altar on the model of the previous one. They rebuilt the Temple and restored its interior, and consecrated the Temple courts. . . .

Then early on the twenty-fifth day of the ninth month, the month Kislev, in the year 148 [164 B.C.], sacrifice was offered as the law commands on the newly made altar of burnt offerings. On the anniversary of the day when the Gentiles had profaned it, on that very day, it was rededicated, with hymns of thanksgiving, to the music of harps and lutes and cymbals. All the people prostrated themselves, worshipping and praising Heaven that their cause had prospered.[21] *(1 Maccabees 4:36-55)*

Negotiated Survival

The Maccabees had won the effective independence through the force of arms; what now remained was to negotiate that effective control into recognized and juridical sovereignty, something that could be bestowed only by the Seleucid sovereigns with whom they were at war. But the Seleucids were even more deeply engaged in a war among themselves, and in the context of this rivalry the new Judean state appeared not so much a rebellious vassal as an ally to be wooed and won, first by the pretender Alexander Balas and then by his rival Demetrius, and on terms acceptable to new Maccabean leader Jonathan:

King Alexander [Balas] to his brother Jonathan, greetings.

We have heard about you, what a valiant man you are and how fit to be our friend. Now therefore we do appoint you this day to be high priest and of your nation with the title of "King's Friend," to support our cause and to keep friendship with us. . . .

Thus with the blessings of Alexander Balas, Jonathan assumed the vestments of high priest and ruler of the Jewish state on the Feast of Tabernacles in 152 B.C.

When this news reached Demetrius, he was mortified. "How did we come to let Alexander forestall us," he asked, "in gaining the friendship and support of the Jews? I too will send them cordial messages and offer honors and gifts to keep them on my side." So he sent a message to the Jews to this effect:

King Demetrius to the Jewish nation, greetings. . . . Jerusalem and all its environs, with its tithes and tolls, shall be sacred and tax-free. I also surrender authority over the citadel in Jerusalem and grant the high priest the right to garrison it with men of his own choice. . . .

Ptolemais and the lands belonging to it I make over to the Temple in Jerusalem, to meet the expenses proper to it. I give 15,000 silver shekels annually, charged on my own royal accounts, to be drawn from such places as may prove convenient. And the arrears of the subsidy, in so far as it has not been paid by the revenue officials, as it formerly was, shall henceforward be paid in for the needs of the Temple. In addition, the 5,000 silver shekels that used to be taken from the annual income of the Temple are also released, because they belong to the ministering priests. . . . The cost of rebuilding and repair of the Temple shall be borne by the royal revenue; also the repair of the walls of Jerusalem and its surrounding fortifications, as well as of the fortresses of Judea, shall be at the expense of the royal revenue. (1 Maccabees 10:18-45)

Simon and the Akra

Jerusalem was now back in traditionalist hands, but despite the promises of Demetrius, the Syrians still lorded it over the city from their fortified enclave in the Akra, which by its strength and position prevented the inhabitants from moving freely in and out of the city and must even to some extent have inhibited the liturgical life of the Temple. Finally the Akra fell in 142 B.C. to Simon, the first perhaps in the history of the Jews to possess simultaneously supreme religious, military, and political control of the state:

The Jews and their priests confirmed Simon as their leader and high priest in perpetuity until a true prophet should appear. He was to be their general and have full charge of the Temple; and in addition to this the supervision of their labor, of the country, and of the arms and fortifications was to be entrusted to him. He was to be obeyed by all; all contracts in the country were to be drawn up in his name. He was to wear the [royal] purple robe and the gold clasp. (1 Maccabees 14:41-42)

If the citadel garrison still in some sense held Jerusalem in thrall, they were themselves captives, a condition that Simon finally managed to exploit:

The men in the citadel in Jerusalem were prevented from going in and out to buy and sell in the country; famine set in and many of them died from starvation. They clamored to Simon to accept their surrender, and he agreed: he expelled them from the citadel and cleansed it from its pollutions. It was on the twenty-third day of the second month in the year 171 [141 B.C.] that he made his entry, with a chorus of praise and the waving of palm branches ... to celebrate Israel's final riddance of a formidable enemy. Simon decreed that this day should be celebrated as an annual festival. He fortified the Temple hill opposite the citadel and he and his men took up residence there. (1 Maccabees 13:49-52)

He (Simon) also took the citadel at Jerusalem by siege, razing it to the ground that it might not serve his foes as a base to occupy and do mischief from it, as they were then doing. Having done this, he thought it would be an excellent thing and to his advantage to level also the hill on which the citadel stood, in order that the Temple might be higher than this. . . . He persuaded the people since he was recommending something that was to their advantage. And so they all set to and began to work to level the hill, and without stopping work night and day, after three whole years brought it down to the ground and the surface of the plain. And thereafter the Temple stood high above everything else, once the citadel and the hill on which it stood had been demolished.[22] *(Josephus, Ant. XIII, 6, 7)*

Glory and the End

The Seleucids were by no means quit of Judea nor the new Jewish monarchy of the Maccabees. The House of Hasmon, as the Maccabees were now known, was deeply involved in Syrian politics, whether in the Seleucid succession or in supplying mercenaries and federate troops for the expeditions of those monarchs. And on an even wider stage, Simon sent an embassy to Rome in 139 or 138 B.C. requesting recognition and alliance, which was granted by the Roman Senate. A new Seleucid monarch, Antiochus VII (140-129 B.C.), felt assured enough on his own throne to demand of Simon the return to Syrian control of the Jerusalem Akra. The request was refused, and though Antiochus was sufficiently distracted by other affairs not to press the matter too strongly at that point, by 135 B.C., when there was a new king in Judea, John Hyrcanus (135-104 B.C.), Antiochus mounted a full-scale invasion of Judea and lay Jerusalem under siege. As the net tightened but before there was an assault on the city, Hyrcanus chose to buy off the Seleucid, with silver, Josephus reports (*Ant.* VII, 15, 3), taken from the tomb of David.

According to Josephus' account of that campaign of 135, one of Antiochus' terms was the demolition of the walls of Jerusalem. This appears to have been done, though later in his reign Hyrcanus may have rebuilt them, since the archeological evidence at the western gate of Jerusalem, where Herod later built his massive citadel, and elsewhere along the southern perimeter of the city shows that in Hasmonean times there was a sturdy wall around Jerusalem. It is likely this wall that Josephus calls the "ancient wall" when describing the fortifications of Jerusalem at the time of Herod. [23]

Jerusalem of the Hasmoneans must have borne many of the physical marks of the *polis* installed there by Antiochus IV. The Upper City, for example, where the Seleucids had installed their agora, or commercial center, remained the secular focus of the city under the Hasmoneans. Their palace was located there, as well as the Xystus, a kind of gymnasium that survived into the days of Herod and the Romans. It is likely too that there remained something of formal street plan on a Hippodamian model in the Upper City. Hellenism had not disappeared from the city; indeed its style became the Hasmoneans' own. And if class distinctions were not as formally institutionalized as they had been by the *polis'* creation of citizen rolls that effectively disenfranchised the poor and the non-Hellenized, they were signalled by the growing separation between the Upper City as the haunt of the wealthy and powerful, and the Lower City in the valley beneath as a commercial and popular quarter. This urban division was probably hastened by the Hasmoneans' construction of a bridge over the valley that linked their palace with the Temple opposite.

During the reigns of the expansionist Judean kings John Hyrcanus and Alexander Janneus (103-76 B.C.) war and even the threat of war was remote from Jerusalem. Abroad it was a time of conquest and at home a period of opulence, reflected in Jerusalem by the splendid palace built somewhere in the Upper City and the magnificent tombs spread through the outskirts. [24] The opulence was also reflected in the Hasmoneans' own lifestyles. And it was precisely the issue of Hasmonean Hellenism and the nagging doubts about the Hasmoneans' right to the hereditary office of the high priesthood that introduced another kind of war into the community and brought to the fore in Jerusalem a group of which we have heard little heretofore, the Pharisees. Josephus supplies the background:

As for Hyrcanus, the envy of the Jews was aroused against him by his own successes and those of his sons; particularly hostile to him were the Pharisees, who were one of the Jewish schools. . . . So great is their influence that even when they speak against a king or high priest, they immediately gain credence.

Hyrcanus too was a disciple of theirs, and was greatly loved by them. And once he invited them to a feast and treated them hospitably, and when he saw that they were having a very good time, he began by saying that they knew he wished to be righteous and in everything he did tried to please God and them—for the Pharisees profess such beliefs—and at the same time he begged them, if they observed him doing anything wrong or straying from the right path, to lead him back to it and correct him. But they testified to his being altogether virtuous and he was delighted with their praise.

One of the guests, however, named Eleazer, who had an evil nature and took pleasure in dissension, said, "Since you have asked to be told the truth, if you wish to be righteous, give up the high priesthood and be content with governing the people [as king]." And when Hyrcanus asked him for what reason he should give up the high priesthood, he replied, "Because we have heard from our elders that your mother was a captive in the reign of Antiochus Epiphanes."

Josephus assures us that the charge was a canard, but Hyrcanus was encouraged to think that the Pharisees were behind it. In the end he decided to break with the Pharisees and "to abrogate the regulations which they had established for the people and punish those who observed them." He explains:

The Pharisees had passed on to the people certain regulations handed down by former generations and not recorded in the Laws of Moses, for which reason they are rejected by the Sadducees, who hold that only those regulations should be considered valid which were written down (in Scripture), and those that were handed down by former generations need not be observed. . . . The Sadducees have the confidence of the wealthy alone but no following among the populace, while the Pharisees have the support of the masses. . . . (Josephus, Ant. XIII, 10, 5-7)

The leaven of the Pharisees' disapproval may be observed at work during the reign of Hyrcanus' son Alexander Janneus:

60

As for Alexander, his own people revolted against him—for the nation was aroused against him—at the festival (of Tabernacles), as he stood beside the altar and was about to sacrifice [in his capacity as high priest], they pelted him with citrons, it being a custom among the Jews that at the festival of Tabernacles everyone holds wands made of palm branches and citrons. . . . And they added insult to insult by saying that he was descended from captives and was unfit to hold (priestly) office and to sacrifice. And being enraged at this he killed some 6,000 of them, and also placed a wooden barrier about the altar and the Temple as far as the coping (of the court) which the priests alone were permitted to enter and by this means blocked the people's way to him. (Josephus, Ant. XIII, 13, 5)

Alexander Janneus had cause to regret this conflict—the Pharisaic influence was too great, he finally conceded—and on his deathbed he commended to his wife Salome Alexandra that she make peace with the Pharisees. She did as he requested and it bought a kind of peace. Other terms of his testament created more serious problems, however:

Now although Alexander had left two sons, Hyrcanus and Aristobulus, he had bequeathed the royal power to Alexandra. Of these sons the one, Hyrcanus, was incompetent to govern, and in addition much preferred a quiet life, while the younger, Aristobulus, was a man of action and high spirit. . . . Alexandra then appointed Hyrcanus as high priest because of his greater age but more especially because of his lack of energy; and she permitted the Pharisees to do as they liked in all matters and also commanded the people to obey them. . . . And so, while she had the title of sovereign, the Pharisees had the power. (Josephus, Ant., XIII, 16, 1-2)

This peculiar formula barely lasted through the queen's reign, and when she died in 67 B.C. the rage and frustration of Aristobulus broke into open warfare. Hyrcanus, now in the competent hands of an Idumean adventurer named Antipater, threw himself upon the mercy of the king of the Arab empire of the Nabateans around Petra in the Transjordan. And by 65 B.C. Hyrcanus, Antipater, and his Arab allies had Aristobulus and his followers pinned and besieged inside the Temple precinct in Jerusalem. It was in fact a charade. The conflict between the two brothers over who would be the ruler of Jerusalem and Judea was settled not by arms in the Holy City but over a table in Damascus. The Romans had come to the Near East.

Pompey in Jerusalem

How the Romans came to be engaged with Jerusalem on this occasion is richly suggestive of all that was to follow. In 63 B.C. the Roman general

Pompey was in the East fulfilling the limited mandate given him by the Senate of the Roman Republic, a pursue and destroy mission in Anatolia where what were perceived to be Roman interests in the eastern Mediterranean were being threatened by a skillful, persistent, and ambitious ruler called Mithridates. The mission, or *imperium*, as it was called, was successful, but it brought in its train long-term consequences that ran directly into Judea. In unseating Mithridates the Romans wittingly or unwittingly sent a shock through the entire political structure in the East, and that flimsy house of cards, which the Romans themselves had been engaged in shoring up for nearly a century, came tumbling down, at the feet, or perhaps more appositely, into the lap of the *imperator* Pompey.

The linchpin of this arrangement was the succession of enfeebled monarchs who had presided in Antioch over the end-time of the empire of Seleucus and Antiochus III. They still held the title, these last Seleucid kings, but the power rested in other hands, those of the local dynasts who did as the Hasmoneans had done in Judea and carved out for themselves from the ruin of the Seleucid Empire a chain of kingdoms that extended from the Euphrates to the Gulf of Aqaba. The Romans were aware of this—very little occurred in the Near East in the last two centuries before the Christian era without Roman information and indeed approval—and had as yet no reason to forestall it. But the rise, and then the fall, of Mithridates had drawn in Armenia and threatened to do the same with an even more powerful Parthia, both at the expense of the enfeebled Seleucids, and as the Romans saw it, to their own detriment as well. In 64 B.C. the Roman Senate annexed Syria as a province to what was becoming in fact, if not yet in name, an empire.

If the Romans were building an empire, there was not as yet an emperor; so it was to the *imperator* Pompey that the former clients, allies, petitioners, and dependents of the Seleucid kingdom came when he sat in Damascus in the spring of 63 B.C. Among these petitioners were the two claimants of the Hasmonean throne in Judea, Alexander Janneus' two sons, Aristobulus and Hyrcanus. Thus it fell to Pompey, since there was none else, to settle who should rule the Jews. Pompey postponed his choice—settling the affairs of the rich Arab caravan empire in the Transjordan had a far higher priority in his order of business—and bade the two men hold their peace until he was ready for them. According to Josephus, who is our chief reporter in these matters, Aristobulus read it as a decision and not a postponement.

On the one hand Aristobulus cherished the hope that he would obtain the kingdom from Pompey and so feigned obedience to everything he commanded, and on the other hand he retired to the stronghold in order not to weaken his force and to prepare for himself supplies for making war, as he feared that Pompey might transfer the royal power to Hyrcanus. Pompey, however, commanded him to deliver up his strongholds and give the order therefore to his garrison commanders in his own handwriting. . . . And so Aristobulus obeyed but retired resentfully to Jerusalem to set about preparing for war. . . .

Pompey then encamped near Jericho, where they cultivate the palm tree and opobalsamum, that most excellent of ointments, . . . and at dawn set out for Jerusalem. And Aristobulus, thinking better of his plan, came to Pompey and promising to give him money and admit him into Jerusalem, begged him to stop the war and do as he liked peacefully. On making this request Pompey pardoned him and sent Gabinius and some soldiers to get the money and take over the city. None of these promises was carried out, however, and Gabinius returned after being shut out of the city and failing to receive the money; for Aristobulus' soldiers had not permitted the agreement to be carried out. And Pompey, being seized with anger at this, placed Aristobulus under arrest and himself went to the city, which was strongly fortified on all sides except on the north, where it was weak. For it is surrounded by a broad and deep ravine which takes in the Temple, and this is very strongly protected by an encircling wall of stone.

The Jews inside the city were divided as to what should be done next. Some wished to deliver the city to Pompey, but the followers of Aristobulus chose to barricade themselves within the Temple area and fight it out with the Romans. Pompey made one last offer of terms and then moved:

At dawn Pompey pitched his camp on the north side of the Temple, where it stood open to attack. But even here stood great towers, [25] and a trench had been dug, and the Temple was surrounded by a deep ravine; for there was a steep slope on the side toward the (Upper) city after the bridge was destroyed, and at this spot Pompey by great labor day by day had caused earthworks to be raised, for which the Romans cut down the timber round about. And when these were high enough, though the trench was filled up with difficulty because of its immense depth, he moved up and set in place the siege engines and instruments of war that had been brought from Tyre, and began to batter the Temple with his catapults. . . .

. . . There was slaughter everywhere. For some of the Jews were slain by the Romans and others by their fellows; and there were some who hurled themselves down the precipices, and setting fire to their houses burned themselves within them, for they could not bear to accept their fate. And so of the Jews there fell 12,000, and of the Romans only a very *few. . . . And not light was the sin committed against the sanctuary, which before that time had never been entered or seen. For Pompey and not a few of his men went into it and saw what was unlawful for any but the high priests to see. But though the golden table was there and the sacred lamp stand and the libation vessels and a great quantity of spices, and besides these in the treasury the sacred moneys amounting to 2,000 talents, he touched none of these because of piety, and in this respect also he acted in a manner worthy of his virtuous character.* [26]

And on the next day he instructed the Temple servants to cleanse the Temple and to offer the customary sacrifices to God, and he restored the high priesthood to Hyrcanus because in various ways he had been useful to him. . . . And he made Jerusalem tributary to the Romans, and he took from its inhabitants the cities of Coele-Syria, which they had formerly subdued, and placed them under his own governor, and the entire nation, which before had raised itself so high, he confined within its own borders. (Josephus, Ant. XIV, 4, 1-4)

Tacitus, writing in his *History* at the very beginning of the second Christian century, has his own, somewhat interested, non-Jewish perspective on the same event:

A great part of Judea consists in scattered villages. They have also towns. Jerusalem is the capital. There stood there a temple of immense wealth. First came the city with its fortifications, then the royal palace, then, within the innermost defenses, the Temple itself. Only the Jew was permitted to approach the gates; all but priests were forbidden to pass the threshhold. . . .

Tacitus then gives a very brief resume of Jewish history from the return from exile through the Maccabees, including his assessment of Antiochus IV Epiphanes who, according to the Roman historian, "strove to destroy the national superstition and to introduce Greek civilization, but was prevented by his war with the Parthians from at all improving this vilest of nations."

Cneius Pompeius was the first of our countrymen to subjugate the Jews. And invoking the right of conquest, he entered the Temple. It was in this manner that it became common knowledge that the place stood empty with no likenesses of gods within, and that the shrine had nothing to reveal. The walls of Jerusalem were destroyed, but the Temple was left standing. (Tacitus, History V, 8, 9)

Josephus was not the only public figure to praise Pompey's restraint with regard to the treasures of the Jewish Temple. A few years later, in 59 B.C.,

Cicero, in whose consulship the event had taken place, was engaged as defense lawyer for a certain Flaccus and had occasion to deal with Pompey's act, which the prosecutor Laelius had contrasted with Flaccus' own behavior in the matter of Jewish gold. He parried the argument by citing the Jews' own behavior:

Next there is the question of the odium connected to Jewish gold. . . . When it was the custom every year to send gold to Jerusalem from Italy and from all our provinces on the order of the Jews, Flaccus issued an edict forbidding its exportation from (the province of) Asia. Who is there, gentlemen, who could not honestly praise this action? On many earlier occasions as well as during my consulship the Senate had most urgently forbade the export of gold. But to resist this barbaric superstition was an act of firmness, to defy the crowd of Jews when sometimes in our assemblies they were heated with passion, to serve the welfare of the state, this was an act of the greatest gravity. "But Gnaeus Pompeius," you say, "on the occasion when Jerusalem was captured [in 63 B.C.], laid his victorious hands on nothing in that shrine." In that he was especially wise—as in many other matters. . . . But I do not think that that celebrated general was so much inhibited by the religious feelings of the Jews and his enemies as by his own sense of honor. . . .

Even while Jerusalem was still standing and the Jews were at peace with us, the practice of their sacred rites was at variance with the glory of our empire, the dignity of our name, the customs of our ancestors. But now it is even more the case, when that nation by its armed resistance, has shown what it thinks of our rule; and just how dear that nation was to the immortal gods may be seen from the fact that it has been conquered, let out for taxes, made a slave. (Cicero, For Flaccus, 28:66-69)

The Rise of Herod

Pompey did not tarry long over the arrangements for Judea. Aristobulus walked a captive in Pompey's triumph in Rome, and a much reduced Judea was attached to the political control of the Roman governor of the new province of Syria, while the purely internal affairs of the former Hasmonean kingdom were committed to the now inevitable high priest, Hyrcanus II. Only for a while however. First Aristobulus' son and then Aristobulus' himself, who managed to escape from his captivity in Rome, resisted the Romans' arrangements in Judea; on two occasions, in 57 and 56 B.C., the governors of Syria, Gabinius and Crassus, had to intervene in their Judean canton. Neither governor showed Pompey's tact, or as Cicero preferred it, his "honor"; the opposition was crushed, the country despoiled, and the ineffective Hyrcanus was restricted to playing out his role of high priest inside the walls of the Temple compound.

In the years that followed, the Romans were more concerned with their own civil wars than with the politics of Judea. For the Jews who had or would have power there, however, these civil wars presented an opportunity to rise or fall on a throw of the Roman dice. In this instance, Hyrcanus won the cast, backing Caesar against Pompey. After the defeat of Pompey, Caesar came to Syria and rewarded his faithful vassals: Hyrcanus had his powers extended, this time to "ethnarch," not yet and not quite "king," while his vizier and mentor, the Idumean Antipater, was granted Roman citizenship.

At this point the future of Jerusalem begins to reveal itself in Josephus' narrative. It was Antipater, it becomes clear, who was the real ruler of Judea for the Romans, and his lieutenants were his own sons, Phasael in Jerusalem and the younger Herod in Galilee. In 44 B.C. Caesar was murdered, and in the following year Antipater suffered the same end. Rome went through another civil upheaval, and now it was Herod who had to navigate the same dangerous choices that had once confronted his father, though with new complexities. The Parthians too sought to make profit of the Romans' internal political problems, while Antony, who was emerging as the principal claimant to Caesar's mantle in the East, dallied in Egypt, the Parthians in 40 B.C. came crashing through the Roman defenses in Syria and marched on Jerusalem, carrying in their van their own candidate for king and high priest, Aristobulus' son Antigonus. Phasael was killed, and Herod fled first to the protection of the Arabs in the Transjordan and then to his only true hope, Antony and the Senate at Rome. Whatever spoke louder, his reasoning or his bribes, in 40 B.C. Herod was nominated and confirmed as king of Judea by the Roman Senate.

It took the Romans two years to rid Palestine of the Parthians for good and Herod another year and the assistance of a Roman army to clear Antigonus out of Jerusalem, the second time in twenty-five years that the Holy City had been subjected to a Roman siege. Herod then accomplished the possibly more difficult task of persuading the Romans to withdraw as well. They took Antigonus with them, and this last Hasmonean was executed in Antioch in that same year of 37 B.C. A new dynasty, the Herodian, had begun, and a new era, the Augustan, was about to begin in Jerusalem.

For the next six years Herod stayed closely attached to Antony, even though it meant suffering the partial dismemberment of some rich parts of his kingdom to be given as lease lands to Cleopatra. Then in 31 B.C., when the hopes of Antony and Cleopatra went down in the waters off

Actium, the agile Herod managed to transfer his allegiance to the victor Octavian and to embrace Rome's new and permanent *imperator* as warmly as he had once held his rival. Octavian, now Augustus, had little choice perhaps, or else he was astute enough to recognize Herod's value to his imperial enterprise; in any event, the embrace was returned and Herod was once again confirmed as king of Judea, where he was to rule for thirty-three years (37-4 B.C.).

Jerusalem Topography

In his *Jewish War* Josephus gives a detailed description of the Roman siege of Jerusalem in A.D. 70. But before he begins, he undertakes to present to the Roman reader for whom the book was intended a sense of the topography of the city as it appeared in the middle decades of the first Christian century. For us it represents the landscape upon which Herodian Jerusalem must be laid out, again chiefly from Josephus: [27]

The city was fortified by three walls, except where it was enclosed by impassable ravines, a single wall there sufficing. It was built in portions facing each other, on two hills separated by a central valley [the Cheesemakers or Tyropean], in which the tiers of houses ended.

Of these hills, that on which the Upper City lay was far higher and had a straighter ridge than the other. Consequently, owing to its strength it was called by King David, the father of Solomon, the first builder of the Temple, "the Stronghold," but we called it the Upper Market.

The notion that the western hill of Jerusalem was the site of the City of David and of the stronghold called Sion certainly did not originate with Josephus, but this is the first we hear of it. Not the last. Henceforward, through late Roman, Byzantine, and Islamic to modern times, David's presence is felt strongly at the western gate of the city, at the Christians' "David's Tower" or the Muslim's "Prayer Niche of David"; David's Sion is put on the western side of Jerusalem; and more specifically, the southern spur of the western hill becomes "Mount Sion" and the tomb of David is eventually and inevitably discovered there. Passing over the Temple mount, Josephus goes on to what we understand from archeological data as the true City of David, the "third hill" in what follows:

The second hill, which bore the name of Akra and supported the Lower City, was a "hog's back." [28] *Opposite this [that is, immediately to the south of it] was a third hill, by nature lower than the Akra and once divided from it by another broad ravine. Afterwards, however, the Hasmoneans, during the period of their reign, both filled up the ravine, with*

Herodian Jerusalem (37 B.C.-A.D. 70).

68

the object of uniting the city with the Temple, and also reduced the elevation of the Akra by reducing its summit, in order that it might not block the view of the Temple. The Valley of the Cheesemakers, as the ravine was called, which, as we have said, divided the hill of the Upper City from that of the Lower, extends down to Siloam; for so we called that fountain of sweet and abundant water. On the exterior the two hills on which the city stood were encompassed by deep ravines, and the precipitous cliffs on either side of it rendered the two nowhere accessible. (Josephus, War V, 4, 1)

The City Walls

Josephus then proceeds to the walls of Jerusalem, likewise critical to an understanding of the siege that will follow in his account:

Of the three walls, the most ancient, owing to the surrounding ravines and the hill above them on which it was reared, was well-nigh impregnable. But besides the advantage of its position, it was also strongly built, David, Solomon, and their successors on the throne having taken pride in the work. Beginning on the north at the tower called Hippicus, [29] it extended to the Xystus, and then joining the Council Chamber terminated at the western portico of the Temple. Beginning at the same point in the other direction, westward, it descended past the place called Bethso to the Gate of the Essenes, then turned southwards above the fountain of Siloam; thence it again inclined east toward Solomon's pool, and after passing a spot called Ophlas [Ophel], finally joined the eastern portico of the Temple.

Thus far we can follow without a great deal of difficulty, though some precise points may escape us. This "ancient wall," which of course had nothing to do with either David or Solomon, was anchored at the tower called Hippicus at what later was called the Citadel by the Jaffa Gate. It went east past the gymnasium called Xystus down in the Tyropean Valley, then to the "Council Chamber," probably the same place where the Sanhedrin met, [30] until it finally joined the Temple enclosure at its western wall. This juncture probably took place somewhere in the vicinity of "Wilson's Arch," and if this is so, this ancient wall likely ran close to the course of the present David Street across the city. [31] We cannot be certain where "Bethso" is or "the Gate of the Essenes," [32] but the wall obviously swept south then east, encompassed the fountain of Siloam and rejoined the Temple at its southeast corner.

The second wall started from the gate in the first (wall) which they called

*Gennath [perhaps the "Garden Gate"], and, enclosing only the northern
district of the town, went up as far as Antonia.*

Here we are in the presence not so much of topography as of theology,
since it is this "second wall" of Josephus that will place the site of the
execution and burial of Jesus inside or outside the city. Or to put it another way, how can the line of this wall, which seems to start east of the
Hippicus Tower and the Jaffa Gate and ends at the Antonia at the northwest corner of the Temple precinct, be drawn in such a way that it passes
east of the Holy Sepulcher? Josephus is not of much help since we have
no idea where the "Gennath Gate" was located. As a result, archeologists,
historians, military strategists, and polemicists have made free to draw the
wall as they will. [33] All that can be said, perhaps, is that so far there is no
archeological evidence to suggest that the area around the Holy Sepulcher
was inside the city anytime before it was rebuilt by Hadrian in A.D. 135,
and therefore a line projecting the "second wall" east of that church is at
least plausible. [34]

Finally Josephus takes up the last built wall of the city, this one put up
by Herod Agrippa on the very eve of the Roman siege in A.D. 70:

*The third (wall) began at the tower Hippicus, whence it stretched north-
wards to the tower Psephinus, and then descending opposite the monuments of Helena (queen of Adiabene and daughter of King Izates), and
proceeding past the royal caverns, it bent round a corner tower and terminated at the valley called Kedron. This wall was built by Agrippa to
enclose the later additions to the city, which were quite unprotected; for
the town, overflowing with inhabitants, had gradually crept beyond the
ramparts. Indeed, the population, uniting to the hill (of the Upper City)
the district north of the Temple, had encroached so far that even a fourth
hill was surrounded with houses.*

*This hill, which is called Bezetha, lay opposite [that is, just to the north
of] Antonia, but was cut off from it by a deep ditch, dug on purpose to
sever the foundations of Antonia from the hill and so render them at once
less easy of access and more elevated, the depth of the trench materially
increasing the height of the towers. The recently built quarter was called
in the vernacular Bezetha, which might be translated into Greek as "New
Town."* [35] *Seeing then the residents of the district in need of defense,
Agrippa [I], the father and namesake of the present king [Agrippa II],
began the above-mentioned wall; but fearing that Claudius Caesar might
suspect from the vast scale of the structure that he had designs of revolution and revolt, he desisted after merely laying the foundations. . . . The
wall itself was ten cubits [15 ft.] broad . . . it rose to a height of twenty
cubits [30 ft.], besides having battlements of two cubits [3 ft.] and bul-*

warks three cubits [4.5 ft.] high, bringing the total height up to twenty-five cubits [37.5 ft.].

Above the wall, however, rose towers, twenty cubits [30 ft.] broad and twenty high. . . . The whole circumference of the city was thirty-three stadia [somewhat more than 6.5 miles]. . . . (Josephus, War V, 4, 2-3)

This third wall, which extended in a loop northwards and then eastwards to enclose the growing northern suburb called Bezetha as well as to defend the vulnerable northern approach to Jerusalem has provoked its own share of controversy, though in this instance it is more likely archeological nationalism rather than theology that has fueled the debate. One school, Kathleen Kenyon at its head, sees evidence for this wall under the present northern wall of the city, while Israeli scholars are strongly in support of two of the earliest Jewish archeologists in Jerusalem, Mayer and Sukenik, who in 1928 claimed that they had identified the remains of Agrippa's wall in their soundings well north of the Turkish wall that still stands on the northern side of the city. [36] The dimensions given by Josephus, for all the notorious inaccuracy of figures in ancient texts, may favor the more northern, and more extensive, hypothesis.

Herodian Jerusalem

If we assemble these somewhat sparse descriptive data, little of them with any archeological verification, we can begin to sketch at least a provisional portrait of the Jerusalem of Herod. From the outset he had resolved to change not only the face of the city and the countryside, but, as Josephus charges, of the Jewish people as well:

For this reason Herod went still further in departing from the native customs, and through foreign practices he gradually corrupted the ancient way of life, which had hitherto been inviolable. As a result of this we suffered considerable harm, because those things were neglected which had formerly induced piety in the masses. For in the first place he established athletic contests every fifth year in honor of Caesar [Augustus], and he built a theater in Jerusalem and after that a very large amphitheater in the plain, [37] both being spectacularly lavish but foreign to Jewish custom, for the use of such buildings and the exhibition of such spectacles have not been traditional (with the Jews).

Herod, however, celebrated the quinquennial festival in the most splendid way, sending notices of it to the neighboring peoples and inviting participants from the whole nation. Athletes and other classes of contestants were invited from every land, being attracted by the hope of winning

71

the prizes offered and by the glory of victory. And the leading men in various fields were assembled, for Herod offered very great prizes not only to the winners in gymnastic games but also to those who engaged in music and those who are called thymelikoi [probably a guild of entertainers]. And an effort was made to have all the most famous people come to the contest. He also offered considerable gifts to drivers of four-horse and two-horse chariots and to those mounted on race-horses. And whatever costly or magnificent efforts had been made by others, all these did Herod imitate in his ambition to see his spectacle become famous. All round the theater there were inscriptions concerning Caesar and trophies of nations which he had won in war, and all of them made for Herod of pure gold and silver. . . . [The Jews were angered by the animal and gladiatorial contests.] But more than all else it was the trophies that irked them, for in the belief that these were images surrounded by weapons, which was against their national custom to worship, they were exceedingly angry. (Josephus, Ant. XV, 7, 1)

This is one perception of Herodian Jerusalem, a city already contaminated by Hellenism and its values, its practices, and its institutions. It was by no means the only view, nor was Hellenism the only ideal being propagated in Jerusalem. The evidence dates from somewhat later, a collection of rabbinic aphorisms that was redacted sometime about A.D. 200. But the "Fathers according to Rabbi Nathan" is an authentic reflection, somewhat idealized perhaps, of what Jerusalem should be and surely to some extent was, a holy city, as pleasing to the Lord as the Temple itself and sharing some of the same strictures against impurity as the very House of the Lord:

Ten things are said of Jerusalem:
Jerusalem's houses do not become unclean through leprosy;
It is not to be declared a condemned city;
Neither beams nor balconies nor sockets may project there over the public thoroughfares lest by overshadowing they give passage to corpse uncleanness;
The dead may not be lodged there overnight;
The bones of a dead man may not be carried through it;
No place is made there for a resident alien;
No graves may be kept there excepting the graves of the house of David and of Huldah the prophetess, which were there since the days of the early prophets;
No plants may be planted there, neither gardens nor orchards may be cultivated there, excepting rose gardens which were there since the days of the early prophets;

Neither geese nor chickens may be raised there, nor, needless to say,
  pigs;
No dunghills may be kept there because of uncleanness;
No trial of a stubborn or rebellious son may be held there; such is the
  view of R. Nathan (Deut. 21:18)
No houses may be sold there save from the ground up [that is, only the
  structure, not the ground];
The sale of houses is not valid there for longer than twelve months;
No payment for a bed is accepted there [from the pilgrims who come on
  festivals]—Rabbi Judah says: Not even payment for beds and
  coverings;
The hides of sacrificial animals are not for sale there.
(Aboth Rabbi Nathan 1955: 143-144)

The City Quarters

When he came to power, Herod found a city defined on the north by the "ancient wall" running west from the Temple mount along present-day David Street, curving southward to include some at least of Mount Sion and David's old city and the Ophel, until it rejoined the Temple enclosure at its southeastern corner. Within this perimeter the topography defined three distinct areas: the Upper City on the west; the Temple mount on the east, with its southern extension of the Ophel and an adjoining hill; and between them, the Lower City, the drainage line of the Tyropean Valley. It was the western hill, Josephus' Upper City or Upper Market, where since Hellenistic times the wealthy and the powerful of the city, its kings and its high priests, chose to live. In those days, as in Herod's, topography also defined class. The Hellenized elite lived in the cooler and airier Upper City or Upper Market on the western hill; the commercial and poorer classes in the Lower City, the valley between the hills, and in the old sections of town south of the Temple. In these older and lower quarters also lay many of Jerusalem's municipal buildings and the tangled bazaars of the wool and cloth merchants and coppersmiths. [38]

In an earlier day the most prominent buildings in the Upper City must have lain close to the ridge line of the western hill, or even somewhat down on its eastern slope. This is our impression of the Xystus, the old Hellenistic gymnasium later used as an open paved area for assemblies, and certainly of the Hasmonean palace, for which Josephus provides some further details drawn from the reign of Agrippa II (A.D. 50-53):

About this time King Agrippa built a chamber of unusual size in his palace in Jerusalem adjoining the [Temple] colonnade. The palace had been erected long before by the Hasmoneans, and being situated on a lofty site, afforded a most delightful view to any who chose to survey the city from it. [39] *(Josephus, War XX, 8, 11)*

Agrippa stayed in the old Hasmonean palace because in his day the Romans had appropriated the building that his great-grandfather Herod had built for himself in Jerusalem. It was at the western gate of the city and formed part of a formidable defense complex that also included the immense towers called Hippicus, Phasael, and Mariamne. Whether intended or not, Herod was moving the center of the Upper City farther west. The palace was, according to Josephus, unmatched in extravagance and fittings, with immense banquet halls and bedchambers for a hundred guests:

The interior fittings are indescribable—the variety of stones, since species rare in every other country were here collected in abundance, ceilings wonderful both for the length of the beams and the splendor of their surface decoration, the host of apartments with their infinite varieties of design. . . . All around were many circular cloisters, leading one into another . . . with their grassy open courts; there were groves of trees intersected by long walks, which were bordered by deep canals, and ponds everywhere studded with bronze figures, through which water was discharged, and around the streams were numerous cots for tame pigeons. (Josephus, War V, 4, 4)

Josephus could barely bring himself to speak of this building since he saw it go up in flames, almost by accident, along with most of the public buildings in Herod's city, in the general conflagration that swept Jerusalem during the siege of A.D. 70. [40]

Fortress Antonia

Among the other buildings brought to ruin in A.D. 70 was one of Herod's most impressive excursions into a form in which he excelled, military architecture. This was the fortified structure named after his good friend Antony and built in the northwest corner of his Temple enclosure. As Josephus constantly stressed and the events bore out, Jerusalem, a city surrounded on three sides by ravines, was most vulnerable to attack from the north. The city's growth was precisely in that direction in Herodian days, and as we have seen, the king attempted to enclose at least part of that growth within the line of the "second wall." But until he pushed that perimeter even further to the north, the northern defense line of the city was the northern edge of the Temple enclosure, and to protect that area he built a fortress on its northern side, as indeed both the Greeks and the Hasmoneans had done before him:

At an angle on the north side there had been built a citadel, well fortified and of unusual strength. It was the kings and princes of the Hasmonean family before Herod who had built it and called it Baris. Here they had deposited the priestly robe which the high priest put on only when he had to offer sacrifice. This robe Herod (too) kept safe in that same place. . . . At the time mentioned, Herod, the king of the Jews, made this Baris stronger for the safety and protection of the Temple, and to gratify Antony, who was his friend and at the same time the ruler of the Romans, he called it Antonia. (Josephus, Ant. XV, 11, 4)

The tower of Antonia lay at the angle where two porticoes, the western and the northern, of the first court of the Temple met; it was built upon a rock fifty cubits high and on all sides precipitous. It was the work of King Herod and a crowning exhibition of the innate grandeur of his genius. For, to begin with, the rock was covered from its base upwards with smooth flagstones, both for ornament and in order that anyone attempting to ascend or descend it might slip off. Next, in front of the actual edifice there was a wall three cubits high; and behind this the tower of Antonia rose majestic to an altitude of forty cubits. The interior resembled a palace in its spaciousness and appointments, being divided into apartments of every description and for every purpose, including cloisters, baths, and broad courtyards for the accommodation of troops; so that from its possession of all conveniences it seemed a town; from its magnificence, a palace.

The general appearance of the whole was of a tower with other towers at each of the four corners; three of these turrets were fifty cubits high, while that at the southeast angle rose to seventy cubits, and so commanded a view of the whole area of the Temple. At the point where it impinged upon the porticoes of the Temple, there were stairs leading down both of them, by which the guards descended. For a Roman cohort was permanently quartered there and at the festivals took up positions in arms around the porticoes to watch the people and repress any insurrectionary movement. For if the Temple lay as a fortress over the city, Antonia dominated the Temple, and the occupants of that post were the guards of all three. The Upper City had its own fortress—Herod's palace. The hill Bezetha was . . . cut off from Antonia; the highest of all the hills, it was encroached on by part of the new town and formed on the north the only obstruction to the view of the Temple. . . . (Josephus, War V, 5, 8)

The protection of the northern approach to the Temple was only one of the purposes of the Antonia. One of the most remarkable things about Herod's buildings was their multifunctionalism. His palace in the Upper City, for all its luxurious, parklike quality, was also a fortress, and the Antonia, the Jerusalem fortress par excellence, had all the appointments of a palace. From its towers he could both observe and control the critical Temple area. Twice within his lifetime the Temple had been used as a redoubt, and on the later of these occasions he himself had to take it. As always in such matters, Herod's judgment was flawless. The Romans later stationed their Jerusalem garrison there, just as the Mamluks would do in the sixteenth century, the Turks in the nineteenth, and as today an Israeli military post watches the same area from a former Muslim madrasa in the southwest corner.

In the northwestern corner of the present Muslim enclosure on the Temple mount is a high rock escarpment, precipitously planed down on its southern side and sloping, only somewhat less sharply, on the north down into what is now called Lady Mary Street. Between those two cuts, there is a flat area, a mesa almost, upon which now sits a Muslim school and which was, as is commonly agreed, the fortified heart of the Antonia. Since this flat area could scarcely have contained the kind of complex described by Josephus, it was once thought that the Antonia's outworks extended beneath Lady Mary Street and were represented by the Roman work, including a large paved area, preserved under buildings like the Convent of the Sisters of Sion on the other side of the street. That work has been identified as Hadrian's, so it now seems highly likely that Lady Mary Street represents the ditch that screened and separated the fortress from the hill of Bezetha to its north. [41] As for Josephus' description, either he was exaggerating wildly or, as seems more plausible, we must extend our vision of the Fortress Antonia complex southward into the greatest of all of Herod's buildings, the new Temple upon Mount Moriah. [42]

Herod's Temple

The effect of Herod's building in Jerusalem was dauntingly impressive, built, as the Roman historian Tacitus put it at the beginning of the second century, in times of peace in a manner more suitable for war:

The commanding position of the city had been strengthened by enormous works which would have been an effective defense even at ground level. Two hills of great height were enclosed by walls which had been skillfully angled or bent inwards in such a manner that the flank of an assailant was exposed to missiles. The rock ended in a precipice; the towers were raised to a height of sixty feet, and where the hill lent its aid to the fortifications, where the ground fell, to a height of 120 feet. The walls had a marvellous appearance, and seemed to someone looking from a distance to have a uniform height. Inside were still other walls surrounding the palace, and, rising to a notable height, the Tower Antonia, so called by Herod in honor of Mark Antony.

The Temple resembled a fortress and had its own walls, which were more laboriously constructed than the others. Even the colonnades with which it was surrounded formed an admirable outer defense. It contained an inexhaustible spring. There were underground cuttings in the hill, and tanks and cisterns for holding rain water. The founders of the state had foreseen that frequent wars would result from the singularity of its customs, and so had taken precautions against even the most protracted siege. After the capture of the city by Pompey, experience and fear taught them much. Availing themselves of the distasteful policy of the Claudian era to purchase the right of fortification, they raised in time of peace such walls as were appropriate for war. (Tacitus, History V, 11-12)

We cannot be certain when the Antonia was built, but it must certainly have been before Actium in 31 B.C., at a time when Herod and Antony were fast friends and political allies. We can be more precise, however, about the beginning of the enormous Herodian building project that so impressed Tacitus, Herod's own new version of the Jewish Temple atop Mount Moriah: [43]

It was at this time [of Augustus' visit to Syria in 20 B.C.], in the eighteenth year of his reign, . . . that Herod undertook an extraordinary work, the reconstructing of the Temple of God at his own expense, enlarging its precincts and raising it to a more imposing height. For he believed that the accomplishment of this task would be the most notable of all the things achieved by him, as indeed it was, and would be great enough to assure his eternal remembrance. . . . (Josephus, Ant. XV, 11, 1)

Herod's announcement that he would rebuild the Temple was not greeted with universal acclaim—little that the unpopular king did found favor with his subjects—but that was not Herod's way in any event. He was playing the traditional role of Hellenistic dynast, humanist, and benefactor on a monumental scale, the builder, at home and abroad, of grandiose public works, many of which, like the Fortress Antonia, spoke directly to another of his concerns, the security of himself and his regime: [44]

And while the unlikelihood of his realizing his hope did not disturb (the people), they were dismayed by the thought that he might tear down the whole edifice and not have sufficient means to bring his project (of rebuilding it) to completion. . . . Since they felt this way, the king spoke encouragingly to them, saying that he would not pull down the Temple (of Zerubbabel) before having ready all the materials needed for its completion. And these assurances he did not belie. For he prepared 1,000 wagons to carry the stones, selected 10,000 of the most skilled workmen, purchased priestly robes for 1,000 priests, and trained some as masons and others as carpenters, and began the construction only after all these preparations had been diligently made by him.

More than that, according to the Mishna, the king arranged that the Temple liturgy was not disturbed at any time during the work:

Rabbi Eliezer said: I have heard a tradition that while they were building the Temple they made curtains for the Temple and curtains for the court-yards, but they built [the walls of] the Temple outside [the curtains], [the walls of the courtyards] they built within [the curtains]. . . . (Danby 1933: 436)

Josephus continues:

After removing the old foundations, he laid down others, and upon these he erected the Temple [that is, the sanctuary proper], which was a hundred cubits in length . . . and twenty more in height, but in the course of time this dropped as the foundations subsided. And this part we de-cided to raise again in the time of Nero. [45] *The Temple was built of hard, white stones. . . . And in the whole of it, as also in the Royal Portico, either side was the lowest, while the middle portion was the highest, so that it was visible at a distance of many stades to those who inhabited the coun-try, especially those who lived opposite or happened to approach it. . . . And he surrounded the Temple with very large porticoes, all of which he made in proportion (to the Temple), and he surpassed his predecessors in spending money, so that it was thought that no one else had adorned the Temple so splendidly.*

[The Temple sanctuary and its porticoes] were supported by a great wall, and the wall itself was the greatest ever heard of by man. The hill was a rocky ascent that sloped gently up toward the eastern part of the city to the topmost peak. The hill our first king Solomon [or "our king Solomon first"] with God-given wisdom surrounded with great works above at the top. Below, beginning at the foot, where a deep ravine runs round it, he [Herod] surrounded it with enormous stones bound together with lead. He cut off more and more of the area within as (the wall) became greater in depth, so that the size and height of the structure, which was square, were immense, and the great size of the stones was seen along the front [outside] surface, while the iron clamps in the inside assured that the joints would remain permanently united.

When the work reached the top of the hill, he leveled off the summit and filled in the hollow spaces near the walls, and made the upper surfaces smooth and even throughout. Such was the whole enclosure, having a circumference of four stades, each side taking up the length of a stade. Within this wall and on the very summit there ran another wall of stone, which had on the eastern ridge a double portico of the same length as the wall, and it faced the doors of the Temple, for this lay within it. This portico many of the earlier kings adorned. [46] *Round about the entire Temple were fixed the spoils taken from the barbarians, and all these King Herod dedicated, adding those which he took from the [Nabatean] Arabs. (Josephus, Ant. XV, 11, 2-4)*

Again, in the *War*:

Though the Temple . . . was seated on a strong hill, the level area on its summit originally barely sufficed for shrine and altar, the ground around it being precipitous and steep. But king Solomon, the actual founder of the Temple, having walled up the eastern side, a single portico was reared on this made ground; on its other sides the sanctuary remained exposed. In the course of the ages, however, through the constant additions of people to the embankment, the hill-top by this process of levelling up was widened. They further broke down the north wall and thus took in an area as large as the whole Temple area subsequently occupied. Then, after having enclosed the hill from its base on (the other) three sides, and accomplished a task greater than they could ever have hoped to achieve—a task upon which long ages were spent by them as well as all their sacred treasures, though replenished by the tributes offered to God from every quarter of the world—they built around the original block the upper courts and the lower Temple enclosure. The latter, where its foundations were lowest, they built up from a depth of three hundred cubits; at some spots this figure was exceeded. The whole depth of the foundations was not, however, apparent, for they filled up a considerable part of the ravines, wishing to level the narrow alleys of the town. Blocks of stone were used in building measuring forty cubits; for lavish funds and popular enthusiasm led to incredible enterprise, and a task seemingly interminable was through perseverance and in time actually achieved. (Josephus, War V, 5, 1)

The work did take a long time to accomplish. According to Josephus (*Ant. XX*, 9, 7), the final touches were not put on the complex until A.D. 60-62, no more than ten years before its destruction by the Romans. And it was immense. The size of the platform upon which the Jerusalem Temple sat far outstripped not only Herod's other building projects but every known temple complex in the Greco-Roman world, particularly if we are to believe, as most do, that the present-day Muslim enclosure around the Dome of the Rock exactly represents the Herodian platform.

And why should we not? For one reason, the enormous size apart, both Josephus and our other literary evidence on Herod's Temple, the Mishna treatise called Middoth, attest that Herod's platform was square—in Josephus a square of one stade or about 600 feet on each side; in Middoth 2:1 about 500 cubits or 750 on each side—while the actual dimensions of the Haram al-Sharif are those of an irregular rectangle measuring 929 feet on the south side, 1,041 feet on the north, 1,556 feet on the east, and 1,596 feet on the west. And the place is highly visible; no one standing on the Mount of Olives and looking down upon it would judge that the Haram al-Sharif was square. The notion must, then, at least be entertained that what Herod built is the southern two-thirds of the present platform, and that the northern third of today's Haram were not part of the Temple but of the large complex of the Fortress Antonia. [47]

The Gates of the Temple

Josephus proceeds to describe the gates into the Temple complex, and the Mishna too names and locates them:

In the western part of the court (of the Temple) there were four gates. The first led to the palace over the intervening ravine [Wilson's Arch?], two others led to the suburbs, and the last led to the other part of the (Upper) city [Robinson's Arch?], from which it was separated by many steps going down into the ravine and from here up again to the hill. For the city lay opposite the Temple, being in the form of a theater and being bordered by a deep ravine along its whole southern side. The fourth front of this (court), facing south, also had gates in the middle, and had over it the Royal Portico, which had three aisles extending in length from the eastern to the western ravine. And it was a structure more noteworthy than any under the sun. For while the depth of the ravine was great, and no one who bent over to look into it from above could bear to look down to the bottom, the height of the portico standing over it was so very great that anyone looking down from its rooftop, combining the two elevations, would become dizzy and his vision would be unable to reach the end of so measureless a depth. (Josephus, Ant. XV, 11, 5)

There are five gates to the Temple Mount: the two Huldah Gates on the south that served for coming in and for going out; the Kiponus Gate on the west that served for coming in and going out; the Tadi Gate on the north which was not used at all; the eastern on which was portrayed [or sculpted] the Palace of Shushan. Through this the high priest who burned the [Red] Heifer and the heifer and all [the priests] who aided him went forth to the Mount of Olives. (Danby 1933: 590)

Some of these gates can be identified without difficulty. The Mishna's two Huldah Gates, mentioned but not named by Josephus, are still visible on the south face of the Herodian platform. Today they are known as the Double and the Triple Gates, and though they have undergone some Byzantine and perhaps Muslim reconstruction, their Herodian origins are clear. In fact, we know a good deal about this area, since unlike the other sides of the Temple enclosure, it has been systematically excavated. We know now there were broad steps here leading up to the Temple entries, a piazza, and facilities for ritual ablution. [48] By all indications, these were the chief gates into the Herodian Temple.

The southeast corner of the platform was likewise the highest point above the valley floor below, as Josephus points out. It was here that one of the Gospel events was traditionally set, and the place, called the "Pinnacle of the Temple," was shown to Christian pilgrims for centuries to come:

Full of the Holy Spirit Jesus returned from the Jordan, and for forty days was led by the Spirit up and down in the wilderness and tempted by the devil. All that time he had nothing to eat, and at the end of it he was famished. The devil said to him, "If you are the Son of God, tell this stone to become bread." Jesus answered, "Scripture says, 'Man cannot live on bread alone.'" . . . The devil took him to Jerusalem and set him on the parapet of the Temple. "If you are the Son of God," he said, "throw yourself down, for Scripture says, 'He will his angels order to take care of you,' and again, 'They will support you in their arms for fear you should strike your foot against a stone.'" Jesus answered him, "It has been said, 'You are not to put the Lord your God to the test.'" So, having come to the end of all his temptations, the devil departed, biding his time. (Luke 4:1-13)

As for the north side, we simply accept the Mishna's statement that there was a single gate here and that it was called Tadi. Though there is no archeological evidence, we can guess that it was in the northeast corner, at or near the Muslim gate called the Gate of the Tribes. There was nearby a pool called the "Sheep Pool" and so we can extend the guess one step further, that the animals for sacrifice in the Temple were kept just outside and brought in through this gate. [49] We know about the Sheep Pool from the Gospels, but there it has quite another use:

Later on Jesus went up to Jerusalem for one of the Jewish festivals. Now at the Sheep Pool in Jerusalem there is a place with five colonnades. Its name in the language of the Jews is Bethesda. In these colonnades there lay a crowd of sick people, blind, lame, and paralyzed. Among them was a man who had been crippled for thirty-eight years. When Jesus saw him lying there and was aware that he had been ill for a long time, he asked him, "Do you want to recover?" "Sir," he replied, "I have no one to put me in the pool when the water is disturbed, but while I am moving, someone else is in the pool before me." Jesus answered, "Rise to your feet, take up your bed and walk." The man recovered instantly, took up his stretcher, and began to walk. (John 5:1-9)

In this instance, we do have material evidence that at a double pool just beyond the northern edge of the Temple there was a curative sanctuary when the Romans redid the city in A.D. 135. John seems to suggest that the place had a somewhat similar association even in the Jewish city of Herod. [50]

In discussing the eastern side of the Temple enclosure, Josephus had earlier said that there was a "double portico of the same length as the wall, and it faced the doors of the Temple, for this lay within it. This portico many of the earlier kings adorned." Here, however, Josephus makes no mention of a gate, though the Mishna is quite specific on the Shushan or Susa Gate and its remarkable decoration, set there, doubtless, to remind the people of the Exile and their release by Cyrus. Both the gate and the portico appear to be mentioned in the New Testament:

It was winter and the festival of the Dedication [Hanukka or the recon-secration of the Temple in 164 B.C.] was being held in Jerusalem. Jesus was walking in the Temple's precincts, in Solomon's Portico. . . . (John 10:21)

One day at three in the afternoon, Peter and John were on their way up to the Temple. Now a man who had been a cripple from birth used to be carried there and laid every day by the gate of the Temple called "Beautiful Gate," to beg from people as they went in. When he saw Peter and John on their way into the Temple he asked for charity. But Peter fixed his eyes on him, as John did also, and said "Look at us." Expecting a gift from them, the man was all attention. And Peter said, "I have no silver or gold, but what I have I give you; in the name of Jesus Christ of Nazareth, walk." Then he grasped him by the right hand and pulled him up; and at once his feet and ankles grew strong. He sprang up, stood on his feet and started to walk. He entered the Temple with them, leaping and praising God, and when they recognized him as the man who used to sit begging at the Beautiful Gate, they were filled with wonder and amazement at what had happened to him. And as he was clutching Peter and John all the people came running in astonishment toward them in Solomon's Portico, as it is called. . . . (Acts 3:1-11)

They [Jesus' disciples] used to meet by common consent in Solomon's Portico, no one from outside their number venturing to join with them. But people in general spoke highly of them, and more than that, numbers of men and women were added to their ranks as believers in the Lord. In the end the sick were actually carried out into the streets and laid there on beds and stretchers so that even the shadow of Peter might fall on one or another as he passed by; and the people of the towns around Jerusalem flocked in, bringing those who were ill or harassed by unclean spirits, and all of them were cured. (Acts 5:12-16)

The nearness of the Beautiful Gate to Solomon's Portico in these accounts strongly suggest that the Beautiful Gate of Acts is the same as the Shushan Gate of the Mishna. The early Christian pilgrims certainly identified the eastern entry to the platform in their day with the Beautiful Gate—the Piacenza pilgrim of A.D. 570, for example—just as a somewhat later generation called the same entry the Golden Gate. The Golden Gate is still standing on the eastern side of the Muslim Haram and it does indeed appear to be in part Herodian in construction, which makes the triple identification of Shushan-Beautiful-Golden Gate a highly likely one. [51]

The gates on the western side of the Temple enclosure, four in Josephus, one in the Mishna, are more problematic. The Temple sanctuary faced, as we shall see, east and west, but the traffic patterns of the entire Temple complex seem to have kept their older orientation toward the south, the site of the original Israelite settlement, even though by Herod's day part of the hill of Sion had been leveled off and cleared and the rest of the City of David was in a state of decline. In the first century B.C. the city's growth was westward and northward from the Temple. The northern approach was blocked by reservoirs and fortifications, the Hasmoneans' Baris and Herod's Antonia. Thus we would expect the western accesses to be the most important. But ceremony and tradition dictated that the southern entries receive the more striking architectural treatment.

We suppose that the Mishna was speaking only of the most important western entry and that it somehow acquired the name of Coponius, the first of the Roman procurators in Judea (ca. A.D. 6-9). Of the four gates mentioned by Josephus, two can be located with some certainty. That which led over the ravine must surely be located near the Muslim Gate of the Chain and atop Wilson's Arch, the underpinning of the bridge that led from the Temple across the Tyropean Valley to the palace and the Upper City. [52] The southernmost entry is even more certainly represented by the remains of Robinson's Arch, which supported a large stairway that led up from the street in the valley to the western face of the Royal Stoa above. [53] As for Josephus' other two entries that led into the suburbs, it seems likely that they were somewhere north of Wilson's Arch, though precisely where cannot even be guessed.

The Inner Courts of the Temple

Josephus now takes us through the Court of the Gentiles, the unrestricted outer perimeter of the Temple platform, into the inner courts of the Temple:

Within it [the Court of the Gentiles] and not far distant was a second one, accessible by a few steps and surrounded by a stone balustrade with an inscription prohibiting the entry of a foreigner under threat of penalty of death. On its southern and northern side the inner court had three-chambered gateways, equally distant from one another, and on the side where the sun rises it had one great gateway [Nicanor's Gate], through which those of us who were ritually clean used to pass with our wives. Within this court was the sacred court where women were forbidden to enter, and still further within was a third court into which only priests were permitted to go. In this (priests' court) was the Temple [naos], and before it was an altar on which we used to sacrifice whole burnt-offerings to God. Into none of these courts did King Herod enter since he was not a priest and was therefore prevented from so doing. But with the construction of the porticoes and the outer courts he did busy himself, and these he finished building in eight years. The Temple [naos] itself was built by the priests in a year and six months, and all the people were filled with joy and offered thanks to God, first of all for the speed (of the work) and next for the king's zeal, and as they celebrated they acclaimed the restoration.

There was also made for the king a secret underground passage which led from the Antonia to the eastern gate of the inner sacred court, and above this he had a tower built for himself in order to be able to go into it through the underground passage and so protect himself should there be a revolt of the people against its kings. (Josephus, Ant. XV, 11, 5-7)

The Mishna treatise Middoth, which has an elaborate treatment of the chambers of the Temple, also supplies some additional information on the courts:

The Temple Mount measured five hundred cubits by five hundred cubits. Its largest open space was to the south, the next largest to the east, the third largest to the north, and its smallest was to the west; the place where its measure was greatest was where its use was greatest.

Inside the Temple Mount was a latticed railing [the soreg], ten hand-breadths high. It had thirteen breaches which the Grecian kings had made; they were fenced up again and over against them thirteen prostrations were decreed. Inside this was the Rampart [the hel], ten cubits broad. . . .

All the walls there were high, save only the eastern wall, because the [high] priest that burns the [Red] Heifer and stands on the top of the Mount of Olives should be able to look directly into the entrance of the Sanctuary when the blood was sprinkled. (Danby 1933: 591)

The careful distinction of the courts, even to the posting a public warning in Greek and Latin threatening death to intruders beyond the stone bal-lustrade called the *soreg*, is the working out in architectural terms of the degrees of holiness focussed in that place. [54] The Mishna treatise Kelim sets them out, as we have already seen (Chapter One), beginning with the Land of Israel and ending in the inner courts of the Temple:

The Temple Mount is still more holy (than the city of Jerusalem), for no man or woman that has the flux, no menstruant, and no woman after childbirth may enter therein. The Rampart is still more holy, for no Gen-tiles and none that have contracted uncleanness from a corpse may enter therein. The Court of the Women is still more holy, for none that has immersed himself the selfsame day (because of uncleanness) may enter therein, yet none would thereby become liable to a sin-offering. The Court of the Israelites is still more holy, for none whose atonement is yet incom-plete may enter therein, and they would thereby become liable to a sin-offering. The Court of the Priests is still more holy, for Israelites may not enter therein, save only when they must perform the laying on of hands, slaughtering, and waving.

Between the Porch and the Altar is still more holy, for none that has a blemish or whose hair is unloosed may enter there. The Sanctuary is still more holy, for none may enter therein with hands or feet unwashed. The Holy of Holies is still more holy, for none may enter therein save only the High Priest on the Day of Atonement at the time of the [Temple] service. R. Jose said: In five things is the space between the Porch and the Altar equal to the Sanctuary: for they may not enter there that have a blemish, or that have drunk wine, or that have hands or feet unwashed, and men must keep far from between the Porch and the Altar at the time of the burning of incense. (Danby 1933: 605-606)

The Sanctuary

And finally, there was the Temple proper, the sanctuary building which housed the Holy of Holies where the presence of God still dwelled among His people:

Passing within one found oneself in the ground floor of the Sanctuary.
This was sixty cubits in height, the same in length, and twenty cubits in
breadth. But the sixty cubits of its length were again divided. The front
portion, partitioned off at forty cubits, contained within it three most
wonderful works of art, universally renowned: a lampstand, a table, and
an altar of incense. The seven lamps, such being the number of the
branches of the lampstand, represented the planets; the loaves on the
table, twelve in number, the circle of the Zodiac and the year; while the
altar of incense, by the thirteen fragrant spices from sea and from land,
both desert and inhabited, with which it was replenished, signified that all
things are of God and for God.

The innermost recess measured twenty cubits, and was screened in like
manner from the outer portion by a veil. In this stood nothing whatever;
unapproachable, inviolable, invisible to all, it was called the Holy of Holy.

In front of it [the Sanctuary] stood the altar, fifteen cubits high, and
with a breadth and length extending alike to fifty cubits, in shape a square
with horn-like projections at the corners, and approached from the south
by a gently sloping acclivity. No iron was used in its construction, nor did
iron ever touch it. (Josephus, War V, 5, 5-6)

Josephus has described the Sanctuary, or *naos*, but he has not located it
for us on the platform. Nor has anyone after him been remarkably successful at the enterprise, even assuming that it stood somewhere near the
center of the enclosure, since there is no certainty, as we have seen, about
the exact dimensions of that enclosure. What has been the starting point
of most of the attempts at answering the question is the dual assumption
that first, the present Haram is identical with Herod's platform, and second, the Sanctuary had some connection with the rock that is presently
enshrined under the Muslim Dome of the Rock. The latter assumption
dates back among the Christians to before the Crusades, though not earlier than the fourth century, and among the Jews likely even earlier. [55]

What is that connection? It has been suggested that the rock was under
either the Holy of Holies or the Altar of Sacrifice, though to put it under
the former would move the entire structure too close to the eastern portico. Indeed to put it under either poses other problems since both structures were very large and the present rock would disappear under either
the Holy of Holies or the Altar. [56] And of course, if the Herodian platform
was actually only the southern two-thirds of the Haram, the Sanctuary
would have been well south of the Dome of the Rock.

Attempts at deducing its appearance from later portraits in art have not
been entirely successful, either. As in the case of the connection of the
Sanctuary with the Rock, there has been a somewhat easy assumption that

the building portrayed on the coins of Bar Kohkba, for example, or in the synagogue frescoes at Dura-Europus on the Euphrates was indeed the already destroyed Temple at Jerusalem and, if so, that the portrait intended to depict the building in a realistic fashion. Neither intention is certain, and for every scholar who has built upon these iconographic foundations, there is another who has cast them into serious dispute. [57]

Josephus, from whom most of information on Hasmonean and Herodian Jerusalem derives, was writing a tragedy wrapped in his history, the city's dizzying fall from a great height into utter ruin. He may have been exaggerating, then, when he described Jerusalem before its fall. From what remains in the fallen stones and the existing foundations of the city before A.D. 70, however, the exaggeration could not have been very great. Jerusalem was indeed a magnificent city in its Greco-Roman heyday, as large and as splendid as it was ever to be in its very long history. Its long paved and colonnaded streets, its carefully managed water resources fed by aqueduct and cistern, its palaces, public buildings, and heroic and dazzling fortifications, the crowning splendor of the Temple atop Mount Moriah with its innumerable priests and impressive daily sacrifices, all presented to the eyes of the perhaps 100,000 visitors who converged upon it from all over the Mediterranean Diaspora for the annual pilgrimage festivals a spectacle of wealth and power, and all of it toppled, in the final rush of Josephus' narrative, into unspeakable ruin. [58]

Not a Stone Upon
a Stone: The Destruction
of the Holy City

*Neither its antiquity nor its ample wealth, nor its people spread over
the whole habitable world, nor yet the great glory of its religious
rites, could aught avail to avert its ruin.*
—*Josephus*

WHATEVER his subjects thought of him, Herod was a useful and obliging
client to his Roman masters, and not least for his capacity and willingness
to maintain order, if not peace, in his turbulent kingdom. He cost the
Romans little and gave a substantial return. How substantial appeared
immediately after his death in 4 B.C. In his own plans for his succession
Herod's choice for Judea fell upon his son Archelaus, but even as the
ineffective Archelaus was preparing to go to Rome to secure his own
appointment as king, "because Caesar was to have control of all the settlements he [Herod] had made," disturbances broke out in Jerusalem, and
at his departure the Roman governor of Syria had to intervene with a
legion to quell them.

Archelaus' appointment did not go uncontested. A delegation of Jews
went to Rome and rehearsed Herod's crimes against the people:

*. . . that in short the Jews had borne more calamities from Herod, in a
few years, than had their forefathers during all that interval of time that
had passed since they had come out of Babylon, and returned home, in
the reign of Xerxes. . . . Whereupon, they prayed that the Romans would
have compassion upon the remains of Judea and not expose what was left
of them to such as would barbarously tear them to pieces, and that they
would join their country to [the province of] Syria and administer the
government by their own commanders. . . . (Josephus, War II, 6, 2)*

The Romans were uncertain, however—uncertain on a policy level and
uncertain of the man Archelaus. Finally, Augustus appointed Archelaus
ethnarch with the promise that he would be named king "if he rendered
himself worthy of that dignity." He did not, and after ten brutal years the
Romans did as the Jewish ambassadors had suggested and added Judea as
a kind of annex to the province of Syria, with its own governor of somewhat lower rank called a procurator or prefect. [1] It was, if anything, an

even unhappier arrangement than the Herodian monarchy. Herod, for all his brutality, was neither stupid nor completely insensitive when it came to the beliefs and cultic practices of his coreligionists, while the Romans soon showed that they could be both.

The Romans and Jerusalem

The Roman governor of Judea had his official residence in Caesarea, as Herod had had, but when his presence was required in Jerusalem, on the occasion of the great Jewish pilgrimage festivals, for example, when tension was always high and the possibility of trouble never very remote, he and his escort troops almost certainly resided in Herod's palace by the Citadel on the western side of the city. [2] Under normal circumstances, however, the security of Roman Jerusalem was in the hands of a commander and cohort stationed in the Fortress Antonia overlooking and giving immediate entrance to the Temple compound. [3]

The Romans generally displayed an easy and almost indifferent tolerance of the religious practices of their subjects, so long, that is, as those practices did not interfere with either the social or political order. They neither retracted nor even modified the protection extended to Jewish cult and religious observances extended by their Seleucid predecessors, and as alien sovereigns had been doing since the days of Antiochus III, or even of Darius, Roman emperors underwrote the expenses of the public sacrifices in the Temple. What they failed to understand, was how far beyond Temple and sacrifice at least some Jews of that day were construing the "traditions from their fathers."

The pages of Josephus are filled with these sometimes comic but more often tragic misunderstandings, but here we need cite only two, both under the prefecture of Pontius Pilate, who governed Judea from A.D. 26 to 36. The first, reported by both Josephus and Philo, [4] seems to have occurred near the beginning of his tenure:

Now Pilate, who was sent as procurator into Judea by Tiberius, sent by night those images of Caesar that are called "standards" into Jerusalem. This excited a great disturbance among the Jews when it became day, for those that were near them were astonished at the sight of them, as an indication that their laws were being spurned, since those laws did not permit any images to be brought into the city.

Jews began to converge from all over the countryside on Pilate's headquarters in Caesarea where they staged a demonstration of passive resistance by lying down immobile before his palace for five days and nights.

He finally agreed to hear their complaint in the marketplace, where the protestors were alarmed to discover they were surrounded by armed soldiers:

Pilate said to them that they would be cut in pieces unless they admitted Caesar's images and signalled the soldiers to draw their swords. Thereupon the Jews, as if upon signal, fell down together and exposed their bared necks, crying out that they would sooner be slain that their law should be broken. At that Pilate was greatly surprised at their extraordinary superstition and ordered that the standards should be removed from Jerusalem. (Josephus, War II, 9, 2-3)

If the first protest surprised Pilate, he must have been even more startled by the second. Jerusalem had grown prodigiously under Herod and the Hasmoneans, and while the city could survive, as it often did, simply by its ample rainfall collected in the great number of underground cisterns it seems always to have possessed, Pilate conceived the highly practical idea of using Roman hydraulic technology to bring additional perennial sources of water to the city by building an aqueduct to Jerusalem from the springs known as Solomon's Pool between Bethlehem and Hebron. [5] The problem was the financing of the project. The Roman prefect certainly had a say in the administration of the Temple, which was not to say, however, that its funds, which were in effect sacred moneys, were available to his purposes, however laudable:

He [Pilate] caused another disturbance by spending that sacred treasure [of the Temple] called the Qorban on the building of aqueducts by which be brought water [to Jerusalem] from a distance of four hundred stadia. The crowd became angry at this, and when Pilate visited Jerusalem they came to his tribunal and raised a clamor about it. He knew about this beforehand and so he had ordered his armored soldiers to mingle with the crowd, though dressed as ordinary citizens, and to use not swords but clubs on whoever made the outcry. He then from his tribunal gave them the signal to begin, and the Jews were so badly beaten that many of them died from the blows, while others were crushed under foot. The rest were so startled at the calamity of the slaughter that they held their peace. (Josephus, War II, 9, 4)

The aqueduct was constructed, in any case, and served the inhabitants of Jerusalem for many centuries. Pilate received no thanks for its completion, however, nor is this the accomplishment for which his governorship is best remembered. The protagonist of that other well-known event was even then perhaps approaching Jerusalem:

They were on the road, going up to Jerusalem, Jesus leading the way; and the disciples were filled with awe, while those who followed behind were afraid. He took the Twelve aside and began to tell them what was to happen to him. "We are now going to Jerusalem," he said, "and the Son of Man will be given up to the chief priests and the doctors of the Law. They will condemn him to death and hand him over to the foreign power. He will be mocked and spat upon, flogged and killed; and three days afterwards he will rise again." (Mark 10:32-34[6])

So begins Jesus' final visit to Jerusalem. Though he had been to the Holy City before on occasion—how often or for how long is difficult to say on the Gospel evidence—he had labored during most of his brief career in his native region of Galilee. Now as the end that he had anticipated approached, sometime about A.D. 30, he came to the heart and center of Judaism, to Jerusalem. With Jesus' final journey up to the Holy City, the focus of the four Gospels that chronicle his ministry and his teaching move there as well. It is not, however, Jesus' teaching or his claims that are at issue in the present context, but the considerable knowledge of both the topography and institutions of Herodian Jerusalem that are displayed in the Gospel accounts of those days.[7] And more important to our purposes here, it is precisely the events during and after the Passover season of the year of Jesus' death that will determine the future shape of the city and its holy places, when Jesus' followers began to visit and enshrine the sites where those events were thought to have taken place.

Jesus in Jerusalem

They were now nearing Jerusalem; and when they reached Bethphage at the Mount of Olives, Jesus sent two disciples with these instructions: "Go to the village opposite, where you will at once find a donkey tethered with her foal beside her; untie them and bring them to me. If anyone speaks to you, say 'Our Master needs them' and he will let you take them at once." This was to fulfill the prophecy which says: "Tell the daughter of Sion, 'Here is your king, who comes to you in gentleness, riding on an ass, riding on the foal of a beast of burden.'"

The disciples went and did as Jesus had directed, and brought the donkey and her foal; they laid their cloaks on them and Jesus mounted. Crowds of people carpeted the road with their cloaks, and some cut branches from the trees to spread in his path. Then the crowd that went ahead and the others that came behind raised the shout: "Hosanna to the Son of David! Blessings on him who comes in the name of the Lord! Hosanna in the heavens!"

When he entered Jerusalem the whole city went wild with excitement. "Who is this?" people asked, and the crowd replied "This is the prophet Jesus, from Nazareth in Galilee."

Jesus then went into the Temple and drove out all who were buying and selling in the Temple precincts; he upset the tables of the money-changers and the seats of the dealers in pigeons; and said to them: "Scripture says, 'My House shall be called a house of prayer,' but you are making it a robbers' cave." (Matthew 21:1-17)

John continues the story:

His disciples recalled the words of Scripture "Zeal for thy house will destroy me." The Jews challenged Jesus: "What sign," they asked, "can you show us as authority for your action?" "Destroy this Temple," Jesus replied, "and in three days I will raise it again." They said, "It has taken forty-six years to build this Temple. Are you going to raise it again in three days?" But the Temple he was speaking of was his body. After his resurrection his disciples recalled what he had said, and they believed the Scripture and the words that Jesus had spoken. (John 2:17-22)

As he was leaving the Temple, one of his disciples exclaimed, "Look, Master, what huge stones! What fine buildings!" Jesus said to him, "You see these great buildings? Not one stone will be left upon another; all will be thrown down." (Mark 13:1-2)

"O Jerusalem, Jerusalem, the city that murders the prophets and stones the messengers sent to her! How often have I longed to gather your children, as a hen gathers her brood under her wings; but you would not let me. Look, look! There is your Temple, forsaken by God. And I tell you, you shall never see me until the time when you say 'Blessings on him who comes in the name of the Lord.'" (Matthew 23:37-39)

The occasion of this last visit of Jesus to Jerusalem was the celebration of the great pilgrimage feast of Passover, when every Jew was obliged to come to the Temple and share in the sacrifices. The year, as closely as we can estimate it, was A.D. 30, and inside the city itself, the Gospels tell us, the powers that would kill him were already drawing up their plans:

The Jewish Passover was now at hand, and many people went up from the country to Jerusalem to purify themselves before the festival. They looked out for Jesus, and as they stood in the Temple, they asked one another, "What do you think? Perhaps he is not coming to the festival." Now the chief priests and the Pharisees had given orders that anyone who knew where he was should give information, so that they might arrest him. (John 11:55-57)

Mark adds:

*"It must not be during the Passover," they said, "or we should have riot-
ing among the people."*

*Now on the first day of Unleavened Bread, when the Passover lambs
were being slaughtered, his [Jesus'] disciples said to him, "Where would
you like us to go and prepare for your Passover supper?" So he sent out
two of his disciples with these instructions: "Go into the city, and a man
will meet you carrying a jar of water. Follow him, and when he enters a
house, give this message to the householder. 'The Master says, Where is
the room reserved for me to eat the Passover with my disciples?' He will
show you a large room upstairs, set out in readiness.* [8] *Make the preparations for us there." Then the disciples went off, and when they came into
the city they found everything just as he told them. (Mark 14:12-16)*

The three Synoptic Gospels all provide us with a brief but highly charged
account of that meal, a traditional Jewish Passover supper by all appearances, which would be so pregnant for the future history of Christianity:

*During supper he took bread, and having said the blessing, broke it and
gave it to them, with the words: "Take this; this is my body." Then he
took a cup, and having offered thanks to God he gave it to them, and
they all drank from it. "This is my blood, the blood of the Covenant, shed
for many. I tell you this; never again shall I drink from the fruit of the
vine until the day I drink it new in the kingdom of God." (Mark 14:22-
25)*

For the Christian this was the institution of the Eucharist, the central
liturgical act of the new faith which in a few years would be reenacted
daily in every corner of the Roman Empire. The Eucharist, the rite and
the notion, transcended Jerusalem, but its original celebration marked the
spot forever. That upper room on Mount Sion, which the Christians later
identified as the same place where the Apostles had received the Holy
Spirit after Jesus' ascension into heaven, likely served as the first assembly
place of the new Christians in Jerusalem, the "mother of all the churches,"
and then, in the century after Constantine, as the site of one of the city's
largest shrine-cathedrals.

But meanwhile the train of events set in motion that night moved rapidly forward:

*After singing the Passover Hymn, they went out to the Mount of Ol-
ives. . . . Jesus then came to a place called Gethsemane. He said to them,
"Sit here while I go over there to pray." . . . Then he came [back] to the
disciples and said to them, "Still sleeping? Still taking your ease? The hour*

has come. *The Son of Man is betrayed to sinful men. Up, let us go for-ward; the traitor is upon us."* While he was still speaking, Judas, one of the Twelve, appeared; with him was a great crowd armed with swords and cudgels, sent by the chief priests and the elders of the nation. The traitor gave them this sign: *"The one I kiss is your man; seize him";* and stepping forward at once he said, *"Hail, Rabbi!"* and kissed him. Jesus replied, *"Friend, do what you are here to do."* Then they came forward, seized Jesus, and held him fast. *(Matthew 26:30-50)*

Jesus was led off under arrest to the house of Caiaphas the high priest where the lawyers and elders were assembled.[9] . . . The chief priests and the elders tried to find some allegation against Jesus on which a death sentence could be based; but they failed to find one, though many came forward with false evidence. Finally two men alleged that he had said *"I can pull down the Temple of God and rebuild it in three days."* At this the high priest rose and said to him, *"Have you no answer to the charge that these witnesses bring against you?"* But Jesus kept silence. The high priest then said, *"By the living God I charge you to tell us: Are you the Messiah, the Son of God?"* Jesus replied, *"The words are yours. But I tell you this: from now on, you will see the Son of Man seated at the right hand of God and coming on the clouds of heaven."* At these words the high priest tore his robes and exclaimed, *"Blasphemy! Need we call further witnesses? You have heard the blasphemy. What is your opinion?"* "He is guilty," they answered; "he should die." Then they spat in his face and struck him with their fists; and others said, *"Now, Messiah, if you are a prophet, tell us who hit you."* *(Matthew 26:30-50)*

When morning came, the chief priests and the elders of the nation met in conference to plan the death of Jesus. They then put him in chains and led him away, to hand him over to Pilate, the Roman governor. . . . *Jesus was now brought before the governor,*[10] and as he stood there the gov-ernor asked, *"Are you the king of the Jews?"* "The words are yours," Jesus said; and to the charges laid against him by the chief priests and elders he made no reply. Then Pilate said to him, *"Do you not hear all this evidence that is brought against you?"* But he still refused to answer one word, to the governor's great astonishment. *(Matthew 27:1-14)*

Pilate then said to the chief priests and the crowd *"I find no case for this man to answer."* But they insisted: *"His teaching is causing disaffection among the people all through Judea. It started in Galilee and has spread as far as this city."* When Pilate heard this, he asked if the man was a Galilean, and on learning that he belonged to Herod's [that is, Herod Antipas] jurisdiction, he remitted the case to him.[11] When Herod saw

Jesus he was greatly pleased; having heard about him, he had long been wanting to see him and and had been hoping to see some miracle performed by him. He questioned him at some length without getting any reply; but the chief priests and lawyers appeared and pressed the case against him vigorously. Then Herod and his troops treated him with contempt and ridicule and sent him back to Pilate dressed in a gorgeous robe. That same day Herod and Pilate became friends; till then there had been a standing feud between them. (Luke 23:4-12)

Pilate, perhaps in an effort to confront the crowd with an unacceptable alternative, offered them the release of either Jesus or a notorious criminal called Bar Abbas. They chose Bar Abbas.

Pilate could see that nothing was being gained and a riot was starting; so he took water and washed his hands in the full view of the people, saying, "My hands are clean of this man's blood; see to that yourselves." And with one voice the people cried, "His blood be upon us and upon our children." He then released Bar Abbas to them; but he had Jesus flogged and handed over to be crucified. Pilate's soldiers then took Jesus into the governor's headquarters, where they collected the whole company round him. They stripped him and dressed him in a scarlet mantle; and plaiting a crown of thorns they placed it on his head, with a cane in his right hand. Falling on their knees before him they jeered at him: "Hail, King of the Jews!" They spat on him, and used the cane to beat him about the head. When they had finished their mockery, they took off the mantle and dressed him in his own clothes. [12] (Matthew 27:24-31)

The Christians of the post-Crusade period made a particular devotion of tracing the various steps in Jesus' final journey from the Pretorium to the place of the crucifixion and burial. [13] Most of the events commemorated along this "Way of the Cross" are derived from the apocryphal tradition, however. The Gospels themselves have in fact little to say: "Then they led him away to be crucified. On their way they met a man from Cyrene, Simon by name, and pressed him into service to carry his cross" (Mt. 27:32); "Great numbers of people followed, many women among them, who mourned and lamented over him. Jesus turned and said to them 'Daughters of Jerusalem, do not weep for me; no, weep for yourselves and your children . . .' " (Lk. 23:27-28).

The Crucifixion

Jesus was now taken in charge and, carrying his own cross, went out to the Place of the Skull, as it is called (or, in the Jews' language "Golgotha"), where they crucified him, and with him two others, one on the right, one on the left, and Jesus between them. And Pilate wrote an inscription to be fastened on the cross; it read, "Jesus of Nazareth, King of the Jews." This inscription was read by many Jews, because the place where Jesus was crucified was not far from the city, and the inscription was in Hebrew, Latin and Greek. . . . (John 19:17-20)

The directions to the place of the crucifixion are no more precise than that: "the Place of the Skull," in the Latin Vulgate *Calvarium,* located outside the city wall of Jerusalem, as we might expect with a place of execution and burial. When late in the 320s A.D. the Christians chose to enshrine the spot that is presently within the Church of the Holy Sepulcher, the local tradition had no other real candidate, and there still is none today. [14] We have no firm archeological grounds for either accepting or rejecting the traditional Golgotha, [15] and the location of the Herodian wall outside of which Golgotha stood, the already noted "second wall" of Josephus, is still being debated apropos of the site in the Church of the Holy Sepulcher rather than vice versa.

The passers-by hurled abuse at him: they wagged their heads and cried, "You would pull the Temple down, would you, and build it in three days? Come down from the cross and save yourself, if you are indeed the Son of God." So too the chief priests with the lawyers and elders mocked at him. "He saved others," they said, "but he cannot save himself. King of Israel indeed! Let him come down now from the cross, and then we will believe him. Did he trust in God? Let God rescue him, if he wants him—for he said he was God's Son." Even the bandits who were crucified with him taunted him in the same way.

From midday a darkness fell over the whole land, which lasted until three in the afternoon; and about three Jesus cried aloud "Eli, Eli, lema sabachthani?" which means "My God, my God, why hast thou forsaken me?" Some of the bystanders, on hearing this, said, "He is calling Elijah." One of the soldiers then ran at once and fetched a sponge, which he soaked in sour wine, and held it to his lips at the end of a cane. But the others said, "Let us see if Elijah will come to save him." Jesus again gave a loud cry and breathed his last. At that moment the curtain of the Temple was torn in two from top to bottom. There was an earthquake, the rocks split, and the graves opened, and many of God's saints were raised from sleep; and coming out of their graves after his resurrection they entered the Holy City where many saw them. . . . (Matthew 27:39-53)

Because it was the eve of Passover, the Jews were anxious that the bodies should not remain on the cross for the coming Sabbath, since that Sabbath was a day of great solemnity. So they requested Pilate to have the legs broken and the bodies taken down. The soldiers accordingly came to the first of his fellow victims and to the second, and they broke their legs. But when they came to Jesus they found that he was already dead, so they did not break his legs. But one of the soldiers stabbed his side with a lance, and at once there was a flow of blood and water. . . . (John 19:31-34)

The Burial

After that, Pilate was approached by Joseph of Arimathea, a disciple of Jesus, but a secret disciple for fear of the Jews, who asked to be allowed to remove the body of Jesus. Pilate gave the permission, so Joseph came and took the body away. He was joined by Nicodemus, the man who had first visited Jesus by night, who brought with him a mixture of myrrh and aloes, more than half a hundredweight. They took the body of Jesus and wrapped it, with the spices, in strips of linen cloth according to Jewish burial customs. Now at the place where he had been crucified there was a garden, and in the garden a new tomb, not yet used for burial. There, because the tomb was near at hand and it was the eve of the Jewish Sabbath, they laid Jesus. (John 19:38-42)

So Joseph bought a linen sheet, took him down from the cross, and wrapped him in the sheet. Then he laid him in a tomb cut out of the rock, and rolled a stone against the entrance. And Mary of Magdala and Mary the mother of Joseph were watching and saw where he was laid. (Mark 15:46-47)

The details appear solid and circumstantial, as if, it has been argued, the tomb was well known and seen by contemporaries, two of whom, Mary of Magdala and Mary the mother of Joseph, had seen the actual deposition of the body of Jesus. [16] The tradition must have been very solid indeed, since in A.D. 58, when Mark's Gospel was probably redacted, the city had already grown to the north and the west and therefore the quarter containing the tomb was inside the walls. A tomb inside the city would have been very improbable if the tradition had not already existed to bear witness, and so precisely, to the authenticity of the venerated site.

The Apostles in Jerusalem

All this must have occurred early in the fourth decade of the present era. The events—a brief popular demonstration and the quick trial and execution of a not very notable criminal on not very notable charges—are unremarked by Josephus, as well they might have been in a time filled with more considerable political and military alarums. Josephus would not more likely have much noted the sequel to these events, either, here presented in recollected resume by Luke, one of the followers of this Jesus of Nazareth:

In the first part of my work, Theophilus, I wrote all that Jesus did and taught from the beginning until the day when, after giving instructions through the Holy Spirit to the apostles whom he had chosen, he was taken up to heaven. He showed himself to these men after his death and gave ample proof that he was alive: over a period of forty days he appeared to them and taught them about the kingdom of God. While he was in their company he told them not to leave Jerusalem. "You must wait," he said, for the promise made by my Father, about which you have heard me speak: John, as you know, baptized with water, but you will be baptized with the Holy Spirit, and within the next few days."

". . . You will bear witness for me in Jerusalem, and all of Judea and Samaria, and away to the ends of the earth." When he had said this, as they watched, he was lifted up, and a cloud removed him from their sight. . . . Then they returned to Jerusalem from the hill called Olivet, which is near Jerusalem, no farther than a Sabbath day's journey. Entering the city they went to the room upstairs where they were lodging: Peter and John and James and Andrew, Philip and Thomas, Bartholomew and Matthew, James son of Alphaeus and Simon the Zealot and Judas son of James. All these were constantly at prayer together, and with them a group of women, including Mary the mother of Jesus, and his brothers. (Acts 1:1-14)

Again we hear of an "upper room," and though there is no suggestion in the text that it was the same in which Jesus had eaten his Passover meal with his followers, the Christians eventually identified the two in the same place on Mount Sion, as the southern spur of the western hill was then called. [17] The account continues:

While the day of Pentecost was running its course they were all together in one place when suddenly there came from the sky a noise like that of a strong driving wind, which filled the whole house where they were sitting. And there appeared to them tongues like flames of fire, dispersed among them and resting on each one. And they were all filled with the Holy Spirit and began to talk in other tongues, as the Spirit gave them power of utterance.

Now there were living in Jerusalem devout Jews drawn from every nation under heaven; and at this sound the crowd gathered, all bewildered because each one heard his own language spoken. They were amazed and in their astonishment exclaimed, "Why these are all Galileans, are they not, these men who are speaking? Parthians, Medes, Elamites; inhabitants of Mesopotamia, of Judea and Cappadocia, of Pontus and Asia, of Phrygia and Pamphylia, of Egypt and the districts of Libya round Cyrene; visitors from Rome, both Jews and proselytes, Cretans and Arabs, we hear them telling in our own tongues the great things God has done." (Acts 2:1-11)

Pentecost, or the Feast of Weeks, was one of the three great Jewish pilgrimage festivals (Deut. 16:1-16), and the mixed company in the city on that occasion is not surprising, nor were the numbers inconsiderable. [18] And as in all pilgrimage centers, the problem of lodging in Jerusalem was difficult. One solution to it may have been the emergence of a relatively new institution, the synagogue.

Jerusalem Synagogues

Most of what we know about ancient synagogues comes from outside Jerusalem, and the bulk of the earliest examples date from well after the destruction of the Temple. But earlier than that, Jesus had preached in a synagogue in Galilee (Lk. 4:16-22). And there is firm evidence that there were indeed synagogues in the Holy City before A.D. 70, at a time when the Temple was still the center, and apparently the unique center, of the liturgical life of the Jewish community. One important piece of that evidence is an inscription discovered on the Ophel in 1914:

Theodotus, son of Vettenus, priest and synagogue chief, son of a synagogue chief, grandson of a synagogue chief, had the synagogue built for the reading of the Law and for the teaching of the commandments, as well as the hospice and the accommodations and the water-works as lodging to those needing it from abroad, [the synagogue] whose foundations had been put down by his fathers and the elders and Simonides.

On the face of it, this Herodian era synagogue, located in the old section of the City of David, had a dual function: as a place of reading and teaching the Law, much as Jesus is shown doing in a synagogue in Nazareth; and as a boarding facility for Diaspora Jews come to the Holy City in fulfillment of the requirements of pilgrimage. We get somewhat the same impression of a synagogue connected with visitors from the Diaspora, perhaps Hellenized visitors, from an incident that occurred in Jerusalem in the 30s of the first Christian century and is reported in the Acts of the Apostles: [19]

During this period, when disciples were growing in number, there was disagreement between those who spoke Greek and those who spoke the language of the Jews. The former party complained that their widows were being overlooked in the daily distribution. . . . [So] they elected Stephen, a man full of faith and the Holy Spirit, Philip, Prochorus, Nicanor, Timon, Parmenas, and Nicolas of Antioch, a former convert to Judaism. These they presented to the apostles, who prayed and laid hands on them. The word of God now spread more and more widely; the number of disciples in Jerusalem went on increasing rapidly, and very many of the priests adhered to the Faith. Stephen, who was full of grace and power, began to work great miracles and signs among the people. But some members of the synagogue called the Synagogue of the Freedmen, comprising Cyrenians and Alexandrians and people from Cilicia and Asia, came forward and argued with Stephen, but could not hold their own against the inspired wisdom with which he spoke. (Acts 6:1-10)

Paul in Jerusalem

It is Stephen, one of the "Hellenists," who provokes the next crisis for the followers of Jesus in Jerusalem. The performance of signs and wonders might excite admiration, astonishment, and even belief, but Stephen's long and critical catechesis of the Jewish elders in Jerusalem aroused somewhat different feelings:

This [speech of Stephen's] touched them to the raw and they ground their teeth with fury. But Stephen, filled with the Holy Spirit, and gazing intently up to heaven, saw the glory of God, and Jesus standing at God's right hand. "Look," he said, "there is a rift in the sky. I can see the Son of Man standing at God's right hand!" At this they gave a great shout and stopped their ears. Then they made one rush at him, and flinging him out of the city, set about stoning him. The witnesses laid their coats at the feet of a young man named Saul. So they stoned Stephen,[20] and as they did so, he called out, "Lord Jesus, receive my spirit." Then he fell on his knees and cried aloud, "Lord, do not hold this sin against them," and with that he died. And Saul was among those who approved of his murder. (Acts 7:54–8:1)

Christianity thus had its first martyr, and more important in a historical sense, there appears dramatically and for the first time the figure of Paul, here still called Saul. His well-known conversion through a vision of Jesus on the road to Damascus followed, and the prosecutor almost immediately became the fugitive:

As the days mounted up, the Jews [of Damascus] hatched a plot against his life; but their plans became known to Saul. They kept watch on the city gates day and night so that they might murder him. But his converts took him one night and let him down by the wall, lowering him in a basket. When he reached Jerusalem he tried to join the body of the disciples there; but they were all afraid of him, because they did not believe that he was really a convert. Barnabas, however, took him by the hand and introduced him to the apostles. . . . Saul now stayed with them, moving about freely in Jerusalem. He spoke out openly and boldly in the name of the Lord, talking and debating with the Greek-speaking Jews. But they planned to murder him, and when the brethren learned of this, they escorted him to Caesarea and saw him off to Tarsus. (Acts 8:23-30)

That is the version of Paul's coming to Jerusalem in Acts, but Paul's own account in his letters is considerably different:

You have heard what my manner of life was when I was still a practicing Jew: how savagely I persecuted the church of God and tried to destroy it; and how in the practice of our national religion I was outstripping many of my Jewish contemporaries in my boundless devotion to the traditions of my ancestors. But then in his good pleasure God, who had set me apart from birth and called me through his grace, chose to reveal his Son to me and through me, in order that I might proclaim him among the Gentiles. When that happened, without consulting any human being, without going up to Jerusalem to see those who were apostles before me, I went off at once to Arabia, and afterwards returned to Damascus. Three years later did I go up Jerusalem to get to know Cephas [Peter]. I stayed with him for a fortnight, without seeing any of the other apostles, except James, the Lord's brother. What I write is plain truth; before God I am not lying. (Galatians 1:13-20)

Paul was once more in Jerusalem during the reign of Agrippa I (A.D. 41-44), when the emperor Claudius again made brief trial of a Jewish monarchy in Judea. Agrippa received rather high marks in the Jewish tradition, as his presence in this brief Mishnaic vignette of the bringing of the first-fruits to Jerusalem shows:

They that were near [to Jerusalem] brought fresh figs and grapes, and they that were far off brought dried figs and raisins. Before them went the ox, having its horns overlaid with gold and a wreath of olive leaves on its head. The flute was played before them until they drew nigh to Jerusalem. When they had drawn nigh to Jerusalem they sent messengers before them and bedecked their first-fruits. The rulers and the prefects and the treasurers of the Temple went out to meet them. . . . And all the crafts-

men in Jerusalem used to rise up before them and greet them, saying, "Brethren, men of such-and-such a place, you are welcome!" The flute used to be played before them until they reached the Temple mount. When they reached the Temple mount even Agrippa the king would take up his basket on his shoulder and enter in as far as the Temple court. . . . (Danby 1933: 96-97)

This pastoral quality is notably lacking in the same monarch's reflection in the Acts of the Apostles:

During this period some prophets [in the Christian community] came down from Jerusalem to Antioch. One of them, Agabus by name, was inspired to stand up and predict a severe and world-wide famine, which in fact occurred in the reign of Claudius. So the disciples [in Antioch] decided to make a contribution, each according to his means, for the relief of their fellow Christians in Judea. This they did and sent it off to the elders [in Jerusalem], in charge of Barnabas and Saul. It was about this time that King Herod [Agrippa I] attacked certain members of the church. He beheaded James, the brother of John, and then, when he saw that the Jews approved, proceeded to arrest Peter also. This happened during the festival of the Unleavened Bread. Having secured him, he put him in prison under a military guard, four squads of four men each, meaning to produce him in public after Passover. (Acts 11:27–12:4)

Peter was miraculously freed on this occasion and the incident passed. There were more serious problems at hand for the Jerusalem Christians, however, and they arose from within the community itself:

Now certain persons who had come down [to Antioch] from Judea began to teach the brotherhood that those who were not circumcised in accordance with the Mosaic practice could not be saved. That brought them into fierce dissension and controversy with Paul and Barnabas. And so it was arranged that these two and some others from Antioch should go up to Jerusalem and see the apostles and elders about this question. . . . When they reached Jerusalem they were welcomed by the church and the apostles and elders, and reported all that God had done through them. Then some of the Pharisaic party who had become believers came forward and said. "They must be circumcised and told to keep the Law of Moses."

The question was discussed at length. Peter expressed a preference for the lenient view, then James, "the brother of the Lord," spoke:

My judgment therefore is that we should impose no irksome restrictions on those of the Gentiles who are turning to God but instruct them by letter to abstain from things polluted by contact with idols, from forni-

cation, from anything that has been strangled, and from blood. Moses, after all, has never lacked for spokesmen in every town for generations past; he is read in the synagogues Sabbath by Sabbath. (Acts 15:1-21[21])

Paul and the Temple

After the community meeting in Jerusalem, Paul departed for a long round of missionary visits around the eastern Mediterranean. Finally, he and Luke, who uses "we" in the account in Acts, reached Jerusalem:

So we reached Jerusalem where the brotherhood welcomed us gladly. Next day Paul paid a visit to James; we were with him, and all the elders attended. He greeted them, and then described in detail all that God had done among the Gentiles through his ministry. When they heard this they [James and the elders] gave praise to God. Then they said to Paul, "You see, brother, how many thousands of converts we have amongst the Jews, all of them staunch upholders of the Law. Now they have been given certain information about you: it is said that you teach all the Jews in the Gentile world to turn their backs on Moses, telling them to give up circumcising their children and following our way of life. What is the position, then? They are sure to hear that you have arrived. You must therefore do as we tell you. We have four men here who are under a vow; take them with you and go through the ritual purification with them, paying their expenses, after which they may shave their heads. Then everyone will know there is nothing in the stories that were told about you, but that you are a practicing Jew and keep the Law yourself." . . . So Paul took the four men and next day, having gone through the ritual purification with them, he went into the Temple to give notice of the date when the period of purification would end and the offering be made for each of them. (Acts 21:15-26)

But just before the seven days were up, the Jews from the province of Asia saw him [Paul] in the Temple. They stirred up the whole crowd, and seized him, shouting, "Men of Israel, help, help! This is the fellow who spreads his doctrine all over the world, attacking our people, our Law, and this sanctuary. On top of all this he has brought Gentiles into the Temple and profaned this holy place." For they had previously seen Trophimus the Ephesian with him in the city and assumed that Paul had brought him into the Temple.

The whole city was in turmoil, and people came running from all directions. They seized Paul and dragged him out of the Temple; and at once the doors [of the Court of the Israelites] were shut. While they were clamoring for his death, a report reached the officer commanding the co-hort [in the Antonia] that all Jerusalem was in an uproar. He immediately took a force of soldiers with their centurions and came down on the rioters at the double. As soon as they [the people] saw the commandant and his troops, they stopped beating Paul. The commandant stepped forward, arrested him [Paul], and ordered him to be shackled with two chains. He then asked who the man was and what he had been doing. Some in the crowd shouted one thing, some another. As he could not get at the truth because of the hubbub, he ordered him [Paul] to be taken into the bar-racks. When Paul reached the steps [up to the Antonia], he had to be carried by the soldiers because of the violence of the crowd. For the whole crowd were at their heels yelling "Kill him!"[22]

Just before Paul was taken into the barracks he said to the commandant, "May I have a word with you?" The commandant said, "So you speak Greek, do you? Then you are not the Egyptian who started a revolt some time ago and led a force of four thousand terrorists into the wilds?" Paul replied, "I am a Jew, a Tarsian from Cilicia, a citizen of no mean city. I ask your permission to speak to the people." When permission had been given, Paul stood on the steps and with a gesture called for the attention of the people. As soon as quiet was restored, he addressed them in the Jewish language: "Brothers and fathers, give me a hearing while I make my defense before you." When they heard him speaking to them in their own language, they listened more quietly. "I am a trueborn Jew," he said, "a native of Tarsus in Cilicia. I was brought up in this city, and as a pupil of Gamaliel I was thoroughly trained in every point of our ancestral law." (Acts 21:27–22:4)

Paul proceeded to describe his conversion and his return from Damascus to Jerusalem, when he had had another vision of Jesus who said "Go, I am sending you far away to the Gentiles."

Up to this point they had given him a hearing but now they began shout-ing, "Down with him! A scoundrel like that is better dead!" And as they were yelling and waving their cloaks and flinging dust in the air, the com-mandant ordered him to be brought into the barracks and gave instruc-tions to examine him by flogging and find out what reason there was for such an outcry against him. But when they tied him up for the lash, Paul said to the centurion who was standing there, "Can you legally flog a man who is a Roman citizen and moreover who has not been found guilty?" When the centurion heard this, he went and reported it to the comman-dant. "What do you mean to do?" he said. "This man is a Roman citizen." The commandant came to Paul. "Tell me, are you a Roman citizen?" he asked. "Yes," said he. The commandant rejoined, "It cost me a large sum to acquire citizenship." Paul said, "But it was mine by birth." Then those who were about to examine him withdrew hastily, and the commandant himself was alarmed when he realized that Paul was a Roman citizen and that he had put him in irons. (Acts 22:22-29)

The commandant of the Antonia garrison planned to have a hearing before the Sanhedrin in Jerusalem, but threats to Paul's life caused him to send the prisoner under heavy escort to Caesarea to the governor Felix. The date was sometime shortly before A.D. 60, and it marks Paul's last association with Jerusalem. [23]

The Death of James

Shortly after the arrest and departure of Paul another graver calamity fell upon the Christians in Jerusalem, the murder of James, the brother of Jesus, and the head of the Church there. A circumstantial account is given in the second book of the *Church History* of Eusebius. This was written in the first decades of the third century, but as the text reveals, it goes back to a much older source:

When Paul appealed to Caesar and was sent to Rome by Festus, the Jews were disappointed in the expectations with which they had plotted against him and so they turned their attention to James, the brother of the Lord, who had been chosen by the Apostles to the episcopal throne in Jerusalem. . . . So they killed him, using the absence of the government to achieve their end, since at that time Festus [A.D. 60-62] had died in Judea, leaving the province without a governor or a procurator [for a brief period in A.D. 62]. How James died has already been shown by the words quoted from Clement, who tells us that he was thrown from the parapet and clubbed to death. But the most detailed account of James is provided by Hegesippus, who was of the first generation after the Apostles. In his fifth book he writes as follows:

"Governance of the Church passed [from Jesus] to the Apostles, together with James, the brother of the Lord, whom everyone from the Lord's time till our own has called the 'Righteous' [Zaddiq]. There were many Jameses, but this one was holy from his birth; he drank no wine or intoxicating liquor and ate no animal food; no razor touched his head; he did not anoint himself with oil and took no baths. He alone was permitted to enter the Holy Place, for his garments were not made of wool but linen. [24] He used to enter the Sanctuary [here possibly the Court of the Priests] alone, and was often found on his knees begging forgiveness for the people. Because of his unsurpassable righteousness he was called the

Righteous and Oblias[?]—which in our own tongue means 'Bulwark of the People and Righteousness'—thus fulfilling the statements of the prophets concerning him.

"Representatives of the seven popular sects already described by me asked him what was the meaning of the expression 'the door of Jesus,' and James answered that Jesus was the Savior. Some of them came to believe that Jesus was the Messiah: the aforementioned sects did not believe in either a resurrection or in One who is To Come to give every man what he deserves by his deeds, but those of them who did come to believe did so because of James. Since many even of the ruling class believed, there was a tumult among the Jews and the Scribes and Pharisees, who said there was a danger that the entire people would come to expect Jesus as the Messiah. So they assembled and said to James: 'Please restrain the people since they have wandered off after Jesus in the belief that he is the Messiah. Please explain the facts about Jesus to all who come for the day of Passover. All of us accept your word: we can vouch for it and so can all the people, that you are a righteous man and take no one at his face value. So make it clear to the crowd that they must not go astray regarding Jesus: the whole people and all of us accept your word. So stand up on the parapet of the Temple, so that from that height you might be easily seen and your words be heard by everyone. Because of the Passover all the tribes have foregathered, and the Gentiles too.'[25]

"So the Scribes and the Pharisees made James stand on the parapet of the sanctuary and they shouted to him: 'Righteous one, whose word we are all obliged to accept, the people are going astray after Jesus who was crucified: so tell us what is meant by "the Door of Jesus."' He replied as loudly as he could: 'Why do you question me about the Son of Man? I tell you, He is sitting in heaven at the right hand of the Great Power, and He will come in the clouds of heaven.' At this many were convinced and they gloried in James' testimony, crying 'Hosanna to the Son of David!' Then the Scribes and Pharisees said to each other: 'We made a serious mistake in permitting such witness to Jesus. We had better go up and throw him down, so that they will be frightened and not believe him.' 'Look, look!' they cried out, 'even the Righteous One has gone astray,' fulfilling the prophecy of Isaiah: 'Let us remove the Righteous One, for he is unprofitable to us. Therefore they shall eat the fruits of their works' [Is. 3:10].

"So they went up and threw down the Righteous One. Then they said to each other, 'Let us stone James the Righteous,' and they began to stone him, since despite his fall he was still alive. . . . Then one of them, a fuller [that is, a bleacher or laundryman], took the club with which he used to beat out the clothes and brought it down on the head of the Righteous

One. James was buried at that place, right by the Sanctuary, and his head-stone is still there by the Sanctuary. . . ."[26] *(Eusebius, Church History II, 23)*

Agrippa II (A.D. 50-53)

The death of Agrippa I in A.D. 44 had ended the Roman experiment with a restored Herodian kingship in Judea; Agrippa's young son Agrippa II was judged too callow for the task, though in A.D. 50 he was given some land in Lebanon, and then in 53 he was promoted to succeed Philip in the lava lands of southern Syria, where he ruled until perhaps 92 or 93. Though Judea and Jerusalem thus passed back under direct Roman control, Agrippa II as the chief Herodian heir did possess some privileges in the Holy City, that of appointing the high priests, for example, [27] and he expended what must have been considerable funds in planning to shore up the sinking foundations of Herod's Temple platform (*Wars* V, 1, 5). Then, when the Temple was finally completed in the time of the prefect Albinus (A.D. 62-64), Agrippa II allocated Temple funds toward a project to pave the streets of Jerusalem in order to ease the unemployment caused by the end of the work on the Temple (*Ant.* XX, 9, 7). [28]

This is all quite Herodian, as is another incident recalled at length by Josephus:

About this time King Agrippa built a chamber of unusual size in his palace in Jerusalem adjoining the colonnade. The palace had been erected long before by the Hasmoneans, and being situated on a lofty site, [29] afforded a most delightful view to any who chose to survey the city from it. The king was enamoured of this view and used to gaze, as he reclined at meals there, at everything that went on in the Temple. The eminent men of Jerusalem, seeing this, were extremely angry; for it was contrary to tradition for proceedings in the Temple—and in particular the sacrifices—to be spied on. [30] They therefore erected a high wall on the arcade that was in the inner Temple facing west. This when built blocked not only the view from the royal dining room but also from the western portico of the outer Temple, where the Romans used to post their guards for the sake of supervising the Temple. (Josephus, War II, 16, 2-3)

The Great War Begins

Albinus was succeeded in A.D. 64 by the last of the Roman prefects for Judea, Gessius Florus, the unwitting *provocateur* of the destruction of the

Holy City. From the beginning Florus had little understanding of or sympathy with his subjects in Judea, who were in fact never very far from sedition. It began when a number of Jews were arrested in Caesarea.

The citizens of Jerusalem, though they took this affair badly, yet they restrained their passion. But Florus acted as if he had been hired to fan the war into flame, and sent some men to take seventeen talents out of the sacred treasure (of the Temple), on the pretense that Caesar required them. At this the people became immediately disturbed and ran in a body to the Temple with great shouting and called upon Caesar by name and begged him to free them from the tyranny of Florus. Some of the more seditious cried out against Florus himself and blamed him severely. They carried about a basket and solicited small change for him, as if he were a poor man without possessions. Far from being ashamed of his greed for money, he became further enraged and was provoked to get even more. Instead of going to Caesarea, as he ought to have done, and damping the flames of war there ... he marched quickly with a force of cavalry and infantry against Jerusalem, that he might gain his objective by force of Roman arms and drain the city dry.

Once in the city, Florus summoned the elders and leaders of the Jews and demanded the guilty be handed over to him. Apologies were made, but they protested, "it was no wonder that in so great a crowd there should be some rasher than they ought to have been and, by reason of their age, foolish as well."

Florus was all the more provoked at this, and called out aloud from his soldiers to loot the Upper Market, [31] *and to slay whomever they met there. The soldiers, who found this order of their commander agreeable to their own sense of greed, plundered not only the (public) place where they were sent but broke into houses and killed the inhabitants. The citizens fled down the alleys and the soldiers killed those they caught and looted in every way conceivable. They also arrested many of the peaceable citizens and brought them before Florus, whom he first had whipped and then crucified. . . . (Josephus, War II, 14, 6-9)*

This was in April or May, A.D. 66, and there was at least one attempt to head off what was beginning to seem like a long-postponed and now increasingly inevitable confrontation between the Romans and the Jews of Jerusalem:

Agrippa [II] thought it altogether too dangerous for them to appoint men to lay accusations against Florus, yet he did not think he should allow the Jews to be provoked into war. So he called the crowd together at the

Xystus and placed his sister Berenice in the Hasmonean Palace so that she might be visible to them as well, since the house was above the Xystus square, on the other side of the Upper City, where the bridge joined the Temple to the Xystus. [32] *(Josephus, War II, 16, 3)*

Agrippa then addressed them. He counselled patience and restraint, and warned that the people might very well fight against Florus but that it would be a tragic mistake to fight against the Romans. It was too late, however. Agrippa's appeal fell upon deaf ears. The critical moment was at hand:

Eleazer, the son of Ananias the high priest, a very bold young man, who was also at that time the superintendent of the Temple, persuaded those who were officiating in the divine services to accept no gift or sacrifice on behalf of any foreigner. And this was the true beginning of our war with the Romans, for they rejected the sacrifice of Caesar on this account. When many of the high priests and leaders begged them not to omit this sacrifice, which was customary for them to offer for their rulers, they would not be persuaded. [33] *(Josephus, War II, 17, 2)*

When the (Jewish) leaders in Jerusalem perceived that the sedition was too difficult for them to put down, and that the danger that would arise from the Romans would descend in the first place upon their shoulders, they tried to clear themselves and sent representatives, some to Florus . . . and others to Agrippa . . . and they requested that both of them should come with an army to the city and cut off the revolt while it was still possible. Now this terrible message was good news to Florus, and since it was his intent that there should be a war, he gave no answer to the delegates. But Agrippa was equally solicitous for the rebels and for those against whom the war would be fought; he wanted to save the Jews for the Romans and the Temple for the Jews. He was also aware that a war would not be to his own advantage and so he sent 2,000 horsemen to the assistance of the people. . . .

At this the (Jewish) leaders and the high priests, as well as those others who wanted peace, took courage and seized the Upper City, since the rebels had already occupied the Lower City and the Temple. . . . [The next day Agrippa's cavalry were driven out of the Upper City by the rebels, who] then set fire to the house of Ananias the high priest and to the palace of Agrippa and Berenice. After which they spread the fire to the place where the archives were kept and quickly burned the due bills belonging to creditors in order to dissolve the obligation of paying debts. This was done to gain the allegiance of the many who profited thereby and to persuade the poorer citizens to join the insurrection with impunity against the wealthy.

The next day they . . . made an assault upon the Antonia and besieged the garrison within it for two days, and then took the garrison and slew them and set the citadel on fire, after which they marched against the palace [that is, Herod's former palace, the Roman pretorium] where the king's soldiers had fled. . . . (Josephus, War II, 17, 4-7)

Finally all the forces of resistance, Roman and Agrippan, were driven from Jerusalem and the city rested entirely in the possession of the rebels. Others had departed as well:

Through an oracle revealed to acceptable persons there, the members of the Jerusalem church were ordered to leave the country before the war [of A.D. 66-70] began and settle in a town in the Peraea [in the Transjordan] called Pella. Those who believed in Christ migrated from Jerusalem to Pella; and it was as if holy men had abandoned the royal capital of the Jews and the entire Jewish land; and the judgment of God at last overtook them for the hateful crimes against Christ and his Apostles, completely blotting out from among men that wicked generation. (Eusebius, Church History III, 5)

Somewhat later in the war:

Now when Vespasian came to destroy Jerusalem, he said to the inhabitants, "Fools, why do you seek to destroy this city and why do you seek to burn the Temple? For what do I ask you but that you send me one bow or one arrow and I shall go away from you?" They then said to him, "Even as we went forth against the first two who were here before you and slew them, so shall we go forth against you and slay you."

And when Rabban Yohanan ben Zakkai heard this, he sent for the men of Jerusalem and said to them, "My children, why do you destroy this city, and why do you seek to destroy the Temple? For what is it that he asks of you?" . . .

Vespasian had men stationed inside the walls of Jerusalem. Every word which they overheard they would write down, attach it to an arrow and shoot it over the wall, saying that Rabban Yohanan ben Zakkai was one of the emperor's friends.

Now after Rabban Yohanan ben Zakkai had spoken to them one day, two days, and three days, and they would still not listen to him, he sent for his disciples, Rabbi Eliezer and Rabbi Joshua.

"My sons," he said, "arise and take me out of here. Make a coffin for me that I may lie in it."

Rabbi Eliezer took the head of the coffin and Rabbi Joshua took hold of the foot, and they began carrying him as the sun set until they reached the gates of Jerusalem. "Who is this?" the gatekeepers demanded. "It is a dead man," they replied. "Do you not know that the dead may not be held overnight in Jerusalem?" "If it is a dead man," the gatekeepers said to them, "take him out." So they took him out. (Aboth Rabbi Nathan 1945: 4)

Thus Rabbi Yohanan ben Zakkai, who eventually went on to Jabneh to found the academy from which much of rabbinic Judaism was later to flow, escaped like the Christian elders from a Jerusalem destined for ruin and so preserved intact institutions that would return there at a later date and shape the city's spiritual reconstruction. [34]

The war now focussed on Jerusalem. The first to intervene there was Cestius Gallus, the governor of Syria, who camped with a considerable force on Mount Scopus. He attacked the city from the north, but after occupying the northern suburb of Jerusalem called Bezetha, he was forced to withdraw. His army was dealt a severe blow as it retreated toward the coast. Nero then appointed his commander Vespasian to take the revolt in hand, and by the end of A.D. 67 all of Galilee was once again in Roman hands. Nero died on June 9, A.D. 68, and Vespasian awaited new orders. Two more emperors came and went in a brief interval until Vespasian himself was proclaimed emperor by the eastern legions and departed for Rome in the summer of A.D. 70. His son Titus was left to pursue the final siege of Jerusalem.

The Siege of Jerusalem

As Gallus before him had done and as the topography of the city required, Titus began his assault on the north side of Jerusalem, where the first barrier to be overcome was the "third wall" hastily put up by Agrippa I, and here called the "first wall" by Josephus, viewing it from Titus' perspective. A classic Roman siege operation was mounted, and on the fifteenth day after it began, one of the rams had battered a hole in the wall:

The Romans thus on the fifteenth day of the siege, being the seventh of the month of Artemisius, became master of the first wall and razed a large part of it along with the northern quarter of the city. . . .

Titus now shifted his camp from the first wall to the so-called "Camp of the Assyrians,"[35] occupying all the ground between it and the Kedron, but keeping far enough back to be out of bowshot of the second wall, which he forthwith proceeded to attack. The Jews dividing their forces, maintained a stubborn defense, John's division fighting from the Antonia, from the north portico of the Temple and in front of the tomb of King Alexander,[36] while Simon's troops occupied the approach alongside the tomb of John (Hyrcanus) the high priest and manned the wall as far as the (Jaffa) gate through which the water was conveyed to the Hippicus tower. . . . *(Josephus, War V, 7, 2-3)*

At this spot [the central tower of the north wall], on the fifth day after the capture of the first wall, Caesar stormed the second; and, as the Jews had fled from it, he made his entry, with a thousand legionaries and his own picked troops, in that district of the new town where lay the wool shops, the braziers' smithies, and the clothes market, and where the narrow alleys descended obliquely to the ramparts. . . . *[Titus offers to allow any out of the defenders who wish to leave the city.] The people indeed had long been ready to act on his advice, but the militants mistook his humanity for weakness and regarded these overtures as due to his inability to capture the rest of the town.* . . . *They attacked the Roman division that had entered. Some confronted them in the streets, some assailed them from the houses, while others, rushing outside the wall by the upper gates caused such a commotion among the sentries on the ramparts that they leapt down from their towers and made off for their camp.* . . . *The Jews, constantly growing in numbers and greatly at an advantage through their knowledge of the streets, wounded multitudes of the enemy and with their assaults thrust them before them. (Josephus, War V, 8, 1)*

The situation was saved by Titus' posting archers at the ends of streets, whose fire covered the retreating Romans until everyone was safely back out of the city.

. . . No overtures for peace having come from the Jews, Titus formed the legions into two divisions and began raising earthworks opposite Antonia and John's [that is, Hyrcanus'] monument, respectively, his intention being to carry the Upper City at the latter point, and the Temple by way of the Antonia, for unless the Temple were secured, to hold even the city would be precarious. The erection of two banks at each of the two quarters was accordingly begun, one being assigned to each legion. . . . *(Josephus, War V, 9, 2)*

Though the Romans had begun their earthworks on the twelfth of the month Artemisius, they were scarcely completed on the twenty-ninth, after seventeen days of continuous toil. For the four embankments were immense. Of the first two, that at Antonia was thrown up by the Fifth Legion over against the middle of the pool called Struthion, the other by the Twelfth Legion about twenty cubits away. The Tenth Legion, at a considerable distance from these, was employed in the northern region and over against the pool termed Amygdalon; [37] *while, thirty cubits from*

them the Fifteenth were at work opposite the high priest's monument.
(Josephus, War V, 11, 4)

These works were undermined and set on fire by the defenders, but before
Titus began again, he adopted a new strategy. He hastily built and
manned his own wall around the city, to keep the defenders in and supplies out. It worked all too well, and starvation set in among the defenders
of Jerusalem.

The Antonia and the Temple

Twenty of the guards on outpost duty on the earthworks came together,
and enlisting the services of the standard-bearer of the Fifth Legion, two
troopers from the auxiliary squadrons and a trumpeter at the ninth hour
of the night advanced noiselessly over the ruins towards Antonia. The first
sentinels they encountered they cut down in their sleep and, taking pos-
session of the wall, ordered the trumpeter to sound. Thereupon the other
guards suddenly started to their feet and fled, before any had noted what
number had ascended. . . . Caesar, hearing the signal, promptly called the
forces to arms, and with generals and his body of picked men, was the
first to mount.

The Jews had fled to the Temple, into which the Romans were also
penetrating. . . . So the armies clashed in desperate struggle around the
entrances, the Romans pressing on to take possession also of the Temple,
the Jews thrusting them back upon Antonia. . . . At length, Jewish fury
prevailing over Roman skill, the whole line began to waver. For they had
been fighting from the ninth hour of the night until the seventh of the
day; the Jews in full strength, with the peril of capture an incentive to
gallantry, the Romans with but a portion of their forces, the legions upon
whom the present combatants were dependent having not yet come up.
It was therefore considered sufficient for the present to hold Antonia.
(Josephus, War VI, 1, 7)

Titus now ordered the troops that were with him to raze the foundations
of the Antonia and to prepare an easy ascent for the whole army. Then,
having learned that on that day—it was on the seventeenth of Panemus—
the so-called continual sacrifice had for lack of men ceased to be offered
to God and that the people were in consequence terribly despondent, [38]
he put Josephus forward to repeat to John the same message as before,
namely, that if he was obsessed by a criminal passion for battle, he was at
liberty to come out with as many as he chose and fight, without involving
the city and sanctuary in his own ruin; but that he should no longer

pollute the Holy Place nor sin against God; and that he had his permission to perform the interrupted sacrifices with the help of such Jews as he might select. (Josephus, War VI, 2, 1)

The offer was refused.

Meanwhile the rest of the Roman army, having in seven days overthrown the foundations of the Antonia, had prepared a broad ascent to the Temple. The legions now approaching the first wall began to raise embankments: one facing the northwest angle of the inner Temple, a second over against the northern hall which stood between the two gates, and two more, one opposite the western portico of the outer court of the Temple, the other outside (or further out) opposite the northern portico. The works, however, did not advance without causing the troops great fatigue and hardship, the timber being conveyed from a distance of a hundred stadia [that, is about a five hours journey]. . . . (Josephus, War VI, 2, 7)

Meanwhile the Jews, sorely suffering from their encounters, as the war slowly yet steadily rose to a climax and crept towards the sanctuary, cut away, as from a fatally diseased body, the limbs already affected, to arrest further ravages of the disease. In other words, they set fire to that portion of the northwest portico that was attached to the Antonia, and afterwards hacked away some twenty cubits, their own hands thus beginning the conflagration of the holy places. Two days later, on the twenty-fourth of the month of Panemus, the Romans set light to the adjoining portico; and when the flames had spread a distance of fifty cubits, it was again the Jews who cut away the roof, and with no reverence whatever for these works of art, severed the connection thereby formed with the Antonia. . . . Thus conflicts around the Temple raged incessantly, and fights between small parties sallying out upon each other were continuous. (Josephus, War VI, 2, 9)

Two of the legions having now completed the earthworks, on the eighth of the month of Lous, Titus ordered the rams to be brought up opposite the western wall of the outer court of the Temple. Before their arrival, the most redoubtable of all the siege engines had battered the wall without effect, the massiveness and nice adjustment of the stones being proof against it as against the rest. Another party endeavored to undermine the foundations of the northern gate, and by great exertions succeeded in extricating the stones in front; but the gate, supported by the inner stones, stood firm. [The Romans then attempted to scale the wall with ladders. That too failed.] Titus, now that he saw that his endeavor to spare a foreign temple led only to the injury and slaughter of his troops, issued orders to set the gates on fire. (Josephus, War VI, 4, 1)

Above, nineteenth-century engraving of the Pool of Siloam, the western outlet of Hezekiah's tunnel from the Gihon spring. *Right*, the entry to the Gihon spring on the eastern slope of the "City of David."

A section of Hezekiah's "broad wall," uncovered during excavations in the Jewish quarter of Jerusalem.

Above, the "seam" on the eastern side of Herod's Temple platform. The stonework on the south (left) is Herodian (*detail below*); that to the north (right) is possibly from the Persian period following the return of the Jews from their Exile in Babylonia.

PICTORIAL ARCHIVE (Near Eastern History) Est., The Old School, P.O. Box 19823, Jerusalem.

Aerial view of the Citadel area and the excavation within; the tower at the upper right is Herodian in its lower courses and was known in the Middle Ages as the "Tower of David."

Above, Jerusalem from the southeast, with the Kedron Valley running along its eastern side. The southeastern corner of the Temple platform marks the traditional site of the "Pinnacle of the Temple" (*close-up, below left*); it is here that the Herodian stonework has survived to its highest point. *Below right*, the "Probatic" Pool, or Sheep Pool, north of the Temple area, with part of the vaulting of the interior walls; on the right are the foundations of a Byzantine church that was built out into the pool.

Above, an aerial view looking southward over Jerusalem from above the Damascus Gate. The lines of the two Roman cardos shown on the Madaba map (*detail below*) are still clearly visible today.

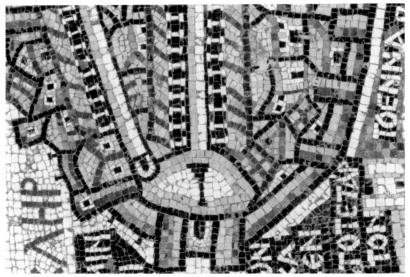

At top, the Damascus Gate in the early nineteenth century, when the rising ground level had covered the remains of the Hadrianic foundations. *Below*, the Damascus Gate in elevation: in the center is the Crusader entry, with Ottoman additions above; at the lower left, the pedestrian arch of Hadrian's gateway.

Top of page, the actual site of Justinian's "Nea" church, visible at the southern end of the Madaba map. The view here is eastward, with the Mount of Olives in the background. *Below*, the massive supporting foundations of the "Nea" described by Procopius (p. 164 of this book). Today they are just outside the city wall, visible on the left, which appears at the center of the above illustration.

The troops were by now setting fire to the gates, and the silver melting all around quickly admitted the flames to the woodwork, whence they spread in dense volumes and caught hold of the porticoes. . . . Throughout that day and the ensuing night the fire prevailed; for they could only set light to portions of the porticoes, and not to the whole range at once. (Josephus, War VI, 4, 2)

On the following day Titus, after giving orders to a division of his army to extinguish the fire and make a road to the gates to facilitate the ascent of the legions, called together his generals. . . . Titus brought forward for debate the subject of the Temple. Some were of the opinion that the law of war should be enforced since the Jews would never cease from rebellion while the Temple remained as the focus for assembly from every quarter. Others advised that if the Jews abandoned it and placed no weapons whatever upon it, it should be saved, but that if they mounted it for purposes of war, it should be burnt, as it would no longer be temple but a fortress, and thenceforward the impiety would be chargeable not to the Romans but to those who forced them to take such measures. Titus, however, declared that, even were the Jews to mount it and fight therefrom, he would not wreak vengeance on inanimate objects instead of men, nor under any circumstances burn down so magnificent a work; for the loss would affect the Romans, inasmuch as it would be an ornament to the empire if it stood.[39] (Josephus, War VI, 4, 3)

The Ninth of Ab

Titus then withdrew to the Antonia, and determined on the following day, at dawn, to attack with his whole force and invest the Temple. That building, however, God long since had sentenced to the flames; but now in the revolution of the years had arrived the fated day, the tenth of the month of Lous, the day on which of old it had been burnt by the king of Babylon.[40] (Josephus, War VI, 4, 5)

The event is later commemorated in the Mishna and so in the entire rabbinic and subsequent Jewish tradition:

Four things befell our fathers on the Seventeenth of Tammuz and five on the Ninth of Ab. On the Seventeenth of Tammuz the Tables [of the Ten Commandments] were broken, and the daily Whole-Offering ceased, and the city [of Jerusalem] was breached, and Apostomus [Posthumus?] burnt [the Scrolls of] the Law, and an idol was set up in the Sanctuary. On the Ninth of Ab it was decreed against our fathers that they should not enter the Land of Israel [Num. 14:29f.], and the Temple was destroyed the first and second time, and Beth Tor [Bethar, presently Bittir, scene of Bar Kokhba's defeat in A.D. 135] and the city was ploughed up. When Ab comes in, gladness must be diminished.

In the week wherein falls the Ninth of Ab it is forbidden to cut the hair or wash the clothes, but it permitted on the Thursday because of the honor due to the Sabbath. On the eve of the Ninth of Ab let none eat of two cooked dishes, let none eat flesh and let none drink wine. . . . (Danby 1933: 200)

The Burning of the Temple

The flames, however, owed their origin and cause to God's own people. [More skirmishing took place inside the precincts.] At that moment, one of the soldiers, awaiting no orders and with no horror of such a dread deed, but moved by some supernatural impulse, snatched a brand from the burning timber and, hoisted up by one of his comrades, flung the fiery missile through a low golden door which gave access on the north side to the chambers surrounding the sanctuary. As the flame shot up, a cry, as poignant as the tragedy, arose from the Jews, who flocked to the rescue, lost to all thought of self-preservation, all husbanding of strength, now that the object of all their past vigilance was vanishing.

Titus was resting in his tent after the engagement when a messenger rushed in with the tidings. Starting up just as he was, he ran to the Temple to arrest the conflagration; behind him followed his whole staff of generals, while in their train came the excited legionaries, and there was all the hubbub and confusion attending the disorderly movement of so large a force. Caesar, both by voice and hand, signalled the combatants to extinguish the fire; but they neither heard his shouts, drowned in the louder din that filled their ears, nor heeded his beckoning hand, distracted as they were by the fight and its fury. The impetuosity of the legionaries, when they joined the fray, neither exhortation nor threat could restrain; passion was for all the only leader. . . . Around the altar a pile of corpses was accumulating; down the steps of the sanctuary flowed a stream of blood, and the bodies of those killed above went sliding to the bottom.

Caesar, finding himself unable to restrain the impetuosity of his frenzied soldiers and the fire gaining the mastery, passed with his generals within the building and beheld the holy place of the sanctuary and all it contained—things far exceeding the reports current among the foreigners and not inferior to their proud reputation among ourselves. As the flames had nowhere yet penetrated to the interior, but were consuming the chambers surrounding the Temple, Titus, correctly assuming that the structure

116

might still be saved, rushed out and by personal appeals endeavored to induce the soldiers to quench the fire. . . . But their respect for Caesar . . . [was] overpowered by their rage, their hatred of the Jews, and a lust for battle more unruly still. Most of them were further stimulated by the hope of plunder, believing that the interior was full of money and actually seeing that all the surroundings were made of gold. However, the end was precipitated by one of those who had entered the building and who, when Caesar rushed outside to restrain the troops, thrust a firebrand into the darkness, into the hinges of the gate. At once a flame shot up from the interior, Caesar and his generals withdrew and there was none left to prevent those outside from kindling a blaze. Thus, against Caesar's wishes, was the Temple on fire. (Josephus, War VI, 4, 5-7)

While the Temple blazed, the victors plundered everything that fell in their way and slaughtered wholesale all who were caught. No pity was shown for age, no reverence for rank; children and greybeards, laity and priests alike were massacred. The roar of the flames streaming far and wide mingled with the groans of the falling victims; and owing to the height of the hill and the mass of the burning pile, one would have thought that the whole city was ablaze. . . .

The Romans, thinking it useless, now that the Temple was on fire, to spare the surrounding buildings, set them all alight, both the remnants of the porticoes and the gates, excepting two, one on the east and the other on the south; these also they subsequently razed to the ground. They further burnt the treasury-chambers, in which lay vast sums of money, vast piles of raiment and other valuables; for this, in short, was the general repository of Jewish wealth, to which the rich had consigned the contents of their dismantled houses. . . . (Josephus, War VI, 5, 1-2)

The Romans, now that the rebels had fled into the city, and the sanctuary itself and all around it were in flames, carried their standards into the Temple court, and setting them up opposite the eastern gate, they sacrificed to them, and with rousing acclamations hailed Titus as supreme commander [imperator]. So glutted with plunder were the troops, one and all, that throughout the whole of Syria, the standard of gold was depreciated by half its value. . . . (Josephus, War VI, 6, 1)

The Jerusalem Temple and its treasures, like all the other sumptuous "Houses of God" across the Near East, excited the imagination and greed of every ruler and adventurer who passed that way. Assyrians, Babylonians, Greeks, and Romans had all earlier helped themselves to its riches, but now there would be no more "vast sums of money and vast piles of raiment and other valuables" atop Mount Moriah. The Temple, Herod's more expansive and magnificent echo of Solomon's splendor, lay gutted and in ruins, a desolation that would last for six centuries.

As the Romans stood sacrificing amid the flames that were consuming the ruined Temple, the insurgents showed signs of losing heart; the rebellion, it appeared, might soon be over:

The tyrants and their followers, beaten on all sides in the war and surrounded by a wall preventing any possibility of escape, now invited Titus to a parlay. Anxious, with his innate humanity, at all events to save the town, and instigated by his friends, who supposed that the brigands had at length been brought to reason, Titus took up a position on the west of the outer court of the Temple; there being at this point gates opening above the Xystus and the bridge which connected the Upper City with the Temple and now parted the tyrants from Caesar. The multitude stood in crowds on either side: the Jews around Simon and John, excited by hopes of pardon, the Romans beside Caesar eagerly waiting to hear their claim. . . . (Josephus, War VI, 6, 2-3)

The negotiations broke down when the rebels presented demands instead of offering concessions.

. . . Thereupon Titus, indignant that men in the position of captives should proffer proposals to him as victors, ordered proclamation to be made to them neither to desert nor to hope for terms any longer, for he would spare none. . . . He then gave his troops permission to burn and sack the city. For that day they refrained, but on the next day they set fire to the Archives [to Archaeion], the Akra, the Council Chamber, and the region called Ophlas [that is, the Ophel], the flames spreading as far as the palace of Queen Helena [of Adiabene], which was in the center of the Akra. The streets were also burned and the houses, packed with the bodies of the victims of the famine. (Josephus, War VI, 6, 3)

The rebels now rushed to the royal palace [of Herod], in which owing to its solidity, many had deposited their property; and having beaten off the Romans, they slew the whole mass of people who had congregated there, to the number of 8,400, and looted the money. . . . (Josephus, War VI, 7, 1)

The Burning of the Lower City

In the final stages of the campaign against Jerusalem, the Roman troops, who were by now as much inspired by frustration as by greed, turned to the business of looting; for the rebels, on the other hand, their mood swung vertiginously from a shuddering joy in the utter destruction they had brought about to desperate thoughts of how to survive the ruin of the city that was collapsing about them:

On the following day, the Romans, having routed the brigands from the Lower City, set the whole on fire as far as Siloam; the consuming of the city rejoiced their hearts, but they were disappointed of plunder, the rebels having cleared out everything before they retired to the Upper City. For the rebels showed no remorse for their evils, but rather bragged of them as blessings. Indeed, when they beheld the city burning, they declared with beaming faces that they cheerfully awaited the end, seeing that, with the people slaughtered, the Temple in ashes, and the town in flames, they were leaving nothing to their foes. . . .

A last and cherished hope of the tyrants and their brigand comrades lay in the underground passages, as a place of refuge where they expected no search would be made for them, intending after the complete capture of the city and the departure of the Romans to come forth and make their escape. But this proved to be but a dream: for they were not destined to elude either God or the Romans. . . . (Josephus, War VI, 7, 2-3)

Caesar, finding it impractical to reduce the Upper City without earth-works, owing to the precipitous nature of the site, on the twentieth of the month Lous apportioned the task among his forces. The conveyance of timber was arduous, however, since all the environs of the city to a distance of a hundred furlongs had, as I said, been stripped bare for the former embankments. The works raised by the four legions were on the west side of the city, opposite the royal palace (of Herod); while the auxiliaries and other units threw up embankments adjoining the Xystus, the bridge, and the tower that Simon had built as a fortress for himself when he was at war with John.

The earthworks having now been completed after eighteen days labor, on the seventh day of the month Gorpiaeus the Romans brought up the engines. Of the rebels, some already despairing of the city retired from the ramparts to the Citadel, others slunk down into the mines. . . . And when a portion of the wall broke down and some of the towers succumbed to the battering of the rams, the defenders at once took flight, and even the tyrants were seized with needlessly serious alarm. . . . For the three (Herodian) towers, which we have described above, would have defied every engine of war. . . . The Romans, now masters of the walls, planted their standards on the towers, and with clapping of hands and jubilation raised a paean in honor of their victory. . . . Pouring into the alleys, sword in hand, they massacred indiscriminately all whom they met, and burnt the houses of all who had taken refuge within. . . . Towards evening they ceased slaughtering, but when night fell fire gained the mastery, and the dawn of the eighth day of the month Gorpiaeus broke upon Jerusalem in flames. . . . (Josephus, War VI, 8, 1, 4-5)

Titus, on entering the town, was amazed at its strength, but chiefly at the towers, which the tyrants, in their infatuation, had abandoned. Indeed, when he beheld their solid lofty mass, the magnitude of each block and the accuracy of the joinings, and how great was their breadth, how vast their height, "God indeed," he exclaimed, "has been with us in the war. God it was who brought the Jews down from these strongholds; for what power have human hands or engines against these towers?" . . . (Josephus, War VI, 9, 1)

The End, from the Beginning

Thus was Jerusalem taken in the second year of the reign of Vespasian on the eighth of the month of Gorpiaeus [September 26, A.D. 70]. Captured on five previous occasions, it was now for the second time devastated. Asochaeus,[41] *king of Egypt, and after him Antiochus, then Pompey, and subsequently Sossius in league with Herod [in 37 B.C.: War I, 345] took the city but preserved it. But before their days the king of Babylon had subdued it and laid it waste, fourteen hundred and sixty-eight years and six months after its foundation. Its original founder was a Canaanite chief, called in the native tongue "Righteous King";*[42] *for such indeed he was. In virtue thereof he was the first to officiate as priest of God and, being the first to build the Temple, gave the city, previously called Solyma, the name of Jerusalem. The Canaanite population was expelled by David, the king of the Jews, who established his own people there. And four hundred and seventy-seven years and six months after his time it was razed to the ground by the Babylonians. The period from King David, its first Jewish sovereign, to its destruction by Titus was one thousand one hundred and seventy-nine years; and from its first foundation until its final overthrow, two thousand one hundred and seventy-seven. Howbeit, neither its antiquity nor nor its ample wealth, nor its people spread over the whole habitable world, nor yet the great glory of its religious rites, could aught avail to avert its ruin. Thus ended the siege of Jerusalem. (Josephus, War VI, 9, 1)*

The City Razed and Occupied

The army, now having no victims either for slaughter or plunder, through lack of all objects on which to vent their rage—for they would assuredly never have desisted from a desire to spare anything so long as there was work to be done—Caesar ordered the whole city and the Temple to be razed to the ground, leaving only the loftiest of the towers, Phasael, Hippicus, and Mariamne, and the portion of the wall enclosing the city from the west: the latter as an encampment for the garrison that was to remain, and the towers to indicate to posterity the nature of the city and the strong defenses which had yet yielded to Roman prowess.[43] *All the rest of the wall encompassing the city was so completely levelled to the ground as to leave future visitors to the spot no ground for believing that it had ever been inhabited. Such was the end to which the frenzy of revolutionaries brought Jerusalem, that splendid city of world-wide renown.*

As the local garrison Caesar decided to leave the Tenth Legion, along with some squadrons of cavalry and companies of infantry. . . . (Josephus, War VII, 1, 1-2)

The Spiritual Restoration of Jerusalem and the Temple

Some sense, and some recompense, had to be made of a disaster of such magnitude. One response is found among Yohanan ben Zakkai's spiritual descendants at Yabneh and the other schools where the rituals and injunctions of post-Temple Judaism were shaped. In the new age every Jew was required to pray the the eighteen blessings or benedictions, the *Shemoneh Esreh* or Tefillah, three times daily (Berekoth 4:1), and:

If [a man] was riding on an ass [when the time of prayer is upon him], he should dismount [to say the Tefillah]. If he cannot dismount he should turn his face [toward Jerusalem]; and if he cannot turn his face, he should direct his heart toward the Holy of Holies. (Danby 1933: 5)

Among the blessings of the Tefillah, three are directed precisely at the question of Jerusalem, a city destroyed but still gloriously flourishing in another, more spiritual dimension:

BENEDICTION 14 *Be merciful, O Lord our God, in Thy great mercy, towards Israel Thy people, and towards Jerusalem Thy city, and towards Sion the abiding place of Thy glory, and towards the Temple and Thy habitation, and towards the kingdom of the house of David, Thy righteous anointed one. Blessed art Thou, O Lord God of David, the builder of Jerusalem.*

BENEDICTION 16 *Accept [us], O Lord our God, and dwell in Sion; and may Thy servants serve Thee in Jerusalem. Blessed art Thou, O Lord, who makest peace.*

BENEDICTION 18   *Bestow Thy peace upon Israel Thy people and upon Thy city and upon Thine inheritance, and bless us, all of us together. Blessed art Thou, O Lord, who makest peace.* [44]

There were other responses as well, some of which we have already seen in another context. The city and its Temple were permanently and untouchably enshrined in the Mishna more than a century after their destruction, where in the tractate Middoth the Temple's buildings and rituals were as lovingly and as carefully detailed as if there were still Jews passing daily in and out of those precincts. And in Kelim 1:6-9 (see Chapter Two) the holiness of Jerusalem and the Temple are mapped and guaranteed. In both texts the conviction is enormous that in reality neither Jerusalem nor the House of the Lord had been destroyed, as in fact they had not, in the sense that the rabbis intended and that many subsequent generations of Jews understood.

The Christian Response

The Christians also required a response, though in their case the task was considerably easier since Jesus had repeatedly predicted the destruction of the Temple, and however he may have intended the prophecy, its literal fulfillment brought a centuries-long satisfaction to the Christians. There was in fact a double satisfaction since by the fourth century Christians like Eusebius and Jerome had transferred the responsibility for the deed from the Romans to the Jews themselves: it was their killing of Jesus that brought about the destruction of their city.

It was of course merely the earthly city that had been destroyed. The Christians too looked toward a heavenly Jerusalem, though for very different reasons than did the contemporary Jews. The notion, and its motives are already present in Paul writing before the destruction:

Tell me now, you who are you so anxious to be under law, will you not listen to what the Law says? It is written there that Abraham had two sons, one by his slave and the other by his free-born wife. The slave-woman's son was born in the course of nature, the free woman's through God's promise. This is an allegory. The two women stand for two covenants. The one bearing children into slavery is the covenant that comes from Mount Sinai: that is Hagar. Sinai is a mountain in Arabia and it represents the Jerusalem of today, for she and her children are in slavery. But the heavenly Jerusalem is the free woman; she is our mother. For Scripture says: "Rejoice, O barren woman who never bore child; break into a shout of joy, you who never knew a mother's pangs; for the deserted wife shall have more children than she who lives with the husband." (Galatians 4:21-27)

The theme is announced again in Revelation or the Apocalypse, the final book of the Christians' New Testament, composed after the events of A.D. 70:

Then I saw a new heaven and a new earth and the first earth had vanished and there was no longer any sea. I saw the Holy City, new Jerusalem, coming down from out of heaven from God, made ready like a bride adorned for her husband. I heard a voice proclaiming from the throne: "Now at last God has his dwelling among men! He will dwell among them and they shall be his people, and God himself will be with them. . . . " (Revelation: 21:1-4)

Then one of the seven angels that held the seven bowls full of the seven last plagues came and spoke to me and said, "Come, and I will show you the bride, the wife of the Lamb." So in the Spirit he carried me away to a great high mountain and showed me the city of Jerusalem coming down out of from God. It shone with the glory of God; it had the radiance of some priceless jewel, like a jasper, clear as a crystal. It had a great high wall, with twelve gates, at which were twelve angels; and on the gates were inscribed the names of the twelve tribes of Israel. There were three gates to the east, three to the north, three to the south and three to the west. The city wall had twelve foundation stones, and on them were the names of the twelve apostles of the Lamb. (Revelation 21:9-14)

If this sounds like Ezekiel, there is a profound difference between the Jewish prophet of the Exile and his later Christian counterpart:

But I saw no Temple in the city; for its Temple was the sovereign Lord God and the Lamb. And the city had no need of sun or moon to shine upon it; for the glory of God gave it light, and its lamp was the Lamb. By its light shall the nations [Gentiles] walk and the kings of the earth shall bring into it all their splendor. The gates of the city shall never be shut by day, and there will be no night. The wealth and splendor of the nations shall be brought into it; but nothing unclean shall enter, nor anyone whose ways are false or foul, but only those who are inscribed in the Lamb's roll of the living. (Revelation 21:22-27)

There was, then, a Jerusalem in the Christian future, but no longer a Temple. Like much else in the Jewish past of the new faith, that too had been superseded, and the author of the letter attributed to Barnabas but likely written sometime about A.D. 130 proceeds to its allegorical dismantling with as much vigor as the Romans took to its physical destruction:

As for the matter of the Temple, I shall show you how mistaken were those miserable people who pinned their hopes to the building itself, as if that were the house of God, instead of on God Himself, their own Creator. Indeed, they were scarcely less misguided than the heathen in the way they attributed divine holiness to their Temple. For note how completely the words of the Lord Himself do away with that notion: "Who is it who can span the whole heaven with the breadth of one hand, or the earth with the flat of his palm? Is it not I?" says the Lord. "The heaven is my throne, and the earth a stool for my feet. What sort of house then will you build for Me, and where is the spot on earth that can serve Me for a resting place?" [Isaiah 66:1] You can see that their hope was the purest folly. Besides, He also says "Behold, those who pulled the Temple down will not rebuild it" [Isaiah 49:17], the very thing which is now in the course of fulfillment; for after their armed rebellion it was demolished by their enemies, and now they themselves are about to build it up again, as subjects of their foemen. Nonetheless, it has been revealed that city, Temple, and Jewish people are all alike doomed to one day be destroyed, for Scripture says, "it will come to pass in the last days that the Lord will deliver up to destruction the sheep of the pasture, with their sheepfold and their watchtower" [Enoch 89:56]. And for the Lord to say such a thing is for that thing to come about.

But what we must next inquire into is whether there can be any such thing as a temple to God at all? To be sure there can, but in the place where He Himself tells us that He is building and perfecting it. For it is written, "when the Week draws near its close, then a temple of God will be built gloriously in the Name of the Lord." And from this I must infer that there is indeed such a thing as a temple. Note, however, that it is to be "built in the Name of the Lord"; for in the days before we believed in God, our hearts were a corrupt and flimsy abode, and a temple only too truly built with hands, since by our constant opposition to God we had made them into a house of idolatry and a home for demons. . . . But when we were granted remission for our sins and put our hope in His Name, we were made new men, created all over again from the beginning; and as a consequence of that, God is actually dwelling within us in that poor house of ours. . . . It is in these ways that He admits us, the slaves of mortality, into the Temple that is immortal. . . . (Letter of Barnabas, 16)

Jerusalem Between the Wars

We now enter a dark phase in the history of Jerusalem, where most of our sources, literary and archeological, desert us. Jerusalem was undoubtedly

124

a ruined city after A.D. 70, but it was not an abandoned one. The Tenth Legion put there by Titus still had its station there where Herod once had his palace along the western city wall, and at least some of the Christians returned from their self-imposed exile to Pella. The Jewish evidence is far less direct, but since there was as yet no ban on their living in Jerusalem, there is not reason to think that some Jews did not choose to do so. There were certainly Jewish pilgrims to the city, and it has been argued that that fact, when added to the evidence for reburial, makes plausible some kind of Jewish settlement in Jerusalem after A.D. 70. [45]

We are on even less certain ground if we ask what kind of religious and cultic life went on in the city. The Christians surely did as they continued to do for years thereafter, worship and celebrate the Eucharistic liturgy in private homes. The Christian pilgrim Egeria, visiting Mount Sion in the 380s, gives the impression that the church there had only recently been converted from a private house. [46] As for the Jews, if they were to worship on the Temple mount as before, and no one was preventing them from doing so, as far as we know, the place would have had to have been repurified and resacralized. Its barriers against impurity had been broken, as had earlier happened at the hand of Antiochus Epiphanes, and if there had been a reconsecration, which also would have necessitated some kind of rebuilding, the act would surely have left some trace in the Jewish tradition, which it has not.

But the Jews had by then another institution in which some form of prayer worship might be conducted and the study of the law pursued, the synagogue, and one source at least, the Christian Epiphanius writing late in the fourth century, suggests that there were such in Jerusalem between the wars:

[Hadrian] found the city completely leveled to the ground and God's temple trodden down, except for a few small houses and the church of God, which was quite small. To it the disciples returned after the Savior's ascension from the Mount of Olives. They went up to the Upper Room, for it had been built there—that is, in the part of the city called Sion, which part was exempted from destruction, as also were some of the dwellings around Sion and seven synagogues, the only ones which existed in Sion, like monks' cells. One of these survived until the time of the Bishop Maximus and King Constantine. It was like a tent in a vineyard, to quote the Scriptures. In the midst of these Hadrian took thought to rebuild only the city, not the Temple, and he put in charge of the reconstruction Aquila, whom we have already mentioned as the Greek translator of Scripture and his brother-in-law, a native of Sinope in Pontus. Since he wished to call the city after himself and his reign, he named it Aelia since he himself was named Aelius Hadrianus. (Baldi 1955: 477-478)

An earlier Christian visitor, a pilgrim from Bordeaux who was in Jerusalem in A.D. 333, has it somewhat differently:

Inside Sion, within the wall, you can see where David had his palace. Seven synagogues were there, but only one is left, the rest have been "ploughed down and sown," as was said by the Prophet Isaiah. (Wilkinson 1981: 157-158)

In 1947, after the place called "David's Tomb" on Mount Sion had been taken by the Israelis, a systematic investigation of the site was begun by J. Pinkerfeld, who discovered three of the original walls and late Roman stonework in a niche facing the Temple mount, from which he concluded that this was indeed a synagogue, and of a date that would render it a likely candidate for the surviving synagogue mentioned by both the Bordeaux pilgrim and Epiphanius. [47]

Hadrian and the Second Jewish War

According to Epiphanius, Hadrian's visit to Jerusalem took place in A.D. 117, and it was then that the emperor laid his plans to rebuild "only the city but not the Temple." The date is almost certainly wrong: Hadrian made his grand progress through Syria, Palestine, and Egypt in A.D. 129-130, when a number of cities were rebuilt at the imperial command and expense. [48] But the question remains whether those plans to rebuild Jerusalem were in fact the cause of the second Jewish revolt against Roman authority, which broke out in A.D. 132 and is associated with the name of its leader Bar Kokhba. [49] The historian Dio Cassius, who has a brief account of the revolt, was convinced that it was:

But (Hadrian) stirred up a war of no small extent or duration by founding a city at Jerusalem in place of that which had been destroyed, which city he named Aelia Capitolina, and by setting up another temple to Jupiter on the site of the Lord's Temple, for the Jews thought it an outrage that any foreigners should be made citizens of their city and that foreign temples should be set up in it. And so, for as long as Hadrian was present in their country and in Syria and Egypt, they remained quiet, except that they made the arms which they were required to furnish of deliberately bad workmanship so that the arms might be rejected and then they might have them themselves for their own use. And then in his absence far from the country they began their insurrection. They did not dare to meet the Romans in pitched battle, but they seized upon all the strategic positions in the country and strengthened them with walls and underground passages so that they might have ways of escape when overpowered, and they might pass unobserved underground from one of their strong places to another. Moreover, they made holes in the upper part of their subterranean galleries to give them light and air.

At first the Romans took no notice of them; but when the whole of Judea became moved and all the Jews throughout the land were stirred up and gathered together and did the Romans much mischief both by treachery and in open war, and many people belonging to other nations were led by hopes of plunder to join them, and nearly all the world was in an uproar about it, then at last Hadrian sent his best generals against them. Of these the first was Julius Severus, who was transferred from his governorship of Britain and sent against the Jews. At first he did not venture to make any direct attack upon them on account of their numbers and their desperation; but he did cut off various groups of them by the numbers of his soldiers and officers, and straitened them for provisions, and shut them up in fortresses. Thus he was able slowly but surely to wear them out and destroy them.

Very few Jews survived; Julius Severus took fifty of their most notable forts, 985 of their chiefest villages were laid in ruins, and 580,000 men were slain in skirmishes and battles, while the number of those who perished by starvation, plague, or fire cannot be reckoned. Thus almost the whole of Judea was laid waste, even as had been foretold to the its people before the war. For Solomon's tomb, which they regard as one of their holy places, fell to pieces and was scattered abroad of its own accord, and many wolves and hyenas came howling into their cities. Many of the Romans also perished in this war; and so Hadrian, when he wrote to the Senate, did not use the usual imperial preface, to wit, "If you and your children are well, it is well; I and the army are well." (Dio Cassius, History LXIX, 12)

Dio makes no mention of Bar Kokhba nor of the question that concerns us here, whether the rebels took Jerusalem from the Romans. No other text says that they did, but a number of others mention in passing that in suppressing the revolt Hadrian captured or destroyed Jerusalem, something that would obviously not have taken place if the rebels had not driven the Romans out in the first place. [50] Another piece of evidence often adduced for the rebels' occupation of Jerusalem are the rebels' coins, which, during all three years in which they were struck, bear the name of Jerusalem on them; in addition, those from the third year of the revolt have the legend "for the liberation of Jerusalem," a sign, it is argued, that Jerusalem was being used as the Jewish insurrectionists' mint. [51]

If this seems at least plausible on the evidence, the ground becomes far less certain when we approach the question of whether or not the Temple was rebuilt or even whether sacrifice was resumed on the Temple mount. Here the evidence is entirely numismatic, the appearance on the Bar Kokhba coins of a building that is alleged to have been the Temple, indeed the rebuilt Temple, particularly since the name of "the priest Eleazer" also appears there. Neither argument, nor even their combination, appears entirely convincing. [52]

The end was bitter for Jerusalem, even when seen through Eusebius' retributive theology:

The climax of the war came in Hadrian's eighteenth year, in Betthera [probably Bittir, seven miles southwest of Jerusalem], an almost impregnable village not very far from Jerusalem. The blockade lasted so long that hunger and thirst brought the revolutionaries to complete destruction, and the instigator of their crazy folly paid the penalty he deserved. From that time onward the entire [Jewish] race has been forbidden to set foot anywhere near Jerusalem, according to the conditions and ordinances of the law of Hadrian which ensured that not even from a distance might Jews have a view of their ancestral soil. Aristo of Pella tells the whole story. When in this way the city was thus interdicted to the Jewish race and suffered the total destruction of its former inhabitants, it was colonized by an alien race, and the Roman city which later arose there changed its name, so that it is now, in honor of the then reigning emperor, Aelius Hadrianus, it is known as Aelia. Furthermore, as the church in the city was now composed of Gentiles, the first after the bishops of the Circumcision to be put in charge of the Christians was Mark. (Eusebius, Church History IV, 6)

In the same *Church History* Eusebius supplies further information on the Christian community in Jerusalem, both before and after the revolt of A.D. 132-135:

After the martyrdom of James [in A.D. 62] and the capture of Jerusalem which followed immediately [in A.D. 70], there is a firm tradition that those of the Apostles and disciples of the Lord who were still alive assembled from all parts together with those who were the mortal blood relatives of the Lord, for most of them were still living. Then they all discussed whom they should choose as a fit person to succeed James, and they voted as one that Symeon, son of the Clopas mentioned in the Gospel narrative [Jn. 19:25] was a fit person to occupy the throne of the Jerusalem see. He was, so it is said, a cousin of the Savior, for Hegesippus tells us that Clopas was Joseph's brother. (Eusebius, Church History III, 11)

I have not found any written evidence on the dates of the bishops of Jerusalem—it is known that they did not live very long—but I do have documentary evidence of this, that up to Hadrian's siege of the Jews [in A.D. 135] there had been a series of fifteen bishops there. All are said to have been Hebrews in origin, who had received the knowledge of Christ with all sincerity, and consequently those who had the authority to decide such matters judged them worthy of the episcopal office. For at that time the whole church was made up of Hebrew believers who had continued from apostolic times down to the later siege in which the Jews, after a second revolt against the Romans, were overcome in a full-scale war. (Eusebius, Church History IV, 5)

Aelia Capitolina

Once the revolt was quelled and Jerusalem back in Roman hands, Hadrian could put into effect the plans for the rebuilding of the city that may have triggered the insurrection in the first place. Jerusalem was in fact refounded and given a new name, Colonia Aelia Capitolina, celebrating both the emperor's name and that of the deity under whose protection it was being placed, Jupiter Capitolinus. Of that much we are certain; nor do we have any reason to doubt the testimony of an anonymous sixth-century work called the "Paschal Chronicle" that says the emperor installed there two public baths; colonnaded steps, probably down to the Siloam pool, where there was a four-porticoed monumental fountain; a *trikameron*, which may mean a triple-aisled temple; and something mysteriously called in the chronicle's Greek *kodra*, in Latin, *quadra*, "something square," which few have been able to resist seeing as the ruined and deserted Temple platform of Herod. [53]

This is little enough to go on, and there were no visitors or historians of the era between A.D. 135 and 330 to assist us with a description of Hadrian's Jerusalem. We know what his other cities looked like and so perhaps can fill in some of the broad strokes; and archeological investigation, or in some cases reevaluation, has supplied others. We know, for example, that Aelia Capitolina had two forums, one on its eastern side, just north of the Temple mount and inside the gate today called St. Stephen's or the Lion Gate; [54] and another, the chief commercial center of Hadrianic Jerusalem, just south of what is now the Church of the Holy Sepulcher and beneath the square in the Upper City today called the Muristan. [55] Again, excavated and visible under the present Damascus Gate is the pedestrian walkway of what was Hadrian's monumental northern gate—or triumphal arch—into the city. [56]

We were once far more certain about Aelia Capitolina than we are today. There was, after all, the Madaba map, a mosaic portrait of the city drawn in about A.D. 580, showing two prominent colonnaded streets running north and south through the city, one along the ridge of the western hill and the other down through Valley Street, which surely were Hadrianic, it was thought. Now it seems not: a southern section of the Upper City street has been excavated by Nahum Avigad, and it is Byzantine, *with no Roman remains beneath it.* Nor indeed are there Roman remains anywhere else in the southern part of the Old City; the stratum here dating from before A.D. 70 is followed directly by Byzantine remains. The evidence seems convincing, then, that Hadrianic Jerusalem extended no further south than the present line of King David and Gate of the Chain Street, and that all of its southward extension, as reflected on the Madaba map, for example, was a purely Byzantine phenomenon, a reflex of the revival and expansion of the city under Christian auspices from the fourth century onward. [57]

Finally, there is the problem of the Temple mount and of Hadrian's own temple to Jupiter Capitolinus. Christian pilgrims were up on the Temple mount early in the fourth century A.D., and though there were statues visible there, [58] no one remarks on seeing a temple. We must conclude then that no attempt was made by Hadrian or any other to resacralize the Temple mount—it is for all practical purposes invisible on the Madaba map—and that Hadrian's Capitolium was where we might naturally expect it, on his forum in the Upper City. [59]

The Romans had no great interest in Jerusalem: they occupied it because they had to; they incorporated it and surrounding Judea into their empire because they could find no one to rule it; and they destroyed it because rebels chose it as the place of their last stand. They destroyed far more than they built in the city, and when they did choose to rebuild it in A.D. 135, it was as an object lesson to their defiant Jewish subjects. For the Romans, as for many after them, Jerusalem was a problem. For those who followed them there were at times compensations in their stewardship of the Holy City; but for the Romans there was no profit—material, spiritual, or political—to be had from being masters of that place.

4

Mother of All the Churches

*So was the New Jerusalem built, over against
the one so famous of old. . . .*
—*Eusebius*

THE CONVERSION of Palestine, a province of the Roman Empire, into
a Christian Holy Land begins with Emperor Constantine. Constantine's
embrace of Christianity, at a time when only a relatively small number of
his subjects were adherents of that recently persecuted faith, was his personal statement; but given his position as emperor and the monotheistic,
exclusionary nature of the Christian faith, the consequences, political and
theological, had inevitably to follow. The most important of them was
undoubtedly the emperor's summoning the bishops of the entire Church
to the city of Nicea in A.D. 325 to sit in conclave and attempt, under his
guidance and direction, to restore the unity of the Christian community
that had been shattered by the teachings of the Alexandrian priest Arius.
Their task was accomplished to Constantine's satisfaction, but their deliberations there, and the celebratory mood that followed set other sentiments and other projects in train. The bishops had in fact addressed themselves to other questions as well, among them the city still known as Aelia.
They decreed in the seventh of the canons passed by that council: "Since
custom and ancient tradition have established that the bishop of Aelia
should be honored, let him have the next place of honor [after the bishop
of Rome], with all due recognition, however, of the domestic right of the
Metropolitan See of that province [of Palestine]."

The issue of Jerusalem's position vis-à-vis its own Metropolitan See of
Caesarea would arise later; for the moment, the focus was on the Holy
City itself. In the wake of the council at Nicea, Constantine embarked
upon a prodigious program of church building and endowment. Its intent
was to give Christianity the same public and political visability enjoyed by
the other cults of the Empire. No longer would the Christians' churches
be modest or disguised buildings, underground chapels in cemeteries outside the city or private houses within; henceforward they would stand,
large and magnificent, at the heart of Rome's metropolises in both the
East and the West.

Jerusalem was a somewhat different case, however. It was not a metropolis, even within its own region: in the fourth century it was still
much as Hadrian had left it two centuries earlier: a provincial city in the

high empire style, somewhat too glittering for its actual commercial and political importance. And the governor of the province still continued to reside in Herod's city of Caesarea on the coast. In Christian eyes it was somewhat more, of course: Jerusalem, Bethlehem, Nazareth, the land around the Sea of Galilee were all places sanctified by the presence of Jesus. No one had forgotten that, not the bishops at Nicea who formally recognized the special place of Jerusalem in the Christian community, and not the Christians who went to Palestine to see the holy places, to study and to meditate upon the mysteries of Salvation. [1]

Constantine and Jerusalem

What the bishops of Nicea intended by decree, Constantine resolved to do in a more imperial, more political fashion. Our reporter is Eusebius, himself a Palestinian, a scholar of biblical and early Christian history in Palestine, [2] and the emperor's biographer. According to his *Life of Constantine*, the chief target of the emperor's interest was the place of Jesus' burial:

This cave of salvation [in Jerusalem] certain ungodly and impious persons had determined to hide from the eyes of men. . . . Having expended much labor in bringing in earth from outside, they covered up the whole place. Then, when they had raised this [fill] to a certain height and paved it with stone, they entirely concealed the divine cave beneath a great mound. Next, as if nothing further were left for them to do, they prepared above ground a dreadful thing, a veritable sepulcher of souls, building to the impure demon called Aphrodite a dark shrine of lifeless idols and offering their foul oblations on profane and accursed altars. . . . He [Constantine] gave orders that the place should be purified, counting it especially fitting that a spot that had been polluted by his enemies should enjoy the mighty working of the All-Good at his hands. And as soon as his orders were given, the contrivances of deceit were cast down from on high to the ground, and the dwelling-places of error, images, and demons and all, were overthrown and utterly destroyed.

Nor did his zeal stop here. The emperor gave further directions that the materials of the destroyed structure, both wood and stone, should be removed and taken as far from the spot as possible, which was done in accordance with his command. . . . Again, inspired with holy zeal, he issued orders that, after the soil had been excavated to a considerable depth, they should transport to a far distant spot the actual ground, earth and all, inasmuch as it had been polluted by the defilements of demon-worship.

This was done without delay. And as one layer after another was laid bare, the place which was beneath the earth appeared; directly as this was done, contrary to all expectation, the venerable and hallowed monument of our Savior's resurrection become visible, and the most holy cave received what was an emblem of his coming to life. (Eusebius, Life of Constantine III, 26-28)

Thus Constantine discovered, under the temple of Jupiter Capitolinus on Hadrian's forum in the Upper City, the place of Jesus' burial. The site, it is clear from the account, was known, and indeed it is unlikely that the local Christian community in the city would have forgotten where the Savior of Mankind had died and been buried, and this despite the fact that the shape and topography of the city had been considerably altered since the days when Pontius Pilate sat in the Roman pretorium in Jerusalem. Jesus had been executed and buried outside the western city wall; that same place was now in the center of the Upper City, at the commercial and political heart of the Aelia designed by Hadrian's builders. It was a place, Constantine must have thought, for a monumental public statement. Eusebius continues:

Thereupon the emperor issued sacred edicts and, when he had provided an abundant supply of all the things required for the project, he gave orders that a house of prayer worthy of God should be erected round about the Cave of Salvation, and on a scale of rich and imperial costliness. . . . To the governors of the provinces in the East [he gave instructions] that by providing liberal and abundant grants they should make the work exceedingly large, great, and costly; and to the bishop who at that time presided over the Church in Jerusalem [Macarius] he sent the following letter . . . :

It is a truly miraculous event that the symbol of the most holy Passion, which was long ago buried underground and remained unknown for so many cycles of years, should now be made to shine forth to His servants, who are themselves freed by the removal of that man who was the common enemy of all.[3] . . . It is my wish, then, that you should be especially convinced of this, which I suppose is clear to everyone, that of all things it is my chief concern how we may splendidly adorn with buildings that sacred place which, under divine direction, I freed, as it were, from the heavy burden pressing down upon it, yes, even from the disgraceful addition of an idol—a place holy indeed from the beginning of God's judgment, but which has been made to appear still more holy since it brought to light the assurance of the Savior's Passion.

It is fitting, then, that in your wisdom you order and make provision for everything necessary, that not only shall this basilica be the finest in

Byzantine Jerusalem (330-638).

Permission Carta, Jerusalem

134

the world, but that the details also shall be such that all the most beautiful structures in every city may be surpassed by it. Concerning the building and beautification of the walls, know that my intention has been entrusted to my friend Dracilianus, deputy of the pretorian prefects, and to the governor of the province. For by my piety has it been commanded them that craftsmen and workers and all things which they may learn from Your Wisdom might be necessary for the building shall be furnished by them. As for the columns and marbles, have a care to tell us in writing, after you have inspected the plan, whatever you judge to be most precious and serviceable, so that those materials, of whatever sort and in whatever quantity, may be procured from every quarter. . . .

As to the vaulted roof I wish to know from you whether you think it should have a panelled ceiling or be finished in some other fashion. If it is to be panelled, it may also be ornamented in gold. It remains for Your Holiness to make it known to the aforesaid magistrates with all speed how many workers and craftsmen and how much money will be needed. Be careful to report straightway to me, not only concerning the marbles and the columns, but also about the panelled ceiling, if you should judge this the more beautiful. God guard you, beloved brother. . . . (Eusebius, Life of Constantine III, 29-32)

The public and state resources of the empire, as well as the emperor's private fortune, were thus being mobilized for this work in Jerusalem, all overseen by the local bishops and, it is evident, by the emperor himself, who provides specific construction details. Eusebius proceeds to describe the results, beginning with the cave-tomb:

And first of all the emperor adorned the sacred cave, which was, so to speak, the chief part of the whole work, and the generosity of the emperor beautified it with choice columns and with much ornament, decorating it with all kinds of adornments.

In front of the cave, that is, toward the east:

. . . one crossed over to a very large space of ground, to wit, the atrium, which was open to the pure air of heaven; its floor was a polished stone pavement, and it was bounded by long porticoes which ran round continuously on three sides.

Finally, there was the most striking architectural feature of the whole complex, a huge basilica that stretched eastward from the site of Calvary until its monumental entryway touched upon Hadrian's north-south *cardo*, or market street, through the Upper City:

The basilica was constructed adjoining the site opposite the cave, which *looked toward the rising sun, a truly extraordinary work, reared to an immense height, and enormous in both length and breadth. Slabs of variegated marble lined the inside of the building, and the appearance of the walls outside exhibited a spectacle of extraordinary beauty, in no way inferior to the appearance of marble, shining brightly with polished stones which fitted exactly into each other. . . . (Eusebius, Life of Constantine III, 34-36)*

There were, according to Eusebius, twin colonnades along the northern and southern sides of this building, with three entries on the east "to admit the entering crowds." Eastward of these three entries lay an open court or atrium and, beyond that, a monumental propyleum:

As you go toward the entrances which lie in front of the sanctuary, you first come upon an atrium. There were here on each side first a court, then porticoes, and lastly the gates of the court. And after these, in the midst of the wide marketplace [or market street, the Roman cardo], the exquisitely worked main entrance of the whole building presented to the passers-by on the outside a striking view of the interior. (Eusebius, Life of Constantine III, 39)

Not all the details of Eusebius' elaborate description are entirely clear, though they can be glossed by some archeological evidence, by the remarks of later visitors to Constantine's church complex around Calvary and the sepulcher of Jesus, and by one quite extraordinary picture we have of the church. [4] The central nave was flanked by double aisles on either side, and these in turn had above them galleries supported on high columns. The walls of the aisles were covered with marble facing. The nave ended at its western side in a structure covered by what Eusebius calls a *hemisphairion*, a half-dome, apparently some kind of rotunda, which had within it twelve columns.

If many of the details must be conjectured, the emperor's intent in putting up such a complex of buildings is quite explicit:

So on the monument of salvation itself was the new Jerusalem built, over against the one so famous of old which, after the pollution caused by the murder of the Lord, experienced the last extremity of desolation and paid the penalty for the crime of its impious inhabitants. Opposite this the emperor raised, at great and lavish expense, the trophy of the Savior's victory over death. . . . (Eusebius, Life of Constantine III, 33)

Thus the New Jerusalem came into existence, the Holy City to replace the earthly one destroyed by God's vengeance against the Jews for their crime of "the murder of the Lord." This is Eusebius' theology of the event, and perhaps it was Constantine's as well, but the site and the building strongly suggest that the emperor, who knew and cared more for politics than theology, had something additional in mind. These large and sumptuous buildings set down right in the very heart of Roman Jerusalem spoke not so much to the Jews—there were, in any event, no Jews resident in Jerusalem; they were still under Hadrian's ban from the city—as to the pretensions of Roman paganism. The city's pagan cathedral had been replaced by a Christian one, a monumental basilica built from state funds and in the recognized imperial style. [5]

Helena and the Invention of the Cross

In his summing up, Eusebius touches upon another character in the drama of Christian Jerusalem, the emperor's mother Helena, herself a convert to Christianity even before her son:

After he had selected other places in the same region which were held in honor on account of two sacred caves [at Bethlehem and on the Mount of Olives], the emperor adorned them as well at great expense. . . . He granted those places extraordinary honors and thus immortalized the memory of his mother. . . . For though she was advanced in years, she . . . came with all the energy of youth to acquaint herself with this land worthy of all veneration. . . . And when she had bestowed fitting worship on the footprints of the Savior . . . she immediately bequeathed to those who were to come after her the fruit of her personal piety. She dedicated two sanctuaries to the God whom she worshipped, one at the Cave of the Nativity and the other at the Mount of the Ascension. . . . Wherefore the most pious empress Helena adorned the scene of the birth-pains of the Mother of God [at Bethlehem] with rare monuments, beautifying in every way the sacred cave [of the Nativity]; and then a short time later the emperor too bestowed imperial gifts upon it, gold and silver treasures and brocaded curtains, and so enhanced the artistic designs of his mother. Again, the empress-mother erected a stately edifice on the Mount of Olives as a monument, . . . raising a sacred church and sanctuary on the mountain ridge, at the very summit of the hill. Here, in this cave, a true account has it that the Savior of all mankind had initiated His disciples into sacred mysteries. (Eusebius, Life of Constantine III, 41-43)

For all his brevity, Eusebius does not scant Helena's accomplishments in Jerusalem and Palestine, though he does omit the single event for which a somewhat later Christian tradition best remembered her. [6] The following is the account from the *Church History* of Sozomen, a native of Palestine from the next century and someone well acquainted with the local Jerusalem tradition:

When the business at Nicea was finished, the priests returned home. The emperor rejoiced greatly at the restoration of unity of opinion in the Catholic Church, and in his desire to express, on behalf of himself, his children and the empire, the gratitude towards God which the unanimity of the bishops inspired, he directed that a house of prayer should be erected to God at Jerusalem near the place called Calvary. At the same time his mother Helena went to the city for the purpose of offering up prayer and of visiting the sacred places. Her zeal for Christianity made her anxious to find the wood which formed the adorable Cross. But it was no easy matter to discover either this relic or the Lord's sepulcher; for the pagans, who in former times had persecuted the Church and who, at the first promulgation of Christianity, had had recourse to every artifice to exterminate it, had concealed that spot under much heaped-up earth and built up what before had been a depression, the way it appears now, and the more effectively to conceal them had enclosed the entire place of the Resurrection and Mount Calvary within a wall and had moreover ornamented the whole area and paved it with stone. . . .

At length, however, the place was discovered, and the fraud about it that had been so zealously maintained was detected; some say that the facts were first disclosed by a Hebrew who dwelt in the East and who derived his information from some documents which had come to him by paternal inheritance; but it seems more likely to suppose that God revealed the fact by means of signs and dreams. . . . When by command of the emperor the place was excavated deeply, the cave whence our Lord arose from the dead was discovered; and at no great distance three crosses were found and another separate piece of wood on which were inscribed in white letters in Hebrew, Greek, and Latin the following words: "Jesus of Nazareth, the king of the Jews." These words, as the sacred book of the Gospels relates, were placed by command of Pilate, governor of Judea, over the head of Christ.

There remained a difficulty, however, in distinguishing the Divine Cross from the others, for the inscription had been wrenched from it and thrown aside and the cross itself had been cast aside with the others, without any distinction, when the bodies of the crucified were taken down. . . . It was no concern of theirs [the Roman executioners] to deposit the crosses in their original order, since it was growing late, and as the men were dead they did not think it worthwhile to remain to attend to the crosses. A more divine indication than could be furnished by man was therefore necessary in order to distinguish the Divine Cross from the others and this revelation was given in the following manner. There was a certain lady of rank in Jerusalem who was afflicted with a most grievous and incurable disease. Macarius, bishop of Jerusalem, accompanied by the mother of the emperor and her attendants, went to her bedside. After engaging in prayer, Macarius signalled the spectators that the Divine Cross would be the one which, on being brought in contact with the invalid, would cure the disease. He approached her with each of the three crosses in turn, but when two of the crosses were laid upon her, it seemed but folly and mockery to her for she was at the gates of death. When, however, the third cross was in like manner brought to her, she suddenly opened her eyes, regained her strength, and immediately sprang from her bed well. It is said that a dead person was, in the same way, restored to life. The venerated wood having thus been identified, the greater portion of it was deposited in a silver case, in which it is still preserved in Jerusalem; but the empress sent part of it to her son Constantine, together with the nails by which the body of Christ had been fastened. . . . (Sozomen, Church History II, 1)

The Dedication, or Encaenia

The Holy Sepulcher complex—actually the rotunda-shrine over the tomb of Jesus, which was named the *Anastasis*, or Resurrection; the shrine at Calvary; and the immense basilica, the "Martyrium," as Eusebius had already begun to call it—rapidly became the center and focus of Christian Jerusalem. And the feast of its dedication took its place in the liturgical and commercial life of Jerusalem. Sozomen takes us back to the consecration day:

The temple called the "Great Martyrium" [the basilica] which was built in the place of the skull at Jerusalem, was completed about the thirtieth year of the reign of Constantine [A.D. 335]; and Marianus, an official who was a shorthand writer of the emperor came to Tyre and delivered a letter from the emperor to the council (convened there), commanding them to repair quickly to Jerusalem in order to consecrate the temple. Although this had been previously determined upon, the emperor still deemed it necessary that the disputes that had prevailed among the bishops who had been convened at Tyre should be first adjusted and that they should be purged of all discord and grief before going to the consecration of the temple. . . . When the bishops arrived in Jerusalem, the temple was therefore consecrated, as likewise numerous ornaments and gifts which were sent to the emperor and are still preserved in the sacred edifice; their costliness and magnificence is such that they cannot be looked upon with-

out exciting wonder. Since that period the anniversary of the consecration has been celebrated with great pomp by the church of Jerusalem; the festival continues for eight days, initiation by baptism is administered, and people from every region under the sun resort to Jerusalem during this festival and visit the holy places. (Sozomen, Church History II, 26)

Among the earliest witnesses to this feast was the pilgrim Egeria, who describes it as it was about A.D. 380, when she was in the city:

The days commemorating the consecration of both the church on Golgotha, which is called the Martyrium, and the holy church of the Anastasis, where the Lord rose again after his passion, are called the Encaenia.[7] The dedication feast of these holy churches is celebrated with special magnificence since it is on this very date that the cross of the Lord was discovered. So they arranged that this day should be observed with all possible joy by making the original dedication of these holy churches the same as the day when the cross was found. And you will also find in Scripture that the day of Encaenia was when the House of God was consecrated, when holy Solomon stood before God's altar in prayer, as we read in the Books of Chronicles [2 Chr. 6:12].

When the time of the Encaenia has come, they keep festival for eight days, and many days beforehand the crowds begin to assemble. Monks and apotactites[8] come not only from the provinces such as Mesopotamia, Syria, Egypt, and the Thebaid, where there are large numbers of them, but from every place and province. No one of them fails to make for Jerusalem to share the celebrations of this honorable festival. There are even laymen and women who assemble in Jerusalem from every province at this time to observe the festival. There are at least forty or fifty bishops in Jerusalem at this time, all accompanied by many of their clergy. In fact, people say that it is a grave sin to miss taking part in this feast, unless anyone had been prevented from coming by an emergency.

During Encaenia they decorate the churches in the same way they do on Easter and the Epiphany, and each day they assemble in the same holy places as on those days. On the first and second day of the feast they go to the Great Church, the Martyrium; on the third day to the Mount of Olives, to the church on the mountain itself, from which the Lord ascended into heaven after his Passion. . . . (Egeria, Pilgrimage, 74)

Hebron / Mamre

Constantine's program in Jerusalem had to do with what were exclusively Christian holy places, but outside the city Christians and Jews, and in some cases pagans, shared a veneration for cult centers that went back into remote biblical times. One such was Hebron, south of Jerusalem, the reputed grave site of Abraham and other of the biblical patriarchs. Nearby was Mamre, a village where the local tradition showed an ancient oak and a well that were connected with Abraham's stay in that place; indeed the very place was visited by God's angels beneath the terebinths (Gen. 18:1-33).

Such were the emperor's most notable sacred buildings. But when he heard that the same Savior who had lately appeared on earth had also long before manifested his divine presence to pious men in Palestine near the oak of Mamre,[9] he ordered that a house of prayer should be raised there to the God who was seen. And to the rulers of the provinces went an imperial order through letters sent to each, commanding them bring to finish what had been proposed; but to us who write this history he sent other instruction on the matter, and provided the specific reasons. . . .

[A letter to Eusebius and other bishops of Palestine:] A singular benefit has been conferred on me by that most pious lady, my wife's mother [Eutropia], in writing to me and describing the mad folly of abandoned men, which has hitherto escaped your notice. And in this way the error that has been overlooked may receive at my hands that fitting correction and attention which, if somewhat late in coming, is nonetheless necessary. . . .

She informs me that the place which is called after the oak of Mamre, where we are told that Abraham had his home, is defiled in every possible way by certain superstitious people; for she has told me that idols worthy of complete destruction are being erected next to it, and that an altar stands near, and that impure sacrifices are continually offered. Now . . . we wish to inform your reverences that we have written to the illustrious Count Acacius our friend that the idols, as many as may be found in that place, are to be immediately put to the torch and that the altar is to be completely demolished. . . . We have given further orders that the place itself should be adorned with an unpolluted building, a basilica, that it may be made place fit for the assembly of holy men. . . .[10] (Eusebius, Life of Constantine III, 51-53)

Sozomen repeats the story in the next century, though with far more detail on the local festival and an almost apologetic air, as if to say that the emperor had somewhat overreacted:

I consider it necessary to detail the proceedings of Constantine in relation to what is called the oak of Mamre. This place is now called Terebinthus and is about fifteen stadia distant from Hebron, which lies to the south, but is two hundred and fifty stadia from Jerusalem. It is recorded that here the Son of God appeared to Abraham, with two angels who had been sent against Sodom, and foretold the birth of Abraham's son. Here the inhabitants of the country and of the regions around Palestine, the Phoenicians and the Arabians, assemble annually during the summer season to keep a brilliant feast; and many others, both buyers and sellers, resort thither on account of the fair. Indeed, this feast is diligently frequented by all nations; by the Jews because they boast of their descent from the Patriarch Abraham; by the pagans because angels appeared there to men; and by Christians because He who for the salvation of mankind was born of a virgin manifested Himself there to a godly man.

This place was moreover honored fittingly with religious exercises. Here some prayed to the God of all; some called upon the angels, made libations of wine, burnt incense, or offered an ox, a he-goat, a sheep, or a cock. Each one made some beautiful product of his labor and after husbanding it through an entire year, he offered it according to a promise as provision for the feast, both for himself and his dependents. And either from honor to the place or from fear of the divine wrath, they all abstained from coming near their wives, although during the feast these were more than ordinarily studious of their beauty and adornment. Nor if they chanced to appear and to take part in the public processions, did they act at all licentiously. Nor did they behave imprudently in any other respect, although the tents were contiguous to each other and they all lay promiscuously together.

The place is open country, and arable, and without houses, with the exception of the buildings around Abraham's old oak and the well he prepared. No one during the feast drew water from that well; for according to pagan usage, some placed burning lamps near it; some made libation of wine or cast in cakes; and others, coins, myrrh, or incense. Hence, as I suppose, the water was rendered useless by commixture with the things cast into it.

Once while these customs were being celebrated by the pagans, after the aforesaid manner, (Eutropia) the mother-in-law of Constantine was present for prayer, and apprised the emperor of what was being done. On receiving this information, he rebuked the bishops of Palestine in no measured terms because they had neglected their duty and had permitted a holy place to be defiled by impure libations and sacrifices. And he expressed his godly censure in a letter which he wrote on the subject to Macarius, bishop of Jerusalem, to Eusebius of Pamphylia, and to the bishops of Palestine. He commanded these bishops to hold a conference on this subject with the Phoenician bishops and to issue directions for the demolition, from the foundations, of the altar earlier erected there, the *destruction of the carved images by fire, and the erection of a church worthy of so ancient and so holy a place.* . . . *(Sozomen, Church History II, 4)*

The Bordeaux Pilgrim (A.D. 333)

Egeria was not the first pilgrim to the newly defined and adorned Christian Holy Land in Palestine to have left behind an account of the place. That distinction belongs to an anonymous visitor from Bordeaux who travelled about the Near East sometime around A.D. 333, thus while the Constantinian project was still abuilding. We are now *seeing* Jerusalem, present at the side of a traveller who not only describes what he is seeing but provides topographical details that amount in effect to directions, as if he realized that he was merely the first of many who would be coming to those places. The pilgrim is standing on or near the Temple mount:

In Jerusalem there are two large pools at the side of the Temple, one to the right and the other to the left, which were built by Solomon, and in addition there are inside the city twin pools with five porticoes, which are called Bethsaida. There people who had been sick for many years are cured. The water of these pools is red when it is stirred up.

There is also a crypt there where Solomon used to torture devils, and the corner of a very high tower, which was where the Lord ascended and the tempter said to him, "If you are the Son of God, cast yourself down from here." And the Lord answered, "You shall not tempt the Lord your God, but him only shalt you serve." And there also is the great cornerstone of which it was said, "The stone which the builders rejected has become the head of the corner."

Below the pinnacle of this tower are many chambers, and here Solomon had his palace. There too is the chamber where he wrote (the Book of) Wisdom, and it is roofed with a single stone. Below ground there are some great reservoirs for water and pools built with great labor.

And in the sanctuary itself, where the Temple stood which Solomon built, they say that the blood of Zacharias, which was shed upon the stone pavement before the altar, remains to this day. There are also visible all through the enclosure the marks of the hobnails of the soldiers who killed him, as plainly as if they had been pressed into wax. There are two statues of Hadrian, and, not far from them, a pierced stone to which the Jews come every year and anoint. They mourn and rend their garments, and then depart. There too is the house of Hezekiah, king of Judah. (Bordeaux Pilgrim, Itinerary 589-591)

143

This is our first real view of the Temple area since it was destroyed by Titus in A.D. 70, and it is filled with interesting, if sometimes puzzling, details. We can immediately recognize the twin probatic pools of the Gospel account (Jn. 5:2), the site of the later Church of St. Anne, then the underground chambers under the southeast corner of Herod's Temple platform which later generations more confidently identified as "the Stables of Solomon," and perhaps in that same corner, above, the pilgrim had the surviving stonework pointed out to him as "the pinnacle of the Temple" of the Gospels, where the construction reached, as Josephus had already described, its greatest height from the valley floor. It is somewhat less certain what the pilgrim was being shown atop the platform itself. There were no buildings there, as is clear, but he did see two statues, one of Hadrian and another perhaps of his successor Antoninus, whom the pilgrim took as both of the same emperor. [11] Coloring on some of the stones of the platform was shown to him as the blood of Zacharias, [12] a common belief of the "simple folk," as Jerome somewhat disapprovingly remarks. Finally, and most startlingly, we are told, as the pilgrim was or may even have seen, the Jews were permitted to return to Jerusalem and commemorate the destruction of the Temple with an annual ritual around a "pierced stone," which is unmistakably located on the Temple platform.

It is not our only piece of information on this cult. Jerome, who lived in Bethlehem at the end of the same century, goes on at some length on the subject, and draws all the terrible theological conclusions:

Right to this present day those faithless people who killed the servant of God and even, most terribly, the Son of God himself, are banned from entering Jerusalem except for weeping, to let them attempt to buy back at the price of their tears the city they once sold for the blood of Christ and that not even their tears be free. You can see with your own eyes on [the anniversary of] the day that Jerusalem was captured and destroyed by the Romans, a piteous crowd that comes together, woebegone women and old men weighed down with rags and years, all of them showing forth in their clothes and their bodies the wrath of God. That mob of wretches congregates, and while the manger of the Lord sparkles, the Church of His Resurrection glows, and the banner of His Cross shines forth from the Mount of Olives, those miserable people groan over the ruins of their Temple. . . . A soldier asks money to allow them to weep a little longer. Can anyone harbor doubts, when he looks upon this scene, about the Day of Tribulation and Suffering, . . . the Day of the Trumpet and the Shout? They indeed trumpet forth their grief, and what the Prophet called the "Voice of Solemnity" is heard in their wailing. They groan over the ashes of the sanctuary, the destroyed altar, over the high pinnacles of the Temple from which they once threw down James, the brother of the Lord. (Jerome, On Zephania I, 15-16)

We return to the Bordeaux pilgrim, now on Mount Sion, outside the city walls in the southwest corner of Jerusalem:

As you come down from Jerusalem to climb Sion, on your left hand, down in the valley, beside the wall, is the pool called Siloam. It has four porticoes and there is another large pool outside it. This spring flows for six days and six nights; but the seventh day, which is the Sabbath, it does not flow at all, either by night or by day.

Climbing Sion from there you can see the place where the house of Caiaphas the priest was, and the column against which Christ was scourged still stands there. Inside Sion, within the wall, you can see where David's palace was. Of seven synagogues which were once there, only one is left—the rest are "ploughed over and sown," as was said by the Prophet Isaiah. As you leave there and pass through the wall of Sion towards the Gate of Neapolis, on the right down in the valley are some walls where Pontius Pilate had his house, the Pretorium where the Lord was tried before his Passion. (Bordeaux Pilgrim, Itinerary 592-593)

Despite the directions, it is impossible to follow this itinerary exactly, but at its end we find ourselves standing before Constantine's still unfinished buildings around the Hadrian's forum:

On your left is the little hill of Golgotha where the Lord was crucified. About a stone's throw from it is the crypt where they laid his body, and [from where he] rose again on the third day. There at present, by order of the Emperor Constantine, there has been built a "basilica," that is, a church of wondrous beauty, which has beside it cisterns from which water is raised and beside them a baptistry where children are baptized. (Bordeaux Pilgrim, Itinerary, 593-594)

The "crypt" in this passage seems to refer not to the somewhat later open-domed structure over the tomb but to the tomb building, or edicule. It is also noteworthy that the pilgrim is still somewhat uncomfortable with the word "basilica" and must explain it to his readers. [13]

Julian and the Rebuilding
of the Temple

For the Bordeaux pilgrim, as for Egeria about a half-century after him, Jerusalem was a thoroughly Christian place. Its Roman associations and monuments and what must have still been a considerable non-Christian population find no place in their accounts. Pilgrims came to the city to visit the Christian holy places; the rest was of no interest to them. But though the moment was surely not far off, in the mid-fourth century neither Jerusalem nor the Roman Empire was yet Christian in any absolutely irreversible sense. The truth of that must have become apparent to many with the accession to the throne in A.D. 361 of the Hellenophile and rabidly anti-Christian emperor Julian.

Elsewhere Julian confronted Christianity directly, but in Jerusalem he followed a somewhat different tactic. [14] The account is from Sozomen's *Church History*:

Though the emperor [Julian] hated and oppressed the Christians, he manifested benevolence and humanity toward the Jews. He wrote to the Jewish patriarchs and leaders requesting them to pray for him and for the prosperity of the empire. In taking this step he was not actuated, I am convinced, by any respect for their religion . . . but he thought to grieve the Christians by favoring the Jews, who are their most inveterate enemies. . . . Events proved that this was his real motive, for he sent for some of the chiefs of the race and exhorted them to return to the observance of the laws of Moses and the customs of their fathers. On their replying that because the Temple in Jerusalem was overturned, it was neither lawful nor ancestral to do this in any place other than the metropolis out of which they had been cast, he gave them public money, commanded them to rebuild the temple, and to practice the cult similar to that of their ancestors by sacrificing in the ancient way.

The Jews entered upon the undertaking without reflecting that, according to the prediction of the holy prophets, it could not be accomplished. They sought out the most skillful artisans, collected materials, cleared the ground, and entered so earnestly upon the task that even the women carried heaps of earth and brought their necklaces and female ornaments toward defraying the expense. The emperor, the other pagans, and all the Jews regarded every other undertaking as secondary in importance to this. Although the pagans were not well-disposed toward the Jews, yet they assisted them in this enterprise because they reckoned upon its ultimate success and hoped by this means to falsify the prophecies of Christ. Besides this motive, the Jews themselves were impelled by the consideration that the time had arrived for rebuilding their Temple.

When they had removed the remains of the former building, they dug up the ground and cleared away its foundation. It is said that on the following day, when they were about to lay the first foundation, a great earthquake occurred, and by the violent agitation of the earth stones were thrown up from the depths, by which those of the Jews who were engaged in the work were wounded, as likewise those who were merely looking on since the houses and the public porticoes near the site of the Temple, in which they had diverted themselves, were suddenly thrown down. Many were caught thereby, some perished immediately, others were found half-dead and mutilated of hands or legs or other parts of the body. When God caused the earthquake to cease, the workmen who survived again returned to their task, partly because such was the edict of the emperor and partly because they were themselves interested in the undertaking. . . .

All parties relate that they had scarcely returned to the undertaking when fire burst suddenly from the foundations of the Temple and consumed several of the workmen. [15] This fact is fearlessly stated and believed by all; the only discrepancy in the narrative is that some maintain that flame burst from the interior of the Temple, as the workmen were striving to force an entrance, while others say that fire issued directly from the earth. In whichever way the phenomenon might have occurred, it is equally wonderful. A more tangible and still more extraordinary prodigy ensued: suddenly the sign of the cross appeared spontaneously on the garments of the persons engaged in the undertaking. These crosses were disposed like stars, and appeared the work of art. Many were hence led to confess that Christ is God and that the rebuilding of the Temple was not pleasing to Him. . . . If one does not feel disposed to believe my narrative, let him go and be convinced by those who heard the facts I have related from the eyewitnesses, for they are still alive. Let him inquire also of the Jews and pagans who left the work in an incomplete state. . . . (Sozomen, Church History V, 22)

By the Christians' scenario, where the work was halted by a miracle, the project was doomed to failure. But we may add another, more natural cause: even as these events were taking place in Jerusalem, Emperor Julian was murdered while campaigning against the Persians deep within Mesopotamia. That too the Christians regarded as a miracle. No other pagan was ever to wear the imperial purple, and with that support gone, we hear of no other attempts at restoring the Temple for nearly three hundred years, when another quite unexpected opportunity presented itself.

Egeria, ca. A.D. 380

Egeria in A.D. 380 seems blissfully unaware of either Julian or the Temple mount project. She was no more a historian than the Bordeaux pilgrim was; her eyes were fixed on the holy places, though she could not help but note that Jerusalem, and indeed all of Palestine, was a remarkably cosmopolitan place, with Christians attracted to it from all over the Empire, and beyond:

In this province [of Syria-Palestine] some people know both Greek and Syriac, but others know Greek alone or Syriac only. The bishop [of Jerusalem], though he may know Syriac, never uses it. He always speaks in Greek and never Syriac, and he always has a presbyter standing beside him translates the Greek into Syriac so that everyone can understand what he means. And since the lessons read in church have to be read in Greek, there is always someone standing by to translate into Syriac so that the people are instructed. And so that the Latins who know neither Syriac nor Greek may not be disheartened, since some of the brothers or sisters present who understand both Greek and Latin will explain things to them. (Egeria, Pilgrimage, 73-74)

What most interested Egeria in Jerusalem was the sometimes spectacular liturgy that had already developed around the primary Christian holy places, and this a scant half-century after Constantine had begun the conversion of Jerusalem from a Roman into a Christian city. The center of that liturgical life was, naturally, the Church of the Anastasis or the Resurrection:

Loving sisters, [she writes for those back home, probably in a convent somewhere in France] since I know you are eager to know about the services they have daily in the holy places, I shall tell you about them. All the doors of the Anastasis are opened before cock-crow each day, and the monks and virgins, monazontes and parthenae, as they call them here, [16] *come in, and also some lay men and women, at least those who wish to make an early vigil. From that hour to daybreak hymns are sung and psalms and antiphons sung in response. And after each hymn a prayer is offered, since there are two or three presbyters or deacons each day by turn, who are there with the monazontes, and they say prayers after each hymn or antiphon.*

When day begins to break, they begin to sing the matin hymns. Then the bishop with his clergy comes and joins them. He goes straight into the cave [that is, the Holy Sepulcher], and inside the screen he first says a prayer for all, mentioning any names he wishes, and blesses the catechumens. Then he says another prayer and blesses the faithful. And next, when he comes outside the screen, everyone comes up to kiss his hands. He blesses them one by one and then goes out, and by the time the dismissal takes place it is already dawn. . . .

But on the seventh day, the Lord's Day, there gather in the courtyard before cock-crow all the people, as many as the place will hold. . . . Those who are afraid they may not arrive in time for the cock-crow come early, and sit waiting there singing hymns and antiphons, and after each hymn or antiphon a prayer is offered, since there are always presbyters and deacons there ready for the vigil, because so many people assemble there, and it is not the custom to open the holy places before cock-crow.

But when the first cock has crowed, the bishop straightway enters and goes into the cave in the Anastasis, and the whole crowd streams into the Anastasis, which is already ablaze with many lamps. When they are inside, a psalm is said by one of the presbyters, and they all respond. . . . After these . . . prayers they take censers into the cave of the Anastasis so that the whole basilica is filled with the smell. [17] *Then the bishop, standing inside the screen, takes the Gospel and advances to the door, where he himself reads the account of the Lord's Resurrection. At the beginning of the reading the whole assembly groans and laments at all the grievous things that the Lord underwent for us. . . . When the Gospel is finished, the bishop comes out and is taken with hymns to the Cross, and they all go with him. They say one psalm there and a prayer, then he blesses the faithful and the dismissal is given. . . .*

At daybreak, because it is the Lord's day, the people assemble in the Great Church built by Constantine on Golgotha behind the Cross. And they do what is everywhere the custom on the Lord's Day. But they have this custom, that any presbyter who is seated there may preach, if he so wishes, and when they have finished, the bishop preaches. The reason why they have this preaching every Lord's day is to make sure that the people will continually be learning about the Scriptures and the love of God. Because of all this preaching it is a long time before they are dismissed from the church, which takes place not before ten or even eleven o'clock. (Egeria, *Pilgrimage*, 57-58)

The primary liturgical season in Jerusalem was of course Easter week, when the events of the Gospels could be commemorated on the actual spot where they had taken place. Thus Egeria describes the "Good Friday" before Easter, when the relics discovered by Helena are brought forth:

The people are dismissed at the Cross [after the dawn service] even before the sun is up, and those who are more ardent go to Sion to pray at the pillar at which the Lord was scourged. The then go home for a short rest, but it was not long before everyone is assembled for the next service. The bishop's chair is placed on Golgotha behind the Cross, which stands there now. He takes his seat and a table is placed before him with a linen cloth on it. The deacons stand round, and there is brought to him a gold and silver box in which is the Holy Wood of the Cross. It is opened and the Wood of the Cross and the Title are taken out and placed on the table.

As long as the Holy Wood is on the table, the bishop sits with his hands resting on either end of it and holds it down, and the deacons round him keep watch over it. They guard it like this because the custom is that all the people, catechumens as well as the faithful, come up one by one to the table. They lean down over it, kiss the Wood and move on. And it is said that on one occasion one of them bit off a piece of the Holy Wood and stole it away, and for this reason the deacons stand round and keep watch in case anyone dares to do the same again.

Thus all the people go past one by one. They stoop down, touch the Holy Wood and the inscription with their forehead and then their eyes, then kiss it, but no one dares put out his hand to touch it. When they have kissed the Cross they go to a deacon who stands holding the Ring of Solomon, and the Horn with which the kings were anointed. [18] *These they venerate by kissing them, and they start around about eight o'clock, with everyone going by, entering by one door and going out by the other, until midday. . . . (Egeria, Pilgrimage, 67)*

Pentecost in Jerusalem

And finally, Pentecost, fifty days after Easter, the day on which the Holy Spirit descended on Jesus' disciples who were patiently and fearfully collected in an upper room, as it was believed, on Mount Sion:

When it is the morning [of Pentecost Sunday] all the people assemble in their usual way in the Great Church, the Martyrium, and have sermons from the presbyters and then the bishop, and the offering is duly made in the way that is usual on the Lord's day, except that the dismissal at the Martyrium is hurried, so that it is over before nine o'clock. And soon after the dismissal at the Martyrium all the people escort the bishop with singing to Sion, where they arrive in time for nine o'clock. When they arrive, they have a reading of the passage from the Acts of the Apostles where the Spirit descends so that all nations might understand the things that were spoken, after which the Mass proceeds as usual.

The presbyters read this passage from the Acts of the Apostles because this place on Sion, though it has now been altered into a church, is the very spot where what I have mentioned was done by the multitude who were assembled with the Apostles after the Lord's Passion.

After that the service proceeds as usual, and they make the offering there. Then as the people are dismissed the archdeacon makes this announcement: "Let us all be ready today on the Mount of Eleona [that is, of Olives] at the Imbomon immediately after midday." [19]

So all the people return home for a rest. And as soon as they have had their meal, they go up to Eleona, the Mount of Olives, each at his own pace, till there is not a Christian left in the city. Once they have climbed Eleona, the Mount of Olives, they go first to the Imbomon, the place from which the Lord ascended into heaven, where the bishop and the presbyters take their seats, and likewise all the people. They have readings, and between them hymns and antiphons suitable to this day and to the place. . . . When this has been done, the catechumens are blessed, and also the faithful.

It is now already three o'clock, and they go down singing hymns from there to another church, also on Olivet, and in it is the cave where the Lord used to sit and teach the Apostles. By the time they get there it is after four, and they have vespers. The prayer is said, the catechumens are blessed, and then the faithful.

Thence all the people go down with their bishop, singing hymns and antiphons suitable to the day, and so, very slowly and gently, they make their way to the Martyrium. When they arrive at the city gate it is already night, and the people are brought hundreds of church candles to help them. But since it is quite a way from the gate to the Great Church, the Martyrium, they arrive there at about eight at night, going very slowly all the way so that the walk does not weary the people. The great doors which face the market street are opened, and the bishop and all the people enter the Martyrium with hymns.

Once inside the church they have hymns and a prayer, and the catechumens are blessed, and also the faithful. Then they set off once more with hymns to the Anastasis. Again in the Anastasis they have more hymns and antiphons and a prayer, and the catechumens are blessed, and also the faithful. Then the same is done again at the Cross. And once more all the Christian community conducts the bishop with hymns to Sion. Once there, they have suitable readings, psalms, and antiphons, a prayer, the blessing of the catechumens and the faithful, and so they are dismissed. After the dismissal everyone goes to have the bishop's hand laid on him, and about midnight everybody returns to his home. Thus this is a very tiring day for them, for they have never stopped all day since they kept vigil in the Anastasis at cock-crow, and the services have taken so long that it is midnight by the time they are dismissed at Sion and all return to their homes. (Egeria, *Pilgrimage, 70-71*)

Jerome and Paula in Palestine

Egeria and the Bordeaux pilgrim marked merely a beginning. Their accounts of the Holy Land and what might be seen there were doubtless

151

copied and read in the Christian circles, but a more potent force by far in inducing Latin Christians to leave their homes and convents in Europe and make the long and dangerous voyage to the Near East was Jerome, the translator of the Old and New Testaments into Latin, a redoubtable biblical scholar, and himself a monastic resident of Palestine from A.D. 385 to his death in 420.

Jerome's firsthand knowledge of the land shines through all the learning of his Bible commentaries, but the spiritual flavor of a religious pilgrimage to Jerusalem is caught most directly in the account of his first trip to Jerusalem in company with two of his friends and pupils from Rome, a woman named Paula and her daughter Eustochium. The narrative occurs in one of his letters in the form of a eulogy of Paula, who died in 404:

She [Paula] passed on her left the tomb of Helena, Queen of Adiabene, who in the time of famine helped the people with a gift of grain [Josephus, Ant. XX, 5], and entered Jerusalem, the city of three names—Jebus, Salem, and Jerusalem—which was later named Aelia when Aelius Hadrian rebuilt it out of ruins and ashes. When the Proconsul of Palestine, who knew her [Paula's] family well, sent his chamberlain on ahead to make the Pretorium ready for her, she chose a humble cell, and visited all the places with such ardent fervor that, had she not been in a hurry to see the rest, there would have been no taking her away from the first. She fell down and worshipped before the Cross as though she saw the Lord hanging upon it. On entering the Tomb of the Resurrection she kissed the stone which the angel removed from the sepulcher door, then like a thirsty man who had waited long and at last comes to water, she faithfully kissed the very place where the Lord had lain. Her tears and lamentations were known to all Jerusalem, or to the Lord himself whom she called upon.

Leaving that place, she ascended Sion, a name which means "citadel" or "watchtower." David once took this city by storm and rebuilt it. . . . She was shown the pillar of the church which supports the portico and is stained with the Lord's blood. He is said to have been bound to it when he was scourged. She was also shown the place where the Holy Spirit descended upon the souls of more than a hundred and twenty people, that the prophecy of Joel might be fulfilled. (Jerome, letter no. 108, 6-7)

The Spread of Christian Pilgrimage

Jerome's influence was spread through a variety of channels into the western parts of Christendom. His Bible commentaries added an assured and concrete note to the general knowledge of the Holy Land, its places, peoples, and customs, which he did not always view in a kindly light. Jerome had, in fact, serious reservations about the growing practice of pilgrimage. The question of the spiritual value of such visits had been raised somewhat earlier by Gregory of Nyssa, who had been to Jerusalem and reported on the Holy City in his *Letter on Pilgrimages*:

If God's grace were more plentiful in the vicinity of Jerusalem than it is elsewhere, then the people who live there would not make sin so much their custom. But in fact there is no sort of shameful practices in which they do not indulge and cheating, adultery, theft, idolatry, poisoning, quarrels, and murder are everyday occurrences. . . . What proof is there, then, in a place where things like that occur, of the abundance of God's grace?

Jerome did not disagree with this late fourth century characterization of Jerusalem, and he warned one prospective pilgrim, Paulinus of Nola, that he should expect "a crowded city with the whole variety of people you find in such centers, prostitutes, actors, and clowns. . . ."[20] But on balance he approved of pilgrimage to the Holy Land, and in fact his letters on the subject must have persuaded others to follow in the footsteps of the blessed Paula, and even, like Jerome himself, to settle permanently in the Holy Land as monks. By the fifth century Christian ascetics, many of them from Egypt, were swiftly converting the Judean wilderness region stretching east and south of Jerusalem and Bethlehem into a new center of Christian monasticism.[21] As a result, descriptions of the city grew denser in topographical detail, as in the letter written by Eucherius, bishop of Lyons, who visited the city sometime in the second or third decade of the fifth century, an older contemporary of Jerome, a younger one of the historian Sozomen:

I have briefly put together an account of the situation of the city of Jerusalem and of Judea, to the extent I have learned about it through conversation or reading, and have described it in a brief preface, because it is by no means fitting that a work of no length have a lengthy introduction. . . .

Jerusalem, they say, is naturally lofty, so that you must ascend to it from all sides; it rises by a long but gentle slope. The site of the city is almost circular in shape, enclosed by a lengthy wall, which now includes Mount Sion, though this was once outside. It is on the south and overlooks the city like a citadel. The greater part of the city lies on the flat top of a hill which is lower than this mount. Mount Sion on its northern slope is set aside for the dwellings of priests and monks, and its summit, which is level, is covered by monks' cells surrounding a church which, it is said, built there by the Apostles in honor of the place of the Lord's resurrection; because, as promised previously by the Lord, it was there that they were filled with the Spirit.

The three most frequented city gates are those on the west, east, and north. [If you enter from the north] the direction of the streets must bring you to visit the Martyrium, built with great magnificence by Constantine. Next to this and to the west one visits the sites of Golgotha and the Anastasis. . . . The Temple, which was situated in the lower city near the eastern wall, was once a world's wonder, but of its ruins there stands today only the pinnacle of one wall, and the rest are destroyed down to their foundations.

A few water cisterns can be seen on the northern side of the city near the Temple. The Pool of Bethsaida is there, distinguished by its twin pools. One is usually filled with winter rains, while the other is filled with red-colored water. On the steep rocky side of Mount Sion which faces east, below the city walls and at the bottom of the hill, gushes forth the fountain of Siloam. It does not flow continuously, but only on certain days and at certain hours, and it flows with an intermittent stream toward the south.

Beside the east wall of Jerusalem, which is also the wall of the Temple, is Gehenna, the Valley of Jehoshaphat. It runs from north to south, and a torrent runs through it whenever there has been rain to provide it with water.

Round Jerusalem the country has a rough, hilly appearance, and the Mount of Olives is to be seen on the east at about a mile's distance. On this there are two very famous churches, one sited on the spot where Jesus spoke to his disciples and the other at the spot where he is said to have ascended to heaven. (Eucherius, Letter to Faustus, 1-7)

Two Byzantine Guidebooks to the Holy Land

A sure sign that Western pilgrimage to the Holy Land was not only becoming common but had, for some, commercial possibilities that might be exploited is the preservation from the sixth century of two works that might fairly be called guidebooks to the area. [22] Neither the anonymous *Breviarius* nor the *Topography of the Holy Land* attributed to a certain Theodosius, the latter accompanied by maps, [23] makes claim to be a learned work nor even a personal or religious statement, but both had their use and each contributed to the fund of information that was accumulating in the West and being passed on, copied, and reintegrated into newer accounts. Pilgrims, it appears, were beginning to read up on the subject before setting out for the Holy City:

The city itself is set on a mountain. In the center of the city is the basilica of Constantine. As one goes into the basilica there is on the left a chamber in which the Cross of the Lord is kept. Beyond this, as you go into the Church of the Holy Constantine, there is a great apse to the west, and there the three crosses were found. And above it is an altar of pure silver and gold. It is supported by nine columns and around the apse stand twelve quite marvellous columns of marble, and on these columns are twelve silver bowls. And in the center of the basilica is the lance with which they pierced the Lord, and from this has been made a cross: at night it shines like the sun in full daylight.

And going from there into Golgotha there is a great court, on the site where the Lord was crucified. There is a silver railing around this mount and a kind of flint is noticeable there. It has silver doors where the Cross of the Lord is displayed, all adorned with gold and jewels, with the open sky above. . . . There Adam was formed out of clay; there Abraham offered his own son Isaac in the very place where our Lord Jesus Christ was crucified.

Beyond this, on the west, you enter the [Church of the] Holy Resurrection, which contains the Tomb of the Lord. In front of it is a stone, a kind of flint. Above it has been built a round-shaped church. Over the roof of the actual tomb is a roof of gold and silver, and everything round it is gold. In front of this Tomb is the altar where Holy Zacharias was killed, and where his blood dried there may still be seen. . . .

You go from there to the very large basilica on Holy Sion, containing the column at which the Lord Jesus was scourged. There is a mark where his hands grasped it, like an impression on wax. From there you go to the place of sacrifice. It contains the stone with which St. Stephen was stoned. In the center of the basilica is the crown of thorns which they gave the Lord. There too is the Upper Room where the Lord taught His disciples when He had the Supper. There too is the rod enclosed in silver.

From there you go to the house of Caiaphas, where St. Peter made his denial. A large basilica of St. Peter is there. From there you go to the house of Pilate, where he had the Lord scourged and handed over to the Jews. There is a large basilica there, and in it the chamber where they stripped Him and He was scourged. It is called Holy Wisdom.

From there you come to the Temple built by Solomon, but there is nothing left there apart from a single cave. From there you come to the pinnacle on which Satan set the Lord. (Breviarius)

There is nothing very remarkable in this, though we note that the place of Adam's "shaping," more often connected with a certain clay in a field near Bethlehem, has found its way into the Holy Sepulcher complex, as have certain other events earlier associated with the Temple mount, like the blood of Zacharias and the site of the altar upon which Abraham was bade sacrifice Isaac. The Jewish holy places, it is clear, were slowly being drawn into a Christian orbit.

Another version of the same work ends somewhat differently, however:

From there you come to the pinnacle of the Temple on which Satan tempted Our Lord Jesus Christ. A cross-shaped basilica is there.

At one time this was read by some as evidence that there was a Christian church *atop* the Temple mount. This did not find a great deal of support, since no one else seems to have noticed such a building. What is far more likely is that the author of the *Breviarius* was referring to the same complex that Theodosius described just *below* the pinnacle at the southeast corner of the Temple:

Below the Pinnacle of the Temple is a convent of virgins, and whenever one of them departs this life, she is buried there inside the convent, and from the day that they enter its walls they never go out as long as they live. The door is opened only for a nun or a penitent who wishes to join the convent, but otherwise the gates are kept shut. Their food is let down to them from the walls, but they have their water inside in cisterns. (Theodosius, Topography of the Holy Land, 52)

This too seems somewhat curious and otherwise unattested, but the excavations begun south of the Temple mount in 1967 by Benjamin Mazar have confirmed the accuracy of Theodosius in a quite unexpected fashion: there was a convent, however short-lived, below the southeast corner of the Temple platform. [24]

Theodosius' modest narrative reveals something else, what Wilkinson has called "the beginning of the Jerusalem circuit." As the numbers of pilgrims grew, so too did the formality of their moving from site to site within the Holy City, a tendency born of the liturgy, the historical progression of the events of Jesus' last days in the city, and, doubtless, a simple matter of convenience. This "Jerusalem circle," as it came to be called, came to full maturity only after the Crusades in the "Way of the Cross," but here perhaps, in Theodosius' sixth-century *Topography*, we can already see its beginnings:

In the city of Jerusalem, at the Sepulcher of the Lord, is the place of Calvary. There Abraham offered up his son for a burnt-offering, and because it is a hill of rock, it was in the hill itself—at its foot to be exact— that Abraham made the altar. Above the altar rises the hill; one climbs to the top of it by steps. There the Lord was crucified. . . .

From the Tomb of the Lord it is fifteen paces to the place of Calvary. It is all under one roof. From the place of Calvary it is fifteen paces to

Golgotha, where the Lord's cross was discovered. From Golgotha it is two hundred paces to Holy Sion, which is the Mother of All Churches: this Sion our Lord Christ founded with his Apostles. It was the house of St. Mark the Evangelist. From Holy Sion to the House of Caiaphas which is now the Church of St. Peter, it is about fifty paces. From the House of Caiaphas to the Pretorium of Pilate it is about a hundred paces; the Church of St. Sophia [or Holy Wisdom] is there. Beside it St. Jeremiah was cast into the pit [Jer. 38:6]. The column which was in the House of Caiaphas, at which the Lord Christ was scourged, is now in Holy Sion. This pillar by the Lord's command followed him. And you can see the way He clung to it when He was being scourged as if the marks were in wax. His arms, hands and fingers clove to it, as it shows even today. Also He made on it the impression of His whole face, chin, nose and eyes as if it had been wax. . . . The Pool of Siloam is a hundred paces from the pit where they cast the Prophet Jeremiah; the pool is inside the wall. From the house of Pilate it is about a hundred paces to the Sheep Pool. There the Lord Christ cured the paralyzed man, whose couch is still there. Beside the Sheep Pool is the Church of St. Mary. (Theodosius, Topography, 40-45)

Jerusalem in the Fifth Century

James, "the brother of the Lord," was accounted by the Christian tradition as the first bishop of Jerusalem, and Eusebius' careful tracing of the episcopal succession in the Holy City has already been cited in Chapter Three. But when the lines of episcopal *jurisdiction* begin to appear in the Church, Christian Jerusalem, like secular Roman Jerusalem, was subject to the higher authority of Caesarea in Palestine. The Council of Nicea in honoring the Holy City in its Seventh Canon had already made that clear, and following Roman administrative practice, Jerusalem continued to be subject in Church matters to Caesarea, and Caesarea in turn to Antioch, the capital of the Diocese of the East.

In A.D. 421 Jerusalem had a new bishop, Juvenal, who would reign there until his death in 458, and the theological difficulties that began to beset the Eastern sees in the third decade of that same century gave this ambitious pastor of the Jerusalem Church an opportunity to advance his position vis-à-vis both Caesarea and Antioch. The Antiochene Church sided with the theologian Nestorius in the Ecumenical Council that was convened at Ephesus in A.D. 431 to discuss Nestorius' teachings, while Juvenal took his position with Alexandria and Rome. It was a politically wise decision, and when Nestorius was condemned and "Nestorianism" anathematized, Juvenal took advantage of his wisdom and declared his jurisdictional independence of Antioch. Sometime later, probably at a synod held in Constantinople in A.D. 450, Juvenal got what he wanted, the absolute and autonomous jurisdiction over the three provinces of Palestine: thus within twenty years Juvenal had freed himself of the ecclesiastical fetters of both Caesarea and, more impressively, of Antioch.

One further piece of theological agility was required of Juvenal, however. In 451 a new council was convoked at Chalcedon. At issue now was the theology emanating from Juvenal's old allies in Alexandria. In their zeal against Nestorius they had gone beyond what some—the bishop of Rome, for one—thought orthodox. And their "Monophysitism," as it was called, was condemned at Chalcedon, with the yardstick of orthodoxy being provided on this occasion by Leo, bishop of Rome. Juvenal hesitated no longer than the blinking of a theological eye; he renounced Alexandria and put his name, and his see's, to Leo's new definition of the faith. It saved his earlier gains, but it sowed the seeds of immense problems to come since most of the faithful of the East, and of Jerusalem, were Monophysites by persuasion. [25]

The Affair of Barsauma, A.D. 439

This bare resume of the events of the middle decades of the fifth century masks beneath its surface a cast of imperial, episcopal, and monastic characters who pass in and out of the career of Juvenal and profoundly affect the life of the Holy City: Empress Eudocia, for example, who lived in Jerusalem and was responsible for changing the physical face of the city; and the monk Barsauma, an outsider who rubbed raw the always delicate relations between the Christians and the Jews of Palestine. Eudocia we know both from her building projects and from the chroniclers who followed, and sensationalized, her remarkable career. In the case of Barsauma, we have a *Life* written in Syriac and filled with circumstantial detail. [26]

The choice of Syriac for Barsauma's *Life* is appropriate. A form of Aramaic, Syriac was the language of the non-Hellenized Christians of Syria-Palestine—one recalls Egeria's remarking that the bishop of Jerusalem knew Syriac but would not speak it and insisted on delivering the homily in Greek, even though it then had to be translated into Syriac so that everyone could understand it. By the mid-fifth century these local Syriac-speaking Christians constituted the bulk of the growing monastic population throughout Syria and Palestine, and though these monks, many of them unlettered in anything other than the Scriptures and the Spirit, played little part in the high theology of that century of high theology, their presence in the countryside, and frequently in the streets of a city like Jerusalem, left its mark on the politics of the Church councils. Among those frequently fanatic Christians of the countryside, anti-Jewish feelings ran deep and strong, and by the time of his second visit to Jerusalem in A.D. 438, Barsauma, the monk of northern Syria who never sat and never lay down, already had a reputation as a destroyer of synagogues, an act expressly forbidden by imperial edicts of A.D. 423. For their part, the Jews were beginning to take advantage of what they construed as a more sympathetic attitude in imperial circles, and particularly on the part of Eudocia, née Athenais, the pagan daughter of a professor of rhetoric in Athens who converted to Christianity to marry Emperor Theodosius II in A.D. 421. The Jews may well have been correct in their assessment of at least the empress' intentions; she granted their request to be permitted to return once again to Jerusalem and at least pray at the site of their former Temple. But an encyclical letter sent in 438 to all the Jews of the Roman and Persian Empires held out something more:

To the great and powerful people of the Jews. From the priests and the leaders of Galilee, greetings. Know that the time of the dispersion of our people has ended and the day of the reunion of our tribes is at hand. For the kings of the Romans have ordered that our city of Jerusalem be returned to us. Hasten and come to Jerusalem for the Feast of the Tabernacles, for our kingdom will be reestablished in Jerusalem. (Nau 1927: 196)

Barsauma was also in Jerusalem on that Feast of the Tabernacles in 438, and though the Syriac *Life* puts him innocently in the convent at which he was lodging, his disciples at least were at the Temple mount when the Jews convened there, dressed in black and covered with ashes. Then there occurred, according to that same source, another of those miracles so often associated with the site: the Jews were stoned with missiles coming, as it were, from heaven. A number were killed. The Jews who were struck read the act somewhat differently, however: they seized eighteen of the followers of Barsauma on the site, handed them over to the local police and charged them with murder before the Roman magistrates. The case was obviously politically sensitive, and it almost immediately landed on the doorstep of Eudocia:

The Romans, the police officers, and the Jews came together, broke off olive branches and went and surrounded the palace of the empress (Eudocia), who was in Bethlehem, at a distance of six miles from Jerusalem, and there they celebrated her with the olive branches and they cried out again, saying to her: "Many brigands have come from Mesopotamia, dressed in the respectable habits of monks; they have made a great war in the city and have devastated it. Many people have been put to death and lie in the public places and in the courtyards of homes and the cisterns are filled with the corpses of the murdered." (Nau 1927: 198)

The monks, now faced with execution, implicated their master Barsauma. This added a new dimension, and even the empress had some hesitation in moving against so powerful and popular a holy man. The Byzantine governor was summoned from Caesarea to hear the case, and in the time it took him to come, public sentiment, which was originally with the Jews who were murdered at the Temple mount, began to veer around toward the monks:

The (Jerusalem) Christians said to one another: the empress is looking for a pretext to put the Christians to death. Then they added: We will burn the empress and all those with her. There were then several bishops assembled in Jerusalem. They sent out to their cities and villages letters requiring people's presence and so assembled a crowd. Everyone came to Jerusalem and the city was filled to its limits and could not contain the great number of people who had assembled there. They were waiting for the empress to announce the sentence so they could then put her to the fire. On the sixth day the governor arrived (from Caesarea) with many attendants, but he lived at some distance outside the city since he hesitated coming into Jerusalem for fear of being stoned. (Nau 1927: 198)

The governor soon caught the drift of events, particularly when his own prisoners finally gave him permission to visit them in prison, but only in the presence of Barsauma. It was on the occasion of one of those "interrogations" that an earthquake occurred. Barsauma quickly took the governor by the hand and assured him that God did not yet intend that he should die. While the governor was digesting this piece of doubtful consolation, the medical examiner's report arrived: the Jews at the Temple mount showed no signs of wounds; they had perished from natural causes!

And Barsauma ordered the public herald to announce throughout the city "The Cross has triumphed!" and then all the people in turn, those inside and outside the city, took up the cry "The Cross has triumphed!" And the voice of the people swelled and spread, like the roar of a wave of the sea, to the point that the children of the city trembled at the force of the clamor.

The Christians formed five hundred groups, since all the monks of the desert had come with the people of the towns and villages. When the blessed Barsauma went around the places of the city in the midst of his brethren many spread before him excellent perfumes and choice ungents, and as he advanced they threw at his feet incense and agreeable aromatics. And they conducted the blessed one to the great church that had been built on Sion and there the blessed one offered the Holy Sacrifice. (Nau 1927: 199)

The bishop of Jerusalem during this extraordinary demonstration of the power of Barsauma over the people was, of course, Juvenal, and we are not surprised to learn that the bishop had Barsauma positioned comfortably at his side when he attended the ecumenical council convened at Ephesus in A.D. 449.

Eudocia in Jerusalem

In 438-439, when the incident involving Barsauma occurred, Eudocia was merely visiting Jerusalem in fulfillment of a vow, and the unpleasantness there apparently did not affect her enthusiasm for the Holy City. She returned to Constantinople weighed down with relics and in the intervening years arranged for many buildings to be put up in Jerusalem, including the church called St. Sophia, or Holy Wisdom, at Pilate's Pretorium, a church in honor of St. Peter at the site of Caiaphas' house, one to St. John near the Holy Sepulcher and another at the pool of Siloam. In A.D. 415 there had been a miraculous "invention" of the remains of St. Stephen, the first Christian martyr, at the village of Kafr Gamla just outside the north wall of Jerusalem, [27] and Eudocia had the honor of inaugurating a martyrium to the saint on the spot. But things did not go well for her in Constantinople either, and there was a public break between Eudocia and her husband Theodosius and her sisters-in-law. In 443 or 444 she returned to Jerusalem, now to live in the Holy City and its environs until her death in 460, her rank and income intact, but in effect an empress in exile, with Palestine as her kingdom. [28]

Eudocia continued her generosity toward the Holy City during her exile. It was she, for example, who built the first Patriarchal Palace in Jerusalem—the bishops had had to live till then in upper apartments in the Church of the Holy Sepulcher—and a large hospice to lodge the increasing numbers of pilgrims coming to Jerusalem. [29] It was the same empress who extended Jerusalem's city wall to embrace the newer Christian suburbs of the city that had been developing on the south around Mount Sion and the Pool of Siloam since the mid-fourth century. [30] Finally, in the last days of her life she urged on the completion of a great basilica to replace the more modest martyrium that she herself had dedicated at the site of the martyrdom of St. Stephen in 439. The urgency was personal since she intended that she herself be buried there, as she was in the consecrated building in A.D. 460.

Justinian and Jerusalem

The last great imperial benefactor of Christian Jerusalem before the Crusades was Emperor Justinian (A.D. 527-565). His interest was not so personal perhaps as that of Constantine or Helena or Eudocia, but it was moved by the same combination of political opportunism and genuine religious philanthropy that has motivated most of the rulers of the Holy City. [31] In the first instance the initiative came from within the city, from the holy man Sabas, a more sober man than Barsauma but the most charismatic and influential figure in the monastic communities that by the sixth century not only ringed Jerusalem to the south and east but had branches and hospices within the city itself. [32] The year is A.D. 531 and the source is Cyril of Scythpolis, a disciple and biographer of the Blessed Sabas:

Some days after this the emperor (Justinian) sent for St. Sabas and said to him, "Father, I hear many monasteries have been organized in the wilderness, but if you wish, ask for public funds for the use of those who dwell there and we will provide them, that you may pray for us and for the commonwealth committed to our charge." He answered: "Those who pray for your holiness need no revenues of this sort, for the Lord is their portion and revenue, who in the wilderness rained bread from heaven and gushed forth quails upon a stiff-necked and rebellious people. But, Most Holy Emperor, we beg of you for the restoration of the holy churches throughout Palestine; we ask you for a grant from the public funds and for the rebuilding of the holy houses which have been burnt by the Samaritans, a subsidy to the Christians of Palestine who have been made few and robbed. Moreover, we entreat you to establish a hospital in the Holy City for the nursing of sick strangers, and that you should build and adorn the New Church of St. Mary, whose foundations were laid some time ago by Archbishop Elias [A.D. 494-516], for this is a task which especially becomes Your Holiness. And because of the inroads of the Saracens, we beseech Your Serenity to give orders to His Highness Summus to build a castle at the public expense beyond the monasteries which my insignificance has established in the wilderness. . . ."

Now those things which Father Sabas asked our most pious emperor were carried out without delay. . . . First of all, imperial rescripts were sent to Archbishop Peter [of Jerusalem] and to all those who bore office throughout Palestine, bidding Anthony, Bishop of Ascalon, and Zachary,

Bishop of Pella, to view the villages in First and Second Palestine which had been burned by the Samaritans, [33] and to subscribe from the public funds of the Ninth and Tenth Indiction, [34] in proportion to the injury done to each place, the sum of 1,300 gold pieces. He also bade them view the burned chapels and reckon how much money the restoration of each holy place would cost, and provide this money either from the public funds or the property of the Samaritans, by means of the Illustrious Count Stephen, who was also bidden to protect the bishops with as large an escort as they might need.

Moreover, in accordance with the holy man's third request, he founded a hospital in the middle of Jerusalem. [35] It contained at first one hundred beds, and he set apart for it a clear annual revenue of 1,850 gold nomismata. Afterwards, he ordered that the hospital should contain two hundred beds and he added as much more clear and inalienable revenue to it. He also most zealously fulfilled the old man's fourth request and sent to Jerusalem one Theodorus, an engineer, to the end that he might build the New Church of the Holy Mother of God, the ever-Virgin Mary; and he gave orders to the farmers of the tax revenue of Palestine to provide money for the building. He gave supreme authority over the matter to Archbishop Peter, but he ordered Baruch, the Bishop of Bacatha, to overlook the work of building. Thus, through much zeal and many hands the New Church of the Holy Virgin was in twelve years built and fitted with all due ornament. It is needless to dilate upon the size of this holy temple, its radiant glory, and its costly ornament, seeing that it is present before our eyes and excels all the ancient spectacles and wonders which man used to admire of old, and of which the Greeks have told us in their histories. This, then, was the fruit of St. Sabas' fourth petition.

Lastly, the Most Holy Emperor, having respect for the fifth petition of St. Sabas, sent a rescript to Summus bidding him take a sum of 1,000 gold pieces out of the revenues of Palestine to build a fort for Father Sabas and to provide a garrison of soldiers kept at the public expense to protect his monasteries. (*Life of Sabas, 72-73, trans. E. Waller*)

Cyril of Scythopolis was a hagiographer and so not greatly interested in the details of these new constructions. But there was a contemporary writer who was and who had, in addition, a personal investment in that interest. Procopius too was a hagiographer, in this case of Justinian. His *Wars* was the authorized version of the emperor's military campaigns, and he devoted a special monograph *On Buildings* to Justinian's building projects across the Empire. From Procopius' perspective, with its emphasis on the monumental and the grandiose, it was the "New Church" that crowned the emperor's benefactions in the Holy City, and he describes its building in great detail:

At Jerusalem Justinian built to the Mother of God a sanctuary which is incomparable. The people who live there call it "The New Church," and I shall describe what it is like, prefacing my account with the remark that this city is built mostly on hills: they are not covered with soil but are rough and precipitous, so that the connecting streets run down from the top to the valley like ladders. The buildings which were already there were all in one place, either completely on hill-tops or on level ground in the valleys, but this church alone stands in a different position. Emperor Justinian had given orders to build it on a prominent hill and among other things had specified its breadth and length.

The hill was not, however, spacious enough for the building the emperor wanted, and a quarter of the site was missing on the south, and also on the east at the very place where it is the custom for the priests to celebrate sacred mysteries. Those in charge of the work therefore contrived this plan: they laid their foundations right out to the edge of the flat ground, and then added to the hill an artificial platform of the same height as the rock. After they had built this up to the level of the hill-top, they placed vaults on the walls and joined this building onto the rest of the sanctuary buildings. Thus this church had its foundations partly on solid rock and partly on air, on account of the extension that the power of the emperor had added to the area of the hill.

The stones used for this substructure were unusually large. The builders of the work had to overcome the natural disadvantages of the site and to build a construction the height of a mountain. All the ordinary measures proved useless, and they had to resort to unconventional, indeed, unprecedented measures. They quarried blocks of enormous size from the mountains which rise to vast heights in the neighborhood of the city; then they deftly squared them off and transported them to the site in the following manner. They made special wagons the size of the stones, put a stone in each wagon and had it drawn up by forty oxen which the emperor had specially selected for their strength. Since the roads leading into the city were not wide enough to take the wagons, they cut away large sections of the mountains to give access to the wagons coming in, and that is how they succeeded in building the church to the dimensions that the emperor wished.

Even though they had made it the correct width, they could not roof it, and so they went round inspecting all the groves and woods where they were told that there were specially tall trees. And they discovered a thick forest containing some cedars of unusual height. Using these to construct the roof of the church they succeeded in making its height proportionate to its length and breadth.

These were the works which the emperor accomplished by human strength and skill. He was also assisted by his pious faith, which both brought him honor and enabled him to carry out his design. The church had to be surrounded by columns as beautiful as the rest of the building and large enough to support the weight which was to rest upon them. But the site was far inland, away from the sea, and sealed off by the steep mountains which I have described, which made it impossible for the engineers to transport columns from abroad. Then, as the emperor was beginning to despair at the difficulties of the task, God revealed in the mountains nearby a bed of stone exactly suited to this purpose. Perhaps the stone had long been there unnoticed, or perhaps it was created by God there and then. In either case, we must ascribe its provision to God. Judging by human standards we regard a great many things as impossible, but with the God of all nothing is difficult or impossible.

The church was throughout supported on huge flame-colored columns from this source, a vast number of them. Some were inside, some above, and some in the porticoes which ran all round the sanctuary, except on the side facing east. Of these columns the two which stood in front of the church doors were so enormous that they may be the largest in the whole world. Next to this place is another colonnaded area called "by the narthex" because it is narrow. Beyond this there is a court surrounded by columns of the same type on all four sides. Leading out of the court are magnificent doors which give the people passing outside some indication of the kind of things they will see if they go in. The gateway attached to them is also remarkable, and there is an arch [apse] rising from two columns to a great height. Further on, on one side of the way which leads into the church, are two semicircular recesses facing each other, and facing each other on the other side of the street are two hospices built by Emperor Justinian. One is intended for foreign visitors and the other to be an infirmary for the sick poor. Emperor Justinian also endowed this Church of the Mother of God with large revenues. This, then, was what Emperor Justinian achieved in Jerusalem. [36] (Procopius, *On Buildings V, 6*)

All the external indices—there are few clues in Procopius' account—suggested that this massive complex of church, cloisters, and hospices was located at the southern edge of Jerusalem, at the southern limits of the present Jewish quarter, and in 1973 this was confirmed by archeological excavations begun by Nahum Avigad of the Hebrew University. [37] Procopius, it turned out, had been more than accurate: the building was shored up—the terrain drops away sharply—by an immense vaulted construction not unlike the so-called Solomon's Stables that rest under the southeast corner of the Temple platform. More, in May of 1977, as the excavations continued, there was found among those subterranean vaults and cisterns the dedication inscription of the church:

This is the work which our most pious Emperor Flavius Justinianus carried out with munificence, under the care and devotion of the most holy Constantinus, priest and abbot, in the thirteenth year of the Indiction.†

A Pilgrim and a Map, A.D. 570

The "New Church" of the Mother of God, the *Theotokos*—begun by Bishop Elias sometime in the beginning of the sixth century, the subject of a petition from Sabas in 531, and completed and dedicated by Justinian on November 20, A.D. 543—was somewhat of an anomaly in Jerusalem in that it commemorated no holy site or event, either in the life of Jesus or one of the saints. This may explain why it was never rebuilt after its destruction by an earthquake, probably in A.D. 746 since it is described as being in ruins in an inventory of the Jerusalem churches made about 800. [38] A hospice or convent might be constructed anywhere in the city, but churches were normally built at shrines, sited at a holy place, and blessed by both the increasing number of relics pointed out there and the miracles that inevitably took place in connection with them:

Coming down from the Mount of Olives we arrived at the Valley of Gethsemane, to the place where our Lord was betrayed. There are there three couches on which he reclined and where we also reclined to gain a blessing. . . .

After we had bowed to the earth and and kissed the ground, we entered the Holy City, through which we prayerfully proceeded to the Lord's Tomb. . . . Earth is brought to the Tomb from the outside, and those who go in take some as a blessing when they leave. The stone which closed the Tomb lies in front of the Tomb door and is made of the same colored rock as the rock of Golgotha, though the color is not visible since the stone is decorated with gold and precious stones. The rock of the Tomb is like a millstone. There are ornaments in vast numbers, and there are hung from iron rods armlets, bracelets, necklaces, rings, tiaras, waistbands, sword belts, imperial crowns of gold and precious stones, and many ornaments given by empresses. . . .

From there [that is, the Tower of David] we went to the basilica of Holy Sion, which contains many remarkable things, among them the cornerstone which the Scripture tells us was "rejected by the builders." When the Lord Jesus entered this church, which used to be the house of St. James, he found this ugly stone lying about somewhere; he lifted it up and placed it in the corner. You can hold it in your hands and lift it. Then if you put your ear in the corner, the sound is like the murmuring of many men. In this same church is the pillar at which the Lord was scourged, and it has on it a miraculous mark. When he clasped it, his chest imprinted itself on the stone, and you can see the marks of both his hands, his fingers, and his palms. They are so clear that you can use them to take "measures" for any kind of disease, and people who wear those measures around their necks are cured. . . . [39]

From Sion we came to [Justinian's] basilica of the Blessed Mary, where there is a large congregation of monks and hospices for both men and women visitors. There I was received as a pilgrim; there were countless tables, and more than three thousand beds for sick persons. We also prayed in the Pretorium, where the Lord was tried, and which is now the basilica of St. Sophia. It is in front of the Temple of Solomon, below the street which runs down to the Spring of Siloam. Near Solomon's porch, in this basilica, is the seat where Pilate sat to hear the Lord's case. There is also a square stone which used to be in the center of the Pretorium, and upon which the accused who was being tried was made to mount so that everyone could hear and see him. The Lord mounted it when He was tried by Pilate, and his footprints are still on it. *The portrait, which was painted during his lifetime and placed in the Pretorium, shows a well-shaped foot, small and delicate, a person of ordinary height, with a handsome face, curly hair, and a beautiful hand with long fingers.* From this stone where He stood come many blessings. People take measures from the footprints and wear them on their bodies for their various diseases, and they are all cured. The stone itself is decorated with gold and silver. . . .

From there [that is, the tomb of Rachel, three miles south of Jerusalem] it is three (more) miles to Bethlehem, which is a most magnificent place and there are many servants of God there. There is the cave in which the Lord was born, and inside it there is a manger decorated gold and silver, at which lamps burn day and night. As you go in, the mouth of the cave is very narrow. The priest Jerome hewed out the rock at the very mouth of the cave and made himself a tomb, where he was in fact buried. Further on, half a mile from Bethlehem, in the suburb, David's body lies buried with that of his son Solomon, and they have separate tombs. [40] The basilica is called St. David's. The children slaughtered by Herod also have their tomb there, and they all lie buried together. When their tomb is opened you can look at their bones. . . .

From Bethlehem it is twenty-three miles to the Oak of Mamre, the resting-place of Abraham, Isaac, Jacob, and Sarah and also of Joseph's bones. The basilica has four porticoes, and there is an unroofed central atrium. *Down the middle runs a partition, and the Christians come in on one side and Jews on the other, and they use much incense. On the day following Christ's birthday the people of this area celebrate the burial of Jacob with much devotion, and Jews from all over the country congregate for this, too great a crowd to count. They offer much incense and lights, and give presents to those who minister in the church.* [41] *(Piacenza Pilgrim, 17-18, 22-23, 29-30)*

The author of this tour of the holy places of Jerusalem and vicinity is an anonymous pilgrim from Piacenza who made his pilgrimage to the Holy Land about A.D. 570, to "see and touch," as Paulinus of Nola had expressed it in the opening years of the fifth century "the places where Christ was present in the body," [42] to gain the "blessings" attached to such visits, and finally to collect and bring home relics and souvenirs of the Holy City and the Holy Land. Already Helena had sent fragments of the Cross to her son in Constantinople, together with the nails by which Christ was fastened to it. The ordinary pilgrim had no such imperial opportunity, of course, but there was a rich harvest to be had, nonetheless, bones and other remains of the saints and, even for the most humble, in addition to the "measures" mentioned by the Piacenza pilgrim, water from the Jordan, oil or palms from Jericho, and even the dust upon which the feet of Jesus had trod. [43]

Like many others before and after him, the Piacenza pilgrim continued on to make the perilous journey across Sinai to visit the Mountain of Moses and the monastery of St. Catherine at its foot, and perhaps even the home of the holy family when they fled from Herod into Egypt. And amidst the glowing accounts of shrines and relics and miracles there also appear pieces of information to fit into our mosaic of the landscape of Byzantine Jerusalem. We can follow the pilgrim, for example, on his way from the Pretorium and St. Sophia, "which is in front of the Temple of Solomon," southward toward Siloam:

We went on from there to an arch on the site of an ancient city gate. At that place are the stagnant waters into which they put Jeremiah. From that arch you descend many steps to the fountain of Siloam, and above Siloam is a round basilica beneath which the water of Siloam rises. Siloam has two basins constructed of marble, which are separated from each other by a partition. Men wash in one and women in the other, to gain a blessing. In these waters many cures take place, and lepers are cleansed. In front of the court is a large man-made pool and people are continually bathing there; for at certain hours the spring pours forth a great deal of water into the basins, which runs down the valley of Gethsemane, which they also call Jehoshaphat, as far as the Jordan; it enters the Jordan at a place where the Jordan drains into the Salt Sea below Sodom and Gomorrah. (Piacenza Pilgrim, 24)

We also have an eyewitness to some of the building activity of Empress Eudocia in the city, chiefly her extension of the city wall southward from the line of Hadrian's wall—the "ancient city gate" mentioned above is probably one of Hadrian's, then after Eudocia's construction left *within* the city—and her construction of a basilica to St. Stephen outside the northern gate of the city, a church in which the empress herself found her final resting place:

Siloam is presently inside the city since Empress Eudocia herself added these walls to the city. She also built the basilica and tomb of St. Stephen, and her own tomb is next to St. Stephen's, with six paces between the two. St. Stephen's resting place is outside the gate and a bowshot from the road which descends to Joppa, Caesarea Palestinae, and Diospolis, which in ancient times was called Azotus, where St. George the martyr rests. . . . (Piacenza Pilgrim, 25)

The Piacenza pilgrim also touches briefly and provocatively upon one of the great puzzles of Jerusalem, the sealed gate called the Golden Gate, which is located in the eastern wall of what is now the Haram, somewhat to the north of the east-west axis of the Muslim Dome of the Rock. [44] The visitor has come down from Olivet, through Gethsemane:

From Gethsemane we climbed by many steps to the gate of Jerusalem. There is an olive grove on the right of the gate; in it is the fig tree from which Judas hanged himself, and its trunk still stands there, protected by stones. This gate of the city is next to [or possibly "joined to"] the Beautiful Gate, which was part of the Temple, and its threshold and entablature are still standing there. (Piacenza Pilgrim, 17)

The reference to the Beautiful Gate recalls a miracle performed by the Apostles at that entry to the Temple, described in Acts 3:1-11 and cited in Chapter Three. How the Beautiful came to be the Golden Gate is unknown, but the change must have occurred shortly after this period (see Chapter Five). The Piacenza pilgrim, at any rate, recognized it as being of ancient construction, possibly Herodian according to modern estimates, [45] and that it was part of the Temple. We cannot be quite so certain on this last, however, since we are unsure of the dimensions of the Herodian platform. The critical point, then, is whether or not the "gate of the city" mentioned in the same breath is a totally different entry, near the present St. Stephen's Gate, for example, or one of the two entries that today exist in what is called the Golden Gate.

169

Almost exactly contemporary, as far as we can tell, with the account of the Piacenza pilgrim is a remarkable piece of visual evidence on the topography of Jerusalem. At about that time the bishop of the town of Madaba in the Transjordan had laid on the floor of the transept of his principal church there a mosaic map of the Holy Land. The chief pilgrim sites are both illustrated and identified, none more remarkably than Jerusalem, which is depicted in a large cartouche near the center of the map. The artist has taken wing in his imagination and given us a bird's-eye view of the city from the west, with all of its principal streets and buildings and gates clearly set out in a variety of colors. We see, for example, the two columned streets that crossed the city from north to south and a number of the east-west transverses. And we are shown, for the last time and in all their magnificence, churches long since destroyed: Constantine's Church and Basilica of the Holy Sepulcher, the cathedral on Mount Sion, and Justinian's enormous Nea, or New Church. [46] The city was surely as the Jerusalem liturgy par excellence, the "St. James," described it in words repeated daily in the Holy City's own churches:

We make offering to Thee also, O Lord, for the Holy Places, which Thou has glorified by the divine appearance of Thy Christ and by the visitation of Thy All-Holy Spirit; especially for the glorious Sion, the Mother of all the Churches; and for Thy Holy, Catholic and Apostolic Church throughout the world: even now, O Lord, bestow upon her the rich gifts of Thy All-Holy Spirit.

The Persian Conquest of Jerusalem

In A.D. 614 the Christian Jerusalem of Constantine, Helena, Eudocia, and Justinian was visited by catastrophe. The state of hostilities between the Byzantine and the Persian Empires had by then become endemic, though most of the fighting took place far to the north, across the open plains of Mesopotamia. In 614, however, during the reign of Emperor Heraclius, the Persians shattered the entire Byzantine defense perimeter across their eastern provinces and came flooding into Jerusalem. We have an eyewitness report of what followed:

The beginning of the struggle of the Persians with the Christians of Jerusalem was on the fifteenth of April, in the second Indiction, in the fourth year of Emperor Heraclius. They spent twenty days in the struggle. And they shot from their ballistas with such violence that on the twenty-first day they broke down the city wall. Thereupon the evil foemen entered the city in great fury, like infuriated wild beasts and irritated serpents. The men however who defended the city wall fled and hid themselves in caverns, fosses, and cisterns in order to save themselves; and the people in crowds fled into churches and altars; and there they destroyed them. For the enemy entered in mighty wrath, gnashing their teeth in violent fury; like evil beasts they roared, bellowed like lions, hissed like ferocious serpents, and slew all whom they found. Like mad dogs they tore with their teeth the flesh of the faithful, and respected none at all, neither male nor female, neither young nor old, neither child nor baby, neither priest nor monk, neither virgin nor widow. . . .

When the Persians had entered the city and slain countless souls and blood ran deep in all places, the enemy in consequence no longer had the strength to slay, and much Christian population remained that was unslain. So when the ferocity of the wrath of the Persians was appeased, then their leader, whom they called Rasmi Ozdan, ordered the public criers to go forth and to make proclamation saying "Come out, all of you that are in hiding. Fear not. For the sword is put away from you and by me is granted peace." Then, as soon as they heard that, a very numerous crowd came forth that had been hidden in cisterns and fosses. But many of them were already dead within them, some owing to the darkness, others from hunger and thirst. Who can count the number of those who died? For many tens of thousands were destroyed by the number of privations and diversity of hardships, before those in hiding came out owing to the number of their privations; and they abandoned themselves to death when they heard the chief's command, as if he was encouraging them for their good and they would get alleviation by coming out. But when those in hiding came out, the prince summoned them and began to question the whole people as to what they knew of the art of building. When they had one by one specified their crafts, he bade those be picked out on one side who were skilled in architecture, that they might be carried captive to Persia; but he seized the remainder of the people and shut them up in the reservoir of Mamel, which lies outside the city at a distance of about two stades from the tower of David. And he ordered sentinels to guard those thus confined in the moat. . . .

After all this evil-doing they captured the good shepherd, the patriarch Zachariah, and conducted him to Sion through the gate through which Our Lord Jesus Christ came in; and he was conducted cautiously, like a brigand, pinioned with cords. . . . Then went forth the blessed pastor with the people by the gate called Probatic, from which also went forth the Savior for His Passion; and he sat down on the Mount of Olives, and as for a widowed bride, so he wept for the holy church. Then there came up before him all the people. They fell prone on their faces furrowed with excess of mourning. He gazed upon them, and beheld the numbers of his *flock, that weakened with lamentation, overcast with grief, and beset with perils, were brought nigh unto death. Then he began to console them. . . .*

Once more they raised up their eyes, and gazed upon Jerusalem and the holy churches. A flame, as out of a furnace, reached up to the clouds and it was burning. Then they fell to sobbing and lamenting all at once and loudly. Some smote themselves upon the face, others strewed ashes upon their heads, others rubbed their faces in the dust, and some tore their hair, when they beheld the holy Anastasis afire, Sion in smoke and flames, and Jerusalem devastated. (Conybeare 1910: 506-513)

In many of the other Byzantine cities of the East dissident and disaffected groups of Christians had cooperated in betraying the imperial defenses to the Persians, but in Jerusalem the role of villainy fell on other shoulders:

Thereupon the Jews, enemies of the truth and haters of Christ, when they perceived that the Christians were given over into the hands of the enemy, rejoiced exceedingly because they detested the Christians; and they conceived an evil plan in keeping with their vileness about the people. For in the eyes of the Persians their importance was great because they were betrayers of the Christians. In this season, when the Jews approached the edge of the reservoir and called out to the children of God, while they were shut up therein, and said to them: "If you would escape from death, become Jews and deny Christ; and then you shall step up from your place and join us. We will ransom you with our money and you will be benefited by us." But their plot and desire were not fulfilled, their labors proved to be in vain; because the children of the Holy Church chose death for Christ's sake rather than to live in godlessness; and they reckoned it better for their flesh to be punished rather than their souls ruined, so that their portion was not with the Jews. And when the unclean Jews saw the steadfast uprightness of the Christians and their immovable faith, they were agitated with lively ire, like evil beasts, and thereupon imagined another plot. As of old they bought the Lord from the Jews with silver, so they purchased Christians out of the reservoir; for they gave the Persians silver and they bought a Christian and slew him like a sheep. The Christians, however, rejoiced because they were being slain for Christ's sake and shed their blood for His Blood, and took on themselves death for His death. . . .

When the people were carried into Persia, and the Jews were left in Jerusalem, they began with their own hands to demolish and burn such of the holy churches as were left standing. . . . (Conybeare 1910: 508))

That much seems certain, but thereafter the sources grow fragmentary and late. What emerges from them, for all their uncertainty, is that the Jews, left in control of Jerusalem for a few brief years, resumed their liturgical rituals. As the *Book of Zerubbabel* laconically remarks, the Jewish leader "made sacrifices," and we can only assume that that occurred in the only place possible, atop the Temple mount. [47] It was an event that had a profound effect on what happened in that same place no more than twenty-odd years later.

The Jewish hegemony in Jerusalem lasted no more than three years at most, from A.D. 614 to 617. The Persian shah then suffered a change of heart, whether for personal or policy reasons—the number and influence of Christians at the Persian court in Iraq was considerable, while the few Jews who returned to Jerusalem after an absence of nearly five hundred years would have had an extremely tenuous grasp on the Holy City and its decimated but still overwhelmingly Christian population. The Jews were thus expelled from the city, and the Persians installed their own governor. [48]

The Restoration of the Cross to Jerusalem

We hear little more of Jerusalem during this era. The important events were taking place elsewhere, in Armenia where Heraclius was raising a new army, and then in Iraq where the Byzantines pursued the shah and his forces and regained Christendom's most sacred relic, carried off by the Persians to their capital in 614. Antiochus is once again the source:

In the fifteenth year of the capture of Jerusalem, in the nineteenth year of the reign of Heraclius, the Tenth Indiction, Khusraw the Persian king was slain by his son, Siron by name, in the month of March. Now about that time King Heraclius with his forces had already reached Persia and took possession of many of his cities and of the royal palace, slew thousands of Persian soldiers, and led back again the Greeks who had been carried into captivity and liberated the Christians from slavery by force. But King Siron, who had taken possession of his father's kingdom, died in the month of September; and his son Ardashir took the kingdom. He was only a child and his reign lasted three months. Between the Greeks and the Persians was then concluded a written peace through the mediation of Rasmi Ozdan, who was the Persian commander-in-chief. But before this King Heraclius sent a eunuch whose name was Narses, his principal chamberlain. He advanced with a numerous army to fight the Persians. The multitude of Persians drawn up in battle was defeated and they fled in terror. . . .

But in the seventeenth year, however, after the capture of Jerusalem, in the third year of the murder of Khusraw, in the twenty-first year after the accession of Heraclius, the Third Indiction, the Persian general Rasmi Ozdan slew the Persian king Ardashir, whom we mentioned above. He seized the kingdom, became the ally of the Greeks, and bestowed on King Heraclius the life-giving tree, the Cross of Christ, as the treasure of the whole world and as the richest of gifts, and he gave it to him. But King Heraclius took it to Jerusalem on the occasion of his going there with Martina, who was the daughter of his father's brother; and he had married her against the law and therefore was very much afraid that the high priests would rebuke him on the score of that indecent action. And when he had entered Jerusalem on the twenty-first of the month of March he reestablished in its own place the glorious and precious tree of the Cross, sealed as before in a chest, just as it had been carried away. It was set up altogether unopened; for just as the Ark of the Covenant was left unopened among strangers, so was left the life-giving tree of the Cross, which had vanquished death and trampled on Hell. Then King Heraclius, seeing the glorious event—namely the restoration of the holy places, which had been rebuilt by the blessed Modestus, was much rejoiced and ordered him to be consecrated patriarch over Jerusalem; for the blessed Zachariah had died in Persia and the church was widowed. In the Fourth Indiction, in the twenty-first year of the reign of Heraclius, the blessed Modestus assumed the patriarchate of Jerusalem. . . . (Conybeare 1910: 516)

The Coming of the Muslims

The reconquest of Jerusalem and the restoration of the Holy Cross to the Holy City was an act of enormous consequence. The name of Heraclius was still echoing on Crusaders' tongues four and a half centuries later when they marched to the reconquest of Jerusalem, and the news of what had occurred reached even to remote Medina in Arabia, where a still obscure Prophet, cast out of his native Mecca, was tasting the first fruits of success. This Prophet saw in the Byzantines' defeat of 614, and their subsequent victory, as in all else, the hand of God:

The Romans have been defeated
In the nearer land, and they, after their defeat will be victorious
Within a few years. God is the Commander in the past and in the
    future. And on that day believers will rejoice
In God's help to victory. He helps to victory whom He wills. He is the
    Mighty, the Merciful. (Quran 30:1-5)

Muhammad died in A.D. 632, the armies of his and God's commonwealth already on the roads leading north toward Palestine and the Holy City.

In December 634 the Muslims were camped around Bethlehem, cutting it off from Jerusalem and preventing the Christians of the city from journeying out and celebrating the Christmas Eve liturgy in the town of Jesus' birth. The newcomers, called then and ever thereafter "Saracens," [49] though as yet with no awareness that the "Saracens," once simply "Arabs," represented a new religious movement, were the subject of Patriarch Sophronius' Christmas Eve sermon of that year:

Because of countless sins and very serious faults, we have become unworthy of the sight of these things [the Holy Places of Bethlehem] and are prevented from entering Bethlehem by way of the roads. Unwillingly, indeed contrary to our wishes, we are required to stay at home, not bound closely by bodily bonds, but bound by fear of the Saracens, and we are prevented from experiencing such heavenly joy, and are engulfed by a grief suited to our wretchedness, which is unworthy of blessings.

But we have the Davidic desire and thirst to see, just as David famous in song, the water, and we are prevented from feasting our souls through fear of the Saracens alone. For now the slime of the godless Saracens, like the gentiles at the time [of David], has captured Bethlehem and does not yield the passage but threatens slaughter and destruction if we leave this Holy City and if we dare to approach our beloved and sacred Bethlehem.

Therefore I call on and I command and I beg you for the love of Christ the Lord, in so far as it is in our power, let us correct ourselves, let us shine forth with repentance, let us be purified with conversion and let us curb our performance of acts which are hateful to God. If we constrain ourselves, as friendly and beloved of God, we would laugh at the fall of our Saracen adversaries and we would view their not distant death and we would see their final destruction. For their blood-loving blade will enter their hearts, their bows will be shattered and their shafts will be fixed in them. They will furnish a clear way for us having neither hills nor thorns nor impassable points so that we, running boldly and dauntlessly, may possess the child of life, may love the God-receiving chamber, may prostrate ourselves before the Holy Manger. We shall embrace the God-producing city [of Bethlehem], dancing with lambs, shouting with the Magi, giving glory with the angels: "Glory to God in the Highest and on earth, peace and good will to men." (Kaegi 1969: 139-141)

The Holy House: The Muslims
Come to Jerusalem

. . . to the distant shrine whose
precincts We have blessed.
—*Quran*

The Muslim Conquest of Jerusalem

THOUGH there is some small disagreement about the date, the Muslims took Jerusalem in an almost matter-of-fact manner, apparently in A.D. 638. As may be seen in the two following accounts by early authorities—there are no eyewitness reports—the city, still called by its Roman name of Aelia, was not a primary strategic or psychological target of the advancing Muslim armies:

After he had conquered Qinnisrin and its districts [in northern Syria] in 16 [A.D. 637], Abu Ubaydah came to Amr ibn al-As while this latter was besieging Aelia, which was the same city as the Holy House. It is said that from Aelia, Amr had sent him to Antioch whose inhabitants had defaulted in its terms of submission. After Antioch was retaken, Abu Ubaydah returned to stay two or three days. Then the people of Aelia requested of Abu Ubaydah security and peace according to the conditions offered to the (other) cities of Syria, that is to say, of paying tribute, the tax, and being treated the same as others like them. With this special condition that the chief present at the conclusion of the treaty be Umar ibn al-Khattab himself. Abu Ubaydah wrote to Umar on this subject. Umar came to the camp of Jabiya of Damascus. From there he journeyed to Aelia and concluded peace with the inhabitants by a written document. The conquest of Aelia took place in 17 [A.D. 638]. (Baladhuri, Conquest of the Countries, 138)

On his return into Jordan, Abu Ubaydah besieged the people of Aelia, which is the Holy House. They prolonged their resistance and Abu Ubaydah wrote to Umar to inform him of the delays and of the patience of the people of Aelia. Some say that the people of Aelia requested of him that it be the caliph himself who concluded peace with them. Abu Ubaydah assured himself of their sincerity by demanding of them promises by a solemn treaty, and then he informed Umar, who left for Syria after nam-

ing Uthman ibn Affan as his deputy in Medina. He honored Khalid in joining the latter to himself and by conferring the command upon him.

This latter put himself at the head of the advance guard. That was in Rajab of the year 16 [A.D. 637]. Umar came to the region of Damascus, then he went to the Holy House, took it without struggle and sent the inhabitants the following written message. "In the name of God, the Compassionate, the Merciful. This is a writing of Umar ibn al-Khattab to the inhabitants of the Holy House. You are guaranteed your life, your goods, and your churches, which will be neither occupied nor destroyed, as long as you do not initiate anything blameworthy." He had it confirmed by witnesses. . . . (Ya'qubi, History II, 161, 167)

If Sophronius' Christmas Eve sermon of A.D. 634 is an accurate reflection of what the Christian residents of Jerusalem thought they might expect at the hands of the approaching "Saracens," there must have been thanksgiving and relief when the Muslims took the city without bloodshed and imposed what can only be construed as generous terms on the conquered. But the Christians' uncertainty ran deeper. By all reports, there was a great deal of confusion in Christian minds on the precise religious beliefs of the invaders, a confusion that became only more densely virulent with time.

The Bible and the Quran

The new Muslims did not enter Jerusalem brandishing copies of the Quran over their heads—the standard text of the Muslim Book of Revelations was not completely codified for another decade—so Christians might well have wondered at the increasingly apparent connection of Islam with their own Holy City of Jerusalem. A connection there assuredly was: we shall see it in the Muslims' own actions in the city, and we, unlike the seventh-century Christians in Jerusalem, can attempt to puzzle it out from the pages of the Quran. Here, in the Quran's classic oblique style, almost devoid of context and referents, is what the later Islamic tradition unanimously understood to be an allusion to the twin destructions of the Jewish Temple in the Holy City:

And We gave guidance to the Children of Israel in the Scripture: Truly, twice will you work evil on the earth, and you will become mightily arrogant.

So when the time of the first of the two came to pass, We sent against you Our slaves of great might who ravaged (your) country, and it was a threat fulfilled.

Then We granted you once again your turn against them. We gave you wealth and children and made you more numerous in manpower.

If you do well, you do well of yourselves, and if you do evil, (you do it) against yourselves. So, when the time of the second (of the warnings) came, (We sent against you others of Our slaves) to ravage you, and to enter the Temple, even as they entered it the first time, and to lay waste all that they conquered with an utter wasting. (Quran 17:4-7)

Thus the Muslims of Muhammad's generation knew of the Jewish Temple in Jerusalem and knew that it had suffered a quite exemplary destruction because, as the Quran itself suggests, of the sins of the Jews. It was not, however, the Romans who were recalled as the agents of God's displeasure by the later commentators on this passage but rather "Bukhnassar," the redoubtable Nebuchadnezzar of the Bible. [1] Thus when the tenth-century Muslim scholar Biruni comes in his *Chronology* to discuss the significance of the Ninth of Ab for the Jews, he notes:

Ninth of Ab: Fasting, because on this day they were told in the desert that they should not enter Jerusalem and they were sorry in consequence. On this day Jerusalem was conquered and entered by Nebuchadnezzar, who destroyed it by fire. On this day it was destroyed a second time, and its soil ploughed over.

Twenty-fifth of Ab: Fasting, because the fire was extinguished in the Temple. On this day Nebuchadnezzar left Jerusalem and the conflagration in its storehouses and temples was put an end to. (Biruni 1879: 276)

It is not, then, Herod's Temple that lived on in the mind of the early Muslims—indeed Jewish history of the postbiblical period was largely unknown or ignored by them—but Solomon's. Solomon himself has an important place in the Quran, a true prophet given by God control over the supernaturally gifted *jinn*, who "made for him what he willed, prayer niches and statues, basins like wells, and boilers built into the ground" (Quran 34:13), which is possibly a composite picture of the Temple. [2]

Later generations of Muslims fleshed out their knowledge of the Temple site and its importance in the careers of Abraham, Jacob, David, and Jesus, but Muhammad, or at least the Quran, is far more allusive. Syria and Palestine did constitute a "Holy Land" (Quran 5:21), but chiefly, as later commentators explained, because it was the principal home of prophecy, and Jerusalem was "the Holy House" or "the City of the Holy House," phrases which by the tenth century at least were being abbreviated as simply "the Holy," in Arabic, then as today, *al-Quds*. The usage is almost certainly Jewish rather than Christian, [3] a conclusion we can draw not only from parallel literary usage but from the Muslims' very first acts in the newly conquered city.

178

The Change in the *Qibla*

Muhammad and his Muslim contemporaries or his pagan audience were thus at least generally aware of the biblical role of Jerusalem, whether they derived that knowledge from the Bible itself or from oral traditions circulating in Jewish circles in western Arabia in the early seventh century. But for Muhammad at least there was more than a simple awareness involved. Early in his career, certainly before he made his celebrated "emigration" (*hijra*) to Medina in A.D. 622, he followed the Jewish custom, though assuredly not the Christian one, of turning toward Jerusalem in prayer. [4] We know this not because the Quran tells us so but because it notes an important *change* in the direction of prayer, in Arabic *qibla*, likely a year or so after he arrived at Medina:

The foolish among the people will say: What has turned them from the qibla which they formerly observed? Say: to God belong the east and the west. He guides whom He will in a straight path.

So we have appointed you a middle nation, that you may be witnesses for mankind, and that the messenger may be a witness for you. And we have appointed the qibla which you formerly observed only that we might test him who follows the messenger from him who turns on his heels. In truth, it was a hard (test), save for those whom God guided. But it was not God's purpose that your faith should be in vain, for God is full of kindness, Most Merciful.

We see the turning of your face to heaven (for guidance, O Muhammad). And now We shall make you turn (in prayer) toward a qibla which will please you. So turn your face toward the Inviolable Sanctuary, and you (O Muslims), wheresoever you may be, turn your faces (when you pray) toward it. The People of the Book know that (this Revelation) is the truth from their Lord. And God is not unaware of what they do.

And even if you were to bring to the People of the Book all kinds of signs, they would not follow your qibla, nor can you be a follower of their qibla; nor are some of them followers of the qibla of others. And if you should follow their desires after the knowledge which has come to you, then surely you are one of the evil-doers. (Quran 2:142-145)

There was a substantial Jewish community at Medina, and Muhammad's decision to change the qibla of prayer from Jerusalem to the Ka'ba in Mecca may have been the result of a falling out with the Medinan Jews. Or, as the Muslim commentators suggest, it may have been done to placate or reconcile the Jews, though this would appear unlikely if it had been Muhammed's custom at Mecca, where there were no Jews that we know of, to pray toward Jerusalem. We are given only a tantalizing glance at that practice in the eighth-century *Life of the Prophet*, from which most of our biographical information on Muhammad derives. In this passage some of the early converts to Islam at Medina set out to Mecca to make the ritual *hajj* or pilgrimage to the Ka'ba there. The time is sometime before 622, since Muhammad is still residing in Mecca:

We went out with the polytheist pilgrims of our people, having prayed and learned the customs of the pilgrimage. With us was al-Bara' ibn Ma'rur, our chief and senior. When we had started our journey from Medina, al-Bara' said: "I have come to a conclusion and I don't know whether you will agree with me or not. I think that I will not turn my back on this building [the Ka'ba] and that I shall pray toward it." We replied that as far as we knew our prophet prayed toward Syria and we did not wish to act differently. He said: "I am going to pray toward the Ka'ba." We said: "But we will not." When the time for prayer came we prayed toward Syria and he prayed toward the Ka'ba until we came to Mecca. We blamed him for what he was doing, but he refused to change.

When we came to Mecca, he said to me: "Nephew, let us go to the Apostle and ask him about what I did on our journey. For I feel some misgivings since I have seen your opposition." So we went to ask the Apostle. We did not know him and had never seen him before. We met a man of Mecca and we asked him about the Apostle; he asked if we knew him and we said we did not. Then do you know his uncle, al-Abbas? We said we did because he was always coming to us as a merchant. He said: "When you enter the mosque he is the man sitting next to al-Abbas." So we went into the mosque and there was al-Abbas with the Apostle beside him; we saluted them and sat down. . . . al-Bara' said: "O Prophet of God, I came on this journey, God having guided me to Islam, and I felt I could not turn my back on this building [the Ka'ba], so I prayed toward it; but when my companions opposed me, I felt some misgivings. What is your opinion, O Apostle of God?" He replied: "You would have had a qibla if you kept to it." So al-Bara' returned to the Apostle's qibla and prayed with us toward Syria. But his own people assert rather that he prayed toward the Ka'ba until the day of his death. But this was not so. We know more about it than they. (Ibn Ishaq 1955: 202)

There was no great agreement among the Muslim quranic commentators on how to construe this verse on the change of the qibla from Jerusalem. The classical *Commentary* of Tabari (d. 923), for example, gives the reader a number of choices, no one of them greatly different from the other:

On the authority of Ikrima and Hasan al-Basri: The first injunction which was abrogated in the Quran was that concerning the qibla. This is because the Prophet used to prefer the Rock of the Holy House of Jerusalem, which was the qibla of the Jews. The Prophet faced it for seventeen months [after his arrival in Medina] in the hope that they would believe in him and follow him. Then God said: "Say, 'To God belong the east and the west. . . .' "

Al-Rabi' ibn Anas relates on the authority of Abu al-Aliya: The Prophet of God was given his choice of turning his face in whatever direction he wished. He chose the Holy House in Jerusalem in order that the People of the Book would be conciliated. This was his qibla for sixteen months; all the while, however, he was turning his face towards the heavens until God turned him toward the House [that is, the Ka'ba].

It is related, on the other hand, on the authority of Ibn Abbas: When the Apostle of God migrated to Medina, most of whose inhabitants were Jews, God commanded him to face Jerusalem, and the Jews were glad. The Prophet faced it for some time beyond ten months, but he loved the qibla of Abraham [the Ka'ba]. Thus he used to pray to God and gaze into the heavens until God sent down (the verse) "We have seen you turning your face toward heaven" (2:144). The Jews became suspicious and said, "What has turned them away from their qibla, toward which they formerly prayed?" Thus God sent down (the verse) "Say, 'To God belongs the east and the west. . . .' " (Ayoub 1984: 168-169)

All these reports attempt to reconcile the quranic verses with what was understood to be the position of Muhammad vis-à-vis the Jews of Medina. It was not the only way of approaching the problem, of course, and the following from Nisaburi (d. 1327) illustrates the more "spiritual" reading of history favored by Sufi authors: [5]

It is that the servant must turn his face toward the king and serve him. It is also in order that unity and harmony among the people of faith may be established. It is as though the Exalted One says, "O man of faith! You are my servant, the Ka'ba is my House and the prayers are my service. Your heart is my throne and Paradise is my noble abode. Turn your face toward my house and your heart to me, so that I may grant you my noble abode." The Jews faced the west, which is the direction of the setting of lights. . . . The Christians faced the east, which is the direction of the rising of lights . . . but the people of faith faced the manifestation of lights, which is Mecca. From Mecca is Muhammad, and from him were lights created, and for his sake the circling spheres were set on their course. The west is the qibla of Moses and the east is the qibla of Jesus; between them is the qibla of Abraham and Muhammad, for the best of things is that which is in the middle position. . . ." (Ayoub 1984: 169)

Muhammad's Night Journey
and Ascension

For us, as for those early Muslim authorities, there are no readily apparent answers to why Muhammad in the early years of his religious calling prayed facing Jerusalem, or, as the Ibn Ishaq narrative put it, "toward Syria," that is, the Holy Land. The later Muslim response, when there was a far greater familiarity with Jerusalem, was that the earlier prophets, most notably David, had prayed toward the Jewish Temple. But the custom of facing Jerusalem in prayer was, in any event, abrogated for Muslims in 623 or thereabouts, as we have seen, and Muhammad's early practice was not much reflected upon by later generations. What attracted far more notice, however, was another, more singular and dramatic connection of the Prophet with the Holy City. The event is mentioned quite briefly at the opening verse of Sura 17 of the Quran:

Glory be to Him who carried His servant by night from the holy shrine to the distant shrine, the precincts of which We have blessed, that We might show him some of our (miraculous) signs. He is the One who hears, the One who sees.

The verse seems straightforward enough: God transported His servant Muhammad by night from one holy shrine to another in order to show him some miraculous signs. Difficulties arose, however, as soon as Muslims began to identify those two shrines mentioned in the text. The following is derived from another of the classical Muslim commentaries on the Quran, that by al-Zamakhshari (d. 1144), who lived in an age when there was at least a popular consensus on the problem but whose commentary still reflects the early uncertainties of the community:

". . . Who carried His servant by night. . . ." One may ask: Since the (word) "carried" in itself already means "to undertake a Night Journey," then what does the stipulation "by night" add to the meaning of the statement? To this I reply: With the expression "by night" God wishes to indicate the duration of the Night Journey as short, saying that within a (single) night He and His servant accomplished the journey from Mecca to the Syrian lands, which usually required forty nights. . . . There is disagreement regarding the place from which the Night Journey originated. Some say it was the holy mosque (of Mecca) itself. This is likely since it is mentioned in the following account from the Prophet: "While I was between being asleep and awake in the apartments near the Ka'ba at the holy mosque, Gabriel came to me with the steed Buraq." Others say, however, that the journey of Muhammad originated from the dwell-

ing of (his cousin) Umm Hani, the daughter of Abu Talib. In this case the expression "holy mosque" would indicate the holy precinct of Mecca, since this area includes the mosque and can thus be referred to by this designation. According to Ibn Abbas, the entire *haram* is a mosque. . . .

Zamakhshari then goes on to show how the Night Journey is connected with another event mentioned in the Quran (53:4-10), Muhammad's Ascension into heaven:

In the same night (in which the journey to Jerusalem occurred), Muhammad was (also) raised up to heaven, that is, his Ascension took its departure from Jerusalem. Muhammad told the Quraysh also of the wonderful things he had seen in heaven, that he met the prophets there and went as far as the house visited (by the pilgrims) and the Zizyphus tree at the far end of heaven.

There is also disagreement concerning the date of the Night Journey. While some say that it occurred one year after the hijra, according to Anas ibn Malik and al-Hasan al-Basri, it took place (even) before the mission (of Muhammad as a Prophet). (Furthermore), there is disagreement concerning whether the Night Journey occurred (while Muhammad was) in the state of being awake or asleep. The following is (related) from A'isha: "By God, the body of the Messenger of God was not missed (during the Night Journey); rather, the Ascension to heaven occurred with his spirit." According to Mu'awiya (also) it took place only with the spirit. On the other hand, according to al-Hasan (al-Basri) it was a vision which Muhammad had in his sleep; yet most traditions stand in opposition to this contention.

". . . the distant shrine . . .": This is Jerusalem. At that time no mosque existed farther away (from Mecca) than the one at Jerusalem.

". . . The precincts of which We have blessed . . .": God means the blessing of religion and of the present world, for Jerusalem had been since the time of Moses the place of worship of the prophets and the place to which (divine) inspiration was restricted (before the time of Muhammad), and it is surrounded with flowing rivers and fruit-bearing trees. (Gätje 1976: 75-77)

Though Zamakhshari and the tradition he represents had already settled on Jerusalem as the site of this "distant shrine" or "farthest mosque" (*al-masjid al-aqsa*) to which Muhammad was taken by God at night, that interpretation had by no means been unanimous. If the Night Journey was combined with the Ascension as a single event, as here, then it was plausible that the "distant shrine" was a reference to "heaven," as a number of early Muslims in fact understood it. The identification with Jerusalem,

183

which is presently the standard interpretation of the phrase, was a secondary and somewhat later one. [6] By the eighth century, however, the Jerusalem connection prevailed, as it does in the account preserved in the *Life of the Prophet*, though with reservations expressed by its author Ibn Ishaq at the very outset:

The following account reached me from Abdullah b. Mas'ud and Abu Sa'id al-Khudri and A'isha the Prophet's wife and Mu'awiya b. Abi Sufyan and al-Hasan al-Basri and Ibn Shihab al-Zuhri and Qatada and other traditionists as well as Umm Hani, daughter of Abu Talib. It is pieced together in the story that follows, each one contributing something of what he was told about what had happened when the Prophet was taken on the Night Journey. The matter of the place of the journey and what is said about it is a searching test and a matter of God's power and authority wherein is a lesson for the intelligent; and guidance and mercy and strengthening to those who believe. It was certainly an act of God by which He took him by night in whatever way He pleased to show him signs which He willed him to see so that he witnessed His mighty sovereignty and power by which He does what He wills to do.

I was told that al-Hasan al-Basri [A.D. 642-728] said that the Apostle of God said: "While I was sleeping in the Hijr [a kind of semicircular stone porch close by the Ka'ba], Gabriel came and stirred me with his foot. I sat up but saw nothing and lay down again. He came a second time and stirred me with his foot. I sat up but saw nothing and lay down again. He came to me the third time and stirred me with his foot. I sat up and he took hold of my arm and I stood beside him and he brought me out to the door of the shrine and there was a white animal, half mule and half donkey with wings on its side with which it propelled its feet, putting down each forefoot at the limit of its sight, and he mounted me on it. Then he went out with me, keeping close by my side."

In his story al-Hasan continued: "The Apostle and Gabriel went their way until they arrived at the shrine at Jerusalem. There he found Abraham, Moses and Jesus among a company of the prophets. The Apostle acted as their leader in prayer. . . . Then the Apostle returned to Mecca and in the morning he told the Quraysh what had happened. Most of them said: 'By God, this is a plain absurdity! A caravan takes a month to go to Syria and a month to return and can Muhammad do the return journey in one night?' At this many Muslims gave up their faith; some went to Abu Bakr and said: 'What do you think of your friend now, Abu Bakr? He alleges he went to Jerusalem last night and prayed there and came back to Mecca.' Abu Bakr replied that they were lying about the Apostle. But they replied that he was at that very moment in the shrine

184

telling the people about it. Abu Bakr said: 'If he says so, then it must be true. And what is so surprising in that? He tells me that communications from God from heaven to earth come to him in an hour of a day or night and I believe him, and that is more extraordinary than that at which you boggle!'"

"Abu Bakr then went to the Apostle and asked him if these reports were true, and when he said they were, he asked him to describe Jerusalem to him." Al-Hasan said that [as a small child] he was lifted up so that he could see the Apostle speaking as he told Abu Bakr what Jerusalem was like. Whenever Muhammad described a part of it, Abu Bakr said: "That's true. I testify that you are the Apostle of God!" until he had completed the description, and then the Apostle said: "And you, Abu Bakr, are the Witness to Truth."

Al-Hasan continued: "God sent down the verse (Quran 13:62) concerning those who had left Islam on this account: 'We made you a vision which we showed you only for a test to men and the accursed tree in the Quran. We put them in fear, but it only adds to their heinous error.'" *Such is al-Hasan's story. . . . (Ibn Ishaq 1955: 181-182)*

Umar in Jerusalem

It may be assumed likely, then, if not entirely certain, that the Muslims who took Jerusalem in 638 knew at least some of the biblical associations of the city but not yet of the city's connection with Muhummad's Night Journey. There are a number of different accounts of what happened next. Umar, the second caliph, or Successor of the Prophet (A.D. 634-644), figures prominently in many of them, although some Western scholars have wondered if he was ever in Jerusalem at all, [7] just as they have wondered at the authenticity of a document incorporated in some of those same accounts which purports to be the surrender terms given to Jerusalem, more specifically to the Christians of Jerusalem, by Caliph Umar himself. The Christians, at any rate, subsequently flourished it when their interests in Jerusalem appeared threatened. This is the so-called Covenant of Umar, and it appears in one of its fullest forms in a text by the tenth-century Muslim historian Tabari (d. A.D. 923): [8]

In the name of God, the Merciful Benefactor!

This is the guarantee granted the inhabitants of Aelia by the servant of God Umar, Commander of the Believers.

He grants them the surety of their persons, their goods, their churches, their crosses—whether these are in a good or a bad condition—and the cult in general.

185

Their churches will not be expropriated for residences nor destroyed; they and their annexes will suffer no harm and the same will be true of their crosses and their goods.

No constraint will be imposed upon them in the matter of religion and no one of them will be annoyed.

No Jew will be authorized to live in Jerusalem with them.

The inhabitants of Jerusalem will pay the poll-tax in the same manner as those in other cities.

It will be left to them to expel from their city the Byzantines (Rûm) and the brigands. Those of the latter who leave will have safe-conduct. Those who wish to stay will be authorized to do so, on condition of paying the same poll-tax as the residents of Aelia.

Those among the inhabitants of Aelia who wish to leave with the By-zantines, take with them their goods, leave behind their churches and their crosses, will likewise have a safe-conduct for themselves, their churches, and their crosses. . . .

The peasants who are presently in the city . . . can remain and pay the poll-tax on the same basis as the inhabitants of Aelia, or, if they prefer, can leave with the Byzantines and return to their families. They will not be taxed until they have gathered their harvest.

This writing is placed under the guarantee of God and the covenant [dhimma] of the Prophet, of the caliphs, and the Believers, on condition that the inhabitants of Aelia pay the poll-tax that is incumbent upon them.

Witnessed by: Khalid ibn al-Walid, Amr ibn al-As, Abd al-Rahman ibn Awf, Mu'awiya ibn Abi Sufyan, who have signed it, here, in the year 15. (Tabari, Annals I, 2405)

We need not comment here on the authenticity of this document except to note that the clause excluding the Jews from Jerusalem—or better, con-tinuing to exclude, since the Christians themselves had long banned the Jews from the city—is contradicted by all the other evidence we possess. The Jews, it seems certain, were not only permitted to reside in Jerusalem but were shown certain signs of favor by the Muslim conquerors.

On the Temple Mount

The center of the action in all the accounts of the Muslim occupation of Jerusalem is the Temple mount on the eastern side of the city. At first it appears an odd landscape; there are now different names and different evocations for the area and its buildings, many of which will be explained on the pages that follow. When we look at the sources, the reasons for this precipitously changed perspective become immediately apparent; all our informants on this important event are Muslims, and more to the point, they all date from an era much later than the events they are describing. We have no immediate eyewitnesses, no contemporaries, Muslim or otherwise, through whom we can trace the passage from a Christian to a Muslim holy place, the appropriation and renaming of shrines, the rethinking and recasting of traditions. Our historians are all fully accustomed to a thoroughly Muslim Jerusalem. For them, Herod's platform was nothing else but the "Noble Sanctuary," the Haram al-Sharif, and atop it there had already stood for hundreds of years the centrally located shrine called the "Dome of the Rock" and, at its southern end, the mosque called al-Aqsa, both wrapped in centuries-old Muslim traditions.

But the accounts are not worthless for that. The names and later sensibilities apart, they embody traditions that may well go back to Muslims of the first generation to live in Jerusalem. The following, for example, is a late and "classical" account of the Muslims' arrival in the Holy City, eclectic in its details and the product of many centuries of refinement; it appears to embody, nonetheless, some very early Muslim perceptions about Jerusalem. It is reported here as it appears in a fourteenth-century work entitled *Muthîr al-Ghirâm*, which was then copied almost verbatim by most later authors:

Al-Walid states on the authority of Saʾid ibn Abd al-Aziz that the letter of the Prophet [calling on world leaders to acknowledge his prophethood] had come to the emperor (Heraclius) while he was residing in the Holy City. Now at that time there was over the Rock in the Holy City a great dungheap which completely masked the prayer niche of David and which the Christians had put there in order to offend the Jews; and further, even the Christian women were wont to throw their (menstrual) cloths and clouts in the place so that there was a pile of them there. Now when the emperor had read the letter of the Prophet, he cried out: "O men of Rum, you are the ones who will be slain on this dungheap because you have desecrated the sanctity of this sanctuary. It will be with you just as it was with the Children of Israel who were slain because of the blood of John, son of Zakariyya."

Then the emperor commanded them to clear the place, as they began to do, but when the Muslims invaded Syria only a third of it had been cleared. Now when Umar came to the Holy City and conquered it, and saw how there was a dungheap over the Rock, he regarded it as horrible and ordered that the place be entirely cleaned. To accomplish this they forced the Nabateans [or native peasantry] of Palestine to labor without pay. On the authority of Jabir ibn Nafir, it is related that when Umar first exposed the Rock to view by removing the dungheap, he commanded them not to pray there until three showers of heavy rain should have fallen.

It is related as coming from Shadad ibn Aws, who accompanied Umar when he entered the Noble Sanctuary of the Holy City on the day when God caused it to be reduced by capitulation, that Umar entered by the Gate of Muhammad, crawling on his hands and his knees, he and all those who were with him, until he came up to the court of the Sanctuary. Then looking around to the right and the left and glorifying God, he said: "By God, in whose hand is my soul, this must be the sanctuary of David of which the Apostle spoke to us when he said 'I was conducted there in the Night Journey.'" Then Umar advancing to the front (or southern) part of the Haram area and to the western part thereof, said: "Let us make this the place for the sanctuary [masjid]."

On the authority of al-Walid ibn Muslim, it is reported as coming from a shaykh of the sons of Shadad ibn Aws, who had heard it from his father, who held it from his grandfather, that Umar, as soon as he was at leisure from the writing of the Treaty of Capitulation made between him and the people of the Holy City, said to (Sophronius) the patriarch of Jerusalem: "Take us to the sanctuary of David." And the patriarch agreed to do so. Then Umar went forth girt with a sword and with four thousand of the Companions (of the Prophet) who had come to Jerusalem with him, all likewise wearing swords, and a crowd of us Arabs who had come up to the Holy City followed them, none of us bearing any weapons except our swords. And the patriarch walked before Umar among the Companions, and we came behind the caliph. Thus we entered the Holy City.

And the patriarch took us to the church which is called the "Dung Heap,"[9] and he said: "This is David's sanctuary." Umar looked around and pondered, then he answered the patriarch: "You are lying, for the Apostle described to me the Sanctuary of David and this is not it." Then the patriarch went with us to the Church of Sion and again he said: "This is the Sanctuary of David." But the caliph replied to him: "You are lying." So the patriarch went on till he came to the Noble Sanctuary of the Holy City and reached the gate later called the Gate of Muhammad. Now the dung which was then all about the Noble Sanctuary had settled on the steps of this gate so that it even came out into the street in which the gate opened, and it had accumulated so greatly on the steps as to reach almost up to the ceiling of the gateway. The patriarch said to Umar: "It is impossible to go on further and enter, except crawling on one's hands and knees." So the patriarch went down on hands and knees, preceding Umar and we all crawled after him, until he had brought us out in the court of the Noble Sanctuary of the Holy City. Then we arose from our knees and stood upright. Umar looked around him, pondering for a long time. Then *he said: "By Him in whose hands is my soul, this is the place described to us by the Apostle of God."*

It is (also) reported . . . that when Umar was caliph he went to visit the people of Syria. Umar halted first at the village of al-Jabiya, while he dispatched a man of the Jadila tribe to the Holy City, and shortly after Umar possessed the Holy City by capitulation. Then the caliph himself went there, and Ka'b [al-Ahbar] with him. Umar said to Ka'b: "O Abu Ishaq, do you know the position of the Rock?" Ka'b answered: "Measure from the well which is in the Valley of Gehenna so and so many ells; there dig and you will discover it," adding, "at this present day it is a dung-heap." So they dug there and the rock was laid bare. Then Umar said to Ka'b: "Where do you say we should place the sanctuary, or rather, the qibla?" Ka'b replied: "Lay out a place for it behind [that is, to the north of] the Rock and so you will make two qiblas, that, namely, of Moses and that of Muhammad." And Umar answered him: "You still lean toward the Jews, O Abu Ishaq. The sanctuary will be in front [that is, to the south of] the Rock." Thus was the Mosque (of al-Aqsa) erected in the front part of the Haram area.

Al-Walid relates further, as coming from Kulthum ibn Ziyad, that Umar asked of Ka'b; "Where do you think we should put the place of prayer for Muslims in this Holy Sanctuary?" Ka'b answered: "In the further (northern) part of it, near the Gate of the Tribes." But Umar said: "No, since the fore part of the Sanctuary belongs to us." . . . Al-Walid relates again, on the authority of Ibn Shaddad, who had it from his father, that Umar proceeded to the fore part of the Sanctuary, to the side adjoining the west, and there began to throw the dung by handfuls into his cloak, and all of us who were with him did likewise. Then he went with it, and we followed along and did likewise, and threw the dung into the wadi which is called the Wadi Jahannam. Then we returned to do it again and yet again, both Umar and the rest of us, until we had cleared the whole of the place where the mosque (of al-Aqsa) now stands. And there we all made our prayers, Umar himself praying in our midst. (Le Strange 1890: 139-143)

Sophronius is already known to us, and it is the Jerusalem patriarch who quite naturally looms large in two Christian accounts of the same events in Jerusalem in 638. The first, from about A.D. 876, is by the Christian historian Eutychius, the later patriarch of Alexandria, who lived under Islam and was well instructed on the Arab tradition:

Then Umar said to him [Sophronius]: "You owe me a rightful debt. Give me a place in which I might build a sanctuary [masjid]." The patriarch said to him: "I will give to the Commander of the Faithful a place to build a sanctuary where the kings of Rum were unable to build. It is the rock where God spoke to Jacob and which Jacob called the Gate of Heaven and the Israelites the Holy of Holies. It is in the center of the world and was a Temple for the Israelites, who held it in great veneration and wherever they were they turned their faces toward it during prayer. But on this condition, that you promise in a written document that no other sanctuary will be built inside of Jerusalem."

Therefore Umar ibn al-Khattab wrote him the document on this matter and handed it over to him. They were Romans when they embraced the Christian religion, and Helena, the mother of Constantine, built the churches of Jerusalem. The place of the rock and the area around it were deserted ruins and they [the Romans] poured dirt over the rock so that great was the filth above it. The Byzantines [Rûm], however, neglected it and did not hold it in veneration, nor did they build a church over it because Christ our Lord said in his Holy Gospel "Not a stone will be left upon a stone which will not be ruined and devastated." For this reason the Christians left it as a ruin and did not build a church over it. So Sophronius took Umar ibn al-Khattab by the hand and stood him over the filth. Umar, taking hold of his cloak filled it with dirt and threw it into the Valley of Gehenna. When the Muslims saw Umar ibn al-Khattab carrying dirt with his own hands, they all immediately began carrying dirt in their cloaks and shields and what have you until the whole place was cleansed and the rock was revealed. Then they all said: "Let us build a sanctuary and let us place the stone at its heart." "No," Umar responded. "We will build a sanctuary and place the stone at the end of the sanctuary." Therefore Umar built a sanctuary and put the stone at the end of it. (Baldi 1955: 447-448)

The other Christian version comes from the Byzantine chronicler Theophanes, writing in the safer and more polemical atmosphere of early ninth century Constantinople:

In this year Umar undertook his expedition into Palestine, where the Holy City having been continuously besieged for two years (by the Arab armies), he at length became possessed of it by capitulation. Sophronius, the leader of Jerusalem, obtained from Umar a treaty in favor of all the inhabitants of Palestine, after which Umar entered the Holy City in camel-hair garments all soiled and torn, and making a show of piety as a cloak for his diabolical hypocrisy, demanded to be taken to what in former times had been the Temple built by Solomon. This he straightway converted into an oratory for blasphemy and impiety. When Sophronius saw this he exclaimed, "Truly this is the Abomination of Desolation spoken of by

190

Daniel the Prophet, and it now stands in the Holy Place," and he shed many tears. [10] *(Le Strange 1890: 140n)*

Jewish Informants, Jewish Memories

Umar's other informant in the Muslim accounts of the capitulation of Jerusalem is the notorious Ka'b al-Ahbar, or "the Rabbi," an early Jewish convert to Islam into whose mouth are put many of the traditions concerning the history and the practices of the Jews of which the Muslims were becoming increasingly aware. In the text already cited, the context is a polemical one: Ka'b counsels Umar to build his mosque north of the rock so that the Jerusalem Muslims will be willy-nilly facing the Temple site when they pray toward Mecca. Umar scents Ka'b's advice for the Judaizing ploy it is and commands the Muslim prayer hall, the Aqsa Mosque, to be built south of the newly uncovered rock. The story represents possibly a conscious Muslim repudiation of its Jewish antecedents, and in the very place it most needed doing, atop Mount Moriah.

The Jewish tradition had, however, quite another recollection. This version comes from Isaac ben Joseph, a visitor to Jerusalem in A.D. 1334:

It was on Mount Moriah that in the olden days the Temple of Solomon (to whom be salvation) was reared; and from that august Temple it received its name of the Mountain of the Temple. Alas, by reason of our sins, where the sacred building once stood, its place is taken today by a profane temple, built by the king of the Ishmaelites when he conquered Palestine and Jerusalem from the uncircumcised. The history of the event was in this wise.

The king, who had made a vow to build up again the ruins of the sacred edifice, if God put the Holy City into his power, demanded of the Jews that they should make known the ruins to him. For the uncircumcised [that is, the Christians] in their hate against the people of God, had heaped rubbish and filth over the spot, so that no one knew exactly where the ruins stood. Now there was an old man then living who said: "If the king will take an oath to preserve the wall, [11] *I will discover unto him the place where the ruins of the Temple were." So the king straightway placed his hand on the thigh of the old man and swore an oath to do what he demanded. When he had shown him the ruins of the Temple under a mound of defilements, the king had the ruins cleared and cleansed, taking part in the cleansing himself, until they were all fair and clean. After that he had them all set up again, with the exception of the wall, and made them a very beautiful temple, which he consecrated to his God.* [12]

It is this wall which stands before the temple of Umar ibn al-Khattab, and which is called the Gate of Mercy.[13] *The Jews resort thither to say their prayers, as Rabbi Benjamin [of Tudela] has already related.*[14] *(Adler 1966: 130-131)*

This is history recollected, the setting down of an oral tradition still in circulation among the Jews of fourteenth-century Jerusalem. It is possible to get much closer to the event, however. Among the debris of documents preserved in the storeroom of the medieval synagogue of Cairo is a poem that provides an apocalyptic vision of what it was like when the Arabs, here as often the "Ishmaelites," suddenly descended on the Holy City in the seventh century. It is couched in the familiar opaque language of apocalypses, but the references are sufficiently clear—to the Byzantines or Romans as "Edomites," for example—to enable us to date it very close to A.D. 638:

> On that day when the Messiah, son of David, will come
> To a downtrodden people
> These signs will be seen in the world and will be brought forth:
> Earth and heaven will wither,
> And the sun and the moon will be blemished,
> And the dwellers in the Land [of Israel] will be struck silent.
>
> The king of the West and the king of the East
> Will be ground one against the other,
> And the armies of the king of the West will hold firm in the Land.
> And a king will go forth from the land of Yoqtan [Arabia]
> And his armies will seize the Land,
> The dwellers of the world will be judged
> And the heavens will rain dust on the earth,
> And winds will spread in the Land.
> Gog and Magog will incite one another
> And kindle fear in the heart of the Gentiles.
> And Israel will be freed of all their sins
> And will no more be kept far from the house of prayer.
>
> Blessings and consolations will be showered on them,
> And they will be engraved on the Book of Life.
> The Kings from the land of Edom will be no more,
> And the people of Antioch will rebel and make peace
> And Maʿuziya [Tiberias] and Samaria will be consoled,
> And Acre and Galilee will be shown mercy.
> Edomites and Ishmael will fight in the valley of Acre
> Till the horses sink in blood and panic.

Gaza and her daughters will be stoned
And Ascalon and Ashod will be terror-stricken.

Israel will go forth from the City and turn eastwards,
And taste no bread for five and four days.
And their Messiah will be revealed and they will be consoled.
And they will share pleasant secrets with their King
And they will raise praises to their King;
And all the wicked will not rise up in the Judgment.

(Lewis 1974: 198)

Jews on the Temple Mount?

The happy optimism of this poem grew somewhat tempered in time, but if we are to believe the testimony of Salman ben Yeruham, a Karaite author writing about A.D. 950, the Muslims, like Antiochus III many centuries before, repaid Jewish cooperation by granting access not merely to Jerusalem but to the Temple mount itself:

As it is known, Jerusalem remained under the rule of the Rûm [the Byzantines] for more than 500 years, during which they [the Jews] were not able to enter Jerusalem. Anyone who was discovered entering was killed. When by the mercy of the God of Israel the Rûm departed from us and the kingdom of Ishmael [the Arabs] appeared, the Jews were granted permission to enter and reside there. The courts of the (House of) the Lord were handed over to them, where they prayed for a number of years.

There was, of course, a condition already familiar to us, as Salman explains in another place:

There were men of the Children of Israel among them who showed them [the Muslims] the place of the Temple and settled in with them from then until the present day. The Muslims stipulated that if the Children of Israel would keep the Temple [precinct] in a clean state, they would be entitled to pray at its gates and no one would prevent them from doing so.

Later a change took place, caused, according to Salman, by reports brought to the caliph of "insolent behavior . . . the drinking of wine and intoxicants" by certain Jews, and for the Karaite Salman that could mean only his arch-foes, the Rabbanite Jews of Jerusalem. [15]

So he [the caliph] ordered their expulsion from all but one of the Temple compound gates, where they prayed; they were not, however, enjoined from using the other gates [for going in and out]. This practice lasted for a number of years. When they stepped up their acts of disobedience, a ruler turned on us and expelled us from the [one permitted] Temple compound gate. . . . (Mann 1935: 18, trans. R. Brann)

Then in Salman's own time, worse threatened to follow:

They [the Muslims] pray in its courts for the dead, and five times daily they recall the memory of the idol and of the false prophet; Israelites, priests and Levites and singers, of blessed memory, are expelled from it. After all this, they [the Christians?] now want to expel us from Jerusalem and impose an iron yoke upon our necks. (Mann 1931: 20, trans. R. Harari)

According to this extraordinary report, then, the Jews of Jerusalem were at one time permitted, and availed themselves of the opportunity, to pray on the Temple mount itself. [16] This was in the earliest days of the Muslim occupation of the city, perhaps before Abd al-Malik's construction of the Dome of the Rock and the subsequent consecration of the entire Temple mount as the "Noble Sanctuary." Once the Dome was constructed, the character of the area must have changed substantially; it was more likely *that* change, rather than the depraved practices of the rabbis, which excluded the Jews from the Haram and confined them to prayer at one of its gates.

Sacred History

For all three groups who claimed descent from Father Abraham—Jews, Christians, and Muslims—the fall of Jerusalem in 638 was a theological event, and all three read it as the Christians' chastisement for sin. In the Christian version the sin was rather generalized, a falling-off from the Christian ideal by the Christian people; the Jews, for their part, needed no citation by chapter and verse on the wickedness of the "Edomites." But the Muslim theology of the event was considerably more pointed, as we have seen, and spoke directly to the condition of the Temple mount in pre-Islamic times: the Christians had not destroyed the Temple, but it was they who had defiled it by heaping rubbish and filth of the most degrading kind on the place where the Temple had once stood. It is all spelled out, now with convincing historical detail, by medieval Jerusalem's chief Muslim historian, Mujir al-Din, writing in A.D. 1496:

After the ascension of Jesus into heaven, the city of the Holy House remained prosperous for forty more years. The Israelites were governed by a series of Roman kings down to the time of Titus the Roman. The capital of his kingdom was Rome, in the land of the Franks. In the first year of his reign he came to the city of the Holy House, fell upon the Jews, massacred them and took the survivors captive, all save those who managed to hide themselves. He destroyed the Holy City and gave it over to plunder. He put the Temple to the torch and burnt their sacred books. The Israelites were banished from the Holy City, which was in a state where it could no longer be inhabited. From this time onward the Jews no longer had the power to govern.

Destroyed by Titus, the city of the Holy House was, after the persecution of the Jews, rebuilt little by little. It remained prosperous until the departure of Helena, mother of Constantine the Victorious, for this city of Jerusalem. Her son was first king at Rome, then he transferred his capital to Constantinople, had its wall constructed and became a Christian. The name of this city was Byzantium but he gave it that of Constantinople. Helena, the mother of Constantine, thus left for Jerusalem in search of the cross of Christ, the cross on which the Christians pretend that Jesus was crucified. Once she was in Jerusalem she had the wood of the cross discovered and to this end instituted the Feast of the Cross and had built the church of al-Qumama over the tomb in which, according to the Christians' pretensions, Jesus had been buried. She also had built the place opposite the Qumama known to this day as the Dargah [probably the patriarchal residence]; the church at Bethlehem; the one on the Mount of Olives at the place of the ascension of Jesus; and among others the one in Gethsemene where the tomb of Mary is located. She had the Temple of Jerusalem leveled down to the ground—it was that which was in the sanctuary—and she ordered that the filth and scourings of the city be thrown on its place. The place of the Noble Rock was transformed into a stable. That state of affairs remained until the arrival of Umar ibn al-Khattab, who took the noble city of Jerusalem. (Marmadji 1951: 35-36)

The Rock and the Dome

When Umar had cleared the area at the top of the Temple mount, he built the first assembly-mosque for the Jerusalem Muslims at the southern end of Herod's platform. It was not an exceedingly impressive structure, as we are told by the Christian pilgrim Arculf, who saw the original Aqsa when he was in Jerusalem in 680. [17] It was, however, large enough to hold what must have been the total Muslim population of Jerusalem at the time:

In that famous place where the Temple once stood, near the (city) wall on the east, the Saracens now frequent an oblong house of prayer, which they pieced together with upright planks and large beams over some ru-

ined remains. It is said that the building can hold three thousand people. (Arculf I, 1)

The debate between Umar and Ka'b about the positioning of the Muslim place of congregational prayer in Jerusalem assumed it would be on the Temple platform; it was simply a question of where. And that question was debated not in terms of any particular holy place but simply in terms of where the mosque would stand in relation to the chief, and perhaps at that stage the only genuine, holy place atop the platform, the outcropping of bedrock situated near the center of the present Haram al-Sharif. [18] We have heard mention of a rock before, but not in connection with Herod's Temple: the already cited descriptions of that complex by both Josephus and the Mishnaic tractate Middoth make no mention of it; moreover, the Holy of Holies and the altar of Herod's Temple were both so large that they would have totally concealed the Muslims' Rock. Where such a rock does appear, however, is in the account of the fourth-century Bordeaux pilgrim cited in Chapter Four, where it is related that the Jews came annually to Jerusalem to mourn the destruction on the Temple and that their ceremonies centered around a "pierced rock."

We know little more than that, except for the obvious fact that when the first Muslims arrived in Jerusalem they were quickly drawn to a rock atop the Temple mount and that it was identified for them as connected in some fashion with the Jewish Temple, Solomon's, as they thought. [19] Who first made that identification or when, we simply do not know. The second-century A.D. Mishnaic treatise Yoma already cited in Chapter One briefly mentions a stone connected with Solomon's Temple. Although neither the Bible nor Josephus mentions it, the Mishna claims to know that it went back to the time of the "early Prophets," that is, to David and Solomon. The account is not clear, however, about whether this "stone of foundation" was still in place after the destruction of the Temple:

After the Ark was taken away, a stone remained there (in the Temple) from the time of the early Prophets, and it was called "foundation" (she-tiyah). It was higher than the ground by three fingerbreadths. . . . (Danby 1933: 167)

The passage in Yoma was an obvious invitation to exegetical embroidery, and the Jewish mystical and midrashic tradition responded avidly, feeding upon and into the parallel Muslim mythology about the stone under Abd al-Malik's magnificent dome atop the Temple mount: that it marked the navel of the world, that the tablets of the Ten Commandments were hewn from it, that the Divine Name was inscribed upon it, and more. [20]

Why Was the Dome Built?

Whatever the history of the rock, the Muslims built over that outcropping an extraordinary octagonal shrine. According to the inscription preserved within, this shrine was the work of Caliph Abd al-Malik and was completed in A.D. 692. [21] We have, moreover, an explanation of the caliph's motives offered about A.D. 874 by the historian Ya'qubi. Abd al-Malik was faced by a serious challenge to his power by the rebel Ibn al-Zubayr, who then controlled Mecca:

Then Abd al-Malik forbade the people of Syria to make the pilgrimage [to Mecca], and this by reason that Abdullah ibn Zubayr was wont to seize on them during the time of the pilgrimage and force them to pay him allegiance—which, Abd al-Malik having knowledge of, forbade the people to journey forth to Mecca. But the people murmured thereat, saying "How do you forbid us to make the pilgrimage to God's house, seeing that the same is a commandment of God upon us?" But the caliph answered them, "Has not Ibn Shihab al-Zuhri [the traditionist who knew many of the Companions of the Prophet] told you how the Apostle of God did say 'Men shall journey to but three mosques, the Holy Shrine (at Mecca), my mosque (at Medina) and the mosque of the Holy City (of Jerusalem)'? So this last is now appointed to you (as a place of worship) in place of the Holy Shrine of Mecca. And this Rock, of which it is reported that the Apostle of God set his foot when he ascended into heaven, shall be to you in the place of the Ka'ba." Then Abd al-Malik built above the rock a dome and hung it around with curtains of brocade, and he instituted doorkeepers for the same, and the people took up the custom of circumambulating the rock, even as they had paced around the Ka'ba, and the usage continued thus all the remaining days of the dynasty of the Umayyads [from A.D. 692 to 750]. (Le Strange 1890: 116)

This explanation for the construction of the Dome of the Rock, which is repeated by a number of later Muslim authors and has become canonized in all Western accounts, suffers from a number of fatal flaws that render it extremely suspect. [22] Not the least of them is that no other contemporary or near contemporary authorities seem aware of this singular piece of religious blasphemy on the part of the caliph, to wit, the usurpation of the quranically mandated hajj to Mecca, with its prescribed circumambulation of the Ka'ba, by a similar ritual to be held in the Dome of the Rock in Jerusalem. Indeed, one who was distinctly in a position to know, the historian Muqaddasi, himself a native of Jerusalem, not only is ignorant of this extraordinary act on Abd al-Malik's part but offers an entirely different explanation. He tells of discussing with his uncle the Great Mosque of Damascus, built by Abd al-Malik's son al-Walid:

Now one day I said, speaking to my father's brother, "O my uncle, truly it was not well of Caliph al-Walid to spend so much of the wealth of the Muslims on the mosque at Damascus. Had he expended the same on making roads or for caravanserais or in the restoration of fortresses, it would have been more fitting and more excellent of him." But my uncle said to me in answer, "O my little son, you have not understanding! Truly al-Walid was right and he was prompted to do a worthy work. For he beheld Syria to be a country that had long been occupied by the Christians, and he noted herein the beautiful churches still belonging to them, so enchantingly fair and so renowned for their splendor; even as are the Holy Sepulcher and the churches of Lydda and Edessa. So he sought to build for the Muslims a mosque that should prevent their admiring these and should be unique and a wonder to the world. And in like manner, is it not evident how Caliph Abd al-Malik, noting the greatness of the Dome of the Holy Sepulcher and its magnificence, was moved lest it should dazzle the minds of Muslims and so erected, above the Rock, the Dome which is now seen there." (Muqaddasi 1896: 22-23)

What Muqaddasi here suggests is a more likely motive, if not nearly so dramatic as Ya'qubi's charge, for Abd al-Malik's construction of the singular shrine that yet stands atop the Temple mount, and in much the same form he built it. [23] But the Caliph did more than simply put up the building; he also endowed it with attendants:

The shrine is served by special attendants; their service was instituted by Caliph Abd al-Malik, the men being chosen from among the fifth owed to the sovereign out of the captives taken in war and hence they are called "the Fifths." None besides these are employed in the service and they take their watch in turn beside the Rock. (Muqaddasi 1896: 48.)

All of that [construction] took place during the reign of Abd al-Malik ibn Marwan. This prince appointed to guard the shrine three hundred black slaves in residence whom he had bought for the sanctuary out of the funds belonging to the "fifth" of the Community Treasury. Whenever one of them died he was replaced in his duties by his son, by his grandson, or someone else of his family, and that was the procedure to be followed for as long as they had offspring. . . . Ten Jews, who were exempted from the poll-tax, were also employed in its service, and they and their children numbered twenty in all. They were charged with cleaning up whatever filth occurred at the time of the pilgrimage, summer and winter, and to keep in order the public places around the shrine. Ten Christians, mem-

bers of the same family who had this as a hereditary charge, were attached to the shrine to remove the rubbish and to take care of the conduits that brought water to the cisterns [of the Haram] and the cisterns themselves. There were also a certain number of Jewish servants who busied themselves with the glasswork, the various types of lamps, and other such. They were not subject to the poll-tax, nor were those who prepared wicks for the lamps. This exemption applied to themselves and their families in perpetuity, as long as they had descendents, from the period of Abd al-Malik onward. *(Mujir 1876: 56-57)*

The Umayyads and Jerusalem

One Jewish apocalyptic poem has already been cited in connection with the Muslim conquest of Jerusalem. There is another such "unveiling," which probably dates from around the end of the Umayyad dynasty in A.D. 750, the dynasty of which Caliph Mu'awiya (661-681), the fifth of the Successors of the Prophet, was the effective founder and to which Abd al-Malik also belonged. This text takes the form of a vision of the future given to Simon ben Yohai, an early rabbinic sage whose grave is still shown near Merom in Galilee:

He saw the Kenite. When he saw the kingdom of Ishmael [the Arabs] that was coming, he [Simon] began to say: "Was it not enough what the wicked kingdom of Edom [Rome / Byzantium] did to us, but must we have the kingdom of Ishmael too?" At once (the angelic prince) Metatron, the prince of the countenance, answered and said: "Do not fear, son of man, for the Holy One, blessed be He, only brings the kingdom of Ishmael in order to save you from this wickedness (of Edom). He raises up over them a Prophet [Muhammad] according to His will and will conquer the land for them and they will come and restore it in greatness, and there will be great terror between them and the sons of Esau." Rabbi Simon answered and said: "How do we know that they are our salvation?" He answered: "Did not the Prophet Isaiah say thus [21:13], that he saw a troop with horsemen in pairs, etc. Why did he put the troop of asses before the troop of camels, when he need only have said: 'A troop of camels and a troop of asses'? But when he goes forth riding a camel the dominion will arise through the rider on an ass. Again 'a troop of asses,' since he rides on an ass, shows that they are the salvation of Israel, like the salvation of the rider on an ass [i.e., the Messiah]." . . .

The second king who arises from Ishmael [Mu'awiya] will be a lover of Israel; he restores their breaches and the breaches of the Temple. He hews Mount Moriah and makes it all straight and builds a mosque there on the

Temple rock ["eben shetiya"], as it was said: "Thy nest is set in the rock" *[Num. 24:21]. He makes war against the sons of Esau and kills his armies* *and takes many captives from them, and he will die in peace and great* *honor. And a great king will rise from Hazarmaveth [Gen. 10: 27] [Ha-* *dramawt?: a reference to Ali?] and rule for a short time, and the strong* *men of the sons of Kedar will rise up against him and kill him.*

They will raise up another king whose name is Marwan, and they will *take him from the sheep and the asses and raise him to the kingship, and* *for arms will rise from him and they will repair the Temple [the Dome of* *the Rock and Aqsa]. At the end of the kingdom of the four arms another* *king will arise and reduce the weights and measures and spend three years* *in peace. And there will be great strife in the world in his days and he will* *send great armies against the Edomites and there they will die in hunger* *and they will have much food with them and he withholds from them and* *none will he give them, and the sons of Edom will rise up against the* *sons of Marwan and kill them and the sons of Ishmael will rise up and* *burn the food and those who remain will flee and go forth.*

Then the great king [Hisham] will arise and will rule nineteen years. *These are his signs: reddish, cross-eyed, and with three birthmarks, one* *on his brow, one on his right hand, and one on his left arm. He will plant* *young trees and build ruined towns and burst open the abysses to raise* *the water to irrigate his trees. The grandsons of his sons will eat much,* *and whoever rise up against him will be delivered into his hand. The land* *will be quiet in his days and he will die in peace. . . .*[24] *(Lewis 1950: 321-* *326)*

Not all the identifications offered here are either easy or certain,[25] though the reference to Marwan by name makes it certain that we are dealing with members of the Umayyad house. What chiefly concerns us here is the beginning of that house and the "second king" from Ishmael— Mu'awiya was long governor of Syria and Jerusalem before he became caliph in 661—who is "a lover of Israel" and who "hews Mount Moriah and makes it all straight and builds a mosque there on the Temple rock ['eben shetiya']."

Neither Muslim tradition nor the dedication inscription preserved inside the Dome of the Rock credits him with such, but it is not inconceivable that Mu'awiya at least began the Muslims' work on and around the Temple platform,[26] particularly if the extension of the Haram platform northward from an original Herodian square was an early Muslim undertaking. It would have been an immense and time-consuming labor, that leveling off of the northern scarp upon which the Fortress Antonia once sat, and one that had necessarily to be completed before the Dome could be begun.

The argument that the present platform of the Haram al-Sharif was not entirely the work of Herod is simply put: the Jewish testimony that the Herodian Temple platform was square, while the Haram is an immense irregular rectangle; the certainty that the southern edge of the present platform is Herodian, corner to corner, which enables us to construct such a square, whose dimensions, in turn, correspond more closely, though by no means exactly, to those offered by Josephus and the Mishna; and finally, the absence of definite evidence that would establish that the northern side of the present Haram, like the southern, is Herodian in construction. [27]

The hypothesis for the Muslim extension of the Herodian platform has gained support since excavations were begun outside the southern wall of the platform in 1967. What was unearthed there was a large palace complex, unmistakably Muslim and dated by its excavators to the Umayyad period. [28] The palace was connected at roof and ground levels with the Aqsa mosque which it abutted on the south; and it quite obviously formed part of a single religio-administrative complex together with the buildings atop the Haram. Someone, it is clear, had rather grandiose plans for Muslim Jerusalem, and they were not simply religious. If this person intended to rule the entire Abode of Islam from Jerusalem, Mu'awiya is a highly likely candidate.

Mu'awiya, it appears, changed his mind and chose Damascus over Jerusalem as his political capital, but the idea did not entirely disappear from Umayyad consciousness. The following is a late report—it comes from the fifteenth-century Jerusalem historian Mujir al-Din—but we have no reason to doubt its authenticity:

When Sulayman, son of Abd al-Malik, succeeded his brother al-Walid on throne of the caliphate in the year 96 [A.D. 715], he came to Jerusalem where numerous deputations came to recognize him. Never had one seen a richness so considerable than that which hastened to greet the new caliph. Seated under one of the domes that ornament the platform of the sanctuary around the Rock in Jerusalem, perhaps that called the Dome of Sulayman by the Gate of the Dawardiyya, it is there that he held audience. They extended before the dome where he was a carpet on which they placed cushions and lounges. As soon as he had taken his place, he ordered his attendants to seat themselves. These latter took their places on the cushions and the lounges; at his side were sums of money and the pension registers. Sulayman had conceived the plan of living in Jerusalem, of making it his capital and bringing together there great wealth and a considerable population. . . . (Mujir 1876: 57-58)

Seventh-Century Jerusalem Through
Christian Eyes

There are few actual eyewitness reports of the Muslims' establishing residence in Jerusalem in the seventh and early eighth centuries. Most of what
we have, whether from Muslim, Christian, or Jewish sources, are later
recollections, often and transparently edited to serve the political and religious needs of a later generation. One exception is the European pilgrim
Arculf who has already been cited in connection with the earliest version
of the al-Aqsa Mosque. He was in Jerusalem and the Holy Land sometime
about 680, and if his interests are chiefly in the Christian holy places,
which were the goal of his journey, his narrative does reveal something of
the topography of Jerusalem in the era of the Umayyads and perhaps
something as well, if only by silence or implication, of the Muslim attitude
toward the still predominantly Christian population.

The narrative is often in the third person because Arculf's recollections
were set down by another, Adomnan, abbot of Iona, who was visited by
Arculf on the latter's return to Britain:

*In the great wall which surrounds the city [of Jerusalem] Arculf counted
eighty-four towers and six gates, which are situated in this order around
the city: first, the Gate of David on the west side of Mount Sion; second
is the gate of the Fuller's Field; third is St. Stephen's Gate; fourth, the
Gate of Benjamin; fifth is a portula or "Little Gate" from which one descends by stairway to the Valley of Jehoshaphat; and the sixth is the Gate
of Tekoa.*

*This then is the order as one goes around the wall connecting these
gates and towers. From this Gate of David it turns northwards and then
to the east. Though there are six gates in the wall, only three are reckoned
to be important as main thoroughfares, the one on the west, the one on
the north, and the last on the east. Thus we see that one section of the
wall with its towers has no gates, the section that extends across the northern edge of Mount Sion (which overlooks the city from the south), from
the above mentioned Gate of David as far as the face of the mountain
which looks eastward and ends in a cliff. (Arculf I, 1)*

We cannot make complete sense of this, but at least some of the landmarks
are clear: David's Gate, now called the Jaffa Gate, the main entry on the
western side of the city; St. Stephen's Gate, the present Damascus Gate,
on the northern side, not far from the place where Stephen was martyred
and Eudocia built her church; and the Gate of Benjamin, likely the gate
currently and mistakenly called St. Stephen's on the eastern side of the city

just north of the Haram. These are, as the text comments, the entries into the chief thoroughfares of the city. Following the sequence as Adomnan or Arculf sets it out, the Fuller's Field Gate would be somewhere in the northwest corner of the city, though a persistent tradition places the Fuller's Field in the southeast, near the Pool of Siloam, and the "little gate" somewhere along the eastern side of the city. Since this "portula" has no name in the text and yet fulfills the topographical definition of the Golden Gate—"descends by a stairway to the Valley of Jehoshaphat"—it is possible to think that at this stage the Golden Gate, which now entered directly into the enlarged Haram, was already sealed closed except for the small postern referred to here. The Tekoa Gate, finally, must have been somewhere on the south side of the city, probably in the southwestern corner.

Some additional details are supplied on an area that seems to be just inside the Damascus Gate. This gate was commonly known in the Muslim tradition as the Gate of the Column by reason of the tall column set up there in Roman days and still visible on the Madaba mosaic. It is to that well-known landmark that Arculf appears to be referring in the following passage:

We must speak briefly here of a very tall column which stands in the middle of the city, where it is seen by every passer-by coming northward from the holy places. This column was set up in the place where the Cross of the Lord was placed on a dead man and he returned to life. At the summer solstice when it is noon a marvelous event occurs. When the sun reaches mid-heaven, the column casts no shadow, but as soon as the solstice, that is, the twenty-fourth of June, is past, and after three days the day begins to get shorter, it first casts a short shadow and then as the days pass a longer one. . . . Which demonstrates that the city of Jerusalem is situated in the center of the earth. This explains why the Psalmist used these words to sing his prophecy of the holy places of the Passion and Resurrection which are in this Aelia, "But God, our King, before the ages worked salvation in the midst of the earth," that is, in Jerusalem, which is called the "Navel of the Earth."[29] (Arculf I, 13)

What follows from Arculf is far clearer, a description of the same feast of the Encaenia or the Dedication of the Church of the Holy Sepulcher noted by Egeria in the fourth century (Chapter Four). It appears to have been a major market day in Jerusalem, even under the Muslims:

Each year on the fifteenth of the month of September a great crowd always comes to Jerusalem. They come from almost every country and many nationalities to hold a fair, to buy and sell to each other. Thus these crowds from various countries have necessarily to spend some days in the inns of the city, while a great many of their camels and horses, asses and oxen, for their various baggages, cover the city streets with their revolting dung. Not only does the smell of this clogging filth cause a considerable nuisance to the citizens, but it even makes walking about difficult.

Then a truly wonderful thing occurs. On the night after this aforementioned festival an immense abundance of rain pours down on the city and washes all the disgusting dirt off the streets and makes them free of filth. For God made the terrain of Jerusalem a slope going gradually down from the northern ridge of Mount Sion towards the lower ground by the northern and eastern walls. In this way it is impossible for the heavy rain to collect in the streets but it rushes downhill from the higher to the lower ground. The flood of water from the heavens flows out through the eastern gates and down into the Valley of Jehoshaphat and the Brook Kedron, taking with it all that revolting dung. And once Jerusalem has been thus "baptized" the downpour stops. . . . (Arculf I, 1)

The Church of the Holy Sepulcher in A.D. 680

Arculf is at his explicit best on the subject of the Church of the Holy Sepulcher, even supplying sketches of its plan. [30] This is our first literary view of the church since its reconstruction by Patriarch Modestus after the Persian destruction of A.D. 614:

When I asked Arculf about the houses in that city, he replied: "I remember how often I used to see and visit many buildings in the city and look at the numerous large stone houses filling the space within the city walls. They are wonderfully well built. But for the present let us pass them all over except the marvelous buildings in the holy places, to wit, of the Cross and the Resurrection." I carefully questioned Arculf about those places, and especially about the Lord's Sepulcher and the church built over it, and Arculf drew its shape for me on a wax tablet.

This is a very large church made entirely of stone and built on a remarkable round plan. Three walls rise from the foundations, and they have a single lofty roof, with a broad pathway between one wall and the next. There are also three altars arranged in particular emplacements in the middle wall. This lofty round church, with the above mentioned altars, one looking toward the south, another to the north, and a third on the west, rests on twelve columns of remarkable size. It has eight doors, or entries, in the three walls divided by the width of a street. Four of them are on the northeast, also called the Caecias wind, while the other four are on the southeast.

In the center of the round space enclosed by this church there is a small building cut out of a single rock. Nine men can stand praying inside it, and a man of ordinary height has one and a half feet clearance between his head and its roof. The entrance to this small building faces east. Its whole exterior is covered with choice marble, and the roof is decorated on the outside with gold and supports a large gold cross.

Inside this small building is the Lord's Tomb, which has been cut into the same rock on the north side. The pavement of this building is, however, lower than the position of the Tomb, and the distance between the floor and the edge of the Sepulcher on the side is about three palms. This information was given me by Arculf, who had often been to visit the Lord's Tomb and measured it accurately. (Arculf I, 2-3)

Further to the east has been built another very large church on the site which in Hebrew is called Golgotha. From the roof hangs a large bronze chandelier with lamps suspended from it by ropes. Below it stands a great silver cross, fixed in the same socket as the wooden cross on which the Savior of mankind once suffered. [31] *There is a cave in this same church, which has been cut into the rock below the place of the Lord's Cross. Here there is an altar on which sacrifice is offered for the souls of certain specially honored persons. Their bodies are laid in the court in front of the door of this Church of Golgotha, until the Holy Mysteries for the dead are completed. (Arculf I, 6)*

This rectangular stone construction built on the site of Calvary has adjoining it on the east the stone basilica built with great reverence by King Constantine. It is also called the Martyrium, and people say it was built on the site where, by the permission of the Lord, after 233 years had gone by, the Cross of the Lord was discovered hidden underground, together with the two crosses of the thieves. Between these two churches comes the renowned spot where the patriarch Abraham set up an altar, and arranged a pile of wood on it, and took up his drawn sword to sacrifice his own son Isaac. Now a large wooden table stands there, on which the alms for the poor are offered by the people. I questioned Arculf further and he added: "There is a small court between the Anastasis, that is, the round church we have described above, and the Basilica of Constantine. It extends as far as the Church of Golgotha and lamps are burning continuously in it day and night." (Arculf I, 7-8)

Somewhat more direct, though considerably less circumstantial, is the account of the Holy Sepulcher / Calvary complex incorporated in the *Life of St. Willibald*, the biography of a German cleric who was in Jerusalem in A.D. 724:

From there he [Willibald] came on to Jerusalem, to that place where the Lord's Holy Cross was found. That place is called "The Place of Calvary" and there is now a church there. Earlier this place was outside Jerusalem, but Helena put the place inside Jerusalem after she discovered the Cross. Now there are three wooden crosses standing there outside the church, on the east of it near the wall, in memory of the Holy Cross of our Lord and of the others who were crucified with him. At present they are not inside the church, but stand outside under a roof. Nearby there is that garden in which was the Savior's tomb. The tomb had been carved out of a rock, and the rock juts up out of the ground; at the bottom it is square but it is tapered toward the top. The tomb is now surmounted by a cross, and there is now a remarkable house over it. On the east of the rock of the tomb a door has been made, through which people enter the tomb to pray. Inside there is a bed [or shelf] on which the Lord's body lay. Fifteen golden bowls stand on the shelf. They are filled with oil and burn day and night. The shelf on which the Lord's body lay is inside the rock of the tomb on the north side, that is, on the the right side of the tomb as one enters the tomb to pray. There also, in front of the tomb door, lies a large square stone, like the earlier stone which the angel rolled away from the tomb door. (Life of Willibald, 18)

The Church of the Ascension

Another church that attracted Arculf's attention, and for which he also provided a sketch plan, was the Imbomon, built over the spot of Jesus' Ascension atop the Mount of Olives. In shape and in purpose it was far closer to the Muslim Dome of the Rock than to the Church of the Resurrection across the city:

Nowhere on the whole of the Mount of Olives is there a higher spot than the one from which it is said that the Lord ascended into the heavens. A great round church stands there, which has round it three porticoes with vaulted roofs. But there is no vault or roof over the central part of the church; it is out of doors open to the sky, though on its eastern side there is an altar with a small roof over it.

There is no roof over the interior of the building so as not to prevent those who pray there from seeing the way from the last place where the Lord's feet were standing when he was carried up to heaven in a cloud. At the time when they were building this church I have just been describing, it was impossible, as you will find written elsewhere, to extend the paved part over the place of the footprints of the Lord. Indeed the earth was unused to bear anything human and cast back the coverings in the face of those who were laying them. Moreover, the footmarks on the dust on which God stood provides a testimony which is permanent, since his footprints are to be seen in it, and even though people flock there, and in their zeal take away the soil where the Lord stood, it never becomes less, and to this day there are marks on the earth like footprints.

The sainted Arculf was an attentive visitor at this place, and he reports that it is situated, as we have explained, inside a large circular bronze railing, which is about the height of a man's neck, according to the measurements. In the center of it there is a sizable opening through which one looks down and sees the uncovered marks of the feet of the Lord plainly and clearly impressed in the dust. On the west of the railing is a kind of door, so that any entering by it can easily approach the sacred dust, reach their hands down through a hole in the railing and take in them some particles of the sacred dust.

Thus the account of our friend Arculf on the place of the Lord's footprints agrees exactly with what others have written, namely, that they could not be covered in any way, either with a roof, nor with any other sort of lower and closer covering, so they can always be seen by all who enter and the prints of the Lord's feet can be clearly pointed out there. A great lamp hangs above the circular railing from pulleys and lights the footprints of the Lord, burning day and night. (Arculf I, 23)

If the Dome of the Rock and the Church of the Ascension were provocatively similar in form and function, each building was also notoriously visible to the worshippers in the other:

On the western side of the round building described above are eight upper windows paned with glass. In these windows, and in corresponding positions, are eight lamps suspended from chains in such a way that each one of them seems to hang neither above nor below its window, but just inside it. These lamps shine out from their windows on the summit of the Mount of Olives with such brilliance that they light up not only the part of the Mount to the west, near this round stone church, but also the steps leading all the way up from the Valley of Jehoshaphat to the city of Jerusalem, which are lighted in a wonderful manner, however dark the night. Most of the nearer part of the city [which would be, of course, the Haram al-Sharif] is lighted as well. The remarkable brilliance of these eight lamps shining out by night from the holy Mount and the place of the Lord's Ascension brings to the hearts of believers a greater readiness for the love of God and strikes awe in their mind and deep compunction in their soul. (Arculf I, 23)

Christians and Muslims in
the Holy Land

Arculf has little to say about Christian-Muslim relations in Jerusalem, but a recent rather curious controversy in the city did catch his interest:

A certain trustworthy Jewish believer, immediately after the Resurrection of the Lord, stole from his Tomb the sacred linen cloth and hid it in his house for many days. But by the grace of the Lord it was found again after the lapse of many years and brought to the notice of the whole people about three years ago. . . .

The original thief had given the cloth to his son, it appears, and it was passed on secretly in the family for generations.

The Cloth of the Lord was handed on from father to son, and from one believer to another it passed on by inheritance until the fifth generation. But many years had gone by, and after the fifth generation there were no more believing [that is, Christian] heirs in the family. So the Holy Cloth was handed on to some Jews who were not believers. Unworthy though they were to receive such a gift, they nevertheless treated it with respect, and by the divine generosity were much blessed with riches of many kinds. But when the believing Jews heard among their people the true story about the Lord's Cloth, they began a violent dispute over it with the non-Christian Jews, seeking with all their might to get possession of it.

This contention, once it started, divided the people of Jerusalem into two factions, one the Christian believers and the other the non-Christian infidels. Both parties appealed to Muʿawiya, king of the Saracens, to adjudicate between them. In the presence of the Christian Jews he addressed as follows the unbelieving Jews, who were still persistently keeping the Lord's Cloth in their possession. "Put the Holy Cloth which you have in my hand!" They obeyed the king, took it out of its box and laid it on his lap. With great reverence the king took it and commanded that a great fire be made in the courtyard in the presence of all the people. When it was fully alight he rose, approached the fire and said to the two contending parties: "Now let Christ, the Savior of the world, who suffered for mankind, whose head, when he was entombed, was covered by this Cloth which I hold to my breast, judge by fire between you. . . ."

The caliph threw the cloth into the fire. It rose up, fluttered, and descended among the Christians.

Then with deep respect they took the Lord's Cloth, a venerable gift from

208

heaven. . . . and placed it in a church casket, wrapped in another cloth. One day our brother Arculf saw it taken out of its box, and among the great many people who kissed it, he did likewise. It measures about eight feet in length. (Arculf I, 11)

Arculf's attention remained strictly focused on the Christian holy places that he had come to visit in the East, but Willibald, who seems to have travelled more widely and in a somewhat more leisurely fashion, has a revealing anecdote on what the early eighth century traveller might expect in that society:

. . . They walked to a city which is called Emesa, twelve miles distant. There is a large church, which St. Helena built in honor of St. John the Baptist, and his head, which is now in Damascus, was there for a long time. There were at that point seven other people making the pilgrimage with Willibald. The Saracens, who had discovered that some strange and unknown men had arrived, suddenly arrested them and took them prisoner. Not knowing what country they had come from, they took them as spies. They took their prisoners along to a rich shaykh so that he could have a look at them and see where they had come from. So the shaykh asked where they had come from and what kind of business they were on. They replied by telling him from the beginning the exact reason for their whole journey. Then the shaykh answered as follows: "Many times have I seen people coming here, fellow-tribesmen of theirs, from those parts of the world. They mean no harm. All they want to do is fulfill their law." Then they left him and went to ask for a permit to go to Jerusalem, but the moment they arrived there, the governor said they had been spying and ordered them to be kept prisoner till he found out from the king what he should do with them.

 . . . There was in the city a merchant who wished to pay their ransom and free them from prison as an act of almsgiving and for the redemption of his own soul, and in that way they might be free to go as they wished. He was not successful, but instead sent them dinner and supper every day, and on Wednesdays and Saturdays sent his son to the prison to take them out to have a bath and bring them back again. And on Sundays he took them to church through the market so that they could see what goods were for sale, and whatever pleased them, these he then bought for them at his own expense, whatever it might be that caught their fancy. All the people of nearby towns were filled with curiosity and came out to look at them there. They were young and handsome men, well turned out and with good clothes. (Life of Willibald, 12)

Willibald in Jerusalem: A.D. 724

The charge, or at least the suspicion, that foreign visitors or pilgrims in the Islamic world were there as spies was to have a long history in the Near East, but Willibald and his companions were eventually released through the intervention of a Spanish merchant—Spain was already in the hands of the Muslims—who was in Emesa and whose brother served as a chamberlain to Hisham (caliph A.D. 724-743), the "Saracen king, whose name was Mirmumnus." This connection with the *Amîr al-Mu'minîn*, or "Commander of the Faithful," as the caliphs were addressed, was more than adequate, and Willibald continued on to Damascus and eventually Jerusalem:

Our bishop [Willibald] arrived there [in Jerusalem] on the feast of St. Martin [November 11]. But as soon as he reached the place he fell ill, and lay sick until a week before the Lord's nativity. Then, when he was feeling somewhat recovered and felt he had got the better of his illness, he got up and went off to visit the church called Holy Sion, which stands in the middle of Jerusalem. He prayed there and went on to Solomon's porch. There is there a pool, and sick people lie there waiting for the water to be moved and for the angel to come and move the water: then the first to get down into it is cured. It is where the Lord said to the paralytic, "Arise, take up your bed and walk."

He [Willibald] also said that there was a great column standing in front of the city gate, which had on top of it a cross as a sign and to remind people of the place where the Jews wanted to carry off the body of St. Mary. For as the eleven Apostles were carrying the body of St. Mary and taking it down from Jerusalem, as soon as they reached the city gate the Jews wanted to seize it from them. But any one of them who reached out to take hold of the bier found that his arms were pinned and stuck to the bier, and that they could not pull them free till, by the grace of God and the prayers of the Apostles, they had been released. Then they left them alone. St. Mary departed this life right in the middle of Jerusalem at the place called Holy Sion. . . .

From there Bishop Willibald went down and came into the Valley of Jehoshaphat. It is situated next to the city of Jerusalem on its eastern side. In the valley is the Church of St. Mary which contains her tomb, not because her body is buried there, but to commemorate her. After he prayed there he went up the Mount of Olives. There is now a church on the Mount of Olives at the place where the Lord prayed before his Passion and said to his disciples, "Watch and pray so you may not enter into temptation." From there he went to the church on the mountain itself, where the Lord ascended into heaven. In the center of it is a square brass thing [candelabrum?] which is beautifully engraved. It is in the center of the church where the Lord ascended into heaven. In the middle of the brass thing is a square lantern with a small candle inside; the lantern encloses the candle on all sides. It is enclosed in this way so it will continue to burn, both in rain and sunshine. That church is open at the top and has no roof. Inside it, against the north and south walls, stand two columns, to remind people of the two men who said "Men of Galilee, why do you gaze into heavenly?" And anyone who can creep between the wall and the column is freed from his sins.

. . . From there he went to Bethlehem, where the Lord was born, seven miles from Jerusalem. The place where Christ was born was originally an underground cave, and now it is a square room cut in the rock. All around it the earth has been dug out and thrown away, and over it a church has now been built. Over the actual place where our Lord was born an altar now stands, and they have also provided a smaller altar, so that when people want to celebrate Mass inside the cave, they can fetch the smaller altar and carry it there for the time when the Mass is being celebrated, and then carry it away again. The church [above the place] where the Lord was born is a splendid building constructed in the form of a cross. (Life of Willibald, 19-22)

Before he departed, Willibald had two more encounters with the Muslim authorities:

From Jerusalem he went more than three hundred miles to the city of Emesa in Syria, and from that came to the city of Salamiyya at the far end of Syria. He spent the whole of Lent there since he fell sick and could not travel. The companions who were travelling with him went to the Saracen king called Mirmumnus, wishing to ask him for a letter giving them permission to travel. But they could not find the king since he had fled abroad from that district to escape the sickness and plague which devastated the district. Failing to find the king, they returned to stay together in Salamiyya till the week before Easter. Then they returned to Emesa and begged the governor to give them a letter. So he divided them into pairs, and gave each pair a letter, since they could not go all together but had to travel in pairs because in that way it would be easier for them to find food. (Life of Willibald, 26)

Eventually the pilgrims reached Tyre, there to await a ship to take them to Constantinople and then home. But first the problem of "customs" had to be faced:

Earlier on, when he was in Jerusalem, Bishop Willibald had bought him-

*self some balsam and put it into a container. Then he took a cane which
was hollow, and put the container down inside, filling it with mineral
oil. . . . And when they came to the city of Tyre the citizens arrested them
and searched their baggage to discover if they had any concealed contraband, and if they had found anything, they would have at once inflicted
on them the death penalty. So they made a thorough search of everything,
but found nothing apart from this one container belonging to Willibald.
They opened it and smelled to find what was inside it. But when they
smelled the mineral oil, which was on top, inside the cane, but failed to
find the balsam, underneath the mineral oil, in the container, they let them
go. (Life of Willibald, 28)*

Though Willibald was unaware of it, the city that had drawn him to the
East had already been dealt a morbid political wound. In A.D. 716, the
same Caliph Sulayman we saw sitting in state in Jerusalem founded out
of the ruins of Christian Lydda the new city at Ramle near the Mediterranean coast and made it the administrative capital of Palestine. It was the
Umayyads' Caesarea, their own place and so a better place from which to
rule Palestine than an all too Christian Jerusalem. The founding of Ramle
did not affect the sanctity of Jerusalem, merely its claim to secular power
and, of course, the secular prosperity that would follow. [32] How prosperity
followed political power is all too clear in Muqaddasi's description of
Ramle in A.D. 875, a mere century and a half after its foundation:

*Al-Ramle is the capital of Palestine. It is a fine city and well built; its water
is good and plentiful; its fruits are abundant. It combines manifold advantages, situated as it is in the midst of beautiful villages and lordly towns,
near to holy places and pleasant hamlets. Commerce here is prosperous
and means of livelihood easy. There is no finer mosque in Islam than the
one in this city. . . . The capital stands among fruitful fields, walled towns,
and serviceable hospices. It possesses magnificent hostelries and pleasant
baths, dainty foods and various condiments, spacious houses, fine mosques
and broad roads. . . . The chief mosque of al-Ramle is in the market, and
it is even more beautiful and graceful than that of Damascus. It is called
al-Abyad (the White Mosque). . . . I have heard my uncle relate that when
the caliph [Hisham, A.D. 724-743] was about to build the minaret, it was
reported to him that the Christians possessed columns of marble, then
lying buried beneath the sand, which they had prepared for the church of
al-Bali'a [the later Abu Gosh]; thereupon Caliph Hisham informed the
Christians that either they must show him where the columns lay or he
would demolish the church at Lydda in order to use its columns for his
mosque. So the Christians pointed out where they had buried their col-*

umns and they were very thick and tall and beautiful. . . . (Muqaddasi 1896: 32-33)

The Umayyad Haram

The earliest Muslim achievement in Jerusalem would be neither eroded nor even dimmed by Ramle or any other place. The Haram al-Sharif is an Umayyad monument as spectacular in its space, arrangement, and principal edifices in the seventeenth century as in the seventh when it was designed and built. Over the course of the Islamic centuries in Jerusalem the Haram platform has been framed on its western and northern sides with graceful porticoes and the attractive facades of schools and convents, but the eye is still drawn to the space they enclose, and within it, the two domes of the Aqsa and the Rock. We have no description of the place from the Umayyads themselves, but the earliest preserved description of the Haram, that written by Ibn al-Faqih in A.D. 903, still reflects the original achievement: [33]

It is said that the length of the Noble Sanctuary at Jerusalem is 1,500 feet, and its width 1,050 feet. There are (in its buildings) 4,000 beams of wood, 700 pillars (of stone), and 500 brass chains. It is lighted every night by 1,600 lamps, and it is served by 140 slaves. The monthly allowance of olive oil is 100 kists [about 150 quarts] and yearly they provide 400,000 yards of matting, also 25,000 water jars. Within the Noble Sanctuary are sixteen chests for volumes of the Quran set apart for public service, and these manuscripts are the admiration of all men. There are four pulpits for volunteer preachers and one set apart for a salaried preacher; and there are also four tanks for ablutions. On the various roofs, in place of clay, are used 45,000 sheets of lead. To the right of the prayer niche (in the Aqsa Mosque) is a slab on which, in a circle, is written the name of Muhammad—God's blessing be upon him—and on a white stone behind the qibla [that is, the southern] wall, is the inscription: "In the name of God, the Compassionate, the Merciful, Muhammad is God's Apostle. Hamzah [the Prophet's uncle] was his helper." Within the mosque are three enclosures for the women, each enclosure being 105 feet in length. There are within and without (the Haram) altogether fifty gates (and doors). (Le Strange 1890: 161)

In the middle of the Haram area is a platform measuring 450 feet in length, 60 feet across, and its height is 13½ feet. It has six flights of stairways leading up to the Dome of the Rock. The Dome rises in the middle of this platform. The ground-plan of the same measures 150 feet

213

by 150 feet, its height is 105 feet, and its circumference is 540 feet.[34] *In the Dome every night they light 300 lamps. It has four gates roofed over, and at each gate are four doors, and over each gate is a portico of marble. The stone of the Rock measures 51 feet by 40½ feet and beneath the Rock is a cavern in which people pray. This cavern is capable of containing sixty-two persons. The [building of the] Dome is covered with white marble and its roof with red gold. In its walls and high in the drum are fifty-six openings, glazed with glass of various hues; each measures 9 feet in height and 6 spans across. The Dome, which was built by Abd al-Malik ibn Marwan, is supported on twelve piers and thirty pillars. It consists of a dome over a dome [that is, an inner and an outer], on which are sheets of lead and white marble.*

To the east of the Dome of the Rock stands the Dome of the Chain. It is supported by twenty marble columns and its roof is covered with sheets of lead. In front of it [again on the east] is the prayer station of al-Khidr. [35] *The platform occupies the middle of the Haram area. To the north is the Dome of the Prophet and the prayer station of Gabriel; near the Rock is the Dome of the Ascension. (Le Strange 1890: 120-121)*

When these lines were written in the opening years of the tenth century, the Muslims had already for a long time enjoyed an untroubled and almost casual possession of their holy city in Palestine, a place which for them, as for the Christians before them, had no particular political significance that we can now discern. But this city which had passed from Christian to Muslim hands was even then taking on a different kind of importance in the minds of other Christians in lands and for reasons far beyond the thoughts and even the imaginings of the present masters of al-Quds.

—————— 6 ——————

The Uncertain Glory:
Jerusalem Under the Abbasids and
the Fatimids, A.D. 750-1000

At the dawn, when the light of the sun first strikes the Dome and the drum catches the rays, then is this edifice a marvellous sight to behold, and one such that in all of Islam I have not seen the equal; neither have I heard tell of anything built in pagan times that could rival in grace this Dome of the Rock.
—*Muqaddasi*

THE FALL of the Umayyad house in A.D. 750 marked a political turning in Islam away from Jerusalem to other centers and other concerns. The exact nature of the Umayyads' plans for the city remain uncertain for us, but their interest in the place and their willingness to invest the resources of empire in the Holy City are still visible in their magnificent religious buildings atop the Haram al-Sharif and in the recently excavated ruins of their ambitious secular constructions at its southern foot. The succeeding dynasty of the Abbasids neither denied nor denigrated the Muslim sanctity of Jerusalem—its religious prestige was already too well established for that—but their acknowledgment often appears to be little more than that, a respectful nod, perfunctory at times, in the direction of Jerusalem from their distant capital of Baghdad.

The Abbasids and the Holy City

The earliest Abbasid caliphs, al-Mansur (A.D. 754-775) and al-Mahdi (A.D. 775-785), visited the Holy City, out of piety perhaps, but surely with political aims in mind as well. Then even this custom ceased, and the caliphs were no longer to be seen in the holy city even as pilgrims, though they continued scrupulously to visit Mecca. [1] Jerusalem sat, after all, in the former Umayyad heartland. If the Abbasids had no political plans for the city, however, as surely they did not, they still could not afford to neglect it or its obvious need for repair on occasion, as when al-Mansur somewhat grudgingly addressed the needs of the crumbling Aqsa Mosque:

Abd al-Rahman ibn Muhammad ibn Mansur ibn Thabit reports from his father who had it from his grandfather that all the gates [of the Aqsa Mosque] were covered with plates of gold and silver at the time of Abd al-Malik. But when Abu Ja'far al-Mansur the Abbasid came, the eastern and western parts [of the Aqsa Mosque] had fallen down. "Commander of the Faithful," they told him, "the eastern and western parts of the sanctuary were thrown down in the earthquake of 130 [A.D. 746]. Will you order the sanctuary to be restored?" "I have no money," he answered. Then he ordered that the plates of gold and silver that covered the doors be removed. It was so done and they converted them into dinars and dirhams which would serve to pay for the reconstruction. . . . (Mujir 1876: 59)

But in the days of the Abbasids occurred the earthquakes that threw down most of the main building; all, in fact, except that portion around the prayer niche. Now when the caliph of that day [al-Mahdi, A.D. 775-785] received news of this, he inquired and learned that the sum at that time in the treasury would in no wise suffice to restore the mosque. So he wrote to the governors of the provinces and to other amirs that each should undertake the building of a colonnade. The order was carried out and the edifice rose firmer and more substantial than it had ever been in former times. The more ancient section remained, however, even like a beauty spot, in the midst of the new; and it extends as far as the limit of the marble columns, for beyond, where the columns are of concrete, the later part begins. . . . (Muqaddasi 1896: 41-42)

The first restoration noted above probably took place in A.D. 771, when Mansur visited Jerusalem and could take personal note of the devastating effect of the earthquake that had occurred in A.D. 746, the same that threw down the New Church put up by Justinian (which, unlike the Muslim shrine, was never rebuilt). Both buildings were constructed over vaulted substructures, but the earthquakes that seemed particularly frequent in Jerusalem from late antiquity into the Middle Ages were especially destructive of the mosque perched on the southern end of Herod's artificially constructed platform. Al-Mahdi made his repairs sometime about A.D. 780, and his son Ma'mun (A.D. 813-833) likewise contributed to rebuilding there, as well as somewhat ungenerously removing Abd al-Malik's name from the dedicatory inscription in the Dome of the Rock and squeezing in his own, though without bothering to change the date. [2]

The fortune of Palestine under the Abbasids was not a happy one. Some of the problems were acts of God or nature—plagues, drought, and famine—but they were enlarged and exaggerated by what can only be construed as Abbasid indifference. The natural disasters were soon followed by political and social ones, including a peasant revolt at the time of Caliph Mu'tasim, whose seriousness is underlined, as Goitein has pointed out, by the mere fact that it was noted by the Muslim chroniclers, who generally ignored the affairs of such a minor provincial outpost as Jerusalem. [3]

Harun and Charlemagne

One Abbasid caliph does, however, loom large in at least the Western perception of Jerusalem during this period, though probably with little foundation in fact. Harun al-Rashid (A.D. 786-809) stands at the height of Abbasid glory, just as his contemporary Charlemagne does in the emerging Roman-Frankish state in Europe. The two rulers likely did have diplomatic contacts, and though they were ignored by Muslim chroniclers, later Latin writers in the West enlarged them to embrace the Holy City of Jerusalem, and indeed brought Charlemagne to the city on pilgrimage. [4] Benedict, writing about the year A.D. 1000, two centuries after the supposed event, reports:

Then Charles came to the Most Holy Tomb of Our Lord and Savior Jesus Christ, which is also the place of the Resurrection. He adorned the holy place with gold and jewels, and he also placed on it a large gold standard. Amongst all the holy places he especially adorned the Manger of the Lord [in Bethlehem] and his Tomb, for King Aaron [Harun] granted him permission to do as he wished. And what garments and spices and wealth of eastern treasures he presented to Charles! Then going on, the Most Wise King went with King Aaron as far as Alexandria, and the Franks and the Hagarenes rejoiced together as if they were blood brothers. So Charles said farewell to King Aaron and returned to his own country. (Benedict, Chronicle, 23)

There is no evidence, certainly not in Eginhard's contemporary *Life of Charlemagne*, to support this reported visit of the emperor to Jerusalem. Eginhard does mention an embassy to Harun, an exchange of gifts, and, as the Crusader historian William of Tyre reports, quoting from Eginhard's *Life*, perhaps something more as well:

. . . That rare and praiseworthy monarch, Harun, surnamed Rashid. He ruled over the entire East, and even to this day his liberality, unusual courtesy, and most excellent character are the subject of deep admiration and undying praise in the East.

The good will between Harun and the Christians [of Jerusalem] rested on an admirable treaty which the devout Emperor Charles, of immortal memory, brought about through the work of frequent envoys who went back and forth between them. The gracious favor of that potentate was a source of much comfort to the faithful, so that they seemed to be living under the rule of Emperor Charles rather than that of Harun. In the life of that famous monarch, we read as follows: "With Harun, king of the Persians, who ruled over almost the entire world except India, his relations were so harmonious that the prince preferred his favor above the friendship of all the kings and potentates of the earth. . . . When the ambassadors sent by Charles to visit the Most Holy Sepulcher and the place of the Resurrection of the Lord and Savior came to Harun with gifts and made known their master's wishes, he not only granted them what they asked but gave them possession of that sacred and blessed place, that it might be regarded as placed under the power of Charles. When they returned, he sent his own ambassadors with them as bearers of magnificent gifts for the king. . . ."

Charles sent frequent and liberal relief to the faithful who were living in Jerusalem under the power of the infidels and likewise extended the work of piety to those who dwelled in Egypt and Africa under the ungodly Saracens. . . . (William of Tyre 1943: 64-65)

In connection with this same exchange, Eginhard mentions that the patriarch of Jerusalem sent as a "blessing" to Charlemagne the keys of the Holy Sepulcher and of Calvary together with a banner. Much has been made of this, even to crediting Charlemagne with a kind of Frankish "protectorate" over the Holy Land, and not coincidentally perhaps, chiefly by French authors writing in the 1920s when France enjoyed a mandate over parts of the Near East, even as they did when William of Tyre was composing his *History*. [5] Even granted the gifts to the Holy City, which we have no reason to doubt, there is no independent evidence from any source to indicate that Harun had surrendered his sovereignty over Palestine, or even Jerusalem, to the distant Frankish monarch. [6]

Charlemagne and Jerusalem

But we are not in the realm of pure legend. Two documents give unmistakable contemporary and eyewitness testimony that Charlemagne had interests, if not jurisdiction, in Jerusalem. [7] The first is an anonymous *Memorandum on the Houses of God and Monasteries in the Holy City*, the so-called *Commemoratorium*, written about A.D. 808 for Charlemagne and intended as a report on the churches and other Christian establishments in Palestine:[8]

Summary of a Memorandum on the Churches and Monasteries in the Holy City of Jerusalem and its neighborhood; also on the bishops, priests, deacons and monks who make up the clergy who serve in these holy places or in monasteries of women.

First at the Holy Sepulcher of the Lord: nine priests, fourteen deacons, six subdeacons, twenty-three canonical clergy, thirteen guardians called fragelites, forty-one monks, twelve attendants who carry candles before the patriarch, seventeen servants of the patriarch, two superiors, two treasurers, two scribes, two guardians. The priests who look after the Lord's Sepulcher: one for Holy Calvary, two for the Lord's Chalice, two for the Holy Cross and the Headcloth, and one deacon. One secretary who orders everything after the patriarch, two cellarers, one treasurer, one guardian of the springs, nine porters. There are 150 people in all, not counting the three guestmasters.

The Holy Sepulcher, then, appears undisturbed and fully staffed a century and a half after the Muslim takeover of Jerusalem. Charlemagne's establishment nearby appears somewhat later on the list, however:

From the empire of the Lord Charles, serving at the Lord's Sepulcher, seventeen women vowed to God, one anchoress from Spain. . . .

Mount Sion too seems to be much as it was before:

At Holy Sion seventeen priests and clergy, not counting two who are vowed to God as hermits. . . .

Not so the Nea of Justinian:

At New St. Mary, built by Emperor Justinian, twelve [attendants]. . . . [to which the anonymous author later adds:] The Church of St. Mary which was [thrown] down by the earthquake and engulfed by the earth has side walls thirty-nine dexteri long and a facade thirty-five dexteri wide; inside it is thirty-two wide and fifty long. . . .

One must assume then that the twelve clerics assigned to the Nea were no longer connected with the church but possibly with surviving parts of the hospice facilities. The document continues:

At St. Mary, where she was born at the Probatica, five and twenty-five women vowed to God as anchoresses. . . .
    At the three churches on the holy Mount of Olives:
    First, the Ascension of Christ [the Imbomon], three priests and clergy.
    Second, the church where Christ taught his disciples [that is, the Eleona], three monks, one priest.
    Third, the church dedicated to St. Mary, two clergy. Of hermits living in cells and holding offices in Greek, eleven; in Georgian, four; in Syriac, six; in Armenian, two; in Latin, five; in the Saracen tongue [Arabic], one.
    Near the steps as you ascend to the Holy Mount [of Olives] two hermits (one Greek, the other Syrian); at the top of the steps in Gethsemane:

*three hermits, a Greek, a Syrian, and a Georgian; in the Valley of Jehosh-
aphat: one hermit and cells for twenty-five women.*

*Descending from Jerusalem into the Valley of Jehoshaphat, at the place
of St. Mary's tomb there are 195 steps, and going up to the Mount of
Olives, 537.*

Thus far Christian Jerusalem appears as we might expect it after its deci-
mation at the hands of the Persians in 614. The churches and convents
were not so many as the sixth-century Madaba map indicates, but those
that were there and open appear to have been functioning normally. It is
only in the final financial summary of the *Commemoratorium* that the fact
of Muslim sovereignty appears:

Annual expenses of the patriarch:
*630 gold solidi among the priests, deacons, monks, clergy and the whole
    congregation of the church.*
540 solidi [for the servants].
300 solidi for church materiel.
140 solidi for the [churches in the city].
580 solidi paid to the Saracens.
[. . . solidi] for Saracen servants. (Commemoratorium)

The Christian community had to pay what appears to be a collective poll-
tax of 580 gold solidi to the Muslims, here collected and paid by the
patriarch, as the principal Christian official in the city, to the qadi, or
Muslim chief justice, of Jerusalem. [9]

The second witness to Charlemagne's contribution to Jerusalem is the
monk Bernard, who was in Jerusalem about A.D. 870:

*From Ramle we pushed on to the village of Emmaus, and from Emmaus
we arrived at the Holy City of Jerusalem, where we stayed in the hospice
of the Most Glorious Emperor Charles. All who come to Jerusalem for
reasons of devotion and who speak the Roman [Latin] language are admitted there. Close to it there is a church in honor of St. Mary, and thanks
to the aforesaid emperor, it has a splendid library, and twelve dwellings
with fields, vineyards, and a garden, in the Valley of Jehoshaphat. In front
of this hospice is the market, and anyone who does his business there pays
the person in charge an annual fee of two gold pieces. (Bernard, Itinerary,
10)*

The Christian Sites under Islam

Thus it appears from the *Commemoratorium* and Bernard's narrative, both
of them ninth-century documents, that Charlemagne had endowed a hos-

pice, church, and convent for the use of Latin pilgrims to Jerusalem. The entire complex was located across from the Church of the Holy Sepulcher in an area that in Hadrian's day had been the imperial forum and was still functioning as a commercial center when Bernard visited the city. It was in this same location, today called the Muristan, that the Latins continued to build facilities down to and through the time of the Latin Kingdom of the Crusaders.

Bernard also gives us a rather careful look at other aspects of Jerusalem in the last quarter of the ninth century—not the whole city, of course, for he was a pilgrim, and in this era at least, Christian visitors confined their attention rather narrowly to the holy places that were the object of their journey. Chief among these was Constantine's fourth-century complex still standing at the site of Jesus' death and burial:

Among the churches inside the city there are four that are particularly notable, and their walls adjoin each other. One is on the east, and inside it are Mount Calvary and the place where the Lord's Cross was found; this one is called the Basilica of Constantine. There is another one to the south and a third on the west, and in the center of this latter is the Lord's Sepulcher. Around the Sepulcher are nine columns and the walls between them are made of the very best stone. . . . It is not necessary to write a great deal about this Sepulcher because Bede says quite enough about it in his history.

These churches [around the Sepulcher] have between them an unroofed court, with its walls ablaze with gold and a paved floor of the most precious stone. From each of the four churches runs a chain, and the point where the four chains join in the center of this garden is said to be the center of the world.

Moreover, in this city there is another church to the south, on Mount Sion, called St. Simeon's, where the Lord washed the feet of his disciples, and in this the Lord's crown of thorns hangs. This is the church where we are told St. Mary died. Nearby on the east is the church in honor of St. Stephen, where he is said to have been stoned. [10] *And further east is the church in honor of blessed Peter, on the spot where he denied the Lord. To the north is the Temple of Solomon, which contains a Saracen synagogue.* [11]

Bernard then visited the eastern side of Jerusalem, down into the Kedron Valley, already identified as the site of the Last Judgment, then went up onto the Mount of Olives:

Going outside of Jerusalem we went down into the Valley of Jehoshaphat, a mile away from the city, which contains the garden of Gethsemane and the place of St. Mary's birth, and a large church has been built there in her honor. In this garden there is also a round church of St. Mary which contains her tomb, but it has no roof and suffers badly from rain. In that same place there is also a church where the Lord was betrayed, with the four round tables at which he had supper. There is another church in the Valley of Jehoshaphat, which is in honor of St. Leontius, and to this the Lord is said to be coming for judgment.

From this we proceeded to the Mount of Olives, on the slopes of which we were shown the place where the Lord made his prayer to the Father [that is, the Eleona]. Also on the mountain side is shown the place where the Pharisees brought the woman taken in adultery; it has a church in honor of St. John where they keep some writing on marble which the Lord wrote on the earth. On the top of this celebrated mountain, a mile away from the Valley of Jehoshaphat, is the place where the Lord ascended to the Father. The church there [the Imbomon] is round and has no roof, and in the middle of it, that is, at the place of the Lord's Ascension, is an open-air altar at which they celebrate the rites of the Mass. . . . As you go down the western slope of the Mount of Olives you are shown a stone from which the Lord mounted the foal of an ass, and nearby to the south, in the Valley of Jehoshaphat, is the pool of Siloam. (Bernard, Itinerary, 11-16)

Muslims and Christians

The Muslims are invisible in this portrait of Jerusalem, which is about holy places, and except for the one passing allusion to the "Saracen synagogue," so are the Muslims' shrines. But Bernard was aware that there was a different political order in the East, and once outside of Jerusalem, where his vision was drawn only to the places of Christian veneration, his account opens up somewhat to provide glimpses of other vistas, like this revealing incident in Egypt:

As soon as we came to Babylon [near the site of Fustat in Egypt], the city guards led us away to the prince, a Saracen called Adelacham,[12] who inquired of us the purpose of our journey and the names of the princes who had given us letters. So we showed him our letters from Suldanus [the sultan] and the chief man of Alexandria. Which availed us nothing: he put us in prison. Then, with the help of God, we each paid a fee of thirteen dinars. He too gave us letters, and all who read them in whatever city or place we visited dared not extort any more from us, and this was because he was the second in authority after the Amarmominus [that is, Amir al-Mu'minin, Commander of the Faithful, the caliph] whom we have mentioned. Even so, whenever we entered any of the cities which we shall be describing, we were never allowed to leave until we had been given a parchment or a sealed document, and this cost us a dinar or two to obtain.

This city has a patriarch, the Lord Michael, who by the grace of God rules over all the bishops, monks, and Christians of Egypt [patriarch of Alexandria, though resident in Fustat, 859-871]. These Christians have this agreement with the heathen, that each one pays for himself every year a tribute to the prince, so they may have the right to live in freedom and security: the payment demanded is three gold pieces [for the wealthy] or two or one or, from poorer persons, thirteen dinars. And anyone who cannot pay the thirteen dinars, whether he is a native Christian or a stranger, is imprisoned either till such time as God in his love sends an angel to set him free, or else until some other good Christians pay for his freedom. (Bernard, Itinerary, 7)

These will all become familiar themes in the later pilgrims' accounts: the poll-tax and the other fees attached, legally or illegally, to entry into cities and shrines; the need for some kind of patronage or protection; and the Muslims' fear, particularly at the outset, that many of these Christian visitors, whose motives for being so far from home may have been inexplicable to them, were actually spies, though for whom and to what end is never made explicit.

Not all of Bernard's impressions of Muslim rule in the East were negative, however:

Finally, I must tell you how Christians observe God's law in Jerusalem and Egypt. The Christians and pagans have this kind of peace between them, such that if I were travelling, and the camel or donkey which bore my poor luggage were to die on the way, and I left all my belongings there without any guardian, and went off to the city for another animal, I would find everything unharmed when I came back. Such is the peace there. But any traveller who stays in a city, or goes on a journey by sea or any other way, and is found walking by night or by day without a paper or a stamp issued by one of the kings or princes of that country, is sent to prison straightway until such time as he can explain that he is not a spy. (Bernard, Itinerary, 23)

Jewish Endowments in Jerusalem

The Jews are as invisible as the Muslims in Bernard's description of Jerusalem, but they were assuredly present from the time of the Muslim conquest, as we have already seen, when they were allowed to resettle in the city for the first time since Hadrian banned their presence in A.D. 135. Their presence becomes more distinct to our eyes about A.D. 800, when references to the Jerusalem community begin to appear in contemporary Jewish documents.[13] Among the first reporting is a Rabbi Ahima'as, an Italian who, like Bernard, was in Jerusalem on pilgrimage, and perhaps no more than two years before the Christian monk:

At that time there was a Jew named Rabbi Ahima'as who went up to Jerusalem, the glorious city, three times with his vowed offerings. Each time he went, he took with him 100 pieces of gold, as he had vowed to the Rock of his salvation, to aid those who were engaged in Torah study and for those who mourned the ruined House of His Glory. . . . (Ahima'as 1924: 65, trans. R. Harari)

In the same source reference is also made to the famous Rabbi Paltiel, the head of the Jewish community in Egypt under the Fatimids:

Once, on the Day of Atonement, when Rabbi Paltiel was summoned to read from the Torah, the whole assembly arose and remained standing in his presence: the sages, the scholars who were in the school, the young students and the elders, boys and children; the entire community was standing. He said to them: "Let the old be seated and the young stand. If you refuse that, then I will sit down and refuse to read, for this does not seem proper to me."

When he had finished the reading, he vowed to the God of his praise 5,000 dinars of genuine and full value: 1,000 for the head of the Yeshiva and sages, 1,000 for the Mourners of the Sanctuary, 1,000 for the Yeshiva of the Geonim at Babylon, 1,000 for the poor and needy in various communities, and 1,000 for the exaltation of the Torah, for the purchase of the necessary oil.

In the morning he arose early and hurried off, for he was always zealous in observing the Law, so that his evil inclination might not prevail over him to prevent him from carrying out his good intention. He hired men, horses, and mules, provided guards, and sent them to accompany the caravans that travelled through the deserts [of Sinai]. They delivered the gold pieces, as Rabbi Paltiel their master had ordered, and they distributed them among the schools and synagogues, and the Mourners of Sion and the poor of the communities of Israel.

In that year Rabbi Paltiel died. He was the leader of the people of God who were settled in Egypt and Palestine, in Palermo [that is, in all of Sicily], and in all the territories of the Ishmaelites. For he ruled over the (ancient) kingdom of the Hebrews, over that of the Syrians and the Egyptians, over the domains of the Ishmaelites and the land of Israel. . . .

His place was taken by his son Rabbi Samuel, a great and respected man in his time, who worthily filled the place of his forefathers. He brought (to Jerusalem) the remains of his father and his mother in caskets, as well as the bones of Rabbi Hananel, his father's uncle, which had been embalmed in balsam. He dedicated in the name of the Most High, so that it might be accounted righteousness for himself by Him who dwells in the clouds, 20,000 gold drachmas for the poor and the afflicted and the scholars and instructors who were teaching the Torah, and for teachers of children and readers (of prayer); and oil for the inner altar of the sanctuary at the western wall; and for the synagogues and communities, far and near; and for those who were mourning the loss of the Temple, those who grieved and mourned for Sion; and for the teachers and their students in the Yeshiva (in Jerusalem); and for the scholars of Babylon in the Yeshiva of the Geonim (there). (Ahima'as 1924: 95-97, trans. R. Harari)

The Paltiel of Ahima'as' *Chronicle* is a familiar figure. Under the Fatimid caliph al-Mu'izz (A.D. 953-975) he enjoyed an officially recognized status as the nagid, or "chief of the Jews," within the Fatimid realms. He appears to have been a powerful figure at court, and it was perhaps he who won permission for the Jews to return for prayer to the Temple precinct. They were banned from that area in Salman ben Yeruham's day, as seen in Chapter Five, but once the Fatimids took Jerusalem in A.D. 970, the Jews were permitted to take up their devotions at that mysterious "inner altar of the sanctuary at the western wall" for which Paltiel's son and successor brought a gift of oil to Jerusalem. Where was this place? Certainly not atop the Haram or Temple mount itself, as was once maintained. [14] A more likely possibility, since there are frequent references in the pre-Crusader Jewish sources to a cave which served as a synagogue somewhere near the Haram, is an underground chamber *within* the western platform wall. It stands behind what is now called Barclay's Gate and was later used by the Muslims as a mosque named after the miraculous steed Buraq who bore Muhammad on his Night Journey. [15]

The Presence of God at the Western Wall

If this suggestion is correct and there was in Fatimid times a synagogue located in the interior of the western wall of Herod's Temple platform, none of the brief and scattered references to it makes any reference to what is today, and has been in a verifiable fashion from the beginning of the sixteenth century onward, the chief site of Jewish public cultus in the Holy City at that same site, the celebrated "Western Wall." This latter is a stretch of massive Herodian stonework on the the western side of his

Temple platform, running, until 1967, for about ninety feet between the Gate of the Chain Street on the north to the Maghrebi Gate entry to the Haram on the south. It was connected by a later generation of Jews with a far older tradition that held that God's presence, in Hebrew his *Shekhinah*, would never leave the Western Wall.

That tradition occurs in its earliest form in those collections of biblical exegesis known as the Midrash Rabbah, in that on the Song of Songs, for example, from the seventh or eighth century, where it is said, reflecting on the verse "There he stands outside our wall" (2:9): "Behold He [God] stands behind our wall, behind the western wall of the Temple, which the Holy One, blessed be He, swore would never be destroyed. The Priest's Gate and the Huldah Gate will also never be destroyed until the Almighty renews them." Or again in the Exodus Rabbah of the tenth century, where a certain Rabbi Aha is reported to have said: "The Presence of God never leaves the Western Wall."

Two of the exegetical works that make up the Midrash Rabbah, that on Lamentations from about the fifth century and that on Ecclesiastes from perhaps the seventh, give extended, identical, and obviously legendary accounts of why the wall in question was not destroyed:

When he [Vespasian] conquered [Jerusalem], he divided its four walls between four commanders, and it was Pengar who got the western gate [pylê] ... and from heaven they decreed that it should not be destroyed. Why? Because the Presence of God (Shekhinah) is in the west. ... They [that is, the other three commanders] destroyed the sections that had been assigned to them but he [Pengar] did not destroy his. Vespasian sent for him and said to him: "Why did you not destroy your section?" He answered: "By your life! I did it for the glory of the empire, because had I destroyed it nobody would ever have known what you had destroyed. Now, people will see and say 'Look at Vespasian's power! what (a strong city) he destroyed!'" Vespasian said to him, "By your life! You have spoken well, but because you did not obey my order, you will go up to the summit and throw yourself down (to your death). If he lives, he lives; if he dies, he dies." Pengar went up and threw himself down and he died. ... (Lamentations Rabbah 1:31, trans. D. Nelson)

This story is a transparent retelling of an incident related by Josephus (*War* VII, 1, 1-2) and already cited in Chapter Three. In the original version Titus himself did indeed spare part of the western side of the city, the three Herodian towers that formed the Citadel; and he did so in order to allow future generations to understand the might of the city he had fought and conquered. What this seventh-century retelling cannot mean, of course, is that the emperor or one of his commanders left one of the

Temple walls standing, which they did not, or that they destroyed three sides of the Herodian platform and spared the fourth; the platform base they left intact on all four sides, as far as we can tell. The tradents of the Midrash Rabbah knew this perfectly well, and we can only assume that God's continued presence was a spiritual one and not precisely localized by them or by any one else of those generations immediately preceding and following the rise of Islam.

This assumption is confirmed by most of the evidence we have at hand until the sixteenth century. When the Jews made public prayer in Jerusalem, they made it atop or around the Mount of Olives or at the eastern gate, which was called by them and the Muslims the "Gate of Mercy" and by the Christians the "Golden Gate." [16]

But all history apart, the traditions were being knit together: Temple, wall, stone, and Ark, as in this text, for example, from the influential codification of Jewish law written about 1180 by one of medieval Judaism's most revered and widely read authors, Maimonides:

There was a stone in the Holy of Holies, at its western wall, upon which the Ark rested. In front of it stood the jar of manna and the staff of Aaron. When Solomon built the Temple, knowing that it was destined to be destroyed, he built underneath, in deep and winding tunnels, a place in which to hide the Ark. It was King Josiah who commanded the Ark be hidden in the place which Solomon had prepared; as it is said: "And he said unto the Levites that taught all Israel, "Put the Holy Ark in the house which Solomon the son of David did build; there shall no more be a burden on your shoulders; now serve the Lord your God" (2 Chron. 35:3). (Maimonides 1957: 17)

The Mourners for Sion

One Jewish group engaged in what appears to be the performance of liturgical prayer in Jerusalem, and likely somewhere in the vicinity of the Temple, are the "Mourners for Sion" already noted in Ahima'as' *Chronicle*. This is not the first time they are mentioned; they occur somewhat earlier, in the midrash written about A.D. 845, possibly by an immigrant to Palestine from Europe, and called *Pesikta Rabbati*: [17]

"Rejoice greatly, O daughter of Sion, shout, O daughter of Jerusalem; behold thy king cometh unto thee, he is submissive, and yet he promises salvation; afflicted and he is riding upon an ass, even upon the colt of the foal of an ass" (Zech. 9:9). . . . What did Isaiah have in mind when he spoke this verse? He spoke it with a view to comforting the Mourners for

Sion, to whom the Holy One, blessed be He, will give victory over their enemies. . . . The Holy One, blessed be He, will stand by them with His arm, in answer to the prayer "O Lord, be gracious unto us; we have waited for Thee; be Thou their arm every morning, our deliverance also in time of distress" (Isa. 33:2).

The phrase "every morning" alludes to those who rise up every morning to beseech mercy, [and] alludes particularly to the Mourners for Sion who yearn for deliverance morning, evening, and noon. Now the Mourners for Sion suffered great distress because it was Children of Israel who both mocked and scorned them. But when these Children of Israel see the afflictions decreed by God for the years immediately preceding that extraordinary year in which the Messiah is to appear amidst Israel, and when they see that the afflictions follow one upon another without ceasing, then at last they will understand that it was because of the unending prayers of the Mourners for Sion that the Messiah will appear. . . .

"All that see them shall acknowledge them" [Isa. 61:9]—all will acknowledge the Mourners for Sion with whom the Holy One, blessed be He, will specially concern Himself. For during the time immediately preceding the appearance of the Messiah, the Holy One, blessed be He, will increase the number of the angels of destruction hovering over His world, and these will take their toll of those Children of Israel who scorned the possibility of redemption. In that time the Mourners for Sion will walk among and beside the angels of destruction like a man visiting with his fellow man, for the angels of destruction will do no harm to the Mourners for Sion. And the Children of Israel, dumbfounded, will say: "Without justification we made sport of the Mourners for Sion. Without justification we mocked their words." . . . (Pesikta Rabbati 1968: 663-665)

It is surely to this same group that Ahima'as, Paltiel, and his son Samuel all made substantial donations. We must assume that early on Jews of not only scholarly and legal interests but those with a pietistic and even apocalyptic bent were assembling in the Holy City, just as Jerusalem had earlier attracted Christian monks and ascetics and even then was beginning to serve as magnet for the Muslim mystics and pietists, like the community in Jerusalem called the Karramites who are mentioned by Muqaddasi in A.D. 985:

There is a community of Karramites at Jerusalem who possess a cloister and a house of assembly. These latter are a sect who make great pretensions in matters of theology, jurisprudence, and piety, but among themselves they dispute, and in their reading of the Quran they adopt the most literal interpretation. (Muqaddasi 1896: 67)

A Call to Aliya

Unlike their Christian and Muslim counterparts, the Mourners for Sion, had something in mind other than their own salvation or perfection in conducting thcir devotions in Jerusalem. They were praying for the restoration of Israel, not in any political sense, of course, which would have been unthinkable at that time and place, but rather in the spirit of what might be called a "spiritual Zionism." How seriously that ideal was taken by some is revealed in the following tract on that subject by Daniel al-Kumisi, written at the end of the ninth century:

You should know that it is the villains of Israel who say to one another "We are not obliged to go to Jerusalem until He gathers us just as He has scattered us." These are the words of those who anger (God) and of fools. Even if God had not commanded us to go to Jerusalem from the countries (of the Disapora) in lamentation and bitterness, we would nevertheless know, by virtue of our own intelligence, that there is an obligation upon all those who suffered from (God's) anger to come to the Gate of the Angry to supplicate Him, as I have written above. . . .

You, God-fearers, must therefore come to Jerusalem, dwell there and become its guardians until the rebuilding of Jerusalem. . . . One should not say: "How can I go up to Jerusalem for fear of bandits and robbers or for fear of not being able to earn a livelihood in Jerusalem? . . ." Are there not nations besides Israel who come from the four corners (of the earth) to Jerusalem every year to be in the awe of the Lord? Why it is that you, our brethren of Israel, do not do as the other nations of the world do and come and pray . . . ? If you do not come because you covet and are obsessed with your merchandise, then (at least) send five men from each city with enough (money) to support them, so that we can become a united group to supplicate our Lord continuously in the mountains of Jerusalem. . . . You will have no excuse before God if you do not return to God's Torah and His commandments, as it is written in His Torah. . . . From the beginning of the Exile the rabbis were officials and judges during the Greek monarchy, the reign of the Greek kings, the Roman monarchy, and the Persian Magus (and so) those who taught the (true) Torah could not open their mouths with God's commandments out of fear of the rabbis . . . until the coming of the Ishmaelites [the Muslims] since they are constantly helpful in aiding the Karaites to observe the Torah of Moses. . . . (Mann 1922: 134-136, trans. R. Harari)

The Karaites in Jerusalem

The Karaites of this text are a group to whose number the writer Daniel himself belonged and who stood in profound disagreement with the prevailing rabbinic teaching in Jerusalem and elsewhere. The Karaites, who originated among the Jews of "Babylonia," that is, in Iraq, arrived early in Jerusalem, probably very early in the ninth century. [18] They were quickly attracted to the Mourners for Sion movement, and the emphasis on a "return" became a powerful element in Karaite preaching, as this tract of Daniel al-Kumisi reveals. Some were willing to go even further. The following piece of audacious Karaite exegesis of Genesis 16 boldly suggests so to a tenth-century reader for whom "Ishmaelite" meant only one people, the Muslim Arabs presently exercising sovereignty over Jerusalem and the entire East:

It says: "And he shall be a man like the wild ass" (Gen. 16:12), that is to say, like an animal that dwells in the desert, so your son Ishmael will find shelter in the desert. And with this, she [Hagar] realized that Ishmael her son would have no portion in the land of Canaan, short of a foothold. With this statement he [God?] disabused her of her view and so obliged her to return and submit to Sarah because the promises (made to Abraham) would not be fulfilled in her son.

When Abraham and Sarah heard this statement from her, they rejoiced, understanding that he [Abraham] would still be blessed by other seed, from her or from another woman, because Sarah was an old woman, and that the promise would be fulfilled. Sarah too was astonished to hear Hagar, imagining that Abraham would have a child from her [Hagar] or from another woman.

Then the announcement was made that Abraham would have another son, and he was Isaac and it was he of whom the promises had been spoken.

And it says: "His hand shall be against every man" (Gen. 16:12), meaning that at the end of his lifetime Ishmael will enter a settled area and will dwell in settlements, and will reign over settlements and rule nations. Of this it is written in Daniel (11:24): "In time of peace he will overrun the richest districts of the province and succeed in doing what his fathers and forefathers failed to do, distributing spoil, booty, and property to his followers, etc." At first he will come forth with only a few people and he will manipulate with plots and cunning, as it says, "he will enter into fraudulent alliances, and although the people behind him are but few, he will rise to power" (Dan. 11:23). And he will stretch his arm upon the nations, as it says: "His hand shall be against every man." This is what Zechariah has said (6:4) "(The chariot) with the roan horse went forth (to the east), and they were eager to go and range over the whole earth." So he said "Go and range over the earth," and they did so.

The roan horses are the Ishmaelites from whom some Arab tribes *emerged with the "Defective."[19] They took the kingship from the Midianites, from (Shah) Yazdgard [A.D. 635-651], of whom it is written: "A contemptible creature will succeed" (Dan. 11:21), and he is called "the Little Horn" (Dan. 7:8), of which it is said, "and three of the first horns were uprooted to make way for it" (ibid.). [20]*

There was no nation in the world that had happen to it what happened to Ishmael. No one spoke like it, as it was written: "And a mouth speaking great things" (Dan. 7:8). Of its leaders it is said "a king shall appear, harsh and grim, a master of strategem" (Dan. 8:23). At first the Ishmaelite nation lived in the desert and did not have the "yoke of kingship," as it is written, "a wild ass used to the wilderness snuffing the wind in her lust." And when this nation grew up it entered the settled areas and imposed its yoke on kingdoms and on deserts. And they did not leave these places and they are in their hands up to this day, a period of 372 years [from the hijrah, that is, A.D. 982]. . . . And just as the saying "His hand shall be against every man's" was fulfilled, so shall the saying "and every man's hand shall be against him" will (also) be fulfilled, as it is written in Habakkuk (2:8) "Because you have plundered many mighty nations, all the rest of the world will plunder you." (Sokolow 1981: 313-316, trans. R. Arav)

The Karaites became a powerful force in Jerusalem, and as the passage from Daniel also suggests, one factor in their growth may have been the sympathy of the Egyptian governor Ahmad ibn Tulun, who also controlled Palestine. In A.D. 878 that ruler effectively declared his independence of the caliph in Baghdad, a step that would make him particularly susceptible to Karaite arguments that the Jerusalem rabbis owed their allegiance to a religious leader, the Jewish exilarch, who resided in caliphal Baghdad, while they, the Karaites, were totally independent of Iraq. [21]

The differences between the two groups, Karaites and the rabbis of the schools, ran through almost every aspect of Jewish life, from a denial of the oral law upon which the Mishna and Talmud rested, through the dietary laws derived from that tradition, down to details of synagogue worship and the hairdressers used by the Rabbanite women[22]—to these popular practices denounced by the Karaite Sahl ibn Masliah, though it is difficult to imagine that they were encouraged by the rabbis:

How can I be silent while idolatrous ways exist among the Jews? They sit by the graves, take up lodgings by the vaults, and speak to the dead, saying: "R. Yose the Galilean, cure me," or "impregnate me." And they light candles at the graves of the saints, burn incense on bricks before them, tie bundles on the palm tree of the graves of the dead saints, make vows to them, call to them and ask them to grant their requests. (Mann 1931: II, 56, trans. R. Harari)

The Jerusalem Yeshiva

The Karaites established themselves in Muslim Jerusalem at a relatively late date, however. The first Jews to take up formal residence there were the rabbis of Tiberias, the spiritual and intellectual descendents of the Yohanan ben Zakkai, whom we saw escape from Jerusalem in A.D. 70 to found an academy at Yabneh. [23] Out of that school, which eventually found a more or less permanent home in Tiberias in Galilee, came the literary and legal foundations of rabbinic Judaism, namely, the oral law redacted about A.D. 200 into the Mishna and the commentaries of succeeding generations of rabbis that constitute the "Jerusalem Talmud." [24] As far as authorship is concerned, the latter name is singularly inappropriate since none of those scholars who contributed to it could live, study, or teach in Jerusalem.

In 638 that situation changed, and shortly after the Muslim conquest, the Yeshiva, as it was subsequently called, moved from Tiberias to its natural home in Jerusalem. Though in modern usage the word "yeshiva" most generally means "school," the newly constituted Jerusalem Yeshiva was hardly that; it was rather, as Goitein has defined it, "a council of learned men who discussed and decided questions of religious belief, law, and ritual addressed to them or questions which arose during their own study of the sacred texts." [25] The Yeshiva was, then, part curia, part tribunal, school, and legislative body; and its head, the "gaon," had acknowledged jurisdiction over all the Jews of the "Western" Diaspora, while his counterparts in Iraq were the chief legal authority for the Jews of the Muslim "East."

Thanks to the documents uncovered in that rich storehouse of medieval Jewish life called the Cairo Geniza, we have a detailed picture of the structure of both the Palestinian Yeshiva and the community that it served. [26] The gaon, together with the president of the court and a board of five "international" notables, constituted the "council" of the Yeshiva. Though its judicial sessions often took place in the Muslims' political capital of Ramle, the Yeshiva itself was located in Jerusalem, and its administrative and educational activities took place there: the fixing of the annual calendar, the liturgy in the community synagogue, study of the law in the "house of study," and a good deal else in the house of the gaon or the president of the court. [27]

The Jerusalem Yeshiva in the period before the Crusades produced few luminaries comparable to the scholars of the earlier Galilean yeshiva or even to the contemporary scholars who were at that time shaping a parallel religious and legal tradition in the Iraqi yeshiva. The energies of the Jerusalem community, and particularly of the activists who guided and supported the more insouciant saints who prayed for the restoration of Israel, were chiefly directed toward survival. The Jerusalem Jews were not notably persecuted; like their Christian contemporaries in Jerusalem, they appear to have suffered mainly from the oppression normally associated with a greedy and inept administration. But the Geniza documents reveal that the gaon and his emissaries engaged in almost continuous begging expeditions for funds abroad, primarily among the better-off Jews of Fatimid Fustat and Cairo, but also in Europe. Most of these were for cash contributions. But there was also some endowment, and in much the same form that it later manifested itself in Islam. [28] It is possible, for example, to trace across two centuries the fortunes of blocks of buildings in Old Cairo whose income had been designated in trust for "the poor of Jerusalem"; [29] and there likewise appear to have been Jewish-owned shops in Ramle whose income had been settled on the Jerusalem community, just as the income from shops in the bazaar of Jerusalem had been designated for Christian churches by the Crusaders and then for law schools by the Muslims who followed them. [30]

Poverty and Prayer in Jerusalem

The following is a letter written from Jerusalem to the Jews of the Diaspora at the end of the tenth century, thus early in the Fatimid takeover of Jerusalem. Its purpose is to introduce a fund-raiser who will be visiting those communities, and it sounds themes that appear again and again in Jewish accounts of life in Jerusalem during this period: mixed feelings about the Arab regime, tempered by a rejoicing in the new freedom of cultus under Islam; complaints about Karaite interference; and, finally, the inevitable request for funds for the chronically impoverished community in the Holy City:

Greetings to you from the faithful Lord, the eternal city, and from the head of Sion's yeshivas, from the city in which the seventy-one members of the Sanhedrin sat with their students before them . . . the city which is now widowed, orphaned, deserted, and impoverished with its few scholars. . . . Many competitors and rebels have arisen [the Karaites], yet it yearns for the day when the All-Merciful Lord will redeem it.

We, the Rabbanite community, a pitiful assembly living in the vicinity of the Temple site, regret to inform you that we are constantly harassed by those foreigners who overrun the Temple grounds. We pray, "How long, O Lord, shall the adversary reproach? Shall the adversary blaspheme Your name forever?" (Ps. 74:10). Our sole comfort shall be when we are once again permitted to walk freely about its gates, to prostrate ourselves in prayer for Jerusalem's total liberation with its Temple restored. . . . Yes, there is a synagogue on the Mount of Olives to which our Jewish confreres gather during the month of Tishri. There they weep upon its stones, roll in its dust, encircle its walls, and pray. [31]

It was God's will that we found favor with the Ishmaelite rulers. At the time of their invasion and conquest of Palestine from the Edomites [the Romans / Byzantines], the Arabs came to Jerusalem and some Jews showed them the location of the Temple. This group of Jews has lived among them ever since. The Jews agree to keep the site clear of refuse, in return for which they were granted the privilege of praying at its gates. They then also purchased the Mount of Olives, where the Shekhinah is said to have rested, as we read in Ezekiel 11:23: "The glory of God went up from the midst of the city and stood upon the mountain which is on the east side of the city." . . . Here we worship on holy days facing the Lord's Temple, especially on Hoshana Rabba. We entreat the Lord's blessing for all of Israel wherever they might reside. All who remember Jerusalem will merit a share in its joy. . . . Everyone can partake of it by supporting Jerusalem's residents. Life here is extremely hard, food is scarce, and opportunities for work very limited. Yet our wicked neighbors exact exorbitant taxes and other "fees." Were we not to pay them, we would be denied the right to pray on Mount Olivet. . . . These intolerable levies and the necessary frequent bribes compel us to borrow money at high rates of interest in order to avoid imprisonment or expulsion.

Help us, save us, redeem us. It is for your benefit too, for we pray for your welfare. (Holtz 1971: 122-123)

As the letter indicates, the Mount of Olives had become the chief place of Jewish public prayer in Jerusalem; it was there too that was held the great annual assembly during the feast of Hoshana Rabba, the last day of the Sukkoth festival.[32] Whereas on this day during the period of the Temple the community had circled the great altar before the Sanctuary, now under the Fatimid dispensation they circled the Mount of Olives seven times with song and prayer. On that same day the gaon of the Jerusalem Yeshiva made public proclamation concerning the dates of the new moons, the festivals, and the intercalation of the calendar. Then he appointed members of the "Great Sanhedrin" and bestowed titles of honor on those who had worked on behalf of the Palestinian Yeshiva. Finally, he pronounced bans of excommunication on the unobservant and on those who rebelled against authority, especially the intransigent Karaites.[33]

A Muslim Native Son

If Jews and Christians loom so large in this account, it is simply because Jerusalem in the tenth century was still a city dominated by those two groups. We have in fact to look no further than our chief Muslim authority on Jerusalem of that era, the traveller and geographer Muqaddasi, himself a native of Jerusalem, to confirm our impression. "Her streets are never empty of strangers," he writes about A.D. 985. "Everywhere the Christians and Jews have the upper hand." So it appeared to one who lived there. If we have our own grounds for thinking that the Jews of Jerusalem, whatever their numbers, were not exceedingly prosperous, such was not the case with the Christians. As Muqaddasi explains, speaking more generally of Syria, of which Jerusalem was reckoned a part, the literate class was still made up chiefly of Christians:

It is seldom recorded that any jurisprudent of Syria propounds any new doctrines, or that any Muslim here is the writer of anything, except only at Tiberias where the scribes have always been in repute. Truly, the scribes here in Syria, as in the case of Egypt, are all Christians, for the Muslims abandon to them entirely this business, and unlike the men of other nations do not hold letters a profitable subject of study. . . . In this province of Syria also it is the Jews who are for the most part the assayers of coins, the dyers, bankers, and tanners, while it is most usual for the physicians and scribes to be Christians. (Muqaddasi 1896: 77)

More, the cycle of feasts and festivals observed by the Muslims of Jerusalem, and indeed in all of Syria, in the tenth century was still closely tied to those celebrated by the Christians, whether seasonal or purely religious holidays:

Of Christian feasts that are also observed by the Muslims of Syria by reason of the division of the seasons of the year there are the following: Easter, [which falls] at the New Year; Whitsuntide, at the time of the heat; Christmas as the time of the cold; the Feast of St. Barbara [December 4] in the rainy season. . . . The Feast of the Kalends [January 1] . . . the Feast of the [Invention of the] Cross [January 13 or 14] at the time of the grape harvest;[34] and the feast of Lydda [or St. George; April 23]. (Muqaddasi 1896: 76-77)

Muqaddasi is an observant and scrupulous reporter, experienced in the lands of the tenth-century Islamic empire by reason of his broad travels and his acquaintance with almost all the classes of Islamic society. He could be dazzled on occasion—when he described the mosaic work in the great Ummayad mosque in Damascus, for example—but when he comes to speak of Jerusalem, Muqaddasi is not the awe-struck visitor or pilgrim seeing the Holy City for the first time. It was his city—virtues, faults, and all:

Bayt al-Maqdis [the Holy House], also known as Iliya [Aelia], and al-Balat [the Palace or Pretorium]. Among provincial towns, none is larger than Jerusalem, and many capitals are in fact smaller. . . . The buildings of the Holy City are of stone, and you will find nowhere finer or more solid constructions. And in no place will you meet with people more chaste. Provisions are most excellent here; the markets are clean, the mosque is among the largest, and nowhere are holy places more numerous. . . . In Jerusalem are all manner of learned men and doctors, and for this reason the heart of every man of intelligence yearns toward her. All the year round, never are her streets empty of strangers. . . . As to the saying that Jerusalem is the most illustrious of cities, is she not the one that unites the advantages of This World with those of the Next? [35] *He who is of the children of This World and yet is ardent in the matters of the Next may find here a market for his wares; while he who would be of those of the Next World, though his soul clings to the good things of This World as well, he too may find them here. . . .*

As to the excellence of the city, why is this not to be the plain [sahira] of marshalling on the Day of Judgment, where the Gathering Together and the Appointment will take place? Truly Mecca and Medina have their superiority by reason of the Ka'ba and the Prophet—the blessings of God upon him and his family—but truly on the Day of Judgment they will both come to Jerusalem and the excellence of them all will be united there. As to Jerusalem being the most spacious of cities, since all created things are to assemble there, what place on earth can be more extensive than this? (Muqaddasi 1896: 34-37)

Jerusalem's virtues, then, are both of this world and the next, and if Muqaddasi seems a little concerned with the apparently great eminence of Mecca and Medina—"Jerusalem is smaller than Mecca but larger than Medina," he says in another place—on the Last Day the palm will be delivered to Jerusalem. In the meantime, however, Jerusalem has its more mundane attractions:

From Jerusalem come cheeses, cotton, the celebrated raisins of the species known as Aynuni and Duri, excellent apples, bananas—which is a fruit of the form of the cucumber, but the skin peels off and the interior is not unlike that of the watermelon, only finer flavored and more luscious—also pine nuts of the kind called "Quraysh-bite" and their equal is not to be found elsewhere; also mirrors, lamps, jars and needles. (Muqaddasi 1896: 69)

Still [he continues], Jerusalem has some disadvantages. . . . You will not find anywhere baths more filthy than those in the Holy City; nor anywhere heavier fees for their use. Learned men are few, and the Christians numerous, and the latter are unmannerly in the public places. In the hostelries the taxes are heavy on all that is sold; there are guards at every gate, and no one is allowed to sell the necessities of life except in the appointed places. In this city the oppressed have no succor; the meek are molested, and the rich are envied. Jurisconsults remain unvisited, and erudite men have no renown; also the schools are unattended, for there are no lectures. Everywhere the Christians and Jews have the upper hand, and the mosque is void of either congregation or assembly of learned men. (Muqaddasi 1896: 37)

As one who lived there, Muqaddasi shows concern, and pride, in the water supply of Jerusalem:

There is water in Jerusalem in plenty. Thus it is a common saying that "There is no place in Jerusalem where you cannot get water or hear the call to prayer," and few are the houses that have not cisterns, one or more. Within the city are three great birkehs [cisterns], namely the Birkeh of the Children of Israel, the Birkeh of Solomon, and the Birkeh Iyad. In the vicinity of each of these there are baths, and to them lead water channels from the streets. In the Haram area there are twenty underground cisterns of vast size, and there are few quarters in the city that have not public cisterns, though the contents of these last is only the rain water that drains into them from the streets. At a certain valley, about a stage from the city, they have gathered together the waters and made two pools into which the torrents of the winter rains flow. From these two reservoirs there are channels bringing the water to the city which are opened in the Spring in order to fill the cisterns in the Haram area and those in other places. [36] (Muqaddasi 1896: 39-41)

In a few brief lines Muqaddasi sketches the extent of the tenth-century city:

Jerusalem has eight iron gates. The Sion Gate, the Nea Gate, [37] the Gate of the Palace [or possibly Pretorium], [38] the Gate of Jeremiah's Pit, the Gate of Siloam, the Gate of Jericho, the Gate of the Column, and the Gate of the Prayer Niche of David. (Muqaddasi 1896: 38)

Some of these are easily identified. "Gate of the Column" is the consistent Arab name for the gate presently called the Damascus Gate, and the Prayer Niche of David, Sion, and Jericho Gates are likely quite close to the present Jaffa, Sion, and St. Stephen's Gates on the western, southern, and eastern sides of the city, respectively. [39] So too would the Nea Gate stand near the remains of the church of that name, where the old Byzantine cardo left the city on its southern side (see Chapter Four). We cannot be absolutely certain about the remaining gates on the southern side of the city—the Palace, Jeremiah's Pit, and Siloam Gates—though it should be recalled that Christian pilgrims located the Pretorium of Pilate, like the Pit of Jeremiah, west of the Temple in the Tyropean Valley. Also, in both Muqaddasi's account and that of Nasir-i Khusraw written in 1047, the Pool of Siloam was *outside* the city. One may conclude, then, with Tsafrir, "that the wall which Muqaddasi saw was, in its general delineation, more or less the same as the [sixteenth-century] Turkish wall which now encloses the Old City of Jerusalem."[40]

The Noble Sanctuary

It was, of course, the enshrined holy places of Muqaddasi's city that claimed the largest share of his attention, and chief among them the Aqsa Mosque, where the familiar theme of Christian emulation reappears:

The Aqsa Mosque lies in the southeastern corner of the Holy City. The stones of the foundation [that is, of the Herodian Temple platform], which were laid by David, are fifteen feet or a little less in length. They are chiselled, finely faced and jointed, and of the hardest material. On those Caliph Abd al-Malik subsequently built, using smaller but well-shaped stones, and battlements are added above. This mosque is even more beautiful than that of Damascus, for during the building of it they had for a rival and as a comparison the great church [of the Holy Sepulcher] belonging to the Christians of Jerusalem, and they built this [al-Aqsa] to be even more beautiful than that other.

The Haram court is paved in its entirety, and in its center arises a platform, like that in the mosque at Medina, up to which ascend on all sides broad flights of steps. There are four domes on the platform. Of these, the Dome of the Chain and the Dome of the Ascension of the Prophet and the Dome of the Prophet are small in size. They have lead covered cupolas and stand supported on marble pillars without exterior walls. (Muqaddasi 1896: 41-44)

Among the holy places within [the Haram area] are the prayer niches of Mary, Zakariyya, Jacob, and al-Khidr, [41] the prayer stations of the Prophet and of Gabriel, the Places of the Ant and of the Fire and of the Ka'ba, and also the Bridge al-Sirat, which shall divide Heaven and Hell. The dimensions of the Haram area are 1,500 feet in length and 1,050 feet in width.[42] *The measurement of the Rock itself is 49½ feet by 40½ feet, and the cavern which lies beneath will hold sixty-nine persons. . . . The mosque is served by special attendants; their service was instituted by Caliph Abd al-Malik, the men being chosen out of the one-fifth share owed to the sovereign out of the captives taken in war and hence they are called "The Fifths." None besides these are employed in the service and they take their watch in turn beside the Rock. (Muqaddasi 1896: 47-48)*

Muqaddasi next turns his fine eye for architectural and decorative detail to the Dome of the Rock:

In the center of the platform is the Dome of the Rock, rising above an octagonal building with four entrances, each opposite to one of the flights of stairs leading up from the courtyard. . . . All (the entrances) are adorned with gold, and each is closed by a beautiful door of cedar wood worked with fine designs. . . . Over each of the entrances is a marble porch, decorated with cedar wood and brass work. Each entry porch likewise has a door, but these are not decorated.

Inside the building are three concentric colonnades with beautiful polished marble columns that are visible, and above them is a low vaulted roof. Inside the colonnades is the central hall over the Rock. This space is circular, not octagonal, and is encircled by polished marble columns supporting circular arches. Built above these and rising high into the air is the drum of the dome with large windows running round it. And above the drum is the cupola itself, rising from the floor to the top to a height of 150 feet. . . . The outside of the dome is completely covered with gilded brass plates, while the whole of the building proper—floor, walls, and drum, inside and out—is decorated with marble and mosaics in the manner we have already described in speaking of the mosque of Damascus. . . . At the dawn, when the light of the sun first strikes the dome and the drum catches the rays, then is this edifice a marvellous sight to behold, and one such that in all of Islam I have not seen the equal; neither have I heard tell of anything built in pagan times that could rival in grace this Dome of the Rock. (Muqaddasi 1896: 44-46)

Siloam and Hebron

South of the Haram, or the Temple mount, at the southern edge of the old City of David, was the pool called Siloam. The Christians had made it into a hospice and holy place (see Chapter Four). And from Muqaddasi we learn that the Muslims had done the same, at the very beginning of their occupation of the city:

Sulwan [Siloam] is a place on the outskirts of the city. Below the village is Ayn Sulwan, of fairly good water, which irrigates the large gardens which were given as an endowment by Caliph Uthman ibn Affan [A.D. 644-656] for the poor of the city. Lower down than this, again, is Jabob's Well. It is said that on the Night of Arafat the water of the Zamzam at Mecca comes underground to the pool of Sulwan. The people hold a festival here on that evening. (Muqaddasi 1896: 48-49)

Nasir-i Khusraw, a Persian visitor to Jerusalem in 1047, supplies additional details on the Muslim installation at Siloam:

Going southward of the city half a league and down the gorge (of the Kedron), you come to a fountain of water gushing out from the rock, which they call Ayn Sulwan. There are all around the spring numerous buildings; and the water flows from there on down to a village where there are many houses and gardens. It is said that when anyone washes from head to foot in this water he obtains relief from his pains and will even recover from chronic illnesses. There are at this spring many buildings for charitable purposes, richly endowed. And the Holy City itself possesses an excellent hospital which is provided for by considerable sums that were given for that purpose. Great numbers of (sick) people are served there with potions and lotions, for there are physicians who receive a fixed stipend and attend at the hospital. (Nasir-i Khusraw 1893: 26)

Another more famous charitable endowment of the Muslims was located at Hebron south of Bethlehem, where lay the tombs of Abraham and the Jewish patriarchs. We shall hear more of this in Chapter Ten, but Muqaddasi here gives us one of the earliest views of the Hebron establishment under Muslim auspices:

Hebron, the village of Abraham, the Friend of God. Within is a strong fortress which, it is said, was the work of jinns [demons], [43] *being of great squared stones. In the middle of this place rises the dome built of stone since the time of Islam, which covers the sepulcher of Abraham. . . . The garden round about it has become the mosque-court, and built about it are rest houses for pilgrims, which thus adjoin the [Hebron] haram. . . .*

In the haram of Hebron is a public guest house, with a kitchener, a baker, and servants attached to it. These present a dish of lentils and olive oil to every poor person who arrives, and it is even set before the rich if perchance they desire to partake of it. Most men erroneously imagine that this dole is of the original guest-house of Abraham, but in truth the funds come from the bequests of Tamim al-Dari and others. . . . Also there was once an amir of Khurasan—may God have confirmed his dominion—who assigned to this charity 1,000 dirhams yearly; and further, al-Adil, the shah, the sultan of Ghurjistan, gave great benefits to this house. At the present day in all of Islam I know of no charity or almsgiving better regulated than this one; for those who travel and are hungry eat here of good food, and thus is the custom of Abraham continued, for he during his lifetime rejoiced in giving hospitality, and after his death, God—may He be exalted—had allowed the custom to be perpetuated. Thus I myself, in my experiences, have become partaker of the hospitality of Abraham, the Friend of God. (Muqaddasi 1896: 50-52)

And Nasir-i Khusraw in 1047 on the same place:

The people of Syria and the inhabitants of the Holy City call the shrine at Hebron "Khalil" [or the Friend of God], and they never make use of the real name of the village. . . . This shrine has many villages belonging to it that provide revenues for pious purposes. . . . The shrine stands at the southern border of the town and extends towards the southeast. The shrine is enclosed by four walls built of square masonry. . . . The shrine and the closed prayer hall stand in the width [that is, the southern end] of the building. In the prayer hall there are many fine prayer niches. There are two tombs within the prayer hall, laid with their heads facing south. Both are covered with cenotaphs built of squared stones as high as a man. The one on the right is the grave of Isaac, son of Abraham, and that on the left is the grave of his wife Rebecca. . . . (Nasir-i Khusraw 1893: 53-54)

On the (western) side, where the ground is level, that is, beyond the tomb of Joseph and the shrine, lies a great cemetery to which the dead are brought from many places. On the flat roof of the prayer hall in the shrine compound they have built cells for the reception of pilgrims who come here. The revenues for this charity are considerable, being derived from villages and from houses in the Holy City. In Hebron they grow for the most part barley, wheat being rare, but olives are in abundance. The pilgrims and travellers and other guests are given bread and olives. There are very many mills here, worked by oxen and mules, that all day long grind the flour. And further, there are slave girls who during the entire day are engaged in baking the bread. The loaves they make here are each a mann weight [about three pounds], and to every person who arrives they give a loaf of bread daily and a dish of lentils cooked in olive oil, also some raisins. This practice has been in use since the days of (Abraham) the Friend of the Merciful—peace be upon him—down to the present, and there are some days when as many as five hundred pilgrims arrive, to each of whom this hospitality is offered. (Nasir-i Khusraw 1893: 57)

The Byzantine "Holy War" in Syria

Muqaddasi's is a general work that ranges widely over the Near East, and when he comes to speak of the Syrian coastal cities, we begin to sense some of the nuances of Mediterranean politics absent from the account of the Holy City:

All along the seacoast of the province of Syria are the watch stations where the levies assemble. The warships and galleys of the Greeks also come into these ports, bringing on board the captives taken from the Muslims. These they offer for ransom, three for a hundred dinars. In each one of these ports there are men who know the Greek tongue, for they go on missions to the Greeks and trade with them in diverse wares. At the watch stations, whenever a Greek vessel appears, they sound horns. And if it is night, they light a beacon on the tower there, or if it is day, they make a great smoke. . . . [At that signal the local levies collect on the coast.] Then the ransoming begins. One prisoner will be given in exchange for another, or money or jewels will be offered; until at length all the prisoners on the Greek ships have been set free. . . . (Muqaddasi 1896: 61-62)

This brief but lively sketch leaves a mixed impression: there was some trading going on between the Muslims in Syria and the Byzantine power in the eastern Mediterranean in the late tenth century, but there was war and the threat of war in the air as well, alarms, calls to arms, the ransoming of captives. It was more than mere coastal raiding. By the ninth century the Byzantines had recovered from the loss of most of their eastern provinces to the Muslims, and by the tenth a powerful counteroffensive was under way in northern Syria.

The time was ripe in every respect. In A.D. 969 a new Muslim power had conquered Egypt, the radically anticaliphal dynasty that called itself the Fatimids. [44] And from Egypt they proceeded in 970 to the conquest of Palestine and much of Syria. They did not bring better times in their wake, however. The Abbasid caliphs had not ruled well in Palestine, and the Fatimids were incapable of stemming the forces of anarchy that now shook the land from one decade to the next. As usually happened when the normal instruments of government and order failed, the bedouin were abroad in Palestine, often with Byzantine and indeed with local Christian connivance, and the Fatimids were hard put simply to hold Jerusalem. [45]

It was under these circumstances that the Byzantines began their counteroffensive. First, Nicephorus Phocas in 964, and then his imperial successor John Tzimisces in 972 and 974, took the field successfully in Syria against the armies of Islam in what appears to have been regarded as a "holy war." [46] In 975 Tzimisces sent this letter describing his Syrian campaign of 974 to his ally, Ashot III, king of Armenia. The text begins after Tzimisces' capture of Damascus: [47]

We went to the Sea of Galilee, where our Lord Jesus Christ had performed a miracle with one hundred and fifty-three fish. We were intent on laying siege to the town of Tiberias also, but the townspeople came in submission to Our Imperial Majesty and brought us many gifts as the Damascenes had done and also tribute in the amount of 30,000 dehekans, not counting many other valuable presents. They requested that one of our commanders be put over them and gave us an affirmation of loyalty as had the Damascenes, promising to be subject to us perpetually and to give us tribute ceaselessly. On that basis we left them free of enslavement and did not devastate the town or the region; moreover, we did not plunder them because the region was the native land of the Holy Apostles. We felt the same way about Nazareth where the Theotokos, the holy Virgin Mary, heard the good tidings from the angel. We also went up to Mount Tabor and climbed up to that place where Christ our Lord was transfigured.

While we remained in that place, people came to us from Ramle and Jerusalem to beseech Our Imperial Majesty, looking for compassion from us. They asked for a commander to be appointed over them and become tributary to us, swearing to serve us; all these things which they asked we indeed did. We also were intent on delivering the Holy Sepulcher of Christ our God from the bondage of the Muslims. We established military commanders in all the areas which had submitted and become tributary to Our Imperial Majesty; these were Baisan called Decapolis [Scythpolis], Genesareth, and Acre, also called Ptolemais, and by a written statement they undertook to give tribute ceaselessly from year to year and to serve us. We went up to Caesarea which is on the coast of the great Mediterranean Sea, and they also submitted and came under our rule. If the abominable Africans [the Berber troops in the Fatimid army] had not fled to the coastal fortresses where they had taken refuge because they feared us, by the assistance of God we would have gone to the Holy City of Jerusalem and would have stood in prayer at the Holy Places of God. When we heard that the coastal inhabitants had fled, then we brought into submission the upper part of the country, subjecting it to the rule of the Romans and establishing a commander there. We brought under our control many towns, besieging and assaulting those which did not submit; having captured them we went by the coastal route which leads directly to the famous, renowned, and heavily fortified town of Berytus, which is today called Beirut. (Walker 1977: 319-320)

This account by the emperor of his own conquest of Galilee, and indeed Caesarea and all but Jerusalem itself, was once taken at face value. [48] But there now seems to be little reason to do so since there is not a solitary confirmation from any other source, contemporary or later, particularly among the Muslim historians who would certainly have at least noted this powerful Byzantine thrust into the very heart of Palestine. [49] That Tzimisces took Damascus, however briefly, is beyond doubt, and that he shook the Fatimid control of the region is likewise certain. Jerusalem was never seriously threatened, but the tone of the letter, which was probably written to encourage the assistance of Ashot of Armenia, shows that such a campaign was at least feasible, and that it might have been promoted on religious grounds—"delivering the Holy Sepulcher of Christ our God from the bondage of the Muslims," as Tzimisces put it.

Jerusalem Before the Crusades

It would be another century and more before the goal proposed by Tzimisces would be attained, and then not by the Byzantines but by Franks from the West. But we have a final, full-scale description of Jerusalem before that occurred, written by Nasir-i Khusraw after his visit of 1047. A careful and detailed portrait, it displays the city and its holy places before the Crusaders occupied and rebuilt it. It is also filled with interesting and at times surprising religious observations, like the following:

It was the fifth of Ramadan of the year 458 [March 5, A.D. 1047] that I thus came to the Holy City; and the full space of a solar year had elapsed since I had set out from home, having all that time never ceased to journey onward, for in no place had I yet sojourned to enjoy repose. Now the men of Syria and of the neighboring parts call the Holy City [Bayt al-Muqaddas] by the name of al-Quds ["the Holy"]. And the people of these provinces, if they are unable to make the hajj, will go up at the appointed season to Jerusalem and there perform their rites, and upon the feast day slay the sacrifice, as it is customary to do (at Mecca on that same day). There are years when as many as 20,000 people will be present in Jerusalem during the the first days of (the pilgrimage month of) Dhu al-Hajj; for they bring their children also with them to celebrate their circumcision. From all the countries of the Greeks too, and from other lands, the Christians and the Jews come up to Jerusalem in great numbers in order to make their visitation of the Church (of the Resurrection) and the synagogue that is there. . . . (Nasir-i Khusraw 1893: 23)

We have heard the complaint before and we shall hear it again, that Jerusalem threatened to replace Mecca as a religious center; on the basis of this report of Nasir-i Khusraw, the complaint had some substance. We note too the continued presence of large numbers of Christian and Jewish pilgrims, and this only slightly more than fifty years before the arrival of the Crusaders. Nasir continues, now concerned with more mundane matters:

The country and the villages around the Holy City are situated upon hill-sides. The land is well cultivated, and they grow grain, olives, and figs; there are also many kinds of trees here. In all the country around there is no (spring) water for irrigation, and yet the produce is very abundant and the prices are moderate. Many of the chief men harvest as much as 50,000 mann weight [about 16,000 gallons] of olive oil (in season). It is kept in tanks and they export it to other countries.

Jerusalem is a very great city, and at the time of my visit there were in it 20,000 men. [50] *It has high, well-built, and clean bazaars. All the streets are paved with slabs of stone; and wheresoever there is a height, they have cut it down and made it level, so that as soon as the rain falls the place is washed clean. There are in the city numerous artisans, and each craft has a separate bazaar. The mosque lies in the southeast quarter of the city so that the eastern city wall also forms the wall of the mosque (court). (Nasir-i Khusraw 1893: 23-24)*

The Direction of Muslims' Prayer

Nasir's account of the Haram and its buildings begins with a rehearsal of the pre-Islamic, that is, the biblical history of the place, and particularly its choice as the focus of prayer:

The Friday Mosque lies on the east side of the city, and one of the walls of the mosque (area) is the Wadi Jahannam [Gehenna.]. When you examine this wall, which is on the wadi, from the outside of the mosque (area), you see that for the space of a hundred cubits it is built up of huge stones set without mortar or cement. . . . The mosque occupies the position it does because of the Rock. This Rock is that which God—may He be exalted and glorified—commanded Moses to institute as the qibla (or direction of prayer). After this command had come down, and Moses had instituted it as the qibla, he himself lived but for a brief time since of sudden his life was cut short. Then came the days of Solomon—upon him be peace—who, seeing the Rock was the qibla point, built a mosque about the Rock in such a way that the Rock stood in the middle of the mosque, which became the oratory of the people. So it remained down to the days of our Prophet Muhammad, the Chosen One—upon him be blessings and peace—who likewise at first recognized this to be the qibla and turned toward it in his prayers. But God—be He exalted and glorified—afterwards commanded him to institute the House of the Ka'ba as the qibla. (Nasir-i Khusraw 1893: 26-27)

The Haram al-Sharif

Nasir enters the Haram through its chief western portal, later called the Gate of the Chain but referred to in his day as David's Gate:

The Haram area lies in the eastern part of the city, and through the bazaar of this (quarter) you enter the Haram by a great and beautiful gateway that measures thirty ells in height and twenty across. The gateway (the Gate of the Chain) has two wings with open halls, and the walls of both gateways and halls are adorned with colored enamels set in plaster and cut in patterns, so beautiful that the eye becomes dazzled in contemplating them. Over the gateway is an inscription, which is set in enamels, giving the titles of the sultan of Egypt. . . . There is also a great dome that crowns this gateway, which is built of squared stones. . . . The gateway we have just described is called the David Gate—peace be upon him.

After passing [through] this gateway, you have on the right two great colonnades. . . . These colonnades lead down to near the prayer hall (of the Aqsa Mosque); on your left and toward the north there is likewise a long colonnade, with sixty-four arches supported by marble pillars. . . . Running along the north side of the Haram area and between the two gateways just mentioned [Gate of the Tribes and Gate of Gates] is a colonnade with arches that rest on solid pillars, and adjacent to it is a dome supported by tall columns and adorned with lamps and lanterns. This is called the Dome of Jacob—peace be upon him—since this spot was his place of prayer. And further along the breadth (or northern wall) of the Haram is (another) colonnade, in the wall of which is a gate which leads to two cloisters belonging to the Sufis who have their place of prayer there and have built a fine prayer niche. There are always in residence a number of Sufis who make this oratory the place of their daily devotions, except on Friday when they go into the Haram al-Sharif to attend the prayer service there. (Nasir-i Khusraw 1893: 29-32)

There were no colonnades on the eastern side of the Haram, but Nasir's attention was drawn there by an extraordinary monument that elicited some comment from almost every visitor to the Haram, the Golden Gate.

In the eastern wall of the Haram area there is a great gateway so skillfully built of squared stones that one might almost say that the whole was carved out of a single block. Its height is fifty ells and its width thirty, and it is sculpted and ornamented throughout. There are ten beautiful doors in this gateway (set so close) that between any two of them there is not the space of a foot. The doors are all most skillfully wrought in iron and Damascus brass work, set in with bolts and rings. They say that this gateway was constructed by Solomon, son of David—peace be upon him—to please his father. When you enter this gateway facing east there are on your right hand two great doors. One of them is called the Gate of Mercy and the other the Gate of Repentance, and they say of this last that it is the gate where God—may He be exalted and glorified—accepted the repentance of David—upon whom be peace. Near the gateway is a beautiful mosque. [51] *In former times it was only a hall, but they turned the hall into a mosque. It is spread with all manner of beautiful carpets and there are servants especially appointed to it. (Nasir-i Khusraw 1893: 32-33)*

There follows a long and circumstantial description of the Aqsa Mosque, which Nasir saw shortly after its Fatimid reconstruction after the destructive earthquake of A.D. 1033. It was now on a different scale from the building Muqaddasi had seen in 985. The earlier visitor counted fifteen doorways opening into the mosque on the north and eleven on the east, while Nasir counted ten on the east but a mere five across the northern facade. The building must have been considerably narrowed in the interval.[52]

One of the most illuminating parts of Nasir-i Khusraw's description of the Haram area is that which has to do with the area immediately to the south of the platform, the former site of a large Umayyad palace, as we have seen, and still apparently frequented in Nasir's day:

In the south wall of the Haram area is a gate leading to places for ablution, where there is running water. When a person has need to make ablution, he goes down to this place and accomplishes what is prescribed; for had the place of the ablution been set outside the walls, because of the size of the Haram area no one could have gone and returned in time and before the appointed hours for prayer had gone by. (Nasir-i Khusraw 1893: 39)

This suggests that the platform above was still accessible from this southern side, as it no longer is today, and likely through or within the Huldah Gates of Herod's Temple, as appears below:

. . . As I have written above, the Holy City stands on the summit of a hill and its site is not on level ground. The place, however, where the Haram al-Sharif stands is flat and on the level, but outside the area the enclosing wall varies in height in different places by reason that where the fall is abrupt, the Haram wall is at its highest, for the foundation of the wall lies at the bottom of the slope; and where the ground rises, the wall has no

need of being so high. Wherever in the city itself, or in its suburbs, the ground level is below that of the (surface of the) Haram area, there they have made gateways like tunnels cut through, that lead up into the court of the Haram. One of these is called Gate of the Prophet—peace and blessing be upon him—which opens toward the qibla-point, that is, toward the south. [The passageway of this gate] is ten ells broad and the height varies by reason of the steps. . . .

Nasir is filled with awe, as we still are today, at the Herodian stonework in the platform construction, and like many another, attributed it to Solomon, who was alone thought to be capable of such architectural wonders:

Over this passageway has been erected the main building of the (Aqsa) mosque, for the masonry is so solidly laid that they have been able to raise the enormous building that is seen here without any damage occurring to what is beneath it. They have made use of stones of such size that the mind cannot conceive how, by human power, they were carried up and set in place. It is said, however, that the construction was accomplished by Solomon, the son of David—peace be upon him. The Prophet—peace and blessing be upon him—on the night of his Ascent into Heaven passed into the Haram al-Sharif through this passageway, for the (lower) gateway opens onto the road to Mecca. . . . This gateway of the Haram leading into the tunnelled passageway is closed by a double door, and the wall of the Haram outside it is nearly fifty ells high. The reason for piercing this gateway was to enable those inhabitants of the suburb lying obliquely beyond to enter the Haram area at their pleasure, without having to pass through the other quarters of the city. . . . (Nasir-i Khusraw 1893: 40-42)

The Dome and the Rock

In the middle of the court of the Haram is the platform, and set in the midst of it is the Rock, which before the revelation of Islam was the Qibla. The platform was constructed because the height of the Rock made it impossible to bring it within the compass of the main building. (Nasir-i Khusraw 1893: 43)

The Rock itself rises out of the floor to the height of a man, and a balustrade of marble goes around it in order that none may lay his hand on it. The Rock inclines on the side that is toward the qibla-point [the south], and it appears as if someone had walked heavily on the stone when it was soft like clay and the imprint of his toes had remained there. There are on the

Rock seven such footmarks, and I have heard it stated that Abraham—peace be upon him—was once there with Isaac—peace be upon him—when he was a boy, and that he had walked over this place and that the footprints were his.

In the house of the Dome of the Rock men are always congregated, pilgrims and worshippers. The place is laid with fine carpets of silks and other stuffs. In the middle of the Dome and over the Rock there hangs a silver lamp from a silver chain, and there are in other parts of the building great numbers of silver lamps, each inscribed with its own weight. These lamps are all gifts of the sultan of Egypt, and according to the calculation I made, there must be here various silver utensils to a weight of a thousand mann [about a ton and a half]. I saw there a huge wax candle that was seven cubits high and three spans in diameter. . . . They told me that the sultan of Egypt every year sent here a great number of candles, the large one just described among them, and on it was written the name of the sultan in golden letters. (Nasir-i Khusraw 1893: 47-48)

Other Holy Places on the Haram

Also on the platform is another dome that sits atop four marble columns. This too is closed in on the qibla-side to form a fine prayer niche. It is called the Dome of Gabriel and there are no carpets spread there for its floor is formed by the living rock that has here been made smooth. They say that on the night of the Ascension the steed Buraq was tied up at this spot, until the Prophet—peace and blessing upon him—was ready to mount. Lastly there is another dome lying twenty cubits distant from the Dome of Gabriel and it is called the Dome of the Prophet—peace and blessings be upon him. This dome is likewise set upon four pillars.

They say that on the night of his Ascension into Heaven the Prophet—peace and blessing be upon him—prayed first at the Dome of the Rock, laying his hand upon the Rock. As he went out, the Rock, to do him honor, rose up, but he laid his hand on it to keep it in its place and firmly fixed it there. But by reason of this rising up, it is even to this present day partly detached [from the ground beneath]. The Prophet—peace and blessing be upon him—went out from that place and came to the dome now named after him and there he mounted Buraq; and for this reason is that dome venerated. Beneath the Rock is a large cavern, where candles burn continually, and they say that when the Rock moved in order to rise up [in honor of the Prophet], this space below was left empty. . . . (Nasir-i Khusraw 1893: 49-50)

By the time Nasir-i Khusraw was writing those lines, the chief parties of the tenth-century struggle, the Byzantines and the Fatimids, were being moved aside by another power that was even then beginning to make itself felt in Palestine, that of the Turks. The Turks were already everywhere present in the caliphal armies as commanders in the ninth century, and by the beginning of the tenth their chieftains were carving out principalities for themselves from the possessions of both the Sunni caliph in Baghdad and the Fatimid ruler in Cairo. In A.D. 1071 they took Jerusalem too, a fact that was noted and reflected upon in Christian circles in Europe:

When the power of the Turks began to flourish, and their sway was extended over the lands of the Egyptians and Persians, matters grew worse again. The Holy City came under their control and, during the twenty-eight years of Turkish domination [A.D. 1071-1098], the people of God endured far greater troubles, so that they came to look back upon as light the woes which they had suffered under the yoke of the Egyptians and the Persians. (William of Tyre 1943: I, 71)

The Turkish occupation of Jerusalem was ephemeral, and the chief effect of their presence in the city was to raise new misgivings in the minds of the Christians of Europe. The Fatimids, in any event, had the city back in 1098, just soon enough to place upon their shoulders the burden of defending it against the eager legions of the First Crusade.

The Coming of the Crusade

From the confines of Jerusalem
a horrible tale has gone forth. . . .
—Urban II

FROM THE beginning, Westerners have looked for the origins of the Crusades in the events and ideology of medieval Europe. That search continues, and still primarily within the West, though no longer with any great conviction that there was a single or even a predominant reason why in the eleventh, twelfth, and thirteenth centuries hundreds of thousands of Europeans vowed themselves to the liberation of the Holy Land from Islam. The Crusades were a complex and long-lasting phenomenon, and even if we confine our attention, as we shall do here, to the first Crusade, the only one that captured and occupied Jerusalem, the unraveling of the chain of causality is no less complex. [1]

Pilgrimage and the Crusade

The concentration on the European aspect of the Crusades, itself a reflex of a continuing Western myopia on the subject of Islam, may well be correct in the matter of causes, since a closer investigation of the Near Eastern milieu on the eve of the first Crusade has revealed little or nothing in the condition of Jerusalem to explain the rather remarkable outburst of European sentiment for its reconquest in the last decade of the eleventh century.[2] There continued to be European Christian pilgrimages to Jerusalem in the eleventh century, some of them substantial enterprises indeed, and if the pilgrims were cheated and harassed at every turn and even threatened with the loss of their goods or even their lives in Palestine, there was nothing new in it. If those were grounds for a Crusade, Christians would have been taking up the Cross from the time of Constantine down to the twentieth century. And yet they were proposed precisely as such. Witness this report of the speech made by Pope Urban II at Clermont in November 1095:

If neither the words of Scripture arouse you, nor our admonitions penetrate your minds, at least let the great suffering of those who desired to go to the Holy Places stir you up. Think of those who made the pilgrimage across the sea! Even if they were more wealthy, consider what taxes, what violence they underwent, since they were forced to make payments and tribute almost every mile, to purchase at every gate of the city, at the entrance of churches and shrines, at every side journey from place to place; also, if any accusation whatsoever was made against them, they were compelled to purchase their release; but if they refused to pay money, the prefects of the Gentiles, according to their custom, urged them fiercely with blows. What shall we say of those who took up the journey without anything more than trust in their barren poverty, since they seemed to have nothing except their bodies to lose? They not only demanded money of them, which is not an unendurable punishment, but also examined the calluses of their heels, cutting them open and cutting the skin back, lest, perchance, they had sewed something there. Their unspeakable cruelty was carried on even to the point of giving them scammony to drink until they vomited, or even burst their bowels, because they thought the wretches had swallowed gold or silver; or, horrible to say, they cut open their bowels with a sword and, spreading out the folds of the intestines, with frightful mutilation disclosed whatever nature held there in secret. . . . (Krey 1921: 39-40)

As the texts cited in previous chapters have already testified, travel was a risky business at best in the ancient and medieval world, long-distance travel to a strange locale even more risky, and for an unarmed traveller moving under the impulse of religious enthusiasm, as the pilgrims were, notably so. The Near East, likely more highly urbanized than the European milieu from which the pilgrims came, had also between its towns and cities a nomadic population whose enthusiasm for booty was as high as the pilgrims' own enthusiasm to reach the holy places. Bedouin were an endemic problem for travellers in the Near East, and they made no nice distinctions. Themselves Muslims after the seventh or eighth century, the bedouin then and later had as few qualms about falling upon a hajj caravan bound to or from Mecca as they had about attacking pilgrim bands heading from Jaffa to Jerusalem or caught in the wildernesses around Bethlehem or marooned in the wastes of Sinai. If the hajj caravan promised the looter richer spoils by far, it was also likely to be more heavily armed and escorted to and from the Islamic holy cities of the Hejaz.

The Christian pilgrim to the Holy Land was forbidden to carry arms and was counselled to take nothing with him but purse and staff. As long as he was in Europe, the presumably poor and defenseless pilgrim was exempted from tolls and protected by a series of ecclesiastical calls for "sacred truces" as well as by heavy penalties for attacks on pilgrims. [3] None of these measures had the slightest effect in Islamic territory, of course. As a matter of fact, pilgrimage was not only a dangerous but an expensive business, and the European visitor who came without the means to pay the tolls and charges levied against him, was likely to spend a great deal of his pilgrimage in a Muslim jail in Jaffa or Cairo. So there was gold sewn into those rough cloaks, as the bedouin were well aware, and sometimes more besides. The great German pilgrimage of 1064 led by Arnold, bishop of Bamberg, was an immense affair of many thousands of pilgrims and appears to have made a public spectacle of the magnificence of its grandees and the sumptuousness of their appointments. It was, in effect, an open invitation to plunder issued to the coveteous bedouin of Palestine, and they responded with alacrity and in great numbers. The results were predictable: the rich and pious pilgrims had to choose between their goods and their lives, and the consequence was a sinister bloodbath with great loss of life almost within sight of the Holy City. [4]

It had no sequel. There was, as far as we can tell, no popular outcry or call for vengeance. And pilgrims continued to come to Jerusalem, whether or not with greater circumspection than Arnold of Bamberg and his charges, we cannot tell. To put it as pointedly as possible: no one in Jerusalem summoned a Crusade, neither the local Christians nor the Latin visitors to the city, and nothing in the status or conditions of Jerusalem had so altered as to make an international expedition for the conquest of Jerusalem intelligible. This is our perception, at any rate, as we look at the internal affairs of the Holy City in the eleventh century: the Crusade had more to do with Europe than it did with anything happening in Jerusalem.

This was not, however, the Crusaders' version, or at least what was being put out in the generation immediately following the taking of the city when there was a chance to reflect on the event, and indeed on its long-range causes. Our chief informant among those historians is William, Latin archbishop of Tyre in the middle of the twelfth century, who has been somewhat ungenerously called "the great and only luminary of the kingdom [of Jerusalem]," and who possessed the considerable advantage of familiarity with Islamic history and indeed had a working knowledge of Arabic as well.[5] In his view there had been a change for Christians in Jerusalem, a considerable change for the worse. The first blow to Christianity was the very coming of Islam, as the opening lines of his great *History of Deeds Done Beyond the Sea* set forth for the reader:

In the time of the Roman emperor Heraclius, according to ancient histories and the Oriental tradition, the pernicious doctrines of Muhammad had gained a firm foothold in the East. This first-born son of Satan falsely declared that he was a prophet sent by God and thereby led astray the lands of the East, especially Arabia. The poisonous seed which he sowed so permeated the provinces that his successors employed sword and vio-

lence, instead of preaching and exhortation, to compel the people, however reluctant, to embrace the erroneous tenets of the prophet. . . . (William of Tyre 1943: I, 60-61)

The Christian Condition in Jerusalem

William briefly describes the Muslim conquest of Jerusalem, and the construction of the Dome of the Rock, "just as one might see it today in Jerusalem." Then he proceeds to an important distinction between Sunni and Shi'ite Muslims hardly within the capacities of most Western historians down to the nineteenth century:

There existed at this time a persistent strife between the Egyptians and the Persians, induced by a bitter rivalry over the supremacy (in Islam). The fact that these nations held diametrically opposed doctrines contributed largely to the feeling of hatred between them. Even at the present day [the 1170s] this difference of religious views is the subject of such controversy between the two nations that they hold no communication, for each looks upon the other as sacrilegious. This feeling is carried so far that they wish to be different even in name. Hence, those who follow the tenets of the East are called in their tongue Sunnites, while those who prefer the tradition of Egypt, which apparently inclines more toward our own faith, are known as Shi'ites. But to explain the difference of error between them does not lie within the province of this work.

As the kingdom of Egypt gradually became more powerful, it seized the provinces and countries as far as Antioch; and the Holy City, among others, fell under its sway, subject to the same laws. Under this headship the troubles of the Christians were slightly relieved, just as prisoners are ofttimes allowed to enjoy some measure of relaxation. Finally, however, as a just punishment for the wickedness of man, al-Hakim became caliph of that realm [A.D. 996-1021]. The sin of this ruler so far exceeded those of his predecessors and successors alike that his name has become proverbial to later generations who read of his madness. This man was so notorious for every form of impiety and wickedness that his life, hateful to the sight of both God and man, deserves a special treatise. Conspicuous among the many other impious acts for which he was responsible was that of the total demolition of the church of the Lord's Resurrection. . . .

Yaruk, the governor of Ramle, one of Hakim's officers, took it upon himself to carry out the imperial command and immediately razed the edifice to the very ground. The head of the church at the time was the venerable Orestus, a maternal uncle of that same wicked ruler. Report says that the caliph used this extreme measure to prove to the infidels that he was loyal to them. For the name of Christian was used as a reproach against him, because he was born of a Christian mother. Hence, desiring to clear himself of that charge, he ventured to perpetrate that crime. In the belief that thereafter no reproaches could be cast against his person and that his rivals would have opportunity for no further malicious attacks, he had overthrown the cradle of the Catholic faith, the fount from which the Christian religion flows. (William of Tyre 1943: I, 65-67)

We shall return to this signal event of the destruction of the Church of the Holy Sepulcher, which took place in A.D. 1009, ninety years before the coming of the Crusaders. But for now, William continues his narrative:

From that time the condition of Christians in Jerusalem became far worse, not alone because of the righteous sorrow they felt over the destruction of the Church of the Holy Resurrection, but also on account of the increased burdens arising from manifold services. Enormous tribute and taxes were demanded from them, contrary to custom and the privileges granted by their former lords. In addition, they were forbidden to observe the religious rites which, under their various masters, they had been free to practice, both openly and in secret. The more solemn the day, the more strictly were they forced to remain within their own houses. They dared not come forth in public. Even home, however, proved no safe refuge for them. The enemy threw stones and filth and made fierce attacks upon them. On their solemn feast days especially they were annoyed beyond measure. For the slightest trivial word, at the demand of any chance accuser, they were dragged away to punishment and torture, without due process of law. Their goods were confiscated, their possessions stolen. Their sons and daughters were snatched away from home and forced, either by the lash or by soft words and promises, to forswear their faith or suffer on the gibbet.

He who was at this time their patriarch at first bore these injuries and insults, then exhorted his people both secretly and openly to show forbearance; he promised that, in return for the temporal evils which they were suffering, they should have crowns in the life hereafter. Inspired by his words and example, they comforted one another with mutual affection and, for Christ's sake, scorned temporary evils. . . .

At length divine mercy and compassion visited the afflicted people and brought no slight assistance for their desperate situation. For when that wicked prince [al-Hakim] was removed from earthly affairs [A.D. 1021] and his son Zahir succeeded to the royal power, persecution from that source ceased. Zahir renewed the treaty which his father had broken, and entered into alliance with Romanus [III] [A.D. 1028-1034], the emperor of Constantinople, surnamed of Heliopolis. At the request of the latter, Zahir granted the Christians the privilege of restoring the church. Yet although they had received this permission, the faithful at Jerusalem well knew that their own means alone were not adequate for the restoration of so important an edifice. They therefore sent an embassy to Constantine [IX] Monomachus [A.D. 1042-1055], the successor of Romanus, who was wielding the scepter at that time. With many humble entreaties, the envoys described the deep sorrow and desolation in which the people had lived since the destruction of their church. Most lovingly they besought him that he should extend the generous hand of imperial munificence toward the rebuilding of the church.

. . . Since permission had been granted and the expenses were assured from the imperial treasury, they built the Church of the Holy Resurrection, the same that is now at Jerusalem. This was in the year 1048 of the Incarnation of the Lord, fifty-one years before the liberation of the city, but the thirty-seventh after the destruction of the church. 6 When the building was completed, the people were comforted for the many deadly perils and imminent dangers to which they were exposed.

Yet repeated wrongs and tribulations under new forms did not cease to afflict that faithful people. They were spit upon and cuffed; they were thrown into chains and prisons; in fact, they suffered incessantly every sort of punishment. This persecution was practiced not only upon Christians who dwelt in Jerusalem but also upon the true believers who lived in Bethlehem and Tekoah. Whenever a new governor came or the caliph sent a representative, fresh insults were devised for God's people and various methods of extortion invented. When their oppressors desired to exact anything by force from either the patriarch or the people, any delay in rendering obedience was immediately followed by the threat that the church would be pulled down. Nearly every year they endured the same treatment. The overseers pretended that his imperial majesty had given strict orders that, if they ventured to make any delay in the payment of tribute or taxes, their churches were to be razed immediately. (William of Tyre 1943: I, 67-71)

The Turks

William backtracks to instruct his readers on the origin and nature of the Turks, both in their organized political form as the dynasty of the Seljuqs and in those other tribes "which still retained their rude and primitive mode of life . . . known by their original name as Turkomans" (I, 7). Then he returns to the plight of the Christians:

In the midst of the insidious perils of these times, it happened that a numerous company of Greeks and Latins, after risking death in a thousand forms in hostile lands, arrived in Jerusalem. They had come for the purpose of worshipping at the venerated places, but the keepers of the gates refused them admittance until they should pay the gold piece that was fixed as tribute money. Those who had lost their all upon the way, however, and had with extreme difficulty arrived in physical safety at their longed-for goal, had nothing with which to pay tribute.

So it happened that more than a thousand pilgrims, who had gathered before the city to await the privilege of entering, died of hunger and nakedness. These people, whether living or dead, were an intolerable burden to the local citizens. They attempted to keep alive those who survived by furnishing them with such food as they could. They also made an effort to bury the dead, although their own affairs were beyond their strength. Those pilgrims who paid the usual tribute and received permission to enter Jerusalem brought still greater responsibility upon the citizens. For there was danger, as they wandered about incautiously in their eagerness to visit the holy places, that they would be spit upon, or boxed on the ears or, worst of all, be furtively smothered to death. Consequently, as the pilgrims hastened to the holy places, the [local Christian] citizens followed them in brotherly kindness. Anxious for their life and safety and full of terror lest some unlucky accident befall them, they hoped in this way to prevent such mishaps. (William of Tyre 1943: I, 79-80)

No one, medieval or modern, has disputed the events William describes: the persecution by al-Hakim, the razing of the Church of the Holy Sepulcher, the request and permission to rebuild it, the hard and frequently vexatious conditions imposed on pilgrims to the Holy City. The heart of the question lies in the implication that something generally new had occurred in Jerusalem, which was, as William himself expressed quite explicitly and as we have seen in Chapter Six, the result of the Seljuq Turks' wresting Jerusalem from the Fatimids.

It is precisely this that we cannot verify. The Turkish occupation of Jerusalem lasted from 1071 to 1098, when the city was retaken for the Fatimids even as the first Crusade was getting under way, and there is absolutely no evidence to suggest that things were any better or any worse in Jerusalem than they had been under the Fatimids.[7] Where the Turks were a threat was, of course in Anatolia, where in their progress toward Constantinople they were swallowing up lands that had never been part of the "Abode of Islam." The Byzantines indeed had reason to fear the Turks, a fear they actively proselytized in the West,[8] and William may have extrapolated the sentiment to Jerusalem. The new conquest of old

Christian lands and the treatment of Christians who had lived under Islam for four centuries, as those in Jerusalem had, were two very different matters, however.

William of Tyre's account makes clear something else, however, that is far more consequential. It was not the decline in Christian pilgrimage to Jerusalem but precisely its increase in the eleventh century that brought home to the Muslim rulers of the city—the local governor or the absentee caliph or sultan in Cairo or Damascus or eventually Istanbul—that here was a considerable source of revenue. Palestine, whether ruled by the Fatimids before the Crusades or a succession of Islamic dynasties after it, was a poor place with few sources of tax revenue. But by the eleventh century it had become clear to those rulers that Palestine had at least one commodity that could be taxed in the form of duties, dues, admission fees, protection money, the sale of privileges, or simply extortion: the Christian pilgrims who annually came from Europe to visit the holy places. In other words, the Muslims discovered the Jerusalem tourist industry, and the raw edges of its transactions already sprawl across William of Tyre's account, as they will on other pages into modern times.

Al-Hakim and the Holy Sepulcher

One event cited by William was indeed unique in the piebald story of the relations of the Muslims and their Christian, and Jewish, subjects: the destruction in 1009 of the Church of the Anastasis—the Christians' *Kanisat al-Qiyama*, or Church of the Resurrection, which the Muslims derisively called "the Church of the Dungheap," *Kanisat al-Qumâma*. And here at last we can begin to invoke Muslim witnesses as well. The Muslims never meditated upon the causes of the Crusades, since, to put it only slightly hyperbolically, they never understood there had been a Crusade, a Christian holy war directed specifically at Jerusalem and the Holy Land. But al-Hakim was a well-known figure across the Islamic world, and his actions in Jerusalem provoked both comment and meditation. The most detailed account is given by Ibn al-Qalanisi, the Syrian historian who died in 1160:

It is told in the history of al-Hakim bi-amri'llah that in 398 [A.D. 1007-1008] he ordered the destruction of the Church of al-Qumama in Jerusalem, a church that had a considerable importance for the Christians and which they venerated. The reason for the destruction of this church and of the related measures to destroy the synagogues and churches in Syria and Egypt and the obligation that he imposed on the dhimmis [9] *to wear distinctive signs is as follows. It was the current custom of the Christians* of Egypt to go every year to Jerusalem in great camel-litters to celebrate Easter there in the Church of the Qumama. This year they departed in the customary way, with a great and expensive display, much in the fashion of the pilgrims departing for Mecca. Al-Hakim requested of the missionary Qutekin al-Adudi, [10] who was present at court, information on why the Christians went to that church, on their beliefs in this matter and to tell him what value they placed on it.

Qutekin knew about the matter by reason of the frequent trips he had made to Syria and his frequent correspondence in al-Hakim's name with the governors there. "This church," he told him, "is near the al-Aqsa Mosque. The Christians are extremely devoted to it and go there every Easter from every land. Sometimes the Byzantine emperors and the most important of their patricians go there, incognito of course. They carry there immense sums of silver, [priestly] vestments, dyed cloths, and tapestries. They have lamps made for it, crosses and chalices of gold and silver, and over the course of a long period of time there has been amassed there a considerable number of objects of great value and of the most various types. When the Christians go there on the day of their Easter, and their metropolitan appears in public and they all raise their crosses and perform their prayers and ceremonies, all that makes a great impression on their spirits and introduces confusion in their hearts. They hang their lamps on the altar, and then by a trick they cause fire to appear in the balsam oil in their lamps, since this oil has the property of igniting with the oil of jasmine and it produces a flame of remarkable whiteness and brilliance. . . . Those who see it imagine that the fire has come down from heaven and lit the lamps."

When al-Hakim had heard this explanation, he summoned Bish ibn Sawar [or Severus], the secretary of the chancery and ordered him to write to the prefect of Ramle and to Ya'qub the missionary agent and tell them to go to Jerusalem with the nobles, qadis, witnesses, and local notables, to take up quarters in Jerusalem, go to the Church of al-Qumama, remove everything there and demolish it. When they had done this they should make an official report, sign it, and send it to Cairo.

As soon as they got this letter, they left to execute the order they had received. The Christians of Egypt meanwhile had been informed of what was going on and hastened to the patriarch of the church [in Jerusalem], informed him of the matter and put him on guard. They took the precaution of removing the gold and silver objects, the jewels, and the vestments in the church. Al-Hakim's agents then arrived, surrounded the church and gave the order to loot it and had carried away whatever was left, which was of considerable value. Then the building was destroyed stone by stone. A report was drawn up, signed as he had ordered, and sent to al-

Hakim. News of the event spread in Egypt. The Muslims rejoiced at hearing it and showered al-Hakim with gratitude for what he had done. His information agents reported on the public reaction, which pleased him a great deal and he ordered the destruction of churches and synagogues in the various provinces. (Ibn al-Qalanisi 1932: 66)

Some additional details from still another perspective are supplied by Yahya ibn Sa'id, an eleventh-century Christian historian from Antioch:

[After the destruction of churches in Cairo] al-Hakim likewise sent to Syria, to Yarukh, governor of Ramle, written orders to destroy the Church of the Holy Resurrection, to get rid of the Christian emblems and to destroy completely the Christian relics. Yarukh sent to Jerusalem his son Yusuf and Husayn ibn Zahir, the inspector of currency, with Abu al-Fawaris al-Dayf. They confiscated all the furnishings that were in the church, after which they razed it completely, except those parts that were impossible to destroy or would have been too difficult to carry away. The Cranion [Golgotha] was destroyed, as well as the Church of St. Constantine and everything that was found in the precinct. The complete destruction of the relics was accomplished. Ibn Zahir bent every effort to demolish the Holy Sepulcher and to remove its every trace; he broke up the greater part of it and removed it. In the neighborhood of the Holy Sepulcher there was a convent of women called Dayr al-Sari, which he likewise destroyed. The demolition began on 5 Safar 400/28 [September 1009]. All the goods and endowed possessions belonging to the church were seized, as well as all the cult objects and gold ornaments. (Yahya ibn Sa'id, 491-492)

Al-Hakim did not much puzzle medieval historians, Jewish, Christian, or Muslim, most of whom branded him mad, as did William of Tyre. Perhaps he was, at least in the extravagance of his policy, since it was not simply the Holy Sepulcher that was destroyed—many other churches and synagogues suffered the same fate. Nor was it only the Christians and Jews who were persecuted by the Fatimid caliph; his repressive measures against Muslims in Cairo provoked such a reaction that by 1020 he had to reconcile himself to the Jews and the Christians to find any support. In the end, he outraged even his own followers with the proclamation of his own divinity. Perhaps he was reacting against the strong Christian influences in his own upbringing, and perhaps too there was some calculated anti-Byzantine purpose in his provocations in Jerusalem. [11] But the events surrounding the destruction of Christendom's central shrine, and their sequel, remain extraordinary.

The Descent of the Holy Fire

According to Ibn al-Qalanisi, though not to the Christians Yahya or William of Tyre, there was at least a provocation for the burning of the Holy Sepulcher in the presence there of the remarkable annual miracle called "the Descent of the Holy Fire," an act that dazzled—and later appalled—Christian visitors to the Holy Sepulcher down to the twentieth century [12] and elicited among Muslim witnesses a curious mixture of admiration and disdain. It is clear that the Muslims did view it, in both an official and an unofficial capacity, and that the experience gave rise to a number of reactions, among them stunned outrage, that still shook the native Jerusalem historian Mujir al-Din at the end of the fifteenth century:

> The practice [of the Descent of the Holy Fire] is still going on in our time in the Qumama, and the day is called "the Saturday of the Light." There occur under the very eyes of the Muslims a number of hateful things which are not right to hear or look upon. Making public manifestation of their infidel faith, the Christians cry out in a loud voice "Hasten to the religion of the Cross!" They recite their books aloud, raise their crosses above their heads, and give themselves over to other abominations which make one shudder with horror. (Mujir 1876: 67-689)

The point, it appears, was that the Christians could annually and publicly stage an apparent miracle at their chief shrine in Jerusalem that seemed to proclaim the validity of both the place and the event it celebrated, the resurrection of the Christian Messiah Jesus. The Muslims were unable to deny the evidence of their own senses, but they had other ways of attacking the problem. What might be called a "political solution" is detailed in a report written from Jerusalem to the Byzantine emperor Constantine Porphyrogenitus in 947:

> Early on Holy Saturday an amir arrived here from Baghdad with the governor of the province and went to the Pretorium, filled with fury and rage. Cruel messengers soon made his arrival known to Patriarch Christodoulos, whom they brought to the Pretorium. [The amir told Christodoulos that he had come to prohibit the future celebration of the Holy Saturday feast] . . . since, in performing your celebrated miracle with magic artifices, you have filled all of Syria with the religion of the Christians and you have all but destroyed all of our customs; you have made of it a "Romania."

The patriarch protested this accusation of magic and assured the amir that his predecessor had replaced with metal the wick in the lamp placed before the Holy Sepulcher but that the divine breath had nonetheless lit it of a sudden like a taper. The Christian secretaries in the employ of the amir took up the defense of the patriarch by pointing out that he could not pay the heavy public assessments if they prohibited this annual feast, and they threatened to report the amir to the caliph if he persisted in his interference.

Following upon this intervention, the amir had recourse to another plot. He demanded of the patriarch, under the threat of prohibiting the popular feast of the Resurrection of Christ, a payment of 7,000 gold pieces. This payment would not have been made except for an immediate disbursement by the secretaries of 2,000 gold pieces with a guarantee of the remaining 5,000. While the patriarch was being held in custody in the Pretorium, the God of miracles filled two of the lamps of the triple lamp suspended at the place where they said the body of Christ was taken down from the cross to be washed. When the news of this wonder came to the Pretorium, Christians and Muslims ran pell-mell to the church. But the Muslims came filled with bloody thoughts and murderous designs, armed and ready to slay every Christian carrying a lighted lamp. The patriarch arrived, followed by the clergy, and having determined that the illumination of the sacred fire had not yet taken place, with the help of the Muslims had the Holy Sepulcher closed and began to pray with the Christians. Toward the sixth hour, fixing his gaze on the Holy Sepulcher, he saw the supernatural appearance of the light. He entered the Holy Sepulcher whose entry was shown to him by an angel. At the moment when he took a taper to give of the divine fire to all of those in the church who had torches, scarcely had he come out of the tomb, when he saw the church suddenly filled with a divine light. The faithful were standing on the right and the left, some near the door, some by Calvary, others near the cruciform chain suspended from the ceiling and all around which they had hung their lamps, the chain, that is, which passes for representing the center of the world and which is hung there as a sign, so that all men might be astonished at the apparition of the divine fire. The Muslims themselves were filled with astonishment since up to that point the apparition of this light annually occurred at only one of the lamps inside the Holy Sepulcher, while on this day the entire church was filled with light. The amir, who was looking on from above on one of the tribunes, was witness to an even greater miracle. The largest of the lamps suspended in front of him let escape the oil and water which it contained and was suddenly filled with a divine fire even though it had no wick at all. (Canard 1965: 30-33)

The tale told the emperor had, not unnaturally, a happy Christian ending, this despite the fact that the cotton wicks in the lamps were replaced by nonflammable metal. We hear elsewhere of similar efforts to prevent the

"Descent of the Fire." Here, for example, is a passage from al-Biruni's work on the holidays of various religious groups in the Islamic world, which concludes with obvious bafflement:

A story is told in connection with the Saturday of the Resurrection that astonishes the investigator of the physical sciences and whose basis is impossible to uncover. If it were not for the agreement on the phenomenon of persons with differing views who report that it is based on eyewitness testimony and has been perpetuated by excellent scholars and other people in their books, one would give it no credence. I have learned of it in books and heard of it from al-Faraj ibn Salih of Baghdad. . . . A report is made on the subject which is sent to the capital of the caliphs as soon as the fire has descended. They say that if the fire comes down quickly and at a time close to midday, that presages a fertile year and that, on the contrary, the occurrence is delayed until the evening or afterwards, that that presages a year of famine. The one who told me of this reported that some of the [Muslim] authorities had the wick of the lamp replaced by a copper wire to the end that it would not take light and the ceremony thus be disrupted. But when the fire descended it was lit nonetheless. (Canard 1965: 36-37)

Al-Biruni's account, written in the early eleventh century, goes back to a source in the tenth, and the story of this famous miracle can be traced back to Muslim authors in the tenth and even ninth centuries.[13] The Christian Bernard, who was in Jerusalem in 870, gives the first sketchy but unmistakable description of the event:

It is unnecessary to write a great deal about the sepulcher (of the Lord) since Bede describes it at length in his history. But it is worth telling what happens (in that church) on Holy Saturday, the Vigil of Easter. The office begins early in the morning in this church, and when it is finished they go on singing the Kyrie eleison till an angel comes in and kindles light in the lamps which hang above the aforementioned sepulcher. The patriarch passes some of this fire to the bishops and the rest of the people, that each may light his home with it. . . . (Bernard, Itinerary, 11)

Bernard does not dwell on what was by all accounts a startling event and an emotional occasion. One of the fullest of the early descriptions is that of an authentic eyewitness, and one who had no doubts as to the authenticity of what he saw, the abbot Daniel who was in Jerusalem in 1106—that is, just shortly after the Crusaders took the city. It is thus no longer the Muslim amir but the Latin king Baldwin who is the official presence in the church:

The following is a description of the Holy Light which descends upon the Holy Sepulcher, as the Lord vouchsafed to show me, his wicked and unworthy servant. For in truth I have seen with my own sinful eyes how the Holy Light descends upon the redeeming Tomb of our Lord Jesus Christ. Many pilgrims relate incorrectly the details about the Holy Light. Some say that the Holy Spirit descends upon the Holy Sepulcher in the form of a dove; others that it is lightning from heaven that kindles the lamps above the Sepulcher of the Lord. This is all untrue for neither dove nor lightning is to be seen at that moment; but the divine grace comes down unseen from heaven and lights the lamps in the Sepulcher of our Lord. I will only describe it in perfect truth as I have seen it.

On Holy Friday, after Vespers, they clean the Holy Sepulcher and wash all the lamps there and fill them with pure oil, unmixed with water, and having put wicks in them, they do not light them. Seals are put on the Tomb at two in the morning and at the same time all the lamps and candles are extinguished in all the churches of Jerusalem. . . .

I went joyfully to buy a large glass lamp, and when I had filled it with virgin oil, I brought it to the Holy Sepulcher toward evening and asked for the guardian, who was alone in the chapel of the Tomb and had myself announced to him. He opened the holy door for me, told me to take off my shoes, and with bare feet, alone with my lamp, which I was carrying, he let me enter the Holy Sepulcher and bade me put the lamp down on the Tomb of the Lord. I did so, with my own sinful hands, there where reposed the blessed feet of Our Savior Jesus Christ, since the lamp of the Greeks was placed toward the head and that of St. Sabas and the other monasteries near the breast, since this is the annual custom. By the grace of God all three of these lamps were subsequently lit, while none of the lamps of the Franks, which were suspended above the Tomb, was lit.

After I had put my lamp on the Holy Tomb and venerated this holy place with kisses of compunction and the tears of piety, I left the Holy Tomb with great excitement and retired to my cell. The next day, at the sixth hour of Holy Saturday, everyone assembles at the Church of the Holy Resurrection, people from everywhere, foreigners, natives of the place, even from Babylon and Egypt and all points of the earth, in numbers that are difficult to estimate. The crowd filled the space around the church and around the place of the Crucifixion. The press of people became terrible and the pain so great that many people were crushed in this compact mass of humanity, all standing with unlit tapers in their hands and awaiting the opening of the doors of the church. Only the priests were inside, and everyone, clergy and laity, awaited the arrival of the prince and his court.

When they arrived, the doors were opened and the crowd rushed in, jostling and elbowing each other in terrible fashion and filled the entire church and its galleries. And since the church itself was not large enough to accommodate all of them, a large number were left outside, round about Golgotha and from the Place of the Skull as far as the spot where the Cross had been raised. People were everywhere, and all they could cry was "Lord, have mercy on us," and the cry was so powerful that the whole building shook with it. The faithful wept torrents of tears; even someone with a heart of stone would have wept. Hearts were scrutinized and sins recalled. "Will my sins prevent the Holy Fire from descending?" So the crowd stood there weeping and contrite; even Prince Baldwin had a contrite and humble countenance. Torrents of tears rolled from his eyes, and his courtiers, who surrounded him, stood in great recollection near the main altar before the Tomb.

Earlier, about the seventh hour of Saturday, Prince Baldwin had left his residence and going on foot toward the Church of the Holy Sepulcher, he sent to the monastery-hospice of St. Sabas to get the abbot and the monks there, and the abbot, followed by the monks, likewise went to the Holy Sepulcher, and I, unworthy sinner, I went with them. When we met the prince, we all saluted him. He returned our greeting and requested us, the abbot and myself to walk at his side. The other monks went ahead and his entourage brought up the rear. Thus we reached the western door of the Church of the Resurrection, but the crowd was massed so tightly there that we could not enter. Then Baldwin ordered his soldiers to disperse the crowd and open a passage. So they did and made a path to the Tomb, and that is how we got through the crowd.

We reached the eastern entrance of the Holy Sepulcher of the Lord, and the prince, following after, took his place on the right, near the great altar facing the eastern side of the Holy Sepulcher, where there was a raised place for him. The prince ordered the abbot of St. Sabas, together with his monks and the orthodox clergy, to arrange themselves above the Tomb, and as for unworthy me, he ordered me to go higher still, above the doors of the Holy Sepulcher, opposite the great altar, so that I could see past the doors of the Tomb, three of them, all sealed with the royal seal. As for the Latin clergy, they remained at the great altar.

At the eighth hour the orthodox clergy, which was above the Holy Sepulcher, together with all the other clerics, monks, and hermits, began to chant vespers; on their side, the Latin clergy muttered along in their peculiar fashion. While this chanting was in progress, I stood in my place and kept my gaze on the doors of the Tomb. When the chanting reached the lections for Holy Saturday, the bishop [the Latin patriarch], followed by the deacon, left the great altar during the initial lesson and approached the doors, looked through the grillwork into the interior, and when he did not see the light, returned to his place. He returned at the sixth lesson and still saw nothing. Then everyone began to cry out "Kyrie, eleison," which means "Lord, have mercy." At the end of the ninth hour, when they began to sing the passage "Cantabo Domino," a small cloud coming from the east suddenly came to rest over the open dome of the church and a light rain fell upon the Holy Sepulcher, and upon us too who were above the Tomb. It was then that the Holy Light suddenly illumined the Holy Sepulcher, stunningly bright and splendid. The bishop, followed by four deacons, then opened the doors of the Holy Sepulcher and went in with the candle he had taken from Prince Baldwin, the first to be lit from this holy fire. He then returned to replace it in the hands of the prince, who resumed his place once again, candle in hand and joy in his heart. It was from the prince's candle that we lit ours, which were then used to pass on the fire to the rest of the people in the church.

This holy fire is not like an ordinary flame but burns in a quite extraordinary way and with an indescribable brightness and with a red color the likes of cinnamon. Thus all the people then stood with lit candles in their hands and repeated loudly and with excitement "Lord, have mercy on us!" No one can experience the kind of joy that invades the heart of every Christian at that moment, when they see the Holy Light of God. Someone who has not shared in the excitement of that day cannot possibly believe that all that I saw is true. Only the truly wise and believing who bring a full faith to the truth of this narrative will hear with delight the details of the event. Even the lukewarm will be somewhat moved, but to the evil man and the doubter, the truth always seems distorted. As for my account and my lowly person, God and His Holy Sepulcher are my witnesses, as well as my companions from Russia and Novgorod and Kiev: Iziaslav, Ivanovitch, Gorodislav, Mikhailovitch, the two Kashkitches, and many others who were there that day.

But let us return to where I digressed. Scarcely had the light shone out in the Holy Sepulcher than the chanting ceased and the whole crowd, crying "Kyrie, eleison" and cupping the candles in their hand against the draft, ran out of the church in great excitement. Everyone went back to his own place and with his candle lit the lamps of the churches and completed vespers there, while only the clergy stayed behind and finished vespers in the great church of the Holy Sepulcher. Carrying our lit candles we returned to the convent with the abbot and the monks. We finished vespers there and then retired to our cells, praising God for having deigned to allow us to witness, unworthy though we were, His divine favor. (Daniel the Abbot 1895: 74-79)

The Holy Sepulcher Rebuilt

This, then, was the public and notorious miracle that, on the testimony of the Muslim historians, so exercised al-Hakim that he commanded the destruction of the Church of the Holy Sepulcher. From there William of Tyre passes, as we have seen, to the account of the reconstruction of the church, a work that was probably begun in 1030 and completed in 1048 under the auspices and at the expense of the Byzantine emperor Constantine IX Monomachus. But it was not constructed as it had been before. Al-Hakim's destruction changed the face of the church forever. The Byzantine architects saved the lines of the rotunda over the Sepulcher—the entire western circuit of that building appears to have survived the Fatimid demolition—but what was gone and never rebuilt was all of Constantine the Great's immense basilica that had stretched from Calvary eastward to the main market street of the city; it remained nothing more than a field of ruins for a half-century until the coming of the Crusaders. At the place where it had joined the rotunda, the Byzantines constructed a large archway and, slightly beyond it, an eastern apse. [14]

The results of the reconstruction were not altogether unworthy, at least if we credit this account by a Muslim visitor, Nasir-i Khusraw, who saw the Church of the Holy Sepulcher in 1047, that is, when the new structure was all but complete. The Muslim, whose own religion forbade figurative religious art, was naturally most curious about the pictures there, and in their preservation:

The present day church [of the Holy Sepulcher] is a most spacious building and is capable of holding 8,000 people. The edifice is built most skillfully of colored marbles, with ornamentation and sculptures. Inside, the church is everywhere adorned with Byzantine brocade worked in gold with pictures. And they have portrayed Jesus—peace be upon him—who at times is shown riding an ass. There are also pictures representing others of the Prophets, Abraham, for example, and Ishmael and Isaac, and Jacob with his son—peace be upon them all. These pictures they have overlaid with a varnish of the oil of Sandaracha [or red juniper], and for the face of each portrait they have made a plate of thin glass to cover it, and it is perfectly transparent. This dispenses with the need of a curtain and prevents any dust or dirt from settling on the painting, for the glass is cleaned daily by the servants [of the church]. . . . In the church there is a picture divided into two parts representing Heaven and Hell. One part shows the saved in Paradise, while the other depicts the damned in Hell, with all that there is there. Assuredly there is in no other place in the world a picture like this. There are seated in this church great numbers of priests and monks who read the Gospel and say prayers, for day and night they are occupied in this manner. (Nasir-i Khusraw 1893: 60)

William of Tyre on the Causes
of the Crusade

The destruction of the Church of Holy Sepulcher did not bring on the Crusade. It figures in William of Tyre's analysis, but chiefly, one suspects, because he not only enjoyed the historian's hindsight but was exceedingly well informed on what had happened in the Holy Land prior to the coming of the Latins; the event is unmarked, on the other hand, in our preserved accounts of the pre-Crusade preaching and rhetoric in Europe. But even William does not give al-Hakim's act undue prominence. This, for example, is his summing up of the events that led to the Crusade:

Thus neither at home nor abroad was there any rest for the [Christian] citizens [of Jerusalem]. Death threatened them every day and, what was worse than death, the fear of servitude, harsh and intolerable, ever lowered before them. Another thing caused them extreme distress. Even while they were in the very act of celebrating the holy rites, the enemy would violently force an entrance into the churches which had been restored and preserved with such infinite difficulty. Utterly without reverence for the consecrated places, they sat upon the very altars and struck terror to the heart of the worshippers with their mad cries and whistlings. They overturned the chalices, trod underfoot the utensils devoted to the divine offices, broke the marble statues and showered blows and insults upon the clergy. The Lord Patriarch then in office was dragged from his seat by hair and beard and thrown to the ground like a mean and abject person. Again and again he was seized and thrust into prison without cause. Treatment fit only for the lowest slave was inflicted upon him in order to torture his people, who suffered with him as with a father. . . .

For 490 years, as has been stated, this devoted people of God endured cruel bondage with pious long-suffering. With tearful groans and sighs, ever constant in prayer, they cried to God, begging that he would spare them now that their sins were corrected and that, in His great mercy, He would turn away from them the source of His wrath. . . . Finally, the Lord looked with pity upon them from His seat of glory, and desiring to end such tribulation, determined with fatherly care to comfort them as they desired. In the present work it is our intention to set down, as a perpetual memorial to the faithful in Christ, the method and ordering of this divine plan by which He purposed to relieve the long-continued affliction of His people. (William of Tyre 1943: I, 81)

The Walls Rebuilt

William's attention is drawn, not unnaturally, to the plight of Latin visitors to Jerusalem in the eleventh century, but he does provide some information on the local Christian community, as for example, in his account of the origins of the Christian quarter in the city:

At this period the kingdom of the [Fatimid] Egyptians surpassed all other kingdoms of the East and the South, not alone in strength and riches, but also in worldly wisdom. Desiring to enlarge the limits of his empire and expand his sovereignty far and wide, the caliph of Egypt sent out his armies and seized by force the whole of Syria even to Laodicea, a city which lies next to Antioch and is the boundary of Coele Syria. . . . Moreover, he ordered each city to rebuild its walls and raise strong towers around about it. In accordance with this general edict, the procurator in charge of Jerusalem compelled the inhabitants of the place to obey the common orders and restore the walls and towers to their former condition.

Unless William is telescoping different events, this was not the first attempt to rebuild the walls of Jerusalem. The tenth-century Christian historian from the East, Yahya ibn Saʿid, tells us how the walls were earlier damaged by a series of shattering earthquakes that struck not only Jerusalem but the entire area of Syria-Palestine:

In this year, after he had built the wall of Ramle, [Caliph] al-Zahir began work on the wall of the city of Jerusalem. Those who were in charge of the construction had destroyed many churches outside the city and used the stones from them. [15] *They had even decided to tear down the Church of Mount Sion to carry off its stones for the wall. But there occurred in the land a terrible earthquake, the likes of which had never been seen or heard, late on Thursday, the tenth of Safar in the year 424 [A.D. 1033] A great number of people perished. The city of Jericho fell in ruins upon its inhabitants, and similarly the city of Nablus and the towns in its vicinity. A part of the mosque of Jerusalem collapsed, as did a number of convents and churches around the city. Buildings also collapsed in the city of Acre and a great number of people died. The water drained out of the harbor there for a whole hour then returned to its normal state. (Yahya ibn Sa'id 2:272)*

This natural disaster made a deep impression on the cities struck by it. When Nasir-i Khusraw visited Ramle, the Muslim administrative center for Palestine not far from Jerusalem, he saw in the Great Mosque there an inscription dated December 10, 1033, declaring that on that day "there came an earthquake of great violence, which threw down a large number of buildings. . . ." Another inscription, which a Muslim read and recorded in the Aqsa Mosque during the Crusader occupation, likewise bears witness to the damage in Jerusalem: the reconstruction of the Aqsa dome at the Fatimid caliph's expense:

In the name of God, the Compassionate, the Merciful. Glory to Him who "transported by night His servant from the Sacred Mosque to the Further Mosque whose environs We have blessed" [Quran 17:1]. May God grant His support to His servant and friend Abu'l-Hasan Ali, the Imam al-Zahir li-i'zâz dini llâh, Commander of the Faithful. May the blessings of God be upon him, on his pure ancestors and his most noble descendents. The order to construct and gild this dome was given by our lord, the most illustrious vizier, the intimate and sincere friend of the Commander of the Faithful, Abu'l-Qasim Ali b. Ahmad, may God assist and sustain him. All was completed by the end of Dhu al-Qa'da of the year 426 [October 1035]. The work of Abdullah b. al-Hasan al-Misri the mosaicist.[16] (Harawi 1957: 64)

We return to William of Tyre's discussion of the rebuilding of the walls:

In the distribution of this work, it happened, rather by malice afore-thought than by a just parcelling out, that a fourth part of this construction work was assigned to the wretched Christians who were living in Jerusalem. These faithful people, however, were already so ground down by corvées and extra corvées, by tributes and taxes, and by the rendering of various ignominious services that the wealth of the entire community was scarcely sufficient to enable them to restore even one or two of these towers. Perceiving, therefore, that their enemies were seeking occasion against them and having no other resort, they betook themselves to the governor. . . . Through the intervention of many mediators and the free use of gifts, they finally succeeded in obtaining a stay of sentence from the governor until envoys should be sent to the emperor in Constantinople to implore alms from him for the accomplishment of their task.

At that time Constantine [X, 1059-1067], a wise and splendid man, was wielding the scepter and administering with vigorous energy the empire of Constantinople. He gave a ready assent to the pitiful petitions of Christ's faithful ones and promised them money with which to accomplish the task laid upon them, for he felt full and loving sympathy with their continuing troubles and afflictions. He added this condition, however: the money should be given if they could obtain a promise from the lord of the land that none but Christians should be permitted to dwell within the circuit of the wall which they proposed to erect by means of the imperial donation. Forthwith, the emperor wrote to Cyprus directing the people of that island, in the event of the Christians' obtaining the necessary concession at Jerusalem, to supply them, from taxes and money due the treasury, with a sum sufficient to pay for the said work.

[The caliph in Cairo] Having at last brought the matter to a successful end, the [Jerusalem] deputies returned home and the Christians, with the help of God, completed the portion of the wall allotted to them. This was in the year . . . 1063, in the thirty-sixth year before the liberation of the city, under the reign of the Egyptian caliph Mustansir [A.D. 1035-1094].

Up to that time the Saracens and Christians dwelt together indifferently. Thenceforward, by order of the prince, the Saracens were forced to remove to other parts of Jerusalem, leaving the quarter named to the faithful without dispute. By this change the condition of the servants of God was materially improved. Because of their enforced association with the men of Belial, quarrels had often arisen, which greatly increased their troubles. When at last they were able to dwell by themselves, without the disturbance of discord, their lives flowed more tranquilly. Any disagreements which arose were referred to the church, and the controversy was settled by the decision of the patriarch then ruling as sole mediator.

From that day, then, and in the manner just described, this quarter of the city had no other judge or lord than the patriarch, and the church therefore laid claim to that section as its own in perpetuity. (William of Tyre 1943: I, 405-406)

Protection and Concessions

The true significance of the destruction of the Holy Sepulcher with regard to the Crusades lay in its political consequences, and chiefly in the direct intervention of Christian powers abroad, in this case the Byzantines in the person of their emperor, on behalf of the Jerusalem Christians. The Byzantine protectorate in Jerusalem appears to have been at least tacitly recognized by even the Egyptian caliphs in that the Jerusalem Christians were permitted to subsidize themselves from the emperor's purse, harmlessly enough perhaps in the case of the rebuilding of the Anastasis, but with certain concessions in the case of the reconstruction of the wall. The Christian Quarter, also called the Patriarch's Quarter, which was partially enclosed by the wall, had, as William of Tyre just put it, "no other judge or lord than the patriarch. . . ." The Jerusalem Christians discovered they could buy autonomy, and the price of the purchase was sustained, and some of its rewards collected, in Constantinople.

The prototype of this "protectorate" arrangement was, as we have seen in Chapter Six, that modestly pioneered by Charlemagne. With the earlier ruler it was perhaps no more than the recognition of an "interest" in Jerusalem, but with Constantine IX and X, that interest became more formal and more urgent. [17] The distant Charlemagne posed no threat to his far more powerful and affluent contemporaries in Baghdad, but in the tenth century Byzantium demonstrated both its capacity and its will to retake some of the Islamic possessions, and in the eleventh the two powers—Byzantine and Fatimid—were joined by both the threat of military aggression and the promise of mutual gain in the growing world of Mediterranean commerce. Both the threat and the promise are captured in one visitor's brief impressions of the Syrian port of Tripoli some time about 1047, a little over half a century after Muqaddasi described the situation there (see Chapter Six). The reporter is now the Persian Shiʿite, Nasir-i Khusraw:

The city of Tripoli belongs to the [Fatimid] sultan of Egypt. The origin of this, as I was told, is that when, a certain time ago, an army of infidels from Byzantium had come against the city, the Muslims from Egypt came and fought them and put them to flight. The sultan of Egypt has remitted his right to the land tax in the city. There is always a body of the sultan's troops in garrison here, with a commander set over them, to keep the city safe from the enemy. The city too is a place for customs dues, where all ships that come from the coasts of the Greeks and the Franks and from Andalusia and the Maghreb have to pay a tithe to the sultan, which sums are used for the rations of the garrison. The sultan also has ships of his own here, which sail to Byzantium and Sicily and the West to carry merchandise.

The people of Tripoli are all of the Shiʿa sect. The Shiʿites in all countries have built fine mosques for themselves. There are in this place houses like watch stations,[18] only no one lives there as a garrison, and they call them mashhads *or "shrines." There are no houses outside the city of Tripoli, except two or three of the* mashhads *just mentioned. (Nasir-i Khusraw 1893: 8)*

The Origins of the Hospital

As Nasir's text suggests, it was not merely the Byzantines who were conducting trade in and with the East; there were Europeans involved there as well, and they too expressed an interest in Jerusalem, according to William of Tyre. Just as William's interest in the Patriarch's Quarter arose not so much from a curiosity about the topography of Fatimid Jerusalem as from an interest in establishing precedent for the jurisdictional claims of the Latin patriarchs once the Crusaders had taken Jerusalem, so his interest in another Latin institution there led him back into the eleventh- and eventually into the ninth-century past of the city. William's reflections on Charlemagne's half-historical, half-legendary connection with the Holy City have already been cited in Chapter Six. One of that emperor's beneficiaries was, as we have seen, the hospice located near the Holy Sepulcher on the site of what was once Hadrian's forum in the Upper City of Jerusalem. Its history after Charlemagne is unknown, but in the eleventh century it emerges once more, and now into the more certain light of history:

There was a monastery in the city belonging to the people of Amalfi, which was called, as it is even yet, St. Mary of the Latins. Close by, also, was a hospital with a modest chapel in honor of St. John the Almoner. This was under the charge of the abbot of the monastery just mentioned. Here aid was given at any time to wretched pilgrims who arrived under such circumstances, the expense being defrayed either by the monastery or from the offerings of the faithful. Scarcely one out of a thousand pilgrims who came was able to provide for himself. Many had lost their travelling money and were so exhausted by dreadful hardships that they were barely able to reach their destination in safety. (William of Tyre 1943: I, 80-81)

Although the holy places were thus under the power of the enemy [Saracens], from time to time many people from the West visited them for the sake of devotion or business, possibly for both. Among those from the West who ventured at that time to go to the holy places for purposes of trade were certain men from Italy who were known as Amalfitani from the name of their city. . . . The people of Amalfi . . . were the first who, for the sake of gain, attempted to carry to the Orient foreign wares hitherto unknown to the East. Because of the necessary articles which they brought thither, they obtained very advantageous terms from the principal men of those lands and were permitted to come there freely. The people were also favorably disposed toward them. . . . The Amalfitani enjoyed the full favor of the king [of Egypt] as well as of his nobles and were able to travel in perfect safety all over the country as traders and dealers in the useful articles which they carried. Faithful to the traditions of their fathers and the Christian profession, these merchants were in the habit of visiting the holy places whenever opportunity offered. They had no house of their own in Jerusalem, however, where they might remain for a while, as they had in the coast cities. To carry out a long-cherished plan, therefore, they assembled as many people of their own city as possible and visited the caliph of Egypt. They gained the good will of the people of his household, presented a petition in writing, and received a favorable response, in accordance with their desires.

A written order was accordingly sent to the governor of Jerusalem, directing that a very ample area of Jerusalem, in that part of the city occupied by Christians, be designated at their request for the people of Amalfi, friends and carriers of useful articles. There they were to erect such a building as they desired. The city was divided at that time, as it is today, into four almost equal parts; of these that quarter alone which contains the Sepulcher of the Lord had been granted to the faithful as their abode. The rest of the city, with the Temple of the Lord, was occupied exclusively by infidels.

In accordance with the caliph's command, a place sufficiently large for the necessary buildings was set aside for the people of Amalfi. Offerings of money were collected from the merchants, and before the door of the church of the Resurrection of the Lord, barely a stone's throw away, they built a monastery in honor of the holy and glorious mother of God, the Ever Virgin Mary. In connection with this there were suitable offices for the use of the monks and for the entertainment of guests from their own city. When the place was finished, they brought an abbot and monks from Amalfi and established the monastery under a regular rule as a place of holy life acceptable to the Lord. Since those who had founded the place and maintained it in religion were men of the Latin race, it has been called from that time to this the monastery of the Latins.

Even in those days it happened that chaste and holy widows came to Jerusalem to kiss the revered places. Regardless of natural timidity, they had met without fear the numberless dangers of the way. Since there was no place within the portals of the monastery where such pilgrims might be honorably received, the same pious men who had founded the monastery made a suitable provision for these people also, that when devout women came they might not lack a chapel, a house, and separate quarters of their own. A little convent was finally established there, by divine mercy, in honor of that pious sinner, Mary Magdalen, and a regular number of sisters placed there to minister to women pilgrims.

During these same perilous times there also flocked thither people of other nations, both nobles and those of the middle class. As there was no approach to the Holy City except through hostile lands, pilgrims had usually exhausted their travelling money by the time they reached Jerusalem. Wretched and helpless, a prey to all the hardships of hunger, thirst, and nakedness, such pilgrims were forced to wait before the city gates until they had paid a gold coin, when they were permitted to enter the city. Even after they had finally gained admission and had visited the holy

Above, the Chapel of the Ascension with flanking minaret. *Right*, inside the present chapel; the interior was considerably more elaborate in Arculf's day (pp. 206-207).

An aerial view of the summit of the Mount of Olives. The chapel of the Ascension is inside the walled enclosure at the center; lower down the slope on the left, the remains of the Eleona, later called the Church of the Pater Noster.

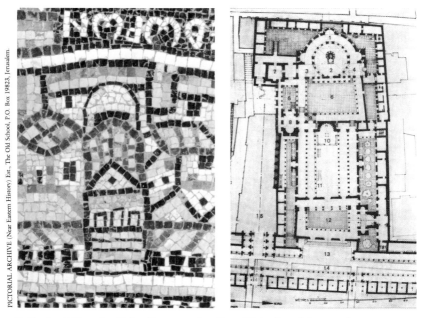

Left, the "Church of the Resurrection," or Holy Sepulcher, as it appears on the sixth-century Madaba map. *Right*, the plan of Constantine's Holy Sepulcher (2) and Calvary (8) complex in its finished, late fourth century version.

PICTORIAL ARCHIVE (Near Eastern History) Est., The Old School, P.O. Box 19823, Jerusalem.

Above, the Haram al-Sharif, or Noble Sanctuary (actually the platform of Herod's Temple), from the northeast, with the Dome of the Rock in the center and the Aqsa Mosque just beyond. *Below*, the Rock under the Dome.

Above left, the Dome of the Prophet, shown here directly in front of the Dome of the Rock; and *above right*, the Dome of the Ascension, south and west of the Dome of the Rock on the Haram platform. *Below*, the often rebuilt Aqsa Mosque at the southern end of the Haram. As in most mosques, the dome is over the prayer niche signalling the direction toward Mecca.

Above, the Haram from the south, with excavations of the seventh-century palace built by the Umayyad caliphs in the foreground on the left. *Below*, the partially restored western facade of the Umayyad palace. Rising directly behind is the southwest corner of Herod's Temple platform.

The facade of the southern entrance to the Church of the Holy Sepulcher as it appears today, on the right, the Crusaders' direct entry to the site of Calvary.

Top left, the southern entrance to the Church of the Holy Sepulcher in the nineteenth century, with (*top right*) a detail of the Crusader facade decoration. *Lower left*, the same facade, as depicted by Von Breydenback in 1483; to the right is his version of the edicule enclosing Jesus' tomb inside the church.

PICTORIAL ARCHIVE (Near Eastern History) Est., The Old School, P.O. Box 19823.

Above, the Crusader church of St. Anne, with the remains of the Probatic Pool in the lower foreground. *Left*, the "Stables of Solomon," the vaulted structure supporting the southeastern end of the Herodian Temple platform.

places one after another, they had no means of resting even for a single day, except as it was offered in fraternal spirit by the brothers of the monastery. All the other dwellers in Jerusalem were Saracens and infidels with the exception of the patriarch, the clergy, and the miserable Syrian people. These latter were so overburdened by daily exactions of manifold corvées and extra services, and by work of the most menial nature, that they could scarcely breathe. They lived in the direst poverty and in continual fear of death.

Since there was no one to offer shelter to the wretched pilgrims of our faith, thus afflicted and needy to the last degree, the holy men who dwelt in the monastery of the Latins in pity took from their own means and, within the space allotted to them, built a hospital for the relief of such pilgrims. There they received these people, whether sick or well, lest they be found strangled by night on the streets. In addition to offering shelter in the hospital, they arranged that the fragments remaining from the food supplies of the two monasteries, namely of the monks and the nuns, should be spared for the daily sustenance of such people.

Furthermore, they erected in that place an altar in honor of St. John the Almoner. [19] *This venerable foundation which thus stretched out the hand of charity to its fellow men had neither revenues nor possessions; but each year the citizens of Amalfi, both those at home and those who followed the business of trading abroad, collected money from their own number as a voluntary offering. This they sent to the abbot of the hospital, whoever he might be at the time, by the hands of those who were going to Jerusalem. From this money food and shelter were provided for the brethren and the sisters and the remainder was used to extend some assistance to the Christian pilgrims who came to the hospital. (William of Tyre 1943: II, 241-245)*

On the scant archeological evidence available from the much built-upon place at the center of Jerusalem, the area today called the Muristan, William appears to be generally correct. [20] There were in fact three large buildings in the area: the Hospital of St. John and the church-hospices called by the Crusaders, and perhaps by others before them, Sancta Maria Latina and Sancta Maria Majora. Indeed, there is good reason to think that either the church or the monastery called St. Mary's went back to Charlemagne's own foundation, and that what the Amalfitani did was restore a much older structure that had been destroyed during al-Hakim's rampage through and around the Holy Sepulcher area. A likely time for that rebuilding would have been the period of 1063-1071 when, under Caliph al-Mustansir, the Christians repaired the walls of the city. [21]

The presence of this large hospital complex within the Patriarch's

Quarter in Jerusalem would later cause problems for the Latin Church in the city, but in the eleventh century the hospital was still a relatively modest affair and enjoyed none of the exemptions of its Crusader successor: like all the other Christian institutions of Fatimid Jerusalem it fell under the jurisdiction of the patriarch of the city. Christians were still numerous in the city, at least as numerous as Muqaddasi found them at the end of the tenth century, and it is likely that despite William of Tyre's dark portrait, the more aggressive Byzantine attitude toward the Muslims very probably strengthened the Christians' hand. Al-Hakim's persecution did permanent damage to the physical fabric of Christianity in Jerusalem—churches going back to Constantine, or at least to the reconstruction after the Persian invasion of 614, were destroyed and never rebuilt—but the city still had very much a Christian cast, and an increasingly variegated ethnic mix: Greeks, Armenians, Egyptian Copts, Syrian Jacobites, and now, increasingly, Latins from Europe.

The Jews and Jerusalem

The Jerusalem Jews likewise had their protectors, though within the Muslim world. The circumstances are obscure, but at some point the Fatimid government had begun to pay a subsidy to the Jewish Yeshiva in Jerusalem, probably by reason of the highly placed Jewish officials in court circles in Cairo and Fustat. We know about this subsidy only because we discover that in the wake of al-Hakim's persecution, which struck the Jews as forcibly as it did the Christians, it had been discontinued. [22] Not only was the subsidy lost but synagogues were closed or destroyed and the gaonate likely transferred from Jerusalem to Ramle. The latter was no safer a place to escape al-Hakim than Jerusalem, but it was certainly a more prosperous one, at least until the earthquake of 1033, which almost totally levelled that city. The Jerusalem Jews, who depended on the Ramle community, had then to turn to the only place left, Fustat. [23]

In 1020 al-Hakim's measures against the Jews and Christians were rescinded, and in the following year the Fatimid "God Made Manifest" mysteriously disappeared into the hills above Cairo. Almost at once the old antagonisms between Rabbanite and Karaite Jews resurfaced in the Holy City. The former had had the upper hand for many years, including the satisfaction of pronouncing an annual excommunication on the Karaites on the Mount of Olives, and almost certainly because the Fatimid caliph in Cairo preferred it so, as we have seen. But in 1024 there was a somewhat abrupt reversal, and al-Hakim's successor al-Zahir issued an edict to the Jerusalem Jews. Its beginning is missing, but the intent is clear:

. . . from following your custom and continuing in the traditions which you have learned in your religions, without any hindrance being raised by one party against the other or any harsh treatment being meted out by either of the two factions against the other; permitting the followers [of each party] to live up to their beliefs; enabling you and them [to prevent] any molestation [one from the other] in regard to that which is necessary in the ordinary course of buying and selling as they either follow or neglect upon their festivals [such business] according to their choice and free will. . . . Security is accorded both to you and to them so that you might restrain any evildoer among you from disputing that which ought ordinarily to be avoided. . . . At the same time [all] are prohibited from interfering with the sect of the Karaites in their synagogue which belongs to them to the exclusion of all others. . . . (Mann 1920-1922: I, 134-135)

This charter of freedom or even of equality to the Karaites of Jerusalem vis-à-vis the Rabbanites brought satisfaction but no real relief from the deeper economic woes of either Jewish community in the Holy City. The disappearance of the Ramle support struck both groups alike, and the Cairo Geniza documents from the last half of the eleventh century are filled with urgent appeals to Fustat to save their coreligionists in Jerusalem from an unceasingly heavy burden of taxation. [24] Then in 1071 the Turks took the city. The Palestinian Christians had from time to time allied themselves with the enemies of the Fatimids, whether bedouin or Byzantines, but whatever influence the Jews possessed lay in Cairo, and whatever hopes they might entertain rested on the good will of the Fatimid caliphs. The Jerusalem gaon and the Yeshiva officials there had little choice but to follow the receding Fatimid tide: after 1071 the Yeshiva is reported in Haifa, then in Tyre, both still in Fatimid hands, and then finally where it had inevitably to go, in Fustat-Cairo.

The Enduring Vision

These are in a sense provincial concerns. The fears and hopes concerning Jerusalem in this era extended far beyond the orbit of Syria, Palestine, and Egypt; they echoed, for Jew and Christian alike, throughout the Mediterranean world. The Christian response to those fears eventually came to term in a Crusade for the recapture of the city. And while such an act was far beyond either the capability or even the imagining of the Jews, the fate and future of Jerusalem was not forgotten, whether expressed in poetry by Judah ha-Levi (ca. 1085-1140), whose chief desire was to visit the Holy City, or in the more matter-of-fact, though as deeply experienced, legal brief presented in 1180 by Maimonides in his *Misnheh Torah*, medieval Judaism's most influential codification of law:

Sion, will you not ask if peace be with your captives
That seek your peace, that are the remnants of your flocks?
From west and east, from north and south, the greeting "Peace" from
    far and near, take from every side.
And greeting from the captive of desire, giving his tears like dew of
    Hermon
And longing to let them fall on your hills.
To wail for your affliction I am like the jackals;
But when I dream of the return of your captivity, I am a harp for your
    songs. . . .

Would that I might be wandering in the places where
God has revealed unto your seers and messengers.
O who will make me wings, that I may fly afar,
And lay the ruins of my cleft heart among your broken cliffs?
I would fall, with my face upon your earth,
and take delight in your stones and be tender to your dust. . . .
The life of souls is the air of your land; and of pure myrhh the grains of
    your dust, and honey from the comb your rivers.
Sweet would it be to my soul to walk naked and barefoot upon the des-
    olate ruins where your holiest dwellings were. . . .
Sion, perfect in beauty! Love and grace did bend on to you of olden
    time;
and still the soul of your companions are bound up with you. . . .
Your God has desired you as a dwelling place,
and happy is the man whom He chooses and brings near that he may
    rest within your courts. (Halevi 1924: 3-7)

In the "Book of the Temple Service," the eighth section of the *Mishneh Torah*, Maimonides devotes considerable attention to the question of the long-disappeared Temple and its ritual, including the question, not entirely academic perhaps in those expectant times,[25] of the reconsecration of the Temple mount:

If at any time the rite of hallowing did not include all of the above pro-
visions and in the order stated, the hallowing (of the Temple site) was not
complete. And when Ezra prepared two thank-offerings, he did so merely
as a memorial (of the rite). The (Temple) site was not hallowed by his
ceremony, since neither a king was present nor did the Urim and the
Thummim function. How then was the site hallowed? By the first sancti-

fication which Solomon had made, for he had hallowed the Court (of the Temple) and Jerusalem for both his own time and for all time to come.

Therefore it is permissible to offer all manner of sacrifice (upon the hallowed site), even though there was as yet no Temple erected, and to eat most holy offerings in any part of the Court even though it had been destroyed and was no longer surrounded by an enclosure; also to eat less holy offerings and the Second Tithe in Jerusalem, even though there were no walls enclosing the city—because the first sanctification (under Solomon) had hallowed these sites for his own time and for all time to come.

Now why is it my contention that as far as the Sanctuary and Jerusalem were concerned, the first sanctification hallowed them for all time to come, whereas the sanctification of the rest of the Land of Israel, which involved the laws of the Sabbatical year and tithes and like matters, did not hallow the land for all time to come? *Because the sanctity of the Sanctuary and of Jerusalem derives from the Divine Presence, which could not be banished.* Does it not say "and I will bring your sanctuaries unto desolation" [Lev. 26:31], wherefrom the Sages have averred: even though they are desolate, the sanctuaries retain their pristine holiness.

Even though the Sanctuary is today in ruins because of our iniquities, we are obliged to reverence it in the same manner as when it was standing. One should not enter save where it was permissible; nor should anyone sit down in the the Court or act irreverently while facing the East Gate; for it is said: "You shall keep My sabbaths and reverence My sanctuary" [Lev. 19:30]. Now just as we are obliged to keep the Sabbath for all time to come, so must we reverence the Sanctuary for all time to come; *for even though it is in ruins, its sanctity endures.* (Maimonides 1957: 28-30)

A Muslim Refugee in Jerusalem

The Jerusalem Jews' preference for the Fatimids over the Turks was not universally shared. If the Fatimids showed themselves to be generally tolerant and liberal in Cairo or even Jerusalem, their Ismaʿili ideology and tactics gave them the look of revolutionaries and terrorists inside the Iraqi and Iranian domains of the Abbasid caliph. The Shiʿite Fatimids posed a serious threat to the legitimacy of that caliph and to the stability of those Muslims who called themselves "traditionalists," or Sunnis. We shall hear more of this threat, but if it was to be met, the Sunni house had itself to be put in order, as it was; the rulers and intellectuals of Sunni Islam cooperated in what became a genuine revival. In the eleventh century those rulers were effectively the Seljuq Turks, and a major landmark in that revival was the decision of the Seljuqs' grand vizier Nizam al-Mulk to invest his interest, his wealth, and his prestige in opening in the capital of Baghdad in 1068 the first Sunni madrasa, or law school, which bore his name. It was not the end of the struggle by any means. In 1092 Nizam al-Mulk died at the hand of an Isma'ili *fidawi*, or terrorist, disguised as a Sufi; and three years later, al-Ghazali, the brightest star on the faculty of the Nizamiyya Madrasa and the chief spokesman for Sunni traditionalism, bolted Baghdad and fled in what was close to panic—he had written extensively against the Isma'ilis and may have felt that he too was marked for assassination—into the safe confines of a Sufi convent in Jerusalem, which the Turks had recently, and briefly, reacquired in the caliph's name.

Ghazali's stay in Jerusalem lasted less than a year and he devotes but a single line to it in his autobiography, at the end of his sojourn in Damascus:

In due course I entered Damascus, and there I remained for nearly two years with no other occupation than pursuing retirement and solitude, together with religious exercises, as I busied myself purifying my soul, improving my character and freeing my heart for the constant recollection of God most, as I had learnt to do from my study of mysticism. I used to go into retreat for a period on the mosque of Damascus, going up to the minaret of the mosque for the whole day and shutting myself in so as to be alone. From Damascus I went to Jerusalem where every day I shut myself up in the precinct of the Dome of the Rock. (Ghazali, Deliverer from Error)

Like much else in that autobiography, it is not the whole story we are being told, at least according to a later tradition. Mujir al-Din in his fifteenth-century history of the Holy City has considerably more detail:

The Imam Zayn al-Din Hujjat al-Islam Abu Hamid Muhammad al-Ghazali al-Tusi, the Safi'ite. . . . The community of the Shafi'ites had no one, toward the end of his century, who can be compared to him. He began his work in Tus, then he went to Nishapur where he raised himself to the ranks of the notables and acquired a high position. After having resided for some time in Damascus, he took himself to Jerusalem, burning with the desire to commit himself to the life of devotion and to visit the tombs of the martyrs and the holy places. It was in the Holy City that he worked on his most celebrated compositions, and it is said that it was in Jerusalem that he wrote the book called The Revivification of the Sciences of Religion. He took up residence in the convent which is above the Gate of Mercy [the Golden Gate] and which was previously known as the Nasiriyya, on the eastern side of the Haram of Jerusalem. It was renamed in his honor the Ghazaliyya. Today it is in ruins and all traces have disappeared. . . . (Mujir 1876: 66)

The Call Goes Out from Clermont

The European movement toward a Crusade was a gradual one and, as was suggested at the outset of this chapter, arose out of not one but many causes. But we can at least pinpoint its formal beginning: the Church council convoked at Clermont in November 1095. It lasted for ten days, and at its final session on November 28, Pope Urban II delivered an impassioned address, which was, in effect, the proclamation of the Crusade. We have a number of different versions of what he said on that occasion written down by witnesses to the event. They are by no means identical, but one at least, that from the the monk called simply Robert, touches on most of the themes and most of the motives that were invoked that day on the Holy City of Jerusalem:

From the confines of Jerusalem and the city of Constantinople a horrible tale has gone forth and very frequently has been brought to our ears; namely, that a race from the kingdom of the Persians, an accursed race, a race utterly alienated from God, a generation indeed which has neither directed its heart nor entrusted its spirit to God, has invaded the lands of those Christians and has depopulated them by the sword, pillage, and fire; it has led away a part of the captives into its own country, and a part it has destroyed by cruel tortures; it has either entirely destroyed the churches of God or appropriated them for the rites of its own religion. They destroy the altars, after having defiled them with their own uncleanness. They circumcise the Christians, and the blood of the circumcision they either spread upon the altars or pour into the vases of the baptismal font. . . . On whom, therefore, is the task of avenging these wrongs and of recovering this territory [lost by the Byzantine Christians] incumbent, if not upon you? You, upon whom above other nations God has conferred remarkable glory in arms, great courage, bodily energy, and the strength to humble the hairy scalp of those who resist you. . . .

Let therefore hatred depart from among you, let your quarrels end, let wars cease, and let all dissensions and controversies slumber. Enter upon the road to the Holy Sepulcher; wrest that land from the wicked race, and subject it to yourselves. The land which, as the Scripture says, "flows with milk and honey," was given by God into the possession of the Children of Israel.

Jerusalem is the navel of the world; the land is fruitful above all others, like another paradise of delights. This the Redeemer of the human race has made illustrious by His coming, has beautified by His presence, has consecrated by suffering, has redeemed by death, has glorified by burial. This royal city, therefore, situated at the center of the world, is now held captive by His enemies, and is in subjection to those who do not know God, to the worship of the heathen. Therefore she seeks and desires to be liberated and does not cease to implore you to come to her aid.... Accordingly, undertake this journey for the remission of your sins, with the assurance of the imperishable glory of the kingdom of heaven. (Krey 1921: 30-32)

The Taking of the Cross

The sequel to Urban's stirring discourse is described by Guibert of Nogent, who was also present at Clermont that day in November:

The most excellent man [Urban II] concluded his oration and by the power of the blessed Apostle Peter absolved all who vowed to go and confirmed those acts with apostolic blessing. He instituted a sign well suited to so honorable a profession by making the figure of the Cross, the stigma of the Lord's Passion, the emblem of the soldiery, or rather, of what was to be the soldiery of God. This, made of any kind of cloth, he ordered to be sewed upon the shirts, cloaks, and byrra of those who were about to go. He commanded that anyone, after receiving this emblem, or after openly taking this vow, who should shrink from his good intent through base change of heart, or any affection for his parents, he should be regarded an outlaw forever, unless he repented and again undertook whatever of his pledge he had omitted. Furthermore, the Pope condemned with a fearful anathema all those who dared to molest the wives, children, and possessions of those who were going on this journey for God. (Krey 1921: 40)

Fortified by papal promises and protected by papal anathemas, the Frankish Crusaders thus set out, under the sign and emblem of the Cross, for that city "at the center of the world," which was being held, they were assured, in a most fearful captivity by the heathen.

282

Jerusalem Under the
Latin Cross

There came at last a Christian people. . . .
—William of Tyre

NEITHER the high politics of the papal and Byzantine courts nor the increasingly fervent popular sentiment for a Western Christian pilgrimage in arms to Jerusalem appears to have made any impression on the Islamic world—not in Cairo or Damascus certainly, nor even in the very object of this attention, Jerusalem. The Muslims were apparently little informed on European affairs, either past or present, and showed even less interest, then or later, in trying to understand the military and religious phenomenon that was being mounted against them in the late eleventh century.[1] When the Crusaders arrived, their onslaught was not so much inexplicable as too easily understood; it was one more attack upon a city that had long been a helpless pawn in Near Eastern power politics. So it appeared to the two chief Muslim chroniclers, not of the "Crusades"—that word appears nowhere in the Muslim histories—but of the attack of the Franks:

In this year [490/1096-1097] a series of reports began to come in concerning the appearance of the armies of the Franks from the direction of the Sea of Constantinople, with forces so numerous that their numbers cannot be reckoned. These reports followed one another, and as they were spread and made known, people became anxious and disquieted. . . . (Ibn al-Qalanisi 1932: 41)

The first appearance of the Empire of the Franks, the rise of their power, their invasion of the lands of Islam and occupation of some of them occurred in the year 478 [1085-1086], when they took the city of Toledo and others in the land of Andalus, as has already been set forth. Then in the year 484 [1091-1092] they attacked the island of Sicily, and conquered it, and this too I have related before. Then they forced their way even to the shore of Africa, where they seized a few places, which were however recovered from them. Then they conquered other places, as you will now see. When the year 490 [1096-1097] came, they invaded the land of Syria. . . . (Ibn al-Athir X, 185)

The Capture of Jerusalem

The Crusaders' objectives were not, in 1098-1099 at least, "the land of Syria" but the Holy City of Jerusalem, which they reached, without great difficulty, in the summer of 1099. A siege was mounted, and its conclusion was foregone. According to Ibn al-Athir, "it was discord among the Muslim princes . . . that enabled the Franks to overrun the country." So it may have been, but perhaps somewhat more to the point, the Fatimids, who had driven out the Turcomans and were now once again briefly installed as its masters, had the will but not the capacity to defend Jerusalem against the urgent fanatics who stood poised outside the walls. The end is described by one who was there, the anonymous knight who fought at Jerusalem and later wrote *The Deeds of the Franks*:

From Acre we came to a castle named Haifa, and afterwards we encamped near Caesarea, where we celebrated Whitsunday on May 30. Thence we came to the city of Ramle, which the Saracens had evacuated for fear of the Franks. Near Ramle [at Lydda] is a church worthy of great reverence, for in it rests the precious body of St. George, who there suffered blessed martyrdom at the hands of the treacherous pagans in the name of Christ. While we were there our leaders took counsel together to choose a bishop who might protect and build up this church, and they paid him tithes and endowed him with gold and silver, horses and other animals, so that he and his household might live in a proper and religious manner.

He stayed there gladly, but we, rejoicing and exalting, came to the city of Jerusalem on Tuesday June 6 and established a very thorough siege. Robert the Norman took up his station in the north (outside the Damascus Gate), next to the Church of St. Stephen the Protomartyr, who was stoned there in the name of Christ, and Robert count of Flanders was next to him. Duke Godfrey and Tancred besieged the city from the west. The count of St. Gilles was on the south, that is to say on Mount Sion, near the Church of St. Mary, the Mother of the Lord, where the Lord shared the Last Supper with his disciples. . . .

On the Monday (following) we pressed upon the city in such a vigorous assault that if our scaling ladders had been ready, we should have taken it. We did indeed destroy the curtain-wall and against the great wall we set up one ladder, up which our knights climbed and fought hand-to-hand with the Saracens and those who were defending the city, using swords and spears. We lost many men, but the enemy lost more. During this siege we could not buy bread for nearly ten days, until a messenger arrived from our ships, and we suffered so badly from thirst that we had to take our horses and other beasts six miles to water, enduring great terror and apprehension on the way. The Pool of Siloam, at the foot of Mount Sion, kept us going, but water was sold very dearly in the army. . . . We sewed up the skins of oxen and buffaloes, and we used to carry water in them for the distance of nearly six miles. We drank the water from these vessels, although it stank, and what with foul water and barley bread we suffered great distress and affliction every day, for the Saracens used to lie in wait for our men by every spring and pool, where they killed them and cut them to pieces; moreover, they used to carry off the beasts into their caves and secret places in the rocks.

Our leaders then decided to attack the city with siege engines, so that they might enter it and worship at our Savior's Sepulcher. . . . When the Saracens saw our men making these machines, they built up the city wall and its towers by night, so that they were exceedingly strong. When, however, our leaders saw which was the weakest spot in the city's defenses, they had a machine and a siege-tower transported round to the eastern side one Saturday night. They set up these engines at dawn and spent Sunday, Monday, and Tuesday in preparing the siege-tower and fitting it out. . . . On Wednesday and Thursday we launched a fierce attack upon the city, both by day and by night, from all sides, but before we attacked our bishops and priests preached to us, and told us to go in procession round Jerusalem to the glory of God, and to pray and give alms and fast, as faithful men should do. On Friday at dawn we attacked the city from all sides but could achieve nothing, so that we were all astounded and very much afraid. Yet, when the hour came when Our Lord Jesus Christ deigned to suffer for us on the cross, our knights were fighting bravely on the siege tower, led by Duke Godfrey and Count Eustace his brother. At that moment one of our knights, called Lethold, succeeded in getting onto the wall. As soon as he reached it, all the defenders fled along the walls and through the city. . . . (Gesta Francorum 1962: 87-91)

Thus the fortifications were breached, and the Crusaders streamed into the city. The eyewitnesses, Christian and Muslim, leave little doubt as to what followed:

Now that our men had possession of the walls and the towers, wonderful sights were to be seen. Some of our men—and this was the more merciful course—cut off the heads of their enemies; others shot them with arrows so that they fell from the towers; others tortured them longer by casting them into the flames. Piles of heads, hands, and feet were to be seen in the streets of the city. It was necessary to pick one's way over the bodies of men and horses. But these were small matters compared to what happened in the Temple of Solomon [that is, the al-Aqsa Mosque], a place where religious services were ordinarily chanted. What happened there? If I tell the truth, it will exceed your powers of belief. So let it suffice to say this much at least, that in the Temple and porch of Solomon men rode in blood up to their knees and bridle reins. Indeed, it was a just and splendid judgment of God that this place should be filled with the blood of unbe-

lievers, since it had suffered so long from their blasphemies. The city was filled with corpses and blood. Some of the enemy took refuge in the Tower of David, and petitioning Count Raymond for protection, surrendered the tower into his hands. (Krey 1921: 261)

In fact Jerusalem was taken from the north on the morning of . . . July 15, 1099. The population was put to the sword by the Franks, who pillaged the area for a week. A band of Muslims barricaded themselves in the Oratory of David [near the Citadel] and fought on for several days. They were granted their lives in return for surrendering. The Franks honored their word, and the group left by night for Ascalon. In the al-Aqsa Mosque the Franks slaughtered more than 70,000 people, among them a large number of Imams and Muslim scholars, devout and ascetic men who had left their homelands to live lives of pious seclusion in the Holy Place. The Franks stripped the Dome of the Rock of more than forty silver candelabra, each of them weighing 3,600 drams, and a great silver lamp weighing 44 Syrian pounds, as well as 150 smaller silver candelabra and more than 20 gold ones, and a great deal more booty. (Gabrieli 1969: 11)

After this great slaughter they [the Crusaders] entered the houses of the citizens, seizing whatever they found there. This was done in such a way that whoever first entered a house, whether he was rich or poor, was not challenged by any other Frank. He was to occupy and own the house or palace and whatever he found in it as if it were entirely his own. In this way many poor people became wealthy. Then the clergy and the laity, going to the Lord's Sepulcher and His most glorious Temple, singing a new canticle to the Lord in a resounding voice of exaltation, and making offerings and most humble supplications, joyously visited the holy places as they had long desired to do. (Fulcher of Chartres 1969: I, xxix)

Jerusalem fell to the Frankish forces on July 15, 1099, but when Fulcher returned to the city at Christmas of the same year, the signs of the massacre were still everywhere around the city:

Oh what a stench there was around the walls of the city, both within and without, from the rotting bodies of the Saracens slain by our comrades at the time of the capture of the city, lying wherever they had been hunted down! (Fulcher of Chartres 1969: I, xxxiii)

The City Desolate

William of Tyre was not present at the fall of Jerusalem, but his own highly circumstantial and dramatic account also derives from what are clearly eyewitness sources:

It was impossible to look upon the vast numbers of the slain without horror; everywhere lay fragments of human bodies, and the very ground was covered with the blood of the slain. It was not alone the spectacle of headless bodies and mutilated limbs strewn in all directions that roused horror in all who looked upon them. Still more dreadful was it to gaze upon the victors themselves, dripping with blood from head to foot, an ominous sight that brought terror to all who met them. It is reported that within the Temple enclosure alone about 10,000 infidels perished, in addition to those who lay slain everywhere throughout the city in the streets and squares, the number of whom was estimated as no less.

The rest of the soldiers roved the city in search of wretched survivors who might be hiding in the narrow portals and byways to escape death. These were dragged out into public view and slain like sheep. Some formed into bands and broke into houses where they laid violent hands on the heads of families, on their wives, children, and their entire households. The victims were either put to the sword or dashed headlong to the ground from some elevated place so that they perished miserably. Each marauder claimed as his own in perpetuity the particular house which he had entered, together with all it contained. For before the capture of the city the pilgrims had agreed that, after it had been taken by force, whatever each man might win for himself should be his by right of possession, without molestation. Consequently, the pilgrims searched the city most carefully and boldly killed the citizens. They penetrated into the most retired and out-of-the-way places and broke open the most private apartments of the foe. At the entrance of each house, as it was taken, the victor hung up his shield and arms, as a sign to all who approached not to pause there but to pass by as that place was already in the possession of another.

Arms were then laid down, and the conquerors, now washed and purified, approached the Church of the Holy Sepulcher.

Here the leaders were met by the clergy and the faithful citizens of Jerusalem. These Christians who for so many years had borne the heavy yoke of undeserved bondage were eager to show their gratitude to the Redeemer for their restoration to liberty. Bearing in their hands crosses and relics of the saints, they led the way into the church to the accompaniment of hymns and sacred songs.

When their prayers had been completed and the venerable places visited in the spirit of sincere devotion, the chiefs deemed it necessary, before all else, to cleanse the city and especially the temple precincts, lest pestilence should arise from the air tainted by the stench from the corpses of the slain. This task was imposed on those captured citizens who, though cast into prison, had by chance escaped death. But since their number was not sufficient to accomplish so great a work without aid, the poor of the army were offered a daily wage to give assistance in cleaning up the city without delay.

. . . The city was found to be full to overflowing with goods of all kinds, so that all, from the least to the greatest, had an abundance of everything. In the houses that had been were discovered vast treasures of gold and silver, besides gems and valuable raiment. There were stores of grain, wine, and oil, as well as a plentiful supply of water, the lack of which had caused great suffering among the Christians during the siege. Consequently those who had appropriated the residences were able to supply their needy brethren in all affection. On the second day after the occupation of Jerusalem and again on the third, a public market of goods for sale was held under the best conditions. Even the common people had all they needed in abundance. The days passed in joyous celebration, as the pilgrims refreshed themselves to some extent with the rest and food they all so greatly needed.

Those who had undertaken to cleanse the city showed great diligence and zeal in the work. Some of the bodies were burned and others buried, according as the exigency of the time permitted. Quickly, within a few days, all was finished and the city restored to its usual state of cleanliness. The people then flocked with greater confidence to the venerated places and were able to meet more fully and enjoy pleasant converse with one another in the city streets and squares.

Jerusalem was taken in the year of the Incarnation of the Lord 1099 on Friday, July 15, about the ninth hour of the day. It was the third year from the one in which the faithful had assumed the burden of this great pilgrimage. Pope Urban II was presiding over the Holy Roman Church and Henry IV was administering the empire of the Romans. King Philip· was reigning in France, and Alexius was wielding the scepter over the Greeks. Guiding and directing all was the merciful hand of God, to whom be honor and glory for ever and ever. (William of Tyre 1943: I, 372-378)

The Jews and the Fall of Jerusalem

It is clear from all the accounts we possess that the Muslim population of Jerusalem either fled the city, were captured and sold into slavery, or were simply slaughtered where they stood and fought. What was less certain was the fate of the Jewish population. The Jewish family chronicles and "scrolls" of the time did concern themselves with the events of the world outside the Jewish community, but oddly, they make no mention of either the fall of Jerusalem or what happened to the Jews who lived there at the time. A report from a Muslim historian, the same Ibn al-Qalanisi cited above, suggests that the Jews too were massacred by the Franks, down to the last woman and child. At least some of the Latin sources indicate that the Jews were treated somewhat differently from the Muslims: they were set to cleaning up the Temple mount and then either sold into slavery or deported. [2]

Now, however, we possess accounts from contemporary Jews. Among the many letters preserved in the Cairo Geniza is one written in the summer of 1100 attempting to raise money among the Jews of Cairo to defray the expenses borne by the community in Ascalon in connection with the fall of Jerusalem. It was they who had to feed and succor the refugees who had managed to escape the city and to ransom not only the Jewish captives but even the sacred books looted by the Crusaders from the Jerusalem synagogues.

A second letter was written at about the same time from Egypt back to Spain or North Africa by an elderly Jewish pilgrim who had earlier set out for Jerusalem but had been overtaken, and forestalled, by events:

In Your name, You, Merciful.

If I attempted to describe my longing for you, my Lord, my brother and cousin—may God prolong your days and make permanent your honor, success, happiness, health, and welfare; and . . . subdue your enemies—all the paper in the world would not suffice. . . .

You may remember, my Lord, that many years ago I left our country to seek God's mercy and help in my poverty, to behold Jerusalem and return thereupon. However, when I was in Alexandria, God brought about circumstances which caused a slight delay. Afterwards, however, "the sea grew stormy," and many armed bands made their appearance in Palestine; "and he who went forth and he who came had no peace," so that hardly one survivor out of a whole group came back to us from Palestine and told us that scarcely anyone could save himself from those armed bands, since they were so numerous and were gathered round . . . every town. There was further the journey through the desert, among [the bedouin], and whoever escaped from one, fell into the hands of the other. Moreover, mutinies [spread throughout the country and reached] even Alexandria, so that we ourselves were besieged several times and the city was ruined; . . . the end, however, was good, for the sultan [Al-Afdal]— may God bestow glory upon his victories—conquered the city and caused justice to abound in it in a manner unprecedented in the history of any king in the world; not even a dirham was looted from anyone. Thus I had come to hope that because of his justice and strength God would give the land into his hands, and I should thereupon go to Jerusalem in safety and

*tranquillity. For this reason I proceeded from Alexandria to Cairo, in or-
der to start my journey from there.*

*When, however, God had given Jerusalem, the blessed, into his hands,
this state of affairs continued for too short a time to allow for making a
journey there. The Franks arrived and killed everybody in the city,
whether of Ishmael or of Israel; and the few who survived the slaughter
were made prisoners. Some of those have been ransomed since, while
others are still in captivity in all parts of the world.*

*Now, all of us had anticipated that our sultan—may God bestow glory
upon his victories—would set out against them [the Franks] with his
troops and chase them away. But time after time our hope failed. Yet, to
this very present moment we do hope that God will give his [the sultan's]
enemies into his hands. For it is inevitable that the armies will join in
battle this year [1100]; and, if God grants us victory through him [the
sultan] and he conquers Jerusalem—and so may it be with God's will—I
for one shall not be among those who linger, but shall go there to behold
the city; and shall afterwards return straight to you—if God wills it. My
salvation is in God, for this [is unlike] the other previous occasions [of
making pilgrimage to Jerusalem]. God indeed will exonerate me, since at
my age I cannot afford to delay and wait any longer. I want to return
home under any circumstances, if I still remain alive—whether I shall have
seen Jerusalem or have given up hope of doing it—both of which are
possible. (Goitein 1952: 175-177)*

The first letter reveals that the fate of the Jews of Jerusalem was somewhat
more complex than we had imagined: some indeed had been slaughtered
in the city at the side of the Muslims, but others had been led into captivity, some of them later ransomed, while at least some of the community
had managed to flee Jerusalem for Ascalon and other places before the
Crusaders arrived. The second letter, cited above, tells us something else.
The Jewish pilgrim reflects what must have been a prevalent attitude in
the Islamic world, that the Frankish presence was both unremarkable and
likely ephemeral—hence the silence of the Jewish chronicles and the reti-
cence of the Muslim ones—and that it was merely a question of time
before the Fatimid caliph, here al-Afdal, would drive them out. Here too
there is no sense of the Crusade as such or the strength of the Frankish
conviction that would keep them in Jerusalem for a century.

The Latin Patriarchate

The Latin conquest brought a new order to Jerusalem—in the secular
sphere, an autonomous Frankish monarch in place of the Fatimid gover-

nor who had ruled the city in the name of the caliph in Cairo; and in the religious, a new Latin patriarch to replace the Byzantine prelate who had ruled there as far back as the time of Constantine. The city was filled with religious minorities like the Armenians, Copts, and Syrian Jacobites even before the coming of the Crusades, but the supreme ecclesiastical jurisdiction as well as the control of all the major shrines of the city rested in the hands of the Byzantine bishop and clergy, known to the Crusaders as "Greeks" and to the Muslims as "Rumi" or "Romans." With the coming of the Latins, the order of precedence changed. At the death of the Greek patriarch of Jerusalem on Cyprus, the Frank Daimbert became Jerusalem's "metropolitan archbishop"—the office called "patriarch" since the time of Juvenal in the fifth century—and in 1101 Latins replaced the Greeks as the resident clergy in the Church of the Anastasis, or as the Crusaders called it, the Holy Sepulcher. [3]

As William of Tyre's account cited above makes clear, among the first orders of business for the Crusaders was the distribution of properties in the newly possessed city. The homes and lots of the dead or dislodged Muslims were there simply for the taking, first come, first served; but more overarching questions of property, and indeed of sovereignty, had also to be settled between king and bishop in the Holy City:

A few days after Godfrey was elected head of the kingdom, he began to offer the first fruits of his responsibility to the Lord. He established canons in the church of the Lord's Sepulcher and in the Temple of the Lord; and upon them he bestowed ample benefices known as prebends. At the same time also he gave them noble houses in the vicinity of these same churches beloved of God. He preserved the rule and regulations observed by the great and wealthy churches founded by pious princes beyond the mountains, and he would have conferred still greater gifts, had not death prevented.

When about to start out on his pilgrimage, this man [Godfrey] beloved of God led with him in his train monks from well-regulated cloisters, religious men notable for their holy lives. During the entire pilgrimage, at the regular hours, night and day, these monks celebrated the divine offices for him after the custom of the church. After Godfrey acquired the royal power, he located them at their own request in the Valley of Jehoshaphat and conferred upon them there, as a reward for their services, lands of wide extent.

As soon as Daimbert, the man of God, had been installed in the patriarchal chair, both Duke Godfrey and Prince Bohemond humbly received from his hand, the former the investiture of the kingdom, and the latter that of the principality [of Antioch], thus showing honor to Him whose viceregent on earth they believed the patriarch to be. The ceremony over, revenues were assigned to the Lord Patriarch, from which his establishment might be honorably supported, as was due to his office. Into his hands were given not only those possessions which had belonged to the Greek patriarch from the days of the Greeks in the time of the Gentiles, but new ones as well. . . .

   In the meantime, a question had arisen at Jerusalem between the patriarch and the duke. . . . The patriarch demanded that the new duke give over to him the Holy City of God with its citadel and likewise the city of Jaffa with its appurtenances. [4] For some time the question was under vigorous discussion. Finally, on the day of the Purification of the Blessed Mary [February 2, 1100], in the presence of the clergy and all the people, the duke, a man of humble and gentle nature, who stood in fear of the rebuke of the Lord, resigned a fourth part of the city of Jaffa to the Church of the Holy Resurrection.

   Later, on the holy day of the following Easter, again in the presence of the clergy and the people who had assembled for the feast day, he gave into the hand of the patriarch the city of Jerusalem with the Tower of David and all that pertained to it. The following condition was attached to the gift, however—that he himself should enjoy and have the use of the aforesaid city, with its territories, until the Lord should permit him to take one or two other cities and thus enlarge the kingdom. But if, in the meantime, he should die without legitimate heir, all the aforesaid possessions should pass without difficulty or contradiction into the jurisdiction of the Lord Patriarch. . . . (William of Tyre 1943: I, 392-404)

Godfrey's refusal of the crown of Jerusalem—he would not wear a crown of gold where his Savior had worn one of thorns—soon became part of the Crusader legend of Jerusalem. A German pilgrim visited the site of Calvary in 1350, long after the Muslims had retaken the city, and saw there the tombs of the first two Latin rulers of the Holy City:

Also in this same chapel are buried those right glorious princes Godfrey, Duke of Bouillon, and Baldwin, his brother, the first Christian kings of Jerusalem. . . . It is a great wonder that the Saracens suffer their sepulchers and bodies to rest undisturbed in such honor seeing how much harm they did them and how they even took away from them the whole of the Holy Land. . . . These same glorious princes made a rule that no king of Jerusalem should wear a golden crown but a crown of thorns, which rule their successors observe even to this day. (Ludolph von Suchem 1895: 103-104)

Godfrey's generous gift of the city of Jerusalem to the Holy See and its episcopal representative there was an ephemeral one. Godfrey's successor

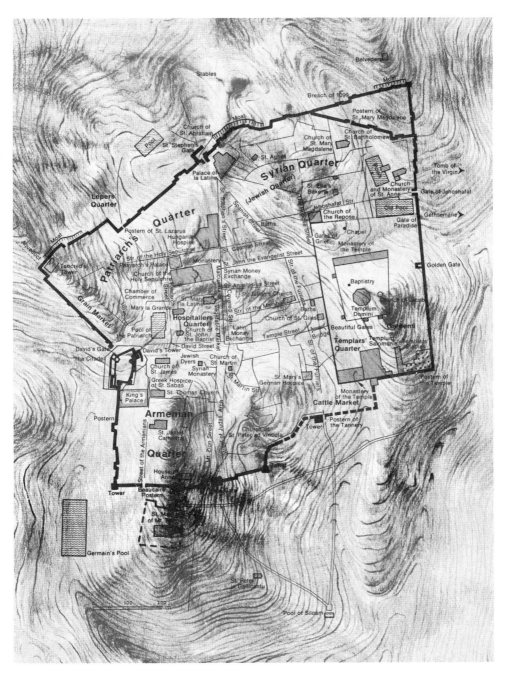

Crusader Jerusalem (1099-1187).

Permission Carta, Jerusalem

293

Baldwin did not, as Godfrey did, content himself with the rank of baron and title of "Protector of the Holy Sepulcher," but claimed and assumed the full royal privilege of king of Jerusalem. Jerusalem was not to be a papal state but a secular kingdom, though the patriarch was given autonomous legal and fiscal jurisdiction over the Christian Quarter in the northwest quadrant of the city.

Early Visitors to Latin Jerusalem

Jerusalem, the center of a tiny new Latin kingdom still gradually expanding over northern and central Palestine, had been visited by European pilgrims since Constantine began his work of converting it into a Christian holy city. The journey had always been perilous, and it was no less so under Latin sovereignty, as may be seen from the testimony of Saewulf, who visited the city less than three years after it had been taken from the Muslims:

We went up from Joppa [Jaffa] to the city of Jerusalem, a journey of two days, along a mountainous road, rocky and very dangerous. For the Saracens, always laying snares for the Christians, lie hidden in the hollow places of the mountains and the caves in the rocks, watching day and night and always on the lookout for those whom they can attack because of the fewness of the party or those who have lagged behind their party from weariness. At one moment they seem all around everywhere, and all at once they disappear entirely. Anyone who makes the journey may see this. Oh, what a number of human bodies, both in the road and by the side of it, lie all torn by wild beasts. Some may perhaps wonder that the bodies of Christians should lie unburied. But it is not to be wondered at at all; for there is very little earth and the rocks are not easy to dig into. And besides, if there were earth, who would be so foolish as to leave his party and go off on his own and dig a grave for his companion? If he did so he would be digging a grave for himself rather than for his companion. On that road not only the poor and the weak but even the rich and the strong are in danger. Many are cut off by the Saracens, but more by heat and thirst; many die through scarcity of drink but many more perish from drinking too much. (Saewulf 1896: 8-9)

Saewulf was followed, some four years later, by the Russian abbot Daniel, who by preference chose to lodge with the Eastern Christians and to select a guide from among their number:

I, the unworthy Abbot Daniel, on arriving in Jerusalem, stayed for sixteen months in the Hospice of the Laura of St. Sabas and was thus able to visit and explore all the holy places. Now it is impossible to visit and explore all the holy places without a good guide and an interpreter. I therefore gave all that I could out of my small means as a reward to those who were thoroughly acquainted with and able to show me the holy places of the city and other localities so that I might see every detail. In this, accordingly, I was successful. By God's grace I found in the Laura of St. Sabas a very pious man of advanced age who was well versed in the Scriptures. God inclined the heart of this holy man to love unworthy me, and it was he who, with great care, showed me all the holy places, both in Jerusalem and the whole country; and who took me to the Lake of Tiberias, Tabor, Nazareth, Hebron, and the Jordan. And out of affection for me, although suffering great fatigue, he conducted me to the large number of holy places of which I shall speak later. (Daniel the Abbot 1895: 3)

A little later he reflects once more upon this same guide:

I have faithfully described these holy places without lying, just as I saw them. Many who have visited these places have been unable to explore them thoroughly, and others, without reaching the holy places have told lies and fables. As for me, a sinner, God granted me the acquaintance of a holy man of great age, very erudite and devout, and who had spent thirty years in Galilee and twenty in the Laura of St. Sabas [near Jerusalem]; and this man gave me all the explanations contained in Holy Scripture. How can I, sinner that I am, be grateful enough for the favor shown to me. (Daniel the Abbot 1895: 61)

The City of Jerusalem

Daniel came to Jerusalem not as a Crusader but as a pilgrim, as many before him had, and he saw the city through pilgrim's eyes. But not only this: the Crusaders' possession of the place brought to the travellers' accounts a new and different awareness of Jerusalem *as a city*, and what had once been merely the setting of holy places now took on a degree of physical and social reality that was present in earlier Muslim accounts of the city but only rarely in the Christian ones. The new attitude toward the physical setting and qualities of Jerusalem is immediately evident in the accounts by the soldier Fulcher, the pilgrim Daniel, and the historian William of Tyre:

The city of Jerusalem is located in a mountainous region which is devoid of trees, streams, and springs excepting only the Pool of Siloam, which is a bowshot from the city. Sometimes it has enough water, and sometimes a deficiency due to a slight drainage. This little spring is in the valley at the foot of Mount Sion in the course of the Brook Kedron which, in winter time, is accustomed to flow through the center of the Valley of Jehoshaphat. The many cisterns inside the city, reserved for winter rains, have a sufficiency of water. More, at which men and beasts are refreshed, are found outside the city. It is generally conceded that the city is laid out in such proper proportion that it seems neither too small nor too large. Its width from wall to wall is that of four bowshots. To the west is the Tower of David with the city wall on each flank; to the south is Mount Sion a little closer than a bowshot; and to the east, the Mount of Olives a thousand paces outside the city. The aforesaid Tower of David is of solid masonry half-way up, of large squared blocks sealed with molten lead. Fifteen or twenty men, if well supplied with food, could defend it from all assaults of an enemy. . . . There were gutters in the streets of the city through which in times of rain all filth was washed away. Emperor Aelius Hadrian decorated this city magnificently and fittingly adorned the streets and squares with pavement. In his honor Jerusalem was called Ae-lia. For these and other reasons Jerusalem is a most renowned and glorious city. (Fulcher of Chartres 1969: I, xxxi)

Jerusalem is a large city, protected by very solid walls, and built in the form of a square, whose four sides are of equal length: it is surrounded by many arid valleys and rocky mountains. It is a place absolutely destitute of water; one finds neither river nor wells nor springs near Jerusalem, with the exception of the Pool of Siloam. The inhabitants of the town, and cattle, have therefore nothing but rainwater for their use. In spite of that, grain thrives well in that rocky land which lacks rain. By sowing one measure, ninety and a hundredfold is reaped. Does not God's blessing rest upon this hallowed land? In the neighborhood of Jerusalem there are plenty of vineyards and fruit trees; fig trees, sycamores, olive trees, carob trees and an infinite number of other trees. (Daniel the Abbot 1895: 25-26)

And again on the Tower of David located near the Citadel:

It is two hundred fathoms thence to the tower and house of David. The tower, where was also his house, is the one in which the holy prophet composed and wrote his Psalter. It is curiously built in massive stone, is very high, and of square, solid, and impregnable form; it is like one single stone from its base up. It contains plenty of water, five iron gates, and two hundred steps lead to the summit. It is very difficult to take, and forms the main defense of the city. It is very carefully guarded and no one is allowed to enter, except under supervision. . . . (Daniel the Abbot 1895: 17)

William too begins with a panoranic view:

Jerusalem lies upon two hills. . . . The summits of these hills lie almost entirely inside the circuit of the walls and are separated from each other by a little valley which divides the city into two parts. The peak on the west is called Sion, whence the city also is so designated. . . . The other hill to the east is called Mount Moriah. . . . On the west, almost on the very summit of the mount is the church which is called Sion; and, not very far from it, is the Tower of David. This is a very massive construction. With its towers, walls, and outworks attached to it, it rises high above the city below and forms the citadel.

On the same height, but on the slope facing the east, is situated the Church of the Holy Resurrection, circular in shape. As this church lies on the slope of the hill just mentioned, which towers above in close proximity to it, the interior would have been very dark. Its roof, however, built of beams rising aloft and interwoven with the most skillful workmanship in the form of a crown, is so constructed that it is always open to the sky, which arrangement provides the necessary light for the interior. Under this wide opening lies the Sepulcher of the Savior. . . . (William of Tyre 1943: I, 343)

History and the Holy Places

The emphasis on the physical face of Jerusalem raised in its train certain grave historical questions for the new visitors, among them the question of the true location of Jesus' tomb. The Gospels unmistakably locate both it and the site of the Crucifixion outside the walls of Jerusalem, but now, in the eleventh century, the visitor to Calvary and the Holy Sepulcher found himself facing an elaborate building complex set down at the very heart of the city:

We know that our Lord suffered outside the (city) gate. But Emperor Hadrian, who was called Helias, rebuilt the city and the Temple of the Lord and extended the city as far as the Tower of David, which formerly had been some distance from the city. Anyone can see from the Mount of Olives where the extreme west walls of the city formerly were and how much the city was afterwards extended. The emperor called the city by his own name, Aelia, which means "The House of God." Some, however, say that it was Emperor Justinian who restored the city, and the Temple of the Lord, just as it is now; but they say this according to their own private opinion and not according to the truth. For the Assyrians [i.e., the local Syrian Christians], whose fathers were the settlers of that country from the first persecution, say that after Our Lord's Passion the city was seven times captured and destroyed, together with all the churches, but not wholly leveled to the ground. (Saewulf 1896: 10)

The more general question of the changes in historical sites is addressed by John of Wurzburg, who visited the city sometime between 1160 and 1170:

I am well aware that long before modern times these same (holy) places, not only those in the aforesaid city (of Jerusalem) but even those at a great distance from it, have been described in writing by a reverend man; [5] *however, since during the long period that has elapsed since that time, the city having been captured and destroyed by enemies, these same holy places of which we think so much, both those within the walls and those at a short distance without them, have been overthrown and perhaps afterwards altered in form. For this reason our pious care about these sites, which we have described as an eyewitness, must not be thought unnecessary or superfluous. . . . (John of Wurzburg 1896: 2)*

Urban Topography

In most of the preserved accounts the physical description of the city is incidental to other concerns, but in one work, which exists in a number of slightly different manuscript variants, the topography of Jerusalem—its secular, not sacred, topography—is the precise point of the narrative. This work, generally entitled "The Condition of the City of Jerusalem," was composed sometime not too long after the Muslims retook their prize in 1187, as is immediately apparent; but it still reflects, in detail unmatched in any other work, the layout of Crusader Jerusalem:

Because most good Christians willingly speak and hear spoken about the Holy City of Jerusalem and the holy places where Jesus Christ lived and died, we shall tell how it was at the time when Saladin and the Saracens took it from the Christians. . . .

The great street which goes from the Tower of David straight to the Golden Gate is called David Street. On the left hand (or north) of the Tower of David there is a large area where they sell grain. Going a little further on David Street you come to a street on the left which is called Patriarch Street because the patriarch has his residence at the top of it. There is an entry to the right from Patriarch Street by which one can enter the Hospital and after it another into the Church of the Sepulcher, though this is not the main entrance.

Almost all the post-Crusade visitors to Jerusalem comment on the markets of the city, but the description given by the anonymous author of "The City of Jerusalem" is the most complete that we possess down to the time of Mujir al-Din in the late fifteenth century. [6] The three covered bazaars described below still exist in the Old City of Jerusalem, seated on the track of the old Roman north-south cardo at the place where it crosses David Street and in the immediate vicinity of what is today called the Muristan and was once Hadrian's chief commercial forum in Aelia Capitolina, then the site of the Crusader's Hospital:

When you come to the Exchange, where David Street proper ends, there is a street [on the right] called Mount Sion Street since it goes straight to Mount Sion; and on the left of the Exchange is a covered street, vaulted over, called the Greengrocers' Street, where they sell all the vegetables, fruits, and spices of the city. At the top of this street is a place where they sell fish. Behind the fish market is a large area on the left where cheese, chickens, and eggs are sold. To the right of this market are the shops of the Syrian goldworkers; and here they also sell the palms which the pilgrims carry overseas. On the left of the market are the shops of the Latin goldsmiths, and at the end of these shops there is a convent of nuns which is called St. Mary the Great; and next a monastery of Blackfriars called St. Mary the Latin. Then comes the residence of the Hospital, where the chief entry into the Hospital is located. To the right of the Hospital is the main entry of the Sepulcher.

. . . Now I shall return to the Exchange. Just before the Exchange and close to Greengrocers' Street is a street called Malquisinat, or "Cooking Smells." In this street food is cooked and sold to pilgrims, and there are washing facilities since they go from this street to the Sepulcher. In front of Malquisinat Street there is a street called Covered Street, which is entirely vaulted over and where cloth goods are sold. And one goes by this street to the Sepulcher. (City of Jerusalem 1896: 7-11)

This was the commercial heart of the city and the chief internal source of its revenues. Much of the revenue went to the patriarch or to other religious endowments since the Church owned or controlled the income of many commercial establishments—bakeries and ovens, for example—outside the Patriarch's Quarter proper. These endowments are duly registered in the charters of the ecclesiastical establishments in question, [7] but a nineteenth-century discovery by the French archeologist Clermont-Ganneau provided a remarkable confirmation:

I have made there a small discovery proving positively that this market [along the ancient cardo] in its present state and in all essential particulars dates at least from the time of the Crusades. At the spring of the cross-rib which covers the main and central alley, which is called Suq al-ʿAttârîn (the Market of the Druggists), I noticed one day, at a place where the old plaster had peeled off, short inscriptions, several times repeated, engraved on the stone in fine large Gothic letters, whose period does not admit of any doubt. . . .

There is no difficulty about reading the name ANNA, either when by itself or preceded by the epithet Sancta, represented by its usual abbreviation SCA; I have noted a considerable number of them; there must be more besides which I have not seen. . . . The great size and regularity of the letters, and the symmetry of the inscription, which are all placed at the same height and at evidently equal intervals, the dressing of the stone, and the appearance of the courses on which they are engraved, all unite to disabuse us of the idea that we have to do with either mere masons' marks, trivial graffiti, or even with stones which have been moved hither from their original positions. On the other hand, both history and paleography teach us that this Christian Latin formula, of an official and public nature, as we shall see, is necessarily earlier in date than the taking of Jerusalem by Saladin in 1187, and consequently belongs to the period of Frank rule in Palestine.

St. Anne's Abbey rose to great importance in the days of Baldwin I, when the second king of Jerusalem immured therein his wife Arda, the daughter of the Armenian prince Tafnuz. . . . A short time afterwards the convent of St. Anne had the honor of receiving a princess of the blood-royal, Joye [a.k.a. Joette, Juette, Judith], the daughter of Baldwin II who subsequently became Abbess of the convent of St. Lazarus at Bethany. We may assume that the presence of these noble ladies procured high favors for St. Anne's Abbey, which had previously contained only a few poor women; quibus ampliavit possessiones et patrimonium dilatavit, says William of Tyre [XI, 1], indeed, when speaking of Baldwin I and of our abbey.

This is confirmed by the Estoire de Eracles in the following terms: "il enrichit le leu de rentes et de teneures." Unfortunately, among the authorities to which I have had access I have not been able to find the actual list of names of these "rentes" and "teneures." The name of St. Anne's Abbey appears sometimes on the exchanges of land between it and other religious houses, but that is all. In spite, however, of the absence of any express mention of it, I am willing to believe that among those "rentes" and "teneures" which were granted to St. Anne's Abbey, there was a share of the revenues of the Jerusalem market, and that the name Sancta Anna carved all along one of the alleys of this market was the sign of the abbatial right to which the market was subject. (Clermont-Ganneau 1899: 116-120)

The secular lord of the Holy City also derived income from those same markets. The king ruled Jerusalem through and with two major courts or assemblies, a "high court," which dealt with all civil and criminal cases concerning the knightly class, and a "court of the bourgeois," whose jurisdiction in similar matters extended over the free, non-noble Frankish citizenry of the city; in both cases, their competence was purely secular. [8] The chief officer of the court of the bourgeois was called the "viscount," and to him fell the duty of collecting the rents and dues owed the crown by householders and tradesmen in the market and of maintaining fair trade practices in that same commercial center. He was, in effect, the chief tax agent and police officer of Jerusalem.

Elsewhere in the Crusader cities the viscount was assisted in his duties by an agent called a *methessep*, and though there is no direct attestation for Jerusalem, it seems likely to conclude there was such a one in the Holy City as well. Here we have a genuine Crusader adaptation of an Islamic functionary, the *muhtasib*, one of the very few such adaptations in the Islamic East. [9] The Muslim muhtasib, or market inspector, was a religious official whose mandate was founded in Islamic law, while in the strict Latin separation of secular and ecclesiastical powers, the methessep fell into the secular jurisdiction of the viscount and the court of the bourgeois. Yet the latter's duties as described in a later resume of Crusader law appear in part identical to those of his Muslim counterpart, though with somewhat broader police powers:

The duty of the methessep is to go every morning to the public places, that is to say, to the butcher shops and the places where bread and wine and other things are sold. There he should take care that no fraud takes place among the sellers and that there be no shortage of bread, as the court has ordered, and that the published prices should be observed, particularly for bread, wine, cartage, and fish. . . . Thus he should go around the city supervising these affairs. . . . To that end he should have inspectors to report to him the malpractices that he cannot detect on his own. . . . He in turn should report to the viscount whatever he has discovered. And if he discovers anyone acting improperly or charged with such, he should have him taken into custody by one or two sergeants whom he should have with him as often as possible and have the accused brought before the viscount and explain the crime or the accusation. If the viscount cannot for any reason hear the charge, the methessep can and should remand the person to prison and bring the case to the attention of the viscount on the earliest possible occasion. Thus he can arrest anyone and put him in prison, but he cannot and should not release anyone from prison without an order from the viscount or the court. . . . He is also

301

responsible for conducting, in the company of sergeants, the convicted to the place of their punishment, likewise those condemned to be broken or to lose their life or a limb. . . . (Recueil Lois 2:243-244)

We return to the narrative "City of Jerusalem":

Now we will leave the Exchange and go toward the Golden Gate [and the Temple mount]. The street that goes from the Exchange to the Golden Gate [thus the eastward continuation of David Street] is called Temple Street, because you go this way not only to the Golden Gate but also to the Temple. As you go down this street, you encounter on the left the Butchers' Marketplace, where the city's meat is sold. On the right is another street which leads to the German Hospital, and this is called Germans' Street. On the left hand, on the bridge, [10] is the Church of St. Giles. At the top of this street there is a gate, called the Gate Beautiful, because by this gate Jesus Christ entered the city when He was on earth. The gate is in a wall between the wall of the city and the Golden Gate.

The exact situation of the Church of St. Giles is unknown, but the Gate Beautiful, mentioned in Acts 3:2, is identified by the Christian tradition with one of the two portals of the Muslim Gate of the Chain in the western wall of the Haram. Opposite it, in the eastern wall of the enclosure, was the Golden Gate, and it is to that complex subject that the narrative now turns:

At the end of this pavement, towards the rising sun, one goes down some steps to get to the Golden Gate. After descending these, is found a broad space reaching the Golden Gate. This is the court which Solomon made. No one passed through these gates, which were walled up, except twice a year, when the walling was removed, to wit, on Palm Sunday, when they went in procession because Jesus Christ passed there on this day and was received in procession; and on the Day of the Feast of the Holy Cross in September because the Cross was brought into Jerusalem through these gates when Heraclius, the emperor of Rome, made his conquests in Persia and brought it back through this gate into the city, being met in procession. Because no one ever went out of the city through this gate there was a postern at the side called the Gate of Jehoshaphat. Those who wished to get out of the city from this part went through this postern, and this postern is on the left of the Golden Gate.

This postern is today called St. Stephen's Gate, but that name was in Crusader times reserved, as below, for the principal northern gate of the city, the one called by the Muslims the Gate of the Column and known today as the Damascus Gate. The Crusaders' nomenclature goes back to the fifth century, when, as we have seen (Chapter Four), Eudocia built her church to house the saint's remains outside the northern gate of the city:

On entering the city by St. Stephen's Gate, you come to two streets, one on the right [Khan al-Zayt Street], which goes to the Gate of Mount Sion, which is due south. . . . The street on the left [Valley Street] goes straight to a postern called the Tannery and goes straight under the bridge [of Wilson's Arch]. The (first) street, which goes to the Gate of Mount Sion, is called the Street of St. Stephen until you come to the Syrian Exchange.

As one comes to the Syrian Exchange, there is on the right the Street of the Sepulcher. Here is the Gate of the House of the Sepulcher, from which those belonging to the Sepulcher entered their dwellings. In front of this exchange, turning toward the right, there is a covered vaulted street by which one goes to the Church of the Sepulcher. In this street the Syrians sell their stuffs and make wax candles. In front of the Exchange they also sell fish. To that Exchange the three streets join which also join the Latin Exchange. One of these is called the Covered Street. There the Latins sell their stuffs. The other is called the Street of Herbs, and the third, Malquisinat.

Now I return to the Gate of St. Stephen to the street on the left [Valley Street], which reaches to the Tannery Postern. After going some way along this street, you find a street on the left hand called Jehoshaphat Street [Bab Sitti Maryam], (and) a little further on one finds crossroads, where the road on the left comes from the Temple and goes to the Sepulcher. . . . Between the Street of Jehoshaphat and the walls of the city on the left [i.e., north of the street] there are streets as far as the Gate of Jehoshaphat, like a city. There dwelt most of the Syrians of Jerusalem, and the streets were called "Jewry" (Juiverie). In this Jewry was a Church of St. Mary Magdalen, and near to the church was a postern, by which one could not go outside to the fields but one went between two walls. . . . (City of Jerusalem 1896: 17-25)

Other Christians

As is repeated several times, the northeast quarter of the city was called "the Jewry," and the not unnatural assumption was that the area had, before the Crusades, a Jewish population. But we have no other evidence whatsoever to support that assumption, [11] thus we must look elsewhere for an explanation of the name—perhaps to the Syrian Christians who took up their residence there and who were, in Crusader eyes, almost indistinguishable from the Muslims among whom they had lived for so many centuries. It is not inconceivable that the name "la Juiverie" was used contemptuously of that quarter whose entire "Oriental" way of life, for all its professed Christianity, was so different from the Crusaders' own.

Another Christian community present in Crusader Jerusalem, and one somewhat more intelligible and congenial to the Latins was that of the Armenians, who likewise had their own quarter in the southwest quadrant of the city:

In the street that leads from the Gate of David down the hill toward the Temple, on the right hand side, near the tower of David, is a convent of Armenian monks in honor of St. Sabas, the most reverent abbot, for whom, while he was yet alive, the Blessed Virgin Mary wrought many miracles.[12] In this same quarter, nor far away, down the descent beyond another street, there is a large church built in honor of St. James the Great, inhabited by Armenian monks, and they have in the same place a large hospice for the reception of the poor of their nation. . . . (John of Wurzburg 1896: 45)

The Latin Quarter

The Armenian quarter in the south of the city abutting on Mount Sion was a venerable and well-defined one in Jerusalem; but the most carefully delimited, because it fell not among the properties of the kingdom but of the Church, was the so-called Patriarch's Quarter around the Church of the Holy Sepulcher. It was, as William of Tyre has already pointed out, under the autonomous sovereignty of the Latin patriarch, who immediately after the conquest had claimed the entire city for the Church, but was, from Baldwin onward, limited to a jurisdiction that William now proceeds to define:

This quarter is described as follows: the outer boundary is formed by the wall which extends from the west gate, or Gate of David, past the [northwest] corner tower known as the Tower of Tancred as far as the north gate known by the name of the first martyr Stephen [now the Damascus Gate]. The inner boundary is formed by the public street which runs from the Gate of Stephen straight to the tables of the money-changers, thence back again to the west gate. Within these boundaries are contained the sacred places of the Lord's passion and resurrection, the house of the Hospital, and two monasteries, one of monks and the other of holy women. Both these cloisters are known as the monasteries of the Latins. The house of the patriarch and the cloister of the canons of the Holy

Sepulcher with their appurtenances also lie within its limits. (William of Tyre 1943: I, 406-407)

The Population of Jerusalem

Even when the properties and jurisdictions in Jerusalem were sorted out, the question remained: who would live in the city? The conquest had destroyed or dispersed the entire population of Jerusalem living there before 1099. And there were few indeed of the newcomers to replace them:

Up to that time [1099] the land route [to Jerusalem] was completely blocked to our pilgrims. Meanwhile they, French as well as English, or Italians and Venetians, came by sea as far as Jaffa. At first we had no other port. These pilgrims came very timidly in single ships, or in squadrons of three or four, through the midst of hostile pirates and past the ports of the Saracens, with the Lord showing the way. . . . They came on to Jerusalem; they visited the Holy of Holies, for which purpose they had come. Following that, some remained in the Holy Land and others went back to their native countries. For this reason the land of Jerusalem remained depopulated. There were not enough people to defend it from the Saracens if only the latter dared attack us. . . . For we did not have at that time more than three hundred knights and as many footmen to defend Jerusalem, Jaffa, Ramle, and also the stronghold of Haifa. We scarcely dared assemble our knights when we wished to plan some feat against our enemies. We feared that in the meantime they would do some damage against our deserted fortifications. (Fulcher of Chartres 1969: II, vi, 5-9)

A city with a population of such dimensions could neither defend itself nor perhaps even survive, situated as it was deep within a hostile environment. Steps had to be taken to repeople the city, and they were put in train by Baldwin I:

At this time the king realized with great concern that the Holy City, beloved of God, was almost destitute of inhabitants. . . . The Gentiles who were living there at the time the city was taken by force had perished by the sword, almost to a man; and if any had by chance escaped, they were not permitted to remain in the city. For to allow anyone not belonging to the Christian faith to live in so venerated a place seemed like a sacrilege to the chiefs in their devotion to God. The people of our country were so few in number and so needy that they scarcely filled one street, while the Syrians who had originally been citizens of the city had been so reduced through the many tribulations and trials endured in the time of hostilities that their number was as nothing. From the time that the Latins came into Syria, and particularly when the army began to march toward Jerusalem after the capture of Antioch, their infidel fellow citizens began to abuse these servants of God greatly. Many were slain for the most trivial remarks, and neither age nor condition was spared. The Gentiles distrusted them intensely, for they believed that it was these people who, through their messengers and letters, had summoned the princes of the West who, it was said, were coming to destroy the infidels.

The king felt that the responsibility for relieving the desolation of the city rested upon him. Accordingly, he made careful investigations in regard to some source whence he might obtain citizens. Finally he learned that beyond the Jordan in Arabia there were many Christians living in villages under hard conditions of servitude and forced tribute. He sent for these people and promised improved conditions. Within a short time he had the satisfaction of receiving them with their wives and children, flocks and herds, and all their households. They were attracted thither not only by reverence for the place but also by affection for our people and the love of liberty. Many, even without being invited, cast off the harsh yoke of servitude and came that they might dwell in the city worthy of God. To these the king granted those sections of the city which seemed to need this assistance most and filled the houses with them. (William of Tyre 1943: I, 507-508)

Another step was taken in 1120 when Baldwin II, at the request of the patriarch, remitted one of the most burdensome of Jerusalem's taxes, one that had a direct and harmful effect on the growing business in pilgrims:

I, Baldwin II . . . yielding to the prayers of our father, Patriarch Guarmund, to the clergy and chapter of the Holy City of Jerusalem, do, with the approval of the nobles, now and in the future remit the customs duties which have previously been demanded and given at the city gate by those bringing grain and vegetables into the city. [13] . . . Those dues seemed indeed burdensome and damaging not only to those coming to visit the Church of the Sepulcher of the Lord as well as to the residents of the Holy City. I therefore free of all exaction all those who wish to bring in grain or vegetables, beans, lentils, or peas through the gates of Jerusalem. Let them have free license to go in and go out and sell without molestation where and to whom they wish, whether they are Christians or Muslims. (Cartulaire Sepulchre 1849: 83-85)

An Introduction to the Inhabitants
of the Holy City

Baldwin's measures must have worked, for the population of the Holy City began to climb back to and eventually surpass its pre-Crusader levels.

One estimate puts it as high as 30,000 during the Latin Kingdom. [14] The local Christians probably needed little urging to move from the countryside, whose population was overwhelmingly Muslim and now unalterably hostile, to the safer confines of Jerusalem. But eventually even a few Jews settled in Jerusalem—Benjamin of Tudela found a handful of poor Jewish dyers there in 1170—along with Muslims, merchants likely, who performed useful services for the Crusaders, this despite William of Tyre's sense that their presence in the Holy City would be "sacrilegious." The population, for all that, remained overwhelmingly Christian, though of very different stripes and persuasions. This is how they appeared to one anonymous pilgrim who recorded his impressions for his Latin compatriots back in Europe:

Of these (who presently live in Jerusalem) some are Christians and some are not. There are divers races of Christians, and they are divided into various sects. Of these, the first are Franks, who are more properly called Latins. They are warlike men, practiced in arms, are bareheaded, and are the only ones who shave the beard. They are called Latins because they use the Latin tongue. They are pure Catholics.

Others are Greeks, who are separated from the Church of Rome. They are cunning men, not much practiced in arms, and they err from the true faith and the articles thereof, especially in that they say that the Holy Spirit does not proceed from the Father and the Son but from the Father alone. They also use leaven in the Eucharist; and they err in many other matters and have an alphabet of their own.

Others are Syrians. These are useless in war. For the most part they do not let their beards grow like the Greeks but trim them somewhat. They do not follow either the Latin or the Greek rite. They are everywhere tributary to other nations. In their faith and sacraments they are in all respects with the Greeks. They use the Saracenic alphabet. . . .

Others are Armenians. They have some slight skill in arms, and differ in many respects from the Latins and the Greeks. They hold their forty days' fast at the time of Christ's nativity, and they celebrate Christ's nativity at the Epiphany, and do many other things contrary to the rule of the Church. They have a language of their own and there is an irreconcilable hatred between them and the Greeks. But of late they have promised obedience to the Church of Rome, since their king has received his crown from the hands of the archbishop of Mainz, the Legate of the Holy See [A.D. 1198].

Others are Georgians and venerate St. George with solemn ritual. They let their hair and beard grow long and wear hats a cubit high. All of them, both churchmen and laymen, wear the tonsure: the clergy wear it round and the laity square. They use leaven in the Mass and imitate the Greeks in almost all respects, but they have their own alphabet.

Others are Jacobites, who have been led astray by one James [Baradaeus] into the Nestorian heresy and do greatly err. They use the Chaldean alphabet.

Others are Nestorians, who are heretical in their faith, saying that the Blessed Mary was only the mother of a man and erring in many other matters. They use the Chaldean alphabet.

Moreover, the Latins are divided into various nations, to wit, Germans, Spaniards, Gauls, Italians, and the other nations which Europe produces. Three Italian peoples are especially powerful and useful in the land of Jerusalem, to wit, the Genoese, the Venetians, and the Pisans. They are skilled in the use of arms, invincible at sea, practiced in every kind of warfare, cunning in the arts of trading, and altogether free from all tribute and toll whatsoever, and exempt from all jurisdiction, making their own laws for themselves. But among themselves they are jealous and quarrelsome, so that the Saracens are safer with them than they are with one another. (Anonymous Pilgrims 1894: 25-29)

National Rivalries

In his final reflections the anonymous author of this account probably had in mind the Latin population of a place like Acre in the late twelfth or even thirteenth century. There the Italian mercantile communities pursued their deadly feuds from inside walled enclaves within the city. Jerusalem during its brief history had no such communes, and its accents were thoroughly and perhaps even overwhelmingly French, as John of Wurzburg sadly reflected sometime about 1160:

Three days afterwards [i.e., after July 15, the anniversary of the recapture of Jerusalem] is the anniversary of noble Duke Godfrey of happy memory, the chief and leader of that holy expedition, who was born of a German family. His anniversary is solemnly observed by the city with plenteous giving of alms in the great church, according as he himself arranged while yet alive.

But although he is there honored in this way for himself, yet the taking of the city is not credited to him with his Germans, who bore no small share in the toils of that expedition, but is attributed to the French alone. Wherefore some disparagers of our nation have actually obliterated the epitaph of the famous Wigger [or Wicker, of Swabia] made glorious by so many deeds, because they could not deny that he was a German, and *have written over it the epitaph of some French knight or other, as may at this day be seen on the spot. . . .*

Although Duke Godfrey and his brother Baldwin, who was made king of Jerusalem after him, . . . were men of our country, yet since only a few of our people remained there with them, and very many of the others with great haste and homesickness returned to their native land, the entire city has fallen into the hands of other nations—Frenchmen, Lorrainers, Normans, Provençals, Auvergnats, Italians, Spaniards, and Burgundians—who took part in the Crusade; and also no part of the city, not even the smallest street, was set apart for the Germans. As they themselves took no care of the matter, and had no intention of remaining there, their names were never mentioned and the glory of delivering the Holy City was ascribed to the Franks alone. . . . (John of Wurzburg 1896: 40-41)

There was in Latin Jerusalem, whether or not it was so called in John's day, a "Germans' Street," as the "City of Jerusalem" has already testified, and John himself undoubtedly walked down it on his way to another familiar institution where he had the opportunity to speak German:

As you descend this same street, beside the gate which leads to the Temple, on the right-hand side, there is a kind of passage through a long portico, in which street is a hospice and a church, which has been newly built in honor of St. Mary, and which is called the House of the Germans, upon which hardly any men who speak any other language bestow benefactions. (John of Wurzburg 1896: 45-46)

Orientalization

John's was one perception of life in Latin Palestine, a realistic one no doubt; but the situation appeared somewhat differently in others' eyes, Fulcher of Chartres for one, who knew the land well:

. . . Consider, I pray, and reflect how in our time [ca. A.D. 1124] God has transformed the Occident into the Orient. For we who were Occidentals have now become Orientals. He who was a Roman or a Frank has in this land been made into a Galilean or a Palestinian. He who was of Rheims or Chartres has now become a citizen of Tyre or Antioch. We have already forgotten the places of our birth; already these are unknown to many of us and not mentioned anymore. Some already possess homes or households by inheritance. Some have taken wives not only from among their own people but Syrians and Armenians and even Saracens who have received the grace of baptism. One has his father-in-law as well as his daughter-in-law living with him, or his own child if not his stepchild or step-

father. Out here there are grandchildren and great-grandchildren. Some tend vineyards, others till fields. People use the eloquence and idioms of diverse languages in conversing back and forth. Words of different languages have become common property known to each nationality, and mutual faith unites those who are ignorant of their descent. Indeed it is written, "The lion and the ox shall eat straw together" [Is. 62:25]. He who was born a stranger is now as one born here; he who was born an alien has become as a native. Our relatives and parents join us from time to time, sacrificing, even though reluctantly, all that they formerly possessed. Those who were poor in the Occident, God makes rich in this land. Those who had little money there have countless bezants here, and those who did not have a villa possess here by the gift of God a city. (Fulcher of Chartres 1969: III, xxxvii)

There is special pleading in this account, surely, particularly in its closing lines with their scarcely disguised invitation to join the Crusaders in their new Sion. But there is as surely some truth to the claims of assimilation, though if it took place in Jerusalem, it was through the agency of the local "Oriental" Christians who had returned to the city. Jerusalem fell, after all, in a Holy War whose stated aim was to free Jerusalem of Muslim domination and ended with eradicating the Muslim presence in the city. There was no Muslim urban bourgeoisie in the Holy City, no surviving merchant or artisan class to form the basis of a new society.

In Jerusalem through the eastern Christians, who lived much as the Muslims did, and elsewhere through contact with the Muslims themselves, the Franks did acquire some taste for the local style of life, even though it probably remained on the somewhat superficial level described by Usama ibn Munqidh, a sophisticated Muslim traveller who knew the land and its ways every bit as well as Fulcher did:

There are some Franks who have settled in our land and taken to living like Muslims. These are better than those who have just arrived from their homelands, but they are the exception, and cannot be taken as typical. I came across one of them once when I sent a friend on business to Antioch, which was governed by Todros ibn al-Safi [Theodore Sophianos], a friend of mine. One day he said to my friend. "A Frankish friend has invited me to visit him; come with me so you can see how they live." "I went with him," said my friend, "and we came to the house of one of the old knights who came with the first expedition. This man had retired from the army and was living on the income of property he owned in Antioch. He had a fine table brought out, spread with a splendid selection of appetizing food. He saw that I was not eating and said: 'Don't worry, please. Eat what you like, for I don't eat Frankish food. I have Egyptian cooks and eat only what they serve. No pig's flesh ever comes into my house.' So I ate, though cautiously, and then we left." (Gabrieli 1969: 78-79)

Church of the Holy Sepulcher

The heart of the Crusader city was the Church of the Holy Sepulcher, as the Latins preferred to call the Anastasis. Destroyed by al-Hakim in 1009 and rebuilt by the Byzantines in 1048 under the patronage of Constantine IX Monomachus, it was refurbished once again by the Crusaders once they had taken possession of the city. [15] There are numerous accounts of the church dating from Crusader times, but only two of the most systematic and circumstantial will be cited here: the first from the anonymous author of "The Condition of the City of Jerusalem," and the second from the Russian abbot Daniel, who visited the city in 1106:

In front of this (main) entry of the Sepulcher is a very beautiful open space paved with marble. To the left of the (entry to the) Sepulcher is a church called St. James of the Jacobites. On the right, close to this entry to the Sepulcher, there are steps by which one ascends Mount Calvary. On the top of the mount is a very beautiful chapel. There is another door in this chapel by which one enters and descends into the Church of the Sepulcher by other steps which are there, just as one enters the church.

On the right, below Mount Calvary, is Golgotha. On the left (of the church) is the bell tower of the Sepulcher, and a chapel which is called Holy Trinity. This chapel is very large, being the place where all the women of the city are married. And there is the font where they baptized all the children of the city. . . .

At the place where the Tomb is the church is quite round, and it is open from above without any covering; and within the monument is the Stone of the Sepulcher. And the monument is vaulted over. . . . There is a beautiful place all around the Tomb, completely paved, so that they can walk in procession around the tomb. Beyond, towards the east, is the choir of the Sepulcher, where the canons chant; it is long. . . . At the head of the choir there is a door by which the canons entered into their places. On the right, between this door and Mount Calvary, there is a very deep moat, into which one descends by steps. Here there is a chapel called St. Helena, where St. Helena found the cross, the nails, the hammer, and the crown. . . . When the canons come out from the (Church of the) Sepulcher, on the left is their dormitory; on the right, their refectory, which is close to Mount Calvary. Between these two offices is their cloister and walking ground. And in the midst of this court there is a large opening

311

from which one could see into the chamber of Helena below. . . . (City of Jerusalem 1896: 7-10)

The Church of the Resurrection is of circular form; it contains twelve monolithic columns and six pillars and is paved with very beautiful marble slabs. There are six entrances and galleries with sixteen columns. Under the ceilings, above the galleries, the holy prophets are represented in mosaic as if they were alive; the altar is surmounted by a figure of Christ in mosaic. At the high altar there is an "Exaltation of Adam" in mosaic, and the mosaic above the arch represents the "Ascension of our Lord." There is an "Annunciation" in mosaic on the pillars on either side of the altar. The dome of the church is not closed by stone vault, but is formed of a framework of wooden beams, so that the church is open at the top. The Holy Sepulcher is beneath this open dome. . . .

The Church of the Resurrection is round in form and measures 280 feet each way. It contains spacious apartments in the upper part, in which the patriarch lives [var. "lived"]. They count 84 feet from the entrance to the tomb to the wall of the high altar. . . .

The place of the crucifixion is toward the east, upon a rounded rock, like a little hill, higher than a lance. On the summit of it, in the middle, a socket-hole is excavated, one cubit deep, and less than a foot in circumference; it is here that the cross of the Lord was erected. Beneath this rock lies the skull of the first man, Adam. At the time of our Lord's crucifixion, when He gave up the ghost on the cross, the veil of the Temple was rent and the rock clave asunder, and the rock above Adam's skull opened, and the blood and water which flowed from Christ's side ran down through the fissures upon the skull, thus washing away the sins of men. The fissure exists to this day, and this holy token is seen to be to the right of the place of the crucifixion.

The holy rock and place of crucifixion are enclosed by a wall, and they are covered by a building ornamented with marvellous mosaics. On the eastern wall there is a wonderful lifelike representation of the crucified Christ, but larger and higher than nature; and on the south side an equally marvellous Descent from the Cross. There are two doors; one mounts seven steps to the doors, and as many after; the floor is paved with beautiful marble. Beneath the place of crucifixion, where the skull lies, there is a small chapel, beautifully decorated with mosaic, and paved with fine marble, which is called Calvary, signifying the place of the skull. The upper part, the place of the crucifixion, is called Golgotha. . . . (Daniel the Abbot 1895: 11-15)

The church appeared quite different in Muslim eyes, for it memorialized the two events in the life of Jesus to which Muslims took the most strenuous exception, his alleged death and resurrection. The Quran maintained quite specifically that Jesus had not died on the cross and so stood in no need of a miracle of resurrection. A Church of the Resurrection, then, got scant theological respect from al-Harawi, who visited the city during the Crusader occupation, though he was quite willing to marvel at its architecture:

As for the places of pilgrimage of the Christians, the most important of them is the Church called al-Qumama which, from the point of view of its construction, is one of the wonders mentioned as such and so I shall describe it [in my work on] the description of the monuments. As far as the Christians are concerned, there is found the tomb which they call the Tomb of the Resurrection [al-Qiyama] because the resurrection of the Messiah took place there; actually the place is called Qumama, the Dung-heap, because they used to throw all the filth of the city there. It was outside the city and the hands of criminals were cut off and thieves crucified there. That is what the Gospel says, and God alone knows the truth. For them there is also in that place the rock which was split, they say, because it was under the cross and Adam was below it. There too is the Garden of Joseph the Just, to which they make pilgrimage. As for the descent of the fire, I lived long enough in Jerusalem at the time of the Franks to know how it was done. (Harawi 1957: 68-69)

The "descent of the fire" is of course a reference to the sometimes famous, sometimes notorious, Christian miracle that occurred in the Holy Sepulcher every year on the eve of Easter.[16] Daniel the Abbot's account of the miracle has already been cited in Chapter Seven, but the Russian monk also used his entree into the Sepulcher to achieve other, not uncommon objectives in visiting the holy places: a bit of scientific research and, more importantly, the procurement of a relic from this, the most sacred spot in Christendom:

On the third day after the Resurrection of Our Lord, I went after my mass to the Guardian of the Keys of the Holy Sepulcher and said: "I want to retrieve my lamp." He received me with affection and let me go alone into the Sepulcher. There I saw my lamp still burning brilliantly with the flame of the Holy Light. I prostrated myself before the Tomb and covered with tears and kisses the place where the pure body of Our Lord Jesus Christ had lain. Then I measured the length and the width and the height of the Tomb as it is presently, an act no one can do when there are people about. I honored the Guardian as much as was in my power and offered, as my means permitted, my small and poor gift. When he saw my devotion to the Holy Sepulcher, he pushed back the stone that covered the Tomb at the place where the head would have been, broke off a piece of the sacred stone, and gave it to me as a blessing, adjuring me not to mention it to anyone in Jerusalem. . . . (Daniel the Abbot 1895: 40-41)

The Haram and Its Buildings

East of the Holy Sepulcher, the Dome of the Rock and the Aqsa Mosque still stood in their glory atop the Haram. The Crusaders did not destroy either building, but they immediately appropriated both to their own purposes, and began to introduce some structural modifications. Before those latter changes occurred, however, at least three visitors—Fulcher, Saewulf, and Daniel—saw the buildings in their original Muslim condition and have given us their impressions of not only what they saw but what they thought they saw. For almost all the Crusader and post-Crusade Christian visitors to the Haram, the Rock stood on the site of—and indeed often represented—the *Templum Domini*, the "House of the Lord" originally built by Solomon, while the Aqsa Mosque to the south marked the place of the "Palace of Solomon," the *Templum Solomonis*. The identifications are already evident in Fulcher of Chartres:

In the same city is the Temple of the Lord, round in shape where Solomon in ancient times erected the earlier magnificent Temple. Although it can in no way be compared in appearance to the former building [i.e., the Church of the Holy Sepulcher], still this one [the Dome of the Rock] is of marvelous workmanship and most splendid appearance. . . . In the middle of the Temple, when we first entered it and for fifteen years thereafter,[17] was a certain native rock. It was said that the Ark of the Lord's Covenant along with the urn and tables of Moses was sealed inside of it, that Josiah, king of Judah, ordered it to be placed there saying "You shall never carry it from this place" [2 Chron. 35:3]. For he foresaw the future captivity. But this contradicts what we read in the descriptions of Jeremiah, in the second Book of Maccabees, that he himself hid it in Arabia, saying that it should not be found until many people should be gathered together.[18] Moreover, this rock, because it disfigured the Temple of the Lord, was afterwards covered over and paved with marble. Now an altar is placed above it, and there the clergy have fitted up a choir. All the Saracens hold the Temple of the Lord in great veneration. Here rather than elsewhere they preferred to say the prayers of their faith, although such prayers were wasted because offered to an idol [the Rock?] set up in the name of Muhammad. They allowed no Christian to enter the Temple.

Another temple, called the Temple of Solomon, is large and wonderful, but it is not the one Solomon built. This one, because of our poverty, could not be maintained in the condition in which we found it.[19] Wherefore it is already in large part destroyed. (Fulcher of Chartres 1969: I, xxxi, 5-10)

You go down [the street] from our Lord's Sepulcher twice as far as a bow can shoot, to the Temple of the Lord, which is to the east side of the Holy Sepulcher. Its court is of great length and breadth and has many gates. But the principal gate is the one which faces the Temple [on the west] and is called Beautiful by reason of the character of the workmanship and the variety of colors. There it was that Peter healed the cripple when he and John went up to the Temple at the ninth hour, the hour of prayer, as we read in the Acts of the Apostles [Acts 3:1-8]. The place where Solomon built the Temple of the Lord was anciently called Bethel, whither, at the Lord's command, Jacob went on his journey and rested there, and saw in the same place the ladder whose top touched the heavens, and he saw angels ascending and descending upon it and said: "Truly, this place is holy," as we read in Genesis [Gen. 28:17-18]. There he set up the stone for the title and built an altar, pouring oil on it. In the same place, afterwards, by divine inspiration, Solomon made a Temple for the Lord. . . .

[Solomon's] Temple of the Lord was of magnificent and incomparable workmanship, and wonderfully decorated with every ornament, as you read in Book of Kings. . . . In the middle of the Temple there was seen a rock, lofty and large and scooped out beneath, on which was the Holy of Holies. . . . [There follows a list of sacred events from both the Old and New Testaments connected with that place.]

There is the gate of the city at the eastern part of the Temple which is called the Golden Gate, where Joachim, the father of the Blessed Mary, by the command of the angel met his wife Anna. Through the same gate the Lord Jesus coming from Bethany on Palm Sunday entered the city sitting on an ass. . . . By that same gate Emperor Heraclius returned triumphant from Persia with Our Lord's Cross; but at first the stones fell down against each other and stopped up the gate, and the gate was made as it were a whole mass of rubbish, until, at the admonition of an angel, the emperor humbled himself and alighted from his horse, and thus an entrance cleared itself for him. (Saewulf 1896: 15-17)

The Church of the Holy of Holies [that is, the Dome of the Rock] is about two bow-shots from the Church of the Resurrection of Christ. The interior of the Holy of Holies is wonderfully and artistically decorated with mosaics, and its beauty is indescribable. It is round in form, and the exterior is covered with magnificent paintings, of whose beauty it is impossible to give any idea. The walls, as well as the floor, are faced with *beautiful slabs of precious marble. Under the roof there is a circle of twelve monolithic columns and eight pillars. There are four doors covered with plates of gilded copper. Beneath this same dome is a grotto cut in the rock. It is there that the prophet Zachariah was killed; formerly his tomb and the marks of his blood were to be seen, but no longer. . . . The ancient Church of the Holy of Holies has been destroyed. Nothing is left of the ancient building of Solomon except the original foundations of the Temple which the prophet David began to lay. The cavern and the stone beneath the cupola are the sole remains of the ancient buildings; as for the present church, it was built by a chief of the Saracens named Umar.*

There also was the house of Solomon. It was an imposing edifice of surprising beauty and grandeur, paved with marble slabs, supported on arches and furnished with copious cisterns. The apartments were artistically decorated with mosaic and superb rows of beautiful marble columns. Chambers rest upon these columns in a very ingenious manner, and the entire house is overlaid with tin.

The gate of this palace, richly and artistically overlaid with tin and ornamented with mosaic and gilded copper, is called the Beautiful Gate. It is there that Peter and John cured the halt, and this place exists to the present day near the gate. There are three other gates, and the fifth is called the Gate of the Apostles. [20] *It was solidly and cleverly constructed by the prophet David, decorated internally with artistic paintings upon copper and externally solidly covered with iron plates. There are four entrances to this gate, which, with the Tower of David, is all that remains of the ancient town; all the rest is modern, the ancient city of Jerusalem having been destroyed more than once. It is through this gate that Christ entered Jerusalem when he came from Bethany. . . . (Daniel the Abbot 1895: 19-21)*

The Dome of the Rock as a
Christian Church

Though the Muslims were immediately driven off the Haram, it must have taken some time before all the Christians' adaptations were made in the two main Muslim buildings atop Mount Moriah: the Dome of the Rock, which the Latins regarded as the site of Solomon's Temple and so called the *Templum Domini*; and the Aqsa Mosque, identified as the place of Solomon's palace. According to William of Tyre (VIII, 3), speaking of the rock under the Dome, "before the Latins came, and in fact for fifteen years afterward, this place lay bare and exposed. Later it was covered with white marble by those who held it and an altar and a choir built above, and there a priest celebrates the sacred offices." [21] Thus the work of conversion did not begin until 1114 or 1115, and if the erection of the altar atop the Rock was completed within a year or so, the formal consecration of the Dome of the Rock as a Christian church did not take place until 1142. [22] In addition, there was a cloister and conventual buildings erected north of the Dome to serve the canons attached to the church of the *Templum Domini*.

The new Christian cathedral atop the Haram was not intended to displace the Church of the Holy Sepulcher, nor did it ever do so. Rather, it was a showplace, the enshrinement of a place associated with a great variety of events in both the Old and New Testaments. Its size and shape ill suited it to Christian liturgical practice, but it was at least expensively adorned by the new Latin masters of Jerusalem, as seen in John of Wurzburg's detailed description of the place as it appeared in 1160 or 1170:

Now this same Templum Domini [whose connections with Jesus, John has just traced], which has been adorned by someone both within and without with a wondrous casing of marble, has the form of a beautiful rotunda, or rather, a circular octagon, that is, having eight angles disposed in a circle, with a wall decorated on the outside from the middle upwards with the finest mosaic work, for the remainder is of marble. This same lower wall is continuous, save that it is pierced by four doors, having one door toward the east, which adjoins a chapel dedicated to St. James. [23] ... On the north side is a door leading to the canons' cloisters, [24] upon the lintel whereof many Saracen letters are inscribed. ... At the entrance to the Temple towards the west, above the vestibule, is an image of Christ with this inscription around it: "My house shall be called the house of prayer." It also has a door on the south looking towards the building of Solomon. The western door also looks towards the Sepulcher of the Lord, where also is the Beautiful Gate through which Peter was passing with John when he answered the lame man begging for alms, "Silver and gold I have none, etc." Each of these two doorways, I mean that on the north and on the west side, have six doors arranged in pairs of leaves; that on the south side has four and that on the east only two. Each of the doorways has a handsome porch.

[There follows a description of the upper portion of the Dome of the Rock.] ... Above this narrower wall is raised on high a round vault, painted within, and covered on the outside with lead, on the summit of which the figure of the Holy Cross has been placed by the Christians, which is very offensive to the Saracens and many of them would be willing to expend much gold to have it taken away; for although they do not believe in Christ's Passion, nevertheless they respect this Temple because they adore their Creator therein, which nevertheless must be regarded as idolatry [by Christians] on the authority of St. Augustine, who declares that everything is idolatry which is done without faith in Christ.

This Temple, so beautifully built and adorned, has on all sides a wide and level platform, paved with stones fitted together, which platform is of a square shape, and is ascended on three sides by many steps. Indeed, this platform is very ingeniously built up because of the nature of the ground. It has on its east wall [i.e., side] a wide entrance through five arches which are linked by four great columns, and this [side] opens thus toward the Golden Gate through which Our Lord on the fifth day before His Passion rode in triumph, sitting upon an ass. . . . This gate by the divine protection has always remained unharmed, though since that time Jerusalem has often been captured and destroyed by hostile armies. This gate, moreover, in pious remembrance of Our Lord's divine and mystic entrance when he came up from Bethany over the Mount of Olives, is closed within and blocked up with stones within and is never opened to anyone except on Palm Sunday, on which day every year, in memory of what took place there, it is solemnly opened to a procession and to the whole people, whether they be citizens or strangers. After the patriarch has preached a sermon to the people at the foot of the Mount of Olives and when the service for that day is over, it is closed again for a whole year as before, except on the day after the exaltation of the Holy Cross, when it is also opened.[25] At the foot of the city walls near this gate is a famous burial place.[26] (John of Wurzburg 1896: 15-19)

The Dome of the Rock was a primary Muslim shrine, and we are fortunate to have preserved the reactions of two Muslims who visited the shrine while it was in Crusader hands and had been adapted as a Christian church. The first is from Ali al-Harawi, the author of a Muslim guide to places of pilgrimage, who not unnaturally was particularly struck by the new figurative art:

The Dome of the Rock has four entrances. I went in there at the time of the Franks in A.D. 1173, and I saw, opposite the entry that leads to the Grotto of the Spirits [Maghârat al-arwâh] and close to the iron grille [that surrounded the Rock], an image of Solomon, son of David, and further to the west, atop a lead doorway, a representation of the Messiah in gold and encrusted with precious stones. On the arch that is atop the eastern doorway, next to the Dome of the Chain, there are written the name of al-Qa'im, Commander of the Faithful, the Sura of Sincerity and the formulae "Praise be to God" and "Glory be to God." The same is true of all the other entries without the Franks having changed anything. Close to this monument on the east is the Dome of the Chain, under which Solomon the son of David rendered justice, and to the north, the residence of the priests, which contains columns and other artistic wonders which I shall indicate, God willing, [in the work] devoted to monuments and antiquities. (Harawi 1957: 63-64)

The second observer was Usama, who made a career of observing the Franks in their new habitat and whose reaction was somewhat more heated and considerably more pointed than al-Harawi's:

I was present myself when one of them came up to Amir Mu'în al-Din— God have mercy on him—in the Dome of the Rock and said to him: "Would you like to see God as a baby?" The amir said that he would, and the fellow proceeded to show us a picture of Mary with the infant Messiah on her lap. "This," he said, "is God as a baby." Almighty God is greater than the infidels' concept of Him! (Gabrieli 1969: 80)

A History Lesson

A greater familiarity with the site did not bring much new information about its history. The Muslims, of course, knew who built the Dome of the Rock and were unanimous in affirming it as the place of Solomon's Temple as well as a stop on Muhammad's Night Journey. But the destruction of the Temple always remained vague to them; and Helena and Constantine were somehow bound up with it, chiefly as the desecrators of the Temple mount. Some Christians, like William of Tyre, for example, knew that the Dome was a Muslim building, erected, according to William, by Umar, but many others thought that it dated from an earlier Christian regime. The following summary account of the history of the Temple, and of the Dome, from the pen of an anonymous pilgrim of the time is not untypical, except perhaps for its epigraphical sophistication:

When his father died, King Solomon built a Temple thereon [i.e., on the threshing floor of Ornan purchased by David] in Bethel, and an altar. . . . This Temple, I say, was profaned and spoiled by Pharaoh Necho, king of Egypt, in the time of Rehoboam, the aforesaid Solomon's son. In the days of Zedekiah, Nebuchadnezzar, by the hands of his chief cook, Nabuzardan, ultimately destroyed both the Temple and the city. . . . Afterwards, in the reign of King Cyrus, the Temple was rebuilt by Ezra the scribe and Nehemiah the priest, and the people were brought back, led by Zerubbabel and Joshua, the chief high priest. The Temple was again profaned by Antiochus and rebuilt in Maccabean times. [27] *It was also profaned by Pompey, who lodged therein when he was fleeing before the face of Julius Caesar. Lastly, the Temple was destroyed for the third time and overthrown down to its very foundations in the reigns of Titus and Vespasian.*

Of a truth I will essay, as well as I am able, to set forth to all the readers of this book the truth of this present Bethel, albeit no man knows for certain by what prince or in whose reign it was restored. Some say that it was rebuilt in the reign of Emperor Constantine by his mother Helena, out of reverence for the Holy Cross which she found there. Others say that it was rebuilt by Emperor Heraclius, out of reverence for the Lord's Cross, which he had gloriously brought back in triumph from Persia. Others say that it was built by Emperor Justinian; others that it was built by a certain Admiral Memphis [Alii a quodam ammiraldo Memphis] [28] *in honor of Allah Kabir [in honore Alla chiberti], that is, God Most High, which the Saracenic inscription thereon proves to me most like the truth. Wherefore this Temple, which is devoutly venerated by men of all tongues alike, is called the fourth Temple. (Anonymous Pilgrims 1894: 64-65)*

The Aqsa Mosque and the Templars

Al-Harawi also went into the al-Aqsa, the former cathedral mosque of Jerusalem, when he visited the Haram in 1073, and he curiously has little to remark upon except the Muslim dedicatory inscriptions, which the Crusaders had left intact. We know as a matter of fact, from both Christian sources and from Muslim accounts of the retaking of the city cited in Chapter Nine, that the Christian modifications of the Aqsa Mosque were extensive. Originally it had been put at the disposal of the new Latin sovereign of Jerusalem—it had been, after all, Solomon's palace—but its use as a royal residence was relatively brief, [29] less than twenty years, according to William of Tyre, who traces the next stage in its history under the Latins:

In this same year [1118], certain pious and God-fearing nobles of knightly rank, devoted to the Lord, professed the wish to live perpetually in poverty, chastity, and obedience. In the hands of the patriarch they vowed themselves to the service of God as regular canons. Foremost and most distinguished among these men were the venerable Hugh de Payens and Godfrey of St. Omer. Since they had neither a church nor a fixed place of abode, the king granted them a temporary dwelling place in his own palace, on the north[?] side of the Temple of the Lord. Under certain definite conditions, the Canons of the Temple of the Lord also gave them a square belonging to the canons near the same place where the new order might exercise the duties of its religion.

The king [Baldwin II] and his nobles, as well as the patriarch and the prelates of the churches, also provided from their own holdings certain benefices, the income of which was to provide these knights with food and clothing. Some of these gifts were for a limited time, other in perpe-

tuity. The main duty of this order—that which was enjoined upon them by the patriarch and the other bishops for the remission of sins—was "that as far as their strength permitted, they should keep the roads and highways safe from the menace of robbers and highwaymen, with especial regard for the protection of pilgrims." (William of Tyre 1943: I, 524-525)

Thus came into existence the Order of the Knights Templars. Their beginning was modest enough. At a Church council held at Troyes in 1128, when there were still only nine members, they were given a Rule, and a white habit was assigned to them. They also found an important sponsor in Bernard of Clairvaux. Knightly recruitment began to increase, and at some point they began to sew a red cross on their white habit, as William continues,

that they might be distinguished from others. Not only the knights but also the inferior brothers called sergeants wore this sign. The Templars prospered so greatly that today there are in the order about three hundred knights who wear the white mantle and, in addition, an almost countless number of lesser brothers. They are said to have vast possessions, both on this side of the sea and beyond. There is not a province in the Christian world today which does not bestow some part of its possessions upon these brethren, and their property is reported to be equal to the riches of kings. They are called Brethren of the Soldiery of the Temple because, as we have said, they had their residence in the royal palace near the Temple of the Lord.

For a long time they kept intact their noble purpose and carried out their profession wisely enough. At length, however, they . . . withdrew from the Patriarch of Jerusalem, from whom they had received the establishment of their order and their first privileges, and refused him the obedience which their predecessors had shown him. To the churches of God they also became very troublesome, for they drew away from them their tithes and first fruits and unjustly disturbed their possessions. (William of Tyre 1943: I, 526-527)

The rapid growth in their wealth and power commented upon by William of Tyre, their freedom from any but papal supervision, and eventually the kingdom's almost total dependence upon them and upon the Hospitallers for its security and indeed its survival gave the Templars an immense importance in Latin Jerusalem and Crusader Palestine, an importance reflected in the changes they began to effect in their headquarters in what had once been the Aqsa Mosque. [30] The reporter is Theoderich, a visitor to Jerusalem in 1172:

Next comes, on the south [of the Templum Domini], the palace of Solo-

mon, which is oblong and supported by columns within like a church. The end is round like a sanctuary and covered by a great round dome so that, as I have said, it resembles a church. This building, with all its appurtenances, has passed into the hands of the Knights Templars who dwell in it and all the other buildings connected with it, having many stores of arms, clothing, and food in it, and are ever on the watch to guard and protect the country. They have below them stables for horses built by King Solomon himself in the days of old. This stable adjoins the palace, a wondrous and intricate building resting on piers and containing an endless complication of arches and vaults. . . . No man could send an arrow from one end of the [Templars'] building to the other, either lengthways or crossways, at one shot with a Balearic bow. Above it abounds with rooms, solar chambers, and buildings suitable for all manner of uses. Those who walk on the roof of it find an abundance of gardens, courtyards, antechambers, vestibules, and rainwater cisterns; while down below it contains a wonderful number of baths, storehouses, granaries, and storehouses for wood and other needful provisions.

On another side of the palace, that is to say, on the western side, the Templars have erected a new building. I could give the measurements of its height, length, and breadth of its cellars, refectories, staircases, and roof, which rises with a high pitch unlike the flat roofs of that country; but even if I did so, my hearers would hardly be able to believe me. They have built a new cloister there in addition to the old one which they had in another part of the building. Moreover, they are laying the foundations of a new church of wonderful size and workmanship in this place, by the side of the great court. It is not easy for anyone to gain an idea of the power and wealth of the Templars, for they and the Hospitallers have taken possession of almost all of the cities and villages with which Judea was once enriched, which were destroyed by the Romans, and have built castles everywhere and filled them with garrisons, besides the very many and indeed numberless estates which they are well known to possess in other lands. (Theoderich 1896: 30-32)

Al-Harawi, as we have seen, mentioned none of this, though he was in the mosque at almost exactly the same time as Theoderich. Usama too visited the Aqsa, but his attention was as usual directed more toward the Latins, in this instance a newly arrived Templar, than toward their buildings:

This is an example of Frankish barbarism, God damn them! When I was in Jerusalem I used to go up to the Aqsa Mosque, beside which is a small oratory which the Franks have made into a church. Whenever I went into the mosque, which was in the hands of Templars who were friends of mine, they would put the little oratory at my disposal so that I could say my prayers there. One day I had gone in, said the *Allah akbar* and risen to begin my prayers, when a Frank threw himself on me from behind, lifted me up and turned me so that I was facing east. "That is the way to pray!" he said. Some Templars at once intervened, seized the man and took him out of my way, while I resumed my prayer. But the moment they stopped watching him, he seized me again and forced me to face east, repeating that this was the way to pray. Again the Templars intervened and took him away. They apologized and said: "He is a foreigner who has just arrived today from his homeland in the north and he has never seen anyone pray facing any other direction than east." "I have finished my prayers," I said and left, stupefied by the fanatic who had been so perturbed and upset to see anyone praying facing the qibla! (Gabrieli 1969: 79-80)

Usama kept his true feelings about the Templars carefully concealed, whether from prudence or merely from ambivalence, but there is no doubt what position the Templars held in the minds of those who lived in or visited the Latin Kingdom. If their wealth excited envy, their military deeds aroused only admiration, as in this account from an unnamed pilgrim to the Holy Land in Crusader times:

In this land there are two religious houses, to wit, the Temple and the Hospital. They have an exceeding great abundance of riches, for they have property in and draw revenues from every part of Europe. When they go to the wars, the Templars fight on the right wing and the Hospitallers on the left.

The Templars are most excellent soldiers. They wear white mantles with a red cross, and when they go to the wars a standard of two colors called balzaus is borne before them. They go in silence. Their first attack is the most terrible. In going, they are the first, in returning, the last. They await the orders of their Master. When they think fit to make war and the trumpet has sounded, they sing in chorus the Psalm of David, Non nobis, Domine, non nobis [Ps. 115], kneeling on the blood and necks of the enemy, unless they have forced the troops of the enemy to retire altogether or utterly broken them in pieces. Should any one of them for any reason turn his back on the enemy, or come forth alive [from a defeat], or bear arms against the Christians, he is severely punished: the white mantle with the red cross, which is the sign of his knighthood, is taken away with ignominy, he is cast out from the society of the brethren and eats his food on the floor without a cloth for the space of one year. . . . The Templars live under strict religious Rule, obeying humbly, having no private property, eating sparingly, dressing meanly, and dwelling in tents.

The Hospitallers bear a white cross on their mantles and are good knights, who, besides their service in the field, take care of the sick and the needy. They live under a Rule and discipline of their own. (Anonymous Pilgrims 1894: 29-30)

The Hospital

The mention of the Hospitallers appears almost like an afterthought in this pilgrim's reflections, and this other religious order of knights doubtless did live somewhat in the shadow of their more aggressive brethren on the Haram. But they enjoyed many of the same privileges and in the end performed many of the same military tasks as the Templars, although their origins were quite different. William of Tyre, who, as we have seen in Chapter Six, traced the origins of the Hospitallers back to the Amalfi hospice in Jerusalem, resumes his narrative at that point:

For many years this place [the Amalfi hospice] existed under these conditions, until it pleased the Supreme Maker of the world to purge from the superstition of the Gentiles that city He had made clean with His own blood. There came at last a Christian people, led by chiefs under the protection of God, to whom the Savior willed that the kingdom be surrendered. At that time there was found in the convent for women, serving as abbess, a certain holy woman devoted to God, named Agnes. This noble woman, a Roman by birth and of high lineage according to the flesh, continued to live in Jerusalem for some years after the city was restored to the Christian faith. In the hospital also was found one Gerald, a man of upright life who, under the orders of the abbots and monks, had long rendered devoted service to the poor in the enemy. Gerald was later succeeded by Raymond. . . . (William of Tyre 1943: II, 245)

Gerald, the first master of the Latin Hospital, is a somewhat shadowy figure, but we are considerably better informed about his successor and the true founder of the Hospital, Raymond du Puy (1120-1160), who lobbied tirelessly and aggressively to acquire both funding and privilege for his fledgling order. It had a formal Rule sometime before 1153, and in the following year was formally recognized as an exempt order of the Church. [31] It was also about this same time that it began to participate in military activities.

The matter of exemptions brought the Order of the Hospital into direct conflict with the patriarch, since the Hospitallers were, in effect, exempt from *his* legal and fiscal jurisdiction, and likely far richer in the bargain since their rapidly growing endowment holdings extended, like the Templars', into all parts of Europe. William of Tyre, himself an archbishop, was no great admirer of exempt orders, and he held the Hospital chiefly responsible for the scandalous disorders that broke out between Raymond and the patriarch in the very heart of Crusader Jerusalem. The matter began with the question of the patriarch's tithes and Raymond's refusal to pay them, but it soon escalated:

The most intolerable wrong of all, however, a thing abhorrent to all Christians, was done to the patriarch and the Holy Church at Jerusalem. For, before the very doors of the Church of the Holy Resurrection, to show their insolent contempt for the church itself, they [the Hospitallers] began to erect an edifice far higher and more costly than that church that had been consecrated by the precious blood of our Savior, who hung upon the cross—the church which afforded him an acceptable sepulcher within its walls after the agony of the crucifixion.

Moreover, whenever the Lord Patriarch went up to speak to the people, according to custom, from the place where the Savior of mankind hung for our salvation and thus bought complete redemption for the whole world, they endeavored to hinder the celebration of the office entrusted to him. With intentional malice they set their many great bells ringing so loudly and so persistently that the voice of the patriarch could not rise above the din, nor could the people, in spite of all his efforts, hear him. The patriarch often complained to the citizens of the outrageous conduct of the Hospitallers, which was perfectly obvious. Yet, though many besought them to cease, they remained incorrigible, and even threatened that eventually they would use measures still more strenuous. This threat they carried out; for they carried their presumption to such extremes that, in a spirit of audacious fury, they armed themselves and breaking into the church beloved of God as into the house of a common person, hurled forth showers of arrows, as if against a den of robbers. The arrows were later collected and tied into a bundle, and we ourselves as well as many others saw them hanging from a rope before the place of Calvary where the Lord was crucified.

Those who have made a careful study of the subject believe that the Roman Church was primarily responsible for this great evil. . . . For it was the Church which unjustly removed the house of the Hospital from the jurisdiction of the patriarch of Jerusalem, to whom it had been rightly subject. . . . (William of Tyre 1943: II, 240-241)

The nerve center of this international operation, and indeed its very reason for being, was the Hospital of St. John, built for the care, treatment, and lodging of pilgrims, which was located on what was earlier Hadrian's forum and is today the Muristan just south of the Church of the Holy

Sepulcher. Today there is nothing to be seen above ground of the elaborate Hospitaller complex, [32] but both John of Wurzburg and Theoderich provide some sense of its size and complexity, and of the expense of maintaining it: [33]

Opposite the Church of the Holy Sepulcher . . . on the opposite side [of the street] to the south, is a beautiful church built in honor of John the Baptist, annexed to which is a hospital in which are collected in various rooms an enormous multitude of sick people, both men and women, who are tended and restored to health daily at a very great expense. When I was there I learned that the whole number of these sick people amounted to two thousand, of whom sometimes in the course of one day and night fifty were carried out dead, while many other newcomers keep continually arriving. What more can I say? This same house supplies as many people outside it with food as it does those inside, in addition to the boundless charity which is daily bestowed upon poor people who beg their bread from door to door and do not lodge in the house, so that the whole sum of its expenses can surely never be calculated, even by the managers and stewards thereof. In addition to all these moneys expended upon the sick and upon other poor people, this same house also maintains in its various castles many persons trained to all kinds of military exercises for the defense of the land of the Christians against the invasion of the Saracens.

Close to this Church of St. John is a convent of nuns built in honor of the Blessed Mary, which at its head almost touches the buildings of the aforesaid church, and is called the Convent of St. Mary the Great. Not far from here, on the same side of the same street, is a convent of monks, which also is built in honor of the Blessed Mary, and is called the Convent of St. Mary the Latin. . . . (John of Wurzburg 1896: 44-45)

As one leaves the Church of the Holy Sepulcher towards the south, one finds a kind of square courtyard paved with square stones. . . . As one comes out of this open space [the parvis of the Holy Sepulcher], there is on the left a vaulted street full of goods for sale. Opposite the church is the marketplace. Here, in front of the church, stand six columns with arches above them; and here, on the south side of the church, stands the Church and Hospital of St. John the Baptist. As for this [complex], no one can credibly tell another how beautiful its buildings are, how abundantly it is supplied with rooms and beds and other material for the use of poor and sick people, how rich it is in the means of refreshing the poor, and how devotedly it labors to maintain the needy. . . . Indeed, we passed through this residence and were unable by any means to discover the number of sick people lying there; but we saw that the beds numbered more than one thousand. It is not every one even of the most powerful kings and despots who could maintain as many people as that house does every day. And no wonder, for in addition to its possessions in other countries, whose sum total is not easily arrived at, the Hospitallers and the Templars have conquered almost all the cities and villages that once belonged to Judea . . . for they have troops stationed throughout the entire country, and castles well fortified against the infidels. Next to this, to the east as one stands there, comes the Church of St. Mary, in which nuns, under the rule of an abbess, celebrate the divine service daily. . . . Moreover there closely follows another church to the east of this, which is also dedicated to Our Lady because while Our Lord was enduring His sufferings for our salvation, Mary fainted from excess of sorrow and was carried by men's hands thither into a subterranean grotto where, in the indulgence of her grief, she tore out her hair from her head, which hair is to this day preserved in a glass vessel in that church. (Theoderich 1896: 21-23)

The two military-monastic orders of the Temple and the Hospital were authentic Crusader creations, previously unknown in a world that regarded the vocation of the monk and the knight as profoundly different. But just as the Crusade had accomplished the conceptually unlikely feat of putting arms in the hands of pilgrims, so too it put them in the hands of monks, or perhaps better, it reconstrued the role of the soldier-knight as a religious vocation. It was an odd birth sprung directly from need. As the texts already cited indicate, there was a manpower crisis in the Latin Kingdom of Jerusalem. Though Italian commercial interests might be willing to invest funds and personnel in Mediterranean port cities like Acre, new colonists could not, in the end, be persuaded to settle in the Holy City. It was a city without defenders.

It found its defenders in the Knights Templars and Hospitallers, military and monastic elites, which, like all such, did not easily suffer control. The two orders prospered because they succeeded in converting European enthusiasm for the Crusade idea into financial support for their own work, the kind of religiously motivated international support that the secular Latin monarchy of Jerusalem never succeeded in promoting on its own behalf. The Templars and Hospitallers were never the king's men. They were the liegemen of the pope; and the Roman Church, as William pointed out, responded by making them independent of the patriarch as well.

Jewish Visitors

There is another interesting perspective on the Hospital from the Crusader era, interesting in that it comes from a Jewish visitor, the celebrated traveller Benjamin of Tudela. The three groups of monotheists who laid spiritual claim to Jerusalem were not overly generous in recognizing or even noting each other's shrines and holy places. Benjamin does, however, comment on the Hospital, then the Templars, and finally, but briefly, on the Holy Sepulcher:

The city [of Jerusalem] also contains two buildings, from one of which, the Hospital, there issue forth four hundred knights; and therein all the sick who come thither are lodged and cared for in life and death. The other building is called the Temple of Solomon; it is the palace built by Solomon the king of Israel. Three hundred knights are quartered there, and issue forth every day for military exercises, besides those who come from the land of the Franks and other parts of Christendom, having taken upon themselves to serve there a year or two until a vow is fulfilled. In Jerusalem there is a great church called the Sepulcher, and here is the burial place of Jesus, unto which the Christians make pilgrimages. (Benjamin of Tudela 1907: 23)

Benjamin does not have a great deal more to say about Jerusalem, but what he does say is filled with arresting details:

Jerusalem . . . is a small city, fortified by three walls. It is full of people whom the Mohammadans call Jacobites, Syrians, Greeks, Georgians, and Franks, and of people of all tongues. It contains a dyeing-house, for which the Jews pay a small rent annually to the king, on condition that besides the Jews no other dyers be allowed in Jerusalem. There are about 200 Jews who dwell under the Tower of David in one corner of the city.[34] The lower portion of the wall of the Tower of David, to the extent of about ten cubits, is part of the ancient foundation set up by our ancestors, the remaining portion having been built by the Mohammadans. There is no structure in the whole city stronger than the Tower of David.

Jerusalem has four gates—the Gate of Abraham, the Gate of David, the Gate of Sion, and the Gate of Gushpat, which is the Gate of Jehoshaphat, facing our ancient Temple, now called the Templum Domini. Upon the site of the sanctuary Umar ibn al-Khattab erected an edifice with a very large and magnificent cupola, into which the Gentiles do not bring any image or effigy, but they merely come there to pray. In front of the place is the wall, which is one of the walls of the Holy of Holies. This is called the Gate of Mercy, and thither come all the Jews to pray before the wall of the court of the Temple. In Jerusalem, attached to the palace which belonged to Solomon, are the stables built by him, forming a very substantial structure composed of large stones, and the like of it is not to be seen anywhere in the world. There is also visible up to this day the pool used by the priests before offering their sacrifices, and the Jews coming thither write their names upon the wall. The Gate of Jehoshaphat leads to the Valley of Jehoshaphat, which is the gathering place of nations. Here is the pillar called Absolom's Hand and the sepulcher of King Uziah.

In front of Jerusalem is Mount Sion, on which there is no building, except a place of worship belonging to the Christians. Facing Jerusalem for a distance of three miles are the cemeteries belonging to the Israelites, who in the days of old buried their dead in caves, and upon each sepulcher is a dated inscription, but the Christians destroy the sepulchers, employing the stones thereof in building their houses. These sepulchers reach as far as Zelzah in the territory of Benjamin. Around Jerusalem are high mountains. (Benjamin of Tudela 1907: 21-23)

If the Gate of Mercy of this text has its usual Muslim identification with what the Christians called the Golden Gate, then it appears that the Jews of this period collected at the *eastern* wall of the Haram to offer prayers— and to write their names, as another text from Petachia of Ratisbon, who visited Jerusalem just before, or after, the Muslims regained the city, also suggests. [35]

Mount Sion and the Tomb of David

There were a number of holy places in Jerusalem where Jews, Muslims, and Christians were in direct competition over one and the same sacred association. One was the Tower of David, at the Citadel, which does not appear to have generated a very heated rivalry even though all three groups accepted its association with David. Another was on Mount Sion, the southwestern hill of Jerusalem, which, as we have seen, the Christians came to identify with Sion or "the City of David" actually located on the eastern hill opposite. The Muslims and Jews eventually took the identification as authentic, but though the Crusaders put up a rather imposing church and monastery on Mount Sion, [36] no real contest developed until the inevitable localization there of the tomb of David. Benjamin of Tudela, the most famous of Jewish medieval travellers to Jerusalem, was in the city about A.D. 1170, and though he ignores the Crusader church on Mount Sion, he is one of our earliest witnesses to the localization of the tomb of David:

On Mount Sion are the sepulchers of the House of David, and the sepulchers of the kings who ruled after him. The exact place cannot be identified, inasmuch as fifteen years ago a wall of the church of Mount

Sion fell in. The patriarch commanded the overseer to take the stones of the old walls and restore therewith the church. . . .

Two workmen discovered a cave, however, and in it was the golden crown and scepter of David and Solomon and other kings.

. . . So the men rushed forth in terror and they came unto the patriarch and related these things to him. Thereupon the patriarch sent for Rabbi Abraham al-Constantini, the pious recluse, who was one of the Mourners of Jerusalem, and to him he related all these things according to the report of the two men who had come forth. Then Rabbi Abraham replied, "These are the sepulchers of the House of David; they belong to the kings of Judah, and on the morrow let us enter, you and I and these men, and find out what is there." On the morrow they sent for the two men and found each of them lying on his bed in terror, and the men said, "We will not enter there, for the Lord doth not desire to show it to any man." Then the patriarch gave orders that the place be closed up and hidden from the sight of man unto this day. These things were told to me by the said Rabbi Abraham. (Benjamin of Tudela 1907: 24-25)

The contest for the holy places on Mount Sion reached its climax in the fourteenth century when the Mamluks exercised sovereignty over the Holy City.

Hebron

Christian interest in purely biblical sites has cooled somewhat over the centuries, and Eusebius' attempt to construct a Christian typology around Abraham's presence at Hebron did not provoke much enthusiasm. Byzantine and medieval Christian pilgrims to the Holy Land visited Hebron, to be sure, but their attachment never equalled that still felt, and fought for, by Muslims and Jews toward the burial ground of Abraham and the Patriarchs.

Though the town lay not very far from Jerusalem toward the south, the journey to Hebron was not an easy one, as we can observe from Daniel the Abbot, who ventured there shortly after the Crusaders had taken Jerusalem:

On the other side of the stream there is a high rocky mountain covered with a large thick forest. The road over this frightful mountain is dangerous. The Saracens profit by this pass to fall upon those who risk the danger in small numbers. As for me, God provided me with a good and numerous company, and I was able to cross this terrible place without hindrance. . . .

Later on, returning from Hebron via Bethlehem, the pilgrim has a further comment:

The Saracen chief, armed, escorted us as far as Bethlehem and accompanied us everywhere: without him we could not have traversed those places, on account of the large numbers of Saracens who carry on brigandage in those mountains. (Daniel the Abbot 1896: 42-43, 50)

Benjamin of Tudela tells of the place in 1170, when the Crusaders held Hebron:

At a distance of six parasangs is St. Abram de Bron, which is Hebron; the old city stood on a mountain, but is now in ruins; and in the valley by the field of Machpelah lies the present city. Here there is a great church called St. Abram, and this was a Jewish place of worship at the time of the Muhammadan rule, but the Gentiles have erected there six tombs, respectively called those of Abraham and Sarah, Isaac and Rebecca, Jacob and Leah. The custodian tells the pilgrims that these are the tombs of the Patriarchs, for which information the pilgrims give them money. If a Jew comes, however, and gives a special reward, the custodian of the cave opens unto him a gate of iron, which was constructed by our forefathers, and he is able to descend below by means of steps, holding a lighted candle in his hand. He then reaches a cave, in which nothing is to be found, and a cave beyond, which is likewise empty, but when he reaches the third cave behold there are six sepulchers, those of Abraham, Isaac, and Jacob, respectively facing those of Sarah, Rebecca, and Leah. Upon the graves are inscriptions cut in stone. . . . [37] (Benjamin of Tudela 1907: 26)

The Crusades left a profound mark on Jerusalem. They changed the physical face of the city, for one thing—not radically, to be sure, but to a far greater extent than the brief period of the Crusader presence might lead us to expect. Still, it was the change in the spiritual and religious climate that had the more deep-seated effects. Christians and Muslims in Jerusalem—there were too few Jews there, and those few were far too poor, to have had much influence—had always experienced a certain amount of friction: the Muslims possessed the sovereignty of the Holy City; but the Christians were numerous, wealthy, and powerful. After the Crusades that friction turned into a systematic hostility, in the first instance between the Christians and the now enduringly suspicious Muslims, and secondly between the Latins on the one side and the Greeks and "Oriental" Christians on the other.

Much of this hostility stemmed from the Latins' behavior during their possession of the city, but some too arose from deeper and wider issues, particularly the paradoxical state of commercial and religious competition in which the Western Christian and Muslim world now found themselves. They were tied to each other by trade far more closely than before the Crusades—and at a time when Europe was still actively pursuing the ideal of a Crusade against Islam. And the Muslims, for their part, were rediscovering their own attachment to the Holy City which the Latin Christians still hungrily coveted.

The Holy War of Islam

It is the second Hijra of Islam,
but this time to Jerusalem.
—Imad al-Din

THE FALL of Jerusalem to the Franks created, as we have seen, little stir in the Islamic world at large, nor even in the neighboring regions of Egypt and Syria. The Muslim dynasts of Syria had been at war with their Byzantine Christian neighbors over the frontiers in Anatolia for generations, and the Egyptians too were accustomed to relations, now friendly, now hostile, with that Christian empire. Nor were the Franks unknown in the Near East before the Crusades, either as merchants or as mercenaries. Finally, Jerusalem itself, whatever religious allure it might have held for Muslim ascetics and mystics in the opening years of the twelfth century, hardly seemed worth the effort of mounting a general war for its recovery. It was then what it had always been, a provincial city with little or no commercial, strategic, or political value.

This attitude may first have begun to change on a popular rather than an official level. Those directly involved as targets or victims of the Frankish assault on Jerusalem and the coastal cities of Palestine could hardly have mistaken what was occurring for simply another series of raids or another change of political sovereignty in an area all too familiar with erratic changes of regime. The Frankish religious slogans and emblems, the presence in their ranks of clerics and monks as fanatic as the warriors themselves, their haste to desecrate mosques, tear down the symbols of Islam, and substitute crosses in their stead all added to the sense of outrage and, in the end, of understanding something of the nature of the Christian Crusade. The historians had not the historical awareness to analyze the Crusade, but the local populations had no need to: they had experienced it.

On the first Friday of Sha'ban [in A.D. 1111] a Hashimite Sharif from Aleppo appeared in the sultan's mosque at Baghdad with a group of Sufis, merchants, and lawyers and began to beseech aid for Syria. They made the preacher come down from the pulpit and then smashed it to pieces. They wept and groaned for the disaster that had befallen Islam with the arrival of the Franks, for the men who had died, and for the women and children who had been sold into slavery. They made such a commotion that the people could not offer the obligatory prayers. To calm them, the servers and imams promised, on behalf of the caliph, that troops would be sent to support Islam against the infidel. On the following Friday the men came back and repeated their noisy laments and cries for help, (this time) in the caliph's mosque. Not long after this the sister of the sultan [Muhammad ibn Malikshah], who was the wife of the caliph, arrived in Baghdad from Isfahan, bringing a train of endless and indescribable splendor: jewels, rich furnishings, horses and trappings, clothes and equippage, slaves and pages, handmaids and servants. The sharif's cries for help disturbed the gaiety and joyousness of this occasion. The caliph, the Prince of the Faithful al-Mustazhir bi-llah, was extremely annoyed and wanted to arrest the offenders and punish them severely. But the sultan intervened, pardoned the offenders and ordered the amirs and army commanders to return to their posts and prepare to march in the Holy War against the infidel enemies of God. (Gabrieli 1969: 29)

Despite the sultan's assurances, nothing came of this somewhat untoward interruption of the festivities in Baghdad. The protest, it will be noted, came from Aleppo, not Jerusalem, and it may well have been the threat to these other, more important centers—both Aleppo and Damascus were repeatedly under siege by the Franks through the early decades of the twelfth century—that contributed to the growing uneasiness. It is also noteworthy that it was the Turkish sultan and not the Arab caliph who reacted positively to the demonstration, and it was precisely the alliance of interest, in most cases a genuine religious interest, between the loyalist Turkish military and the Arab religious intelligentsia, particularly in Syria, that finally mounted the Counter-Crusade.

The Sunni Revival

The Counter-Crusade was really two movements forged into one: a Sunni counteroffensive against the rising tide of Shi'ism in the Islamic world, and particularly the aggressive, anticaliphal brand being propagated by the Fatimid dynasty in Egypt, yoked to the revival of an older notion of a *jihad*, a holy war waged against the infidels who presently held not only Jerusalem but the entire Muslim Holy Land of Palestine. The ideology for the first struggle was already in place before the Franks appeared in Jerusalem. It had been forged in the mid-eleventh century in Baghdad and eastern Islam by the Sunni clerisy and supported by the Turkish dynasts who held the effective political power under the caliphs; and it was spread in both its ideological and institutional form into Syria by the rising Turkish regimes who had dislodged the Fatimids and promoted themselves to power there, principally the line of Zengi, who ruled first in Mosul and then Aleppo from 1127 to 1146, and particularly his son, Nur al-Din, master of Damascus, in the name of the Sunni caliph, to be sure, from 1146 to 1174.

The image of the new Sunni ruler is apparent in its full splendor in Nur al-Din:

He had a good knowledge of Muslim law of the Hanafite school, but he was not a fanatic. He had heard prophetic traditions being transmitted, and had himself transmitted them, which is a meritorious act in God's eyes. As an example of his justice, he would not permit the imposition of any illegal duty or tax anywhere in his domains, but abolished them all, in Egypt, Syria, the Jazira, and Mosul. He held the Holy Law in the deepest respect and applied its precepts. . . . He set up "houses of justice" throughout his realm, and with his chief justice sat to administer justice to the oppressed, Jew or Muslim, at the expense of the oppressor, even if it were his own son or his chief amir. . . . He built numerous Hanafite and Shafi'ite law schools, the Great Mosque of Nur al-Din at Mosul, hospitals and caravanserais along the great roads, dervish monasteries in each town, and left generous endowments to each. I have heard that the monthly income of all his endowments amounted to 9,000 Tyrian dinars. He honored scholars and men of religion, and had the deepest respect for them. He would rise to his feet in their presence and invite them to sit next to him. He was always courteous to them and never contested what they said. He used to conduct correspondence with them in his own hand. . . . (Gabrieli 1969: 71-72)

Nur al-Din's devotion to the revival of Sunnism is apparent in Ibn al-Athir's emphasis on his foundations, particularly the endowed madrasas, or law schools, and the Sufi convents, both instruments for the training of a new generation of teachers, preachers, and intellectuals as effective in the popular spread of the gospel of Sunnism as the Fatimid missionaries had been in the cause of Isma'ili Shi'ism. [1] And it was the "men of religion" so honored by Nur al-Din, the ulama who taught and trained in those schools, who were beginning to preach the Jihad once again.

The Jihad, or Holy War, had been a vital idea in early Islam, when the new faith was being spread in the wake of Muslim arms around the Mediterranean basin and into Further Asia, but it had not been much invoked in the more recent history of Islam. [2] In the beginning of the twelfth century, however, it began to stir once again under the hammer blows administered by the Franks in the name of their own religious convictions. [3] It might have remained simply an ideal but for two things: an event, and a man. The event was the stunning reversal of the fortunes of Islam in Zengi's recapture of the major Crusader stronghold of Edessa in A.D. 1144. The initial loss of the city, like the loss of Jerusalem, had been simply that, another shift in the fortunes of war. But its reconquest had another quality: it was read as a religious conquest, and its very success, all the more for its being unexpected, pointed to another, even richer religious idea, the reconquest of Jerusalem.

It is certain that Nur al-Din intended that; [4] by his day the tide of Jihad propaganda in pietistic circles in Aleppo and Damascus had risen high indeed—"Purify Jerusalem from the pollution of the cross!" Imad al-Din had cried—and after Nur's overthrow of the Fatimids in their own stronghold of Egypt in 1169, he wrote to the caliph of his intent "to banish the worshippers of the cross from the al-Aqsa Mosque, . . . to reconquer Jerusalem and exercise sovereignty over the Sahil," that is, the entire coastal plain of Palestine. [5] In anticipation of that hour he had built a grandiose pulpit for installation in the newly reconsecrated al-Aqsa. It was in fact installed there, where it remained until destroyed by arson in 1969, but it was not Nur al-Din who presided over the installation. Rather it was his successor in both Syria and Egypt, and the successful prosecutor of the Holy War, Salah al-Din ibn Ayyub.

On the Merits of Jerusalem

Before turning our regard to Salah al-Din, or Saladin, as he is more familiarly known, we must first look at a new literary genre that was the chief vehicle for raising Muslim religious sensibilities about Jerusalem. We have these works "On the Merits of Jerusalem" in literary form, but it should be remembered that in that society they were more often recited than read, and generally in the great mosques of Aleppo and Damascus, where they would have a maximum popular effect. The type itself is not new. Works on the "merits" of this city or that were not uncommon compositions among Muslim rhetoricians, but the genre was oddly not put to the service of Jerusalem until relatively late, at the beginning of the eleventh century. [6]

What a work "On the Merits of Jerusalem" generally consisted of was a collection of traditions attributed to the Prophet, in this case in praise of Jerusalem, often with attached rewards for pious acts performed there, and arranged under certain topical headings. [7] The results are often stereotypical, one collection repeating another or one tradition refining another, and it is sufficient to cite here one of the classic examples, albeit somewhat later than this period, to illustrate the tone and approach. The author is one al-Fazari, who died in 1329, and his work is entitled *The Book of Arousing Souls*:

It is related of Abdullah ibn Amr ibn al-As that he said: I heard the Apos-

tle of God say that prayer in Jerusalem is better than a thousand prayers elsewhere, except in the Sacred Mosque (in Mecca) and this my mosque (in Medina).

On the authority of Abu al-Darda it is related of the Prophet that he said: the merit of prayer in the Sacred Mosque (in Mecca) exceeds all else by a hundred thousand prayers, and my mosque (in Medina) by a thousand prayers, and in the Holy Temple (in Jerusalem) by five hundred prayers.

In another tradition on the authority of Abu al-Mujahir it is reported: the Apostle of God said that prayer in Jerusalem is worth five hundred prayers (said elsewhere), and that joining in prayer with the faithful there increases it by twenty-five.

On the authority of Abu Hurayrah it is related: the Apostle of God said that whoever prays in Jerusalem, all his guilt is forgiven him.

On the authority of Abu Umamah al-Bahili it is reported: the Apostle of God said that whoever makes pilgrimage to Jerusalem and performs the ceremonies and prays, and engages in the Jihad, and perseveres, he has become perfect in fulfilling my laws.

On the authority of Mahkul it is reported: whoever goes forth to Jerusalem, not for any ordinary necessity, but rather to pray there, and prays five prayers—in the morning, at noon, in the afternoon, at sunset, and at nightfall—he is absolved from his guilt as on the day his mother bore him.

Also on the authority of Mahkul it is reported: whoever makes pilgrimage to Jerusalem by riding there (that is, from a distance), he shall enter Paradise carefully guided, and shall visit all the prophets in Paradise; and they shall envy him his relationship with God. Whatever company sets forth to go to Jerusalem, there shall attend them ten thousand angels, interceding for them and praying for them, and serving as their agents when they set out for Jerusalem. They shall have for every day in which they steadfastly stand in prayer seventy kingdoms. And whoever enters Jerusalem cleansed from grievous sin, God will meet him with a hundred mercies, not a one of them but is a mercy so great that had it been vouchsafed to all creatures, it would have enriched all of them.

On the authority of Abu Salimah it is related: the Apostle of God said that whoever goes on pilgrimage or pious visitation from the mosque of al-Aqsa to the Sacred Mosque (in Mecca), there shall be covered for him the faults he has committed and those he may later; and he shall be duly granted Paradise.

On the authority of Hasan al-Basri it is related: whoever gives alms in Jerusalem to the value of a dirham, it is his ransom from the Fire (of Hell). Who gives alms to the value of a loaf of bread (in Jerusalem), he is as one who who gives alms (elsewhere) to the value of mountains of gold.

On the authority of Muqatil it is related: whoever fasts in Jerusalem for the space of a day, he has freedom from Hell. (Matthews 1949: 10-14)

The motif that is usually dwelled upon at some length in these works, as it is in the complementary Jewish and Christian traditions, [8] is that of the sanctity of the rock beneath Abd al-Malik's great dome on the Haram:

On the authority of Ali ibn Abu Talib, he [Muhammad] used to say: "The greatest of places is Jerusalem, and the greatest of rocks is the Rock of Jerusalem." And on the authority of Ibn Abbas it is said: The Rock of Jerusalem is from Paradise.

On the authority of Ka'b it is said: Verily the Ka'aba is in the equivalent position to the Frequented House in the Seventh Heaven, to which the Angels of God make pilgrimage. And if rocks fell from this latter, they would have fallen on the place of the rocks of the Temple of Mecca. And indeed, Paradise is in the Seventh Heaven in an equivalent position to the Holy Temple (in Jerusalem) and the Rock; and if a rock had fallen from it, it would have fallen upon the place of the Rock in Jerusalem. For this reason the city is called Urushalim, and the Paradise is called Dar al-Salam.

On the authority of Wahb it is related: God said to the Rock in Jerusalem, "In you is my Paradise and my Hell; and in you is my reward and my punishment. And blessed is he who visits you! Again, blessed is he who visits you! Again, blessed is he who visits you!" . . .

On the authority of Abdullah ibn Sallam it is related: Who prays in Jerusalem a thousand prostrations on the right of the Rock and on the left of it, he shall enter Paradise before his death. Meaning, he shall see it in his dreams.

Abu al-Ma'ali al-Mushrif ibn al-Murajja says in his chapter "What is Fitting for the Worshipper When He Comes in to the Rock": It is considered fitting for him who comes in to the Rock that he place it on his right, so that he is in the reverse position to the circuit around the Sacred House of God (in Mecca). And let him come in to where the people pray and put his hands upon it, but not kiss it; then pray. [9] Then he says: It is indeed most fitting that he descend underneath the Rock; and let him do so. He must fortify himself and repent toward God, and be constant in prayer and sincere in invocation. And when he goes beneath, let him pray as long as he may wish, using the invocations mentioned above. And it is necessary that he be instant in his prayer underneath the Rock; for verily, prayer in that place will be answered, if God the Exalted wills it. . . .

On the authority Ka'b it is related: The most beloved thing about Syria in the sight of God is Jerusalem; and the most beloved thing about Jerusalem in the sight of God are the Rock and the Mount of Olives. . . .

On the authority of Ja'far ibn Musafir it is related: I saw Mu'amil ibn

Isma'il in Jerusalem, as he presented something to the people and they performed the circuit with it and around these places. And his son said to him, "O father, Waki'ibn al-Jarrah entered here, and he did not perform the circuit." He replied: "O son, every man does about it as he wishes." (Matthews 1949: 14-17, 26)

Some of these traditions may in fact be quite old, originating in the first or second century of Islam and here collected and used for more pointed ends. So too with the traditions concerning the "Holy Land." The phrase already occurs in the Quran (5:21) referring to the land promised to the Children of Israel. Muslim traditionists could not agree on its exact definition, but in general they took the larger view, that it embraced all of Syria-Palestine or even, echoing Genesis, all the land "between al-Arish and the Euphrates." [10] Mujir al-Din, writing at the end of the fifteenth century spells it out in detail:

The boundaries of the Holy Land. Its boundaries are as follows:

On the south, the noble Hejaz from which it is separated by the mountains of Shura, which are inaccessible mountains, situated about a day's journey from Aela [Aqaba]. The plateau of Aela forms the limits of the Hejaz. This was part of the desert of the Children of Israel and is about eight days' journey from Jerusalem, measured by pack animals.

On the east, after Dumat al-Jandal [al-Jawf], the great desert of the Simawa which extends to Iraq and is inhabited by the Arab [bedouin] of Syria. Its distance from Jerusalem is about the same as that from Aela.

On the northeast, it is the Euphrates, according to the narrator Muhammad Shams al-Din al-Dhahabi, the author of a history of Syria. The distance from the Euphrates to Jerusalem is about twenty days' journey with pack animal. Thus the entire principality of Syria falls into this definition (of the Holy Land).

On the west, the Sea of the Romans [Rûm], which is the salt sea. It is about two days' journey distant from Ramle in Palestine.

On the south, the sands of Egypt and of al-Arish, about five days' journey from Jerusalem by pack animal. Then comes the desert of the Children of Israel and Mount Sinai. The frontier extends from there to Tabuk and Dumat al-Jandal, where it joins the eastern border. (Mujir 1876: 229-230)

Throughout, however, there is a special emphasis on Palestine, the theater of the Holy War: "The All Highest blessed the country between the Euphrates and al-Arish, giving to Palestine in particular the quality of sanctity, that is, purity." [11] It was the "Abode of the Prophets" and the "Land of Resurrection." And it was not enough to drive the infidels from the

Holy House that was Jerusalem; they had also to be extirpated from the Sahil, the entire coastal plain of Palestine.

Saladin

The heir to Nur al-Din's intentions for the liberation of the Holy Land was the Kurdish general Saladin (A.D. 1174-1193), who succeeded the son of Zengi as ruler of Syria and Egypt and put into action not merely the Jihad against the Franks but the more encompassing crusade against Isma'ili Shi'ism. Saladin's image among the Western historians and memorialists of the Crusades was often that of a cultured and humane foe, but it was not such qualities that mounted and led the Islamic Counter-Crusade. This, for example, is how he appeared to one of his admiring Muslim contemporaries:

Now Saladin was a man of firm faith, one who often had God's name on his lips. He drew his faith from the evidence duly studied in the company of the most authoritative scholars and the greatest lawyers, acquiring sufficient competence to take his part in a theological discussion should one arise in his presence, although of course he did not adopt the technical language used by the specialists. The result of this was that his faith was free of any taint of heterodoxy, and speculation never led him into any theological error or heresy. His faith was firm, within the bounds of healthy speculation, and it had the approval of the highest authorities. The Imam Qutb al-Din al-Nishaburi compiled for him a catechism containing all the essential elements of dogma, and he was so deeply attached to this that he taught it all to his little sons so that it should be impressed on their minds from earliest childhood. I myself have heard him instructing them and heard them repeat it before him. (Gabrieli 1969: 87-88)

However liberally Saladin may have treated his Frankish enemies on occasion, the same liberality of spirit did not extend to his own faith, where he had little tolerance of innovators of any stripe:

He venerated deeply the laws of the Faith, believed in the resurrection of the body, the reward of Paradise for the virtuous and of Hell for sinners, and accepted the teaching of Holy Scripture with an open heart. He hated philosophers, heretics, materialists, and all the opponents of the Law. For this reason he commanded his son al-Malik al-Zahir, prince of Aleppo, to punish a young man named al-Suhrawardi who called himself an enemy of the Law and a heretic. His son had the man arrested for what he had heard of him and informed the sultan, who commanded that he be put to

340

death. So he was killed, and left hanging on the cross for several days [A.D. 1191]. (Gabrieli 1969: 90)

Saladin's energetic and expensive campaign to restore traditionalist Sunnism in the domains just recently under the sway of the Fatimids does not directly concern us here, but rather his single-minded devotion to the ideal of liberating Jerusalem: [12]

The Holy War and the suffering involved in it weighed heavily on his heart and his whole being in every limb; he spoke of nothing else, thought only about equipment for the fight, was interested only in those who had taken up arms, had little sympathy with anyone who spoke of anything else or encouraged any other activity. . . . Anyone who wanted to ingratiate himself with him had only to encourage him in his efforts and recount some anecdote of the war. Several books on the subject were written for him; I was one of those who compiled one for his use, containing all the Laws, Quranic verses, and traditions relating to the subject, with elucidation of the obscure terms. . . .

And Ibn Shaddad records this almost wistful conversation aboard ship en route to Acre in A.D. 1189:

While I was thus standing Saladin turned to me and said "I think that when God grants me victory over the rest of Palestine, I shall divide my territories, make a will stating my wishes, then set sail on this sea for the far-off lands and pursue the Franks there, so as to free the earth of anyone who does not believe in God, or die in the attempt." . . . (Gabrieli 1969: 100-101)

The Holy War Begins

The weapons were forged in the mosques of Syria, the forces were collected, and the Holy War began. It was fought, and won, at least as far as Jerusalem was concerned, not in the Holy City itself, but in a defile in Galilee called Hattin, where on July 4, 1187, the main Frankish and Muslim armies faced each other across a narrow plain. The first reporter is an eyewitness, though unfortunately a somewhat overblown prose stylist as well:

The Franks meanwhile had ranged their standards at Safuriyya and unfurled their banners. . . . They had mustered their hordes, drawn up their army, and with spirits strengthened, . . . the champions of error assembled, the "True Cross" elevated, with the adorers of the false God gathered around it, the delirious madmen of human and divine nature. . . . Night separated the two sides and the cavalry barred both the roads. Islam passed the night face to face with unbelief, monotheism at war with Trinitarianism, the way of righteousness looking down upon error, faith opposing polytheism. . . . (Gabrieli 1969: 128, 131)

From another, the more sober historian Ibn al-Athir:

The Muslims fell upon them, pulled down the king's tent and captured every one of them, including the king [Guy of Lusignan], his brother [Godfrey], and Prince Arnat of Karak, Islam's most hated enemy. They also took the ruler of Jubayl, the son of Humphrey of Toron, the Grand Master of the Templars, one of the Franks' greatest dignitaries, and a band of Templars and Hospitallers. The number of dead and captured was so large that those who saw the slain could not believe that anyone could have been taken alive, and those who saw the prisoners could not believe that anyone had been killed. From the time of their first assault on Palestine in 1098 until now the Franks have not suffered such a defeat. . . . (Gabrieli 1969: 123)

The inflamed religious passions of the occasion are caught by Imad al-Din when he comes to speak of the relic of the True Cross, which the Crusaders had brought from Jerusalem and carried into battle:

At the same time as the (Frankish) king was taken, the "True Cross" was also captured, and the idolaters who were trying to defend it were routed. It was this cross, brought into position and raised on high, to which all Christians prostrated themselves and bowed their heads. Indeed, they maintain that it is made of the wood of the cross on which, they say, he whom they adore was hung, and so they venerate it and prostrate themselves before it. They had housed it in a casing of gold adorned with pearls and gems, and kept it ready for the festival of the Passion, for the observance of their yearly ceremony. When the priests exposed it to view and the heads (of the bearers) bore it along all would run and cast themselves down around it, and no one was allowed to lag behind or hang back without forfeiting his liberty. Its capture was for them more important than the loss of the king and was the gravest blow they had sustained in that battle. The cross was a prize without equal, for it was the supreme object of their faith. To venerate it was their prescribed duty, for it was their God, before whom they would bow their foreheads to the ground and to which their mouths sang hymns. They fainted at its appearance, they raised their eyes to contemplate it, they were consumed with passion when it was exhibited and boasted of nothing else when they had seen it. They went into ecstasies at its reappearance, they offered up their lives for it and sought comfort from it, so much so that they had copies made of it which they worshipped, before which they prostrated themselves in their houses and on which they called when they gave evidence. So when the Great Cross was taken, great was the calamity that befell them, and the strength drained from their loins. Great was the number of the defeated, exalted the feelings of the victorious army. It seemed as if, once they knew of the capture of the Cross, none of them would survive that day of ill omen. They perished in death or imprisonment, and were overcome by force and violence. The Sultan camped on the plain of Tiberias like a lion in the desert or a moon in its full splendor. (Gabrieli 1969: 136-137)

A special fate was reserved for the most implacable of the Franks, the Knights Templars and Hospitallers who were the main military force of the Latin Kingdom of Jerusalem:

When Saladin had brought about the downfall of the Franks, he stayed at the site of the battle for the rest of the day, and on the Sunday he returned to the siege of Tiberias. . . . At the sultan's command, the king and a few of the most distinguished prisoners were sent to Damascus, while the Templars and Hospitallers were rounded up to be killed. The sultan realized that those who had taken them prisoner were not going to hand them over, for they hoped to obtain ransoms for them, so he offered fifty Egyptian dinars for each prisoner in these two categories. Immediately he got two hundred prisoners, who were decapitated at his command. He had these particular men killed because they were the fiercest of all the Frankish warriors, and in this way he rid the Muslim people of them. He sent an order to Damascus to kill all those [Templars and Hospitallers] found in his territory, whoever they belonged to, and this was done. (Gabrieli 1969: 124-125)

The same scene is described by Imad al-Din in his own fashion:

With (Saladin on the plain of Tiberias) was a whole band of scholars and Sufis and a certain number of devout men and ascetics; each begged to be allowed to kill one of them (the Templars and Hospitallers), and drew his sword and rolled back his sleeve. Saladin, his face joyful, was sitting on his dais; the unbelievers showed black despair; the troops were drawn up in their ranks, the Amirs stood in double file. There were some who slashed and cut cleanly and were thanked for it; some who failed and refused to act and were excused; some who made fools of themselves and others took their places. I saw there the man who laughed scornfully and slaughtered, who spoke and acted; how many promises he fulfilled, how much praise he won, the eternal rewards he secured with the blood he had shed, the pious works added to his account with a neck severed! . . .

I saw how he killed unbelief to give life to Islam, and destroyed polythe-
ism to build monotheism, and drove decisions to their conclusion to sat-
isfy the community of the faithful, and cut down enemies in the defense
of friends! (Gabrieli 1969: 138-139)

The Fall of Jerusalem

The Muslim army then marched against Jerusalem and invested the city,
now short on defenders and swollen by refugees from the collapsing Crusader enterprise throughout Palestine. As the siege of Jerusalem grew in
intensity and the hopelessness of their situation came home to the Franks
inside the city, there was some thought given to a final stand at the Holy
Sepulcher, much as the Muslims had made theirs at the al-Aqsa in 1099.
The possibility gave Imad al-Din an opportunity to reflect on that church
and the Franks' devotion to the place the Muslims called the Dungheap,
or Qumama:

The Franks said: "Here our heads will fall, we will pour forth our souls,
spill our blood, give up our lives. . . . This is our Church of the Qumama,
here we will take up our position and make our sorties. . . . We love this
place, we are bound to it, our honor lies in honoring it, its salvation is
ours, its survival is ours. If we go far from it, we shall surely be branded
with shame and just censure, for here is the place of the crucifixion and
our goal, the altar and the place of sacrifice . . . the works of marble and
intaglio, the permitted and the forbidden places, the pictures and the
sculptures, the views and configurations, the lions and the lion cubs, the
portraits and the likenesses, the columns and the slabs of marble, the bod-
ies and souls. Here are pictures of the Apostles conversing, popes with
their histories, monks in their cells, priests in their councils, the Magi with
their ropes [Quran 20:69], priests and their imaginings; here the effigies
of the Madonna and the Lord, of the Temple and the Birthplace, of the
Table and the fishes, and what is described and sculpted of the Disciples
and the Master, of the cradle and the infant speaking.[13] *Here are the*
effigies of the ox and the ass, of Paradise and Hell, the clappers [summon-
ing Christians to the liturgy] and the divine laws. Here, they say, the
Messiah was crucified, the sacrificial victim slain, divinity made incarnate,
humanity deified. Here the dual nature was united, the cross was raised,
light was extinguished, and darkness covered the land. Here the nature
was united with the person, the existent mingled with the nonexistent, the
adored Being was baptized and the Virgin gave birth to her Son." (Ga-
brieli 1969: 148)

The notion of a suicidal last stand in the Church of the Holy Sepulcher was abandoned, however, and the Frankish leader, Balian of Ibelin, lord of Nablus, and now at the capture of the king responsible for the defense of the city, attempted to negotiate:

When the Franks saw how violently the Muslims were attacking . . . they grew desperate, and their leaders assembled to take counsel. They decided to ask for safe-conduct out of the city and to hand Jerusalem over to Saladin. They sent a deputation of their lords and nobles to ask for terms, but when they spoke of it to Saladin, he refused to grant their request. "We shall deal with you," he said, "just as you dealt with the population of Jerusalem when you took it in 1099, with murder and enslavement and other savageries!" The messengers returned empty handed. Then Balian ibn Barzan asked for safe-conduct that he might appear before Saladin to discuss developments. . . .

He presented himself (before Saladin) and once again began asking for a general amnesty in return for surrender. The sultan still refused his requests and entreaties to show mercy. Finally, despairing of this approach, Balian said: "Know, O Sultan, that there are very many of us in this city. . . . If we see that death is inevitable, then by God we shall kill our children and our wives, burn our possessions so as not to leave you a dinar or a drachma or a single man or woman to enslave. When this is done, we shall pull down the Sanctuary of the Rock and the Masjid al-Aqsa and the other sacred places, slaughtering the Muslim prisoners we hold—5,000 of them—and killing every horse and animal we possess. Then we shall come out to fight you like men fighting for their lives. . . . We shall die with honor or win a noble victory." (Gabrieli 1969: 141-142)

The desperate threat of the destruction of the Muslim holy places in Jerusalem must have been effective, for Saladin decided to accept a ransom of ten dinars per man, five for women, and two for children. Those who could pay within forty days were free to leave the city with their possessions.

The Surrender of the City

The victors swarmed into the city, and the day was filled with sweet moments, none so sweet perhaps as that described by Ibn al-Athir:

At the top of the cupola of the Dome of the Rock there was a great gilded cross. When the Muslims entered the city on the Friday, some of them climbed to the top of the cupola to take down the cross. When they reached the top a great cry went up from the city and from outside the walls, the Muslims crying the Allah akbar in their joy, the Franks groaning in consternation and grief. . . . (Gabrieli 1969: 144)

The city surrendered on Friday, October 2, 1187, a memorable day on which the Muslim flags were hoisted over the walls of Jerusalem. At every gate Saladin set military commanders in charge of taxation to claim the appropriate ransom from the inhabitants. But they cheated in carrying out their duties and divided among themselves money that would otherwise have filled the state treasury for the benefit of all. There were in fact exactly 70,000 cavalry and infantry in Jerusalem, not counting the women and children with them; not a surprising number when you consider that there were people there from Darum, Ramle, Gaza, and elsewhere, so many of them that they filled the streets and walking was impossible.

The grand patriarch of the Franks left the city with the treasures from the Dome of the Rock, the Masjid al-Aqsa, the Church of the Resurrection, and others, God alone knows the amount of the treasure; he also took an equal quantity of money. Saladin made no difficulties, and when he was advised to sequestrate the whole lot for Islam, he replied that he would not go back on his word. He took only the ten dinars from the patriarch and let him go, heavily escorted, to Tyre. (Gabrieli 1969: 142-144)

When the Crusaders took the city in 1099, the prevailing sentiment appears to have been one of satisfied but bloodied bewilderment at being at last in such an awesome yet exotic place. The Muslim mood, on the other hand, was the unbridled jubilation of a people who had destroyed their hated enemy and come home:

By a striking coincidence, the date of the conquest of Jerusalem was the anniversary of the Prophet's Ascension into Heaven. Great joy reigned for the brilliant victory won, and words of prayer and invocation were on every tongue. The sultan gave an audience to receive congratulations, and received the great amirs and dignitaries, sufis and scholars. His manner was at once humble and majestic as he sat among the lawyers and scholars, his pious courtiers. His face shone with joy, his door was wide open, his benevolence spread far and wide. There was free access to him, his words were heard, his actions prospered, his carpet was kissed, his face glowed, his perfume was sweet, his affection all embracing, his authority intimidating. His city radiated light, his person emanated sweetness, his hand was employed in pouring out waters of liberality and opening the lips of gifts; the back of his hand was the qibla of kisses and the palm of his hand the Ka'ba of hope.

Sweet was it for him to be victorious; his throne seemed as if sur-rounded by a lunar halo. Quranic reciters sat there reciting and admonish-ing in the orthodox tradition. Poets stood up to declaim and demand, banners advanced to be displayed, pens scribbled to spread the joyful news, eyes wept with great joy, hearts felt too small to contain their joy at the victory, tongues humbled themselves in the invocation of God. The secretaries prepared long and ornate dispatches; eloquent stylists, both prolix and concise, tightened up or opened out their style.

Among those who opened out their style was Imad al-Din himself:

I could not compare my own pen to anything but the collector of the honey of good news, nor liken my words to anything other than the messengers of the divine graces, nor make my pen run except to apply itself to letters, to accompany virtue, divulge benefits, give widespread accounts and lengthy divulgence of superiority. . . . It is indeed the pen that brings armies together, elevates thrones, alarms the confident and gives confidence to the discouraged, raises up the stumbler and causes the upright to stumble, sets the army against the enemy for the benefit of friends. . . . The world of Islam was ready and adorned for a festival to the fall of Jerusalem. Her merits were illustrated and described and the duty to visit her explained and specified to everyone. (Gabrieli 1969: 160-161)

The fate of the unransomed prisoners was of course grim, and Imad al-Din, for one, could scarcely contain his satisfaction at what awaited them, even the most innocent of them:

Most of them [the ransomed prisoners] went to Tyre, to swell shadow with shadow. About 15,000 were unable to pay the (ransom) tax, and slavery was their lot. There were about 7,000 men who had to accustom themselves to an unaccustomed humiliation, and whom slavery split up and dispersed as their buyers scattered through the hills and valleys. Women and children came together to 8,000 and were quickly divided up among us, bringing a smile to Muslim faces at their lamentations. How many well-guarded women were profaned, how many queens were ruled and nubile girls married, and noble women given away, and miserly women forced to yield themselves, and women who had been kept hidden stripped of their modesty, and serious women made ridiculous, and women kept in private now set in public, and free women occupied, and precious ones used for hard work, and pretty things put to the test, and virgins dishonored, and proud women deflowered, and lovely women's red lips kissed, and dark women prostrated, and untamed ones tamed, and happy ones made to weep! How many noblemen took them as concu-

bines, how many ardent men blazed for one of them, and celibates were satisfied by them, and turbulent men able to give vent to their passion. How many lovely women were the exclusive property of one man, how many great ladies were sold at low prices, and close ones set at a distance, and lofty ones abased, and savage ones captured, and those accustomed to thrones dragged down! (Gabrieli 1969: 162-163)

There is an interesting later reflex of this narrative told by a later Christian pilgrim, one Master Thietmar, who doubtless heard the archetypical Christian tale when he was in Jerusalem in A.D. 1217:

Between Bethlehem and Jerusalem there is a monastery where there were nuns living when the Holy Land was lost. They were extremely beautiful women, and when the sultan (Saladin) heard of their beauty, he wanted to have sex with them and gave orders that they put on their their most attractive clothes and bangles. Their abbess, however, to avoid becoming a plaything for the flesh and the devil or casting away the merit of a lifetime of spiritual labor by drowning the lily of her chastity in a cesspool of lust, preferred to mutilate herself and her sisters rather than to live, with her body whole and her face supernally radiant, as the whore of a filthy dog.

Thus, as if she had been given instruction from on high, when the tyrant was at the very doorstep, after exhorting and consoling the sisters, she gave the following advice: "My venerable sisters, this is the time of our trial. Saladin, the enemy of our virginal modesty, is champing at the bit. You cannot escape his hand. Follow, then, my advice and do as I shall do." Since they agreed, the abbess was the first and foremost to mutilate her own nose, and then each of them of her own free will was likewise mutilated. When Saladin heard this he was extremely disturbed, but he was lost in admiration of their constancy and prudence and deeply approved of the deed and the tenacious constancy of their faith. (Laurent 1873: 30)

The Muslim Restoration of Jerusalem

Once the city was taken and the Infidels had left, Saladin ordered that the shrines be restored to their original state. The Templars had built their living quarters against the al-Aqsa, with storehouses and latrines and other necessary offices taking up part of the al-Aqsa. This was all restored to its former state. The sultan ordered that the Dome of the Rock be cleansed of all pollution, and this was done. On the following Friday, October 9, the Muslims celebrated the communal prayers there. Among them was the sultan, who also prayed at the mosque of the Rock, with Muhyi al-Din ibn al-Zaki, chief judge of Damascus, as prayer leader and preacher.

Then, suddenly, almost by inadversion, the spirit of Nur al-Din, whose triumph this was in some sense, reappeared on the scene:

Then Saladin appointed a judge and an [ordinary] prayer leader for the five canonical prayers and ordered that a pulpit be built for him. He was told that Nur al-Din had once had one made in Aleppo, which he had commanded the workmen to embellish and construct to the best of their ability, saying: "We have made this to set up in Jerusalem. The carpenters had taken so many years to make it that it had no rival in the whole of Islam. Saladin had it brought from Aleppo and set up in Jerusalem, more than twenty years after it was made. . . ." (Gabrieli 1969: 144-145)

The Crusaders had made structural changes, as we have seen, in the two chief Muslim shrines atop the Haram. Marble slabs had been laid over the rock under Abd al-Malik's Dome, and the Aqsa had been substantially altered since it had served under the Crusaders as the headquarters and residence of the Knights Templars. Both buildings had to be returned to their original form and function as far as was possible. First, the Aqsa:

When Saladin accepted the surrender of Jerusalem, he ordered the prayer niche (in the Aqsa) to be uncovered. . . . The Templars had built a wall before it, reducing it to a granary and, it was said, a latrine, in their evil-minded hostility. East of the qibla they had built a big house and another church. Saladin had the two structures removed and unveiled the bridal face of the prayer niche. Then he had the wall in front of it taken down and the courtyards around it cleared so that the people coming on Friday should have plenty of room. . . . The Quran was raised to the throne and the Testaments cast down. Prayer mats were laid out, and the religious ceremonies performed in their purity; the canonic prayers were heard and pious orations given continually; benedictions were scattered and sorrow was dispersed. The mists dissolved, the true directions came into view, the sacred verses were read, the standards raised, the call to prayer spoken and the clappers [of the Christians] silenced, the muezzins were there and not the priests, corruption and shame ceased, and men's minds and breaths became calm again. (Gabrieli 1969: 164)

Then the Dome of the Rock:

As for the Rock, the Franks built over it a church and an altar, so that there was no longer any room for the hands that wished to seize the blessing from it or the eyes that longed to see it. They had adorned it with images and statues, set up dwellings there for monks and made it

349

into a place for the Gospel, which they venerated and exalted to the heights. Over the place of (the Prophet's holy) foot they set up an ornamental tabernacle with columns of marble, marking it as the place where the Messiah had set his foot; a holy and exalted place, where flocks of animals, among which I saw a species of pig, were carved in marble. The Rock, the object of pilgrimage, was hidden under constructions and submerged in all this sumptuous building. So the sultan ordered that the veil be removed, the curtain raised, the concealments taken away, the marble carried off, the stones broken, the structures demolished, the covers broken into. The Rock was to be brought to light again for visitors and revealed to observers, stripped of its covering and brought forward like a young bride. . . . Before the conquest only a small part of the back of it was exposed, and the Unbelievers had cut it about shamefully; now it appeared in all its beauty, revealed in the loveliest revelations. Candelabra gleamed upon it, light on light, and over it was placed an iron grille.

The Franks had cut pieces from the Rock, some of which they carried to Constantinople and Sicily and sold, they said, for their weight in gold, making it a source of income. When the Rock reappeared to sight the marks of these cuts were seen and men were incensed to see how it had been mutilated. Now it is on view with the wounds it suffered, preserving its honor forever, safe for Islam, within its protection and its fence. (Gabrieli 1969: 168-171)

Rebuilding the City

Jerusalem was taken, but it remained in a highly vulnerable position in the face of the Crusaders who still held the chief coastal cities in force. The problem was not so much in arms and equipment, with which Jerusalem was well supplied, but in the ruined condition of the walls:

Al-Malik al-Aziz Uthman [son of Saladin and later ruler in Egypt, 1193-1198], . . . when he returned to Egypt after having been present at the conquest and the victory he left his whole arsenal of arms to Jerusalem, not thinking to order me to take it away after he returned to Egypt. . . . The city was reinforced with this arsenal and its defenses made secure. In addition, one of the conditions of the surrender was that the Franks should leave their horses and harnesses, and should leave the city without waiting for the rest to exhaust the time limit for paying the ransom. In this way Jerusalem acquired ample munitions and had no need for help (from outside). (Gabrieli 1969: 172-173)

The problem of the walls was addressed somewhat later, when Saladin returned to the city in 1191 after concluding a truce with the Franks:

He (Saladin) stayed at the Priests' House near the Qumama and occupied himself with the fortification of the city. . . . There arrived from Mosul a group of workers sent by the lord of that city, together with his chamberlain, to dig a ditch around the city. He also gave money to be distributed to the workers at the beginning of every month, and they worked there the better part of a year. The sultan gave orders for the digging of a deep ditch and a fortification wall, and he brought two thousand Frankish prisoners to the city, and he himself organized them for this task. He restored the city towers from the Bab al-Amud [the present Damascus Gate] to the West Gate or Bab al-Khalil [the present Jaffa Gate] and spent a considerable sum on the project. He had it built with large stones, which he quarried from the site of the ditch. He gave over the supervision of the construction to his sons and his brother al-Adil and his commanders. Each day, mounted on horseback, Saladin came in person to inspect the work and even carried stones on the bridge of his saddle. . . . (Mujir 1876: 80-81)

The Islamicizing of Jerusalem

Under the Latins, Jerusalem had been a completely Christian city; after 1099 there were no longer any Muslims resident in the city. And the Muslim shrines on the Haram—not only the chief Muslim holy places in the city, but in effect the only ones, excepting a Sufi convent or two near the Haram and a mosque attributed to Umar but probably dating from Fatimid times, which had been built near the Church of the Holy Sepulcher—were converted into ecclesiastical buildings. Saladin reconverted them, as we have seen, and then turned to a larger question, that of putting a distinctive Islamic stamp on the city.

Jerusalem had surrendered voluntarily to the Muslim armies in 638, so the population was guaranteed the undisturbed possession of their properties, religious and otherwise. In 1187, however, the city had fallen by arms, which meant in terms of at least the theory of Islamic law that the conquerors were free to dispose of its shrines and properties as they would. [14] And the largest and most important of them was of course the Church of the Holy Sepulcher. Imad al-Din has preserved the debate that occurred on that difficult subject immediately after the reconquest of the city:

He (Saladin) had the Church of the Resurrection closed to Christian visitors even as a refuge. Many discussions were held with him about its fate.
Some advised him to demolish it and abolish all trace of it, making it
impossible to visit, removing its statues, driving away its errors, extin-
guishing its lights, destroying its Testaments, eliminating its false allure-
ments, declaring its affirmations to be lies. "When its buildings are destroyed," they said, "and it is razed to the ground, and its sepulcher
opened and destroyed, and its fires spent and extinguished, and its traces
rubbed out and removed, and its soil ploughed up, and the Church scattered far and wide, then the people will cease to visit it, and the longings
of those destined for damnation will no longer turn to seeing it, whereas,
if it is left standing, the pilgrimage will go on without end." But the
majority said: "Demolishing and destroying it would serve no purpose,
nor would it prevent the infidels from visiting it or prevent their having
access to it. For it is not the building that appears to the eyes but the
home of the Cross and the Sepulcher that is the object of worship. The
various Christian races would still be making pilgrimages here even if the
earth had been dug up and thrown into the sky. And when Umar, Prince
of the Believers, conquered Jerusalem in the early days of Islam, he confirmed to the Christians the possession of the place, and did not order
them to demolish the building on it." (Gabrieli 1969: 174-175)

In the end the Holy Sepulcher was left in Christian hands—not the Latins', of course, but the Greeks' and Eastern Christians'—but the same was
not true of other places around the city:

The Oratory of David . . . was in a fortified stronghold [the Citadel, or
Tower of David] near the city gate. It was set up on high in a commanding position and was used by the governor. The sultan took charge of its
restoration and established there a prayer leader, muezzins, and guards. It
is a center for the pious, the goal of visitors morning and evening. It was
Saladin who gave it new life and beauty and enabled visitors to enjoy it.
As well as this, he gave orders for all the mosques to be renovated and all
the sanctuaries to be guarded. . . . The place where this fortress was built
had been the house of David and Solomon (God's blessing on both of
them), where people went to find them. Al-Malik al-Adil had encamped
in the Church of Sion and his troops were at its gates. The sultan's household, pious scholars, and men of virtue, spoke to him of establishing a law
school for Shafi'ite lawyers and a convent for Sufis. He set aside for the
use of the law school the church dedicated to St. Anne near the Gate of
the Tribes, and for the convent the patriarch's house near the Church of
the Resurrection. He endowed both liberally, thus benefiting both these

communities. He also set aside sites for law school for the various [other] communities, to add to the benefits they had already received. (Gabrieli 1969: 173-174)

St. Anne's, or the Saladin
Law School

St. Anne's, or "Sand Hanna" as it is called in the text, is the well-preserved Crusader church near the Sheep Pool associated with Jesus' earlier miracle there. The church was turned into a mosque, and the convent that stood next to it, today destroyed and rebuilt, [15] became the law school, which, like most of its kind, had residential facilities for the faculty and students. This was in A.D. 1192, as the dedicatory inscription attests:

In the name of God, the Merciful, the Compassionate: there is no grace for you but that which is from God. Our master al-Malik al-Nasir Salah al-Dunya wal-Din, the sultan of Islam and the Muslims, Abu Muzaffar Yusuf ibn Shadhi, reviver of the empire of the Commander of the Faithful, made this law school a pious foundation—may God strengthen his followers and bring together for him the blessings of this world and the next [and] upon the followers of the Imam Abu Abdullah ibn Idris al-Shafi'i— may God be pleased with him—in the year 588 [A.D. 1192]. (van Berchem 1922: #35, trans. K. Schaefer)

As in most cases like this, the institution was not only founded but set up with an endowment income. This was achieved by a formal contract, the famous Islamic pious foundation called *waqf*, of which more will be seen in Chapter Ten. In this instance, the fifteenth-century Jerusalem historian Mujir al-Din, who was also the chief judge of the city and so had access to the archives, saw the original endowment charter of the Saladin Law School and adds a number of interesting details, including the fact that the St. Anne's property was not simply confiscated by Saladin but purchased from state funds, and that the endowment was supported in precisely the same way that the Crusaders had endowed the church, from the income of one of the central bazaars of Jerusalem:

There are also in addition [to the market of the Cotton Merchants] the three markets side by side not far from the Gate of the Prayer Niche (of David), which is also called the Hebron Gate. They are of Rûm [Byzantine] construction. They extend north and south and communicate with one another by passages. The first of them, that to the west, is the Bazaar of the Druggists, which Saladin gave as an endowment [waqf] to his Ma-

353

drasa Salahiyya. The one by its side, the central market, is for the sale of vegetables, and that which adjoins it on the east is for the sale of cloth. The latter two are endowments of the holy mosque al-Aqsa. Travellers declare that they have never in their life beheld the like of these three markets in other lands, as regards their plan or their execution. They are one of the beauties of Jerusalem.[16]

Sometime about 1350 the Christian pilgrim Ludolph von Suchem visited Jerusalem and left this report on the former St. Anne's:

A little way to the north of the (former) Temple there is a church on the spot where the Blessed Virgin Mary was born, and on that same spot (her mother) St. Anne and St. Joachim her husband lie buried in an underground cave. In front of this church stands the Sheep Pool with five porticos around it, where the sick used to be healed when the waters were troubled by an angel, as the Gospel [Jn. 5:1] bears witness. At this day there is a cave there where, when it rains, all the water from the city collects. Out of this Church of St. Mary the Saracens have now made a church of their own. Yet all the story of Anne and Joachim and the Blessed Mary's birth remains to this day right nobly painted on the front of the church. This painting in my time used to be devoutly and religiously explained to the Christians by an old Saracen woman named Baguta. She used to live next to the church and declared that the picture of Joachim stood for Muhammad, and the painting of the trees for Paradise, where Muhammad kissed girls. And she referred the whole of the painting to Muhammad and set it forth with fervor and would tell many more wondrous stories of Muhammad with tears in her eyes. (Ludolph von Suchem 1895: 100-101)

Ludolph appears not to have gotten inside the converted church and convent, but it could be arranged, as two later visitors discovered, Felix Fabri in 1480 and Arnold von Harff in 1498. Felix prevailed upon the son of his dragoman to take them into the church "which is now a Mahumeria."

We went round about the cloister and saw the cells there, both above and below, which are finely wrought, for this in the time of the Christians was a convent of nuns of the order of St. Benedict. We went into the church which is now a mosque and scanned it narrowly. We noticed that this church had once been beauteous and decorated, for the walls had been painted, but the Saracens have destroyed the paintings by covering them with whitewash. Howbeit, in many places the whitewash has fallen off and the Christians' paintings can again be seen. . . .

Felix as usual had done his homework by reading Ludolph before going on his own pilgrimage:

I have read in a certain pilgrim's book that the Saracens explain these paintings as referring to their own Mahomet's . . . life and his paradise, putting a carnal meaning upon all of them. (Felix Fabri 1893: II, 134-135)

Arnold left the convent on Mount Sion where he was lodging on the pretense that he was spending the night at the home of a Muslim acquaintance:

We went westwards and came to St. Anne's House, which the Christians in former times made into a beautiful church, but now the heathen have turned it into their praying house or mosque, so that the Christians cannot enter. But by means of secret help we were allowed to go in. We went through the transept, and at the side of the church we climbed through a narrow hole in the arch of a large window, being forced to carry lighted candles so that we could see, and came to a little vault in which St. Anne, the mother of our Blessed Lady, departed from this earth. We went then into another vault in which our Blessed Lady was born. Here is forgiveness of all sins, both penalty and guilt. The next day the Mamluk took me from the church back to Mount Sion, and no one knew that I had [not] slept the night at the Mamluk's house. (Arnold von Harff 1946: 211-212)

Felix also saw another of Saladin's conversions, that of the patriarchal residence built by Eudocia in the fifth century into a convent for Muslim ascetics and mystics. It appears to have been a partial conversion, since Felix, who was obviously not permitted to visit the Muslim institution, could still meditate on the dilapidated Christian structure next door:

We went up into a great house with many rooms, in which house, however, only a few poor Greeks dwelt, though a hundred men could dwell there in comfort, because, as I have said before, it is a great and stately house, containing a very great number of vaulted chambers. It adjoins the western side of the Church of the Holy Sepulcher, in such sort that in the chief room there is a window pierced through the wall into the church, through which one can look down upon the sepulcher of the Lord. This house was once the dwelling of the kings of Jerusalem, who dwelt there that they might always be near to the most Holy Sepulcher of our Lord, and in the days of the Latin kings three loaves of bread were given away there every day to pilgrims. When the sultan took the holy city and possessed it, he kept on this dole for many years, but now it has altogether fallen into disuse, and the Greeks who dwell in the royal palace can hardly exist through poverty. The house itself threatens to fall into ruin on every side; in many places it is already in the ruinous parts. It is inhabited by

Greek pilgrims when there are any in Jerusalem who call it the palace of the patriarch of the Greeks. (Felix Fabri 1893: I, 394)

The Hospital and Nearby Buildings

Directly across the street from the Holy Sepulcher, in the area today called the Muristan, was one of the most remarkable Crusader enterprises in Jerusalem, the immense Hospital of St. John, staffed and financed, as we have seen, by the Knights Hospitallers. This too attracted Saladin's attention:

He converted into a hospital the church belonging to the residence of the Hospitallers near the Qumama, granted it several places as endowment, and placed there all the necessary medicines and drugs. He appointed as qadi and inspector of this endowment Baha al-Din Yusuf ... better known under the name of Ibn Shaddad, who was most competent to fill those functions. .... (Mujir 1876: 82-83)

Felix appears not to have noticed the Muslim institution, if it indeed was still functioning in 1480, but to have been struck by the still impressive ruins of the Hospital:

When we came out of that house we went up to the Hospital of St. John, which is opposite it, in which pilgrims sleep and eat. Adjoining this build-ing in which the pilgrims sojourn there was once a great palace, a stately dwelling of the noble knights of St. John ... as may be still seen by its ruins, and by the part which remains only partly ruined, which is so large that four hundred pilgrims can live in it. Opposite the hospital are the ruins of vast walls, the remains of the house of the Teutonic knights, with whom in former times pilgrims from nobles from Germany were quar-tered. Near this same house was another great hall, wherein women pil-grims were wont to sojourn, since they were on no account permitted to live with their husbands in the great hospital. (Felix Fabri 1893: I, 395)

Close by on a street leading westward away from Holy Sepulcher and the Hospital was a mosque whose original foundation was attributed to Umar ibn al-Khattab. It too became one of Saladin's projects in the Holy City, and its rededication inscription still survives:

In the name of God, the Merciful, the Compassionate: Our master al-Malik al-Afdal Nur al-Dunya wal-Din, servant of the Holy House of God and its protector from infidel devils, Abu al-Hasan Ali, the son of our master al-Malik al-Nasir Salah al-Dunya wal-Din Yusif ibn Ayyub—may God sanctify his spirit and light his tomb as a sign of His favor—ordered

*the renovation of this sacred mosque and the blessed staircase in the
months of the year 598 [A.D. 1193], during the administration of one in
need of the mercy of God, Izz al-Din Jurdik, minister of war in Jerusalem.
(van Berchem 1922: #36, trans. K. Schaefer)*

According to Mujir, it was a famous place, or had been once:

*The narrator Ibn Asakir says that he read the following in an ancient
book: "There are in Jerusalem large snakes whose bite is fatal. Once God
in His goodness granted to His servants a mosque located on the upper
part of the street and taken by Umar ibn al-Khattab near a church that is
located there known as al-Qumama. One sees there two great masonry
columns whose capitals are decorated with snakes and which are said to
be talismans against these animals. If a man is bitten by a snake in Jerusalem no harm comes to him; but let him go outside of the city, even a
short way, and he straightway dies. . . . This mosque, as I have said, is
well known. It is located in the Christian quarter, next to the Church of
al-Qumama toward the west, on your left as you go up the stairway of
the Qumama toward the Convent of Saladin. To all appearances the tal-
isman against the snakes has disappeared. God is more knowing." (Sauvaire 1876: 31)*

Felix Fabri was not much moved by the place, however, as might be expected under the circumstances:

*Now by the side of the great hospital the Saracens have built a tall and
costly tower [a minaret], adorned with white polished marble, and close
to the tower they have built a mosque, facing the Church of the Holy
Sepulcher. In this tower they shout and howl day and night according to
the ordinances of their accursed creed. I believe that this mosque and
tower have been built out of disrespect for the Crucified One and as an
offense to the Christians. Next to the tower is a Muslim boys' school
where they sit and chant bowing down their heads and backs, even as the
Jews are wont to do when saying their prayers, La illaha ill'Allah, "There
is no God but Allah." (Felix Fabri 1893: I, 395-396)*

The Endowment of the Moroccan Quarter

Another member of the family, Saladin's son al-Malik af-Afdal, was responsible for the institution of one of the best documented endowments,
the one that embraced the entire quarter of western Muslims or Maghrebis
living close in upon the western wall of the Haram platform, south of the
street called after the Gate of the Chain.

The Afdal Law School, once also known as the Dome, is in the Maghrebi [or Moroccan] quarter. This is an endowment of Al-Malik al-Afdal . . . son of Saladin, may God enfold him in His mercy. He made it for the benefit of the Malikite jurists in Jerusalem. He also endowed as waqf the entire quarter of the Moroccans in favor of the Moroccan community, without distinction of origin, men and women. The donation took place at the time when the prince ruled over Damascus, to which Jerusalem was joined [A.D. 1186-1196]. Nonetheless, since the deeds for this donation were not found, a hearing was convened to establish the endowment of each of the properties and its findings were certified before the court after the death of the founder. Among his other pious legacies is the mosque located near the Qumama, above the police prison. He made this endowment in A.D. 1193, the same year as the death of his father. You can still see there a minaret rebuilt sometime before 1465. (Mujir 1876: 163)

As Mujir explains, the original deed of charter of this endowment had disappeared, so a special inquiry was held in A.D. 1267 to reestablish and reconfirm the terms and properties. This process was repeated once again after Mujir's day, in A.D. 1595, and the latter commission's report on the original deed is still preserved in the archives of the Court of Islamic Law in Jerusalem.[17] The following is a somewhat abridged version, with titles and honorifics omitted:

The stipulation of the benefactor of the Moroccan Quarter was recorded by the permission of our lord . . . Shuja' al-Din Afandi, the qadi of Jerusalem. The stipulation in this record has been continuously valid and operative under the dictates of the Shari'a law up to this our day. Written on 26 Sha'ban 1004 [A.D. 1595].

In the name of God, the Merciful, the Compassionate. Those whose names and evidence are given below this statement being trustworthy witnesses, free, sane, and male Muslims, of exemplary character, well acquainted with what they say, knowing that their evidence is true and based on personal and certain knowledge without any doubt, and aware that that they will account for it to God on the Day of Judgment—testify that they know all the quarters called the Maghrebi [or Moroccan] Quarter in the city of Jerusalem with the following boundaries:

First, the southern boundary reaches to the wall of the city of Jerusalem and to the public thoroughfare to the Siloam spring.

Second, the eastern boundary reaches to the wall of the Haram al-Sharif.

Third, the northern boundary extends to the arch known as the Arcades of Umm al-Banat.

Fourth, the western boundary extends to the residence of Imam Shams al-Din, the qadi of Jerusalem, then to the residence of Amir Imad al-Din ibn Muski, then to the residence of Amir Husam al-Din Qaymaz.

The witnesses testify that this quarter as defined and delimited was made waqf by Sultan Malik al-Afdal Nur al-Din Ali, son of Sultan Malik Salah al-Din Yusuf ibn Ayyub ibn Shadi, may God have mercy on them, for the benefit of all the community of the Moroccans of all description and different occupations, male and female, old and young, the low and the high, to settle on it in its residences and to benefit from its uses according to their different needs. The supervisor over them and over the endowment shall have discretion in all such arrangements, provided that none of the dwellings may become personal property or reserved as such or sold.

This endowment is made in perpetuity, according to the Shari'a law, operative and effective, reserved for the community of the Moroccans.

The witnesses further testify that the administration of this endowment in every matter, in part or as a whole, shall belong to whoever is regarded as the leading shaykh of the Moroccans, residents at all times in Jerusalem. He shall assume the responsibility himself, or through a deputy or substitute of his choice, both removable at his discretion . . . witnessed on the twenty-fourth day of Rajab, the year six hundred and sixty-six. (Tibawi 1978: 13-14)

The Walls of Jerusalem

Saladin attempted, as we have seen, to give his conquered city of Jerusalem some measure of protection by rebuilding the walls. A quarter-century later, that no longer seemed like a good policy since it seemed Jerusalem could not be defended in any event and a walled city might be more useful to the still aggressive Crusaders than a defenseless one:

When al-Malik al-Afdal was dead, the Franks returned toward Cairo and attacked Damietta, which they took by assault on November 19, A.D. 1219. They took captive all they found there and converted the mosque into a church. Thenceforward they were all the more eager to take all of Egypt. When he saw what had happened, al-Malik al-Mu'azzam Isa took fright that they might come against Jerusalem, which he was then incapable of defending. So he brought in miners and sappers who began to dismantle the wall in A.D. 1219. Its ramparts, which had been heavily fortified, were demolished. Many people left the city and the inhabitants fled from fear the Franks might fall on them day or night. They left behind all their goods too heavy to carry with them and dispersed themselves in every direction around the countryside. . . . Everyone rushed to beseech God for help at the Rock and the Aqsa.

Al-Malik al-Mu'azzam was a well-known scholar, very attached to the Hanafite school, whose rite he professed contrary to the other members of his family who were all Shafi'ites. It was he who had constructed in Jerusalem a law school for the Hanafites near the gate to the Aqsa Mosque known today as the Bab Dawâdâriyya. He also had built, on the far south side of the platform of the Rock, a place called al-Nahwiyya for the study of the Arabic language and endowed this establishment with excellent endowments. During his reign the arcades at the top of the south stairway of the Rock, near the cupola called al-Tumar, were rebuilt. . . . He also restored the Mosque of Hebron and gave it as an endowment the two villages of Dura and Kafr Burayk. (Mujir 1876: 85-87)

Pilgrimage Resumes

Christian pilgrimage meanwhile continued. When in 1192, not long before the death of Saladin, a truce was concluded between the sultan and Richard the Lion-Hearted, it stipulated that Christian pilgrims would be free to go up to Jerusalem from the Christian enclaves on the coast and visit the Holy Sepulcher "without the exaction of any charge." [18] The atmosphere of the negotiations was relaxed and high-minded in the narrative of Canon Richard of London, [19] who was one of the first to go to the Holy City under the arrangement, but somewhat less so in Mujir al-Din's account, written long after the event, of course:

(After the conclusion of the truce of September 1192) the sultan (Saladin) returned to Jerusalem where he busied himself with the completion of the wall and the ditch and gave to the Franks liberal privileges for visiting the Qumama. They came to fulfill their pilgrimage. "It was for no other purpose than this," they said, "that we fought." The English king [Richard the Lion-Hearted] sent to the sultan a request that he prohibit from visiting the church all who did not possess a letter from himself, in order that he might oblige them to return to their country filled with regrets that they had not accomplished the pilgrimage and so be all the more eager to fight upon their return. But the sultan used the conclusion of the peace treaty and the armistice as an excuse: "It would be better for you to prohibit them from coming, since when they do come, it will not be permissible for us to reject them." (Mujir 1876: 81-82)

The pilgrims with the English king divided themselves into three groups, each going in turn to Jerusalem under Saladin's personal guarantee. Canon Richard was a member of the second group to go up:

Those who were mounted went quickly on ahead, the more freely to kiss the tomb of the Lord in fulfillment of their vow, and Saladin had shown to them for their kisses and veneration the True Cross over which they had once fought. We who came after on foot saw what we could, namely the Sepulcher of the Lord, on which we left but very few offerings because the Saracens took them, but rather we distributed them to those whom we saw held captive in chains, Franks and Syrians, who labor there in tasks assigned to them.

. . . Afterwards we went to the church on Mount Sion on whose left side is the place where the Blessed Mother of God departed this world to the Father. After we had bathed that place with tearful kisses we went on to see the most holy table at which Christ deigned to sup. Quickly kissing this, we departed in a group without delay. It was not safe to enter there except in groups because of the treachery of that profane people. If the Turks find pilgrims wandering around, three here, four there, they drag them off into the inside of crypts and strangle them.

The third group was led by the bishop of Salisbury, who had a particular request of Saladin:

He requested that at the Tomb of the Lord, which he had visited and where the divine rites were only occasionally celebrated in the barbarous manner of the Syrians, the sacred liturgy be permitted to be celebrated somewhat more becomingly by two Latin priests and the same number of deacons, together with the Syrians, and that they be supported by the offerings of pilgrims; and likewise at Bethlehem and Nazareth. It was a large request, but not, I think, unpleasing to God.

On Saladin's agreement, the bishop appointed the priests and deacons he had requested in the aforesaid places, giving to God an offering that had not existed before. Thus, the license granted, they left Jerusalem and returned to Acre. (De Sandoli 1983: 156-158)

The pilgrim traffic thereafter slowly increased, though the circumstances continued to be uneasy:

The gate toward the north is called the Gate of St. Stephen [today the Damascus Gate]. By this gate entered pilgrims into the city and all those who by way of Acre came into Jerusalem, and by way of land from the river on one side to the Sea of Ascalon on the other. As one enters this gate, there is outside, on the right, the Church of St. Stephen. Here they say St. Stephen was stoned. In front of this church, on the left, there was a large building called the Asses Stables; here the asses and sumpter-horses belonging to the Hospital were accustomed to be stabled, hence its name of Asses Stables. This Church of St. Stephen was pulled down by the Christians of Jerusalem before they were besieged, because the church was close to the walls. The Asses Stables were not pulled down, but were afterwards of service to the pilgrims who came to Jerusalem during truce, when the building was in the hands of the Saracens [after 1187]. For the Saracens would not let them sojourn in the city; for this reason the house of the Asses Stables was of great use to them. On the right [that is, to the west] of the Gate of St. Stephen, near the wall, was the Hospital for the Lepers of Jerusalem. Close to the Hospital was a postern called St. Lazarus Postern. Here the Saracens let the Christians into the city, so that they could go covertly to the Sepulcher. For the Saracens did not wish the Christians to see the business of the city; wherefore they admitted them by gate which is in the street of the Holy Sepulcher, but would not admit them by the main gate.

But understand well that of the Christian pilgrims who wished to go to the Sepulcher and the other Holy Places the Saracens exacted great bargains, gifts, and services. The Saracens charged them each thirty bezants. But they [the ecclesiastical authorities] afterwards excommunicated all the Christians who gave them hire-money, service, bargains, and ransoms in order to visit the Holy Places; wherefore the Saracens did not receive as much as they used to. (City of Jerusalem 1896: 15-17)

Magister Thietmar, as we have seen, was among that first generation of post-Crusade pilgrims to visit Jerusalem. He has recorded his experiences in A.D. 1217:

As I was proceeding through the mountains of Judea toward Bethlehem, when I had come just opposite Jerusalem at a distance of about three miles, I fell into a trap, for, as the poet says, "seeking to avoid Carybdis, he fell into Scylla." Since Bethlehem was near Jerusalem and I was trying to avoid the Holy City and its dangers, I made a detour. All in vain, because what I feared happened, and I was captured by Saracens and taken to Jerusalem. At that moment I thought I was dead, since the difference between my present sufferings and the fear of death or perpetual captivity seemed to me minimal. . . . Thus I was held captive for two days and one night outside the gate of the city, where the Blessed Stephen the Protomartyr was stoned to death. In that place there had once been a church but now it lay destroyed by the Saracens.

When there seemed no hope for me in my straitened captivity, God, who is close to all who call upon Him, visited His desperate servant, restored my hope, and saved me in miraculous fashion. It happened in this way. I had as a companion (in prison) a noble Hungarian who knew that a number of his fellow Hungarians had obtained leave to be in Jerusalem for the purpose of study. He had them summoned. They came, recognized him, and received him in a most friendly manner. When they finally understood the reason for our imprisonment, they used their good offices and after a great deal of effort had us freed. (Laurent 1873: 25-26)

A Poet's Reflections

Under the Latins, Jews were not encouraged to live in Jerusalem, so there may have been only one or two families there, as Benjamin of Tudela described. But with the Muslim repossession of the Holy City the Jews were permitted to return. Those who did were probably drawn at first from nearby Ascalon, then eventually from North Africa, and in 1209-1211 three hundred Jews arrived from France and England. [20] There were simple pilgrims as well. One of them was the Spanish poet Yehuda al-Harizi, who was there the same year as Thietmar. His experience is not described in a simple travelogue but rather under the form of a pica-resquely rambling dialogue between two characters, one of them standing for the author, on a great variety of subjects, one of them post-Crusader Jerusalem:

"I suppose you have arrived at the end of an exile and from a foreign country?" this man said to me. "In effect yes," I replied. "And how long have the Jews lived anew in this capital?" "Since the Muslims have conquered it." "And why was it they did not live here during the Christian domination?" "Since those latter accuse us of being deicides, of having crucified their God, they have not left off persecuting and stoning us when they found us here." "Tell me the circumstances under which our people were able to return here." "God, jealous of the glory of His Name and having compassion on His people, decided that the sanctuary would no longer rest in the hands of the sons of Esau, and that the sons of Jacob would not always be excluded from it. Thus in the year 4950 of Creation [A.D. 1190] God aroused the spirit of the prince of the Ishmaelites [Saladin], a prudent and courageous man, who came with his entire army, besieged Jerusalem, took it and had it proclaimed throughout the country that he would receive and accept the entire race of Ephraim, wherever they came from. And so we came from all corners of the world to take up residence here. We now live here in the shadow of peace, and we would be very happy were it not for the tedious internal problems of the various communities and the spirit of discord which reigns among them, to the point that one could well name this place 'the rock of dissensions.'" [21] (Harizi 1881: 236)

Later in the same work the author resumes his own itinerary:

We left Egypt to see the beauties of Jerusalem. . . . Arriving at Jerusalem we bowed down and knelt to thank God for having guided us to that place, where we stayed for a month. The time passed most agreeably. Every day we visited the tombs and the funerary monuments. We have wept upon Sion in mourning for its children, shed tears upon the ruins of its palaces and its dwellings, and followed the line of the tombs of the just placed all around it. At the end of a few days the desire came upon us to ascend the Mount of Olives to prostrate ourselves before the Eternal One and address new prayers to Him. What torment to see our holy courts converted into an alien temple; we tried to turn our faces away from this great and majestic church now raised on the site of the ancient tabernacle where once Providence had its dwelling. (Harizi 1881: 238-239)

The Crusade of Frederich II

Shortly after occurred most of the most extraordinary events in the history of Jerusalem, a negotiated and peaceful change of sovereignty over the Holy City. In 1225 Frederich II Hohenstaufen married Isabel of Brienne, heiress to the throne of the Holy City and immediately assumed the title of king of Jerusalem and made public announcement that he would lead a Crusade for its recovery. There was, however, a notorious falling out with the pope that resulted in Frederich's excommunication in September 1227. His fleet meanwhile had arrived in Syria in August of that same year, but Frederich was not with it; illness kept him in his kingdom in Sicily.

Even as Frederich was making preparations for departure, envoys arrived in Sicily from al-Malik al-Kamil, sultan of Egypt (A.D. 1218-1238), who was under attack by his brother al-Mu'azzam, then governor of Damascus in a rapidly disintegrating Ayyubid empire. They brought promises that al-Kamil would hand over Jerusalem on condition that Frederich direct his forces against al-Mu'azzam. Frederich agreed. In September of 1228 Frederich finally arrived in Acre to take up what was now a campaign against the ruler of Damascus. The story is taken up by the Muslim historian Ibn Wasil:

In 1228 Emperor Frederich arrived in Acre with a great company of Germans and other Franks. We have already described how Amir Fakhr al-Din, the son of the Shaykh of Shaykhs, was sent to the king emperor from Sultan Al-Malik al-Kamil. This was in the time of al-Malik al-Mu'azzam. The idea of the approaches made to the emperor, the king of the Franks, and his invitation, was to create difficulties for al-Malik al-Mu'azzam . . . in his quarrel with al-Kamil and al-Malik al-Ashraf.

. . . This word ["emperor"] means in the Frankish language "the king

of the princes." His kingdom consisted in the island of Sicily and Apulia and Lombardy in the Long Country [Italy]. It is the author, Jamal al-Din ibn Wasil, who speaks: I saw these parts when I was sent as ambassador of Sultan al-Malik al-Zahir Rukn al-Din Baybars, of blessed memory, to the emperor's son, Manfred by name. The emperor was a Frankish king, distinguished and gifted, a student of philosophy, logic, and medicine and a friend to Muslims, for his original home was Sicily, where he was educated. He, his father, and his grandfather were kings of the island, but its inhabitants were mostly Muslims.

When the emperor reached Acre, al-Malik al-Kamil found him an embarrassment, for his brother al-Malik al-Mu'azzam, who was the reason why he had asked Frederich for help, had died, and al-Kamil had no further need of the emperor. Nor was it possible to turn him away and attack him because of the terms of the earlier agreement.... (Gabrieli 1969: 267-269)

Al-Kamil decided to honor the original agreement, and early in 1229 a treaty was negotiated at Jaffa:

It was finally agreed that he [Frederich] should have Jerusalem on condition that he did not attempt to rebuild the walls, that nothing outside it should be held by the Franks, and that all the other villages within its province should be Muslim, with a Muslim governor resident at al-Bira, actually in the province of Jerusalem. The sacred precincts of the city, with the Dome of the Rock and the Masjid al-Aqsa were to remain in Muslim hands, and the Franks were simply to have the right to visit them, while their administration remained in the hands of those already employed in it, and Muslim worship was to continue there. The Franks excepted from the treaty certain small villages on the road from Acre to Jerusalem, which were to remain in their control unlike the rest of the province of Jerusalem....

After the truce the sultan [al-Malik al-Kamil] sent out a proclamation that the Muslims were to leave Jerusalem and hand it over to the Franks. The Muslims left amid cries and groans and lamentations. The news spread swiftly throughout the Muslim world, which lamented the loss of Jerusalem and disapproved strongly of al-Malik al-Kamil's action as a most dishonorable deed, for the reconquest of that noble city and its recovery from the hand of the infidel had been one of Saladin's most notable achievements—God sanctify his spirit! But al-Malik al-Kamil of noble memory knew that the Muslims could not defend themselves in an unprotected Jerusalem, and that when he had achieved his aim and had the situation well in hand he could purify Jerusalem of the Franks and chase them out. "We have only," he said, "conceded to them some churches and some ruined houses. The sacred precincts, the venerated Rock and all the other sanctuaries to which we make our pilgrimages remain ours as they were; Muslim rites continue to flourish as they did before, and the Muslims have their own governor of the rural provinces and districts." . . . *(Gabrieli 1969: 269-271)*

The Treaty of Jaffa

The terms of the Jaffa agreement of 1229 appear to have been carefully drawn since there was already a newly settled Muslim population in Jerusalem and neither side envisioned their evacuation. Thus al-Kamil attempted to gain them some kind of extraterritorial status under Frankish sovereignty by stipulating that a Muslim qadi, or chief justice, should reside in the city and have legal jurisdiction over the Muslim residents in accordance with the terms of Islamic law. [22] Another reassuring version of the treaty provided by the chief justice of Hama and quoted by H.A.R. Gibb notes that "the cession was limited to Jerusalem alone, 'including neither much nor little of its territories and dependencies,' and on the condition that the Franks should not rebuild in it anything whatsoever, 'neither wall nor dwellings,' nor pass beyond its moat, that Friday prayer should be observed in it for the Muslim population, that no Muslim should be hindered from visiting it at any time, that no money should be extracted from any visitor." [23]

Frederich Visits the Holy City

The excommunicated Frederich, who was still in Jaffa and under as great an attack by the Church as al-Kamil was by his disappointed coreligionists, now requested the sultan's permission to visit the Holy City, which was granted. He arrived in Jerusalem in the company of the chief judge of Nablus, who had been assigned as his guide and was also Ibn Wasil's chief source of information on what happened there.

In Ibn Wasil's account the emperor first visited the Dome of the Rock, then spied a Christian priest heading into the al-Aqsa, Gospel in hand:

The emperor called out to him: "What has brought you here? By God, if one of you comes here again without permission, I shall have his eyes put out! We are the slaves and servants of al-Malik al-Kamil. He has handed over this church to me and you as a gracious gift. I do not want you exceeding your duties."

His visit complete, the emperor went to the house prepared for his stay. Out of what he imagined as respect, the qadi ordered the muezzins not to issue the call to prayer during the night, but in the morning Frederich protested:

"My chief aim in passing the night in Jerusalem was to hear the call to prayer given by the muezzins, and their cries of praise during the night." (Gabrieli 1969: 271-272)

In addition to Ibn Wasil, we have another contemporary report on the visit, that of Sibt Ibn al-Jawzi, one of the clerical eminences at the court of al-Mu'azzam:

The emperor entered Jerusalem while Damascus was under siege (by al-Kamil). During his visit various curious incidents occurred. . . . The (following) scene was described (to me) by one of the custodians of the Dome of the Rock. They said too that the emperor looked at the inscription that runs around the inside of the sanctuary and reads "Saladin purified this city of Jerusalem of the polytheists. . . ." He asked: "Who would these polytheists be?" He also asked the custodians: "What are these nets at the door of the sanctuary for?" They replied: "So that the little sparrows should not come in." Frederich said: "God has brought the giants here instead!"

When time came for the midday prayer and the muezzins' cry rang out, all his pages and valets rose, as well as his tutor, a Sicilian with whom he was reading (Aristotle's) Logic in all its chapters, and they offered the canonic prayer, for they were all Muslims. . . . It was clear from what he said that he was a materialist and that his Christianity was simply a game to him.

Sibt then repeats the story of the silencing of the muezzins, though with a different response from Frederich:

Frederich said, "You did wrong, Qadi; would you alter your rites and law and faith for my sake? If you were staying in my country, would I order the bells to be silenced for your sake?" . . . Then he distributed a sum of money among the muezzins and pious men in the sanctuary, ten dinars to each. He spent only two nights in Jerusalem and then returned to Jaffa, for fear of the Templars, who wanted to kill him. (Gabrieli 1969: 274)

The Muslim Reaction

With great difficulty Saladin and the pietists and divines of his generation had succeeded in raising Muslim sensibilities about their Holy City of

Jerusalem. Now it was being negotiated away. The clerics in Syria in particular were not impressed by al-Kamil's protestations that nothing had really been lost, that Muslims were still free to visit the city and pursue their devotions at the Dome of the Rock and the Aqsa Mosque. There soon began to be a popular reaction among Muslims, as Ibn Wasil reports:

> When news of the loss of Jerusalem reached Damascus, al-Malik al-Nasir [Ayyubid governor of Damascus, A.D. 1227-1229] began to abuse his uncle al-Kamil for alienating the people's sympathies, and ordered the preacher Shams al-Din Yusuf, the grandson of the Shaykh Jamal al-Din ibn al-Jawzi, who was in great public favor as a preacher, to preach a sermon in the Great Mosque of Damascus. He was to recall the history of Jerusalem, the holy traditions and legends associated with it, to make the people grieve for the loss of it, and to speak of the humiliation and disgrace that its loss brought upon the Muslims. By this means al-Malik al-Nasir proposed to alienate the people from al-Kamil and to ensure their loyalty to himself in his contest with his uncle. So Shams al-Din (Sibt ibn al-Jawzi) preached as he was told to, and the people came to hear him. It was a memorable day, one on which there rose up to heaven the cries, sobs, and groans of the crowd. I myself was one of the crowd there. . . . (Gabrieli 1969: 272-273)

We have no need of a witness; Sibt reports his own sermon on that occasion:

> . . . So I ascended (the pulpit) of the Great Mosque of Damascus, in the presence of al-Malik al-Nasir Dawûd, at the gate of Mashhad Ali. It was a memorable day, for not one of the people of Damascus remained outside. In the course of my oration I said: "The road to Jerusalem is closed to the companies of pious visitors! O desolation for those pious men who live there; how many times have they prostrated themselves there in prayer, how many tears have they shed there! By God, if their eyes were living springs they could not pay the whole of their debt of grief; if their hearts burst with grief, they could not diminish their anguish. May God burnish the honor of the believers! O shame upon the Muslim rulers!" . . . (Gabrieli 1969: 273-274)

The treaty of Jaffa was an agreement for ten years only, and when it lapsed in A.D. 1239, the Muslims repossessed Jerusalem, only to be faced in 1244 by a massive onslaught by Khwarezmian Turks from the east who had been invited to join the then sultan of Egypt. The Khwarezmians paused only long enough to take and sack the Holy City, burn down its churches, and reduce the city to a smoking ruin. [24]

The Latins Return to the
Holy Sepulcher

All the Latin clergy left Jerusalem with the vanquished Crusaders in A.D. 1187, and after some apparent hesitation about the disposition of some of the Christian holy places, the greater number of them were restored to the Christians—the Greeks, Armenians, and Syrians whom the Latins had either dispossessed or relegated to a minor role in Jerusalem. But the European Christian clergy was not necessarily identical with the European knights, and one group of them, the newly founded Franciscans, managed in the more relaxed atmosphere of the time of Frederich II to win a tenuous foothold back inside the chief church of Christendom, the Holy Sepulcher. The history of the effort, and of its success, was pieced together by the Franciscan Father Elzear Horn who was assigned to the Franciscan community in the Holy City between 1724 and 1744:

The convent of the Holy Sepulcher is in order the second in Judea, but fifth in the old province of Syria, which our Friars began to occupy, after they erected the first and principal convent on Holy Mount Sion. In which year they took possession is not entirely certain; nevertheless from the letters of the [Mamluk] sultans of Egypt, especially from one to the Guardian of Holy Mount Sion granting permission to repair the ruined Church of the Holy Sepulcher, and from another from Sultan Ashraf [Qaʾit Bay, 1468-1496] which mentions the twelve sultans who were his predecessors and two of whom very much favored our Friars, namely Zahir, who according to the history of the Saracens ruled in 1258 [Al-Zahir Baybars was sultan from 1260 to 1277], and Mansur Qalawun, who ruled in 1272 [sultan from 1280 to 1290]. Whence it can be concluded that the Friars obtained permission to live in the Church of the Holy Tomb shortly after the Latins lost the Holy Land, which took place about the year 1244, at which time Jerusalem (finally) ceased to be Christian and passed to Saracen sovereignty.

Nor is it difficult to believe that Sultan Salahad [Al-Salih Ismaʿil, ruler of Damascus 1245-1249], son of that prince named Meledin [Al-Malik al-Kamil, 1218-1238] to whom our holy father St. Francis preached, gave this place to the Friars as a dwelling and commanded that the Tomb of Christ should be guarded by them. For on account of the special regard which he entertained for them, he used them as legates to the Supreme Pontiff Innocent IV. . . .

Later, that it should be permissible for the Friars to live continuously within the Church of the Holy Sepulcher and live more freely in the convent of Holy Mount Sion, Robert and Sanchia his wife, rulers of Sicily, in the year 1313 obtained from the sultan of Egypt, not without great expense, and under certain conditions of tribute, and by their authority and at their expense they put these two places in a stronger state. Further they petitioned Pope Clement VI that he should confirm their possession by a papal decree. Clement acceded to the just prayers of the monarchs, and it seemed to him that it was almost a gift fallen from heaven, and rejoiced that a shame had been lifted from the Church when those places sanctified by the work of our Redemption had been by the Friars Minor redeemed from the hands of the barbarians. In 1342 he sent the Bull. (Horn 1962: 81-83)

A Project for Another Crusade

After the interlude of Frederich II, Jerusalem was not taken by Europeans again until 1917, and was not to be under European sovereignty again until it was assigned to Great Britain as part of a Palestinian Mandate in the wake of the First World War. But we can see this only by looking back over the course of the events; for contemporaries peering uncertainly forward, the idea of another Christian Crusade for the liberation of Jerusalem did not die so quickly or so easily, particularly since the dream continued to be nourished by the optimistic reports of pilgrims who visited the Holy Land. [25] This, for example, from Burchard of Mount Sion, a visitor to the Holy Land sometime about A.D. 1280:

What more need I say? Well may we groan over the lukewarmness of the Christian people of our time who, having so many and such great examples before their eyes, hesitate to snatch away from the hands of the enemy that land which Jesus Christ hallowed with his Blood and whose praises are daily sung by the Church throughout all the world; for what hour is there in the day or night all the year round wherein every devout Christian does not by singing, reading, chanting, preaching and meditating read what has been done and written in this land and its cities and its holy places? (Burchard of Mount Sion 1896: 3-4)

Now it must be noted that as a matter of fact, though some who like to talk about what they have never seen declare the contrary, that the entire country, that of the whole East beyond the Mediterranean Sea, even unto India and Ethiopia, acknowledges and preaches the name of Christ, save only the Saracens and some Turkomans who dwell in Cappadocia. So that I declare for certain, as I myself have seen and heard from others who know, that always and in every place and kingdom, Egypt and Arabia *excepted, where Saracens and other followers of Muhammad chiefly dwell, you will find thirty Christians and more for every Saracen. . . .*

But the truth is that all the Christians beyond the sea are Easterners by nation, and despite the fact that they are Christians, yet as they are not much practiced in the use of arms, when they are assailed by the Saracens, Turks, or any other people soever, they yield to them and buy peace and quiet by paying tribute, and the Saracens or other lords place their bailiffs and tax gatherers therein. Hence it arises that their kingdom is said to belong to the Saracens, but as a matter of fact all the people are Christians, save those same bailiffs and tax gatherers and their families, as I have seen with my own eyes in Cilicia and Lesser Armenia, which is subject to the rule of the Tartars. . . . (Burchard of Mount Sion 1896: 106)

The fantasy of liberating Jerusalem from the Muslims did dissipate in the end, or rather it was replaced by a more genuine concern to save Europe from the aggressive and rapidly advancing Turks.[26] But before it died, it provoked hard thinking on what had occurred and why. The following is a memorandum written by one Pierre Dubois in A.D. 1306 that addresses what he understood to be the problems of the original Crusade and the means of remedying them when the opportunity next presented itself. First, as regards finances:

For the emperor and other princes to furnish provisions and ships for sending their troops across the sea would involve too great an expense. Hence it is preferable to provide this for the warriors as individuals, whencesoever they come. It appears that this objective may readily be achieved in the following manner, subject to the change and correction by the proper authorities.

The Hospitallers, Templars, and other orders founded to aid and protect the Holy Land have many resources, goods, and property on this side of the Mediterranean, which so far have been of little benefit to the Holy Land. . . . Hence, if they [the knights] are to be of any benefit to the Holy Land, it is desirable and advisable to combine them into one order as regards appearance, habit, rank, and property, as the holy council shall see fit.[27] They ought also to remain in the Holy Land, subsisting from the property which they hold there and in Cyprus. Until they succeed in regaining the peaceful possession of property of this sort sufficient for their needs, provisions may be furnished them from some other source.

The property which they hold anywhere on this side of the Mediterranean should at first be held in trust with its revenues for three or four years; eventually, or even immediately, this should be converted into a perpetual leasehold if satisfactory terms can be arranged. In this way more than 4,000 Tours livres will be realized annually from the Templars and

Hospitallers. . . . These moneys may be used to procure ships, provisions, and other necessities for the warriors who will cross the sea. In this way a free and comfortable passage will be in the future available to all who wish to cross, even the very poorest. The ships can bring back from the Holy Land such of its products as are in demand here, and carry our products thither. . . . (Dubois 1956: 81-82)

Dubois then takes up the question of how the forces should be mobilized:

The Holy Land has until now been ill supplied because of the great conflict of peoples. The Holy Father, who is said to have this matter very much at heart, will there urge each prelate to send thither at his own expense as great a number of warriors as his resources will allow. These should be arrayed in uniforms distinct for cavalry and infantry,[28] *and provided with like arms and the banner of the lord who sends them. The Lord Pope will see to it that [lay] princes do likewise. . . . In this way all natives of the domain of any certain prince, irrespective of the status of those who send them thither, will form a single army. . . . Men of every rank, even women—widows as well as married—should be encouraged to send men adequately equipped with the same uniform and arms. The brilliant send-off, their orderly march, and their passage through cities, towns, and other communities with sound of trumpets and other instruments and songs and gay banners will rouse the hearts and emotions of all and strongly influence them to cross the sea and send others with suitable equipment. This method of mobilization will increase numbers beyond belief. (Dubois 1956: 84)*

A major problem of the First Crusade, as it was of Jerusalem after the Muslims retook it, was how to persuade people to settle in Palestine, enough people at least to defend the place and make it prosper. Dubois speaks to that problem as well:

Every powerful personage of either sex should be induced to promise that after the route has been secured, he will in any subsequent year provide and send at least to the coast as many warriors as possible, together with funds to aid them further. These warriors, together with their wives, are to be conveyed across the sea to populate the Holy Land and fill it with people in so far as they are needed for the conquest and the maintenance of that land. . . .

Every Catholic kingdom, and indeed every other extensive district as well, should be permitted to occupy some city, fortress, or other position of importance there, together with the adjoining territory, the extent of such occupation being in proportion to the number of their own people taking part in the expedition. New arrivals, exhausted by the difficult roads, the variety of sleeping accommodations, and the shortage of other things, may then have the joy and pleasure of familiar surroundings after their sorrows, hardships, and griefs. Even the names of these should be changed; they may select by lot the nomenclature of the kingdom or the principal city whence the new inhabitants came. This will offer great comfort to later arrivals. . . . (Dubois 1956: 84)

There are a number of other interesting proposals in the memorandum:

It would also be of advantage to those at the head of the kingdom of Jerusalem to have many trustworthy secretaries acquainted with the language and writings of the Arabs and the other idioms of the world.[29] (Dubois 1956: 114-115)

And if language study, then might not sex as well be put in the service of the Cross, though with all due caution?

While others are pursuing a policy of inflicting injury on the Saracens, making war upon them, seizing their lands, and plundering their other property, perhaps girls trained in the proposed schools may be given as wives to the Saracen chiefs, although preserving their faith lest they participate in their husbands' idolatry. By their efforts, with the help of God and the preaching disciples so they may have assistance from Catholics— for they cannot rely on the Saracens—their husbands might be persuaded and led to the Catholic faith. Little by little our faith might be made known among them. Their wives would strive the more zealously for this because each of them has many wives. All the powerful and wealthy among them lead a voluptuous life to the disadvantage of their wives, any one of whom would rather have a man to herself than that seven or more wives share one husband. It is on that account, as I have generally heard from merchants who frequent their lands, that the women of that sect would easily be strongly influenced toward our manner of life, so that each man would have only one wife. (Dubois 1956: 124)

The Glorification of the Holy City

Jerusalem meanwhile, once a thriving Muslim city, was trying to right itself. Unwalled and devastated, stripped, as so often in the past, of what had been the majority of its population—this time the Western Franks— it must have been once again a small settlement. We are not even certain who was living there. The Jews returned, as we have seen; and a few local Christians who lived there under the Franks and still had strong ties to the place asked and were allowed to remain. But no Muslim had lived in

Jerusalem for nearly a century, and, the new Moroccan community apart, there must have been few economic or social inducements to persuade Muslims to uproot themselves and relocate in the city. There were religious ones, however. The intensive propaganda for the liberation of the Holy City, now that the city was taken, would doubtless operate in favor of living there, briefly as a pilgrim, or permanently as an ascetic or scholar in one of the number of schools and convents that began to be built and endowed in Jerusalem. [30] Such seems to be the point of certain traditions of the Prophet in circulation at the time: "He who lives in Jerusalem is considered a warrior in the Holy War," "To die in Jerusalem is almost like dying in heaven," and, most pointedly and practically, "Whoever lives for one year in Jerusalem, despite the inconvenience and adversity, for him God will provide his daily bread in this life and happiness in Paradise." [31]

Moreover, now that the city was once again in Muslim hands, pilgrimage could be encouraged, [32] as in this tradition quoted by Mujir al-Din:

According to Khalid ibn Ma'dan, the Prophet said: "Zamzam and the fountain of Siloam at Jerusalem are the springs of Paradise." And after that he said "Let anyone who has visited Jerusalem go to the Prayer Niche of David to make his prayers and bathe himself in the fountain of Siloam, since it comes from Paradise; let him abstain from going into the churches and buying anything there, since a sin committed at Jerusalem is the equivalent of a thousand sins, and a good work there is the equal to a thousand good works." (Mujir 1876: 186-187)

Likewise, the works "On the Merits of Jerusalem," which by no means ceased being written once the city was retaken, emphasize the virtues of pilgrimage to Jerusalem, or at least a "pious journey" (*ziyara*), the term preferred by the traditionalists, who reserved the sacrosanct notion of *Hajj* for the canonical pilgrimage to Mecca. One of these works, the previously cited *Book of Arousing Souls* of al-Fazari (d. 1329), lays out a kind of itinerary around the Haram for the Muslim visitor, somewhat in the manner of the later Christian "Way of the Cross":

Al-Mushrif says: It is fitting that one go to the Dome of the Ascension (of the Prophet) and pray there, being instant in prayer, for it is a place where the answer to prayer is met. And it is fitting that one go to the Dome of the Prophet, behind the Dome of the Ascension and pray there. . . .

He says further: Then one should go to the Gate of Mercy and pray there, inside the wall (of the Haram). Then one should make invocation and ask God in this place for Paradise and seek refuge in Him from Hell; and there will be granted more than that. And verily behind (this eastern wall) is the Valley of Gehenna, and this is the place about which God said: "And there shall be set between them a wall and a gate, on its inside Mercy, and outside, in front of it, Punishment."

He says: Then one should go to the prayer niche of Zachariah and pray there. . . . Then one should go to the Rocks which are to the rear of the mosque, adjacent to the Gate of the Tribes, and pray in the place which is called the Throne of Solomon; and one should face the qibla and be instant in prayer. This is the place where Solomon prayed when he finished building the Temple, and God gave him answer there. Then one should go to the Gate of Sekinah and do likewise; and as well at the Gate of Forgiveness.

Then one should enter the interior, roofed mosque (of al-Aqsa) and go to the prayer niche of Umar and pray there . . . and likewise to the prayer niche of Mu'awiyah and all the prayer niches in the mosque. And he should go down to the Gate of the Prophet and pray there. . . . Then he should go to the prayer niche of Mary and be instant in prayer. And verily, prayer there is answered. So one should pray there and recite the Surah of Mary [Surah 19], for the sake of her connection with it. And he should worship meanwhile, as did Umar, in the prayer niche of David, when he recited there the Surah Sad [Surah 38], worshipping meanwhile because of its connection with David. . . .

And let him go down to the place where Gabriel made a hole with his finger and tied up al-Buraq there. It is outside the Gate of the Prophet.[33] *. . . And one should ascend al-Sahirah, which is the Mount of Olives. . . .*[34] *(Matthews 1949: 19-20)*

Ibn Taymiyya on Jerusalem

Fazari's list is both prescriptive and transparently liturgical, and this "circling" around the Haram, with its echo, however remote, of what went on around the Ka'ba at Mecca, disturbed some Muslims who continued to fear that Jerusalem would usurp the Islamic Holy City par excellence, Mecca. This polemic had been going on since very early in the history of Islamic Jerusalem, as we have already seen in Chapter Five. But it was by no means resolved,[35] and the post-Crusader exaltation of the city may have added new fuel to the debate. One of the most vocal of the critics of the exaggerated claims put forward for Jerusalem was Ibn Taymiyya (d. 1328), a conservative lawyer who wrote a treatise with the disarming title "In Support of Pious Visits to Jerusalem." The clue is, of course, in the phrase "pious visits," ziyarat:

Regarding pious visits to Jerusalem—it is maintained in the Sound Tradi-

*tions of the Prophet—God bless him and grant him salvation—that he said,
"Do not start on a journey unless it is to one of three mosques: the Sacred
Mosque [in Mecca], the al-Aqsa Mosque [in Jerusalem], or my mosque
[in Medina]."*[36] *This is in the Sound Traditions under the tradition transmitted by Abu Said and Abu Hurayra and it is related by other sources as
well. It is a widely accepted tradition approved by all of the knowledgeable
people in regard to its soundness and believability. But it is only the de-
sirability of travel to Jerusalem for the prescribed forms of worship such
as prayer, invocation, Sufi seances, reading the Quran, and private devotions that is agreed upon by the Muslims.*

*The prescribed worship in the al-Aqsa Mosque is of the same type of
prescribed worship [as that performed] in the Mosque of the Prophet (in
Medina)—God bless him and grant him salvation—and as is [performed]
in the rest of the mosques except for the Sacred Mosque (in Mecca). For
in it (the Sacred Mosque in Mecca), the circumambulation [of the Kaʿba]
and the touching of the two southern corners [of the Kaʿba] and the
kissing of the black stone are prescribed in addition to [the rituals per-
formed] in the rest of the mosques. As for the Mosque of the Prophet—
God bless him and grant him salvation—and the al-Aqsa Mosque and the
rest of the mosques, there is nothing in them to circumambulate and nothing in them to anoint and nothing in them to kiss. It is not permitted to
circumambulate the Tomb of the Prophet (in Medina)—God bless him
and grant him salvation—and anything other than this in the way of the
tombs of the prophets and the Companions and not the Rock in Jerusalem
and not anything other than this, and not the dome over Mount Arafat,
nor anything like this.*

*In fact, there is not in the land [i.e., the Holy Land] a place to circu-
mambulate as the Kaʿba is circumambulated. Whoever believes that circumambulation of other objects is permitted is evil, just as whoever believes that praying toward other than the Kaʿba is permitted. Verily, the
Prophet—God bless him and grant him salvation—when he emigrated
from Mecca to Medina prayed with the Muslims toward Jerusalem, for it
was the qibla of the Muslims at this time. Then God changed the qibla to
the Kaʿba. God revealed this in the Quran as is mentioned in Sura of the
Cow [Sura 2:143-144]. The Prophet—God bless him and grant him salvation—and the Muslims prayed toward the Kaʿba and it became the
qibla. It was the qibla of Abraham and other prophets. One who, today,
regards the rock (in Jerusalem) as the qibla and prays toward it is a renegade apostate who must repent. Either he seeks repentance or he is killed.
Though it (Jerusalem) was (once) the qibla, this part of the Quran was
abrogated. So how can there be those who perceive it (Jerusalem) as a
place to be circumambulated as the Kaʿba is circumambulated? For God*

376

*did not prescribe the circumambulation of other than the Ka'ba under
any circumstance.*

*What some of the ignorant ones have mentioned is that there is the
footprint of the Prophet—God bless him and grant him salvation—or a
trace of his turban or the like on it (the Rock). All of this, however, is a
lie. The greatest lie is from those who think that is the place of the footprint of the Lord and likewise that it is the place mentioned as the cradle
of Jesus—Peace be upon him. It is nothing more than the baptismal font
of the Christians. Thus there are those who claimed that there is the
(Judgment) Path and the Scale (to weigh the good and the bad in people),
or that it is the wall that distinguishes between paradise and hell. It is that
eastern foundation wall of the sanctuary. Likewise the glorification of the
chain or its place is not in accordance with the Islamic law.*

*During the days of (the first four) Rightly Guided Caliphs there was
no dome over it (the Rock). In fact, it was not covered during the reigns
of Umar, Uthman, Ali, Mu'awiya, Yazid, and Marwan. But when the
latter's son, Abd al-Malik al-Sham held the office, dissension occurred between him and Ibn al-Zubayr. The people were performing the hajj [to
Mecca] and siding with Ibn al-Zubayr. Abd al-Malik wanted to deter the
people from Ibn al-Zubayr, so that Abd al-Malik built the dome over the
Rock.* [37] *He covered it during the winter and the summer so that the
people would prefer to visit Jerusalem. They were distracted from their
uniting with Ibn al-Zubayr by that. As for knowledgeable people among
the Companions and their successors, they knew better. They did not
glorify the Rock. Its being the qibla was abrogated just as Saturday being
a festival according to the law of Moses—Peace be upon him—was. It was
replaced in the law of Muhammad—God bless him and grant him salvation—by Friday. Saturday is not considered special by the Muslims while
Sunday is for worship just as it is for the Jews and Christians. The Jews
and some of the Christians, likewise, glorified the Rock. . . .*

*And in Jerusalem, there is not a place one calls truly sacred, and the
same holds true for the tombs at Hebron, and for every other place [in
Islam], except for three places. One of them is sacred by a consensus of
the Muslims, and that is the sacred precinct of Mecca—May God Almighty exalt it. The second sacred precinct, upon the agreement of a majority of prominent scholars, is the sacred precinct of the Prophet [at Med-
ina]—God bless him and grant him salvation. . . . The third is Wejj. It is
a wadi in al-Ta'if. . . . There is not a Muslim scholar who attests to a
sacred precinct other than these three. (Ibn Taymiyya 1936: 7-13, trans.
S. Levy)*

The evidence is all indirect, of course, the attitudes that Ibn Taymiyya is
arguing so forcefully against, but it provides some index of Muslim atti-

tudes towards the Holy City of Jerusalem in the final days of the Ayyubids, the line whose founder and hero Saladin had won the city back for Islam. It is unmistakable that Muslims thought differently about Jerusalem after the Crusades than they had before. It remained for the Ayyubids' successors to translate those newly aroused sentiments into architectural and institutional terms.

10

The Face of Medieval
Jerusalem

*A sin committed at Jerusalem is the equivalent of a thousand sins,
and a good work there is the equal to a thousand good works.*
—*A Tradition of Muhammad*

IN A.D. 1250 there was another change of sovereignty in Jerusalem. The Holy City fell not back into Christian hands—the Europeans were penned impotently inside their enclave at Acre—nor even into Shi'ite ones, but to those of the servants and slaves of the Ayyubids themselves. The Ayyubids, for all their services rendered to Islam in Syria, Palestine, and Egypt, had simply proven themselves incapable of ruling an empire. Saladin had managed it by the force of his own personality and the powerful ideological focus of a Holy War. But the management of the spoils of that war proved more difficult than their winning. The enfiefing of sons, for example, however praiseworthy in terms of Ayyubid family piety, succeeded only in creating competitors and converting Cairo and Damascus into rival cities and effectively into the capitals of rival kingdoms.

A Slave Dynasty in Jerusalem

Peoples no longer fought in the thirteenth century; indeed, since the original Arab conquest perhaps, and certainly since the ninth century in Islam, warfare was left to those whose origins or training or ambition suited them for such a task, and these professional warriors were, more often than not, hardy or impoverished steppe peoples, ethnic and cultural and indeed religious newcomers into Islam. The Fatimids, for all their ideological fervor and revolutionary zeal rose to power on the arms of Berber and Sudanese armies. The Ayyubids, too, outsiders to the Perso-Arab elites of the Islamic world, recruited Turks, as many had before them, to fight their battles. And in the end, it was their Turks who overthrew them.

These soldier-slaves were called *mamlûks*, literally "possessions," since they were enslaved by purchase or capture outside the Abode of Islam—Islamic law forbade the enslaving of one Muslim by another—and then raised to be Muslims and soldiers, and fiercely loyal on both scores. They had been the backbone of the Abbasid caliph's armies since the ninth century, and it was they who by the eleventh ruled at the caliph's side in Baghdad and were the military power behind his religious prestige, a power effective enough to stem the tide of Shiʿism that threatened to engulf Sunni Islam in that same century. [1]

In Cairo in the thirteenth century, however, it was not for and at the side of a caliph that the Mamluk regiments served, but rather as the professional army for a dynasty of former soldiers who claimed Saladin as their prestigious father but who were in effect little different from the Mamluks themselves. And when the masters failed—the last prince of the house was murdered by his own troops in A.D. 1250—they were succeeded by the proud military mandarins who were, at least in the eyes of the Islamic law, their "possessions." Those Mamluks never did produce a Saladin, but their accomplishments were nonetheless considerable: they held most of Syria-Palestine and Egypt against the apparently invincible Mongols with a crucial victory at Ayn Jalut in Galilee in 1260; they drove off the last of the Crusaders from the Holy Land with the capture of Acre in 1291; they ruled their Ayyubid inheritance in a remarkably effective way; and finally, it was the Mamluks who put their physical stamp upon Jerusalem as no other Muslim regime before or since.

The Mamluks were first and foremost soldiers, and when the Dominican pilgrim Felix Fabri encountered a troop of them near Gaza toward the end of the fifteenth century, it was precisely their military posture and equipment that most impressed him, and most pleased the Mamluks to show off to him:

On the third day we made ready to depart [from Gaza], but a great obstacle came in our way; for a host of many thousands of Mamluks came from Egypt into that country, so that the whole city and all the land round about was full of armed men. Their tents were pitched all around Gaza and their number was said to be 8,000. These men were sent by the sultan to fight against the Turkomans in Syria to abate their pride. They strolled about the city and many of them came round to look at us. . . . We asked them all to come in and talked familiarly with them, which displeased our dragoman and guide. For the Saracens secretly hate the Mamluks because the Mamluks domineer over them so that they scarce dare raise their heads in their presence. . . . After we had eaten, the Mamluks came again and talked to us and when we told them we would like to see their army and their horses, tents, and war equipment, they took us into the city to their stables, in which stood most beautiful horses, and then they led us outside the city where their tents were pitched. We viewed all this with admiration, neither did anyone look askance at us while they led us since they appeared to us to be the most powerful men in the army. (Felix Fabri 1893: II, 442-443)

These were troopers that Felix met, field campaigners rather than the rulers of what had once been the Ayyubid estate. Those rulers lived securely in an armed camp erected upon the high citadel of Cairo, deliberately remote from their subjects, so fearful indeed of the contamination of ease and luxury that they contrived an administrative mechanism that seems at once implausible and marvelously effective: the Mamluks banned their own sons from succeeding them; their own descendents passed pampered and impotent into the society of Cairo, while an entire generation of newly recruited and severely trained Spartans took over the reigns of power. The Mamluks were, as David Ayalon has called them, a "one-generation aristocracy." [2]

The Mamluks as Benefactors of Islam

The Mamluks were a military caste born and bred, but their training and manner they reserved for themselves, together with the power that flowed from them; they neither militarized nor puritanized Islamic society, and if they acted like soldiers, they also thought like Muslims, or rather, since they were not ideologues, they behaved like Muslims, with pious and traditional generosity toward the institutions of Sunni Islam that the Ayyubids had first spread across their domains. This is the appreciation of Ibn Khaldun, the famous Spanish social philosopher who lived in Mamluk Cairo from A.D. 1383 to 1406, who here in his *Introduction to History* links in praise the Ayyubids and the Mamluks:

We, at this time, notice that science and scientific instruction exist in Cairo in Egypt, because the civilization of Egypt is greatly developed and its sedentary culture has been well established for a thousand years. Therefore the crafts are firmly established there and exist in many varieties. One of them is scientific instruction. This (state of affairs) has been strengthened and preserved in Egypt by the events of the last two hundred years under the Turkish dynasty, from the days of Salah al-Din ibn Ayyub on. This is because the Turkish amirs under the Turkish dynasty [of the Ayyubids and Mamluks] were afraid that their ruler might proceed against the descendents they would leave behind, in as much as they were his slaves [mamlûks] or clients, and because chicanery and confiscation are always to be feared from royal authority. Therefore they built a great many colleges, hermitages, and monasteries and endowed them with waqf endowments that yielded income. They saw to it that their children would participate in these endowments, either as administrators or by having some other share in them. (This was their intention), in addition to the fact that they were inclined to do good deeds and hoped for a (heavenly) reward for their aspirations and actions. As a consequence, waqf endowments became numerous, and the income and profit (from them) increased. Students and teachers increased in numbers, because a large number of stipends became available from the endowments. . . . (Ibn Khaldun 1967: II, 435)

Ibn Khaldun also touched upon the subject in his *Autobiography*, with direct reference to the Mamluks, though with much the same conclusion:

Since the old days of their masters, the Ayyubid rulers, the members of this Turkish [Mamluk] dynasty in Egypt and Syria have been erecting colleges for the teaching of the sciences, and monastic houses for the purpose of enabling the poor (Sufis) to follow the rules for acquiring orthodox Sufi ways of behavior through prayer exercise and supererogatory prayers. They took over that custom from the preceding Caliphal dynasties. They set up buildings for those institutions as waqf gifts and endowed them with lands that yielded income sufficient to provide stipends for students and Sufi ascetics. When there was excess income, they reserved it for their own descendants, because they feared their weak offspring should suffer want. Their example was imitated by men of wealth and high rank under their control. As a result, colleges and monastic houses are numerous in Cairo. They now furnish livings for poor jurists and Sufis. This is one of the good and permanent deeds of this Turkish dynasty. (Ibn Khaldun 1967: II, 435-436 n. 68)

A City Endowed

What lies behind the lines of Ibn Khaldun, and what made the activities he is describing possible, was a financial instrument so commonplace in his time that it required no explanation or comment, the endowment mechanism known in Arabic as *waqf*. Waqf involves the surrender of some property in one's possession, and its income, for the support in perpetuity of some pious cause specified by the donor. Property converted into waqf thus became untaxable and inalienable, whether by the state, as Ibn Khaldun implies, or by simple sale or gift. The agreement was embodied in a waqf charter, a formal legal contract in which the property, usually real estate, was carefully defined, and the donor spelled out, as we shall see in connection with one of the famous waqfs of Jerusalem, both the administration of the endowment and the purposes for which the income was to be used.

The institution of waqf runs back to early in the history of Islam, and perhaps to other prototype institutions in Byzantium, but it was only in twelfth and thirteenth centuries that the practice became widespread across the Abode of Islam. Even as Ibn Khaldun suggests, the motives for committing one's property to waqf might be mixed indeed—to save it from confiscation, or punitive taxation, or simply from being divided and subdivided among one's heirs according to the detailed prescriptions of the Islamic law of inheritance. Whatever the motives, this endowment instrument eased the passage of large sums of capital from the private into the public domain, and most of the monuments and institutions that typ-ify the medieval Muslim city were in fact erected, and then supported, out of just such endowments.

Ibn Khaldun marvelled at the effect of waqf endowments on the cultural and intellectual life of Cairo under the Ayyubids and Mamluks. [3] But their effect ran far deeper and wider than that, into the entire economy of the Islamic world, as Ibn Battuta remarked in A.D. 1335 of Damascus, another place where both the Ayyubids and the Mamluks had been lavish in their endowments:

The varieties of the endowments at Damascus and their expenditure are beyond computation, so numerous are they. There are endowments in aid of persons who cannot undertake the hajj, out of which are paid to those who go in their stead sums sufficient for their needs. There are endow-ments for supplying wedding outfits to girls, to those namely whose fam-ilies are unable to provide them. There are endowments for the freeing of prisoners, and endowments for travellers, out of which they are given food, clothing, and the expenses of conveyance to their countries. There are endowments for the improving and paving of streets, because the lanes in Damascus all have a pavement on either side of which the foot passen-gers walk, while the riders use the roadway in between. Besides these there are endowments for other charitable purposes.

The people of Damascus vie with one another in the building and en-dowment of mosques, religious houses, colleges, and shrines. . . . Every man who comes to the end of his resources in any district of Damascus finds without exception some means of livelihood opened to him, either as a prayer leader in a mosque, or as a reciter in a madrasa, or by occu-pation [of a cell] in a mosque, where his daily requirements are supplied to him, or by recitation of the Quran, or employment as a keeper at one of the blessed sanctuaries, or else he may be included in the company of Sufis who live in the convent, in receipt of a regular allowance for upkeep money and clothing. Anyone who is a stranger there living on charity is always protected from [having to earn it at] the expense of his self-respect and dignity. Those who are manual workers or in domestic service find other means [of livelihood], for example as guardian of an orchard or intendent of a mill or in charge of children, going with them in the morning to their lessons and coming back with them in the evening, and anyone who wishes to pursue a course of studies or devote himself to the religious life receives every aid to the execution of his purpose. (Ibn Battuta 1959-1962: 148-150)

What Ibn Khaldun said of Cairo and Ibn Battuta of Damascus was in one sense truer of Jerusalem and in another not quite apposite. Jerusalem was a city holier in Islam than the capital of either Egypt or Syria and so had, like Mecca and Hebron, a greater claim on moneys given to support pious works. But Jerusalem was also, in the hard world of medieval *Realpolitik*, a less prosperous place than the other two administrative and commercial centers and of only slight political, economic, or strategic importance. The city remained unwalled throughout the Mamluk period, as it had been since 1219, the prey of bedouin who roamed all round it in search of the unwary, as the pilgrims' accounts vividly describe. [4] Under the Mamluks, as under the Ottomans after them, the civil "governor" of Jerusalem was a mere subaltern of the true governor, who resided in Damascus and who was subject in turn to the true wielders of power, the sultan and the royal Mamluks in Cairo. [5] Even the military commandant of the Holy City, the commander of the small garrison in the Citadel at the Jaffa Gate, could hardly muster a faint echo of the martial pomp and circumstance of which the Mamluks were so fond, as a late fifteenth century eyewitness testifies:

The Citadel has its own governor who is different from the [civil] governor of Jerusalem. According to the custom at all the citadels of the empire, there used to be a dress parade there each evening between sunset and the evening prayer, but in our time it is completely neglected and disorganized. The custom of beating the drum has been suppressed and the Governor of the Citadel is like a private citizen because of the general disorganized state of affairs. (Mujir 1876: 181-182)

And for all the endowments of learned institutions there, Jerusalem never became a renowned center of either Muslim law or theology, and what must have been massive infusions of capital into the city's economy never carried in their train either brilliance or even prosperity for the people who lived there. Few Mamluks lived in Jerusalem by choice—the Citadel in Cairo was a far more congenial place—but not all had the choice. Oddly, what brought substantial new endowment wealth to the Holy City was the Mamluk custom of exiling its refractory military aristocrats, wealth and titles and honor intact, to such holy but harmless places as Mecca and Jerusalem, where they repented their political sins and invested in their eternal future. [6]

The Soup Kitchen at Hebron

The reflections of philosophers and historians and lawyers should not conceal the fact that waqf endowment was aimed at, and frequently achieved, philanthropic goals. The most visible instance, since it struck Christian and Jewish visitors there as well, was probably to be found at the shrine of Abraham and the Patriarchs at Hebron, where one of the reputedly oldest endowments in the Islamic world supported a remarkable welfare program for travellers. We have already seen a ninth-century report on this waqf from Muqaddasi cited in Chapter Six; now let us hear Mujir al-Din, the fifteenth-century chronicler of both Jerusalem and Hebron, on the history of the Hebron endowment:

The waqf endowment of Tamim al-Dari at Hebron includes the site of the actual city of our lord [Abraham], al-Khalil, as well as its surrounding territory. The deed of donation was written on a piece of leather coming from the sandal of Ali ibn abi Talib and was written in his hand.

The chroniclers have different accounts of the terms of the gift. But I have seen in the possession of the person in charge of this domain the piece of leather said to come from the sandal of the Commander of the Faithful, Ali ibn abi Talib [caliph, A.D. 655-661]. It is quite worn and shows only traces of writing. At the same time I saw in the same box in which was kept this piece of leather a paper written, one is assured, in the hand of the Commander of the Faithful Al-Mustanjid-billah, the Abbasid [caliph, A.D. 1160-1170], who had copied the deed of donation. Here is the reproduction traced from the hand of al-Mustanjid:

Glory be to God. This is a verbatim copy of the title which the Envoy of God had recorded in favor of Tamim al-Dari and his brothers, in the year 9 of the noble Hijra [A.D. 630-631], after his return from the expedition to Tabuk, on a piece of leather from the sandal of the Prince of the Faith Ali and written on this latter: "In the name of God, the Merciful, the Compassionate. This is what has been given by Muhammad, the Envoy of God, to Tamim al-Dari and his brothers: Hebron, al-Martum, Bayt Aynun, and Bayt Ibrahim, with all included therein. This gift, undivided among them, is absolute. I transmit and give to them this property, to them and their descendents. And whoever harms them, let him be harmed in turn, by God! And may whoever injures them, let him be cursed of God!" Witnessed by Atiq ibn abi Quhafa, Umar ibn al-Khattab, Uthman ibn Affan and Ali ibn abi Talib, who copied this deed and witnessed it.

I copied this matter just as it is, according to the copy of al-Mustanjid-billah. And perhaps that is the most authentic piece of evidence of this subject. God knows best the truth. (Mujir 1876: 227-228)

Mujir al-Din also describes the distribution of food to the poor and travellers, which was the almost exclusive intent of the Hebron endowment:

At the southern side of the Jawali shrine is the kitchen where they prepare the jashisha [a plate of ground and boiled wheat] for those who are on retreat and for travellers. At the door of the kitchen every day after the afternoon prayer the ceremonial drums are sounded to signal the distribution of the meal. This meal is one of the marvels of the world. Both the residents of the town and visitors take part. It consists of bread that is made [fresh] each day and given out on three occasions daily: in the morning and at midday the distribution is for the local residents; after the afternoon prayer the distribution is for both the residents and travellers. The daily quantity of bread distributed reaches to about 14,000 or even sometimes 15,000 small loaves. The endowments set up for this purpose have an almost incalculable income, and no one, rich or poor, is excluded from the meal. . . .

At the entry of the shrine [of the Patriarchs], where they sound the drums, are the buildings where the meal is prepared. They consist of ovens and mills. It is a large complex which encloses three ovens and six mills to grind the grain. Below are the granaries where the wheat and barley are stored. Looking at this place, whether above or below, one is seized with admiration: the wheat that goes in comes out only as bread. As for the eagerness displayed in the preparation of the meal by the great number of people occupied in grinding the grain, kneading the dough, turning it into bread, getting the wood for the fires and other paraphernalia, as well as making all the other necessary preparations, this too is another marvel almost without parallel among the powerful sovereigns of the earth, and yet one of the least miracles of this noble Prophet. (Mujir 1876: 20)

Another astonished observer of both the Hebron and the entire Islamic endowment phenomenon was the German Dominican friar Felix Fabri who was at the shrine in A.D. 1480:

There are many priests in this mosque [of Hebron], both Soquis [Sufis] and Alhages [Al-Hajjis], so that no hour passes either by day or by night without there being singing beside the double cave, for they relieve one another by turns. . . . After we had viewed the mosque and the double cave, we went down a little way and came to the door of the hospice for poor people, which is below the mosque. We were let in and saw its fine offices, and in the kitchen and bakery great preparations were being made for Saracen pilgrims, of whom a great number come every day to visit the double cave, the sepulcher of the Patriarchs. This hospital has annual revenues amounting to more than 24,000 ducats. Every day 1,200 loaves of bread are baked in its ovens and are given to those who ask for them; neither is charity refused to any pilgrim, of whatever nation, faith, or sect he may be. He who asks for food receives a loaf of bread, some oil, and some thick soup which we call pudding. . . . Rich Saracens and Turks daily send alms thither for the support of pilgrims and to show honor to the Patriarchs; also rich people, when they are about to die, set up perpetual memorials of themselves at this place, and leave legacies to the hospice. At the hour when the dole is served out, they make a terrible noise with a drum. . . . In the serving out of the loaves of bread, they sent a basketful to our inn for our use, albeit we had never asked them for anything. (Felix Fabri 1893: II, 417-418)

Waqf: An Islamic Endowment

Felix Fabri is correct in his understanding where the money for this charity came from, "rich Saracens and Turks" who send alms and "rich people" who set up "perpetual memorials," which are undoubtedly waqfs. But the base of this endowment was the original bequest of the farmland of the local villages, and despite the solemn warnings of the charter, it was difficult to prevent these from falling into private hands over the course of time, as indeed happened at Hebron. Louis Massignon, writing about 1951, notes: "Incorporated by the [Ottoman] Turks into the administration of the Haram of Jerusalem, then into that of the two Harams [of Mecca and Medina] of the Hejaz, the Tamimi waqf had lost two-thirds of its income by 1917; in 1947 its revenues amounted to 150,000 Palestinian pounds, fallen to 18,000 in 1951."[7] One can only surmise that its funding has not improved in the last thirty years.

These endowments were delicate and complex mechanisms, as we can see from Mujir's description of a linked commercial and religious endowment just outside the Holy City. It too ran into problems: [8]

He [Al-Malik al-Zahir Baybars, sultan in A.D. 1260-1277] built the khan situated to the northwest, outside the city of Jerusalem, and known as Khan al-Zahir. Its construction took place in 661 [A.D. 1263]. He had brought [and installed] there the gate of the Fatimid palace [in Cairo] and endowed the khan with the income of half the village of Lefta and other villages of the province of Damascus. He installed in the khan an oven and a mill and assigned a prayer leader to the mosque that was located there. He imposed among other conditions for this establishment that bread be distributed at its gate to the poor, that the servants of those who stopped there should be accommodated, that they should be given food, etc. The endowments which he assigned it in Syria are now used up, and the duties he stipulated, like the distribution of food, are no longer in force by reason of the troubled times and public misfortunes. (Mujir 1876: 239)

Mujir had a great number of endowment charters before him when he wrote his history in 1496, and he quotes liberally from them. But the terms were also on occasion inscribed and posted on the building itself, as in this example from Ayyubid times on the north portal of the Gate of the Chain leading into the Jerusalem Haram. Here the income is not agricultural land but rental income from a nearby apartment:

In the name of God, the Merciful, the Compassionate: May God have mercy upon anyone who asks for His mercy upon the Sufi who built this place and made it a public school for Muslim children with the intention of teaching the Quran in it. The house known as the house of Abu Na'ama beneath the vault opposite the gate of the Aqsa Mosque—may Almighty God preserve it—is constituted as a pious endowment for the school. The rental income from the house is to be used to defray the cost of the teacher and the building which he has and for the cost of instructing orphans and the poor. What remains [is for] renovating the school and the house; for lighting candles under the vault and for water for washing the [writing] boards and for drinking, with the condition that [the teacher] be from among those who are of the true faith and pious. This is a permanent endowment, not to be altered or changed. "Whoever changes it . . . " and so on according to the verse [Quran 2:177]. May God make his endeavor praiseworthy and [may He] pardon his sins and may he illumine the resting place of Salah al-Din—may God have mercy on him—and protect his children in glory and strength. This was written in the months of the year 595 [A.D. 1198-1199]. (van Berchem 1922: #39, trans. K. Schaefer)

Panoramas of Jerusalem

Before we look at some of the details of what the Mamluks did during their somewhat less than three centuries of sovereignty over the Holy City, we must move off a space and see the fourteenth- and fifteenth-century city as a whole, somewhat as the maker of the Madaba map did in the sixth century. It is not a difficult task since it is much the same place as the Old City that still stands before us. The streets and buildings can be surveyed with little more than a stroll, taken in with the eye, as Jerusalem's premier historian Mujir al-Din did at the close of the fifteenth century, near the end of the Mamluks' own tenure there. He had lived in the Holy

Jerusalem Under the Ayyubids and Mamluks (1187-1516).
Permission Carta, Jerusalem

389

City most of his life, but the sight of it still provoked in him a feeling of religious awe and affection:

As for the view of Jerusalem from afar, filled with brilliance and beauty, it is one of the famous wonders. The most attractive view is that which one enjoys from the eastern side, from the Mount of Olives. Likewise from the south. But from the west and the north you can see only a small part of the city because of the mountains that conceal it. The cities of Jerusalem and Hebron are in effect situated on steep and rocky mountains where travel is difficult and round-about. The mountains that surround these two cities extend for nearly three days march, calculating with a pack animal, in width and breadth. Nonetheless, when God grants the pilgrim the favor of arriving at the solemn al-Aqsa shrine and the prayer station venerated by Abraham, he experiences an indescribable feeling of joy and well-being and forgets the pains and troubles he has endured. The poet Ibn Hujr improvised the following verses to precisely that point when he came on pilgrimage to Jerusalem:

"We came to Jerusalem with the hope of gaining pardon of our sins from a generous Master.

"For love of Him we have passed through Hell, but after Hell, there is nothing but Paradise." (Mujir 1876: 183-184)

Nearly three centuries earlier, shortly after the Crusaders had been driven out of the city, another observer, this time a German Christian pilgrim, stood in the same place atop the Mount of Olives and saw something quite different:

From there we went up the Mount of Olives. . . . On the top of the mountain we saw two ruined cloisters, one of which [the Eleona] had been built in the place where the Lord prayed. . . . and the other [the Imbomon] atop the place from which "the Lord ascending on high led captivity captive." Here at the present time the infidel Saracen has made his own oratory in honor of Muhammad. There is a perfect view down on the city, and we saw there the Temple of the Lord, which from its former name they call the "Temple of Solomon," paying no heed to the fact that that other Jerusalem with its Temple has been destroyed. In that place the sultan ordered a most solemn oratory be built for him and his followers, into which the citizens of the city are bade assemble every Friday and worship Muhammad. Next to it there was assigned to us the Probatic Pool, which is called in Hebrew Bethsaida, with its five porticoes.

From that same height of Olivet we saw Mount Sion, which is now included in the walls of the city, but which in the time of Our Savior's

Passion was outside. On its top there is a large and beautiful monastery, in which there are still Syrian Christians, tributaries of the Saracens, who show to pilgrims who come there the place in which the Lord supped with His disciples and the very table at which the Lord Jesus Christ handed on for celebration the mysteries of His body and blood. . . . (Laurent 1873: 188)

In the Streets of the City

Let us return to Mujir, who now descends from the Mount of Olives into the streets of his native city:

Jerusalem is a great city, solid in its construction, situated between mountains and valleys, with one part built on a height and the other resting down in a valley. The buildings built on the heights dominate the lower sections beneath. The major streets of the city are either flat or sloped. In the greater number of the buildings you can find underground ancient constructions upon which the recent ones were raised. The houses are so crowded together that if they were to be spaced out in the way they are in most cities in the Islamic world, Jerusalem would occupy more than twice the space that it does now. The city has many cisterns designed to collect water since the city's water supply comes from rainfall. . . . The buildings of Jerusalem are extremely solid, all of them of dressed stone and vaulted. There is no brickwork in the construction and no wood in the roofing. Travellers attest to the fact that there is no place in the empire with more solid buildings or indeed better looking than Jerusalem. Hebron is similar, but the buildings of the Holy City have greater strength and solidity. Those of Nablus come close, and the solidity of the buildings of these three cities arises from the fact that they are all situated in mountainous areas where there is a good deal of stone and it is easily quarried. (Mujir 1876: 170-171, 183)

The solidity of the construction in Jerusalem had impressed visitors almost from the beginning, as we have seen. The same judgment continued to be rendered on the Mamluk city, whether by a native son, like Mujir, or by Christian and Jewish visitors who had seen a great deal of the world. This one dates from A.D. 1350:

All the houses in Jerusalem are vaulted, without any timber, and in like manner were built the piazzas and streets of Jerusalem which rain does not make muddy nor cause annoyance to the people who pass through the city. There are also streets covered with vaulting where foodstuffs are sold and others where drapery is sold. (Niccolo of Poggibonsi 1945: 9)

These sentiments are echoed, though with some editorial comment, by an anonymous disciple of Rabbi Obadiah, who was present in the city even as Mujir al-Din was writing his history of Jerusalem:

The houses of Jerusalem the Holy are all of stone and do not have many floors one above the other as in your land, nor are there rafters in the houses, nor any wooden buildings. Indeed, wood in this city is very expensive and is sold in the shops by weight, which is why I think they do not make upper floors and attics here. But a single courtyard will be surrounded by five or six rooms. Nor does this city have any wells of fresh water. Instead, every house has a courtyard with a single pit full of rain water; and if there is no rain, the water in these pits is used up; and sometimes the Ishmaelites [Muslims] gather together to pour out Jewish wine and smash Jewish vessels, for they say that the rain does not fall on account of the sin of the Jews in drinking wine. Sometimes water reaches the town from a fountain [the Pools of Solomon] which emerges at Hebron, but there is little water from this and in the summertime it ceases to flow. In the city the wheat is ground by beasts, for there are no water mills at all to do the grinding, as in your country. (Wilhelm 1946: 25)

The Quarters

Like other contemporary Islamic cities, Mamluk Jerusalem was divided into quarters. [9] As we have seen in Chapter Eight, the first *formal* division into quarters occurred in the era before the Crusades, when the Christians had bargained for a kind of separation, of autonomy almost, in the northwest quadrant of the city. Mujir provides a kind of quick and not very revealing summary of what those quarters seemed like to a Muslim of fifteenth century Jerusalem:

The principal quarters of Jerusalem are as follows:

   The Maghrebi Quarter, which is near the wall of the Haram on its western side. It is called "Maghrebi" because it constituted a waqf for the benefit of those latter, who live in it.

   The Sharaf Quarter. It is next to the preceding one, to the west, and owes its name to one of the notables of the city called Sharaf al-Din Musa with known descendents who are called the Banu Sharaf. Formerly it was called the Quarter of the Kurds.

   The Quarter of Alam, so called from a certain Alam al-Din Sulayman, better known as Ibn al-Muhaddib who died toward the end of 770 [A.D.

1369]. His descendents enjoyed a certain renown, like his son Umar, who was Inspector of the Two Sanctuaries, [10] and his other son Sharaf al-Din Musa who is buried in the quarter. This quarter is next to the Sharaf quarter to the north. Today it is called the Quarter of the Haydarira, which derives from a convent belonging to the Sufi order of the Haydarira.

The Quarter of the People of al-Salt, next to the Sharaf quarter toward the southwest.

The Jewish Quarter, bordering the preceding on its western side.

The Quarter of the Feather.

The Quarter of Sion inside the walls, which is located to the west of the Jewish quarter.

The Dawiyya Quarter, next to the Sion quarter, on the north.

The Quarter of the Banu Hârith, outside the city, near the citadel.[11] (Mujir 1876: 174-175)

We can get some idea from Mujir on how and where the population of Jerusalem sorted themselves out in the late fifteenth century. A number of the quarters were constituted of tribal, ethnic, or religious groups, as elsewhere in the Islamic world, while the make-up of others remains unknown because they are named simply after famous people who one time lived in the neighborhood. What is odd, perhaps, is that there is no mention here of a Christian quarter, though elsewhere in the work he says that the Christian quarter extends "from the Hebron Gate [the present Jaffa Gate] to the Gate of the Serbs," the latter presumably a postern somewhere in the northwest angle of the city. Moreover, we know from other sources that there was still a Christian population in the city and that groups of them like the Latins, the Greeks, the Armenians, and the Syrians contested among themselves the possession of the holy places, grounds enough, indeed, for assuming that they also lived in distinct neighborhoods where their cultural and linguistic peculiarities could be served and preserved.

For the rest, we can piece together a picture from this and other texts and from the surviving monuments. The Muslims as a group lived around the Haram, extending north and east from its precinct walls along the major arteries of the city, like Valley Street toward the Damascus Gate, and Gate of the Chain Street toward the central market area and the Jaffa Gate beyond. "Muslims as a group" is not their characterization, of course; the Jews might be lumped together in a single category by the Muslims, but their own quarters they more carefully distinguished: the Maghrebi or Western Muslims from Morocco lived around the southwest corner of the Haram, while the "Easterners" from Iran, Afghanistan, and India lived near the northwestern corner. Smaller ethnic groups like "the people of al-Salt" had their own neighborhoods. [12]

The Maghrebi Quarter

The quarter of the "Western," or Maghrebi, Muslims who lived in the vicinity of the southwestern corner of the Haram is of particular interest not merely because of the political problems that will eventually spring forth from it—the quarter enveloped what was later variously known as the "Western Wall" or "Wailing Wall" venerated by the Jews—but because of the detailed charter that established its waqf endowment.[13] The endowment goes back to a scion of a noted family of mystics from Spain and Morocco, a certain Abu Maydan who came to Jerusalem early in the fourteenth century and settled considerable properties on the support of the colony of Moroccan Muslims already long established in the neighborhood of the Haram, and it is his endowment charter of A.D. 1330 that is still extant:

Abu Maydan . . . who declared, while in sound health, that he dedicated as waqf . . . both the two places mentioned, described and delimited below, which are his property, under his control and power up to the date of the waqf. . . .

The first place is a village called Ayn Karim of the villages of Jerusalem,[14] embracing land cultivated and uncultivated . . . rocky and plain . . . and derelict dwelling houses for its cultivators . . . a small orchard, pomegranate and other [fruit] trees, watered from the village fountain, old olive trees, and caroub, fig and oak trees. . . . Its boundary on the south is the lands of al-Maliha al-Kubra [village]; on the north some of the land . . . of Qalunya . . . ; on the west it reaches Ayn al-Shaqqaq, on the east it reaches parts of the land of al-Maliha al-Kubra. . . .

He [made all this land] waqf with all its rights and benefits . . . including the village fountain and the oozing fountain, the trees, the disused wells, the stumps of old vines, and all that is connected with the village and all the rights pertaining thereto . . . with the exception of God's mosque, the thoroughfare used by the Muslims, their cemetery—these are excluded and not included in this waqf.

The second place dedicated as a waqf in Jerusalem is a locality known as Qantarat Umm al-Banat at the Gate of the Chain and comprises a hall, two apartments, a yard, private conveniences, and, on a lower level, a store and a cave—the whole he dedicated as true, absolute, and legal waqf in perpetuity, . . . free from all impediments, for its beneficiaries forever. The site cannot be sold, nor any parts thereof, nor any of its rights, nor its boundaries. It cannot be owned [by others], nor exchanged. None of this waqf's legal provisions can be dissolved, and none but its beneficiaries may enjoy it. . . . Passage of time does not invalidate it nor weaken it, but confirms it . . . for ever and ever until God inherits the earth and all those on it.

The institutor of this waqf . . . assigns it for the benefit of the Moroccan residents of Jerusalem, or coming to reside in it, of whatever description or occupation. . . . None shall dispute it or share it with them. . . . It is for their benefit . . . precedence being given to the newcomers over the old residents, and the more needy come before the less needy. . . . Should the Moroccans all perish and none of them remain in Jerusalem . . . then the beneficiaries of the waqf shall be the Moroccans living near the Two Noble Mosques in Mecca and Medina. If no Moroccans exist in the Two Holy Cities, then the benefit of the waqf should go to these Two Noble Mosques.

The benefactor stipulated that in his lifetime he himself shall be the administrator and supervisor of the trust. Thereafter the post shall be held by that Moroccan in Jerusalem whose wisdom and piety was recognized [by all of them].

The benefactor assigned the second place specified above as a convent-hospice for the residence of newly arrived male Moroccans. . . . Neither the male nor the female Moroccans resident in Jerusalem are eligible. It is incumbent upon him who becomes the administrator to keep the place in a good state of repair. . . .

The benefactor stipulated that after meeting expenses and [cost of] repairs, the supervisor should give [daily] at the convent-hospice two loaves of bread in the months of Rajab, Shaʿban, and Ramadan to every Moroccan, male and female, resident in Jerusalem or newly arrived in the city. The bread should be distributed following the afternoon prayer, and those present should read the *Fatihah* [Sura 1] seven times, *al-Ikhlas* [Sura 112] and the last two Suras each three times, and offer the blessing of the act to the Prophet, his Companions, and Followers, and for the comfort of the soul of the benefactor and all those piously connected with this waqf.

The benefactor stipulated that a meal should be served on the occasion of [the feasts of] Id al-Fitr, Id al-Adha, and the Prophet's Birthday to the poor among the Moroccans in Jerusalem. He likewise stipulated that the supervisor should pay the cost of clothing as a protection against the cold for each new arrival at the convent-hospice from the Maghreb. The supervisor should also pay from the income of the waqf the cost of a funeral and a shroud for all destitute Moroccans [who die in Jerusalem].

Thus was completed this blessed waqf with all its conditions . . . and the terms of its execution by its donor in the proper legal form, free from any provision for its negation or dissolution, because it became an emphatic waqf and perpetual assignment. [The properties covered by it] cannot be owned by others, cannot be given away as alms or gifts; cannot be *mortgaged; cannot be exchanged or compensated for; cannot be usurped. It is unlawful for any governor, official, or tyrant to abolish this waqf or part of it or change it . . . or endeavor to abolish it or part of it. . . . He who does so or assists in it . . . disobeys God and rebels against Him . . . and deserves His curse.*

The benefactor confirmed all that is inscribed in this written document, after it being read to him from beginning to end . . . on this blessed day, the twenty-ninth of Ramadan in the year twenty and seven hundred [October A.D. 1320]. (Tibawi 1978: 11-13)

Subjects and Masters

The Christians lived where they always had in Jerusalem, west of the cardo and north and south of the Holy Sepulcher: the Latins and Greeks to the north of that Church, the Armenians and Jacobites to the south. Some Syrian Christians must likewise have continued to live scattered through the northeast corner of the city, where the Crusaders had resettled them in the twelfth century. The Jews, finally, lived south of the east-west thoroughfare of David Street / Gate of the Chain Street, between the Armenians on their west and the Maghrebi Muslims on their east.

The Muslims, as the sovereigns of Jerusalem, both controlled the city's strong point, the Citadel, and lived clustered around its most prestigious shrine, the Haram al-Sharif. In a departure from Ayyubid times, however, when the governor lived in the center of the city, close to the Church of the Holy Sepulcher, or even in the Citadel, under the Mamluks he had moved to quarters on the northern edge of the Haram:

As for the entries [into the Haram] on the northern side, they extend, from east to west, from the Gate of the Tribes to the Madrasa Jawliyya, which is known in our days as Government House. . . . The Madrasa Jawliyya had as its founder Amir Alam al-Din Sanjar al-Jawli, governor of Gaza, born in 683 [A.D. 1284-1284]. He was a learned man and composed several works. . . . He died in Ramadan of 745 [January-February A.D. 1345]. At the present time this madrasa has become the residence of the governors of Jerusalem. It encloses a tomb where is buried Shaykh Darbas, a Hakkari Kurd, who was a virtuous man and full of faith. . . . (Mujir 1876: 115, 148)

Felix Fabri had a somewhat different perception of the same place some fifteen years earlier than Mujir, in 1480, and incidentally provides a clue as to when the building was converted from a school into an official residence. He is at the start of what was already developing as the Via Dolorosa:

Leaving the aforesaid house [of Pilate] and going further along the street, we came to another street leading upward from it. Here we left the street down which we had come from Mount Calvary, mounted up this street and came to a great house, which was the house of King Herod, to which the Lord Jesus was brought from Pilate up this ascent. Herein he was scoffed at by Herod's army, mocked with a white garment, and tormented in divers ways, as we are told by the Evangelists. . . . During my first pilgrimage I was unable to obtain entrance to this house, because there was there a Saracen school therein, in which boys are taught. In my second pilgrimage we were suddenly driven away from the house because the governor of the city kept his concubines in it, for which reason, even after the departure of the other pilgrims, we could not gain admittance into it. (Felix Fabri 1893: I, 451)

In this year 892 [A.D. 1486-1487] Khidr Bay, the governor of Jerusalem, built in the Government House the room next to the iwan on its north side, where he rendered justice. In making this arrangement he followed the custom common in Egypt for tribunals of justice. The platform was made of varnished wood. Previous to this the governor sat at the back of the iwan, but henceforward he took his place in this room, which is preferable to the older arrangement. (Mujir 1876: 288)

A Walk Along David Street

If Mujir's survey of the quarters appears somewhat mechanical and over-simplified, he does full justice to the urban complexity of medieval Jerusalem in his tour of the streets and neighborhoods of the city. The first is along the major east-west thoroughfare that begins at the entry to the Haram and ends at the western city gate. Mujir proceeds from east to west:

This is the great street, which begins at the gate of the Haram known as the Gate of the Chain and goes to the Gate of the Prayer Niche [of David], and this is the famous city gate now known as the Gate of al-Khalil [or the Friend of God, the normal honorific given to Abraham; this was the major entry from Hebron].

The street is divided into various segments, each of which has its own proper name. From the Haram to the Salamiyya Quran House it is called the Goldsmiths' Bazaar. From the entry of the Salamiyya as far as that of the Sharaf quarter, the Straw Bazaar. From there to the Charcoal Khan as the Bazaar of the Bleachers. From the entry of the khan to the Arcade of al-Jubayli, as the Charcoal Bazaar. The section between the Arcade of al-Jubayli and the Stairway of the Rabble, it is known as the Bazaar of the Cooks. The Bazaar of the Cooks in Jerusalem was constructed with vaulted arcades covering the shops. The work was begun in the month of Rajab of the year 878 [A.D. 1471-1472]. Previous to this time the roofs of the shops consisted of palm branches, a very poor covering in winter by reason of the mud and the rain that fell down from the roof. The construction took place from the Stairway of the Rabble as far as the Arcade of al-Jubayli. [To continue] from the Cooks' Bazaar to the entry of the Jewish quarter, as the Street of the Warehouse. This warehouse is a large khan whose income was endowed for the support of the Aqsa Mosque and is rented for four hundred dinars a year. All kinds of merchandise are sold there. From the entry to the Jewish quarter to the Khan of the Exchange, the street is known as the Bazaar of the Silk Merchants. From there to the city gate it is known as the Street of the Place of the Cereals.

Then follows this somewhat curious postscript:

Taken all together these sections constitute David Street, so called because King David had an underground passage under it that led from the gate of the Haram called the Gate of the Chain to the Citadel, known in ancient times as the Prayer Niche of David and the place where he lived. This passage still exists today and from time to time parts of it are uncovered and can be inspected. It is composed of a series of vaulted chambers of solid construction. David used this passageway to go from his palace to the Sanctuary. (Mujir 1876: 176-177, 289)

The lore of ancient cities is filled with accounts of underground passages, but Mujir's statement has an authoritative ring about it, as if he himself had seen the uncovered portions of it—as indeed he may have. The two British engineers Wilson and Warren surveyed a good deal of the Old City of Jerusalem in 1864. They were standing in an underground chamber next to the west wall of the Herodian platform, with David Street / Gate of the Chain Street passing overhead, when Warren described the following:

We find ourselves in a secret passage leading under the Street of David: it is greatly filled with rubbish and sewage, but the arch is white and clean; this passage is twelve feet wide and the vault is semicircular; its crown is about nine feet below the level of the roadway, and in between must run the aqueduct from the Pools of Solomon. . . . Having traced the passage 220 feet from the Sanctuary wall, we found a thin wall blocking the pas-

*sage; we broke through and dropped down about six feet into a contin-
uation of it stopped up by a wall to the west, but opening with a door to
the south; through this we crept and then saw light, and, getting through
another chamber to the south, we found ourselves in a donkey-stable. . . .
Subsequently we found a further portion of this secret passage used as a
tank, about 250 feet from the Sanctuary wall, and there can be little doubt
but that it can be traced for several yards further up the street, if indeed
it still does not exist right up to the Jaffa Gate.*

*There cannot be a doubt but that the secret passage we have found is
that referred to by Mujir al-Din, but it does not appear to me that its
construction is so ancient a date as the time of David, or even of
Herod. . . .*[15] *(Wilson/Warren 1873: 69)*

Valley Street

Mujir proceeds to another east-west street, Marzuban Street, and then
conducts us along the old Roman colonnaded street running, as it still
does today, southward from the Damascus Gate down through the Tyropean Valley just west of the Haram area. He is at some pains to describe
the side-streets running into this "Valley Street" from both the west and
the east, or Haram, sides, on which were located many of the most splendid Mamluk buildings in Jerusalem. And here at least it is clear that Mujir
is using the word "quarter" in a more confined sense than in the passage cited earlier, closer perhaps to what we might understand as a
"neighborhood":

*The Street of the Valley of the Mills is the great avenue which extends
from south to north from the passageway of the fountain [of Siloam] as
far as the Gate of the Column [the Damascus Gate], one of the city portals. Many roads with their own particular names end in this street. These
are as follows. The Quarter of the Gate of the Cotton Merchants, which
is one of the gates of the Haram and is so called because they sell cotton
in the market situated in front of it. The Quarter of the Gate called al-
Hadid, next to the Gate of the Cotton Merchants to the north. The
Quarter of the Gate of the Inspector, one of the gates of the Haram.
Perpendicular, toward the west, is the Passageway of the Market, actually
known as the Passageway of the Lady because of the very large building
that is found there and that was built by Lady Tunsuq al-Mudaffariyya.
This lady was still living in 793 [A.D. 1391]. Going on toward the west
one finds the Oil Bazaar, in which there is a lane going toward the west
and is called the Lane of Abu Shamma.*

Into Valley Street there enters from the east the Ghawanima Quarter, which is on the west side of the Haram and takes its name from the residence of the Banu Ghanim. Opposite it toward the west is the Zahiriyya Passage, which has taken its name from an ancient convent which is there and is called the Zahiriyya. At the Zahiriyya Passage, on its southern side, ends another called the Passage of the Blacks, into which comes, on its northern side, a lane which is called the Arcades of Khudayr. At the end of the passageway is located, on the western side, the Market of Fakhr, named after Fakhr al-Din, the founder of the Madrasa Fakhriyya; there are soapworks there, where soap is made. . . .

The Quarter of Hitta Gate is at the north of the Haram; it continues toward the north by the Quarter of the Easterners, which runs right up to the city walls. . . .

In addition Jerusalem is crossed by a number of other streets and lanes which it would be pointless to mention since the greater part of them are included in those already mentioned. I have limited myself to mentioning the most noteworthy. One of the most important and largest quarters is that of the Hitta Gate. These quarters, as one can see, surround the Haram on the west and the north; as for the other two sides, they are empty places, as we have already noted. (Mujir 1876: 179-182)

The Markets of Jerusalem

From the streets and neighborhoods of Jerusalem, Mujir next turned his attention, and his instincts as an anecdotalist and a historian, to the markets of the city—its *suqs*, or bazaars—and inevitably to the three covered bazaars that ran down the middle of the former Roman cardo near where David Street met the Gate of the Chain Street:

There are a number of places in Jerusalem remarkable for their solid construction, and among them is the Market of the Cotton Merchants, near the western gate of the Haram. It is a bazaar remarkable for its solidity and height, and there are many cities where one cannot find its equal. Again, there are three suqs situated next to each other near the Western Gate or the Gate of al-Khalil; their construction goes back to Roman days. They run from south to north and connect with each other. The first, on the west, is the Druggists' Bazaar, whose income Saladin made an endowment for the Madrasa Salahiyya. The next or middle bazaar is used for the sale of vegetables. The next, on the east, is used by the textile merchants. The latter two bazaars are endowed for the upkeep of the Aqsa Mosque.

On the testimony of visitors, there are no bazaars anywhere that are the equal of these latter three in arrangement and architecture. They are one of the beautiful things that make Jerusalem distinctive.

It is reported . . . that the caliph [Umar], when he had conquered the Holy City, stopped at the entry of the bazaar, at its highest point. "Who owns this file [of shops]?" he asked, pointing to the row of the bazaar of the cereal sellers. "The Christians," he was told. "And the western row, where the bath of the market is?" he continued. "The Christians," they told him again. "So that this one is theirs and this one is theirs," he said pointing with his hand. "But this section belongs to us." He was referring to the middle section between the other two rows, that is, the great bazaar with the "Lead Dome."

To return, it seems likely that the three markets being referred to are the ones which actually exist today, but that the older designations have given way to the newer constructions that one sees today. God knows best however. (Mujir 1876: 171-172)

Mujir may have been expressing a certain local patriotism, but there were other, more disinterested observers in the 1480s who were equally impressed, though for reasons other than the construction alone. The first is the German Dominican Felix Fabri; the second, the Jewish visitor from Italy, Obadiah da Bertinoro:

On the twenty-eighth of July I went down early with an official into the city, to the marketplace and the street of the cooks, where I saw a great abundance of things for sale, a vast multitude of people, and many kitchens; for men do not cook in their own houses, as they do in our country, but buy their food cooked from the public cooks, who dress meat exceedingly cleanly in open kitchens. There is no woman ever seen near the fire—nay, no woman is so bold as even to enter these kitchens, for the Saracens loathe food cooked by women like poison. Wherefore throughout all the East no woman knows how to bake a cake, but men alone are cooks. In these parts the kitchens must needs be common walls, since owing to the dryness of the land, wood is dear, and there cannot be a kitchen in each house, as with us, because of the want of wood. (Felix Fabri 1893: II, 111)

Jerusalem [writes Obadiah], notwithstanding its destruction, still contains four very beautiful long bazaars, such as I have never seen before, at the foot of Sion. They all have dome-shaped roofs and contain wares of every kind. They are divided into different departments, the merchants' bazaar, the spice bazaar, the vegetable market, and one in which cooked food and bread are sold. [There was a famine when Obadiah arrived, but it had since eased.] Many lived on grass, going out like stags to look for pasture. . . . The soil is excellent but it is difficult to earn a living at a craft unless it's as a shoemaker, weaver, or goldsmith, and even that's hard;

even such artisans as they gain their livelihood with great difficulty. . . .
(Adler 1966: 236-238)

The Market of the Cotton Merchants

Among the streets mentioned by Mujir as connecting the Haram with Valley Street was that called the Market of the Cotton Merchants. There is a good deal of converging information on this short covered street. It was obviously one of the commercial showplaces of Mamluk Jerusalem, though its income was earmarked for pious purposes. [16] And as the street leading up to what was the chief western entry into the Haram, this bazaar street must have been an important and valuable property from the beginning of the Muslim era. Among the first to describe it in its new, reconstructed form—it has been restored once again in recent years [17]—was the historian al-Umari (1347):

[The Gate of the Cotton Merchants is] a large [Haram] gate that was just built and recently opened. There are ten steps down (inside). On each side there are platforms, and the length of each of them is seven and two-thirds pics. The construction of the gate is perfect: its height is eight pics and its width is five. Its arch is of double facing and made of stone which is sculpted and colored. Its inscription is gilt and incised into the stone. Its two portals are covered with plates of gilt and inscribed copper. . . . Through it one arrives at the storehouse recently put up and two rows of shops, one of which is an endowment for the benefit of the Haram and the other for the benefit of the school and the convent built by the pains of the Amir Sayf al-Din Tankiz. (Golvin 1967: 101-102)

Mujir al-Din a century and a half later is briefer:

The Gate of the Market of the Cotton Merchants . . . is so named because it ends in the Market of the Cotton Merchants. It bears an inscription which indicates that it was restored by the Sultan al-Malik al-Nasir Muhammad ibn Qala'un in the year 737 [A.D. 1335], which proves that it was old. [18] (Golvin 1967: 102)

The inquisitive Felix Fabri was drawn to what seems to be the same place, though he does not know or mention its name; he provides as well something of the flavor of an eastern quarter as it appeared to a European Christian of the fifteenth century:

After this we went toward the Temple and in the courtyard thereof we saw many Saracens standing with pails, pots, and pitchers to draw water, which there bursts forth abundantly from a water pipe. . . . From this place we went up towards the Temple to a street covered with a vaulted roof, through which we went to the great gate leading into the court of the Temple. In this street [the Market of the Cotton Merchants?] were many shops and doors for merchants on either side. When they saw us hurrying along towards the gate of the Temple, many people ran up to keep us from going in. We told them by signs that we would not go in, but would only pray to God outside the gate, and so they suffered us to go to the gate where we prayed on our bended knees, looking toward the Temple of the Lord; but even this was annoying to the Saracens and they cried out at us. . . . Thence we came back along the street and making a circuit, came to another vaulted street, through which there is likewise a way to the Temple, and in which there were likewise merchants sitting in shops. . . . (Felix Fabri 1893: II, 124-125)

The literary descriptions do not do justice to the complexity of this single Mamluk vaulted bazaar. In addition to the two rows of shops of varying sizes, twenty-seven on one side, thirty-one on the other, there was a khan with public baths flanking it on each side and, above the shops, rows of residential apartments whose entries were not, however, through the bazaar, which was closed and locked at night for security reasons, but through the mews behind.

The Gate of the Chain Complex

The next Haram entry to the south of the Gate of the Cotton Merchants is that called the Gate of the Chain, the eastern end, as we have seen, of the main east-west artery of Jerusalem, which begins at the Jaffa Gate. The Gate of the Chain is actually a double gate, that on the right as one faces it from the street known as the Gate of the Chain proper (*Bab al-Silsila*), or Gate of the Ark (*Bab al-Sekina*), and that on the left as the Gate of Peace (*Bab al-Salam*). The entire complex is obviously a structural composite, with architectural elements of different eras used and reused in a rich profusion. Where at least some of those pieces came from was first revealed by a first-class piece of archeological detective work done by Clermont-Ganneau in the nineteenth century, when such methods were still in their infancy:

Outside the Haram Gate [the Gate of the Chain] . . . there is a modern building which almost entirely masked the left hand way [the Gate of Peace] of the double gate; there was in that place a little sebil [fountain] with a trough. In 1871 they cleared away this sebil, and the trough, when freed from the stonework wherein it had been so long encased, turned out to be a magnificent antique sarcophagus. This demolition laid bare the base of the central pier [of the gate], which is made of fine blocks of stone, showing medieval tooling with masons' marks. I moreover observed on one of the voussoirs of the left hand arch, still masked by a neighboring house, another mark. *We now have material proof that this gate is entirely of medieval workmanship.*

... Moreover, I think that in the entire mass of building which directly adjoins the Bab al-Silsila [Gate of the Chain] the Mohammadans have used a great quantity of material dating from the period of the Crusaders. Indeed, subsequently, in 1881, I discovered on the south front of the second pier of the portico, which is on the right hand as one enters the Haram from the Bab al-Silsila, a great block of calcareous stone, which displays the medieval tooling in oblique strokes, and the remains of inscription in fine large Gothic letters now reduced to one single line: [HIC JA] CET DROGO DE BUS. ... The rest has been destroyed by the Arab masons who have cut up the original slab to enable it to form part of their pillar. Evidently we have here the epitaph of someone—perhaps a Knight Templar—bearing the Christian name of Drogo, and the surname of Bus. ...

I now return to the sarcophagus which was thus brought to light. ... In the unedited portions of Mujir al-Din's chronicle I find a very interesting piece of evidence on this subject. After having described with enthusiasm the fine Madrasa Ashrafiyya, the building of which, by the order of Sultan al-Malik al-Ashraf, was completed in A.H. 888 [A.D. 1483], he tells us that this prince caused the "basin" which is between the Bab al-Silsila and the Bab al-Sekina to be built.

Evidently this passage alludes to the sebil of which I have just been speaking. ... And thus it appears highly probable that it was in the year 1483 of our era that the sarcophagus was placed where I found it. If, as I suppose, it came from [the cemetery of] Kbur al-Salâtin, it was probably taken away from its original place about that time, and probably others were also brought away with it. ... Mujir indeed tells us that al-Malik al-Ashraf caused many sebils ... to be made, especially in the interior of the Haram. We may therefore conclude from this series of facts that the caves of the Kbur al-Salâtin must have been plundered by the Mussulmans about the year 1483. ... (Clermont-Ganneau 1899: 129-130)

Mujir as an Architectural Historian

Clermont-Ganneau's kind of analysis, first performed in the nineteenth century, was obviously beyond the powers of Mujir al-Din in the fifteenth. But the Mamluk historian did not lack for critical acumen. When he dated monuments, he usually relied on the evidence of a dedicatory inscription, but he was also capable of making a historical identification based on stylistic evidence. In this passage, for example, he is reflecting on the porticoes that run along the northern side of the Haram. He begins on the east:

As for the portico which occupies the space [along the northern edge of the Haram] between the Gate of the Tribes [in the northeast corner] and the Madrasa Ghadiriyya [just east of the Hitta Gate], I was unable to discover the date of its construction, but appearances indicate that it was built at the same time as the minaret there and whose construction took place in the reign of al-Malik al-Ashraf Shaʿban ibn Husayn, in the year 769 [A.D. 1367-1368]. The portico under the Ghadiriyya was constructed at the same time as this madrasa, as well as the assembly hall of the Madrasa Karimiyya. As for the portico extending from the Hitta Gate to the Dawadariyya Gate [today called the Faysal Gate], it gives every appearance of having been built by al-Malik al-Awhad with his tomb, which is located at the Hitta Gate, since certain clauses in the endowment charter of the latter made this hypothesis necessary.

The portico located between the Dawadariyya Gate and the western end of the Haram, which supports five madrasas, was in part an ancient construction. Such, for example, is the section forming the base of the Madrasas Aminiyya and Farisiyya. It [the portico] was later rebuilt during the reign of al-Malik al-Muʿazzam Isa in the year 610 [A.D. 1213]. The remaining part, that under the Madrasas Malikiyya, Asʿardiyya, and Subaybiyya, dates from the same era as those schools, each one of which is constructed in a manner that is congruent with the portico below. That is what an inspection of the sites indicates, in any event, that the architecture of each of these madrasas is harmonious with the gallery which supports it. We shall mention the date of each of these colleges, and thus one will know the date of the construction of the portico underneath.

As for the two lower galleries, on top of which the Government House rises, they were constructed at the same time as the Ghawanima minaret. They bear an inscription indicating the date of their construction and of the minaret, though the characters have been somewhat effaced by time. These two porticoes have two others above them, of a more recent era. We shall cite [only] the date at which the founder of the minaret lived, which will give some idea of the approximate date of their construction. God knows better the truth. (Mujir 1876: 115-117)

The Mamluks and the Haram

The Mamluks invested heavily and consistently in restoring and decorating the Haram area.[19] Sultan Baybars (A.D. 1260-1277), for example, redid the mosaics on the eight exterior faces of the Dome of the Rock building, while Qala'un (A.D. 1280-1290) repaired the roof of the Aqsa; and Qala'un's son al-Nasir Muhammad paid for the regilding of the cupolas of both the Dome of the Rock and the Aqsa Mosque. These tasks have been redone a number of times since, but what is a more lasting testimony to the Mamluk devotion to Jerusalem's chief Islamic holy place is the long portico that still stands along the western side of the Haram, again the work of al-Nasir Muhammad, and what is surely one of the masterpieces of Mamluk architecture, the fountain erected at the command and expense of Sultan Qa'it Bay between the Dome of the Rock and the western wall of the Haram. [20]

All of this is faithfully if somewhat dryly chronicled by Mujir al-Din in his history of Jerusalem. What is more interesting perhaps is to see these same monuments through other, less accustomed eyes, those of Christian and Jewish visitors to Mamluk Jerusalem. They could not visit the Haram in person, of course, except by risking the gravest danger to their life or, for a Jew, we hear for the first time, by promoting a hideous defilement. But the monuments were certainly visible from the outside, and there was a generous number of stories in circulation for the curious. Arnold von Harff, however, who visited Jerusalem in the same year Mujir al-Din was finishing his history of the Holy City, 1496, was one whose curiosity was not satisfied by mere stories:

We came to the Temple of Solomon [the Dome of the Rock] which stands one hundred and sixty paces from the Temple of Christ [the Holy Sepulcher]. By means of gifts and other friendly help, I was taken by a Mamluk into this Temple. But no Christian or Jew is suffered to enter there or draw near, since they say and maintain that we are base dogs and not worthy to go to the holy places on pain of death, at which I was frightened. But this Mamluk instructed me that if I would go with him one evening, dressed in his manner, he would take me into the Temple, and that if I was recognized I was to reply like a heathen [Muslim] with the words and speech, and to use the words and make the signs which I was forced to use when it happened that I was imprisoned at Gaza . . . whereupon the heathen would show me honor and suffer me to go, as indeed happened. The Mamluk fetched me one evening from the monastery at Mount Sion and took me to his house, in the pretense that I should have spent the night with him, where he dressed me in the clothes and appareled me like a Mamluk. Thus we both made our way at evening toward the Temple of Solomon which, by his direction, was opened and forthwith closed so that we should not be crowded; for this I had to give four ducats.

This Temple of Solomon is a fine round and lofty church roofed with lead. Around it is a churchyard, without buildings, which is all paved with large white marble stones, as it is also within. . . . In this Temple, eastwards, is a small round tabernacle or chapel [apparently the dome itself] five feet long and broad, placed on twelve pillars, a spear's height from the ground, in which the heathen priests now pray and hold their services. It is held in great reverence and regarded as a holy place, and many ampullae burn there continuously. Formerly the Jews held this tabernacle or chapel in great honor and reverence and regarded it as a holy place, for on it stood the Ark of God. . . . Beneath this tabernacle is a small piece of rock enclosed with an iron railing, called the Holy Rock, on which many wonders and miracles of God have been performed. . . .

On the left in this Temple there is an altar almost like ours, for it is open on all sides. Here formerly the Jews made their sacrifices, offering doves, hens, and turtledoves to God in heaven. But the heathen have now set a compass [dial] on the rock so that by it, in their manner, they may know the hours. Beside this altar Zacharias was slain.

This Temple of Solomon has four doors by which one may enter. The doors are all made of ancient cypress wood and are carved with ancient histories. By the door to the north is a square cistern in which the heathen wash the members which have sinned by day or night, thinking to cleanse themselves by washing, and they do this before they pray, thinking that otherwise their prayers would not be acceptable to God in heaven. . . . I saw in this Temple no pictures or figures, as we have in our churches, but it is a beautiful Temple with many lamps burning, at least five hundred, as I was in fact told and saw with my own eyes. . . .

. . . We went from this Temple eastwards, some twenty-six paces, into a very fine mosque or church called the Porch of Solomon [the Aqsa Mosque]. When the Christians possessed Jerusalem it was called the Church of Our Blessed Lady, where for a long time she went to school. This church, the Porch of Solomon, is much longer than the Temple of Solomon. It is finely built and roofed with lead, and has within it forty-two marble pillars and eight hundred lamps, which burn there daily. Since the heathen have this church in great reverence, no Christian or Jew may approach it. . . . (Arnold von Harff 1946: 207-210)

Jews in Mamluk Jerusalem

The Jews who looked upon the Haram had somewhat more complex feelings about it than did Arnold von Harff:

In the midst of the city near the [Jewish] House of Study there is an empty place to which all the congregation go after prayers in order to pray facing the Temple, for from there they can see the holy and awesome place. Near this is the al-Aqsa Mosque, the "school of King Solomon," may he rest in peace, but only Ishmaelites enter there. Yet Stella, may she be blessed above all women, amen, the wife of Master Moses of Borgo, may his Rock and Maker guard him, saw it from the outside with the aid of an Ishmaelite townswoman, an important woman who lives near the school. I have heard from Stella that the building is made of extremely beautiful stones, radiant and pure as the very heavens, and covered over with pure gold worked by craftsmen. But she did not see the building itself from the inside. I have heard tell that it is a magnificent building, and the king of Egypt expended immeasurable wealth on it; and the Ishmaelites gather there every Friday at noon and say their prayers. Furthermore, the Ishmaelites refrain from work only during the half hour when they stand in the temple to pray. (Wilhelm 1946: 25-26)

Meshullam of Volterra, who was in Jerusalem sometime about the same time Felix Fabri visited the city in 1480, shows the same kind of mixed feelings. Jerusalem, an unwalled city, he notes, has 10,000 Muslim households and 250 Jewish ones. He was told that the "Stone of Foundation" of Mishna Yoma was in the Haram and that

every year when the Jews go to Synagogue on the eve of the Ninth of Ab all the lamps in the Temple [Haram] court go out of their own accord and cannot be kindled again, and the Muslims know when it is the Ninth of Ab, which they observe somewhat like the Jews because of this.

This annual public miracle does not entirely console him. He notices that it is the Muslims who live all around and overlook the Temple mount and that in front of all the gates of the Haram

there are wide and goodly roads vaulted with houses on either side, in which [Jewish] pilgrims once dwelt, but now through our iniquities the Muslims make them into shops for all kinds of merchandise. (Adler 1966: 189-191)

The famous Obadiah da Bertinoro, a visitor in Jerusalem in 1487-1490, cites the Jews' defilement as the reason for their exclusion from the Temple mount but goes on to describe what he has seen and heard of the enclosure:

No Jew may enter the enclosure of the Temple. Although sometimes the Arabs are anxious to admit carpenters and goldsmiths to perform work there, nobody will go in for we have all been defiled. I do not know whether the Arabs enter the Holy of Holies or not. I also made inquiries relative to the Stone of Foundation where the Ark of the Covenant was placed, and am told that it is under a high and beautiful dome built by the Arabs in the court of the Temple. It is enclosed in this building and none may enter. . . .

The Temple enclosure still has twelve gates. Those which are called the Gates of Mercy [the Golden Gate] are of iron, and are two in number; they look toward the east of the Temple and are always closed. They only reach half-way above the ground, the other half is sunk in the earth. It is said that the Arabs often tried to raise them but were unable to do so.

The western wall, part of which is still standing, is composed of large, thick stones, such as I have never seen before in an old building, either in Rome or in any other country. At the northeast [southeast?] corner is a tower of very large stones. I entered it and found a vast edifice supported by massive and lofty pillars; there are so many pillars that it wearied me to go to the end of the building. Everything is filled with earth which has been thrown down from the ruins of the Temple. The Temple building [i.e., platform] stands on these columns and in each of them is a hole through which a cord may be drawn. It is said that the bulls and rams for sacrifice were bound here. . . . (Adler 1966: 239-240)

The Golden Gate

The Golden Gate obviously interested a great many visitors, and it is instructive to compare interpretations of its history, that of the Christian cleric Niccolo of Poggibonsi (1346-1350), for example, with the one offered by the Muslim cleric Mujir al-Din in 1496:

There is a field above the place of the stoning of St. Stephen. Taking the first path to the left, you reach beside the walls of Jerusalem a Saracen cemetery. Do not enter but go straight ahead, for the Saracens do not wish that Christians enter their churches and either kill them or force them to renounce their faith. And there you find the [exterior wall of the] Golden Gate and of the Temple of the Lord. This gate is very large and consists of two gates, one beside the other. Between the two entries is a wall two feet in width with a vaulted arch. Above the arches is a little house, with a window above the gate. The gate faces east and is all covered with iron attached with stout nails, but now many nails have been removed for the Christians take them, when they can, because they have great power. The wood at the back of the gate is cypress. This gate was never opened, and this not because they did not want to but because they could not since Christ left by it on Palm Sunday.

Once the Tartars conquered a part of the Holy Land and captured Jerusalem, with a great carnage of the Saracens, and when they saw the

Golden Gate was so beautiful, they decided to remove it from its place and take it to their own country, to the great Khan.[21] *But when the Tartars went to remove it, they were unable to do so. So they started to unwall it, but the deeper they dug, the deeper they found the gate ran. Seeing that they could not have it, their leader ordered that it be burned. All those who went to burn it with torches in their hands had the fire turn on them so that they themselves were burned. A little later the Saracens retook and drove the Tartars back as far as Damascus. . . . Therefore the Saracens call it the Gate of Mercy and show it a great reverence. It is the order of the sultan that whosoever, Christian or Saracen, maltreats the gate should pay for it with his head. And that it be not touched it has been walled from the ground up for several arms' lengths. There is a very great indulgence (attached to visiting this spot). (Niccolo of Poggibonsi 1945: 45-46)*

The first [of the gates of the Haram] is the double entry let into the eastern wall. It is of it that the Quran speaks [57:13] "And between them will be erected a wall that will have a gate. Inside will sit mercy; outside and facing it, punishment." In fact, the valley that is behind this gate is that of Gehenna. These two gates are inside the wall and are next to a part of the Haram. One is called the Gate of Repentance, and the other the Gate of Mercy. Presently they are impassable. Over these gates and inside the Haram is a vaulted construction built by Solomon; it is the only building inside the Haram whose construction goes back to Solomon. This place is visited by pilgrims; it has an imposing appearance and commands respect.

One of the older inhabitants of the city once told me that the two gates were sealed by the Commander of the Faithful Umar ibn al-Khattab and that they will not be reopened until the descent of the Lord Jesus, son of Mary, upon whom be blessings. From all appearances they were closed in the fear of an attack on the Haram and the city by the heretic enemy since the gates lead out into the countryside and there would be little use in leaving them open. (Mujir 1876: 127-128)

As usual, Arnold von Harff, who had had to disguise himself as a Muslim to get into the Haram area, is more bitterly pointed and direct in his reactions:

From this church [the al-Aqsa Mosque] we went about thirty paces to the right hand [eastwards] across this fine courtyard which is paved with marble, fifteen paces from the Temple of Solomon. We came then to the Golden Door through which our Lord Jesus rode in on Palm Sunday, sitting on an ass. This gate is of cypress wood covered with copper and is much cut and mutilated. Therefore the heathen guard the doorway closely,

*so that no Christian may approach it. They have also their cemetery out-
side the gate toward the Vale of Jehoshaphat, where they bury their dead.
Therefore they guard the gate closely against Christians and Jews, whom
they regard as more filthy than dogs, lest they should tread upon their
graves. We broke and cut off many pieces of the wood and copper which
I carried back with me. At this gate there is a plenary indulgence, both
penalty and guilt. (Arnold von Harff 1946: 211)*

The Golden Gate enjoyed another, albeit brief, celebrity in Islam. What
must have been an exceedingly small Sufi convent was built atop the gate,
in Niccolo's "little house," and shortly before the Crusaders took the city
it had an exceedingly famous scholar in residence:

*There was on the tower of the Gate of Mercy a school called the Nasiriyya
and named after Shaykh Nasr al-Muqaddasi. It was subsequently known
as the Ghazaliyya after Abu Hamid al-Ghazali.*[22] *Later al-Malik al-
Mu'azzam rebuilt it and made it a convent for the reading of the Quran
and the study of syntax. He gave it gifts of several works, including the
"Thinking Straight" of Abu Yusuf Ya'qub al-Sikkit. . . . This convent has
fallen into ruin in our day: it is no longer occupied and has been abandoned. (Mujir 1876: 140)*

There is a final postscript in the history of this most curious of all the
gates of Jerusalem. The story is told by the Franciscan Elzear Horn, a
resident in Jerusalem between 1724 and 1744, but the event it describes
took place about 1618 when the Ottoman Turks possessed Jerusalem:

*Beneath the Temple of the Lord, there is another gate looking east, which
is called the Golden Gate; formerly in the days of the Christians and the
Saracens, it was opened only on Palm Sunday; at present it is closed by a
permanent wall, for in 1541 the Turks removed the wooden doors and
closed it with a wall, so that it might not be accessible to anyone after
that; for they believed that the Christians would enter by this gate and
capture the city after they had expelled or killed the Muslims. Father Quaresmi, while in Jerusalem as Superior of the Holy Land [A.D. 1618] asked
some Turks rather high in dignity and quite learned in the law, "Why is
it that this gate is not open like the others?" They replied that it was
reserved for some great king to be opened. Who that king would be they
did not wish to state. Every Friday, therefore, about noon, when they
enter their holy place, which is the Temple of Solomon [the al-Aqsa
Mosque], at the hour of prayer, fearing for themselves, they take great
care to have all the city gates closed, in order that they might not be cut
off unawares. And that they use the same precaution on the island of
Rhodes is certain from the reports of trustworthy persons. (Horn 1962:
28-29)*

411

Jerusalem as an Islamic Holy City

The Mamluk work on the Haram was by way of refurbishing or situating minor shrines about the platform, since the overall shape and character of the Noble Sanctuary was fixed almost from the beginning. [23] But on a larger scale, that dynasty changed both the face and the character of the Holy City. The Ayyubids reappropriated what the Crusaders had taken over from Islam, and some more besides, like the patriarch's residence and the Church of St. Anne, but beyond that they were not great builders in Jerusalem. The Mamluks, on the other hand, who inherited the Ayyubids' ideology, *were* such builders, and now for the first time since Muqaddasi's original complaint that the Holy City seemed more like a Christian or even a Jewish city rather than a Muslim one, Jerusalem became a Muslim city.

The bulk of this construction took place, as has already been noted, along the streets leading from the north and the west into the Haram. And what was put up from the generous endowments settled on the city by Mamluk sultans, governors, officials, and even the banished though by no means impoverished colonels who were constrained to live there, were chiefly buildings of a religious character: convents, law schools, and hybrids of the two which were also intended to be the final resting place of the donor. Closer is better in every holy city, so the properties nearest the Haram were obviously choice, and those that faced onto the Haram and looked upon the Dome of the Rock and the Aqsa were the choicest of all. Indeed one foundation, the Jawhar Law School, completed in 1440, climbed up and over the back of its one-storey neighbor, the Convent Kurd, so that its own second floor might open onto the Haram vista. [24]

Amir Sayf al-Din Tashtimur, a former secretary of state in Cairo and former governor of Damascus, was banished to Jerusalem in 1382, where he died three years later. He chose the place of his own mausoleum, a building located fairly far west away from the Haram on Gate of the Chain Street; and in the common manner of the fourteenth century, tomb and law school were to be combined. More, the same edifice also boasted a public fountain facing the street and upstairs a school for the poor and orphans. But Tashtimur's piety was well seasoned with practicality. The building included on its ground floor, also facing the busy commercial thoroughfare of Gate of the Chain Street, a number of commercial boutiques. It was not uncommon to fund endowments out of commercial properties—the Crusaders endowed their markets for the support of St. Anne's, and the Ayyubids did the same with a number of baths and warehouses for the benefit of the Haram—but what is remarkable about the Tashtimuriyya is the sagacious incorporation of those same commercial enterprises into the very edifice whose religious functions they were intended to support. [25]

The Ashrafiyya Law School

One of the most splendid and innovative of the law schools built and endowed by the Mamluks in Jerusalem, and certainly the best known, is that called after its royal benefactor, Sultan al-Malik al-Ashraf Qa'it Bay (A.D. 1468-1496), the Ashrafiyya Madrasa. It sits facing into the Haram between the Gate of the Chain and the Gate of the Cotton Merchants, almost due west and close upon the Dome of the Rock. [26] Completed in its finished version in August 1482, the building is still to some extent preserved, though no longer used as a law school. [27] The dedication inscriptions, still extant, provide basic facts of endowment and construction; more, the school was visited and described during its construction by Felix Fabri in 1480 and analyzed in detail by Mujir al-Din.

Mujir begins with a summary of the construction history of the school:

At the side of the preceding [Madrasa Baladiyya] is the noble Madrasa Sultaniyya Ashrafiyya Qa'it Bay, inside the solemn Haram, near the Gate of the Chain. These are the details of why it was built. Amir Hasan al-Zahiri built the original madrasa for al-Malik al-Zahir Khushqadam [sultan, A.D. 1461-1467], and at the death of this ruler he asked al-Malik al-Ashraf Qa'it Bay to accept its patronage. The sovereign acceded to his request and gave his name to the madrasa where he appointed a superior, Sufis, and lawyers and endowed their stipends. Some time afterward, in the year 880 [A.D. 1475-1476], al-Malik al-Ashraf Qa'it Bay came to Jerusalem and did not find the building to his liking. Thus in 884 [A.D. 1479] he sent one of his personal entourage with the order to demolish it and enlarge it by connecting it to other constructions. They began to dig the foundations of the present madrasa on 14 Sha'ban 885 [October 19, 1480]. The architects threw themselves into the work, and it was completed in Rajab of 887 [August 1482]. They covered its roof in the same manner as that of the al-Aqsa Mosque, with solid sheets of lead. But what constituted its greatest attraction was its position on this noble terrain of which it has become the third jewel; these three jewels [of the Haram] are: The Dome of the Rock, the Dome of the Aqsa, and this madrasa. (Mujir 1876: 143-144)

Later in his work Mujir returns to the subject of the Ashrafiyya and provides an architectural analysis.

We have mentioned earlier the construction of the original madrasa and

413

described the state it was in at first; we have also described the decree of the sultan ordering its demolition and reconstruction, the sending of workers from Cairo for its construction, the care that was lavished on its building until the edifice stood complete, and that, after the putting on the marble and the installation of the wooden doors, it reached that state of perfection which it now displays, with its upper and lower storeys.

The lower storey includes the assembly hall which is connected, on its eastern side, to the portico of the Haram and corresponds to three of the arcades of the portico [built by Sultan al-Nasir Muhammad]. This assembly hall is pierced by two doors, the first of which, on its northern side, is next to a window looking out on the gallery which is the base of the Madrasa Uthmaniyya; the second door is on the east and is flanked, left and right, by two windows. At the [southern] end of the assembly hall is a prayer niche toward the left of center, as well as a window that looks toward the southeast. Adjoining this assembly hall, toward the south, is a dargah, or court, of solid construction and with a door at its western end which leads to the madrasa on the floor above. One goes by this door into a second dargah, all paved with marble, and in which there is, to the right of the entrance, a small private chamber, and, at the end of the dargah, a bench covered with marble. On your left as you go in is the entry by which you go up a broad stairway to the madrasa on the upper floor as well as the minaret of the Gate of the Chain. The staircase ends in a door which goes out onto an open terrace paved in white stone. At the end of this terrace is, toward the north, a square door giving access to a small dargah where, on your right as you enter, there is a vestibule which goes into the madrasa above the assembly hall mentioned earlier.

This madrasa on the upper floor is made up of four iwans, or arched recesses, facing each other. The most southerly [that is, the one facing Mecca], which is the largest, is adorned inside with a prayer niche. Next to this prayer niche, and facing east, are two windows that look out onto the Haram; on the west there are two other windows which look out on the stairway leading up to the madrasa. This aforementioned [eastern] iwan is pierced, on its eastern side, by three windows which open onto the Haram in the direction of the platform of the Dome of the Rock and are opposite three others that overlook the platform of the madrasa. The northern iwan is lit by two windows opening onto the Haram toward the north and by two windows placed on the eastern side. The eastern iwan, which is a kind of lounge, is constituted of three arcades, each resting on two marble columns; its ceiling is composed of round windows of clear glass, beautiful and well constructed. Opposite it is the western iwan with a window opening onto the platform of the madrasa. [28]

The floors of all these rooms are paved in marbles of diverse colors and *their walls are completely lined with marble. The ceilings are of varnished wood, worked with gold leaf and lapis lazuli. They are very strong, solid, and high.*

At the side of the northern iwan is a vaulted chamber into which one goes through the dargah already mentioned. Its door is on your left as you enter. Its floor is decorated with different colored marble, and its walls are lined with marble all around. It has two windows looking into the northern iwan of the madrasa. This room has over it a small chamber lit by two windows, one of which looks into the madrasa and the other out onto the open terrace. This terrace is connected by a door with another terrace off which are the individual rooms [for the residents], which are vaulted, the place for washing and other necessities, the whole resting on the southern and eastern iwans and other parts of the Madrasa Baladiyya.

The madrasa contains furniture and lamps whose beauty surpasses whatever you might find in the other schools. Its roof is covered, like that of the Aqsa Mosque, by strong plates of lead. (Mujir 1876: 286-288)

As Mujir notes, the construction of the final version of the Ashrafiyya Madrasa was being urged forward in 1480 at the specific request of the impatient sultan. It was some⁺ime in that feverish period that the Dominican Felix Fabri visited the site:

Leaving this place we went further through the streets of houses which stand round about the Temple and came to another part of the enclosure, where, beside the wall of the Temple enclosure, a very costly new mosque was being built as an oratory for his Lordship the Sultan, wherein he might pray when he was in Jerusalem. So we went to the place and would have gone up to where the workmen were to see it, but we were told that no man dared to go up to the workmen without leave of the qadi, the bishop of the Saracens' temple. So we entered the house of the qadi, which was hard by, to ask him for leave. The house of this bishop was spacious and lofty, with a vaulted roof, decorated with polished marble, adorned with carpets, like a church, save it has no altars. I now believe that it was a Saracen mosque, into which, however, men of all creeds are admitted because of the bishop, who has his lodging adjoining it, and his household; for I saw women and boys looking at us through an opening in the roof.

Now, the bishop came out to us, and he was a grave and ancient man, reverend and bearded. When he understood what we wished, he consented straightway, and caused us to be taken into the mosque, bidding one of his friends accompany us. We went into the mosque and found many craftsmen and laborers there, making wondrous thin panelling out of polished marble of divers colors, and adorning both the pavement and the walls with designs. Moreover, the upper part was glowing with gold and costly colors, and the windows, which were glazed, lighted the building most excellently well. In that wall which rises from the courtyard of the Temple there are great and tall windows, not as yet glazed, but open, through which we saw the court of the Temple and the Temple itself. . . . When we had seen all these things, we gave the craftsmen a pourboire and came out again. I do not believe that after us any Christian will ever go into that mosque, because they will presently dedicate it by their own accursed rites to the detestable Muhammad and when that has been done, they will let no Christian go in. [29] *(Felix Fabri 1893: II, 125-126)*

The Convents of Jerusalem

As with all such buildings, it was not merely a question of sending architects, masons and craftsmen and subsidizing the construction. Qa'it Bay lavishly endowed his law school on the Haram out of properties he possessed in Gaza, Ludd, Ascalon, Hebron, and elsewhere and arranged for it to have a resident shaykh or spiritual director, with burses for sixty Sufis and an unspecified number of professors and students of law. Thus Sufis and lawyers shared the same quarters and facilities, and the functions associated with each went on under the same roof, instruction in the law in the iwans on the second floor, Sufi seances in the various dargahs throughout the building.

This same mixed function may be read off an endowment inscription fixed to the wall of the Dawadariyya Law School on the street on the northern side of the Haram:

In the name of God, the Merciful, the Compassionate: the devoted servant of Almighty God, Ibn Abd Rabbihi ibn Abd al-Bari Sanjar al-Dawadari al-Salihi ordered the creation of this blessed convent called the House of the Pious. He made it a pious foundation for the sake of Almighty God and for the benefit of thirty members of the Sufi community and their disciples, both Arabs and Persians, of whom twenty are celibate and ten married. They are to reside here and not depart, neither in summer nor winter, neither spring nor fall, except in urgent cases and in order to extend hospitality to those Sufis and disciples who desire it for a period of ten days. He made its endowment [the income of] the village of Bir Nabala [of the territory of] blessed Jerusalem and of the village of Hajla of [the territory of] Jericho; and also [the income of] a bakery and a mill and what is above these two enterprises in Jerusalem; of a soap factory, six shops, and a paper factory in Nablus; of three gardens, three shops, and four mills in Baysan. This is all endowment for the benefit of this convent and for instruction in the Shafi'ite rite; for a professor of pro-

416

phetic tradition and a reader to recite same; for ten persons who will audit traditions and ten who will recite the Book of God in its entirety each day; also for a eulogist who will glorify the Prophet. All of this [latter] is to be done in the Aqsa Mosque.

This [was done] on the first day of the year 695 [A.D. 1295], in the governorship of the devoted servant of God Sanjar al-Qaymari, may God grant him pardon. (van Berchem 1922: #70, trans. K. Schaefer)

Under the Mamluks Jerusalem took on much the aspect of a city of lawyers and ascetics. There were Sufis there in great numbers, many of them merely transients, drawn to Jerusalem by the sanctified allure of the Holy City; many too from distant Islamic lands like Spain in the West, where the Muslims were being driven out before the Spanish Christian reconquest, and Afghanistan and India in the East.[30] They were lodged, all of them, in the various types of convents put up at Mamluk expense in Jerusalem, from tiny "zawiyas," which were little more than a shaykh's room—easily converted into his "blessing"-laden tomb at his death—to elaborate "khanqas," with an internal organization not unlike a European monastery of Benedictines.

We do not as yet have any direct evidence on the life in a Sufi convent in Jerusalem,[31] but we can conveniently extrapolate from Ibn Battuta's eyewitness account of just such a convent in Mamluk Cairo:

Each convent in Cairo is affected to the use of a separate congregation of ascetics, most of whom are Persians, men of good education and adept in the "way" of Sufism. Each has a shaykh and a warden, and the organization of their affairs is admirable. It is one of their customs in the matter of their food that the steward of the house comes in the morning to the faqirs, each of whom then specifies what food he desires. When they assemble for meals, each person is given his bread and soup in a separate dish, none sharing with another. They eat twice a day. They receive winter clothing and summer clothing and a monthly allowance varying from 20 to 30 dirhams each. Every Thursday evening they are given sugar cakes, soap to wash their clothes, the price of admission to the bath house, and oil to feed their lamps. These men are celibate; the married men have separate convents. Among the stipulations required of them are attendance at the five daily prayers, spending the night in the convent, and assembling all together in a chapel within the convent. (Ibn Battuta 1959-1962: 44)

The Appropriation of Christian Buildings

The Ayyubids, caught up in the fervor of a Holy War, had no compunction about appropriating certain Christian buildings in Jerusalem and converting them into Muslim religious institutions, though they did pause, as we have seen, at the confiscation of the Church of the Holy Sepulcher. Most of these takeovers seem to have occurred immediately in the wake of the reconquest of Jerusalem by the sword, as was legally their right. The Mamluks, on the other hand, whose possession of Jerusalem was never threatened by a revived Crusader movement, appear to have been moved to the same acts of appropriation, confiscation, and conversion by a more deeply felt hostility. [32]

Christians and Muslims had always been rivals in Jerusalem, and perhaps a kind of tolerant balance had been achieved by reason of the Muslims' having political sovereignty, though without either the numbers or the prestige or the wealth to use it as they might have wished, while the Christians, who possessed all those advantages, were politically impotent in the face of Muslim power. Under the Mamluks, who built convents and schools all across Jerusalem and filled them with a new population of fervent Muslim ascetics and lawyers, the balance—demographic, social, and economic—shifted for the first time in an obvious way toward the Muslims: the Christians were in Jerusalem by sufferance and not by right. This new state of affairs is written deeply across all the pilgrims' narratives of their experience in the Holy Land, as we shall see in the next chapter, but it can be read as well from the walls of former Christian churches and the somewhat casual, though always approving, accounts of confiscations and conversions given by Mujir al-Din, beginning in the very shadow of the Holy Sepulcher:

The Sufi Convent called the Dargah is near the Hospital of Saladin. This was, at the time of the Franks, the residence of the Hospitallers. It was one of the number of buildings put up by Helena, mother of Constantine, who built the church of the Qumama. It is topped by a minaret partly destroyed. Formerly the governors of the Holy City lived here. It was endowed by al-Malik al-Muzaffar Shihab al-Din Ghazi, son of Sultan al-Malik al-Adil . . . in A.D. 1216. (Mujir 1876: 165)

This is directly to the south of the Holy Sepulcher. Mujir then passes to the northern side of the church, where he notes that there are only two minarets in Jerusalem outside the Haram, a small one on the Madrasa Ma'addamiyya and another atop the convent called after Saladin the Salahiyya. [33] He continues:

Shaykh Burhan al-Din . . . was invested with the office of superior of the Salahiyya Convent in 797 [A.D. 1394-1395] and it was he who constructed the minaret [of the convent], its great entry, the Sufi hall which is inside, as well as the iwan and the lower prayer niche. He died in 839

[A.D. 1435-1436] in Jerusalem. Shaykh Shams al-Din Muhammad . . . told me that when Shaykh Burhan al-Din ibn Ghanim wished to build this minaret, the Christians of Jerusalem were deeply pained because it would be over the Church of the Qumama. They were agreed to offer a great sum of money if he would give up its construction. But he rejected their offer in strong terms. He built the minaret and installed attendants. (Mujir 1876: 69)

The story has a somberly moralistic ending. A man in Jerusalem has a dream, which includes a message from the Prophet Muhammad to Burhan al-Din, to wit: "You will fare well by my intercession on the day of judgment for having built this minaret over the heads of the Christians."

To the south of the Holy Sepulcher there was another oddly hybrid building: the city prison beneath, a mosque above, and another minaret:

Among the other pious bequests of al-Malik al-Afdal [sultan in Damascus A.D. 1186-1196] is the mosque located near the Qumama, above the police prison. He endowed it in 589 [A.D. 1193], which is the year his father [Saladin] died. One can see there a minaret rebuilt prior to 870 [A.D. 1465-1466]. [Later he continues:] There exists another minaret over the mosque we were speaking of earlier in referring to the Afdaliyya Madrasa and which constitutes the upper part of police prison located facing the Qumama on its south side. Its construction is before 870. It seems to have been built on ancient foundations. [34] (Mujir 1876: 163, 170)

Another minaret, finally, rises above a mosque attached to the south side of the synagogue of the Jews. It was rebuilt since 800 [A.D. 1397-1398]. Some good people got together and collected some funds, rebuilt, and endowed it. (Mujir 1876: 170)

The Qalandariyya. In the middle of this cemetery [outside the western wall of Jerusalem] is a large Sufi convent called the Qalandariyya which is of monumental construction. This convent was [originally] a church built by the Byzantines and known as the Red Convent. It was held in great respect by the Christians. But then a man named Shaykh Ibrahim al-Qalandari came to Jerusalem and established himself there with a certain number of ascetics. It is from this shaykh that it takes its name. He was a contemporary of the lady Tansuq, daughter of Abdullah, al-Muzaffariyya [ca. A.D. 1391], the same who had constructed the great palace known as the Palace of the Lady on the hill near [the Haram entry called] the Gate of the Inspector. She was extremely generous to Shaykh Ibrahim and also built in the aforementioned convent, above the tomb of her brother Bihadir, a solid dome which is still there today, as well as an enclosure which surrounds it. This last was built in the year 794 [A.D. 1391-1392]. . . .

There were in the Qalandariyya Convent some people who used to live there. It had substantial income. But not long ago, in 893 [A.D. 1488], the convent fell into ruin and finally collapsed. It has not been rebuilt. It is there that are buried the principal amirs and other important figures who die in Jerusalem. The ground of this Qalandariyya cemetery and the greater part of that of the Mamila is made up of hard rock and it is extremely difficult to cut tombs into it. (Mujir 1876: 198-199)

The initiative for most of these confiscations must have come from the sultans themselves, and on occasion it could be hard-edged indeed, as in this passing remark by Mujir:

In 1262 Sultan Baybars sent troops to destroy the church of Nazareth, one of the most important cult centers of the Christians since it was from this city that the Christian religion came forth. . . . (Mujir 1876: 237)

At times the action had a legal air, as being in violation of the Muslims' contract with their religious minorities that these latter should build no *new* houses of worship. Mujir's account leaves no doubt, however, that what was being done had a great deal of popular support:

During the reign of al-Malik al-Zahir Jaqmaq [A.D. 1438-1453], at the instigation of Shaykh Muhammad al-Mushmar, who belonged to the Sufi order of Shihab al-Din ibn Arslan, the sultan sent [to Jerusalem] a page named Inal-Bay with a royal rescript ordering an inspection of the convents, the destruction of all new constructions built in the one on Sion, and the seizure of the tomb of David from the Christians. As a result the constructions newly built in [the convent of] Sion were destroyed, the tomb of David was taken out of the hands of the Christians, and the bones of the monks buried near the tomb of David were exhumed. These events took place on July 10, 1452, which was a festival day. In this same year there was an outburst against the Christians: the shrine of the Convent of the Syrians was seized, handed over to Shaykh Muhammad al-Mushmar, and converted into a convent. The new buildings at Bethlehem and the Qumama were torn down. The wooden balustrade recently put up in the Qumama was ripped out and taken, amidst shouts of "God is great!" to the Aqsa Mosque. Searches were made in all the convents, and whatever new construction was discovered was destroyed. These events took place toward the end of the life of the sultan: God crowned his deeds by works of devotion and the destruction of impiety. (Mujir 1876: 255-256)

The Christians were not all treated equally, however. The same Sultan Jaqmaq who initiated the pogrom against the Latin Christians on Mount Sion had shortly before expressed his displeasure at the way the Armenians were being treated by his governor in Jerusalem, a displeasure publicly displayed on the walls of the Armenian quarter:

Our master, Sultan al-Malik al-Zahir Abu Saʿid Muhammad Jaqmaq— may his victory be glorious—has posted a decree abolishing the security tax revived by Abu al-Khayr ibn al-Nahhas concerning the Armenian convent in Jerusalem. Sayf al-Din proposed this to his excellency Sharif al-Din al-Ansari. Regarding the repeal of this tax, he demanded that it [the decree] be inscribed on the walls [of the convent]. Dated 854 [A.D. 1450-1451]. Accursed son of an accursed one—and upon him the curse of God—is he who reinstates this tax or renews the injustice. (van Berchem 1922: #100, trans. K. Schaefer)

Mount Sion

The Christian problem in Jerusalem was, for most of the fourteenth and fifteenth centuries, more precisely the Latin problem, and most of its unedifying details unfolded on the slopes of Mount Sion, where we have already seen Sultan Jaqmaq at his furious work. The story properly begins earlier, where Felix Fabri takes it up: [35]

After the driving out of the Latins, the Holy City of Jerusalem remained for many years without any Latin or Roman Christians, for when the Latins left Jerusalem, the Eastern Christians, who are monstrous heretics and schismatics, entered therein in the place of the Latins and became possessed of the churches which the Latins had built. The Latins were not suffered to own any place within the Holy City, nor were they even suffered to enter the Holy Land and the city of Jerusalem without being guarded by Saracens with great precautions, with a safe-conduct and the payment of an exceeding heavy toll. And when they came to Jerusalem, they found no divine service, save that of schismatics and heretics. (Felix Fabri 1893: II, 278)

After the fall of Acre in 1291, Pope Nicholas IV, himself a Franciscan, petitioned the sultan that some Latin clergy be permitted to live in Jerusalem.

The sultan granted this request of the pope and bade him send some clergy, monks, and men of peace to Jerusalem; moreover, he appointed a daily alms to be bestowed on the Christian hospital at Jerusalem. So the pope chose some discreet, learned, and faithful friars from his own order. (Felix Fabri 1893: II, 379)

In 1300 St. Louis, bishop of Toulouse, nephew of St. Louis, king of France, went to his brother, Rupert, king of Apulia, Calabria, Sicily, and Jerusalem, and told him of the sad state of affairs. Rupert went himself to see, as a "simple pilgrim" and with the sultan's safe-conduct. Then he went to Egypt and begged the sultan to give him the church on Mount Sion, the Virgin's Chapel in the Holy Sepulcher, the tomb of St. Mary in Jehoshaphat, and the cave of Nativity in Bethlehem.

King Rupert made a solemn agreement with the sultan about these places, received them from him, and paid the sultan for them 32,000 ducats of ready money. (Felix Fabri 1893: II, 380)

At this point Ludolph von Suchem reports firsthand on what happened and where:

Not far from the Temple of the Lord, on the south side below in the city, is the hill of Sion, which is a little higher than the rest of the ground on which the city stands. It was on this mount that of old stood the City of David, which the Scriptures mention. Upon this Mount Sion, or in this City of David, there once was built [during the period of Crusader control] an exceedingly fair monastery called the Convent of St. Mary on Mount Sion wherein were Canons Regular. . . . In this place also Solomon and David and other kings of Judah were buried, and their sepulchers may be seen at this day. In this monastery there now dwell [Franciscan] Friars Minor who in my time [1336-1341] were amply furnished with the necessaries by Queen Sancea, the wife of King Robert [of Apulia, Calabria, etc., 1309-1343], and there they publicly and devoutly held divine service, except that they were not allowed to preach publicly to Saracens, and they bury their dead without the knowledge of the officers of the city. These brethren were in my time exceedingly prosperous men. Foreign merchants and even Saracens praised them much, for they did good offices to all men. [36] (Ludolph von Suchem 1895: 101-102)

Felix Fabri tells much the same story:

All kings send their alms to them [the Franciscan friars] year by year, some five hundred and some four hundred ducats, some more, some less, according to their custom, or according to the sincerity and depth of their affection for the Holy Land. Many alms likewise are bestowed upon them daily by pilgrims, and by those who receive the ensigns of knighthood in the Lord's sepulcher. And all of these they need, for they gather in no alms from the Easterners, neither from the infidels, nor from the Christians, but get all their means of living from the Westerns. (Felix Fabri 1893: II, 382)

Thus the Franciscans came into legal possession, by actual ownership of the property, of the Church of the Cenacle, or Upper Room, on Mount Sion, and the superior of the Franciscan community on Mount Sion was officially constituted by the pope as "Guardian of Mount Sion," with wide powers over all the Latin Christians in the East.[37] Over the following years the dangers implicit in their situation became clear. In 1365, for example, the Latins on Cyprus attacked Alexandria, and the sultan responded by arresting the Franciscans on Mount Sion, carrying them to Damascus and executing them there. A peace was eventually patched, and a new band of Friars was sent out to replace their murdered brethren, but the Jerusalem Franciscans had become in effect hostage pawns in the ongoing hostilities between the sultanate and the European powers.

The Tomb of David

The next issue was over the Tomb of David, identified at least since Crusader times with a specific place on Mount Sion. It was, as Felix Fabri explains, part of the Franciscans' original purchase on Sion:

The brethren of Mount Sion once counted this place [David's tomb] among those belonging to their convent, and indeed it is part of the Church of Sion, for it is within the same walls, at the head of the choir. . . . The Jews many times begged the sultans to give them that place, that they may make an oratory of it, and they always refused it to them. So at last the sultan [Barsbay, A.D. 1422-1437] inquired wherefore this place was holy. When he was told that David and other kings of Jerusalem of his seed were buried there, he said: "We Saracens also count David as holy, even as the Christians and Jews do, and we believe the Bible as they do. Wherefore, neither the Christians nor the Jews shall have that place, but we will take it for ourselves." He thereupon came to Jerusalem and blocked up the door by which one entered that chapel from inside the monastery, desecrated the chapel, turned out Christ's altars, broke the carved images, blotted out the paintings, and fitted it for the worship of the most abominable Muhammad. . . . And because the place above it, the vaulted roof of the chapel, belonged to the Christians and the brethren, and a great and costly chapel had been founded there by the king of France . . . the sultan caused this chapel also to be destroyed, its vault to be thrown down, and its door blocked, that the Christians might not walk about upon the vaulted roof of the mosque. So the brethren have lost those two precious holy places, through the eagerness of the Jews to possess the lower place [the tomb proper], for which they are

*pleading with the sultan even at this day, and promise to give many thou-
sand talents of silver for it.* [38]

According to Felix, the Jews' interest flowed not from any genuine reverence for David's tomb but from the belief that there was treasure buried
there. At times, he assures us, witchcraft and magic arts were also practiced
there at night. His own curiosity about this famous tomb, now a Muslim
shrine to "the most abominable Muhammad," was obviously piqued. He
managed to sneak inside at night because the lock was broken, but he
found only disappointment:

*The chapel is a long one, with a vaulted roof, and has two windows on
its eastern side and a marble tomb on the north side. The paved floor is
covered with mats. Two lamps hang in it, and there is no altar, no painting, no carved work, only bare whitewashed walls. So also are all Saracen
mosques, empty and void. (Felix Fabri 1893: I, 303-304)*

The Instability of Fortune

There followed in 1453 Jaqmaq's decision to overturn the entire Christian
enterprise on Sion, followed in turn by a period of relative benevolence
during the sultanate of Qa'it Bay (A.D. 1468-1496). Already noted as a
generous patron of Islamic institutions in Jerusalem, Qa'it Bay was also,
as it turned out, a friend of the Friars as well. How that came about is
described by Francesco Suriano, a Jerusalem Franciscan who completed
the first draft of his *Treatise on the Holy Land*, from which this account is
taken, in 1485.

*About 1470, during the guardianship of Friar Francis of Piacenza, at one
time court commissary, the sultan confined as a rebel in Jerusalem an Amir
of a Thousand named Qa'it Bay, who later became sultan and ruled
thirty-eight years, and with him was confined a colleague, who was likewise an Amir of a Thousand, named Amir Isbeq. . . . Since those so confined cannot ride, nor take with them servants, nor go farther from the
city than one mile, nor enter a Muslim house, all under pain of death, . . .
they used to come to Mount Sion for recreation. The guardian, a shrewd
man, knowing too well that the fortune of this unhappy world, lucky or
unlucky as it may be, is not stable but turns as the wheel, and for this
these men could easily return to favor with the sultan, he received them
not as prisoners but as they were, lords. Amir Isbeq [in particular], liking
above all the vegetables and omelettes made by the Friars, came with great
eagerness to the place. . . . In my time the lord of Damascus was confined
in Jerusalem; fascinated by these vegetables, he sent one day for the Friars*

and made them stay with his ladies one day to show them how to cook these vegetables. . . .

To resume our subject, five years later their innocence having been proven, these lords won greater grace with the sultan than formerly. Shortly thereafter, the sultan died and was succeeded by Qa'it Bay, one of these two prisoners, and he made Isbeq, his fellow in misfortune, grand lord of Cairo.

Having entered into this office, the said guardian went to Cairo to visit them. With what joy he was received I cannot relate, as his companions told me. And as long as he lived, whenever the Friars presented themselves, they were given precedence at court. Amir Isbeq after a friendly conversation said to the guardian: "I am much obliged to you, for in my period of anguish and tribulation you have shown me great and cordial kindness. Now I wish to become your protector and defender, only you ask the sultan for the singular privilege of being my vassals and slaves, then you may rest secure." The sultan was content to recommend us cordially to him as his vassals and slaves. And from then on, all the Saracens were afraid to molest us, and he was a sorry man who tried it. (Suriano 1949: 126-127)

This connection worked admirably on an official level. The Friars regained and rebuilt the Church of the Cenacle and made extensive repairs in Bethlehem, but on Mount Sion itself, where the Friars were surrounded by a Muslim population little given to observing official guarantees of protection, the atmosphere was wary, to say the least, as Felix Fabri describes it in 1480:

The precincts of the convent of Mount Sion are very little. Yet albeit the house is small, twenty-four brethren dwell together therein, serving the Lord in a life spent under rule. Because of the insults and rage of the infidels, they have an iron door and beside the same fierce dogs, savage with strangers, and by their barking betray those who come thither to do any mischief, whether by day or by night. (Felix Fabri 1893: I, 340)

Dogs barking savagely into the night on Mount Sion. For some at least, the Holy City had turned into a grim and indeed a deadly abode, but one to which pilgrims and visitors continued to come in pursuit of the elusive "blessings" that all of them, Christians in England, Muslims in Bukhara and Samarqand, Jews in Poland and France, knew must dwell in that holy place:

. . . I left my family, I forsook my house [wrote the elderly Nachmanides in 1267]. There with my sons and daughters, and with the sweet and dear children whom I have brought up on my knees, I left also my soul. My

heart and eyes will dwell with them forever. . . . But the loss of all else which delighted my eyes is compensated by my present joy of a day passed within thy courts, O Jerusalem! visiting the ruins of the Temple and crying over the ruined sanctuary; where it is granted to me to caress thy stones, to fondle thy dust, and to weep over thy ruins. I wept bitterly, but I found joy in my tears. I tore my garments, but I felt solace in it. (Kobler 1978: I, 227)

Piety and Polemic:
The Crusader Legacy in the
Holy City

But since Christians and Saracens cannot agree about this matter, un-
happy Jerusalem has suffered, doth now suffer, and will hereafter suf-
fer sieges, castings down, destructions, and terrors beyond any other
city in the world.
—Felix Fabri

THE PLACE is Ramle, the Muslim administrative center for Palestine, in
a hospice maintained there for Christian pilgrims en route to the Holy
City of Jerusalem. The year is probably A.D. 1480.

In his sermon, [the Franciscan father guardian] delivered to the pilgrims
certain articles wherein were contained the rules and method of seeing the
holy places which they ought to observe while dwelling among the Sara-
cens and infidels in the Holy Land, lest they should run into danger
through ignorance.

The father guardian, the papally appointed and Muslim certified protector
of all Latin pilgrims in the Holy Land, lived in a harsh world of experience—he and the few other Franciscans in residence in Jerusalem were
effectively hostages for the behavior of the collection of saints and sinners,
of fools, knaves, and innocents who stood before him in Ramle awaiting
his instruction. He was nothing if not thorough, and his instructions to
those travellers, reported by one of their number, the Dominican Felix
Fabri of Ulm, is for us the single best introduction to what it was like
being on Christian pilgrimage in the medieval Holy Land under Mamluk
sovereignty:

Instructions to Pilgrims

FIRST ARTICLE. Should any pilgrims come thither without express leave
from the pope, and have thereby incurred the pope's sentence of excom-
munication, such persons must present themselves to the father guardian
after Mass, and he himself would absolve them from their guilt by virtue
of the Apostolic authority committed to him. . . . The cause of this excom-
munication is that after the Christians were driven from out of the Holy
Land some bad Christians remained behind therein, and associated them-

selves with Saracens, swearing allegiance to them. . . . Some also of those who left that country returned thither again to these men and became their subjects, and afterwards sailed to Christian lands and brought from thence ironwork and arms whereof the Easterners were in need. Seeing this, the pope excommunicated all of those who stayed behind in the Holy Land with the Saracens or made common cause with them. He also excommunicated those who carried arms and other needful things to them. Moreover, he excommunicated the land itself, so that whosoever should enter it without his leave might be *anathema*, seeing that he could not dwell therein without consorting with the infidels and heretics. [1]

SECOND ARTICLE. No pilgrim ought to wander alone about the holy places without a Saracen guide, because this is dangerous and unsafe. . . .

THIRD ARTICLE. The pilgrim should beware of stepping over the sepulchers of the Saracens, because they are greatly vexed when they see this done . . . because they believe that our passing over them torments and disturbs the dead.

FOURTH ARTICLE. Should any pilgrim be struck by a Saracen, however unjustly, he must not return the blow, but must complain of him that struck him to the guardian or the dragoman . . . who will see it righted if they are able; if not, seeing that young men are sometimes insolent and stiff-necked, the pilgrims must bear it with patience for the glory of God and their own greater merit.

FIFTH ARTICLE. Let the pilgrim beware of chipping off fragments from the Holy Sepulcher and from the buildings at other places and spoiling the hewn stones thereof, because this is forbidden under pain of excommunication.

SIXTH ARTICLE. Pilgrims of noble birth must not deface walls by drawing their coats-of-arms thereon or by writing their names or by fixing upon the walls papers on which their arms are painted, or by scratching columns and marble slabs or boring holes in them with iron tools to make marks of their having visited them; for such conduct gives great offence to the Saracens and they think those who have done so are fools.

SEVENTH ARTICLE. The pilgrims must proceed to visit the holy places in an orderly manner, without disorder or disagreements, and one must not try to outrun another . . . because the devotion of many is hindered thereby.

EIGHTH ARTICLE. Pilgrims must beware of laughing together as they walk about Jerusalem to see the holy places, but they must be grave and devout, both on account of the holy places and of the example they afford to the infidels, and also lest the latter should suspect that we are laughing at them, which annoys them exceedingly. They are always suspicious about laughter and merriment among pilgrims.

NINTH ARTICLE. Let the pilgrim beware above all of jesting with or laughing at the Saracen boys or men whom they may meet, because how-ever well meant this conduct may be, yet much mischief arises from it. . . .

TENTH ARTICLE. Let the pilgrims beware of gazing upon any women whom they may meet, because all Saracens are exceedingly jealous, and the pilgrim may in ignorance run himself into danger through the fury of some jealous husband.

ELEVENTH ARTICLE. Should any woman beckon to a pilgrim or invite him by signs to enter a house, let him on no account do so, because the woman does this treacherously at the instigation of some in order that the Christian when he enters may be robbed or perhaps slain. . . .

TWELFTH ARTICLE. Let every pilgrim beware of giving a Saracen wine when he asks for a drink, whether on the roadside or elsewhere, because straightway after one single draught thereof he becomes mad, and the first man he attacks is the pilgrim who gave it to him.

THIRTEENTH ARTICLE. Let the pilgrim keep the ass which he first re-ceived from his driver, and let him not change it or exchange it with another, save with the consent of the driver.

FOURTEENTH ARTICLE. Let pilgrims of noble birth beware of revealing their nobility in the presence of Saracens, because it is imprudent to act so for many reasons.

FIFTEENTH ARTICLE. Let no pilgrim put upon his head white turbans or wind white cloths or napkins about his head when there are Saracens present, because they consider themselves alone to be privileged to do this, and it is a sign by which they are distinguished from other nations. Nei-ther will they endure to see Christians clad in white garments, which is nevertheless contrary to the teaching of their Alcoran, wherein Christians are often called "white-robed" . . . as we read in the translation of the Alcoran by Nicolas Cusa. . . .

SIXTEENTH ARTICLE. No pilgrim may wear knives or anything else slung about him, lest they be torn from him and carried off, nor may he bear any arms whatsoever.

SEVENTEENTH ARTICLE. Should any pilgrim form a friendship with any Saracen, he must beware of trusting him too far, for they are treacherous; and he must especially beware of laying his hand on his beard in jest, or touching his turban, even with a light touch and in jest, for this thing is a disgrace among them and all jests are at once forgotten thereat, and they grow angry. . . .

EIGHTEENTH ARTICLE. Let every pilgrim carefully guard his own prop-erty, and never leave it lying about in any place where Saracens are, other-wise it will straightway vanish, whatever it may be.

NINETEENTH ARTICLE. If any pilgrim has a bottle of wine and wishes to drink, let him hide his bottle and drink secretly if Saracens are present. . . . For, because the drinking of wine is forbidden to them, they envy us when they see us drink, and if they can, they molest those who drink.

TWENTIETH ARTICLE. Let no Christian have money dealings with a Saracen except in such sort that he knows he cannot be cheated; for they strive to cheat us, and believe they are serving God by deceiving and cheating us. And, above all, let the pilgrim beware of German Jews and be on his guard against them, for their whole object in life is to cheat us and rob us of our money. Let him also beware of Eastern Christians when he has dealings with them, for they have no conscience, less even than the Jews and Saracens, and will cheat pilgrims if they can.

TWENTY-FIRST ARTICLE. When pilgrims make covenants with Saracens, let them not dispute with them, nor swear at them, nor become angry at them; for they know that their things are contrary to the Christian religion, and when they see anything of this sort they straightway cry out "O thou bad Christian!" for all of them can say this in Italian or German. . . .

TWENTY-SECOND ARTICLE. Let the pilgrim beware of entering mosques, that is, Saracen temples and oratories, because if he be found therein, he will in no case escape unharmed, even should he escape with his life. . . .

TWENTY-THIRD ARTICLE. Let the pilgrim especially beware of laughing to scorn Saracens who are praying and practicing the postures required of their faith, because they cannot bear this at all. For they themselves refrain from molesting or laughing at us when we are at our prayers.

TWENTY-FOURTH ARTICLE. If a pilgrim be detained longer than he wishes at Ramle or elsewhere, let him endure it with patience and not think that it is the fault of the father guardian, but of the Saracens, who do what they please in these matters, not what is convenient to us.

TWENTY-FIFTH ARTICLE. Pilgrims must not begrudge to pay money to save themselves from the many annoyances which beset them, but when money has to be paid they must give it straightway without grumbling. . . .

TWENTY-SIXTH ARTICLE. The pilgrims must give something to the keeper of the hospice in which we stand [in Ramle], to the end that the house may be repaired and raised from its ruins.

TWENTY-SEVENTH ARTICLE. The pilgrims must show respect to the poor convent of the brethren of Mount Sion in Jerusalem, by whose help pilgrims are conducted into and out of the Holy Land and must by their alms cherish this convent and help the brethren thereof, who dwell there among the infidels for the comfort of the pilgrims. . . . (Felix Fabri 1893: I, 248-254)

In going up to Jerusalem, then, the Latin Christian was entering unarmed into what was quite literally a war zone. He was there by sufferance: in the first place of the pope, by whom a special pilgrimage license had to be issued in order to discourage trade in war contraband with the Muslim countries, as Felix explains;[2] and in the second place, of both the Mamluk sovereigns and, more importantly and unpredictably, the Muslim population of that land. Neither the Ayyubid nor the Mamluk sultans banned pilgrimage; indeed, all the evidence points to an *increase* in pilgrimage as a result of the Crusades and the thickening commercial ties that seem to be the only permanent result of those unhappy wars.[3] But the good will of the local population, who had been taught by both experience and the increasingly shrill drumbeat of Muslim propaganda to despise these dangerous Christians, could not be guaranteed. Their behavior must then be extremely circumspect, as the father guardian instructed the newly arrived pilgrims, and beyond that they could only hope for the best.

On the Road

Most of the pilgrims arrived by sea on Venetian galleys and disembarked at Jaffa. It must have become immediately apparent to Felix Fabri and his company, even before the father guardian gave his instruction a few days later, that this was a serious and possibly dangerous enterprise.

As soon as we trod the holy land beneath our feet, we cast ourselves down upon our faces and kissed the sacred earth with great devotion. . . . We went up to higher ground. Above us stood the father guardian of Mount Sion and his brethren, together with the governors of the land, and elders of the Saracens and the Moors, and with a scribe. And they so ranged themselves on either side that the pilgrims must needs pass through the midst of them; nor could two pilgrims pass through them together, but one after another. Nor would they let us pass in a continuous stream, but they laid hold of each man, looked at him narrowly, and demanded his own name and the name of his father, both of which names the scribe wrote down in his documents. . . . [Later, still at Jaffa] our captains stood with some Saracens at this narrow way, holding lights, both lanterns and torches, and asked each pilgrim, one after another, his name and his father's name, and sought for it in the schedule they had drawn up when we disembarked from the ship. When they found the pilgrim's name they allowed him to go down to the asses who stood in a crowd down below near the sea [and continue on the trip]. (Felix Fabri 1893: I, 222-223, 240)

The pilgrims had to bring their own supplies and clothing and, most importantly, enough money to see them through their four- or five-month stay—the pilgrims normally arrived in the late fall and departed promptly after Easter—or to buy them out of whatever scrapes they might get themselves into, with enough left over for an alms for the guardians of the holy places. It was all in all an expensive enterprise,[4] particularly due to the fees that were levied not only for entry into the holy places but also as protection dues along the roads, the notorious *khafara*, or caphars:

Then you return to Jerusalem, and then from Jerusalem to Jaffa, and from Jaffa by sea to Cyprus. But if you wish to go to the noble city of Damascus, it is six days' journey and much tribute to be paid, as you shall hear.

As you set out from Jericho to go to Damascus, you all the time follow a northeasterly direction. Eight miles from Jericho you reach a building, and there you pay a tribute of half a dirham a head. Proceeding over the plain a mile distant from the river Jordan, you find after ten miles, near the bridge over the river [Jisr al-Mujamiah] a house on a hill; and there are Saracens there who collect one dirham a person. One mile past the bridge you pay another dirham. The next day you pass the foot of a big mountain where there is a large stream [the Yarmuk], and there you pay half a dirham. Climbing this mountain, which is very difficult and a journey of two miles, you continue on until you come to a beautiful big city called Zelona. At the entrance to this city there is a strong fortress in the form of a cross, which the Christians built. The city is very prosperous, and there you lodge the night and in tribute pay one dirham. The next day you pass some big mountains, which takes till noon, and then you continue through plains which stretch as far as Damascus. The next night you lodge at an inn open to the sky. The next day you meet a city almost in ruins [Sanamayn], and there you pay, each person, six dirhams. The sixth day you reach a beautiful bridge [near Kiswe] six miles from Damascus, and in that place you pay three dirhams a head. And the next day you enter Damascus, a noble and royal city. The city is very large and not to be compared to any other, except that I have often heard the French say that there are more people in Damascus than in Paris. (Niccolo of Poggibonsi 1945: 76)

On the road or in the city, the pilgrim lodged at some kind of hospice. The first one encountered by Felix Fabri in 1480 was a rather celebrated inn kept by and for Christians at Ramle:

When we were come into the city [of Ramle], at no great distance from the gate, we came to a house with a low and narrow door; . . . within there was a large and beautiful court, with many chambers and vaulted rooms of various kinds, and a fountain full of good and wholesome water. This house was bought long ago by Philip, duke of Burgundy, of blessed memory, for the use of pilgrims and was entrusted by him to the charge of the Brethren of Mount Sion; wherefore it is called the pilgrims' hospice. The Brethren of Mount Sion lease it to an Eastern Christian who dwells therein. (Felix Fabri 1893: I, 246-247)

There were not in Palestine many such places reserved entirely for Christians, as one might suppose, and the pilgrim outside of Jerusalem was more likely to have experience of the khan type of accommodation described by Ibn Battuta in A.D. 1335, though this one had a more official function than most: [5]

At each of these post stations [between Egypt and Syria] there is a funduq, which they call a khan, where travellers alight from their beasts, and outside of each khan there is a public watering place and a shop at which the traveller may buy what he requires for himself and his beast. . . . The place is called qatya, where the poll-tax is collected from the merchants, their goods are examined, and their baggage most rigorously searched. There are government offices here, with officers, clerks, and notaries, and its daily revenue is a thousand gold dinars. No one may pass this place in the direction of Syria[-Palestine] without a passport from Egypt, nor into Egypt without a passport from Syria, as a means of protection for a person's property and of precaution against spies from [Mongol] Iraq. This road is under the guarantee of the bedouin. (Ibn Battuta 1959-1962: 71-72)

The last sentence means to say that the bedouin on the road between Egypt and Palestine have been paid, or bought off, not to attack travellers. This was a major public way, but on the road from Jaffa to Ramle and thence to Jerusalem only unarmed Christian pilgrims passed by, and neither the government nor the bedouin themselves showed much interest in guaranteeing their safety. [6] Early and late, in the sixteenth as well as the sixth century, the greatest threat to the traveller on the road were these nomads, "a naked, miserable, bestial, wandering people, who alone can dwell in the desert which is uninhabitable to all others, attack, harry, and conquer all men alike, even to the king himself, the most puissant sultan of Egypt," as Felix Fabri explains.

The Arabs who at that time were spread abroad throughout many parts of the Holy Land thrice came to meet us [when a medieval author writes "Arabs" in place of "Saracen" he is usually speaking of bedouin]; but seeing that we were well protected by armed defenders, they offered no violence with either stones or cold steel, but secretly joined our host by the side of the pilgrims, and tried to steal scrips, clothes, and the like; for they knew that we were unarmed, and therefore they ran round about us, and snatched up whatever the pilgrims let fall, or did not guard carefully.

Had we not travelled with so great a force, they would have fallen upon us and beaten us with stones, sticks, and staves, as often befalls pilgrims between Jaffa and Ramle. . . . The infidels will not endure that the Christians should enter their cities and towns riding on beasts, unless they come in the dark; by daylight they cannot do so. They consider this city of Rama [Ramle] to be of especial dignity beyond all others because their qadi, that is, their bishop, dwells therein, wherefore they keep watch that no Christian enters it save on foot. (Felix Fabri 1893: I, 245-246)

In the City

Not many pilgrims of that era were likely to complain about having to enter a city on foot, though it became more of an issue later, as we shall see. Additional troubles lay beyond the city gate. The Franciscan friar Niccolo of Poggibonsi had just entered Jerusalem in 1346:

On being presented to the amir of Jerusalem, we caused our interpreter to say, when we were asked for the sultan's tribute, that we were poor, that we had no money, and that as Friars on Mount Sion we carried neither gold nor silver. Because of these words, the amir had our interpreter beaten on the spot. When I saw him so beaten, I expected to have my own share along with him, and in the greatest fear I stood in the corner among those accursed men who held me; and I thought within myself that I was going to die. For one Saracen held me by one arm and another by the other, and they watched the hands of the amir for the signal "Hit him!" But when the beating was finished . . . the interpreter said to us Friars: "I have been caned in your place because I said you had no money to pay. Keep in mind that you will either have to pay or be beaten to death."

Then the amir had me searched, and in truth I could not stand up straight for fear. He asked me if I had any money to pay the tribute, and I replied through the interpreter that I had none but that I would get it for him this same day for sure. Then the amir spoke to the kavasses, and they took hold of me by the arms as if they wished to beat me, and once again fear seized me. Then without relaxing their grip they took us through Jerusalem. I asked the interpreter where they were taking us, and he replied that they were leading us off to prison. That seemed only an increase in evil to me. And while we were being taken through Jerusalem as prisoners, I met a Christian of Cyprus to whom I had delivered a letter, and when he saw me under arrest, asked me what the problem was. I told him of the whole affair, and he had me brought back to the amir and promised to pay for us. Later we were freed, and then we went to our

The eclectic Ottoman fountain facing the Gate of the Chain of the Haram and described by Clermont-Ganneau (pp. 403-404 of this book).

Above and *top of facing page*, Mamluk buildings along the Bab al-Hadid Street leading into the Haram.

Facing page, bottom left and right, entwined columns from Crusader times reused in the doorway of the Nahwiyya on the Haram platform, and a detail of the reused Crusader capitals from the right side of the door.

Above, nineteenth-century engraving of the northwest corner of the Haram, with the Ghawanima minaret. *Top of facing page*, Mamluk-endowed and -built law schools along the northern side of the Haram. The modern building at the upper left is on the site of Herod's Fortress Antonia. *Below*, the steps in the center provide direct access to the Haram from a law school on its northern side; an interior prayer niche architecturally extruded into the Haram is visible at the upper left.

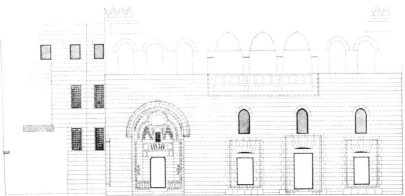

Top of facing page, framing arches atop the steps leading up to the Dome of the Rock platform. *Above left*, the fountain of Qa'it Bay, and *above right*, the pulpit of Burhan al-Din, both on the Haram.

Bottom of facing page, elevation of the Ashrafiyya on the western side of the Haram, and *near left*, the law school's Haram portal.

Above, the Golden Gate from the west, looking from the Haram toward the Mount of Olives behind. *Below*, the sealed Golden Gate from the outside. The graves in the foreground are Muslim.

place on Mount Sion where we lived with those holy Friars. We lost no time in paying the sultan's tribute, which was seventy-two dirhams, which in our money amounts to about four florins a head. (Niccolo of Poggi-bonsi 1945: 8)

At a somewhat later era a visitor subjected to this kind of treatment, particularly if he was not a cleric, would immediately attempt to signal the French consul in Acre or Jaffa. [7] But in the fourteenth and fifteenth centuries he was expected to turn to his official dragoman or guide. This person was not a guide in the sense that he showed sites, though outside of Jerusalem he might lead the visitor to them; rather he was ombudsman. The traveller's official connection to his Muslim environment, government and private, formal and informal, in matters of both life and death, was this franchised official known as the "calinus":

The hospitals and pilgrims have two masters, an upper and a lower. The first is called "sabathytanco," or upper calinus, and the other "elphahallo" [Al-Pahlawan], the lower calinus, that is to say, the master of the hospital and the master of the pilgrims. Both of these calini are called dragomans, that is to say, protectors, conductors, or guardians of the Christian pilgrims. Indeed, in every city there are some men to whom the sultan grants the privilege of guiding Christians through the land and defending them from wrong, which men are officers of the government, having powers granted them by the court of the lord sultan, and are called dragomans. In like manner also the Jews have their own dragomans or calini. [8] (Felix Fabri 1893: II, 105)

The situation became far more complex, of course, if one intended to continue on from Jerusalem, as many of the pilgrims did, and navigate across the Sinai to the Mountain of Moses, and thence to Cairo:

For the advice of others, who like myself may wish to visit this country, I shall say that the custom is to treat with the chief interpreter of Jerusalem, who receives a tax for the Sultan and one for himself, and then sends to inform the interpreter at Gaza, who in his turn negotiates a passage with the Arabians of the [Sinai] desert. These Arabs enjoy the right of conducting pilgrims, and as they are not always under due subjection to the sultan, their camels must be used, which they let to hire at ten ducats a head. The Saracen who at this time held the office of chief interpreter was called "nanchardin." Having received an answer from the Arabs, he called us together before the chapel which is at the entrance and on the left of the Holy Sepulcher; he there took down in writing our ages, names, surnames, and very particular descriptions of our persons, and sent a duplicate of this to the chief interpreter at Cairo. These precautions are taken for the security of travellers and to prevent the Arabs from detaining any of them,; but I am persuaded that it is done likewise through mistrust, and through fear of some exchange or substitution that may make them lose the tribute money. . . . (Bertrandon de la Brocquière 1848: 288)

Lodgings

Inside Jerusalem the European visitor was not offered a choice of lodgings. All the pilgrims were the responsibility of the Franciscan guardian, and they were boarded in either of two places, the laymen in the remains of the Crusader Hospital of St. John across from the Holy Sepulcher, and the clerics on Mount Sion with the Franciscan community there:

When we had finished these our prayers, the guides led us out of the courtyard or square of the Holy Sepulcher, and crossing the road in front of the square, we went up into the Hospital of St. John, which is a large vaulted building, squalid and ruinous. It is only part of the ancient hospital, and is a place like the great refectories of large monasteries where many monks dwell. . . . [The pilgrims settle in there.] Now the father guardian of Mount Sion sent two brethren to the hospital and ordered them to bring all persons in holy orders to Mount Sion: for it is the custom that all persons in orders shall dwell with the Minorite friars on Mount Sion. (Felix Fabri 1893: I, 286-287)

This great Crusader enterprise of the Hospital had fallen on evil days. When the Jewish visitor Jacob of Verona was in Jerusalem, he noted "an ancient building called Solomon's Palace. In the former days, when the uncircumcised [Christians] were in possession, this building was appointed to receive the sick of the holy city. Today a market of considerable importance is held there." That was in 1334, and the entire area is a market today, though its name, the Muristan, still carries some trace of its past as a hospice and hospital. That it survived at all in the fourteenth century was a tribute to a wealthy Christian noblewoman of Sicily, the same already noted in Chapter Ten above as a benefactor of the Franciscans on Mount Sion:

Near the Church of the Holy Sepulcher once dwelt the Brethren of St. John of Jerusalem and their residence is now the common hospital for pilgrims. This hospital is so great that one thousand men can easily live in it and can have everything they want for the buying. It is the custom in this residence or hospital that every pilgrim should pay two Venetian denarii for the use of the hospital. If he stays there for a year, he pays no more; if he stays for only one day, he pays no less. In my day there dwelt

*in this residence or hospital a matron named Margaret of Sicily, who had
a brother named Nicolas who was a canon of the Holy Sepulcher. This
Margaret was of great use and service there, and to my certain knowledge
suffered much misery and trouble for the love of the Christians, and was
always viewed by the sultan with special favor because of her usefulness.
(Ludolph von Suchem 1895: 106-107)*

By the fourteenth and fifteenth centuries pilgrimage had become a flourishing business, not only for the commercial carriers who brought the
visitors to the Holy Land but for the guides, interpreters, and merchants
who did business with them once they arrived, and for the officials of the
Mamluk kingdom who collected tribute, entry fees, and protection money.
The visitors were supplied with food from mobile bazaars that followed
them wherever they collected in groups. These entrepreneurs appear to
have usually been Eastern Christians, as were the translators.[9] The Franciscans themselves served as guides to the holy places within Jerusalem—
where their regular circuit around the city was already developing into the
"Way of the Cross"—and one used whoever was available in a place like
Nazareth or Cana or Bethlehem.[10] Donkeys and drivers had to be hired;
the bedouin had to be bought off. Pilgrimage to Jerusalem had become,
quite simply, a form of tourism, whether one comes to that judgment
through the attitudes of the visitors themselves or by contemplating the
variety of service industries springing up in their wake.[11]

The Holy Sepulcher

Attitudes, numbers, religious and political conditions might change, but
the Church of the Holy Sepulcher continued to be the focus and goal of
Christian pilgrimage to the Holy Land, as it had been since the Bordeaux
pilgrim and Egeria testified to the Constantinian monuments there. The
church of Constantine was long gone, of course, and what the pilgrim of
the fourteenth or fifteenth century saw was a Crusader edifice: a rotunda
over the tomb, extended eastward by a choir and apse; beneath it, the
chapel of Helena's discovery of the cross; and attached to it on the south,
the two-storey chapel of Calvary, with an entry from within and another
built by the Crusaders into the southern courtyard which from that day
to this has served as the main entrance into the church. Outside stood
Muslim guards and dues collectors:

*Now as soon as all the Saracen lords who had to do with the opening of
the church were present at the door of that holy temple, they took their
places gravely and seriously. Before the door on either side thereof great*

stones of polished marble had been placed for benches, upon which these men sat with their faces turned away. They were men of fine presence, well stricken in years, handsome, wearing long beards, and of solemn manners, dressed in linen clothes and with their heads wrapped round and round with countless folds of very fine linen. [The Muslims open the door and let the Christian pilgrims in, two by two.] We went by them with shame and blushing, because it is a great confusion that Christ's faithful worshippers should be let into Christ's church by Christ's blasphemers; and they let in whom they pleased and kept out whom they pleased; for they drove away from the church doors with blows from their staves and fists many Christians of other rites who wanted to come in together with us. (Felix Fabri 1893: I, 341)

The pilgrims were then locked in. Felix was enough of a man of the spirit to be able to respond in print with "Oh how joyous an imprisonment!" but the reaction on the spot must have been somewhat less patient, as Ibn Battuta noticed when he was there in 1335, about a century and a half before the Dominican:

At Jerusalem there is another venerated church [the Holy Sepulcher] to which the Christians come on pilgrimages. This is the church about which they lie and are persuaded that it contains the grave of Jesus—upon whom be peace. All who come on pilgrimage to it are liable to a stipulated tax to the Muslims as well as various humiliations, which they suffer very unwillingly. (Ibn Battuta 1959-1962: 79-80)

Not only were the outer doors of the church guarded; there were guards, and fees, at the Holy Sepulcher edicule itself:

I want to relate how this chapel [of the tomb of Jesus] is guarded, that is to say, locked. As I said, it has three doors. Two are sealed and locked so that they never open; the other door, to the east, opens and is well furnished with key and seal, after our fashion. And these keys and seals are held by Saracens, different from the ones who hold the keys to the door of the church. They open the chapel of the Holy Sepulcher and allow one to stand within for the space of three Our Fathers. Then they throw him out and lock the door again. And if you wish to lease the keys from the Saracen who holds them, you agree on a sum of money and he leaves the door open for you, and if you have paid you can stay there all day and all night, since the Saracens leave the church and lock the door behind them. And the next day the Saracens return and open the door and you can continue on the rest of your pilgrimage stops. (Niccolo of Poggibonsi 1945: 16)

438

Moreover, even with a fee, entry into the church was limited to certain days of the year, and the Christians who paid and entered at those times found the door locked behind them. They were thus constrained to spend the next twenty-four hours in the church, whether they wished to or not. This was the way it was arranged about 1350:

All these (above-mentioned) holy places are enclosed within this church, and the church is like a palace prepared for the various needs of pilgrims and of those locked up in it. For pilgrims who visit it are locked up inside from the first hour of one day till the same hour of the following day and can inspect everything to their hearts' content. But twice a year, that is, from Good Friday to Easter Monday and from the eve of the Feast of the Invention of the Cross till the day after it, the Christians who dwell (in the city) are let into the church without charge and are locked in. Then one finds shops in the church where sundry things and foodstuffs are sold, even as in this country they do at markets and fairs, and on that occasion one hears talk and songs in various tongues. Each nation has its own special place for holding the divine service according to its own rite, and the Latins have the place where Christ appeared to Mary Magdalen in the likeness of a gardener. (Ludolph von Suchem 1895: 106)

Mixed Company

What chiefly bothered Felix Fabri about this arrangement was that it was so indiscriminate: the Muslims let *all* the Christians who paid come in, even the Eastern heretics and schismatics whose "yells and strange outcries . . . fill the church all night long with their discordant clamor" and who were probably responsible as well for the "extraordinary number of fleas" which Felix thought were being fed by the guardians of the church.

At the present day, if there were to come any sect polluted with so atrocious a heresy that none of those already in that holy church would be willing to admit it to their services, yet the sultan would assign the same sect a choir and an abiding place of its own in the church. . . . There is no one who is shut out, no one turned away; whoever pays the Saracens the church fee, five ducats for entrance, he enters in, however unclean he may be. They will not open the church to any Christian without payment of the five ducats and in this regard they do not spare even the Brethren of Mount Sion, whom they will not admit without payment of this fee save at the season when pilgrims visit Jerusalem, with whom they pass in gratis. At the time when the pilgrims are away from Jerusalem, the brethren are not able to change the guardians of the church [the three Franciscans living inside], but those who are sent in thither in charge of pilgrims and are deputed to be guardians of the Holy Sepulcher, remain there unrelieved till the arrival of next season's pilgrims.

How different, Felix could not help but reflect, from the glorious days when the Latin Crusaders held Jerusalem:

... then Catholic Christians were able to enter it free, at any hour, nor was any heretic or schismatic admitted into that church, either free or for a price. But since the Lord's sepulcher has been taken by the enemy, the pilgrims are become prisoners, so that they can do nothing in Jerusalem save what the Saracens please. (Felix Fabri 1893: I, 428-429)

Among those "guardians" who lived in the church and who in effect maintained the Christians' rights of ownership was Niccolo of Poggibonsi:

I have described all the conditions and sights connected with the holy church of Jerusalem, which God gave me the grace to visit and understand, and I lived in that church a full four months. In it there are always men of our order living, that is, the Friars Minor. I spent Palm Sunday [March 25, 1347] there. The reason I had not visited it before was that I had resolved that if I could help it, the Saracens would make no more profit from me, even though I had already paid them a hefty price in tribute. Another reason is that someone who does pay the tribute cannot stay in the church more than one day and one night, as I described above, and it did not appear to my soul that it would be satisfied by one day and one night. Another reason is that I had resolved to stay there for Good Friday and the glorious Easter in order to see all the proceedings, and also to keep the Lenten fast and visit all the Holy Places in order. (Niccolo of Poggibonsi 1945: 22-23)

There were three Franciscans assigned to this duty of living in the church, and each of the other Christian groups that claimed some part of the same property had a similar contingent there to maintain its rights. They had to be fed and supplied from the outside, as Ludolph von Suchem explains, with an audible aside on the Muslims' view of the matter:

There dwell in the Church of the Holy Sepulcher ancient Georgians who have the key to the chapel of the tomb. Food, alms, candles, and oil for lamps to burn round about the holy tomb are given to them by pilgrims through a little window in the south door of the church. And if this should fail, [the tomb] remains without any light whatsoever and it is altogether without respect or honor, for the Saracens have as much respect for Christ's sepulcher as Christians have for a Jewish synagogue. (Ludolph von Suchem 1895: 105)

At the time Ludolph was writing, about A.D. 1350, the Georgian Christians had the possession of the Holy Sepulcher. In this case the possession did not last very long—the Georgians lacked the financial underpinning enjoyed by better organized groups like the Latins, Greeks, and Armenians and ended up selling most of their properties in Jerusalem to other Christian communities. But wherever ownership was established, it was fiercely defended and nowhere more jealously than inside the Church of the Holy Sepulcher itself, where every inch of that sacred real estate was parcelled out among the competing Christian sects. Niccolo's narrative continues:

I wish to tell you about the altars which are inside [the Church of the Holy Sepulcher] and which are twenty in number, for each type of Christian has its own altar. On Palm Sunday and Holy Easter all go there, each Christian group to its own priest, and each priest celebrates for his own people in his own tongue. The Greek patriarch celebrates at the high altar; and on Mount Calvary, the Armenians; beneath Golgotha, the Jacobites; at the altar at the rear of the Holy Sepulcher, the Indians and those of Ethiopia celebrate—and these are all black, darker than ink. Beside them celebrate the Nubians. The Latins, namely the Friars Minor, celebrate at the altar of Mary Magdalen, which belongs to us, the Latin Christians. For in Jerusalem and in all the places overseas, in Syria, Israel, Arabia, and Egypt there are no other [Western] religious, neither secular clergy nor monks, save the Friars Minor, and they are called Latin Christians. At the other altar where Christ appeared to Mary Magdalen, the Georgians celebrate; at the prison of Christ celebrate the "Christians of the Cincture" [i.e., the local Syrian Christians who wore a distinctive woolen cincture]; at the altar which is behind the apse celebrate the Nestorians. (Niccolo of Poggibonsi 1945: 21-22)

The following is the somewhat unedifying result of the ethnic and theological mix as it appeared to Niccolo on one of the highest of Christian holy days, the Holy Saturday before Easter:

On Holy Saturday, one hour before vespers, all the congregations of Christians collect in the square in front of the Church of the Holy Sepulcher, on one side the Greeks and the [local Christians] and the Nestorians; on the other, the Nubians, the Jacobites, the Georgians, and the Latins. And then each congregation begins its own chants in its own tongue, to praise the Lord in a loud voice, and they hoist one another on their shoulders in their joy and approach each other to embrace. There [in their midst] stands the amir of the Saracens, accompanied by his escort who ward off the crowd in front and keep them from approaching too

441

close by administering frequent beatings. This goes on all night, and all the Saracens of Jerusalem, men and women, come to watch. When the Saracen women wish to express their joy, they do so in this fashion: they roll their tongues inside their mouths and produce a sound like that of frogs, and no one who has heard it has not been afrighted. (Niccolo of Poggibonsi 1945: 24)

Pilgrim Behavior

With pilgrims of various persuasions and customs locked together for twenty-four hours within the confines of a relatively small church, the results were predictably chaotic. The Franciscan father guardian attempted to maintain some order among the Latins, instructed doubtless by un-happy experiences. He collected his charges inside the now locked door and gave them the rules of behavior inside the church. There were various items of housekeeping business, distributing altars to the priest for mass and the like, but there were also admonitions to avoid pushing and shoving and to keep an eye on their personal property since there were thieves there as well. He carefully distinguished the various other Christians for them, so that no one should make the mistake of giving alms to a heretic. And finally they were warned against defacing the church in the pursuit of souvenirs and that "we should not make the house of prayer into a house of merchandise and not sit and waste our time trafficking with Eastern Christian merchants."

On their first two nights in the church, Felix noted, the pilgrims were first awed into silence and decorum by the sacredness of the places they were contemplating, and then on the second occasion by the impressive ceremony of the investiture of the new Knights of the Holy Sepulcher. Felix has a detailed description of that ritual (I, 605-610), but we cite here the insouciant account of a less likely candidate invested about 1495, Arnold von Harff, the student of Near Eastern vernaculars who managed to teach himself the useful Arabic phrase for "Good Madam, I am *already* in your bed!":

In this chapel I heard Mass on the Holy Sepulcher, and after Mass I took Communion. After this there came an old knightly brother called Hans of Prussia, who dubs those pilgrims who desired it to be knights. He had already by him a golden sword and two golden spurs, and asked me if I desired to be a knight. I said yes. He asked me if I was well born and of noble parents. I replied that I hoped so. He told me to place foot and then the other on the Holy Sepulcher. Then he fixed on both the golden spurs and girded the sword on my left side, saying: "Draw the sword and kneel before the Holy Sepulcher. Take the sword in your left hand and place two fingers of the right hand on it, and say after me. 'As I, a noble knight, have travelled a long and distant way, and have suffered much pain and misfortune to seek honor in the holy land of Jerusalem, and have now reached the place of martyrdom of our Lord Jesus Christ and the Holy Sepulcher, in order that my sins may be forgiven and I may lead an upright life, so I desire to become here God's knight and promise by my faith and honor to protect the widows, orphans, churches, monasteries, and the poor, and do no man injustice in his goods, money, friendship, or kin, to help right wrongs, and so bear myself as becomes an honorable knight, so help me God and the Holy Sepulcher.'" When I had repeated this, he took the sword from my right hand and struck me with it on my back, saying, "Arise, knight, in honor of the Holy Sepulcher and the Knight St. George." May God in Heaven provide that I and others of my companions who are knights, or may be created knights, may never break their vows. Amen.[12] *(Arnold von Harff 1946: 201-202)*

But on the third night inside the locked Church of the Holy Sepulcher, Felix continues, the novelty had worn off and boredom set in. Some passed the night eating and drinking and endlessly boasting and arguing:

Others spent the whole night bargaining with traders, for to every place to which pilgrims go while they are in the Holy Land they are accompanied by Christian traders of Eastern birth, most cunning and greedy heretics, who never even sleep during the time that the pilgrims are in the Holy Land. Whenever the pilgrims enter the Church of the Holy Sepulcher those traders come in together with them, carrying their wares. They gain admission by payment of a great sum of money and establish themselves straight in front of the door of the church, spread out a cloth on the pavement and set out their wares upon it for sale. Some of the pilgrims, seeing that the time for their departure [from Jerusalem] was at hand, stayed awake all that night bargaining, and bought all kinds of things, for the traders there had for sale not only Pater Noster beads and precious stones, but also cloths of damask, of camlet, and of silk, and round about these merchants there was much disturbance and noise, even as in a marketplace. I saw there some nobly born and illustrious pilgrims, who on their own estates would have thought bargaining with tradesmen, even in a public market, a thing unbecoming to them and beneath their station in life. . . . How great a scandal it must be in the eyes of the infidels . . . is clear from the purity of their own mosques, wherein they will not for anything in the world allow buying and selling to go on, or any talk about the same. . . . (Felix Fabri 1893: II, 84-85)

Nor was the warning about defacing the holy places taken seriously. This was, after all, the holiest spot in Christendom and the temptation to leave there a part of oneself or to take away a part of the place was too overwhelming for some:

Some nobles were led by vanity to write their names, with the symbols of their birth and peerage, on the walls of the church [of the Holy Sepulcher], and painted their coats of arms thereon or pasted up papers on which these matters were inscribed on the walls of this and other churches. Some of them carved their names with iron chisels and mallets on the pillars and marble slabs. . . . [Some of the pilgrims pretended to be praying over the socket-hole of the cross on Calvary, but] within the circle of their arms would secretly scratch with exceeding sharp tools their shields, with the marks, I cannot say of their noble birth but rather of their silliness, for a perpetual memorial of their folly. . . . The same madness moved some to inscribe their names, shields, and armorial bearings with sharp irons on the slab which covers the tomb on the most holy sepulcher of the Lord. . . . I knew one pilgrim who always had a red stone in his purse, with which he used to write his name in every place, on every wall. This fool would sometimes go up to altars and mark the letters of his name at the top of the vacant margins of antiphonals, graduals, missals, and psalters, as though he were the author of the book. . . . He took especial pains to inscribe his name and arms in those places above all others which would be noticed by men passing in and out. (Felix Fabri 1893: II, 86-87)

The Pilgrim Experience

The pilgrim came to Jerusalem and the Holy Land prepared to be moved by a religious experience of the holy places, as others before him had been. Returned travellers spoke of those sites still redolent of the Gospels; books described them in detail and attempted to prepare the newcomer for the *reality* of the event, the *reexperiencing* of the events in the life, death, and resurrection of Jesus:

. . . Thence let [the pilgrim] return to Jerusalem, that he may see and hear Jesus preaching in the Temple, teaching his disciples on the Mount of Olives, supping on Mount Sion, washing his disciples' feet, giving them his Body and his Blood, praying in Gethsemane, sweating blood, kissing his betrayer, being dragged away prisoner, mocked, spat upon, judged, bearing his cross, sinking beneath the weight of his cross before the very gate of the city that is to be seen to this day, helped by Simon of Cyrene, and for our sake celebrating the mysteries of his Passion on Calvary. The mem-

ory of each and every one of these places is still as full and as complete as it was on that day when these things were done therein. Of a truth, there are in the city so many places hallowed by the events of Our Lord's Passion that one day can in no wise suffice for visiting them all profitably. Besides these, there are other things which rouse men in those places to a greater degree of devotional fervor. . . . O Lord God, I see Abraham, as the ancient histories tell us, leaving his country, his family and his father's house and hastening to this land, pitching his tent between Bethel and Ai, sojourning in Gerar, in Beersheba and Hebron. . . . (Burchard of Mount Sion 1896: 2-3)

Then wishing to go to the Sepulcher and seek the Lord whom we had not found on Mount Calvary—for they had already laid Him to rest, since wretched I had arrived too late—I said: "Let us go and seek at the tomb where they have placed Him!" And gathering together the Christians, who then numbered more than a hundred, I organized a procession, and we started out from the column which they say is the center of the world. And we went up the same way the Marys had gone with the spices, going forward and asking each other "Who will roll back the rock for us?" Then as we approached we sang out repeated verses of Victimae paschali laudes etc., someone intoning a verse at each step and all the others responding. We went about here and there around the tomb looking for the Lord and not finding Him, until someone called out "Christ had risen, my hope! He goes before His followers in Galilee!" and the sound of it and the shouting could be heard outside the church by the Saracens. Going into the sepulcher tomb we found there a great stone at the entry into the tomb, but it was already rolled back to the side. We went out, since we did not find the Lord, and they showed us the garden and the place where He had first appeared to Mary Magdalen. . . . (Laurent 1873: 112-113)

Felix Fabri recalled his own first arrival in Jerusalem in 1480:

When we came to the gate which is called the Gate of David, the Gate of the Merchants, or the Fish Gate [that is, the Jaffa Gate], we passed through it with bowed heads, for by the act of so passing we received a plenary indulgence. From the gate we went through a long street and came to a great closed church, before which was a fair large courtyard paved with polished marble, of exceeding whiteness. When we were all standing in the courtyard, one of the brethren of the convent of Mount Sion put himself in a higher place and addressed us, saying that this was the holiest of churches . . . the Sepulcher of the Lord. (Felix Fabri 1893: I, 282-283)

There was a great variety of reactions when the pilgrims realized where they were, the place before which they now stood. Not everyone was as composed as Ludolph of Suchem, whose first reaction on entering the Church of the Holy Sepulcher was that "the inside of this church is very much like the cathedral of Münster in Westphalia, especially in the choir." Some of the pilgrims in Felix's company fell prostrate and lay lifeless on the ground. Others sobbed and wailed. A few lost total control of themselves, it appeared, and wandered about making childish and foolish gestures. Felix looked upon the spectacle as an observer, not a participant, and thought he understood:

It is indeed pleasant to behold the very earnest and yet different behavior of the pilgrims as they prayed at the holy places, which places have a wondrous power of moving to tears, groans, and sighs men who in any other place could not be moved by any speech, advice, or passage of Scripture, by any painting or carving, examples, promise, or threats, by prosperity or adversity. Yet as a rule those who visit the holy places are not affected even to this extent, but merely roused to unusual devotion and piety. Indeed, I have seen some—I would that I had not seen them— whose feelings were acted upon in an exactly contrary direction by the pious behavior of good devotees. I have seen during all the aforesaid devotions of the pilgrims some dull and unprofitable pilgrims, nay rather brute beasts, not having the spirit of God, who stood and smiled mockingly at the prayers, tears, prostrations, beating of breasts, and the like, which were done by the rest. What is even more damnable is that these brutish men . . . hold such devout people to be fools, hypocrites, vainglorious, deceivers, and brain-sick, and ever thereafter treated them with scorn, disdained to converse with them, and disparaged them, calling them fools, hypocrites and Beghards. (Felix Fabri 1893: I, 284)

Relics and Souvenirs

One of the scenes that perhaps Felix wished he had not seen was one that occurred in another holy place inside the Church of the Holy Sepulcher, in the underground chapel where Helena had discovered the Cross of Jesus, and where the actors included Eastern Christians and even Muslims:

In this holy chasm pilgrims are inspired with great devotion, but the Eastern Christians and even the Saracens indulge in vain superstitions about it, and scrape off pieces from these rocks for medicines, for they declare that one sick of a fever will be cured straightway if he drink some wine and water in which a piece of these rocks has been placed. Moreover when anyone suffers with headache, he forthwith causes his head to be shaved and sends the hair which has been cut off to the guardians of the temple that they may place it on the spot where the cross was found; and when this is done, the patient is cured. [So too with toothaches: the beard is shaved.] Hence it comes to pass that all the crannies in the rocks and between the stones are stuffed full of hair. (Felix Fabri 1893: I, 363)

Above all, the experience of making contact with the holy was intensely physical, not merely seeing but touching, as in this scene witnessed by Felix at the site of Calvary, by the hole in the rock where it was said that Jesus' cross had been placed:

. . . each one as best he could crawled to the socket-hole of the cross, kissed the place with exceeding great devotion, and placed his face, eyes, and mouth over the socket-hole, from whence in very truth there breathes forth an exceeding sweet scent, whereby men are visibly refreshed. We put our arms and our hands into the hole down to the very bottom; and by these acts we received plenary indulgence. [13] *(Felix Fabri 1893: I, 365)*

It is little wonder that the pilgrims attempted to pry some fragment of holiness off these holy places and carry them home with them, as Egeria reported was already happening in her day. Relics or souvenirs, "blessings" or physical indulgences, the pilgrims' accounts are full of them, and even the sophisticated Felix, who strongly disapproved of the vandalism he experienced in the holy places, could succumb on occasion to the opportunity for getting hold of a relic or a souvenir. Here he is speaking of the stone that once covered the entry to Jesus' tomb and was in his time pointed out in the house of Caiaphas:

It was once an exceedingly large stone; for after many years the faithful cut the stone in two, and left one part near the Holy Sepulcher, while they brought the other part hither to this church, and appointed it for a slab, or table, for the altar. We kissed the sacred stone and viewed it narrowly. Meanwhile the priests of the church watched us carefully, that none of us should break pieces off the stone with any iron tool, for they greatly reverence the stone. [If it was not for the presence of that stone, Felix continues, the impoverished Armenians would have sold the place to the Franciscans.] But they wanted to sell the place with the condition that they should take the stone away with them, for they were in no wise willing to sell the stone with it. Howbeit this year there came to Jerusalem an exceedingly rich Armenian, who has rebuilt the church [of the House of Caiaphas] and has held out a helping hand to those poor men. During my first pilgrimage a good-sized piece of the stone came into my hands. It was bought by a knight for two ducats from an Armenian priest, who entered there with the knight by stealth, lest the other Armenians should see them, and broke off a piece of the stone. This same knight died at sea and I inherited the piece of stone from him, and brought it with me to Ulm. (Felix Fabri 1893: I, 319)

His relish at the acquisition is evident, though he knew that many were being gulled by the business of relics:

Noblemen who go to Jerusalem take a special interest in the relics of the Holy Innocents [that is, the children killed by Herod in his search for the newborn Jesus], I know not for what reason. There was in our company an exceedingly rich nobleman, who turned over the dust of that cave [near Bethlehem] seeking for relics, and finding none went to the dragoman, the Saracen protector of the pilgrims, and through an interpreter promised that he would give him a hundred ducats if he would procure an entire body for him. The guide told him in reply that the bodies of these children had been removed to Cairo, where the Lord Sultan had them in his own keeping, and sold them to whom he chose, and that there was no man in the whole kingdom save him alone who was permitted to sell the bodies of these children. When the knight heard this he meditated going to St. Catherine [in Sinai] with the rest that he might buy a child when he came to Cairo. Now this bargain struck me as being insulting, tricky, and unjust, wherefore I betook myself to a man of knowledge and inquired of him about this matter, what one was to think about the bodies of children which were sold by the sultan. I was assured by him that it is a fact that Saracens and Mamluks receive the bodies of stillborn children or of children who have died after their birth, slash them with knives, making wounds, then embalm the bodies by pressing balsam, myrrh, and other preservative drugs into the wounds and sell them to Christian kings, princes, and wealthy people as bodies of the Holy Innocents. So they pay great sums of gold and silver and believe they receive the bodies of holy children, whereas they receive the bodies of damned children. Thus are Christ's faithful people mocked and robbed of their money, for these infidels know our ardent desire for the possession of relics and therefore set out for sale wood said to be part of the Holy Cross, and nails and thorns and bones and many other things of the same kind, to delude the unwary and cheat them out of their money. I do not set much value upon new relics brought from parts beyond the sea, especially those that have been purchased from Saracens or from Eastern Christians falsely so-called. It is not so with holy pebbles from the holy places. . . . (Felix Fabri 1893: I, 566-567)

I rose up early, before sunrise, and having said matins, I stole out of the convent alone and rambled off to the holy places. . . . In each of these places I picked up pebbles, marked them, and put them into a bag which

I carried with me for that purpose. Moreover, I gathered up some thorns which grow in the hedges on the side of the Mount of Olives and Mount Sion, and I bound twigs of them together and wove them into a crown of thorns in the way of the thorns wherewith I believe that the Lord Jesus was crowned. All that day I labored at gathering stones and cutting off branches of thorns.... And let no one think it useless or childish of me to bring pebbles to our country with me from the holy places, for I read that the holy men of old did this [Naaman:2 Kgs. 5:17].... By no means, therefore, and in no wise, do pieces of stone brought from that illustrious land deserve to be despised and cast away, but to be gathered up with great devotion and placed among the chief relics of churches. And not only the earth itself and pebbles and bits of stone, but also beads and rosaries, rings and symbols in rosaries, which have touched the holy places are in some sort hallowed and made thereby more venerable and precious.... Neither is it we Western Christians alone who do this thing, but the Eastern Christians from the furthermost parts of the East collect these pebbles in the Holy Land and carry them as it were to the gates of Paradise as most respected relics. (Felix Fabri 1893: II, 214-215)

Felix knew well enough, however, the difference between picking up souvenirs, "holy pebbles from holy places," and taking a chisel to the Holy Sepulcher, an act which led to much graver difficulties than desecration:

Others went round about the church with iron tools hidden in their clothes, and when they came to holy places scratched and picked at the sacred stones, chipping and knocking pieces off them to carry home with them for relics.... Once after the [other] pilgrims had gone home [to Europe] we stayed all night in the Church of the Anastasis, and in the morning it was discovered that pieces had been broken off the rock of Calvary, the slab of the Holy Sepulcher, and the stone of the Lord's unction. When the other Eastern Christians saw this, they cried out in the church against us, calling us thieves and robbers; a dangerous riot was stirred up against us, and they threatened us that they would complain to the Moorish and Saracen lords. Hearing this, the father guardian was afraid, thinking that a great danger was hanging over us. He called us all together into the chapel of the Blessed Virgin, and by his apostolic authority excommunicated those who had broken the stones, nor would he let them go out of the church until the broken pieces were given up to him. (Felix Fabri 1893: II, 90)

The Spirit of Inquiry

There was obviously much credulity in this search for the actual sites of long past events, and some doubts as well. From the beginning of the

Christian pilgrimage tradition, visitors to the Holy Land were confronted with conflicting stories about the site of this or that sacred event, and even a casual reader of the narratives about the city notes that the identifications of some place flutter disconcertingly from one side of Jerusalem to the other, like the place of Stephen's stoning or the spot where Judas hanged himself. These shifts did not seem to bother early visitors, who tended to accept the last word uttered by the local tradition as the true word. The Crusades, however, gave many Christians—those who lived in the Holy Land, those who visited it, and those who read travel books back in Europe—their first real physical familiarity with the Holy City. And from then on, the earthly Jerusalem, the city of the here and now, began to assert its claims more urgently against both its heavenly counterpart and the imagined Jerusalem of Jesus' day.

Any visitor could see that there were some profound differences between what one read of Jerusalem in the Gospels and the city that stood before one's eyes. Most obvious perhaps and certainly most startling, as it continues to startle some today, was that the alleged sites of Jesus' crucifixion and burial, which in the Gospel narrative are explicitly said to lie outside the city walls, were within the Church of the Holy Sepulcher right in the heart of the city. Was this the correct place? Had the city moved? One visitor who attempted to address the question in a serious way, and who thought that he knew the answer to this and a whole series of related topographical questions, was Burchard of Mount Sion. He wrote in 1280:

Jerusalem is a pretty large city, as I shall tell you hereafter, and does not, as some vainly declare, stand in a different place to what it did at the time of the Lord's Passion. The argument on that side is that since the Lord suffered outside the city gate and the place is now within the city walls, therefore the city must stand in a different place. But they do not know what they are saying and want to show what they have not seen. The city now stands where it has always stood, for since the Temple of the Lord stands within the city walls it would be foolish, no, altogether impossible, to move it to another place because of the walls which enclose it on all sides. . . . But as a matter of fact, it has spread itself out, in width though not in length, and the whole of the ancient city, together with Mount Sion, is now within the walls and is inhabited. But at present there are very few inhabitants for so great a city because the people in it live in continual terror.

Burchard then began to build his case:

Mount Moriah, where the Lord's Temple and the king's palace were built, was somewhat higher than the city, as is clearly seen from the position of the Temple and its courts as described by Josephus, since each of them is described in his histories. But all of these places are now utterly levelled, and are almost lower than any other part of the city, for the mount was pulled down by the Romans and cast into the brook Kedron, together with the ruins of the Temple and its courts, as may be clearly seen at this day. The Temple area is square, and is more than a bowshot long and wide. The Temple which is now built on it almost touches the city wall, which the true and ancient Temple did not, because there were four courts between it and the wall; but now it is not more than about a hundred feet away from the wall and the brook Kedron.

The Valley of Jehoshaphat also enclosed the city, passing along its east side at the foot of the Mount of Olives. Though this valley is pretty deep, yet it is much filled up; for the Romans, as Josephus tells us, when they were besieging the city on that side, cut down the olives and other trees, made mounds of them and filled up the valley with the mounds. Moreover, after the city had been taken, Aelius Adrianus caused all the ruins of the courts and the Temple to be cast into the brook Kedron, and Mount Moriah to be levelled, so that the place might not again be fortified, and he had the city sown with salt. All this is obvious to anyone on the spot, for the glorious Virgin's sepulcher, which stands in the Valley of Jehoshaphat, and not at the bottom of it but at the foot of the Mount of Olives, was nevertheless hardly higher than the bottom of the valley, or above the surface, at the time that Jerusalem was inhabited before the destruction. Now it is far beneath the earth, however, so that the whole church, albeit high and vaulted, is now quite underground and entirely covered, and the valley above it is quite smooth, so that there is a road along which one can walk over the top of the church. Whatever the case, on the ground surface there is a building in the form of a chapel, which you enter and go down many steps underground into the church itself, and you will come to the Glorious Virgin's sepulcher. I believe that there are sixty steps. . . . (Burchard of Mount Sion 1896: 66-72)

There is at work here a mind different from that of the ordinary pilgrim. [14] Burchard is reflecting about what he is seeing, as many visitors will begin to do. The objective is still pilgrimage, but now with open eyes as well as an open heart:

Seeing, however, that some are possessed by a desire to picture in their minds those things which they are not able to behold with their own eyes, and wishing to fulfill their longing, as far as I am able, I have, to the best of my ability, thought about, diligently taken note of, and laboriously described that land over which my feet so often passed; for I would have the reader know that I have set down in my own description nothing save *what I have either seen with my own eyes when at the place itself, or, when I could not come to it, what I have seen from some neighboring mountain top or other convenient place and have carefully noted the answers given by the Syrians and the Saracens and the other people of the land, whom I most diligently questioned. . . . Indeed, as I have already said, I have either walked on foot all over the whole land, from Dan to Beersheba, from the Dead Sea to the Mediterranean . . . or else I have carefully made inquiries about the places I could not visit. (Burchard of Mount Sion 1896: 4)*

Local tradition and hearsay from guides still formed the basis of much of what the pilgrim learned, but there was also a somewhat greater insistence on precision, on weighing and balancing what one was told against the physical evidence of one's eyes and the urging of the intelligence. And what was utterly new in Felix Fabri's fifteenth-century account was a self-consciousness totally absent from the pilgrim narratives of the thirteenth and fourteenth centuries. We have earlier seen Felix simultaneously looking at the Holy Sepulcher and observing the reactions of other pilgrims as they looked upon it; here he is looking at himself, measuring his own internal reactions to the pilgrimage experience:

No one should think visiting the places to be a light task; there is the intense heat of the sun, the walking from place to place, kneeling, and prostration: above all, there is the strain that everyone puts on himself in striving with all of his might to rouse himself to earnest piety and comprehension of what is shown to him in the holy places, and to devout prayer and meditation, all of which cannot be done without great fatigue, because to do them fitly a man should be at rest and not rambling about. To struggle after mental abstraction whilst bodily walking from place to place is exceedingly toilsome. (Felix Fabri 1893: I, 299)

One may contrast these two almost contemporary reflections on history and tradition written shortly before the middle of the fourteenth century:

When I met in this town [of Hebron] the pious and aged professor, as well as prayer leader and preacher, Burhan al-Din al-Jaʿbari, one of those saintly men who enjoy the favor of God and of the foremost authorities [in the religious sciences], I questioned him as to the truth of al-Khalil's [Abraham's] grave being there. He replied to me: "All the scholars I have met accept as a certainty that these graves are the very graves of Abraham, Isaac, Jacob, and their wives. No one raises objections to this but the followers of false doctrines; it is a tradition that has passed down from father to son for generations and admits no doubt." (Ibn Battuta 1959-1962: 75)

One should be wise and careful in laying up one's memory, and in order not to fail, should write at once on the places [seen] overseas. But I, Friar Niccolo of Poggibonsi, when I went overseas, I had in mind to visit everything and not return to my own country until I had done so. And what I saw with my eyes and touched with my hands and inquired of others and had assured myself of the particulars, that I wrote on two small tablets which I carried with me. Later, when I was in Jerusalem I procured a measuring rod of one cubit and another of one foot, and going round I measured everything in order, as you will hear. (Niccolo of Poggibonsi 1945: 11)

The Tomb of Jesus, Is It Authentic?

The site of Jesus' tomb presented one type of problem, the actual monument quite another. More than one thoughtful pilgrim must have stood before it and then, just before shedding a tear, entertained the same doubt that Felix Fabri raised:

After having read these [Gospel] accounts, a man who sees the ancient tombs in the Holy Land easily understands what the Lord's sepulcher must have been like; but it cannot possibly now be like what it was then, because of the Church that has been built above it, and because of the decoration. . . . [15] *(Felix Fabri 1893: I, 400)*

For some it was sufficient that the tomb was enclosed:

Christ's sepulcher is cut out of solid rock, but so that it should not be defiled or carried away by pilgrims, it is covered with other stones of white marble. The stone which covers it on the front has three holes pierced through it and through these holes one can kiss the true sepulcher and the true stone thereof. The stone which encases the sepulcher is so cleverly joined to the tomb that to the ignorant it all seems to be one stone. For this reason I do not believe that there is in any church a piece of the true stone of Christ's tomb. . . . It is and ever has been most carefully guarded. Indeed, if Christ's tomb could be carried away only grain by grain like sand, it would have disappeared long ago, even if it had been as big as a mountain, and there would be scarcely a single grain of stone left in that spot. (Ludolph von Suchem 1895: 104-105)

But was what lay beneath that marble sheathing itself authentic? Was is the "true sepulcher and the true stone thereof"?

Some say that under the marble slabs the rock of the monument and the Holy Sepulcher still exists entire, albeit no part of it is visible. Others say that no man knows for certain or can affirm that the true rock is or is not under the slabs. Others plainly assert that there has not been a piece as large as a grain of millet left there of the true stone. For this they allege several reasons. First, the hatred felt for the Christians by the heathen, whose spite against the Christians is so keen that they destroy every single thing which the Christians love and reverence. Now they knew that the sepulcher of Christ was our greatest object of veneration; . . . moreover they knew that as long as the sepulcher existed the Christians would always pant for the recovery of the city of Jerusalem. . . . [Another reason was the capitulation terms of the Crusader departure when they were permitted to leave with everything they could carry with them.] It is believed that in the course of removal they carried away everything which is reputed holy, down to its very foundations—among which things the Holy Sepulcher is the chief—in order that they might leave nothing behind to be trodden under foot by the heathen. Even at the present day the faithful who visit these lands carry off as many pieces of stone and earth as they are able, and if they could they would carry off the whole land, that it might not be trodden under foot by these swine. . . . Another reason why they say that nothing is left of the Holy Sepulcher is the rash zeal of the faithful, who cannot be restrained by any law or ordinance from carrying off pieces of the holy places, if they can. . . .

With regard to this matter I made the following experiment: while keeping my vigil in the Church of the Holy Sepulcher, I took a lighted candle and went to the Lord's monument, which I examined most carefully to see whether I could find any part that was not covered with marble. [He found a place on the wall between the inner and outer cave.] Holding my light near it, I saw a wall cut out of rock, nor made of ashlar work, but all of one piece, with the marks of iron tools plainly to be seen upon it. In the upper part there seemed to have been a fracture, which had been mended with stones and cement. From this it appeared to me that the Lord's sepulcher had once been destroyed but never completely rooted up; that what is now there is a restoration, and that it has stood for more than two hundred years as it appears this day, save that it is now more carefully encased with marble, lest pilgrims should pick pieces off the walls for relics. . . .

In the end, Felix cannot solve the problem. He has given a probable answer, but the real answer is at the same time more spiritual and, he must have thought, more satisfying:

From all that has been said about the Holy Sepulcher, the devout and quiet pilgrim should grasp this fact, that whether the cave as it stands at the present day be the true and entire monument of Christ, or whether a

part of it be there, or whether none of it be there, matters very little either
one way or the other, because the main fact connected with the place
abides there, and cannot by any means be carried away or demolished, the
fact, to wit, that this was the place of the most holy burial and resurrection
of Christ, where, albeit there may not be the very monument wherein
Christ's body was laid, there is nevertheless a monument erected to Christ
and in which the sacrament of His Body has ofttimes been celebrated. . . .
(Felix Fabri 1983: I, 412-415)

Death and Judgment in Jerusalem

The belief that the final judgment of mankind would take place in the
Valley of Jehoshaphat on the eastern side of Jerusalem was an old one
(Joel 3:2), and Jews, Christians, and Muslims alike shared the biblically
derived view that judgment would occur there in that narrow defile between the Temple mount and Olivet. In the course of time, however, it
had been combined or confused with another traditional belief. The biblical Valley of Hinnom, *ge hinnom*, ran south then east around the *western*
side of Jerusalem. It was an unsavory place, associated with human sacrifice—Ahaz had sacrificed his sons and daughters there to the god Moloch
(2 Chron. 28:3; Jer. 7:30-31)—and the "dung gates" of various eras on
the southern side of Jerusalem carried the city's filth and refuse into that
same valley as it curved eastward to join the Kedron south of David's city.
In Jesus' time that same western and southern valley was still "Gehenna,"
the detestable place of filth and hell's fire (Mk. 9:42-49 and elsewhere).
But by at least the fifth century Christian pilgrims were being shown
"Gehenna" on the *eastern* side of the city, that is, in the Kedron Valley. It
is put quite explicitly in Eucherius: "Beside the east wall of Jerusalem,
which is also the wall of the Temple, is Gehenna. This is called the Valley
of Jehoshaphat. It runs from north to south and the brook Kedron runs
through it whenever there has been rain to provide it with water." [16] "Jahannam" often appears in the Quran in the sense of "Hell," just as "Gehenna" does in the Gospels, and the Muslims, like the Christians, localized
it on the *eastern* side of Jerusalem, as is clear already in both Muqaddasi
and Nasir-i Khusraw, on whom the eastern side of Jerusalem exercised a
powerful eschatological appeal as the site of the Last Judgment. And according to Muqaddasi, Muslims were buried there from the very earliest
days of Islam:

The Wadi Jahannam runs from the angle of the Haram area to its farthest
[northern] point and along the eastern side [of the city]. In this valley
there are gardens and vineyards, churches, caverns and cells of anchorites,

tombs and other remarkable spots, also cultivated fields. In its midst stands
the church which covers the sepulcher of Mary, and above, overlooking
the valley, are many tombs, among which are those of Shaddad ibn Aws
ibn Thabit [a Companion of the Prophet] and Ubadah ibn al-Samit [the
first qadi, or chief judge of Jerusalem]. (Muqaddasi 1896: 49-50)

If "Gehenna" is a notion taken over from the Jewish and Christian tradition, the Muslims also had a topographical refinement of their own on the
slopes of the Mount of Olives, the place called *al-Sâhira*, or "the Plain":

The Mount of Olives overlooks the Great Mosque from the eastern side
of the valley [of Jahannam]. On its summit is a mosque built in memory
of Umar, who sojourned here for some days when he came to receive the
capitulation of the Holy City. There is also a church built on the spot
whence Christ ascended into heaven; and further, nearby is the place called
"the Plain" [al-Sâhira], which, as I have been told on the authority of [the
traditionist] Ibn Abbas, will be the scene of the Resurrection. The ground
is white and blood has never been spilt here. (Muqaddasi 1896: 50)

Nasir-i Khusraw elaborates:

When you have passed out of the Haram, there lies before you a great
level plain called al-Sahira, which, it is said, will be the place of the Resurrection, where all mankind shall be gathered together. For this reason
men from all parts of the world come here to live in the Holy City until death
overtakes them, in order that when the day fixed by God—may He be
praised and exalted—shall arrive, they may thus be ready and present at
the appointed place. . . . At the border of this plain of al-Sahira there are
many places of pious renown, where men come to pray and offer up petitions in their need. . . .
  Lying between the Haram and this plain of al-Sahira is a great and steep
valley, and down in this valley, which is like a steep ditch, are many edifices built after the fashion of ancient times. I saw here a dome cut out in
the stone and it is set upon the summit of a building [the Tomb of Ab-
salom]. Nothing can be more curious than it is, and one asks how it came
to be placed in its present position. In the mouths of the common people
it is called the "Pharaoh's House." . . . The common people state that
when you stand at the brink of the valley you may hear the cries of those
in Hell which come up from below. I myself went there to listen but heard
nothing. (Nasir-i Khusraw 1893: 24-26)

"The Plain," then, appears at this point to lie somewhere on the northwestern slope of the Mount of Olives. By the time of Mujir al-Din at the
end of the fifteenth century, however, it had moved across the Kedron

and immediately north of the city where it has since remained. [17] Mujir is well instructed on the Sahira, which he glosses with what was read as an eschatological reference in Quran 79:14: "When behold, they shall be in the state of wakefulness [*bil-sâhira*]":

According to Ibrahim ibn abi Abla, by these words God is referring to the small plain on the slope of the Mount of Olives, near the oratory of Umar and known as the Sahira. A tradition reported by Umar's son says that "the place where God will assemble humankind on the day of the final resurrection is called the Sahira." The original meaning of the word "sahira" is "desert" or "the surface of the land" or even, according to some, "a large plain." In the language of the bedouin "sahira" means "a landscape which the traveller hastens to cross early in the morning," which is to say, "a place where one watches, in wakefulness." (Mujir 1876: 194-195)

As Nasir noted, many came to this place to die and be buried: the simple and the poor, perhaps in the course of fulfilling a pilgrimage, enfeebled or exhausted by the very act; and the rich and powerful, who could make the appropriate arrangements beforehand—and we hear of the Muslim rulers of Egypt doing just that as early as the tenth century. [18] The Crusader kings were buried in the Holy City, many of them in the Church of the Holy Sepulcher itself, where their tombs were still preserved in the eighteenth century. [19]

There was, and is, a certain amount of Muslim and Christian jostling over other grave sites around the city, particularly in the vicinity of the Golden Gate, which overlooked the Valley of Jehoshaphat from the west. Though the poorer Christians who died in the city were buried in the field called Aceldama southwest of the city,[20] Gehenna, or the Valley of Jehoshaphat, was preferred—and not reserved for royalty, either then or later.[21] The site of Gehenna was one of the marvels that no Jerusalem pilgrim might pass up. Ricoldo of Monte Croce descended with his company into Gehenna in 1288 and was powerfully moved:

There in the Valley of Jehoshaphat we sat in tears and trembling contemplating the Place of Judgment. We took counsel where on high the Most Just Judge would take His place and where those would be on His right and His left. And we chose a place on His right hand and each marked a stone there in witness. I too set up and marked a stone there as a testimony and I chose a place on His right hand for myself and for all who heard the Word of God from me, who persevered in the faith and the truth of the Gospel. And there I marked a stone at the behest of all, who stood there weeping. (Laurent 1873: 111)

But the sight of this actual Gehenna raised certain problems, not for Ricoldo perhaps, but for other "simple folk" who grew anxious about reserving a place in that narrow valley which seemed scarcely capable of containing a few thousand people at most. Felix Fabri had a soothing spiritual reply for them:

Now as is commonly believed and taught, all kindreds of the earth will be assembled together in this valley [of Jehoshaphat]. Wherefore men are wont to inquire of those who have been in the Holy Land how large that valley is, whether it is so wide that therein all men can stand on the Day of Judgment. Simple folk care for nothing else, but are anxious about the size of the Valley of Jehoshaphat; and sometimes it has happened, and does still happen, that pilgrims pile up stones for themselves in that valley, wishing before the Day of Judgment to secure a place for themselves whereon they may sit on the Day of Judgment. And sometimes simple folk give money to pilgrims about to set out to Jerusalem to mark a place for them with a stone in the Valley of Jehoshaphat, to which place they believe they will come on the Day of Judgment.

When such men question one about the size of the valley, in truth one is forced to answer that the valley is of no great size, and that in its present form it would hardly be able to take in one nation, for all the Swabians who are now actually alive could barely find standing room in it, without mentioning those who have been or will hereafter be. But on the Day of Judgment the shape of the valley will be different, as will that of the whole earth also. . . . That this valley will be enlarged is evident from Zachariah 14, where we are told that the Mount of Olives shall be riven from the east to the west. . . . One ought likewise to reply to them, and indeed it is a better answer, that those who have spent their lives well, righteously and virtuously, here on earth will have altogether unmolested places to stand in prepared for them by their angels. . . . (Felix Fabri 1893: I, 491-493)

Martyrdom in the Holy City, A.D. 1391

The pious Christian necessarily had his eyes on the world to come, and a visit to the actual site of the Last Judgment must have sharpened that vision. Nonetheless, it was a vision of some incalculable though inevitable future. Among the early Christians, both the vision and the appetite for it had been sharper: men had died for their faith and been accounted martyrs. Indeed, there in Jerusalem was the tomb of the very first of them, St. Stephen. But what had once seemed glorious now seemed merely difficult. The Christians in Jerusalem now lived under a contract drawn up by infidels, and if those infidels were happy to create problems and even sufferings for the Christians on occasion, they showed no inclination to offer them the palm of martyrdom. It had, certain young Friars on Mount Sion decided, to be demanded of them. The text below is from an official ecclesiastical inquiry, held on January 20, 1392, into the consequences of their zeal.

Let all who will inspect these records know that in the year of the Lord 1391, on the eleventh day of November, four Friars Minor resident from various provinces in the convent of Mount Sion in Jerusalem, men adorned with all the virtues, devoted to God and obedient to their prelates, strict in their observance and most experienced and perfect in every virtue of religion, whose names are as follows: Deodatus . . . Nicolas . . . Stephen . . . and Peter, who had lived out of a sense of religious perfection for a number of years either in Bosna or Corsica, finally by reason of their great devotion betook themselves to the Holy City of Jerusalem where they lived a life of regular observance for several more years and underwent a most difficult martyrdom in Christ, as will appear in the sequel.

The above-mentioned brethren had long discussions among themselves on how they might win for Christ souls which the devil was carrying off and offer a rich harvest to God All High in this holy land of Jerusalem. They put aside all timidity and prepared themselves as best they could. They took sound counsel of various theologians and other solid brethren there; they armed themselves with the teachings of Holy Scriptures and of the approved doctors, as they read them in various places; they took counsel how a perfect man might prevail with great merit against carnal and bestial men of the likes of those who live under the law or the sect of Muhammad.

Finally on the day and year already noted, on the feast of St. Martin, about the hour of terce, they set out to fulfill what they had long planned. The aforementioned brethren set out together, each of them carrying with him a parchment or a scroll on which was inscribed in vulgar Italian and in Arabic what is noted below, and first went in procession to the Temple of Solomon [the Aqsa Mosque], where they were prevented from entering as they wished. Asked by the Saracens what they wanted, they replied: "We wish to impart to the qadi (who is their bishop or superior, as we would call him in Latin) much discourse that is useful and healthy for your souls." The others answered: "This is not the qadi's house, but come with us and we will show you the qadi's house." When they came to the qadi's house they took out their scrolls and read aloud to him these words:

"Lord Qadi, and all you others who are here, we ask that you pay close attention to our words since what we will tell you is helpful, true, just,

remote from all trickery, and useful to souls who heed them. Which sentiments are these. You are in a state of eternal damnation since your law is neither the law of God nor given by God nor even a good law; in fact it is evil indeed. There is there neither Old nor New Testament. Further your law contains many lies, impossibilities, laughable matter, contradictions, and other things which lead men not to good or virtue but to evil and a great many vices. . . ."

Next the aforementioned brethren spoke against their prophet, saying that their prophet was not the messenger of God, as they insisted on maintaining, and that he himself says it his law; nor did he perform any miracle, while the prophets of God are attested to by many miracles. . . . Muhammad himself, they said, was a libertine, a murderer, a glutton, a despoiler who put man's end in eating, whoring, and wearing expensive clothes next to running waters. . . .

When the brethren had poured out these words with great fervor and faith, the qadi and his attendants became exceedingly angry, and as their remarks became generally known, a great many other Saracens began to collect there, and the guardian of Mount Sion together with a companion as well as the director of the Jerusalem hospice for pilgrims were summoned. Then the qadi spoke to the four brethren before him as follows: "These words which you just spoke, did you say them in full possession of your faculties or out of stupidity, or madness, or folly? Or tell me, were you sent by your pope or some other king of the Christians?" Then the brethren answered him with confidence, maturity, and discretion, with great zeal, the fervor of faith, and a desire for their own salvation. "We were not sent," they said, "by any creature save by God who deigned to inspire us to preach to you and announce the truth and your salvation. . . ."

Then the qadi asked: "Do you wish to recant everything you said and become Saracens and not die? Because otherwise you must perish." They answered in a clear voice: "In no wise do we wish to recant what we said, but we are prepared to die for that truth and for the Catholic faith in Christ, and by firmly defending it rather to die and put up with every type of torment, because everything we said was true, holy, and Catholic."

When he heard this the qadi and his council pronounced the judgment of death against them. Scarcely had the sentence been uttered when all the Saracens present rose up with the powerful cry: "Let them die! Let them die!" And they struck them so long with different instruments they fell to the ground close to death, and some in fact thought they were dead. This was about the ninth hour. After an hour had passed the brethren began to open their eyes and partially regained their speech. When the qadi saw this he had them bound and locked with chains about their *feet, and they stayed in the same place until about the middle of the night because of the popular clamor. Then toward midnight the qadi had them stripped bare and bound to posts and so cruelly flogged that they were almost skinned alive and could no longer stand. Finally he had them dispatched to underground dungeons and tied to wooden beams so tightly that they could get no rest and were afflicted with countless torments.*

Then on the fourth day they were led out to the public square where criminals were usually punished, in the presence of the amir and the qadi and a countless multitude of Saracens with their swords and daggers drawn. A large bonfire was lit. They asked them once again if they wished to recant what they had said and become Muslims and so avoid death. They answered: "No. We declare to you that you must convert and be baptized; if not, like the children of damnation you are heading for eternal crucifixion in the eternal fire. And you say we should become Saracens! Know that because of Christ and faith in him we fear neither death nor temporal fire."

Thus those holy men mocked them. When the Saracens who were standing there heard this, they became drunk with rage and they savagely rushed as one against the brethren as if they believed that he was most fortunate who struck them the most cruelly. And they so hacked them into pieces that not even a human shape remained. When this was done they tossed them into the raging fire, but the pieces of their bodies did not burn all that day long. The crowd stood there at the spectacle and piled on wood till nightfall, then they scattered the ashes and hid the bones so that no Christians should find them. (Durrieu 1881: 541-542)

Though the text does not say so explicitly, the burning of the Friars most likely took place in the courtyard before the Church of the Holy Sepulcher. It was there, at any rate, that later, similar cases were prosecuted. Elzear Horn, a Franciscan writing in the mid-eighteenth century, recalled three such from the sixteenth century, when the Ottomans were in control of Jerusalem. The first was a certain Maria, a Portuguese of the Third Order of St. Francis who served as a midwife and secretly baptized Muslim infants. One Palm Sunday, "inebriated in spirit, she came into the city abusing the impiety of the Muslims." Whereupon the Turks, "incited by the Jews," dragged her through the city and burned her on a pyre in the Holy Sepulcher courtyard in 1575. The second was Brother Juniper, the Sicilian who twice went into the Aqsa and was slain by the qadi with his own hands and his body burned in the parvis in 1557. And finally there was the instance of Cosmas of St. Damian, a Franciscan lay brother for Granada:

On the feast day of the Assumption of the Blessed Virgin, which then fell

461

on a Friday, he entered the Temple of Solomon, that is, the great mosque
[of al-Aqsa] about midday, when as usual Muslims from the whole city
were congregated for prayer. Raising the crucifix in his hands, he began
with great fervor of spirit courageously to condemn the impure sect of
Muhammad and announce that faith in Christ was necessary for salva-
tion—from long custom and fourteen years stay in the Holy Land he was
fairly proficient in Arabic. The Muslims got angry, and attacking him with
drawn swords, they cruelly slew him. Then they fixed his head, which had
been severed from his body, on a very long pole, and hanging his clothes
on another pole, they bore them away on high; the body, however, with
great derision they brought to this square, and having brought bundles of
wood from all sides, they burned it in the year 1599. (Horn 1962: 89)

Who Are These Peoples?

Confrontations between Friars and Muslims took place often in the Holy
Land and on a variety of levels, though rarely with such murderous results.
The Muslims generally showed no great curiosity or even concern over
these foreign Christians in their midst. [22] Christianity was a known quantity to them on both a social and a theological level. They had ruled Christians since the seventh century, and as for the Christian religion embraced
by their subjects and others, the Quran explained that it was in the end a
perversion of that same revelation represented by Islam in its perfection.

For the Western Christians newly arrived from Europe, on the other
hand, Islam was a new phenomenon on what they had imagined would
be a familiar landscape. Much of that landscape *was* familiar, particularly
when viewed through the eyes of faith, but the Muslims were not, and
these latter now sprawled, as not very genial masters, over a land that had
once been Christendom's own. Perhaps only somewhat less surprisingly,
there were in those same lands believers in Christ whose theology, liturgy,
and customs only vaguely resembled their own but who called themselves,
for all that, Christians.

Almost every author of a pilgrim memoir makes an attempt to explain
the baffling ethnic geography of the Holy Land, whether simply of the
Christian communities in Jerusalem or on the larger scale, as Burchard of
Mount Sion did, taking in the whole panorama of the Near East as it
appeared to him in 1280, each group of its residents appropriately characterized for the European reader. He begins with the people he knows
best, but does not much admire, the Latins who went to the Holy Land
and stayed on to make a home there:

There are dwelling [in the Holy Land] men of every nation under heaven, and each man follows his own rite. To tell the truth, our own people, the *Latins*, are worse than all the other people in the land. The reason for this, I think, is that when a man has been a malefactor, as, for example, a murderer, a robber, a thief, or an adulterer, he crosses the sea as a penitent, or else because he fears for his skin and dares not stay at home. Wherefore men come thither from all parts—from Germany, Italy, France, England, Spain, and Hungary and all other parts of the world; yet they do not but change their climate, not their mind; for when they are here, after they have spent what they brought with them, they have to earn something more and so they return again to their own vomit and do worse than they did before. They lodge pilgrims of their own nation in their houses, and these men, if they do not know how to take care of themselves, trust them and lose both their property and their honor. They also breed children who imitate the crimes of their fathers, and thus bad fathers beget sons worse than themselves, from whom descend most vile grandchildren, who tread upon the holy places with polluted feet. Hence it comes to pass that because of the sins against God of the dwellers in the land, the land itself, and the place of our redemption, is brought into contempt.

Besides the Latins there are many other races there; for example, the *Saracens* who preach Muhammad and keep his law. They call Our Lord Jesus Christ the greatest of the prophets and confess that he was conceived of the Holy Spirit and born of the Virgin Mary. But they deny that He suffered and was buried, but choose to say that He ascended into heaven and sits at the right hand of the Father because they admit Him to be the Son of God. But they declare that Muhammad sits at His left hand. They are very unclean and have as many wives as they can feed; yet, nevertheless, they practice unnatural sins and have boys' brothels in every city. Yet they are very hospitable, courteous, and kindly.

Besides these there are the *Syrians* [or local Christians]. The whole land is full of these. They are Christians but keep no faith with the Latins. They are clothed most wretchedly, and are stingy, giving no alms. They dwell among the Muslims and for the most part are their servants. In dress they are like the Muslims, except that they are distinguished from them by a woolen cincture.

The *Greeks* in like manner are Christians, but schismatics, save that a greater part of them returned to obedience to the Church at the General Council [of Lyons in 1274] held by our Lord Gregory X. In the Greek Church all the prelates are monks and are men of exceeding austerity of life and wondrous virtue.

The Greeks are exceedingly devout, and for the most part greatly honor and esteem their prelates. I have heard one of their patriarchs say in my presence: "We would willingly live in obedience to the Church of Rome and venerate it; but I am much surprised at my being ranked below the inferior clergy, such as archbishops and bishops. Some archbishops and bishops wish to make me, a patriarch, kiss their feet and do them personal service, which I do not hold myself bound to do, albeit I would willingly do so for the pope, but for no one else."

There are also *Armenians, Georgians, Nestorians, Nubians, Jacobites, Chaldeans, Medes, Persians, Ethiopians, Egyptians,* and many other people who are Christians. Of these there are an infinite number. Each of them have their own patriarch and obey him. Their prelates declare that they would most willingly belong to the Church of Rome. Of these, the Nestorians, Jacobites, and the like are so named after certain heretics who were once their chiefs.

Moreover, there are in the Holy Land Midianites, who are now called *bedouin* and *Turkoman,* who apply themselves solely to feeding flocks and camels, of which they have exceedingly great numbers. These people have no fixed dwellings, but wherever they learn there is pasture, thither they go and pitch their tents. They are exceedingly warlike, yet use only swords and lances in battle. They do not use arrows, saying that it is base beyond measure to steal away a man's life with an arrow. They are brave in war but wear only a red shirt, covering their heads only with a cloth. All Syria is full of them. . . . *(Burchard of Mount Sion 1896: 102-105)*

The Muslims at Home

Burchard's description here of the religious beliefs of the "Saracens," as the Arab Muslims were inevitably called by Westerners, is relatively straightforward, and his judgment about their morals and manner of life is typically mixed: they are morally corrupt but in some ways socially admirable. That mixture will reappear many times in many authors, combined with varying degrees of polemic and with a greater or lesser understanding of what they were describing. Some of that understanding came from their own reading done in European libraries, where a Latin translation of the Quran was available, as well as a great many refutations of the errors of the Prophet of Islam and his religion.[23] Some information was supplied by the evidence of the pilgrims' own eyes, much of it favorable, or at least interestingly neutral. There was endless gossip and prurient speculation on the Muslims' notorious polygamy—one pilgrim claims actually to have seen a Muslim and his four wives all lying in the *same* bed! And finally there was the resource of the local Christians and Jews, who had an inexhaustible supply of anecdotes, not only on the holy places but on the Muslims who ruled them. This passage of Magister Thietmar, for example, written not long after the Crusaders were driven from Jerusalem, must have come in part from the Christian community in Damascus and in part from what he himself witnessed in that overwhelmingly Muslim city:

I was in Damascus for six days and I learned a number of things about the Saracens' law and manner of life. Their life is filthy and their law corrupt. The Saracens indulge themselves to the fullest extent possible, whether licitly or illicitly. They have as many wives as possible on the principle that "more is better." At times of fast they fast until nightfall and then they spend the night in eating as often as they wish. They have certain heralds who stand in the towers of the city and call out during the night in the following manner: "Rise, all you who have fasted! Feast happily, refresh yourselves!"

The Saracens converted a large and beautiful monastery which the Greeks had formerly built in honor of St. Paul into one of their mosques, in which they have a pool so that whoever has sinned may wash himself. So it effects a reconciliation with God, and the member by which the sin is committed, that is washed. And these are their beliefs. Four times a day they pray and once during the night. In place of church bells they use a herald, and at his call they are accustomed solemnly to convene at their church. The religious Saracens are wont to wash themselves at any hour, with water or, if there is no water, with sand. Beginning at their head, they wash their faces, then their hands, legs, feet, genitals, and anus. Afterwards they go to pray, and they never pray without prostrations. They make many prostrations. They pray toward the south. They strike their breasts; they pray publicly and audibly. They kneel atop square cloths, which each carried with him under his belt, and on their knees they strike their foreheads upon the ground. Their dead they lay on their right side, and with much chanting they place them in tombs in such a way that they appear to be facing south toward the temple of Muhammad. . . . Their women never enter their temples. The noble women are kept under the supervision of eunuchs and never go out of their homes except on the orders of their husbands. And no one dares go close to a woman without the consent of her husband. (Laurent 1873: 10-11)

Much of Thietmar's information was picked up randomly, more randomly even than his "six days in Damascus" suggests. One pilgrim who had a different and greater opportunity was Ricoldo of Monte Croce, a Dominican who received permission to go to the East not merely to make pilgrimage but to preach, to conduct in effect a mission *in partibus infidelium*. [24] He made his pilgrimage to the Holy City, of course, and left an account of it, but from Jerusalem he went on to Baghdad, a city then in the 1280s still reeling from the Mongol sack of 1258. Ricoldo understood where he was and what he must do:

In Baghdad the Saracens make their studies and have their great teachers, and there too are their religious men and many different sects have come together there. There too are the monasteries of those same Saracens, which are called megiride, [possible masjids, mosques, or madrasas, law schools] which means "contemplatives." For our part, since we wished to bring down the faithlessness of Muhammad and had as our objective attacking them in their own center and the place of their broadest learning, we had necessarily to hold some converse with them. They received us like angels of God in their schools and places of learning and monasteries and in their churches or synagogues and their homes, and we attended carefully to their law and their deeds and we were amazed how in such a perfidious law acts of such perfection were found.

Ricoldo made no attempt to disguise his polemical purpose, neither to his hosts nor to the world at large. In addition to his *Itinerary* he wrote a *Refutation of the Quran*, a *Tract Against the Eastern Nations* directed at Christian schismatics, and finally a *Tract Against the Errors of the Jews*. Ricoldo found much to admire in Islam, at least at first glance: "the Saracens' zeal for learning, their devotion in prayer, their compassion for the poor, their reverence for the name of God and the prophets and the holy places, the generosity in their manner, their friendliness toward outsiders, their internal concord and love of each other, to put it all in a few words." But on closer inspection, even their apparent virtues cloaked a deeper evil within:

What can I say of their prayers? For they have such great care and devotion in their prayers that I was amazed when I saw and experienced it first hand. For I spent three and a half months with the camel nomads in the deserts of Arabia and Persia and never for any reason did I ever see these camel Arabs neglect to pray at the prescribed hours of the day or night, and particularly in the morning and the evening. They manifest such a devotion in their prayers that they put all other things from them. Some grow suddenly and unusually pale; others seem to be rapt. Some of them fall to the ground while others leap about and give out different sounds so that some of them seem to be rapt and others demonic. (Laurent 1873: 131-132)

The Muslims at prayer intrigued Christian visitors, as did their houses of prayer, the mosques all the more so because they were generally closed to Christians. Felix Fabri of course managed to get into one early in his

466

travels, the former church of St. George at Ludd or Lydda, now converted into a mosque.

The rest of the church has been cut off from the choir by a wall and they have made that part of it a fair mosque in honor of Muhammad and adorned it with a lofty tower. The door stood over against us so that we could see into the courtyard of the mosque and into the mosque itself, and it was like Paradise for cleanliness and beauty. (Felix Fabri 1893: I, 256)

Later Felix takes up the question of mosques more systematically. May the Christian enter them, for example for the express purpose of defiling them? The thought must have crossed more than one angry pilgrim's mind, as the discussion itself reveals:

In this there is no service of God, for our holy Mother Church tolerates the synagogues of the Jews and does not destroy them as it might. . . . The same argument applies to the mosques. [He then tells the story of a knight in his company who climbed up to the roof of a mosque and pissed down into it.] Which made us laugh much, for we were all amused at seeing him. But I do not see what virtue there was in what he did, neither could any good follow from it, but much evil; for had the Saracens known of it, we should not have left the country alive. For albeit in mosques God is untruly worshipped, yet they are built in honor of the true God and might be consecrated and made into Christian churches, as often happens when Christians take any town from the Saracens or Turks; and they in like manner make mosques of our churches, wherefore because of this property, not out of any respect for their ritual, one retains a certain respect for the temples of the Gentiles.

If not out of malice, then might one enter there out of simple curiosity?

Although I myself am fond of seeing strange and curious sights, yet I never was tempted to enter the Temple [Dome of the Rock], but was satisfied by the sight of it, by which I confess I have often been troubled and scandalized, when I compared the cleanliness, the beauty, and the decent order of the [Muslim] Temple with our churches, which, O shame, are like stables for beasts of burden. Our churches stand all dirty with people walking through them as though they were inns, and befouled with filth, to our great confusion and to the contempt and reproach of the sacraments. It is a burning shame to see at Jerusalem the church of Christ's Resurrection standing almost without decoration like a smoky hospice and to see the church of Muhammad neat and clean like a king's palace.

There follows a diatribe on the condition of certain European churches, particularly St. John Lateran's and St. Peter's in Rome. Felix then concludes:

O human brother, would you could see at Jerusalem how reverend is the appearance of this Temple of the execrable Muhammad, how pleasant is the approach thereto, . . . how clean and quiet its courtyard, how bright and neat everything is kept, how devoutly the worshippers enter therein, how gravely they bear themselves in praying, how modestly the women show themselves there, with their faces always veiled, and how the men pray in silence apart from them! (Felix Fabri 1893: II, 255-259)

Magumet Unmasked

One of a number of pilgrims who did not confine their efforts to a simple description of the holy places was the German visitor Ludolph von Suchem, who was in the Mamluk domains in the East between 1336 and 1341. [25] His work, composed after his return in 1350, is really two studies. One, on the *Situation of the Places in the Holy Land*, is comfortably within the genre of descriptive narratives on the holy places that pilgrims had been producing for centuries, but the second, his *Geographical and Ethnographical Description*, is more unusual in that it treats of the secular landscape, physical and human, of the Near East. It is in the course of this second part that Ludolph undertakes to provide the reader with a capsule summary of the origins and early development of Islam. Its themes, however, including the allegation of Muhammad's epilepsy, were not novel:

It is a fact that in the year of the Lord 620 the devil did, with God's permission, sow the Muhammadan heresy in the following manner. Earlier he had seduced a monk named Sergius, who was of the Order of St. Benedict but who had been cast out by reason of his Nestorianism, to strive for ecclesiastical honors in the Roman Curia. When he was unable to obtain what he wished, in desperation he went off into Arabia to the Hagarenes or Ishmaelites, who by reason of the nobility of Sarah, who in the first instance had adopted Ishmael as her son, call themselves Saracens. [26] Which indeed they are not; they are better called Magumetans after a certain unholy Magumet through whom so many unlettered wanderers in the desert were deceived.

The aforementioned Sergius, now in disfavor with the Roman Church and moved by self-love, found a rude and foolish man named Magumet, whom he so deluded that he thought himself a prophet. He put a kernel of grain in that latter's right ear and every day he taught a dove to perch on his shoulder and pluck out the kernel. He began to preach to the people that the God of heaven wished to raise up a prophet from the Hagarenes, who of all people were the lowest and most abject, and that God's Holy Spirit would appear in the form of a dove. When the people were convinced of that and when Magumet was standing in their midst, behold, he released the dove which soon was urged by its hunger to fly onto the shoulder of Magumet and seek out the kernel of grain in his ear. In that way Sergius indicated that he was a prophet sent by God to that people. And since he was known to none of them, while he himself knew nothing of his own parentage but had been exposed as an orphan, discovered in the desert, raised by others and eventually became a camel-keeper, thus this man unknown to everyone was thought to have come from heaven.

The fame of Magumet spread widely so that people came to him every day from afar. Then Sergius persuaded an Arab woman named Candugagij [Khadija], who was a widow, to marry him. When this was accomplished, Magumet by his power and deceit subjected the entire people to himself. And when by God's vengeance he became an epileptic and fell down sick, he said he had sustained that disease because of his discourse with an angel. After this he began to lay down his profane laws and to compose the book which they call *Alterianum*, which Sergius dictated but was ascribed to Magumet, who actually was totally ignorant of letters. [27]

The Muhammadans, then, believe in God Almighty, in His law, and in Magumet and St. Michael, to whom they confess their sins in the evening in the mountains. On Thursday they fast until evening but they feast all night, as they do at all their fasts. On Friday they have a feast of Venus, whom they celebrate like Gentiles. They are circumcised and do not eat pork, like the Jews. They wear a habit and shave (their heads) and genuflect like monks. They can have seven or more wives, and the ones they do not want they repudiate, like the pagans. Many of them poison each other because of the mutual hatred they bear. Similarly the men are weak and libidinous, they abuse men, and though they cannot sexually satisfy one wife, they wish to have many and so they are frequently poisoned by their wives. For these reasons they do not produce many offspring, though they spend a lot of time in sexual activities. All of this they were taught by that perfidious, filthy, and unclean Magumet.

The Muhammadans are pusillanimous, to the point that you scarcely hear one case in a century where one has killed or wounded another, and they carry on in their fights and scuffles like women. And so if they have occasionally conquered the Christians, it was accomplished more by cleverness than strength, God all the while imposing His hidden and just judgment. Likewise they are so wretched in the management of their affairs that no one is master of his own property, and the sultan through his amir takes whatever he wishes of their valuables, whether in city or town, and no one dares raise a word of contradiction.

Concerning the bishops of the Saracens, the Saracens have qadis and bishops in the cities, who rule and ordain their profane presbyters. . . . Their qadis are hard on Christians when these latter are accused of entering their shrines and churches or of blaspheming Magumet, for which crimes they are cut in four pieces, and for other reasons they are quick to throw them in prison. For this reason it is a serious business living in their midst. It would, nevertheless, be displeasing to the sultan were this harm to the Christians become known. (Ludolph von Suchem 1884: 371-373)

With his final remark, Ludolph returns us to the real world of Jerusalem and the Holy Land where Christians and Jews were everyday engaged in the "serious business" of living in a Muslim, and sometimes aggressively Muslim, society. If the examples cited by Bertrandon de la Brocquière are random and perhaps trivial, they are at least familiar and convey something of the atmosphere in a Mamluk city in the 1430s:

The Muhammadans have established a peculiar custom for Christians all through Syria, in not permitting them to enter the towns on horseback. None that are known to be such dare do it, and in consequence, our guide made Sir Sanson and myself dismount before we entered any town. Scarcely had we arrived in Damascus when about a dozen Saracens came round to look at us. I wore a broad beaver hat, which is unusual in that country, and one of them gave me a blow with a staff, which knocked it off my head onto the ground. I own that my first movement was to lift my fist at him; but the guide, throwing himself between us, pushed me aside, and very fortunately for me he did so, for in an instant we were surrounded by thirty or forty persons; and if I had delivered a blow, I know not what would have become of us. I mention this circumstance to show that the inhabitants of Damascus are a wicked race, and consequently, care should be taken to avoid quarrels with them. It is the same in other Muhammadan countries. I know by experience that you must not joke with them, nor at the same time seem afraid nor appear poor, for then they will despise you; nor rich, for they are very avaricious, as all who have disembarked at Jaffa know to their cost. (Bertrandon de la Brocquière 1848: 293-294)

The Protection of Christians

Though not all the Mamluk sultans would be so displeased as Ludolph thought at the mistreatment of their non-Muslim subjects, some at least attempted to uphold the prescriptions of Muslim law in their regard. The following inscription was affixed to the wall next to the entry to the Church of the Holy Sepulcher until the middle of the nineteenth century:

In the name of God, the Merciful, the Compassionate: It has been decreed by august, noble executive order of Sultan al-Malik al-Ashraf Sayf al-Dunya wal-Din [A.D. 1501-1517]—may God advance and ennoble him and enable him to carry out [his plan] and to act freely—that the community of Christian monks and nuns, whether Melkites or Jacobites, be compelled to render neither obligation nor payment nor incur any penalty upon their entering the Holy Sepulcher in Jerusalem; likewise the Georgians and the Abyssinians, not upon their entering Jaffa nor upon leaving Jaffa; neither in Gaza nor at Ludd. For the above-mentioned monks and nuns arriving by land or by sea and from every quarter to make a visitation to Jerusalem, this law is valid for all time, without modification or arbitrary change. It is also forbidden for anyone to interfere with them on this occasion nor in their cemetery, that is, the tombs in which they are buried. No one shall interfere with their dead or the guardians thereof.

The monks and nuns of the Greek and Coptic rites are exempt from obligation in the above-mentioned areas on the usual days and on Easter, according to their custom, and [this decree] forestalls whoever would attempt to interfere in this. The present arrangements are supported by previous royal decrees, which are in their [that is, the Christians'] hands and by the royal decree of al-Malik al-Ashraf which they possess and which they observe, to wit, that they are monks, non-Muslim subjects, and that they have firmans, judicial records, and royal decrees attesting to this on their behalf.

They have requested that this royal decree concerning this be carved in marble and affixed to the doorway of the Holy Sepulcher. Let this be a commemoration of the justice of our master al-Maqam al-Sharif—may his victory be glorious—over the course of many ages [and] as an act of charity toward them pursuant to the representation made by the clergyman Sophronius, the Melkite monk, and its submission to the royal government.

The decree was subsequently promulgated in accordance with the account presented by the monks and nuns, was invested with the royal signature by royal order—may God show him honor and make him great. Dated the blessed ninth of this month of Sacred Muharram in the year 919 [March 17, 1513]. Praise be to God alone and safely be kept the Last of the Prophets. (van Berchem 1922: #108, trans. K. Schaefer)

Felix Fabri remarks upon something similar from his own experience of Sultan Qa'it Bay (1468-1496), the builder of the Ashrafiyya Madrasa and benefactor of Muslim Jerusalem, in this case in Bethlehem:

During my first pilgrimage the roof of the church [at Bethlehem], which was of great weight because it is made of lead, was threatening to fall in upon the choir . . . and I have often sorrowed deeply, fearing that the church would fall into irretrievable ruin; for had it fallen down it never would have been rebuilt; for thus are the Saracens charged by Muhammad in his Alcoran, that they suffer not the Christians to build new churches, nor to repair their old ones. So for many years the sultan refused permission to the Christians to repair the breaches of that church. Howbeit, at length being overcome by the constant entreaties of the Minorite brethren of Mount Sion, he relaxed his strictness, and allowed the breaches to be repaired. . . . Not only did the Lord and King of Egypt, Sultan Catube [Qaʾit Bay] grant permission for the repair of this church, but he even allowed much to be set up again among the ruins of the Church of the Holy Sepulcher, contrary to the law of Muhammad his prophet. . . . [A comparison is drawn with Cyrus, who permitted the Jews to rebuild the Temple.] Even so in truth the sultan, moved by the spirit of God, gave leave to repair the holy places, and would give leave to do much more did not the railing enemies of the Christians turn him away from his purposes. . . . Nor should we believe, as many do, that the sultan is chiefly moved by the love of money, and of the gain that he receives from the pilgrims, in that he suffers the churches of the Christians to be re-paired. . . . (Felix Fabri 1893: I, 600-602)

The Jewish Community

In both instances action was taken, as the texts themselves tell us, because of certain representations made within the Christian community; redress was offered and abuses were addressed specifically for the benefit of that community. We are unlikely to hear of such representations made or responded to with regard to the Jews, however. By all reports they were still a very small group in Jerusalem even in the sixteenth century. It is the reports themselves that grow in number since there were assuredly greater numbers of European Jews who were coming to the Holy Land, particularly as the attacks upon Jews in a re-Christianizing Spain picked up after A.D. 1391. As all the Jewish travel accounts of the time attest, moreover, Jewish growth in Palestine was occurring not in Jerusalem but in revived Jewish settlements in Galilee, particularly in Safed and its neighborhood. The tombs there of great scholars and mystics were turning Galilee into a kind of rabbinic holy land within a biblical one. And just as the Crusades, which created a Latin population that lived in Palestine and was not merely visiting it, gave a new concreteness and reality to descriptions of the land and thinking about it, the Jewish migration into Galilee, through the travel literature that reflected it, created a new "realistic" picture of the land of Israel and of its prospects. [28]

The Jerusalem Jews did not possess the kinds of resources that either provoked envy, as the Christians' sometimes did, or could lead to its redress afterwards. [29] Nor were the Jews outspoken on the subject of Islam or Muslims. They ignored or were indifferent to the theological issues between themselves and Islam, just as they were to similar questions regarding Christianity, though at least one author permitted himself some remarks on some of the social differences and similarities, Meshullam of Volterra, who visited Jerusalem in 1481:

The Muslims and also the Jews of this place [Jerusalem] are pigs at their eating. They all eat out of one vessel with their fingers, without a napkin, just as the Cairenes do, but their clothes are clean. . . . The customs of the Muslims are diverse from all people for everyone marries twenty or thirty wives as he pleases, but they do not see them until they go home; and the men give dowries to the women, and from the day of marriage the man is only bound to give her food, but her clothes and all the other things she requires she has to make for herself. And when she is with child the Muslims do not touch her until two months after the child is born, for that would be great sin, and the wife is bound to pay for the food and clothes of all her sons and daughters; therefore they are all openly harlots, and when they do not wish to stay with their husbands they go to the niepo [the na'ib, or governor], the lord of the city, and say that their husband does not give them food and they are believed, and the husband must divorce his wife; for the Muslims give divorce like the Jews. . . . (Adler 1966: 194-195)

These comments do not constitute a model of accuracy, but they are noticeably less pointed and polemical than those of Christians who visited the city. The Jews of Jerusalem constituted no threat to Muslim sovereignty and generally tended to their own community affairs, as far as we can see. The result was that they were generally ignored, though there were of course some occasional conflicts, in this case over shared biblical grave sites:

All round Jerusalem there are many caves and in them are buried many pious and saintly people without number, but we do not know who they are except those marked; it is a tradition among us, however, from mouth to mouth in ancient times, and there is no doubt as to their truth, and we see that the Muslims also honor all these places and that they have the same traditions about them as we. They ask the Jews "Why do you not go to the grave of such a saint or such a prophet?" The Muslims have many a time sought to have these graves closed up or to have them dedicated as waqf in their hands, but God has opposed their intention and would not listen to them, for the keeper of Israel neither sleepeth nor slumbereth. (Adler 1966: 193-194)

Because the Jews who came to Jerusalem were not mere transients and moreover lived inside one of the communities of the city, their accounts are useful barometers of the economic health of the place. The changes are quite noticeable in these three accounts, for example, from Nachmanides in 1267, not long after Jerusalem's brush with the Mongols, the second Isaac ben Joseph in 1334, and finally Obadiah of Bertinoro in about 1487:

But what am I to say to you with regard to this country? Great is the solitude and great the wastes and, to characterize it in short, the more sacred the places, the greater their desolation! Jerusalem is more desolate than the rest of the country; Judea more than Galilee. But even in this destruction it is a blessed land. It [Jerusalem] has about 2,000 inhabitants, about 300 Christians live there who escaped the sword of the sultan. There are no Jews. For since the arrival of the Tartars [Mongols], some fled, others died by the sword. There are only two brothers, dyers by trade, who have to buy their ingredients from the government. There the Ten Men [made up from among visitors] meet and on Sabbaths they hold service at their house. But we encouraged them, and we succeeded in finding a vacant house built on pillars of marble and with a beautiful arch. That we took for a synagogue. For the town is without a master and whoever will take possession of ruins can do so. We gave our offerings towards the repairs of the house. We have sent already to Shechem to fetch some scrolls of the Law from there which had been brought thither from Jerusalem at the invasion of the Tartars. Thus they will organize a synagogue and worship there. For continually people crowd to Jerusalem, men and women, from Damascus, Aleppo, and from all parts of the country to see the Sanctuary and mourn over it. (Kobler 1978: I, 226)

Sixty years later the Mamluks had managed to bring some semblance of stability to the land and the city:

The Jewish community in Jerusalem, God be gracious to her, is quite numerous. It is composed of fathers of families from all parts of the world, principally from France. The leading men of the community, as well as the principal rabbis, came from the latter kingdom. . . . They live there in happiness and tranquillity, each according to his condition and fortune, for the royal authority is just and great. . . . Among the different members of the holy congregation at Jerusalem are many who are engaged in hand-icrafts such as dyers, tailors, shoemakers, etc. Others carry on a rich commerce in all sorts of things and have fine shops. Some are devoted to science, such as medicine, astronomy, and mathematics. But the greater number of their learned men are working day and night at the study of the Holy Law and of the true wisdom, which is Kabbala. These are maintained out of the coffers of the community, because the study of the law is their only calling.

There was even a specialty trade, not entirely inappropriate in the holy city of Jerusalem, the copying of Torah scrolls which were so fine that:

... copies are sought for by strangers who carry them away to their own countries. I have seen a Pentateuch written with so much art that several persons at once wanted to acquire it and it was only for an excessively high price that the chief of the Synagogues of Babylon carried it off with him to Baghdad. (Adler 1966: 133-134)

By the late fifteenth century the situation was grim once again, not now by reason of the Mongols or a Muslim persecution—on the contrary, relations were good—but because the entire Mamluk enterprise was collapsing, and the bedouin of Palestine were as usual among the predators:

Jerusalem is for the most part desolate and in ruins. I need not repeat that it is not surrounded by walls. Its inhabitants, I am told, number about 4,000 families. As for Jews, about seventy families of the poorest class have remained. There is scarcely a family that is not in want of the most common necessaries; one who has bread for a year is called rich. Among the Jewish population there are many aged, forsaken widows from Germany, Spain and Portugal, and other countries, so that there are seven women to one man. . . . The Jews are not persecuted by the Arabs in these parts. I have travelled through the country in its length and breadth, and none of them has put an obstacle in my way. They are not very kind to strangers, particularly to anyone who does not know the language; but if they see many Jews together they are not annoyed by it. In my opinion, an intelligent man versed in political science might easily raise himself to be chief of the Jews as well as of the Arabs; for among the inhabitants there is not a wise or a sensible man who knows how to deal affably with his fellow men; all are ignorant misanthropes intent only on gain. . . .

    The synagogue here is built on columns; it is long narrow and dark. . . . There is a fountain in the middle of it. In the court of the synagogue, quite close to it stands a mosque. The court of the synagogue is very large and contains many houses, all of them buildings devoted by the Ashkenazis to charitable purposes and inhabited by Ashkenazi widows. There

were formerly many courts in the Jewish streets belonging to these buildings, but the elders sold them, so that not a single one remained. . . . The
Jews' street and the houses are very large; some of them dwell also on
Sion. At one time there were more houses, but these are now heaps of
rubbish and cannot be rebuilt because the law of the land is that a Jew
may not rebuild his ruined house without permission, and the permission
often costs more than the whole house is worth.

   Not an inhabited city is to be found there for the bedouin destroy
everything. They come even up to the gates of Jerusalem, steal and plunder in the open roads, and no one can interfere with them, they are so
numerous. For this reason the district is all waste, without inhabitants.
(Adler 1966 234-235, 241)

The situation had not improved materially when a few years later one of
Obadiah's disciples undertook to describe Jerusalem as it was in 1495, a
year before Mujir al-Din wrote his history of the city.

When I saw the desolate and ruined city from a distance, and Mount Sion
lying waste, a habitation for jackals and a lurking place for young lions
which foxes traverse, my spirit overflowed, my heart mourned, and my
eyes filled with tears. I sat down and wept, and rent my garments in two
places as is required; and I prayed facing our Temple. May the Lord in
His loving kindness bring back the captivity of Jacob speedily and in our
days, that we may merit to see the rebuilding of our glorious mansion, so
that it be His will, Amen.

   In Jerusalem the Holy there are about two hundred householders who
refrain from any sin or transgression and are heedful in the performance
of the commandments. Evening and morning and noon they all gather
together, rich and poor alike, to pray with full and complete concentration. . . . Every day after the prayer and the sermon people stay in the
House of Study in order to spend about three hours in the study of the
Mishna and the Talmud; and afterward they "go from strength to
strength," visiting the sick and giving gifts to the poor, each one giving
what his heart counsels him. The people give much alms although they
have little themselves, and there are many poor folk in this city, so that
most of the congregation are supported by charity.

   There is little to be earned here in Jerusalem the Holy from the produce
of the area. Any craftsman, such as a goldsmith or a blacksmith or a flax-
weaver or a tailor, will earn his needs, albeit scantily. But in Damascus
and Egypt, at Alexandria, and at Aleppo, which is Aram Zobah, in all
these places handicraftsmen can earn as much as they desire, particularly
those who know the Arabic language, according to what I have heard.
Here artisans can only earn a meager penny, except possibly goldsmiths.

However, food is not so expensive here, and this year bread and wine are cheap, praise the blessed God. I think a man can sustain himself with ten ducats a year. (Wilhelm 1946: 22-25)

But whatever the physical circumstances were, of poverty or prosperity, assuredly no one had forgotten:

All of these [rabbis] go every year with the congregation behind them to Mount Sion on the Ninth of Ab to mourn and weep, and thence they descend to the Valley of Jehoshaphat and go upon Mount Olivet whence they see the whole of the Temple area and mourn for the destruction of the Temple. . . . Muslims call the whole surroundings of Jerusalem al-Quds, that is, the holy land. May it be the will of our Father in heaven that it may be rebuilt speedily in our days. Amen. (Adler 1966: 196)

The Ecumenical Spirit of
Arnold von Harff

The Christians generally took little notice of these Jews in the Holy Land, and even a professional polemicist like Ricoldo of Monte Croce was more interested in taking on the *idea* of Judaism than debating with the poor tradesmen and pious rabbis who lived in Jerusalem in the thirteenth century. There is one exception, however, Arnold von Harff, whose interest in the local languages and customs brought him into this rather odd contact with some rather odd Jews in the Holy City sometime about 1495:

Within Jerusalem live many Jews, among them certain learned doctors of Christian teaching, born in Lombardy, and two Christian monks who within three years fell away from the Christian faith to the Jewish sect, with whom I had much conversation and questioning, which would take too long to relate. I found also three German Jews in Jerusalem, as also in all heathen and Turkish places. I kept company with them often on account of the language and learnt to write the alphabet and retained also certain words from their daily speech, as they are written here.

He then reproduces the Hebrew alphabet and a list of single words for memorization. Finally, there is a list of useful phrases for the adventuresome traveller whose interests go beyond the holy places:

kamme tetim ly? "How much will you give me?"
anoge etten lachae cambi. "I will give you so much."
ma schemo? "What is his name?"
jehudde atta? "Are you a Jew?"
ken dibarta. "You are right."

planosa anoge tzogeff eitzelga see halegla. *"Woman, let me sleep with you tonight."*

anoge etten lagae zahaff. *"I will give you a gulden."*

(Arnold von Harff 1946: 217-218)

Jerusalem: Sanctity and Sovereignty

In 1331 the Muslim traveller Ibn Battuta found himself in Constantinople, the capital of Eastern Christendom. He met there someone named Georgios who was identified to him as a former emperor who had left the throne and taken up the monastic life. They stopped, Muslim and Christian, and chatted:

The king asked about me, then stopped and said to the Greek [accompanying him], who knew the Arabic tongue, "Say to this Saracen that I clasp the hand that has entered Jerusalem and the foot that has walked within the Dome of the Rock and the great church called Qumama and Bethlehem," and so saying he put his hand on my feet and passed it over his face. I was amazed at their belief in the merits of one who, though not of their religion, had entered those places. He then took me by the hand and as I walked with him asked me about Jerusalem and the Christians living there and he questioned me at length. . . . I said to him: "I should very much like to go into the church with you," but he said to the interpreter, "Tell him that everyone who enters it must prostrate himself before the great cross, for this is a rule laid down by the ancients and cannot be contravened." So I left him and he entered alone, and I did not see him again. (Ibn Battuta 1959-1962: 512-513)

It was, perhaps, quite as simple as Felix Fabri imagined it:

At this present day the Christians would care little about the Saracens' bearing rule in Jerusalem, provided only that we were allowed freedom to pass in and out of our temple of the Lord's sepulcher without fear and without vexations and extortions. Neither would the Saracens mind if the Christians were lords of the Holy City, if we would render up their Temple to them. But since Christians and Saracens cannot agree about this matter, unhappy Jerusalem has suffered, doth now suffer, and will hereafter suffer sieges, castings down, destructions, and terrors beyond any other city in the world. (Felix Fabri 1893: II, 262)

The End of the Middle Ages

. . . superstition on the one side and tyranny on the other endangering
the best pilgrimage, which is the peaceable way of a good conscience
to that Jerusalem which is above.
—Purchas His Pilgrims

IN A.D. 1516 Jerusalem underwent its last change of sovereignty until
modern times. The new masters of the Holy City were the Ottoman
Turks—Muslims and outsiders to the Islamic heartlands like the Mamluks
they replaced. Also like the Mamluks, they chose to rule their new possession from afar, this time from Istanbul, the former Constantinople, once
capital and heart of the Christian Roman Empire in the East.

The Ottomans' takeover of Jerusalem, like that of the Mamluks from
the Ayyubids, was a peaceful affair, and in at least one account appears
marked more by a concern for privileges than for safety:

When Jerusalem was in the possession of the Circassian Mamluks all the
religious scholars and pious men went out to meet [the new conqueror]
Selim Shah in 922 [A.D. 1516]. They handed him the keys to the Mosque
al-Aqsa and the Dome of the Rock of God.[1] *Selim prostrated himself and*
exclaimed "Thanks be to God! I am now the possessor of the Sanctuary
of the first qibla." He then made presents to all the notable people, ex-
empted them from onerous taxes, and confirmed them [in their posts].
He then passed the Documents of Umar,[2] *which were in the possession*
of the Greek and Frankish monks, over his face and eyes and gave them a
Royal Writ, confirming to the monks the contents of the documents, to
wit, that they were exempted from paying taxes[3] *and that the Anastasis*
was to be their prayer place, as before. (Chelebi 1980: 59-60)

The City Renewed

The author of this account was the Ottoman notable Evliye Chelebi, who
was speaking at a distance of more than a century and so reflected the
concerns that still troubled Jerusalem at the time of his own visit in A.D.
1648-1650. There were more immediate reactions to the change of regime, however, like that of the anonymous Jewish resident of the city at
the time of Sultan Suleiman (A.D. 1520-1566), the prodigious ruler called
in the West "the Magnificent."

Jerusalem the Holy City has been destroyed through our sins. Nothing is left of the old structure except for a little of the foundation of the walls. Now in 1537 they have begun to build the walls around the city by order of the king, Sultan Suleiman. They have also put a great fountain in the Temple. . . . [And from another, Joseph ha-Kohen:] In the year 1540 [sic] God aroused the spirit of Suleiman, king of Rumelia and Persia, and he set out to build the walls of Jerusalem, the holy city in the land of Judah. And he sent officials who built its walls and set up its gates as in former times and its towers as in bygone days. And his fame spread throughout the land for he wrought a great deed. And they also extended the tunnel into the town lest the people thirst for water. (Hirschberg et al. 1973: 77)

Thus between 1537 and 1541 Sultan Sulieman undertook the rewalling of the city of Jerusalem, which had been without protection except for the isolated Citadel since al-Mu'azzam razed the walls in 1219, and which was ever the prey of the bedouin who had all but held the city besieged in late Mamluk times. [4] But though the Ottomans were more than generous when it came to maintaining their Syrian cities, this rebuilding of Jerusalem's walls, together with the aqueduct project and the work on the Haram, represents the beginning and almost the end of Ottoman concern and investment in the Holy City. [5] Jerusalem, it appears, continued to suffer from its now chronic condition of spiritual grandeur unaccompanied by the slightest commercial or military importance.

Chelebi takes us on a tour of the rebuilt gates of the city, starting on the southeast corner and proceeding clockwise: [6] the Dung or Maghrebi Gate, so called because of the Moroccan quarter just inside it; a "water tower," David's Gate, also called Sion Gate; then turning north, the Gate of the Friend of the Merciful, that is, Abraham's Gate, today the Jaffa Gate; a "leaning tower" at the northwest corner of the city, the so-called Tower of Goliath, or Tancred; the Bozdoghan Qapu—so called, Chelebi explains, since the recent execution there of a Kurdish wrestler, presumably of that name—also called Gate of the Iron War Mace, our Damascus Gate; a Cave of the Ghosts, where Solomon imprisoned the *jinn*; [7] the Zahira or Sahira Gate; [8] around the corner and to the south, the Gate of the Tribes, presently St. Stephen's Gate; then "an exposed double iron gate," obviously the Golden Gate; and finally the "Shrine of Mary," sometimes called the "Cradle of Jesus," down through the Stables of Solomon.

The Citadel

In Ottoman times, as in all previous eras of the city back to Herod the Great, the Citadel at the western gate was the core of the defensive system of Jerusalem:

The [space enclosed by the Citadel walls] constituted a large fortress, con-structed of ashlars, when it was built by the order of Sultan Selim by Mustafa Lale Pasha with (the revenues of) twelve districts, in an inde-scribable manner. The Citadel, destroyed in olden times, rises to something between forty and fifty Meccan yards from the foundation. It was built outside the city walls, while the mosques of al-Aqsa and of the Rock are within them. It is a square, strong fortress of huge construction, each ashlar having the size of a lion or the hind-parts of an elephant. . . .

Within the Jaffa Gate the Citadel is connected on one side with the main [city] fortress. There is another small, inner fortress [the Citadel proper], four hundred paces in circumference with three exposed iron gates opening into the large fortress. From the first gate one crosses a wooden bridge leading into the Citadel proper. This building, grey with age, has a Council Chamber (or Court of Justice), embellished with very many war implements, situated within the Citadel.

In the Citadel live the commandant, the deputy of the governor, a prayer leader, a preacher, a muezzin, and soldiers. There are altogether seventy stone-built rooms within, and exceedingly small ones at that. The garden of the commandant of the Citadel is a small flourishing one, situ-ated in the moat of the Citadel.

The corner tower of the righthand side of the entrance to the Citadel is the tower and noble dwelling built by David himself. For sentimental reasons it is not inhabited but used as an ammunition depot and treasury. It has an iron door. The tower is built with ashlars measuring five to six yards. Verily, there is no doubt whatever about it having been constructed by spirits. . . . The prayer niche of the mosque of David in the Citadel is directed toward the north [sic] to the mosque of al-Aqsa. When thereafter the verse "Turn your face to the noble sanctuary" [Quran 2:144] was transmitted to Muhammad, the direction during prayers was instituted toward Mecca. Sultan Isa [al-Mu'azzam] of the Ayyubids had this prayer place of David transformed into a mosque and placed a white marble slab in the left wall of it with a dated inscription [from A.D. 1213-1214] (Che-lebi 1980: 64, 66-67)

We are given another, somewhat different view of these fortifications about a century after Chelebi from the pen of Elzear Horn, a member of the Franciscan community in Jerusalem from 1724 to 1744:

The city has an ancient fort, to which to this day the name "Pisan" is attached, on account of its structure, which is quite strong; yet for want of fortifications and ramparts the city can be easily taken from every side without the explosion of the instruments of war. After the Pisans the Saracens occupied this castle, now, however, the Turks: their Sultan Selim, the last one to capture Jerusalem, ordered it to be completely restored with cut and carefully dressed stones, as is evident from the upper part of the structure, which looks new in comparison to the other. He always appointed for it a special commander, who lived there with his Janissaries, without whose permission or gratis no one was given access to it. . . . It has many cannons projecting from the walls, but they are not carefully guarded because the Turks know well that the Christians neglect its recovery owing to dissensions among themselves. It is indeed surrounded by ditches, which do not, however, contain water. Whenever the Turks celebrate a great feast, or some of their principal men come from a distance, they shoot three, six, or nine cannons here. (Horn 1962: 33)

The Ottomans and the Haram

As a new Islamic regime in the city, the Ottomans naturally showed an interest in the Haram, and once again it was Suleiman who was chiefly responsible for the Ottoman construction there. It was not so impressive as what the Mamluks had done there perhaps, but Chelebi could describe the work with justifiable pride:

The Mosque of the Rock of God lies to the north of the Aqsa Mosque already mentioned. From this latter mosque one goes through a meadow over a pavement of two hundred paces of white unhewn marble flagstones laid out by the order of Sultan Suleiman the Magnificent. Thence one directs one's steps to a huge marble water basin [called al-Kas, "the cup"] made of a single block according to Sultan Suleiman's own directions. . . .

In the year 926 [A.D. 1520] Sultan Suleiman the Magnificent acceded to the throne, conquered the fortress of Belgrade, and later on the island of Rhodes and Malta [sic] and thereby accumulated immense wealth. When he became an independent king, the Prophet appeared to him in a "blessed night"[9] and told him: "O Suleiman, you will attain the age forty-eight years (of rule) and will make many conquests. . . . You should spend these spoils on embellishing Mecca and Medina, and for the fortification of the Citadel of Jerusalem, in order to repulse the unbelievers, when they attempt to take possession of Jerusalem during the reign of your followers. You should also embellish its Sanctuary with a water basin and offer annual money gifts to the dervishes there, and also embellish the Rock of God and rebuild Jerusalem."

Such being the order of the Prophet, Suleiman Khan at once rose from his sleep and sent from his spoils 1,000 purses to Medina and another 1,000 to Jerusalem. Together with the required material, he dispatched the master architect Qoja Sinan to Jerusalem and transferred Lale Mustafa

Pasha from the governorship of Egypt to that of Syria. This latter, having been ordered to carry out the restoration of Jerusalem, gathered all the master builders, architects, and sculptors available in Cairo, Damascus, and Aleppo and sent them to Jerusalem to rebuild it and embellish the Holy Rock, so much so that the verse "These are the Gardens of Eden . . . enter ye them . . . " was justly written over the "Gate of Paradise" [the northern gate] in the Dome of the Rock. Verily, it is a replica of a heavenly place. (Chelebi 1980: 73-75)

A New Beginning

The effect of this Ottoman interest and investment in Jerusalem was, at least at the outset, generally positive. There were many new Jewish visitors to Palestine in the early sixteenth century, and though their destination was most often Jerusalem, many of them paused to note a new phenomenon, large-scale Jewish immigration, not in this instance to Jerusalem, but to Galilee. The town of Safed in particular began to enjoy an aura of both holiness and prosperity,[10] in part due to the skills brought by the new migrants, but a functionn also of the overall economic and political stability the Ottomans brought to their new Arab provinces.

Military architecture did not generally impress Jewish visitors to Jerusalem. Many of them came from a mercantile European society, and it was the examples of similar commerce that attracted their attention, and often their admiration, not only in Safed but in Jerusalem itself. Rabbi Moses of Basola was in the Holy City between 1520 and 1523 when it still had not recovered from its last days of Mamluk neglect, but the commercial monuments of earlier Mamluk prosperity, and the still lively activity going on in them, impressed the Italian visitor:

I walked around and circled Jerusalem, peace be unto it, and the Temple, may it be rebuilt speedily in our days. Even though Jerusalem is destroyed and desolate, a little bit of all its beauty can be recognized in lovely buildings and markets. It has four markets covered with domes: one, of the Ishmaelites, who sell wool and linen clothing; one, of Jews, most of whom sell haberdashery and spices; one for vegetables, and one for all kinds of foods and all fruits. There is another market, more beautiful than the others: it is entirely for cotton material. At one end of the market is a gate to the Temple. (Yaʿari 1976: 147, trans. M. Swartz)

The condition of Jerusalem under the Ottomans had in fact materially improved from what it had been in the closing years of the Mamluk era, and what was for Moses of Basola merely an impression can be verified with more objective data. The Ottoman tax registers for Palestine are extant for the years 1525, 1533, and 1553, and the figures for those years reveal the following increases in the tax-paying households of Jerusalem:

1525	Muslims:	3,670	Christians:	714	and Jews:	1,194
1533	Muslims:	7,708	Christians:	884	and Jews:	1,363
1553	Muslims:	11,912	Christians:	1,956	and Jews:	1,958

Thus, if we accept Lewis' calculation of six people to a "household," we reach a total population increase from about 5,600 in 1525 to 9,250 in 1533, and finally in 1553, less than forty years after the Ottoman takeover, to 15,826 souls. [11] This upturn in the economic and social prosperity of Palestine generally and Jerusalem in particular was likewise noted by visitors. Indeed, the conditions of the Jews in the Muslim world in the sixteenth century were appreciably better than in David dei Rossi's native Italy:

Here we are not in exile as in our country [of Italy]. Here, as well as in Alexandria in Egypt, those appointed over the customs and the king's tolls are Jews; and there is no wrongdoing anywhere in the kingdom. There are no special Jewish taxes here, albeit this year, because of the war with the Sophy [i.e., the Sufi, the Safavid Shah of Iran], the Jews were required to lend some money to the princes. Some of the princes gave them pledges in return, and some gave them the sources of the income of the town; and the Jews collect them. But the scholars have no payment to make, saving the poll-tax. (Wilhelm 1946: 35-36)

The same note of optimism is echoed, in a more religious vein, by Solomon ben Hayyim Meinsterl of Ludenburg, a visitor in 1607:

Now the Gentiles who dwell on the soil of Israel are all subject to the holiness of Israel. Even though we stand all day long in the field, wearing our prayer shawls and phylacteries and calling upon the Lord our God in a great voice at the graves of the saint, not a single Gentile would dare approach a congregation of Jews when they are praying, or open his mouth to mock at the prayer, God forbid. On the contrary, they hold the graves of our holy masters in great reverence, as well as the synagogues; and they kindle lights at the graves of the saints and vow to supply the synagogues with oil. (Wilhelm 1946: 60)

Rabbi Moses Basola, 1480-1560

Solomon ben Hayyim's appreciation of life under the new rulers of *Eretz Israel* has a utopian, almost pastoral quality. Other witnesses, though still

484

generally positive, portray the fabric of Jewish life in Jerusalem more concretely. One such writer was Rabbi Moses of Basola, who was in Jerusalem between 1520 and 1523. Here he describes his visit to the holy places in and around the Kedron Valley:

Jerusalem is on one mountain; across from it is the Mount of Olives, and there is a narrow valley between them, the Valley of Jehoshaphat. I went down into it, and at one end there is a large hole which looks like a kind of cave. They say that the mouth of Gehenna is there for the time to come, when Gog comes. Below this there are graves of Jews on the whole slope of the mountain, and a few on the incline of the mountain of Jerusalem. [12] *Half a mile below them are the waters of Siloam, and on the plain there are many beautiful gardens watered by those waters. It goes out from the mountain of Jerusalem, and no one knows from where it flows. On the visible end, there is a building which was once beautiful, with domes. They say that Solomon, may he rest in peace, minted coins there.*

At the bottom of the Mount of Olives I saw the cave of Zachariah the Prophet, which is very lovely: it is all carved as one piece—the mountain is around it—and it is made into twelve columns, and its top is pointed, also all of one piece. Near it is a pit called the "Pit of the Daughters." They say that the daughters of Israel threw themselves into it at the time of the Destruction. There are two fine caves there, one made into niches all around, and one of fingers. Under them is a wide tower pointed at the top, which is Absalom's monument mentioned in the book of Samuel [2 Sam. 18:18].

Above, near the top of the mountain, is the cave of Haggai the Prophet, may he rest in peace, and below are caves large in width and circumference. Above the caves is the cave of Haggai, and below are the caves of his students and others besides. At the top of the Mount of Olives there is a large building, and there in a beautiful pavillion is Huldah the Prophetess in a marble grave. Also, one must pay an Ishmaelite guard there four dirhams to enter, and contribute oil for lighting, for there are perpetual lamps there.

Or his view of the Temple and visit to Mount Sion:

In Jerusalem I rented a room in a large house called the House of Pilate. I lived on an upper storey, and from there I could see the whole Temple enclosure, into the courtyard. There is no house in Jerusalem from which as much can be seen; God has brought it about for me. There, every morning at dawn, I recited the prayer facing the Temple before going to the synagogue. Blessed be the Lord who has found me worthy of this.

When one stands at the top of the Mount of Olives and looks across to

Jerusalem, he sees the whole Temple, the courts and gardens. On that side, the eastern, the Temple has two closed iron gates whose ends are embedded in the earth. They call this the Gates of Mercy [the Golden Gate]. They say that bridegrooms entered through one and mourners through the other. Near the Temple on the south side is a building called Solomon's Academy [the Aqsa Mosque].

Outside Jerusalem on the south side is Mount Sion; the Nagid, may his Rock and Creator preserve him, told me that the place of the Jews also went from Mount Sion up to the Temple; and it stands to reason. And that is the true interpretation of the verse: "Sion, in the far north" [Ps. 48:3]. On Mount Sion there is a place for [Christian] priests, like the conventi of Italy. Adjoining it is a iron door; they say that David and Solomon are buried there. The Ishmaelites never allow anyone to enter these two places. On that side is a well-fortified citadel: they call it David's Tower. The tomb of Jesus is in Jerusalem, to the west: two churches, one opposite the other; a market passes between them, and there is a small square in front of one of the churches. . . .

That much almost any tourist in Jerusalem would have seen, but when it comes to the Jewish quarter and the buildings and population there, we hear new information:

There is only one synagogue in Jerusalem. It is beautiful, with four columns in a row; it is sixty-three feet long and twenty-eight wide. In front of the Ark is a room with Torah scrolls all around—there are more than sixty. They pray towards the east, facing the Temple. The synagogue has no light except from the entrance, which is on the west, and there is a small window over it. They also use the lamps that they light all about for light during the day.

As was already becoming apparent in the Mamluk era, the Jewish population of Jerusalem was not merely growing, it was becoming increasingly diverse. The Christian reconquest of Spain, which had been energetically pursued for centuries and was completed by 1493, set large numbers of Jews in motion, first to the Maghreb, the western provinces of Islam in North Africa, and ever eastward, to Egypt and Palestine.[13] Many who came to the Holy Land settled in Safed and other places in Galilee, but Jerusalem too received its share of new immigrants:

The congregation (in Jerusalem) is of all kinds. There are fifteen Ashkenazi householders, but the majority are Spanish; and there are Arabized (Jews), who are Moorish, long-ago natives of that country, and "westerners" who come from Barbary. In all there are about three hundred householders, excluding widows, who number more than six hundred, and who are well provided for in Jerusalem, for they do not pay any tax or levy. The community is financed because of them, for when they die it receives everything if there is no heir, and from this most public works have been done. Those who receive charity number more than two hundred souls. The Ashkenazi poor are not included in this category because their support comes from Venice.

Men of note in Jerusalem: the father of them all is his Honor Rabbi Isaac Shollal, who is crowned with the crown of Torah, the crown of priesthood, and the crown of royalty and wealth. And the crown of a good name, because of all the good works he does for the poor and students of Torah, rises on top of them all; his Honor Rabbi David ibn Shoshan, physician and head of the Spanish (Sephardic) Yeshiva; and with him an honored and humble man, his Honor Abraham Ha-Levi, who wrote "The Untyer of Knots." Eight or nine Sephardis gather with them and had been learning the tractate Yom Tov; his Honor Rabbi Israel, head of the Yeshiva of the Ashkenazis; and with him Rabbi Peretz who has recently come from Germany. They are learning tractate Baba Metzia. Four or five of the Arabized Jews gather there, as well as Rabbi Judah of Corbeil, who is Spanish, and Rabbi Shlomo of Camerino—twelve or thirteen in all.

Each sage served as judge in Jerusalem for one year, and then a man named Rabbi David Aroch, who is a worker of gold and silver, served as judge; now there is a judge from among the Arabized, who serves permanently. There is also an honored man who teaches beginning students named Rabbi Joseph. Each sage reads from Maimonides in the synagogue after morning prayers for one month. All his fellows listen to him and then go to the Yeshiva. (Ya'ari 1976: 140-145, trans. M. Swartz)

Perilous Times

Life, then, seemed prosperous in early Ottoman Jerusalem, though it was a fragile prosperity at best, shaken not by plague, draught, or natural disaster but by the works of man. The following passage from a Jewish memoir written in 1625-1626 underlines both the prosperity of the city under that generation of Ottomans and the sudden reversal of political fortunes that could strike down Jew, Christian, and Arab Muslim alike:

In the year 1625 under Sultan Murad of Turkey, Muhammad Pasha was the governor of Jerusalem. The city of our God was then more greatly populated than at any time since the first exile when Jews constantly arrived to settle here. In addition pilgrims came to pray to "Him who stands behind our wall." . . . They would not come empty-handed. On the contrary they gave freely for the support of the Jewish community in Jerusa-

lem. Jerusalem's fame spread. It became known that we lived here in peace and tranquility. Many of us purchased homes and fields and rebuilt the ruins; our elders dwelt in the streets of Jerusalem, which were filled with children. From Sion, the fairest of all cities, the Lord appeared, for his teachings spread from the academies. The Torah and the word of God went forth from Sion to all the inhabitants of the world . . . many academies were opened and scholars flocked to the gates . . . and our wealthy brethren in the Diaspora supported them. . . .

One day, however, the most wicked and evil Muhammad ibn Faroukh, blind in one eye, came and entered Jerusalem with three hundred mercenary soldiers who proceeded to depose Muhammad Pasha. Immediately thereafter he set himself against us, and mercilessly tortured us and the Arab and Christian residents as well. Placing guards at the exits of the city, he ordered many of us to be brought bound and tortured before him so he could extort and confiscate their money. . . . For two years we were persecuted, harassed, and molested so that many fled the city. . . . One year later the city was liberated by Hassan Pasha . . but we cannot recount the property losses and personal sufferings endured during those abominable days. (Holtz 1971: 137)

Christian pilgrims and visitors to Palestine usually took little note of the Jews there except to make some stereotyped insult. One who did regard them more closely, however, was John Sanderson, a visitor to the Holy Land in 1601. How he came to be in the company of Jews he explains as follows:

It was determined that Master Best, the captain and master of "the Mermaid," at our arrival in Sidon with three others and myself should have gone for Joppa and so to Jerusalem. But the master, by danger of rocks and rising of wind, thought it not good to leave the ship, and the three other passengers would not. So that I was fain (holding my determination) to post alone without fellow Christian, in company of honorable Jews. In which journey by the principal, named Abraham Coen, who went to accompany his wife's father to Safed, which is at Bethel, and there to end his days, after 2,000 dollars at least distributed to those colleges of Jews, we went to Jerusalem, and in our return we took Tiberias and Capernaum in our way, which was somewhat out of the way direct to Damascus, but this my companion Jew, merchant and dweller in Sio [Chios] and Smyrna, was so respective, kind, and courteous that never in any Christian's company, of what degree soever, I ever did receive better content. (Sanderson 1931: 124)

Travelling widely across Palestine gave Sanderson an opportunity to raise a subject not usually discussed between Christian and Jew:

I noted that in all my pilgrimage the graver and better sort of Jews with whom I travelled would never reason with me of Christ, for offending or being displeasant unto me; for without scoffing they never talk of Him or His followers. Yet one day I had from the mouths of three or four of the meaner sort, aged men who professed knowledge of their Jewish religion, an argument wherein is consideration, and in my opinion, a kind of acknowledgment and confession.

They said that there was a stone in the Lord's House [the Dome of the Rock] in Jerusalem in the midst of the world, called Evenasediya [Eben ha-shetiya, or Stone of Foundation] upon which was written the name of God, and that whosoever could get in thither and return with it written might have what he required and do what he would.[14] *Which they said Jesus, Joseph's the carpenter's son, by extraordinary means got into and wrote it, cutting [it into] his own thigh, so hid it and escaped out of the temple; said: yea afdoni anni [ya abduni 'ammi, or let my people serve me], but was presently answered mamzer bemidatah [bi methâthâ: bastard? in death?]; which interpreted, as the Jews tell me, is: "(Says Christ), let the people serve me." The oracle answered: "After death, not in life."*

Then, they say, first he began to fly and make of earth birds, with many more such works, as these Jews to me confessed in a scornful opprobrious manner, adding further that they marvelled how we Christians could be so led by Peter and Paul, John, Mary, and such like; further adding that it was not possible for the best learned among all the Christians to expound the meaning of the letter A, and that their doctors could, only upon that first letter write whole volumes, to be studied until the world's end; and they knew, they said, that Jerusalem shall be built again and their Messiah come and make them princes, as they have been in time past, but then to govern all the world, and that the other dispersed tribes, who at this day (they say) do live in Ethiopia but cannot come out by reason of a sea of sand which parts Egypt and Ethiopia and is continually troubled. . . . Many other opinions they have . . . that in what parts soever they are die or are buried, their bodies must all rise to judgment in the Holy Land, out of the Valley of Jehoshaphat; which causes that the greater, richer sort have their bones conveyed to some part thereof by their kindred or friends, by which means they are freed of a labor to scrape thither through the ground. . . . Other talk I had from them, offering as little of truth as this last reasonless likelihood. (Sanderson 1931: 118-120)

A Messiah on the Temple Mount

The coming of the Ottomans was indeed a new beginning for Jerusalem, but like other changes of regime in the area, it may have triggered other, deeper sentiments among the Jews. In the summer of 1523, on the very heels of the Ottoman takeover, there appeared in Jerusalem an odd young man named David Reubeni, late of Arabia, who claimed to be the prince of a distant Jewish kingdom, the same, doubtless still being echoed in the story John Sanderson heard in 1601. It was ruled, the young man said, by his brother, and he further maintained that he had discovered the "lost tribes" of Israel. [15] Before passing on to deliver his message to the Jewish congregations of Italy, this Jewish Prester John paid a spectacular visit to the Holy City and its chief shrine, as he himself describes:

I entered it [Jerusalem] on the twenty-fifth of Adar 5283 [A.D. 1523], and that day I went into the house of the Holy of Holies [the Dome of the Rock], and when I came to the sanctuary all the Ishmaelite guardians came to bow before me and kiss my feet, and said to me, "Enter, Oh blessed of the Lord, our lord, the son of our lord," and the two chief among them came and took me to the cavern which is under the Stone of Foundation (Eben Shetiyah), and said to me, "This is the place of Elijah the prophet and this is the place of King Solomon, and this is the place of Abraham and Isaac, and this is the place of Muhammad."[16] I said to the guardians, "Now that I know these places, go you on your way, for I wish to pray and in the morning I will give you charity."

They went away, and I knew at once that their words were false and in vain. I prayed until all the Ishmaelites came to prayer. They left the Temple court after their prayer two hours after dark. I went below the Stone of Foundation. Then the guards extinguished all the lights in the court except four, and before they closed the gates they searched to see if any man were sleeping in the cavern, so as to turn him out. They found me and said, "Leave this place, for we are the guards and may allow no one to remain and sleep here. We have so sworn to the king, and if you will not go we shall ask the governor to remove you against your will." When I heard these words, I came out of the court, and they shut the doors, and I prayed outside the court all night, and fasted, and this was my fourth day.

In the morning, when the Ishmaelites came to pray in the court, I entered with them, and when they finished their prayer, I called out with a loud voice, "Where are the guards? Let them all come before me." And I said to them, "I am your lord, and the son of your Lord, the Prophet. I have come from a distant country to this Holy House and my soul desires to remain here to pray and not to sleep." After that, four of the guards came to expel me, and I said to them, "I am your lord, the son of your Lord, if you wish peace, wish me well and I will bless you; but if not, I will be avenged on you and will write to the king of Turkey your evil deeds." They replied, "Forgive us this time, for we wish to serve you and be your slaves for as long as you remain in the Holy House, and will do your will." Then I gave them ten ducats for charity and stayed in the sanctuary and fasted in the Holy of Holies for five weeks. . . .

The Ishmaelites have a sign on the top of the cupola of the court, and this sign is like a half moon turned westward; and on the first day of Pentecost of 5283, it turned eastward. When the Ishmaelites saw this they cried out in a loud voice, and I said, "Why do you cry?" and they replied, "For our sins this sign of the half moon is turned eastwards, and that is an evil sign for the Ishmaelites." The Ishmaelite workmen went on the Sunday to restore the sign to its place, and on Monday the sign again turned eastward while I was praying, and the Ishmaelites went crying and weeping, and they sought to turn it around and they could not.

Our elders had already told me, "When you see this sign, go to Rome," and I saw the Gates of Mercy and the Gates of Repentance [the Golden Gate] and walked in the sanctuary. It is a big structure like the upper buildings, and I did that which the elders commanded beneath the sanctuary, out of men's reach, and the turning of the sign took place after I had done what the elders commanded beneath the sanctuary.

I went up to the Mount of Olives, and I saw two caves there and returned to Jerusalem and ascended Mount Sion. There are two places of worship there in the town; the upper place [the Cenacle] is in the hands of the Christians, and the lower [the Tomb of David] in that of the Ishmaelites. This the Ishmaelites opened for me and showed me a grave, and told me it was the grave of King David, on whom be peace, and I prayed there. Then I left and went to the upper place of worship, which the Christians opened for me. I entered and prayed there and returned to Jerusalem. . . . I left Jerusalem on the twenty-fourth of Sivan 5283. . . . (Adler 1966: 263-266)

David Reubeni's visit is also dealt with, though in a quite different spirit, in the following letter sent from Jerusalem to Rabbi Abraham in Perugia sometime about 1523.

. . . A short time afterward, an emissary of the Tribes arrived in Jerusalem. His father is of the Tribe of Reuben, and his mother of Dan. He proclaimed wonderful tidings of the forthcoming Redemption. The Tribes would come back with the Tribe of Reuben at their head, as is likewise foretold in the Book of Zohar. [17] He further said that his king had sent him to remove a stone from the Western Wall of the Temple. This stone had been placed in the wall by the infamous Jeroboam, the son of Nebat, king of Israel, and as long as that stone remains in place, Israel cannot be redeemed. He wished to rip the stone from the wall in the presence of our exalted rabbi, the Nagid Isaac ha-Kohen Shohal.

After his departure our honored chief, the nagid, wrote to me from Jerusalem regarding all the youth had said there, and also regarding the removing of the stone in his presence. The youth is all falsehood and deceit, a prattler and a troublemaker, and the nagid required the scholars here, and me in particular, to tell the people so that they might not believe him. How easily the matter could be interpreted in an unfavorable light, and as an incitement against the government!

After this Jews from Egypt and Gaza appeared and reported that messengers from the Tribes had also arrived in Egypt with a message for the Jews, calling upon them to forsake Egypt, for the land would soon totter and he who would not hearken to the message would perish. Arabs from Egypt relate that the Jews there are selling their houses and all their property, at which the people in the Land of Israel wonder greatly. When the Jews are asked why they do this, they explain that they wish to spend the Passover feast in Jerusalem and will then return home. But they are not believed.

This week a letter arrived from Damascus telling of a report from Salonica that a messenger from the king of the Tribe of Reuben had arrived there in Salonica. He is said to have brought a manuscript of his king with the royal seal and the signature of his twelve elders, announcing that the pangs preceding the coming of the Messiah would soon be felt in Galilee, also in the land of Benjamin and in the valley of Jericho. Three hundred families in Salonica will remove here to Jerusalem after the Passover feast.

. . . I have purchased a neglected house, and I wish to restore it, together with a partner. God alone knows that little that is still left to me after the marriage of my daughter. . . . On account of the many people who will come hither from all lands, it is impossible to buy or rent as much as an inch. Therefore I have taken the very bread from my mouth in order to meet the costs, and may God take pity on us. (Wilhelm 1946: 30-31)

The Governance of Ottoman
Jerusalem: 1650

In the seventeenth century the affairs of the Arab provinces of the Near East took a decided turn for the worse. But we are given a detailed overview of the city before that occurred, while the Ottoman system of government was still in place in Jerusalem and functioning with some degree of efficiency, by a traveller who knew something of both the Empire and its administration, Evliye Chelebi. He describes Jerusalem in the years 1648-1650:

The revenues [of the province of Palestine] for the sultan are 357,485 aqtches. . . . The pasha of Jerusalem has 500 soldiers at his command and is the commandant of the pilgrims' caravan of Damascus. He is the leader of the Mecca pilgrims to Damascus and back. [18] *He receives an annuity of 40,000 piasters. It is a prosperous province, yet its fief-holders are not ordered to serve in the field but only to accompany with their banners pilgrims arriving and to conduct them to their place of pilgrimage. Altogether they number 600 men.*

The mulla [chief justice] of Jerusalem receives as much as the pasha, because his district counts altogether 1,600 villages—to all of which deputy judges are appointed, as his is a noble dignity of jurisdiction. And when it sometimes appears that patriarchs, priests and deacons, monks, and married priests leave some money, the mulla and the pasha receive from that money between 40,000 and 50,000 piasters. This is especially the case at the infamous feast of Easter when the mulla and the pasha go to the door of the Anastasis, which would not be opened before their arrival there. The priest [in charge] would take from each of the 5,000 to 10,000 Christians ten to fifteen piasters and give the mulla and the pasha 20[000], which is a considerable sum.

There are in this province some villages that are set aside as waqf, yet the greater part of the villages belong to the . . . fief-holders, the chiefs of the mounted feudal yeomanry. . . . The fief-holders convey the Muslim pilgrims to Hebron and to the birthplace of Jesus at Bethlehem and to the Nebi Musa, as the roads are insecure from the Arab rebels. (Chelebi 1980: 61-62)

Next Chelebi takes up the municipal officials of Ottoman Jerusalem:

There are twenty officers (aghas) under the mulla of Jerusalem, all appointed by imperial rescript. The first is the muhzir bashi, appointed by the sultan on a state occasion. He is the night guardian of the gates and carries on this duty with imperial troops. The second agha is the police inspector appointed especially for Jerusalem, which is a coveted high post. The third agha is the chief architect; the fourth is the chief engineer; the fifth the chief steward; the sixth the chief cashier, who personally pays to the religious scholars the yearly gifts ("purses") from the sultan. The seventh agha is the treasurer, the eighth the police officer, the ninth the market inspector, the tenth the mayor, the eleventh the chief of the brocade bazaar. In fine, the chiefs of all classes of merchants are daily present at the Shari'a Court for duty.

There are seven "resplendent" waqfs in Jerusalem, the director of each attends the court, each coming there with the present for the mulla. It is a large legal administration and judge's court. (Chelebi 1980: 62-63)

And on the buildings of the city:

There are no buildings whatever around the fortress [walls] of Jerusalem, except for the suburb of David [on Mount Sion], which consists of forty houses. Except the gardens, vineyards, and flower gardens, all buildings are within the fortress [walls]. All quarters are Muslim. There are altogether one thousand fortresslike lofty palaces. The buildings within this town are of masonry; there are no wooden constructions at all. Yet the doors are made of wood. The houses are covered with lime as are all the prayer places. (Chelebi 1980: 66-68)

The Muslim Holy Places

Finally, Chelebi turns to the Aqsa and the holy places atop the Noble Sanctuary of Jerusalem:

There are two Friday mosques in Jerusalem, the one within the Citadel, and the other the one which was designated as such by a decisive [Scriptural] text, the Aqsa Mosque, mentioned by the Creator in the Noble Quran [17:1]. Besides these there are no Friday mosques, all others being ordinary ones.

There are eight hundred salaried servants employed at this mosque of al-Aqsa. That is to say, it has prayer leaders for the four schools [of Islamic law] and as many preachers. On Fridays the preacher ascends the pulpit with the sword in his hand.[19] Each preacher is on duty for a week. There are altogether fifty muezzins, reciters of litanies,[20] transmitters,[21] other readers,[22] as well as guardians. All these offices are paid from the private purse of the sultan; the private treasurer comes year by year to distribute to them these gifts and presents. (Chelebi 1980: 72-73)

After a detailed description of the various minor buildings located on the Haram and the legends connected with each, Chelebi offers, much as Fazari had done two centuries earlier, a list of sites to be visited on that holy place:

Sites [or "stations," maqamat] to be visited within the Haram: First comes the Dome of the Rock of God. Between the western and northern gates of the Dome, looking to the north, and close to the outer walls of the building is a red prayer niche, the Dome of the Prophet. A small dome rises over four slender columns. Its prayer niche is low and of natural

494

reddish stones. It was in ancient times ruby-colored. Affected by the black-ness of the primordial waters of the abyss, during the flood in Noah's time, it changed its color and has now a reddish hue.

To the right of this prayer niche is a nice octagonal edifice with a dome, the Dome of the Ascension. It has two alabaster colonnettes at each cor-ner, set by a master mason. Its structure is encased in white marble, and the dome covered by fine lead, with a golden crescent on the top. Its door looks to the north, but it is now closed on all sides. Its contents are un-known. It has no windows. It would seem indiscreet to enter it, as it has been closed.

The Well of the Spirits is in front of the northern gate. [23] The rainwater collected from the shrine flows into the Well of Souls. . . . It is said to be a huge cistern. At the south gate of the Haram is a pulpit [of Burhan al-Din] which the Prophet ascended in the night of his Heavenly Journey to admonish the souls of all the prophets. It is a small pulpit. In times of drought the people of the province gather around it to offer prayers for rain. . . . In front of the eastern gate of the Dome of the Rock, at a dis-tance of some seven paces, is the Judgment Seat of the Prophet David [the Dome of the Chain]. Built below like a palace, its dome rests wholly on columns, there being no wall whatsoever. The outer circle is made of nine precious columns, while the inner circle consists of six columns. The dome rises above them. The interior and exterior of this dome is covered with pure Kashan tiles the color of lapis lazuli. The dome itself is covered with well-wrought lead similar to that of the Suleiymaniyye Mosque in Istanbul. . . . It has a prayer niche where I offered some prayers and praise. . . . (Chelebi 1980: 86-87)

By Chelebi's day the northern and western sides of the Haram enclosure were almost entirely filled with law schools and convents constructed and endowed by the Mamluks, and to these he now turns:

On all sides of the Shrine of the Holy Rock are rooms belonging to forty law schools. [24] In each of them live pious people considered to be wonder-working dervishes. Some of them break their fast only once a week, while others may not have tasted meat for forty or fifty years. Such are these pious souls who lead here a mystical life, while they are at the same time well versed in worldly knowledge and sciences.

All along the southern, western, and northern sides of the Haram en-closures are porticoes with domes, resting on over 360 columns. All the porticoes are lit every night by oil lamps. They become as bright as broad daylight. In these porticoes live dervishes from India, Sind, Balkh, Persia, and Kurds, Tartars, Moghuls, and Turks. They need by night no special candles, for [the oil lamps give so much light that] they can read the Quran [by them] and recite *zikr* and offer God the best prayers.

. . . There are two hundred rooms for law schools around this large enclosure surrounding the lower sections of the Sanctuary of the Rock of God. The total number of law schools in Jerusalem amounts to some 360 law schools and convents, both large and small. Yet the law school that is the most cared for is that of the Hitta Gate. It has a minaret. Then comes that of the al-Nazir Gate. It is just behind the palace of the pasha, in the corner [of the Haram enclosure]. It has a slender minaret. The Ghoraniyye Law School at the Ghawanima Gate has no minaret. The Ashrafiyya Law School at the Mutawadda Gate is the best. It has a minaret with three storeys which is 130 feet high. The humble writer ascended it and enjoyed a complete view over the whole town.

Besides these three there are no other minarets in the Haram area. Neither have the mosques of al-Aqsa and that of the Holy Rock any minarets. The Islamic call for prayer is recited from the heights of this latter minaret [at the Gate of the Chain], as it is near the town. . . .

Inside the Maghrebi Gate [at the southwestern corner of the Haram] stands the massive, beautiful building of the Mosque of the School of the Malikis.[25] It measures three hundred feet from the north door to the prayer niche, and is seventy feet wide. Yet it has no minaret either. But after the first morning prayer a chanting of the zikr and prayers is offered here in such a way as to bewilder lovers of prayer and mystics.[26] (Chelebi 1980: 88-90)

Religious Practices on the Haram

Chelebi's tour around the Haram was concerned almost exclusively with its monuments and the religious legends attached to some of the more prominent among them. But the immense court of the Haram al-Sharif was also the center of the religious life of the Holy City and attracted to it pilgrims and visitors from abroad as well. As might be expected, what occurred there, particularly on popular festivals, was not to everyone's liking. One traditionalist who protested the religious excesses he witnessed in the Noble Sanctuary was Chelebi's contemporary al-Qashashi (d. 1660) from whose *Jewels on the Excellence of Mosques* the following passages on the Haram are taken:

On Friday the men and women would mingle without a partition between them. In fact, some of the women would unveil their faces [displaying] their beauty, their ornaments, and their perfumes. What temptation is stronger than this? By God, they were sitting cheek to jowl among the

men as if they were closely related or members of the same household. . . .
In fact, some of the merchants sat among the women with their goods.
None of his profit is for God. May God kill all of those who are pleased
by this great abomination. Who could be pleased by this except for each
vile tyrant and those who have not even a tiny speck of faith in their
hearts? There is no power and strength except in God Almighty, the Most
High, the Requiter.

In addition, on the festival day of Arafa the men and women gather
together with intermingling [of the sexes] from afternoon until evening. . . . When evening approaches, a man who delivers a sermon appears
before them on the pulpit on the roof of [the Dome of] the Rock in
imitation of the people [celebrating] the [gathering at] Arafa [during the
hajj]. Then upon finishing the sermon, he waves to them with his hand-
kerchief, signalling them to break loose from the [orderly] arrangement
for the Arafa. The women, the men, the girls, and the boys begin to
approach with clamor from beneath the pulpit, the place of the sermons
"as if they were frightened asses fleeing from a lion" [Quran, Sura 74:50-
51]. What kind of terrible innovation is this which has developed on the
Masjid al-Aqsa and in the religion?

In addition, on the Eighth of Shawwal the men and women gather
together. They call this day the Festival of Goodly Devotion, but rather it
is the Festival of the Wicked Devil. They also call it the Festival of My
Lady Mary, but rather it is the Festival of Rebellion. . . . They also call it
the Festival of the Lady, but rather it is the Festival of the Sinful
Woman. . . . Their gathering on this dismal day, which is a bridal feast for
Satan, is the worst and most evil. It causes situations not pleasing to God
and His messenger. Look closely my brother, at the men and women in
small groups and large groups. The young boys jump and shout. . . . The
merchants sell sweets, drums, tambourines, horns, and other things. . . .
Who could approve of these situations which are so horrible? No one
approves of this except for all of those who have a lack of faith in their
hearts and a lack of sense in their minds. There is no strength or power
except in God the Most High, the Mighty.

During the days called "The Days of the Pilgrims" men and women
gather with much mingling [of the sexes] occurring. It [the festival] is the
worst, the most bitter, the most miserable, and the most sinister. Shops
occupy the sanctuary during these days, and selling occurs in them. Each
person has goods and a place in which to sell them. Women are present
among them. These days are the wedding feast of Satan. It is festival of
people of immorality and terror. There is no strength and power except
in God, the Most High, the Mighty.

In addition, on a night in the middle of Shaʿban, the men and women

*gather with a great deal of mingling [of the sexes] occurring. This night
they set aglow the mosque called al-Aqsa which houses the pulpit. On this
night great atrocities happen to all of those who attend and watch it,
except for God Almighty. On this night approximately ten thousand candles are lit for no reason. In fact, that which results because of this setting
aglow are great abominations. In fact, I hear a lot of rumors as to what
happens on that night in the way of reprehensible actions. (Perlmann
1973: 286-289, trans. S. Levy)*

Troubles on Mount Sion

The Franciscans on Mount Sion, as we have already seen in Chapter Ten,
lost to the Muslims in 1452 or 1453 their possession of the place beneath
the Cenacle which was then identified by all as the Tomb of King David.
The population on Sion now became more Muslim and more militant, as
Felix Fabri reported, until finally a Muslim legal tribunal was convened in
Jerusalem and ruled that a Christian presence in the Cenacle in effect pro-
faned the biblical, and Muslim, shrine of David beneath. The decision
was forwarded to Istanbul, where it was effected by an imperial decree of
Suleiman dated March 18, 1523, and addressed to the governor of
Damascus:

*By the receipt of this august and imperial sign, know that by the request
addressed to our Sublime Porte we have been made aware that near to
the noble city of Jerusalem there is the tomb of the Prophet David—may
the blessings and peace of God rest upon our Prophet and upon him—
and that the convent and church of Mount Sion, possessed and inhabited
by the religious Franks, are next to the tomb. These latter, in making the
processions required by their false beliefs, cross the earth which covers the
tomb of the Prophet David—may peace be upon him. It is neither just
nor appropriate that this most noble place remain in the hands of the
infidels and that, in obedience to their impious customs, their feet foul the
places sanctified by the prophets who have a right to our complete veneration. We order, then, upon receipt of this august order, that you expel
from the church and the convent immediately and without delay the religious and all those who reside there. You will have the tomb, the object
of pious visits, purified, and you will put it in the same condition as the
other places sanctified by the prophets for the noble Sayyids, descendants
of our Prophet. We have charged the custodian and the governor of the
Haram the carrying out of this order, the preacher Mahdi al-Hashimi,
column of the faith and arbiter of truth. We have informed him and con-
fided in him the care of taking care of the possessions of the church, the*

gardens and the fields connected to it. We have invested full authority in him and granted him the use of these possessions as well as the power to make all the necessary arrangements to take up residence there. You will make known to our Sublime Porte all that you require, and it will be forthcoming by other decrees.

Written at Istanbul the first day of Jumada I 928 [March 18, 1523]. (Baldi 1955: 524-525[27])

Almost immediately the Franciscans, using the Venetians as their inter-mediaries, attempted to have the order revoked. The maneuver did not succeed—they were expelled in January 1524—nor was an intervention by Francis I of France any more effective. We do not know what the king of France said, but the sultan's lofty denial issued in 1528 is preserved:

You have addressed to my court, the happy residence of the sultans, the qibla of good guidance and happiness, the place where petitions to the sultans are received, a letter by which you have made known to us that there exists in the city of Jerusalem, which is part of my well-guarded domains, a church which was once in the possession of the community of Jesus and later converted into a mosque. I am informed in all its details what you have communicated on this subject.

If it was only a question of property, your desires would have been heeded and granted by our Majesty, the dispenser of felicity, in consider-ation of the friendship and affection which exist between our august Maj-esty and yourself. But this is not at all a question of goods, movable and immovable; it concerns an object of our religious practice. Since, by virtue of the sacred commands of God on high, the Creator of the universe, the benefactor of Adam, and in conformity with the laws of our Prophet, the sun of the two worlds—peace and blessing be upon him—this church has been for a long time converted into a mosque, and the Muslims make their canonical prayer there. But to alter at this date the place which has borne the name of mosque and in which prayer was made would be con-trary to our religion. And if our holy law tolerated it, it would not be possible for me to accept in any manner whatsoever your petition. But with the exception of the places consecrated to canonical prayer, in all those other places in the hands of the Christians, no one, under my reign of justice, can disturb or trouble those who live in them. Enjoying a per-fect repose in the shadow of my sovereign protection, it is permitted them to fulfill the ceremonies and rites of their religion. Since they are estab-lished in full security in the buildings consecrated to their cult as well as in their quarters, it is impossible that there be the slightest trouble or molestation in their regard.

Written in the first decade of the month of Muharram 935 [mid-September 1528]. (Baldi 1955: 525-526)

The Franciscans Get a New Home

The Franciscans' repose on Mount Sion, where the shadow of the sultan's sovereign protection seemed scarcely to reach, was now somewhat less than perfect. From 1524 to 1559 they lived in a bakery near their former church. By then, however, there was a new "Guardian of Mount Sion and the Holy Land," the redoubtable Father Boniface of Ragusa. His response to the crisis is described by another Franciscan, Father Elzear Horn, who served in the community between 1724 and 1744 and had access to the archives:

When Father Boniface of Ragusa, then superior of the Holy Land, saw that the convent of Holy Mount Sion, from which the Friars had been expelled shortly before, would not be recovered, he used the services of the Venetian ambassador at the Ottoman Porte in the last month of the year 960 of the Hijra, or 1551, to obtain a decree from the Turkish sultan (Suleiman) by which he was entitled to acquire another convent in the Holy City. But when he had carefully considered that no other place was more convenient for the Friars than a small monastery of some Georgians, which was somewhat remote from the Muslim quarter and very near to the Christian Catholic quarters and to the Holy Sepulcher, he requested their superior to sell him the place for a just price since it was not so necessary for them seeing that they had seven other monasteries within the city walls.

When, out of his ingrained hate of the Latins he [the Georgian superior] refused, Father Boniface approached the Turkish governor and chief justice and, having shown them the imperial decree, asked them that by virtue of the decree they secure for him that place. These, having accepted some gifts, immediately commanded the Georgian superior through a special order to hand over the place to the Friars after the price had been paid. This took place on July 10, 1559, on which day they took possession of the little monastery, on condition, however, that for the land there should be paid annually to the Muslims the sum of 1,700 aspers, which in Arabic is called waqf.

In the beginning the place was very small, but during the following years by buying up the nearby houses, it grew in such a manner that in time it became a great convent, complete in every respect, although it was not built as regularly as is the custom in Christian lands since in these infidel parts it is not permitted to the Christians without much expense to build how and how much they wish and can, but only as the Muslims decide arbitrarily.

It was hard and painful for the Friars to have lost the convent on Holy Mount Sion, but because for 2,500 pieces of eight [pezzi da otto] they got this [new] place, which formerly in Arabic was called al-Amud, that is, "The Column," they were somewhat consoled and gave most humble thanks to the divine mercy that they had been received into the Holy City as into a safer place and were saved from many persecutions and calumnies of the unbelievers, by which while they lived on Mount Sion outside the city they could be continually annoyed; and for this reason they dropped the old name of the place and called this church that of St. Savior, and yearly they celebrate its principal feast on August 6, on the solemnity of the Lord's Transfiguration. . . . (Horn 1962: 162-163, 165)

The Way of the Cross

Thenceforward the Franciscans performed their tasks in Jerusalem out of the convent in the Christian quarter called St. Savior's, and as Elzear Horn described, it grew from a simple residence into an extensive compound, with a library, an infirmary that was the best medical facility in the city, a school, and facilities for feeding and lodging the pilgrims who were still the chief responsibility of the Friars Minor in the Holy Land. For those pilgrims the services in the Holy Sepulcher during Holy Week continued to be the focus and high point of their visit, but another devotion, whose origins go back to early in Christian times, had come to full maturity in the sixteenth and seventeenth centuries, the so-called Way of the Cross, which traced Jesus' steps across Jerusalem from the place of his trial before Pilate on the eastern side of the city, just inside what is now called St. Stephen's Gate, to his execution and burial at the sites shown inside the Church of the Holy Sepulcher.

The "stations" along this "Via Dolorosa," all of which carried with their veneration the richest possible indulgences, fluctuated in number and site over the centuries, but by the seventeenth century their number, fourteen, as well as their order and place seemed finally settled, chiefly through a widely read work entitled "The Theater of the Holy Land" by a certain Adrichomius. But not for everyone. One of the most learned and prolific of the early Franciscan scholars, Franciscus Quaresmi, attempted to reopen the question in 1626 in his *Historical, Theological, and Moral Study of the Holy Land*, which, like many of the books of the era, was now accompanied by plans, designs, and drawings of the sites in Jerusalem.[28] As Quaresmi carefully explains:

501

Since Adrichomius has very carefully described the memorable places of the Way of the Cross, with its length and the distances between each, I cannot dare contradict him, basing himself, as he did, on the accounts of men famous for their piety of learning who saw the places with their own eyes and walked along in body and spirit. Nonetheless, it would not, I think, be inappropriate to our announced intention nor unwelcome in the future to some reader, if I made a few observations from what I and others know, though not in the same kind of detail. And if they are different from those of Adrichomius, it is not because they are less true, especially since on several occasions while I was living in Jerusalem I went down that same way as those other pilgrims he cites. . . .

The Way of the Cross extends itself in its entirety from the palace of Pilate to Mount Calvary. In older days it was required of the faithful to walk its entire length at one time, but today only one part of it is covered. Wherefore the Via Dolorosa can be divided into two parts: into that part which is within the Holy City, beginning at the palace of Pilate and going continuously to the Gate of Judgments; and that which goes from the Judgment Gate to Mount Calvary. I have divided it thus since the Judgment Gate is closed with a wall [so] it is not possible to go out that way and accompany Christ from it to Mount Calvary. And so it is the first part that in these days the pious faithful follow in the company of our Redeemer. . . . This whole Way is sacred and venerated, consecrated with the footsteps and blood of Christ the Lord; nevertheless, there are eight places that put before our eyes the individual mysteries of our salvation, and I will discourse upon them in the following. (Baldi 1955: 607-608)

Thus he proceeds, tracing the way from place to place and supplying historical and theological considerations for the reader, like this for example on the place where Jesus was reputedly scourged after his condemnation by Pilate:

Going back ten paces from the palace of Pilate . . . on the left side of the street is the place in which, by a common and anciently held tradition in these parts, Christ Jesus was savagely scourged. Long ago the faithful built a small but beautiful church on the spot which by now because of time and the hatred of the infidels has lost its original attractiveness. It is still nonetheless intact and is visited by many of the pilgrim faithful. . . . And that Christ the Lord was scourged in that place is held not merely by the Catholics and the schismatics but even by the Muslims, taught by an ancient tradition. . . .

Toward the end of the year 1618 from the Virgin Birth, the son of the governor of the city took it upon himself to rebuild that place and the church and, one is ashamed to say it, convert it into stable for his horses.

He also ordered a room put above it, but before it could be completed it was destroyed: it fell down on the night of the Feast of the Holy Name of Jesus, January 14, 1619. He did not leave off his plan, however, until he had full experience of the Divine Judgment. After they had brought their horses into that church as if it were a stable, the next day they were all discovered dead, even though the grooms thought they were sleeping. When the governor's son learned of this, and warned by the Christians that they held the place in great veneration, he dropped his plan. . . . Inside and out it once had the form of a church, but now only the inside, so that only by an expert can it be recognized as a church. (Baldi 1955: 611[29])

An individual Christian who followed along the Way of the Cross might go unremarked, but once the practice began to be converted into a public liturgical devotion, and one held openly on the very streets of Jerusalem, trouble had inevitably to follow:

The brethren of the Holy Land, going out from the Convent of St. Savior, devotedly walk the Way of the Cross with bare feet, which the faithful of Jerusalem especially do on Fridays and during Lent, saying at least one "Our Father" and "Hail Mary" at each station. At the time of Father Basil of Caprarola [guardian in 1616] . . . the custom still was in use for the Friars with their superior to march in procession along the Via Dolorosa, without the cross, every Friday in the evening after compline. They went to the House of Pilate and returned by the Gate of Judgment to the vestibule of the Church of the Holy Sepulcher, where they knelt and said the customary prayers before the Cross. But this devotion was stopped on January 22, 1621, because of the anger of a young Turk, which had such an effect on the pasha, the chief justice, and the ministers that the father guardian had unjustly to pay a fine of nine hundred silver pieces. (Horn 1962: 160)

The Restoration of the Church
of the Holy Sepulcher

The Church of the Holy Sepulcher had undergone no thoroughgoing repairs since the time the Crusaders had rebuilt it in the twelfth century. Its state, according to Elzear Horn, was a sorry one when the Franciscan guardian, Father Boniface of Ragusa, undertook its restoration in 1555, followed in 1720 by another overhaul. Of this latter, more thorough reconstruction of the entire church, Horn reports:

The walls of the church are made of square stones . . . ; inside their lower

503

surface was once covered with colored and worked marble slabs, while the upper surfaces were decorated with figures in mosaic and various inscriptions of the Old and New Testament which brought a singular kind of beauty to the brilliant sight. [30] *But when the whole church from the smoke of thuribles and lamps became black and its ornamentation with the injury of time had suffered much, yes, and both the schismatics and the Turks from hate and jealousy had removed thence many precious things, in 1720 the entire mosaic work came loose and fell onto the ground. Christians and Turks everywhere collected gilded or silver coated tesserae; I have seen even up to the present day Turks exhibiting the remains for sale to pilgrims in the courtyard of the Church. To continue the memory of the rich work and of the church of the Redeemer, the Friars left intact the marble slabs and mosaic figures in the place of the crucifixion of Christ above Mount Calvary. (Horn 1962: 60)*

On the earlier occasion, in 1555, the small building under the cupola and over the tomb of Jesus had been rebuilt:

As far as I know, the Most Reverend Father Boniface, then superior of the Holy Land [1551-1560, 1562-1565] and later bishop of Ragusa, was the last one who in 1555, when the exterior structure of the Holy Tomb had collapsed, rebuilt it again in its ancient form, although, for greater ornament, he added marble slabs and columns, a hemisphere or cupola, and perhaps the middle and also the eastern side of the vestibule so that it might receive more persons within itself. (Horn 1962: 36-37)

In the course of restoring the edicule, there occurred an extraordinary event, the opening of the tomb itself. Elzear Horn quotes from Boniface of Ragusa's own account of what happened:

When in the year of our Salvation 1555 that most celebrated structure, once erected by St. Helena, the mother of Constantine the Great, . . . was threatened with ruin and almost about to collapse, Pope Julius III . . . earnestly commanded us, who at that time with the apostolic authority acted as superior of the Convent of St. Francis of the Observance in Jerusalem, that we should undertake as soon as possible to rebuild and restore the sacred place which was collapsing. . . . After having first made great and difficult journeys, and with great labor and expenses, we eventually obtained permission for this from the Ottoman Suleiman, king of the Turks, and then zealously attacked the desired work.

Since it seemed necessary to make that structure level with the ground so that the reconstructed weight might be supported more firmly and last longer, once it was dismantled, our Holy Lord's tomb cut out of the rock was clearly revealed to our eyes. One could make out two painted angels

*set down on top, one with the superscript "He has risen; He is not here,"
and the other, pointing to the tomb [and saying]: "Behold the place where
they laid him." Both images, as soon as they were exposed to the air,
mostly disappeared. Since it seemed required that one of the slabs of alabaster which covered the tomb and which St. Helena had placed there so
that the Most Holy Mystery of the Mass might be celebrated on them had
urgently to be removed, there was revealed to us that ineffable place where
the Son of Man had lain for three days so that we and all who were
present could look upon it with our own eyes. There was the place where
the sacred blood of the Lord Jesus was mixed with the unguents with
which he was anointed for burial and was now gleaming as if with the
shining rays of the sun. And pouring forth pious sobs and a certain spiritual joy of soul, we looked upon it and kissed it, while those who were
with us—there were present not a few Christians of the Eastern and Western nations—in the grip of devotion to this heavenly treasure, some shed
tears from deep within them, some were almost lifeless, all were in the
powerful grip of a kind of ecstasy of the soul.*

*Placed in the middle of that most holy place we found a piece of wood
wrapped in a precious veil. When we took it reverently in our hands and
were kissing it, as soon as it was exposed to the air, the veil completely
dissolved in our hands, except for some golden threads. There were some
inscriptions fixed upon that precious wood, but they were so damaged and
aged by time that no entire sentence could be made out, though at the
head of one parchment these words were legible in Latin capitals:* HELENA
MAGNI. . . .[31] *(Horn 1962: 133-134)*

Horn then continues:

*After that restoration [of 1555], it [the sepulcher] has remained in that
form up to the present day. But when in the course of time that same
tomb again lost its former beauty on the outside . . . our Friars began in
the meantime to decorate the Holy Tomb all around by suspending silk
drapery according to the quality of the feasts, until it would be permissible
to repair it entirely. Up to the present the matter has remained in suspense
because not so much the Turks as the Greeks oppose its repair; the former
do not allow anything to be restored or built in these parts without heavy
expenses; the latter, however, impede its restoration not without injury to
Christian piety, since they unjustly claim in regard to the edifice of the
Most Holy Tomb part of the absolute jurisdiction which the Latins alone
enjoy by right of purchase. (Horn 1962: 36)*

From 1335 onward, as we have seen in Chapter Eleven, the Franciscans
had what Horn calls "absolute jurisdiction" in the chief Christian holy

places in Jerusalem and environs, confirmed by the pope in 1343 as "the Custody of the Holy Land." Though they were dislodged from the Cenacle in 1552 by Suleiman, they continued to exercise the chief control over the Holy Sepulcher, Calvary, the Tomb of the Virgin, and the grotto of the Nativity in Bethlehem. [32] The other Christian groups were not forced to leave those places or to cease conducting services, but it was manifestly the Franciscans who were, or should have been, *padroni principali del tutto*, as Pietro della Valle put it in 1616. But the Greeks "who strive proudly to precede all other nations, by which license I know not," as Elzear Horn complained, had license enough to contest that position by the sixteenth century.

For centuries the Franciscans' own license had been procured through funds and political leverage provided by the Christian powers of Europe. After 1516 that leverage was applied, principally by Venice and then by France, at the Sublime Porte. But the Ottoman conquest of Constantinople in 1453 made the Ecumenical Greek patriarch, and a great many Orthodox Christians, subjects not of a Christian Roman emperor but of the Ottoman sultan. This change in status was a degradation perhaps in some Christians' eyes, but it gave the patriarch his own direct access to the sovereign of Palestine, with effects which were not long in coming. Patriarch Germanus (1534-1579) instituted the Hellenic Confraternity of the Holy Sepulcher whose members were thereafter the guardians of the Jerusalem holy places on behalf of the entire body of Orthodox Christendom.

When challenged, the Franciscans inevitably sustained their case with documents drawn from their archives, the impressive collection of decrees and deeds issued by, or bought from, the sometimes insouciant Mamluk and Ottoman sovereigns who were more than content to sell the Christians back their holy places on as many occasions as seemed necessary or possible. By the seventeenth century the Greeks too were in the game, and with the same instruments, chiefly the Covenant of Umar (see Chapter Five), of which they appeared to be the named beneficiaries in the person of the then Greek patriarch Sophronius. This was duly presented to Sultan Murad for his consideration in 1630. He acceded to the claim, thereby triggering a Christian bidding war for the Holy Sepulcher that lasted for most of the first half of the seventeenth century. [33]

The Franciscan Convent at the Holy Sepulcher

The Franciscans meanwhile lived together with the other Christians in a small residence *inside* the church:

The foundations of our convent are to the north of the adjoining Church of the Holy Sepulcher, the lower part of which is entirely underground, very dark and humid. It is so inconvenient for the Friars living therein that very many contract ills, as headaches, fevers, tumors of the body, diarrhea, dysentery, laryngitis, etc. Formerly they had neither sacristy nor kitchen and vested for Mass in the choir, and were forced to prepare a fire in the refectory for cooking, until they arranged the convent better in 1721 and constructed a sacristy near the chapel and a kitchen near the refectory, together with twenty-two cells, erected partly of wood and partly of stone. Ordinarily there live here eight priests and three lay brothers, which number is rarely increased but very often decreased. . . . There are separate latrines for the Friars and for the schismatics and other seculars and pilgrims of both sexes who come here. In this matter the Friars have greater convenience than the Eastern monks, for these latter do not have privies in their habitations. However, the Friars in the place [chapel] of St. Mary Magdalen suffer much from the smell of these latrines where there is a large crowd of people. (Horn 1962: 75-77)

The sacristy itself, now like the chapel on the northern side of the church, had a somewhat curious history, as Horn explains:

One time [the Franciscan sacristy in the church] was the Chapel of St. Mary Magdalen. . . . After a certain Chaldean archdeacon named Adam sent to Rome made submission to the obedience the Supreme Pontiff Paul V, in the name of his patriarch and his nation, he humbly begged that His Holiness would deign to concede to them for their consolation some place in the Church of the Holy Sepulcher that they might have religious functions there as other nations. The pontiff willingly consented to that petition in order that he and his people might persevere the more firmly in the Catholic faith and sent him to Jerusalem with letters of commendation [dated March 25, 1614] . . . addressed to Friar Angelus of Messina that he might, according to his own judgment, assign some place to this end, while retaining for himself the right to the place. On receiving these letters, he reverently assigned to him this sacristy, which at that time was a chapel. But when in a short time they, like the other Easterners, returned to their own vomit, he rightfully forbade their again approaching this place. (Horn 1962: 77)

The Chaldeans, whether cynically or not, were merely attempting to secure a prayer-hold on the crowded terrain of the holiest of all Christian holy places in Jerusalem, the Church of the Holy Sepulcher. Elzear Horn regards that landscape and its denizens as it appeared sometime about 1740:

In addition to the Latins there were once six other eastern nations of the Christian name who used to exercise jurisdiction in this holy church, each having its own proper chapel and shrines in it so that now this group and now that might worship God day and night with its own liturgy and in its own language. First and principal are the Latins, namely the Friars Minor, popularly called, together with all the Europeans, "Franks." In addition to the Sepulcher of Christ, they have custody of the middle part of Calvary, the Stone of Unction, the Chapel of the Apparition of the B.V.M., the place of the Invention of the Cross, together with the greater part of the upper and lower galleries. . . .

Second are the Greek monks, who have the body of the church, the prison of Christ, the chapel of St. Longinus, the column of the Impropreria, together with certain dark shrines under the lower portico around the Holy Sepulcher and beneath the narrow vaults of Mount Calvary.

Third are the Armenian monks, who possess, in addition to the Chapel of St. Helena and of the Division of the Vestments of Christ, in the upper portico of the church a chapel looking down on the Holy Sepulcher together with some cells made with wooden poles above the vestibule of the church.

Fourth are the Coptic monks, who have a chapel contiguous to the monument of Christ together with some obscure little residences beneath the lower portico of the church. These three aforementioned groups alone live together with us inside the boundaries of the [Church of the] Holy Sepulcher.

The fifth group is the Syrians, who have a chapel near the tomb of Joseph of Arimithea where in certain openings of the door of the church they light several lamps in the course of the year. When the church is closed and they are not there, the Armenians protect the place. . . . The sixth are the Georgians, who hold another part of Calvary and the chapel of Adam. But the aforementioned Greeks have now taken their place because of the overwhelming debts the Georgians have incurred; also their own demerits demanded this.

The seventh were the Abyssinians or Ethiopians, who had a dark chapel around the foundation walls of the church, but reduced to servitude by the Turks, they have left the place and have given over their chapel to the Greek monks for a reception area for pilgrims, for food and drink and other things. (Horn 1962: 60-62)

As we have already seen, these monks had to maintain a continuous residence inside the church or else forfeit their preciously held rights of possession. Sustaining them there was by no means a simple matter for the communities concerned, as appears from the account of Henry Timberlake in 1601:

... At five [in the afternoon] the Turks let us into the Holy Sepulcher, each of us paying nine gold pieces for our entrance. No sooner were we in but they locked the gates; so there I stayed until eleven of the clock the next day, and then came forth. . . . I noted hanging outside the gate [of the church] at least a hundred lines and strings and in the gate a great hole, whereat a little child may easily creep in; whereof demanding the reason, they told me that the hole served to give victuals for them which lie within the church, which are above three hundred persons, men and women, all Christians; and there they live continuously night and day and can have no passage in or out except when the Turks open the doors for some pilgrims, which happeneth not sometimes for fourteen days. Wherefore these Christian lodgers in the church have there their whole household and boarded lodgings there built for them. The strings before spoken of, hanging at the gate, have each one a bell fastened at the lodgings, and when the servants, who are without, bring with them any meat, each rings the bell belonging to his household and so come accordingly [each knowing his own bell] for receipt of their food. . . . (Timberlake 1616: 347)

Elzear Horn discusses the same subject a century and a half later:

Muslims hold the key to the door [of the Church of the Holy Sepulcher] and they do not open it except to those who pay a certain sum of money. In the lower part of the door there are six openings or small doors, closed at night from the inside with moveable boards and two hanging locks, the keys of which are in the hands of the Greek monks. By day, however, they are open, and the Friars and the Eastern monks can speak with other people coming from outside when there is any necessity. Through the central opening, since it is the larger, every day, morning and evening, victuals are handed in to the religious from their respective principal monasteries. . . . The two Copts, seeing that they are poor, hardly succeed in sustaining themselves from an annual stipend; often they are fed from the remains of the food of the other nations in return for services rendered, for example, blowing the bellows of the organ, cleaning the church, drawing water, etc. (Horn 1962: 84)

The Reformation Comes to Jerusalem

The problems of the Franciscans in Jerusalem were those of a community of Latin clerics attempting to maintain a permanent residence in a city whose rulers were growing increasingly impecunious and so increasingly greedy, while events in the larger arena of Ottoman-European politics conspired to alter those circumstances in violently fluctuating ways. The pilgrims themselves faced somewhat different problems, however, and in the seventeenth century they began to pose different problems for their Franciscan hosts as well. Their numbers were not large in any event. As we have seen, Ottoman naval dominance of the Mediterranean made pilgrimage an increasingly perilous venture from the fifteenth century onward, and one which was, on quite different grounds, losing a great deal of its former appeal to European Christians. [34]

Of those who did come, many were of a different sort and with attitudes different from those who had preceded them in the Holy City. A visit to the Holy Land was often included as simply one stage in a larger itinerary across the Levant, and those who undertook it were increasingly merchants en route to or stationed at one or other of the commercial "factories" which the European powers now maintained as a matter of course in the Ottoman and Persian Empires. These new visitors were not so much pilgrims as travellers, and their writings betray the difference. [35] Devotion was yielding to curiosity and faith to skepticism. The tourist was abroad in the Near East and, as the Franciscans discovered to their chagrin, he was often a Protestant.

Two of the new visitors came to Jerusalem in the same year, Henry Timberlake and John Sanderson, and for them, as for us, their arrival in 1601 is an introduction to a new and harsher reality about the Holy City:

Being our Lady-Day in Lent, and nine of the clock before noon, I saw the city of Jerusalem; when kneeling down and saying the Lord's Prayer, I gave God most hearty thanks for conducting me thither, to behold so holy a place with my eyes, whereof I had read so often. Coming within a furlong of the gates, I, with my companion, Mr. John Burrell, went singing and praising God, till we came to the west gate of the city, and there we stayed because it was not lawful for a Christian to enter unadmitted. My companion advised me to say that I was a Greek, only to avoid going to Mass: but I, not having the Greek tongue, refused to do so, telling him even at the entry of the gate that I would neither deny my country nor religion. Whereupon, being demanded who we were, Mr. John Burrell, answering in the Greek tongue, told them that he was a Greek and I am an Englishman. This gave him admittance to the Greek patriarch; but I was seized on and cast into prison before I had stayed a full hour at the gate; for the Turks flatly denied that they had ever heard of either my queen [Elizabeth] or country or that she paid them any tribute. The father guardian, who is the defender of all Christian pilgrims, and the principal procurer of my imprisonment because I did not offer myself under his protection but confidently stood to be rather protected under the Turk than the pope, made the Turk so much my enemy that I was reputed to be a spy and so by no means could I be released from the dungeon.

Now give me favor to tell you how it pleased God that very day to deliver me and grant me to pass as a Protestant without yielding to any other ceremony than carriage of a wax candle only, far beyond my expectation. Here let me remember you that when I stayed in Ramoth, . . . having so good leisure I went to a fountain to wash my foul linen, and being earnest about business suddenly there came a Moor unto me who, taking my clothes out of my hand and calling me by name, said he would help me. [It turned out they had earlier been on the same ship from Algiers and the Moor in question continued on from Ramle to Jerusalem.] When this Moor [now] saw me thus imprisoned in Jerusalem, my dungeon being right up against the Sepulcher of Christ, albeit he wept, yet he bade me be of good comfort and went to the pasha of the city and went to the saniake, before whom he took his oath that I was a mariner of a ship which had brought 250 or 300 Turks and Moors into Egypt from Algiers and Tunis, their journey being unto Mecca.

The Moor, in regard he was a Musselman, prevailed so well with them that, returning with six Turks back to prison, he called me to the door and there said unto me that if I would go to the house of the father guardian and yield myself under his protection, I should be inforced to no religion but mine own, except it were to carry a candle; to the which I willingly condescended.

So paying the charges of the prison, I was presently delivered and brought to the guardian's monastery, where the father [guardian], coming to me, took me by the hand and bade me welcome, marvelling I would so much err from Christianity as to put myself under the Turks' rather than his protection. I told him what I did was because I would not go to mass but keep my conscience to myself. He replied that "many Englishmen had been there but, being Catholics, went to Mass, telling the Turks at the gate's entry that they were Frenchmen, for the Turks know not what you mean by the word Englishman," and advising me further that when any of my countrymen undertook the like travel, at the gates of Jerusalem they should term themselves either Frenchmen or Britons, because they were well known to the Turks.

This or such like conference passed between us; and further he asked me how old our Queen's Majesty was, and what was the reason she gave nothing to the maintenance of the Holy Sepulcher as well as other kings and princes did, with divers other frivolous questions, whereto I answered accordingly. This day being spent even to twilight, Mr. John Burrell, who passed as a Greek without any trouble, came in unto us, being nevertheless constrained to this [same] monastery or else he might not stay in the city; for such sway do the papists carry there that no Christian stranger can

511

have admittance there but that he must be protected under them or not enter the city.

Mr. Burrell and I being together in the court of the monastery, twelve fat-fed friars came forth unto us, each of them carrying a wax candle burning and two spare candles besides, the one for Mr. Burrell and the other for me. Another friar brought a great basin of warm water mingled with roses and other sweet flowers. And a carpet being spread on the ground and cushions in chairs set orderly for us, the father guardian came and sat us down, giving each of us a candle in our hands; then came a friar and pulled off our hose and, setting the basin on the carpet, washed our feet. So soon as the friars began to wash, the twelve friars began to sing, continuing so till our feet were washed; which being done, they went along singing and we with the guardian came to chapel in the monastery where one of them began an oration in the form of a sermon, tending to this effect: "How meritorious it was for us to visit the Holy Land and see those sanctified places where Our Savior's feet had trod."

The sermon being ended, they brought us unto a chamber where our supper was prepared; there we fed somewhat fearfully, in regard that strange cats have as strange qualities; but committing ourselves to God and their outward-appearing Christian kindness, we fell to heartily, supped very bountifully, and, after praising God, were lodged decently. Thus much for my first entertainment in Jerusalem, which was March 25, 1601, being our Lady-in-Lent. (Timberlake 1616: 340-342)

Though John Sanderson was in Jerusalem in the same year as Timberlake, 1601, his *Travels* were not published until 1625 in the miscellany of the Rev. Samuel Purchas entitled *Purchas His Pilgrims*. Purchas himself added further material and documentation, and we begin with his introduction, actually added as a kind of postscript to the *Travels*:

Thus have I given thee the voyage of Master John Sanderson. Touching the difficulties of entrance into Jerusalem, I thought good to add this which follows, the rather that my countrymen may be advised, before they venture this Ierosolymitan pilgrimage; superstition on the one side and tyranny on the other endangering the best pilgrimage, which is the peaceable way of a good conscience to that Jerusalem which is above. For if a man does not give content to the Friars, which a good conscience cannot do, except some of their patrons' and benefactors' letters or other extraordinary provision help, you see these superstitious friars to prove malicious liars, as here they slandered Master Sanderson to be a Jew and Master Timberlake to be a spy; that I mention not four other Englishmen not long before seen to enter their monastery but never seen to come forth, as the [Greek] patriarch of Jerusalem confidently affirmed to Master Sanderson. Hence it is that Master Timberlake affirms that none enter the city but protected by them; which others, having otherwise entered by extraordinary course, disavow. (Sanderson 1931: 121)

The narrative is now Sanderson's, as reported to Samuel Purchas:

Now, Master Purchas, take a memorandum of me, that my first day's entertainment in Jerusalem was somewhat cross, in that I crossed two Friars which came to bid me welcome. I said I had not to use their kindness because I was recommended to the Greek patriarch. So in some choler they left me. But a Turk presently after came, in the name of the bassa [pasha], and took my sword from my side, which had cost me thirty dollars in Damascus, alleging that no Christian ought to enter the city gates with a sword girt about him, but that I might have borne it in my hand; and yet their custom is to privilege the Jews in that case.

Thus I lost my sword and after was led to the Caia [Kethuda] of the bassa, who related to me the error I had committed and further demanded a present for his master and another for himself. Then I showed him the Great Turk's letter, which imparted a command to use me respectfully wheresoever I came into his dominions. He read the letter with great regard and said that he had not, neither would he, offer me any abuse nor any in Jerusalem should do me wrong; and that he would pass over my error concerning the presumption to enter the city gate with a sword at my side, if in courtesy I would bestow a vesture of velvet upon the pasha his master and a garment of satin upon himself; which I denied to do.

He then presently committed me to the subbassie [subashi], a grim and grisly Turk, and his rascally attendants to be laid in prison. But the Jews in whose company I had travelled fell down at his feet and entreated for me, often kissing his hand and garment, praying him to pardon my bold behavior and words of displeasure, with much whispering. They agreed for me that I should give him twelve sequins in gold, wherewith, together also the loss of my sword, I escaped at that time.

But two days later the Friars set upon me again and fed the Turks lustily and largely, thinking to do me some displeasure but effected not their purpose for I still defied them and their father guardian, which in a manner broke their very galls. Only they did put me to some manner and charge. And I in their despite kept company with the patriarch of the Greeks and his colyros, I mean his priests and friars, and I went not at all to the Romish clergy nor visited their father guardian, though the poor Greek patriarch did very much and often entreat me to it, at which they were so exceedingly distempered that my scorn of them was written to Tripoli, they certifying to an old Friar there of all that had passed on my part in Jerusalem. Which Tripoli Friar at my coming ducked very kindly

*and came to our house to bid me welcome from the Holy Land. Yet he
with a fowling piece shot made at me two sundry times, out of an Italian's
house where he kept . . . but, as God would have it, he missed both times.
(Sanderson 1931: 122-123)*

Sanderson of course visited the chief Christian holy place of the city, the
Church of the Holy Sepulcher, though he did not much care for either
the conditions or the outcome:

*In the church [of the Holy Sepulcher], whose distance is twenty or
twenty-five paces, are divers altars of divers sorts of Christians. But first I
noted in the church door two great holes at which is daily given in the
victuals to all sorts of religious persons which keep continually in the said
church; for the Turks never open the door except for some pilgrims who
first pay the cadie [qadi], who is the chief justice, the Great Turk's due:
upon every one under the pope's banner, which they call Franks, nine
sequins in gold, and Greeks under the patriarch four and a half, with other
Christians alike, [or] some less. . . .*

*I had paid these nine sequins and had by the Turks the church door
opened for me, was within and entering the sepulcher, when the Roman
Friars and others fell in an uproar, saying that I was a Jew. The Turks
bade me go in in despite of them, but the babble was so terrible that I
returned to the cadie with the Friars. The padre guardiano sent his dragoman and accused me to be a Jew because I came in company of Jews.
Divers Turks followed to hear the matter. One old Turk came and earnestly exhorted me to become a Musselman in the presence of the cadie.
I gave him the hearing, and told him that I was a Christian and no Jew.
Then he said, in the hearing of all the Jews, Turks, and Christians "Let
him be searched." But the cadie before whom we were, being a very discreet man, did reprove the Turk and also the dragoman and the Friars,
my accusers, and so did dismiss me. But, as I was afterwards told, it cost
my adversaries above two hundred sequins. I spent not past some twenty
in that matter. (Sanderson 1931: 107)*

Sanderson's itinerary also included a visit to Bethlehem where, as it turned
out, it was not only the Franciscan friars who were puzzled by this new
kind of Christian from "the world's end":

*It [the basilica of the Nativity in Bethlehem] hath been a very sumptuous
church, Greek pictured saints yet remaining in the upper end of it, which
is in form round, with large steps to go up to the altar; and on both sides
underneath half round steps to go down to the pope's friars' precinct, who
have the custody of the very place of birth and where the manger stood.
By a gray-headed Greekish priest and a Grecian friar, my attendant, I was*

brought up a pair of stairs going up at the upper end of this great church aloft to a little chapel, where are many pictures according to the Greeks' manner, but especially a large St. George before whom they had a great lamp burning.

Expecting of me great devotion, they unto it making many crosses and told me he was St. George. I answered that I had never seen a bigger. They fixed earnest looks on me at that answer, seeing I regarded it not, and the old man told the other in Greek he thought I was no Christian, because I made no cross nor reverence, neither, as he said, to Our Ladies, Christs, St. Georges, or other saints' pictures. His fellow foolish friar told him that those of my country were Christians on the world's end.

I presently turned them out of their talk by hasting to be gone thence. But they led me up to the top of the church, which is leaded and many Christians had there ingraven their names. . . . Amongst which names I did see Huet Staper's, who, as some said, had travelled from Grand Cairo thither in friar's weeds and, as I have heard, was made a Knight of the Sepulcher by the padre guardiano and the other Romish etc.; so did not I. (Sanderson 1931: 110-111)

The New Learning in an Antique Land

Timberlake and Sanderson were new men in Jerusalem, the products of a revolution against the accepted notions of Church and ecclesiastical authority. They were skeptics about tradition simply because it was tradition, a tradition upheld by representatives of a Roman Church whose bona fides it was impossible for them to accept. And Sanderson, for example, had no hesitation in placing himself under the protection of a Greek patriarch whose authority was more acceptable because it was less Roman. The two Englishmen were shrewd but not learned men, protestors rather than questioners and as opinionated as the men whose views they professed to condemn and whose motives they questioned. But there were others also newly come to the city who were learned as well as skeptical and whose questioning was more profound and conclusions more considered than those of a Henry Timberlake or a John Sanderson.

The effects of a university education are discernible in almost every generation of clerics who came to Jerusalem from the thirteenth century onward. Burchard of Mount Sion and Felix Fabri of Ulm were learned men by any standard of judgment, men who understood evidence and historical process. But they were products of a university formation which was still essentially part of a religious culture. What was different in some of the arrivals in Jerusalem in the seventeenth century was their secular and scientific education in the still fresh European Enlightenment. The past was no longer only the Bible, Josephus and Eusebius, as it had been for earlier savants; it was the entire range of human experience. [36]

Henry Maundrell, the chaplain of the Aleppo factory of the English Levant Company who came to Jerusalem in 1697, is an example of that new learning. Maundrell was closely connected to the guiding spirits of the Royal Society founded in 1660 and to Thomas Sprat, whose *History of the Royal Society* written in 1667 set out the scientific and historical principles of the new learning. Sprat was one of those to whom Maundrell dedicated his *Travels*. He saw his own time as one in which men, "having removed the rubbish of ages" and liberated themselves from "the charms of vain apparitions," could by investigation and experiment finally reach the truth, since now "every man is unshaken at those tales at which his ancestors trembled: the course of things goes quickly along, in its own true channel of causes and effects." [37]

Maundrell and his kindred spirits from the Continent came not so much to the Holy Land as to Palestine, and their quest was for that "channel of causes and effects," which for them ran through the study of secular as well as religious buildings, across a terrain of flora and fauna, into chronology and languages. Even the ideational landscape had changed for these new visitors; where pilgrims, learned and unlearned, from Eusebius onward had seen only holy places in God's Land of Promise, Maundrell could recognize in those same places that antique land in which classical history had also unfolded and in which the lines of that history could still be traced in the Greek and Roman antiquities that were already being studied in Europe and still covered the face of the Near East. [38]

The Levant Company had been organized as a corporate trading company in the 1580s to enable the English to share in what was thought to be the windfall of commerce with the Near East. The Aleppo factory was, after Constantinople, an important center for that trade, a matter of little concern perhaps to Maundrell, whose background and training were ecclesiastical and academic, as were those of most of his predecessors and successors in the chaplaincy there. [39] And an opportunity to visit Jerusalem was not to be missed.

There being several gentlemen of our nation (fourteen in number) determined for a visit to the Holy Land at the approaching Easter, I resolved, though but newly come to Aleppo, to make one in the same design: considering that as it was my purpose to undertake this pilgrimage some time or other before my return to England, so I could never do it, either with less prejudice to my cure or with greater pleasure to myself, than at this juncture, having so large of my congregation abroad at the same time and in my company. Pursuant to this resolution we set out from Aleppo Fri-

day, February 26, 1696, at three in the afternoon, intending to make only a short stop that evening in order to prove how well we were provided with necessaries for our journey.... (Maundrell 1963: 1)

We have already heard Niccolo of Poggibonsi complaining of road tolls in the mid-fourteenth century (Chapter Eleven). On Maundrell's experience, things were not better at the end of the seventeenth century; the cynicism had merely deepened:

These caphars [khafara] are certain duties which travellers are obliged to pay, at several passes upon the road, to officers who attend in their appointed stations to receive them. They were at first levied by Christians to yield recompense to the country for maintaining the ways in good repair and scouring them from Arabs and robbers. The Turks keep up such a gainful usage still, pretending the same causes for it. But under that pretence they take occasion to exact from passengers, especially Franks, arbitrary and unreasonable sums, and instead of being a safeguard, prove the greatest rogues and robbers themselves. (Maundrell 1963: 4-5)

Still on his way to Jerusalem, Maundrell and his company encountered a *zawiya*, a rustic shrine built around the tomb of a local holy man, and it prompted the first of his many reflections on the religion of the country:

At last there being a small shaykh's house or burying place nearby, we comforted ourselves with hopes that we might take sanctuary there. The only difficulty was how to get admission into so reverenced a place, the Turks being generally men of greater zeal than mercy. To negotiate this affair we sent a Turk, whom we had taken with us for such occasions, into the village, ordering him to try first by fair means to gain admittance and, if that failed, to threaten that we would enter it by force.

But the religion of this place was of that kind which supersedes instead of improving humanity. The people absolutely denied us the small charity we demanded and sent us word they would die upon their swords before they would yield to have their faith defiled, adding further that it was their faith to be true to Muhammad and Ali but to hate and renounce Umar and Abu Bakr, and that this principle they were resolved to stand by. We told them that we had as bad an opinion of Umar and Abu Bakr as they could have; that we desired only a little shelter from the present rain and had no intention to defile their faith.

And thus with good words we brought them to consent that we might secure our baggage in the shaykh's house; but as for ourselves and arms, it was our irreversible sentence to be excluded out of the hallowed walls. We were glad however to get the merciless doors open upon any terms, not doubting but that we should be able to make our advantage of it afterwards according to our desire, which we actually did. For when it grew dark and the villagers were gone to sleep, we all got into the place of refuge and there passed a melancholy night among the tombs. . . . They are stone fabrics generally six or eight yards square more or less and roofed with a cupola, erected over the graves of some eminent shaykhs, that is, such persons, as by their long beards, prayers of the same standard, and a kind of pharisaical superciliousness, which are the great virtues of the Ma-hometan religion, have purchased to themselves the reputation of learning and saints.

Of these buildings there are many scattered up and down the country, for you will find among the Turks far more dead saints than living ones. They are situated commonly, though not always, upon the most eminent and conspicuous ascents. To these oratories the people repair with their vows and prayers, in their several distresses, much in the same manner as the Romanists do to the shrines of their saints. Only in this respect the practice of the Turks seems to be more orthodox in regard that though they make their saint's shrine the house of prayer, yet they always make God alone, and not the saint, the object of their addresses. (Maundrell 1963: 12-14)

As he approached Jerusalem, Maundrell began to meditate on the land-scape about him. Like most other pilgrims, he knew of the Bible's praise of that parched and deserted terrain as a "land of milk and honey," but while most simply accepted the paradox, Maundrell reflected:

All along this day's travel from Khan Leban to Bir [about three hours from Jerusalem], and also as far as we could see around, the country dis-covered quite a different face from what it had before, presenting nothing to the view in most places but naked rocks, mountains, and precipices. At sight of which pilgrims are apt to to be much astonished and balked in their expectations, finding that country in such an inhospitable condition, concerning whose pleasantness and plenty they had before formed in their minds such high ideas from the description given of it in the Word of God; inasmuch as it almost startles their faith, when they reflect how it could be possible for a land like this to supply food for so prodigious a number of inhabitants as are said to have been polled in the twelve tribes at one time, the sum given in by Joab in 2 Sam. 24 amounting to no less than thirteen hundred thousand fighting men, besides women and chil-dren. But it is certain that any man who is not a little biased to infidelity before may see, as he passes along, arguments enough to support his faith against such scruples.

For it is obvious for any one to observe that these rocks and hills must have been anciently covered with earth and cultivated and made to con-tribute to the maintenance of the inhabitants, no less than if the country had been all plain. Nay, perhaps more, forasmuch as such a mountainous and uneven surface affords a larger space of ground for cultivation than this country would amount to if were all reduced to a perfect level.

For the husbanding of these mountains their manner was to gather up the stones and place them in several lines, along the sides of hills, in form of a wall. By such borders they supported the mold from tumbling or being washed down; and formed many beds of excellent soil rising gradually one above another, from the bottom to the top of the mountains. Of this form of culture you see evident footsteps wherever you go in all the mountains of Palestine. Thus the very rocks were made fruitful. (Maundrell 1963: 86-87)

Lodging in Jerusalem

Inside the city Maundrell turned to other, perhaps more pressing considerations than agricultural development:

The person who is the French consul at Sidon has also the title of consul of Jerusalem, and is obliged by his master, the French king, to make a visit to the holy city every Easter under pretence of preserving the sanctuary there from violation, and the Friars who have custody of it, from the exactions of the Turks. But the Friars think themselves much safer without this protection. We were desirous to join with Monsieur l'Empereur [Lempereur], the present consul, in this year's pilgrimage and accordingly had sent him a letter from Aleppo on purpose to bespeak that favor, hoping by his protection to pass more securely from the abuses of the Arabs and Turks who are nowhere so insolent as in Palestine and about Jerusalem. . . . (Maundrell 1963: 61)

In one hour more we approached the walls of the holy city, but we could not enter immediately, it being necessary first to send a messenger to acquaint the governor of our arrival and to desire liberty of entrance. Without which preceding ceremony no Frank dares come within the walls. . . . We had not waited above half an hour when he brought us our permission and we entered accordingly at the Bethlehem Gate [the Bab al-Khalil, or Jaffa Gate]. It is required of all Franks, unless they happen to come in with some public minister, to dismount at the gate, to deliver [up] their arms, and enter on foot. But we coming in company with the French consul had the privilege to enter mounted and armed. Just within the gate we turned up a street on the left hand and were conducted by the consul to his own house, with most friendly and generous invitations to make that our home as long as we should continue at Jerusalem. [40] *Having taken a little refreshment, we went to the Latin convent, at which all Frank pilgrims are wont to be entertained. The guardian and the friars received us with many kind welcomes and kept us with them at supper, after which we returned to the French consul's to bed. And thus we continued to take our lodging at the consul's and our board with the Friars during our whole stay in Jerusalem. (Maundrell 1963: 89-90)*

Unless their Protestant sensibilities prevented them, most European visitors stayed with the Franciscans at their Convent of St. Savior's in the Christian quarter, where they enjoyed the protection of the Franciscan guardian. Other nationalities made their own arrangements, as the Franciscan Elzear Horn somewhat maliciously describes toward the middle of the eighteenth century:

Every nation receives in its own hospice the pilgrims who come to Jerusalem either out of devotion or curiosity or any other motive.

The Greek monks distribute the visitors of both sexes here and there in their monasteries, of which they possess thirteen in the Holy City; or separately, putting the men in the monasteries of St. Constantine, St. Abraham, St. Michael, and St. John the Baptist, while the nuns are put up in the nuns' convents; or if they cannot do otherwise, they put husbands and wives in the monasteries of St. Nicholas and St. Demetrius.

The Armenian monks put them up in the very spacious monastery of St. James the Apostle, all in separate cells constructed for that purpose. The Copts, Syrians, and Nestorians do likewise, and on certain days they regale them with a light meal to their own great profit. For following a studied exhortation towards the end of the meal, one of the monks must go round with a silver platter, on which the book of the Gospels has been placed, and with it he collects an appropriate offering of money from each pilgrim, while another monk notes down on a piece of paper the names of the principal benefactors. Likewise, for the first entry into the Church of the Holy Sepulcher, they demand from each pilgrim a candle of fixed weight and about one florin. Besides this they have other ways of making exactions by which they know very well how to empty the purses of pilgrims.

We Friars Minor receive gratis all European pilgrims, not only in Jerusalem but also in other places, wherever they happen to tarry in passing, and supply them with food and drink and a bed. . . . (Horn 1962: 183-184)

Holy War in the Holy Sepulcher

We return to Maundrell's account:

Friday, March 26. The next day being Good Friday in the Latin style, the

*consul was obliged to go into the church of the Sepulcher in order to keep
his feast, whither we accompanied him, although our own Easter was not
till a week after theirs.* [41] *We found the church doors guarded by several
janissaries and other Turkish officers who are placed here to watch that
none may enter in but such as have first paid their caphar. This is more
or less, according to the country or the character of the persons that enter.
For Franks it is ordinarily fourteen dollars per head, unless they are eccle-
siastics, for in that case it is but half as much. . . . (Maundrell 1963: 90)*

Once inside, Maundrell gives the now familiar survey of the Christian sects
who share the premises as regards both living quarters and altars. But, he
continues,

*that which has always been the great prize contended for by the several
sects is the command and appropriation of the Holy Sepulcher, a privilege
contested with so much unchristian fury and animosity, especially between
the Greeks and Latins, that in disputing which party should go in to
celebrate their Mass, they have sometimes proceeded to blows and wounds
even at the very door of the sepulcher, mingling their own blood with
their sacrifices. An evidence of which fury the father guardian showed us
in a great scar upon his arm, which he told us was the mark of a wound
given him by a sturdy Greek priest in one of those unholy wars. Who can
expect ever to see these holy places rescued from the hands of infidels? Or
if they should be recovered, what deplorable contests might be expected
to follow about them, seeing even in their present state of captivity they
are made the occasion of such unchristian rage and animosity.*

*For putting an end to these infamous quarrels the French king inter-
posed, by a letter to the Grand Vizier, about twelve years hence, requesting him to order the Holy Sepulcher to be put into the hands of the
Latins, according to the tenor of the capitulation made in the year 1673.
The consequence of which letter, and of other instances made by the
French king, was that the Holy Sepulcher was appropriated to the Latins:
this was not accomplished till the year 1690, they alone having the privilege to say Mass in it. And though it be permitted to Christians of all
nations to go into it for their private devotions, yet none may solemnize
any public office of religion there but the Latins. (Maundrell 1963: 94-
95)*

Maundrell followed the Latin liturgy, but his observant and sometimes
scornful eye caught much else besides:

*Among the other crucifixes [used in the Good Friday ceremony] there was
one of a very large size, which bore upon it the image of our Lord, as big
as the life. The image was fastened to it with great nails, crowned with*

thorns, besmeared with blood, and so exquisitely was it formed that it represented in a very lively manner the lamentable spectacle of our Lord's body as it hung upon the cross. . . . The ceremony of the Passion being over and the guardian's sermon ended, two Friars, personating the one Joseph of Arimathea, the other Nicodemus, approached the cross, and with most solemn, concerned air, both of aspect and behavior, drew out the great nails and took down the feigned body from the cross. It was an effigy so contrived that its limbs were soft and flexible, as if they had been real flesh. And nothing could be more surprising than to see the two pretended mourners bend down the arms, which were before extended, and dispose them upon the trunk in such a manner as is usual in corpses. . . . They laid down their imaginary corpse, and casting over it several sweet powders and spices, wrapped it up in the winding sheet. While this was doing, they sang their proper hymn and afterward one of the Friars preached in Arabic a funeral sermon. These obsequies being finished, they carried off their fancied corpse and laid it in the sepulcher, shutting up the door till Easter morning. . . . (Maundrell 1963: 97-100)

Saturday, March 27. The next morning nothing extraordinary passed, which gave many of the pilgrims leisure to have their arms marked with the usual ensigns of Jerusalem. The artists who undertake the operation do it in this manner. They have stamps in mood of any figure that you desire, which they first mark off upon your arm with powder of charcoal. Then taking two very fine needles tied close together and dipping them often, like a pen, in certain ink compounded, as I was informed, of gunpowder and ex-gall, they make with them small punctures all along the lines of the figure which they have printed. And then washing the part in wine, they conclude the work. (Maundrell 1963: 100)

There was the usual trip to the Jordan and the expected harassment from the bedouin, though Maundrell saved his heaviest fire for the Franciscans:

No sooner had we arrived at the river and dismounted in order to satisfy that curiosity and devotion which brought us hither, but we were alarmed by some troops of Arabs appearing on the other side and firing at us, but at too great a distance to do any execution. This intervening disturbance hindered the Friars from performing their service prescribed for this place and seemed to put them in terrible fear of their lives, beyond what appeared in the rest of the company, though considering the sordidness of their present condition and the extraordinary rewards which they boast to be their due in the world to come, one would think in reason that they of all men should have the least cause to discover so great a fear of death and so much fondness of a life like theirs. (Maundrell 1963: 110-111)

A Fluttering Pigeon and
Flaming Beards

On April 3, 1696, we witness with Maundrell what was close to the end of a devotional exercise, at least as far as the credulity of Western visitors was concerned, the now notorious Descent of the Holy Fire:

They began their disorders by running round the Holy Sepulcher with all their might and swiftness, crying out as they went Huia! which signifies [in Arabic] "This is he" or "This is it," an expression by which they assert the verity of the Christian religion. After they had by these vertiginous circulations and clamors turned their heads and inflamed their madness, they began to act the most antic tricks and postures, in a thousand shapes of distraction. Sometimes they dragged one another along the floor all round the sepulcher; sometimes they set one man upright on another's shoulders and in this posture marched round; sometimes they took men with their heels upward and hurried them about in such an indecent manner as to expose their nudities; sometimes they tumbled about the sepulcher after the manner of tumblers on the stage.

In this tumultuous frantic humor they continued from twelve to four of the clock. The reason for this delay was because of a suit that was in debate before the [Muslim] chief justice between the Greeks and the Armenians; the former endeavoring to exclude the latter from having any part in this miracle. Both parties having expended, as I was informed, 5,000 dollars between them in this foolish controversy, the judge at last gave sentence that they should enter the Holy Sepulcher together, as had been usual at former times. Sentence being thus given, at four of the clock both nations went on with their ceremony. . . . Toward the end of the procession a pigeon came fluttering into the cupola over the sepulcher, at sight of which there was a greater shout and clamor than before. This bird, the Latins told us, was purposely let fly by the Greeks to deceive the people into an opinion that it was a visible descent of the Holy Ghost.

The two patriarchs then retired as usual, inside the sepulcher, where all the lamps had been quenched, and the doors were fastened and sealed.

The two miracle mongers had not been alone a minute in the Holy Sepulcher when the glimmering of the Holy Fire was seen, or imagined to appear, through some chinks of the door. And certainly Bedlam itself never saw such an unruly transport as was produced in the mob at this sight. Immediately after out came the two priests with blazing torches in their hands, which they held up at the door of the sepulcher, while the people thronged about with inexpressible ardor, everyone striving to ob-

tain a part of the first and purest flame. The Turks in the meantime with huge clubs laid them on without mercy. But all this could not repel them, the excess of their transport making them insensible of pain. Those that got the fire applied it immediately to their beards, faces and bosoms, pretending that it would not burn like an earthly flame. But I plainly saw none of them could endure this experiment long enough to make good that pretension. So many hands being employed, you may be sure it could not be long before innumerable tapers were lighted. The whole church, galleries and every place seemed instantly to be in a flame. And with this illumination the ceremony ended. (Maundrell 1963: 127-130[42])

It must be owned that those two within the sepulcher performed their part with great quickness and dexterity; but the behavior of the rabble without very much discredited the miracle. The Latins take a great deal of pains to expose this ceremony as a most shameful imposture and a scandal to the Christian religion; perhaps out of envy that others should be masters of so gainful a business. But the Greeks and Armenians pin their faith upon it and make their pilgrimages chiefly upon this motive. And it is the deplorable unhappiness of their priests that having acted the cheat so long already, they are forced now to stand to it for fear of endangering the apostasy of their people. (Maundrell 1963: 127[43])

Thursday, April 15. This morning our diplomata were presented us by the father guardian to certify our having visited all the holy places and we presented the convent fifty dollars a man as a gratuity for their trouble; which offices having passed between us, we took our leaves. (Maundrell 1963: 148)

Jewish Immigrants

The Franciscan presence in Jerusalem was both formal and on sufferance: it was a privilege that had been bought and paid for in a sense, and since the Franciscans were, by their own and the Turks' definition, aliens and foreigners in that land and that city, its continuance was the subject of constant negotiation, regulation, and levy. The Jews, on the other hand, had a somewhat different status, one not unlike that of the Greeks or other indigenous Christian groups who lived in Jerusalem. They were a religious minority and so subject to both the regulations of Muslim religious law and the unkind attentions of the tax collector. They were an ethnic minority as well, but of a familiar type, and their existence in Jerusalem, where there had been Jews for as long as there had been Muslims, was by and large unremarkable. Their being there was not, in any event, a political event, as the Franciscan presence in Jerusalem assuredly was: no foreign power as yet spoke for the Jews; no ambassadors at the Sublime Porte intervened on their behalf.

Yet many of the Jews were in effect as foreign as the Franciscans. The Turks, like all their Muslim predecessors, made no distinctions on the matter, however, though they were as careful to distinguish among Christians as the Christians themselves were among themselves: a Jew was simply a Jew, whether Ashkenazi or Sephardic, whether European or "Arabized," and the Jews, who sometimes quarreled among themselves over such things, wisely never instructed their Turkish sovereigns otherwise. Thus the Jews were free to come and go, indifferently visitors, pilgrims, or immigrants, and without, needless to say, a holy place with the public aura and access of the Church of the Holy Sepulcher to draw the unwanted, often unkind, and invariably expensive attentions of Turkish officialdom.

None of this is to suggest that the life of the Jews of Jerusalem was either untroubled or prosperous; it simply did not attract the notice or raise the fears that the European Christians, whether living in or visiting the Holy City, did. The Jews themselves are the best witnesses to their status in the city, and the following piece of advice delivered to prospective immigrants by Abraham Kalisker in the last decade of the eighteenth century contains a gentle warning that was probably true for the entire Ottoman period:

Many, many changes and events, experiences and fates befall every single man who comes to this land, until he adjusts to it, has joy in its stones, and loves its dust, until the ruins of the Land of Israel are dearer to him than a palace abroad, and dry bread in that place dearer than all delicacies elsewhere. But this does not happen in one day nor in two, not in a month and not in a year. Many a year passes before his initiation is over, his initiation into the true life. (Wilhelm 1946: 13)

The advice, as general as it was, was well worth heeding, doubtless, and it could be supplemented by far more specific instructions as the stream of Jewish immigrants and visitors to *Eretz Israel* grew deeper and broader. The following highly practical suggestions, for example, come from a work called "Ways to Sion," written by Moses ben Israel Poryat of Prague in 1650:

The caravan [from Constantinople to Jerusalem] usually remains stationary by day and travels during the night because of the great heat. The only bedding to take along is that which is to be used on the way since feathers can be obtained cheaply at Jerusalem from the German community. You can never bring along a sufficient quantity of sheets, shirts, veils, table-cloths, handkerchiefs, and all other kinds of linen, for in Jerusalem such things are expensive and not very good. Each person should also take along a pair of good shoes as well as woolen winter stockings, for such clothing is not very good in Jerusalem. Apart from this, winter is cold in Jerusalem, even though it does not freeze. Men's clothing should not be brought along in quantity since they are not expensive here.

. . . The baths, thank God, are very good and healthful. Do not take much silver and gold along, even if you are rich, for that only attracts attention. But it is good to bring iron padlocks in order to lock up your rooms and boxes.

In Ofen [the departure point on the Danube] let each man buy something to wrap around his head after the fashion of the Turks, and if the cloth is quite white you should sew a few colored threads in it, but none of green. It is very dangerous to wear anything of green. Sometimes the borders of a prayer shawl are also green and this must be changed in advance. Green, the color of the Prophet, is forbidden to Jews in the whole of Turkey and Jerusalem. (Wilhelm 1946: 68-69)

Some additional instruction and reflections on clothing in Jerusalem was offered in 1716 by the Polish immigrant Gedaliah:

The garments of the Turks are like those of the Poles, but are multi-colored. Round the turban they wrap a cloth or cotton or silk. The Sephardis wear the same garb, but may not wrap their turbans round with green or white. The Jews may wear a white garment. The Sephardis wear a white undergarment and wear over it a black or colored coat even on the Sabbath. The Ashkenazis go in gleaming white on the Sabbath, but the Sephardis wear white only on the Sabbath before the Ninth of Ab. The Christians dress as in the kingdom of Poland. For the Turkish law prescribes that each nation should go in its own costume, in order to make the differences clear to see. . . . (Wilhelm 1946: 80-81)

Poryat even supplies guidance on reading matter for the immigrant and so provides a profile sketch of the religious culture of the seventeenth-century Eastern European Jew en route to the Holy City and, by indirection, of Jerusalem itself:

Books are not expensive in Jerusalem, so you should not burden yourself with them on account of the expense of transportation. Let each person take with him only a thick prayer book, a Pentateuch with commentaries, a Penitential Prayer Book, the Mishna, Rabbi Mordechai Jaffe's "Lavush" ["The Garment," a compendium of Jewish law and religion; Rabbi Jaffe d. 1612 in Posen], A "Shomrim le-Boker" ["Watch till the Morning," dawn service prayers], a Festival Prayer Book according to the Prague usage, a midrash, "En Yaakov" ["The Spring of Jacob," a collection of non-legal material from the Talmud composed in the fifteenth to the sixteenth century], the "Shulhan Aruk" [of Joseph Caro, d. 1575 in Safed] and the "Yalkut" [a compendium of midrashic material put together by Simeon Kara in the thirteenth century]. The womenfolk take with them a "Teutsch Humash" [a Judeo-German translation of the Pentateuch], the Festival Book and "Tehinnah" [a book of vernacular devotions], and other Teutsch books. The prayer books should be small, for there is no lectern in the synagogues and the books must be held in the hand. . . . (Wilhelm 1946: 69)

And once in Jerusalem:

For a large living room an annual rent of eight lion thalers is paid; for a smaller, five or six. Those who dwell in the synagogue court, where the Loeb Synagogue and the two Houses of Study are, live cramped and often lack for water. But on the other hand they can go to the synagogue very early in the morning every day. For the synagogue is locked in the evening as soon as the Evening Prayer is over, and not opened until the break of day. To go through the streets at night is dangerous. Anyone who does not dwell in the Synagogue Court has ample room and also more water at home. The water is good and healthful. He who so desires can drink it with liquorice at twenty kreuzer the rotl. There are some who also drink it with lemonade. The water is only rainwater and not well water. Every house has a large, very well whitewashed cistern under the ground, and up above there is a little hole where the water runs in and is drawn up. In years when there is little water it must be bought from the Turks, who bring it into the house in leather sacks. (Wilhelm 1946: 70-71)

The Western Wall

It was in the Ottoman period too that one of the chief places of Jewish veneration in Jerusalem finally stands forth from legend in the full light of history. Far back in the Jewish tradition, as we have seen in Chapter Six, there was a persistent belief that the "Presence of God," his *Shekhinah*, would not desert Jerusalem, and more specifically, the "western wall of the Temple." Though the tradition is pervasive, there is no evidence that the site mentioned in it was ever localized, assuredly not atop the Temple mount, nor even where it is today, at a stretch of the western side of Herod's Temple *platform* between the Madrasa Tankiziyya on the north and the Maghrebi Gate to the Haram on the south. As is clear from most of the texts cited above, when the Jews prayed outside their synagogues in Jerusalem, the liturgy was performed either atop the Mount of Olives or at the Gate or Mercy, or Golden Gate, on the eastern side of the Haram, or even, on occasion, somewhere on the southern side of the Temple.

With the Ottoman occupation of Jerusalem something must have changed, though we are not sure what or why. Two stories were told by a later generation, one by Moses Hagiz about 1730 of Selim, the Ottoman conqueror of the city, and the other by Eliezer Nahman Poa of Suleiman, the sultan who built its still-standing city walls. In both it was the Turkish ruler who cleared the filth and refuse around the present site of the Western Wall and, at least by implication, first permitted the Jews to pray there. [44] Whatever the case, Jewish visitors from the early sixteenth century on describe what is unmistakably the western wall of Herod's Temple platform and connect it with the earlier tradition of the "Presence of God." Thus in 1658 the Karaite Moses Yerushalmi could write:

Now, everybody knows that one wall and one wall only is left from the Temple, and that we must weep and keen for the destruction of the Temple [there]; this wall is called the Western Wall. . . . Near the Western Wall the Arabs built a house of prayer and surrounded it with a wall, and the Western Wall is also within the [same] wall so that nobody [presumably Christians] may enter. But the Jews are allowed to go there, and they pay a tax of ten paras. The Jews of Jerusalem pay the tax for the whole year and may go there as often as they wish. But you must approach from the outside and not from the inside [that is, from the Haram] for great sanctity rests on the Western Wall, the original sanctity which attached to it then and forever more. (Ben-Dov et al. 1983: 69)

The most complete medieval description of both the site and the wall comes, however, from the gifted observer Gedaliah in the opening years of the eighteenth century:

The Western Wall that remains from the Temple is very long and high. For most of its height it is very ancient and the stones are very large. Some stones are five or six cubits wide and the same is true of their height. But I do not know how thick they are; if I could see them at the end of the Wall I could tell, but a courtyard has been built actually against one [the southern] end of the [exposed section of the] Wall and at the other [northern end] stands the house of an Ishmaelite judge. . . .[45] The Ishmaelites have added to the height of this ancient Wall with new building until it has become very high; in these new walls are also gates to go in and out through them. Only Ishmaelites are permitted to enter the site of the Temple, but not Jews and other peoples unless, God forbid, they convert to Islam. Because they [the Muslims] say that no other religion is worthy enough to enter this holy site. Although God had originally chosen the Jews, because they sinned He deserted them and chose the Ishmaelites. Thus they speak continuously.

When we go to the Wall to pray, we are actually standing "behind our wall" [Cant. 2:9], close by it. On the eve of the New Moon and on the Ninth of Ab and other fasts, [the Jews] go there to pray, and though the women weep bitterly, nobody objects. Even though the Ishmaelite judge lives close by and hears the weeping, he does not object or rebuke them at all. Occasionally a young Arab comes to annoy the Jews, but they give him a small coin and he goes off. If a dignified Ishmaelite or Arab witnesses such impudence, he severely reprimands the child.

The Temple site is far from the streets the Jews live in, and we have to go through markets and other streets to get to the Western Wall. Prayer is generally more desirable by the Wall. (Ben-Dov et al. 1983: 69-70)

Failed Zionists

The city had its Jewish pilgrims and visitors, often under extremely trying circumstances,[46] but immigration, permanent settlement in the Land of Israel, was of far greater concern to those who already lived there. In the mid-seventeenth century that concern was religious and theological rather than political, since, as one author wrote in 1648:

But for the prayer of the men of Jerusalem, who pray at the Wailing Wall with weeping and supplication, and are all great ascetics and saints, the World would—Heaven forfend—no longer exist; and concerning them it is written, "and on Mount Sion there shall be a deliverance," meaning that the Jews that live there and devote themselves to the life of the world to come. (Scholem 1973: 73)

How strongly this was felt may be sensed through the words of Nathan Shapira, who had left his native Cracow to come to Palestine. He spent most of his life there in Jerusalem until he was sent to Italy on one of those fund-raising missions that had characterized the Jewish community in Jerusalem from the beginning. His exposure to the wealthy Jews in the European Diaspora provoked Shapira, and his displeasure at their failure to live in the Land of Promise is apparent in this eschatological passage of "The Goodness of the Land," a work published in 1654:

Know that we possess a tradition that on the day when the Messiah comes to Palestine for the ingathering of the exiles there will be seven thousand

Jews [in Palestine]. On this day the dead in Palestine will arise and the walls of fire will depart from Jerusalem. . . . On this day the dead in Palestine will resume their former lives and will become new spiritual creations. And the seven thousand that were alive there [when the Messiah arrived] will become a new creation, that is, spiritual body like Adam's body before the fall . . . and they will fly in the air like eagles—all this in the sight of the returning exiles.

When the returning exiles see their Palestinian brethren have become a new creation and are flying in the air toward a lower Paradise where they will study the Law from the mouth of God, then their heart will fill with sorrow and dismay and they will complain to the messianic king, saying, "Are we not Jews like the others? And how have they become spiritual kings and we not?" Then the messiah will answer them, "It is known that God dispenses justice measure for measure. Those of the Diaspora who endeavored to come to Palestine to receive a pure soul, who spared neither money nor efforts and came by sea and by land and were not afraid of being drowned in the sea or captured by cruel masters [pirates]: because they were concerned primarily for their spirits and their souls and not for their bodies and money, therefore they were turned into spirits, measure for measure. You, however, who could have come to Palestine like them, but failed to come because of your cupidity, having made a principal concern of your wealth and your bodies, while considering your souls and spirits a lesser concern: you shall remain corporeal, measure for measure."
. . . (Scholem 1973: 73-74)

The Pilgrimage of Rabbi Judah
the Pious, 1700

Nathan Shapira had immigrated to Palestine and survived. His spiritual resources were probably deep and strong enough to transform that ordeal into a spiritual experience, but for many it must have been simply that, an ordeal. We can share the experience with men who went through it, with the earlier-mentioned Gedaliah, for instance, who was a member of a mass migration from Poland to Palestine organized and led by Rabbi Judah surnamed "the Pious." The group, which numbered in the thousands, left the Grodno district in Poland and arrived in Jerusalem the following year. Gedaliah in his "Seek the Peace of Jerusalem" describes what followed:

Our master, Rabbi Judah the Pious, arrived together with his followers in Jerusalem on the New Year's Day of Marheshvan 5461 [A.D. 1700]. He at once acquired a house in the Synagogue Court of the Askenazis, rented dwellings for his faithful ones and distributed money for them to live upon.

Almost immediately afterwards Rabbi Judah fell ill.

In Jerusalem there was a wealthy Sephardic physician. . . . It is dangerous to go out into the streets of Jerusalem at night, even if it is only a half hour after sunset. The Turks do not permit it, and throw every Jew whom they find into prison; and in addition they impose a money fine upon him. Only in order to summon a doctor to a patient or a midwife to a woman in childbirth may a Jew enter the street at night. (Wilhelm 1946: 73)

The rabbi died nonetheless. He was buried on the Mount of Olives, Gedaliah explains, "after the fashion of the Diaspora, not in a sepulchral chamber, as was formerly the custom here."

Immigrant Life in Jerusalem

The followers of Rabbi Judah, now deprived of their leader, attempted to fashion a new life in Jerusalem:

In the late summer of the year, shortly before our arrival [in the fall of 1700], a beginning was made at the building of the new synagogue and of forty dwellings for the poor. A magnificent House of Study containing many books was likewise built. . . . All the houses within the [Ashkenazi] Synagogue Court, including the synagogue and the House of Study, are built of solid hewn stone. . . . These buildings consumed a great deal of money. The Turks in Jerusalem had to be heavily bribed before they permitted the building. Then the Jews of Jerusalem wished to construct the new synagogue on a larger scale than the old one, but the Turkish government permitted them to build it only as high as the previous building. So they had to bribe the pashas heavily again, in order that they might approve a larger building.

The building of a new synagogue was in effect illegal by the terms of Muslim law, as confirmed by a decree of the governor of Damascus in A.D. 1540. [47] Most of the Jews of Jerusalem worshipped in the old Ramban (Nachmanides) Synagogue in the Jewish quarter, next to a mosque, and conflicts between the two congregations led to the tearing down of the synagogue at the end of the fifteenth century. It was rebuilt just before the Ottoman takeover of the city, but the dispute continued to drag on through the Muslim courts and the rebuilt synagogue was closed again sometime before 1587, but as appears from Gedaliah's account below, new synagogues were being built, though at an enormous cost in payoffs and bribes to the local authorities. [48]

Now there is a law in Jerusalem that while building is going on the pasha has to be paid five hundred lion thalers a year for three years. But as the synagogue had been built higher than the old one without permission of the sultan, another pasha came and wished to stop the building. So he also received five hundred lion thalers. Finally a new pasha came from Constantinople to whom five hundred [more] lion thalers had to be given. Thus the Jews were compelled to borrow money from the Turks at a high rate of interest. (Wilhelm 1946: 77-78)

This is little more than extortion, one of the many "special taxes" that the Christians and Jews alike had to pay to a local Ottoman administration, which was turning away from any policy remotely resembling fiscal responsibility to outright extortion.

Gedaliah was close to despair, bitter about fair promises, helpless before prospects impossible to realize, and filled with a profound sense of shame and anger:

But let us return to our great worries, which the synagogue building brought about. Our debts press like a heavy yoke on our necks. We are continually taken into custody, and before one debtor can be redeemed, another has already been detained. One scarcely dares go out in the street, where, to cap it all, the tax collectors lie in wait like wolves and lions to devour us. When we journeyed with our master [Rabbi Judah] to Jerusalem, we passed through the whole of Germany and were promised everywhere that we would receive regular support. At that time be believed we could maintain ourselves in worthy fashion, but now we are oppressed with debts and we have to give money meant for our sustenance to the Turks so that they should not fling us into prison, for prison is the worst of all.

It is hard for us Ashkenazis to begin to trade here, since we lack knowledge of the language. The Sephardic Jews talk Ladino, the Arabs talk Aramaic [that is, Arabic], and the Turks Turkish. None of them understands German. And what should he deal in? There is indeed much wine in the land of Israel, but Turks and Arabs drink neither wine nor brandy. If a Jew sells an Arab even a little wine or brandy and the Arab is seen drunk, then the Jew is imprisoned and beaten and has to pay a money fine. . . .

The Arabs often wrong the Jews publicly. But if the Arab is a respectable man he will cause no injury to the Jew whom he meets on the street. The meeting with common people is often unpleasant for the Jews. We may not raise a hand against a Turk, nor against an Arab either, who has the same religion as the other. If one of them gives a Jew a blow, the Jew goes away cowering and does not dare open his mouth lest he receive worse blows.

That is the way the Sephardis behave, who have become accustomed to the situation. But the Ashkenazi Jews, for whom it is not yet customary to receive blows from Arabs, curse them if they know the language or leap upon them in fury, and then receive even more blows. But if a respectable Turk comes along, he scolds the Arab thoroughly and drives him away; or else he waits until the Jew has gone his way. The Christians must also suffer such indignities. If a Jew makes a Turk angry, then the latter beats him shamefully and dreadfully with his shoe, and nobody delivers the Jew from his hand. Nor is it otherwise with the Christians. They find them-selves under the same oppression, but they have a great deal of money which is sent to them from all over, and they bribe the Turks with it and keep them away. The Jews do not have much money and it is much worse for them. (Wilhelm 1946: 77-80)

Gedaliah's fears were realized soon after those lines were written. The Ashkenazi Synagogue Court in the Jewish quarter was confiscated, looted, and destroyed in 1720 or 1721 for nonpayment of debts. Jewish fortunes in Jerusalem seemed at full ebb by 1766 when Simon van Geldern bade Jerusalem the Holy farewell and cast behind a terrible prophecy:

I had to depart from Jerusalem and flee from the city at night, for dwelling there had become almost impossible. The persecutions and extortions were increasing every day. The Ashkenazi then owed more than 50,000 reichsthaler and the Sephardis about 200,000 gulden. How should we manage to pay off these debts? Every day somebody was flung into prison, either a scholar or a leader, and there was beaten until he gave what was demanded of him. So I fled at night to Hebron on a camel. . . .

In Hebron I dwelt with a scholar, the brother-in-law of Rabbi Isaac Carregal; and I did not have anything to pay him with. I asked people if anybody was prepared to offer me hospitality for six or seven months, until I received some money from abroad. But each one replied that he did not have enough money for himself. Indeed, it is very expensive in Hebron, and it is hard to earn enough to make a living. The Hebron folk also had about 50,000 gulden of debts, and there are only twenty to thirty families to be found there.

On my journeys I saw how contemptible we Ashkenazis are in the eyes of those who dwell in the land. We are, after all, great fools. When they come to us, we think we have to make them rich, while as a matter of fact they collect fortunes. But I can tell you that in fifty years' time no Ash-

kenazis will be living in this land any more. If God had not shown me signs and performed wonders for me, I would have starved here.

More than two hundred families have departed this year from cities like Jerusalem. Life is also difficult in Hebron, Safed, and Tiberias. The legal conditions are hard and are made worse, by reason of our great sins, by persecution, denunciation, and so on. (Wilhelm 1946: 95-97)

Jerusalem Observed:
The Medieval City Through
Modern Eyes

*To see its destroyed walls, its debris-filled moat, its city circuit choked
with ruins, you would scarcely recognize this famous metropolis which
once fought against the most powerful empires in the world; which
for a moment held even Rome at bay; and which, by a bizarre twist
of fate, gains honor and respect in its disgrace. In short,
you would scarcely recognize Jerusalem.*
—*Constantin Volney (1784)*

Jerusalem Enters the Age of Europe

THE MODERN history of Jerusalem begins, it might be argued, in 1535,
when negotiations began between Sultan Suleiman and Francis I of France
to regulate the relations, notably the commercial dealings, between their
two states. What was proposed was the exchange of free-trade privileges,
Ottoman in Europe, French in the Ottoman Empire. It remained only a
proposal at this stage—the draft document was never formally ratified, and
the first effective agreement was not signed until 1569. Moreover, there
was nothing novel in the granting of certain commercial and other privileges between trading partners; the Ottomans had given these privileges,
called "capitulations," to Genoa, Venice, and Florence in the mid-fourteenth century, before they had taken Jerusalem. [1] But the arrangements
under discussion in 1535 ranged far more widely than those earlier agreements and in fact set the tone and issues of almost all that was to follow
in the declining fortunes of the Ottoman Empire and, with them, of
Jerusalem:

*Be it known to everybody that in the year of Jesus Christ one thousand
five hundred and thirty-five, in the month of February, and of Muhammad
941, in the moon of Sha'ban, Sire Jean de Forest, privy counsellor and
ambassador of the most excellent and powerful prince Francis, by the
grace of God, Most Christian King of France, accredited to the most
powerful and invincible Grand Signior, Sultan Suleiman, Emperor of the
Turks, and having discussed with the most powerful and magnificent Signior Ibrahim, serasker of the sultan, the calamities and disadvantages
which are caused by war, and, on the other hand, the tranquility derived
from peace; and knowing how good it is to prefer the one [peace] to the*

other [war], each of them guaranteeing the above mentioned monarchs, their superiors, they have negotiated and agreed upon the following chapters and conventions in the name and on the honor of the said monarchies which are the protectors of their component states and the benefactors of their subjects:

I.   [The conclusion of peace.]

II.   Likewise, the said subjects and tributaries of the said monarchs shall respectively be able to buy, sell, exchange, move, and transport by sea and land from one country to the other all kinds of merchandises not prohibited, by paying only the ordinary customs and taxes, to wit, the Turks, in the dominion of the King, shall pay the same as Frenchmen, and the said Frenchmen in the dominions of the Grand Signior shall pay the same as the Turks, without being obliged to pay any other new tribute, impost, or storage due.

III.   Likewise, whenever the King shall send to Constantinople or Pera or other places a bailiff—just as at present he had a consul at Alexandria—the said bailiff and consul shall be received and maintained in proper authority so that each one of them may in his locality, and without being hindered by any judge, qadi, soubashi, or other, according to his faith and law, hear, judge, and determine all causes, both civil and criminal, which might arise between merchants and other subjects of the King. . . .

IV.   [Limited civil liability.]

V.   [Limited criminal liability.]

VI.   Likewise, as regards religion, it has been expressly promised, concluded, and agreed that the said merchants, their agents and servants, and all other subjects of the King shall never be molested nor tried by the qadis, sanjak-beys, or soubashis, or any person but the Sublime Porte only, and they cannot be made or regarded as Turks [Muhammadans] unless they themselves desire it and profess it openly and without violence. They shall have the right to practice their own religion. . . .

XV.   . . . The King of France has proposed that His Holiness the Pope, the King of England, his brother and perpetual ally, and the King of Scotland shall be entitled to adhere to this treaty of peace, if they please, on condition that when desirous of doing so they shall within eight months from date send their ratifications to the Grand Signior and obtain his. (Hurewitz 1975: 2-3)

It was envisioned that the agreement would be subject to formal review and renewal at the accession of each new sultan; and so it was—until 1740, when as an acknowledgment of the role played by the French ambassador in negotiating peace between the Sublime Porte and its increasingly aggressive neighbors,[2] the capitulation privileges enjoyed by His

Most Christian Majesty were granted in perpetuity. Thus each succeeding sultan was bound beforehand to agreements that had, insistently, more and more to say on the subject of Jerusalem. [3] And as the last cited clause of the agreement of 1535 makes quite explicit, it was not the king of France alone who was invited to address himself to the matter of the treaty. We are not certain what the concerns of the king of Scotland might have been regarding the Holy Land, but the pope had already been long and strenuously engaged there.

The capitulations had a profound effect on the political life of the Ottoman Empire. At the outset the privileges were understood to be mutual, to govern the status of Ottoman merchants in Europe as well as those of the French in the Levant. As a matter of fact, there were no Ottoman traders in France, and the commercial highway between East and West quickly became a one-way street. Eighteenth-century sultans bartered away these privileges, and so mortgaged the economy of the empire, to buy alliances, goods, and cash, all of them in increasingly short supply in the chancelleries of the Sublime Porte. [4]

France and the other nations of Christian Europe that signed such agreements with the Ottoman Empire were not seeking any commercial privileges in Jerusalem, a city that produced or shipped little of value and whose income for its Turkish rulers was limited, as we shall see, to whatever taxes, charges, and fees could be squeezed out of the non-Muslim population of the city and the dwindling numbers of pilgrims who visited it. But this is not to say that France, Austria, and Russia among others were disinterested in the Holy City. Whatever its commercial value and whatever the realities of the desperate life lived by most of its inhabitants, the idea of Jerusalem still exercised a powerful influence in Europe and so constituted an inevitable bargaining chip between the sultan and the Christian sovereigns of Europe.

The Consulship

From the beginning the commercial agreements concluded between the sultan and the rulers of the West usually included the right to appoint consuls to supervise and, more importantly, to protect the rights of the agents of the capitulatory power within the host country. Thus French consular officials were instituted within various commercial centers within the Ottoman Empire, and then finally in 1621 in Jerusalem itself, where both the supervision and the protection had to do with religious rather than commercial matters, and specifically with the Christian holy places.

Among our earliest sources of information on the presence of a French consul in Jerusalem is the Franciscan Eugene Roger who was in the city in 1631 and described the consulship in his work *The Holy Land*, published in Paris in 1664:

The third consulate is that of Jerusalem, which our king, the most Christian of Christians, St. Louis [XIII, 1610-1643], may his memory be blessed, established in 1621 for the protection of our monks, so that through its influence they might establish and strengthen themselves in those places and overcome the insults and inequities inflicted upon them by that barbarous people.

After describing the consul's duties toward the merchants, he turned to the consul's other responsibilities, and here we are at the heart of the European concern for Jerusalem:

The fourth and fifth clauses [of the capitulations] deal only with the holy places and the monks dwelling there, the pilgrims who also come to make visits there, and other Christian transients who are under the protection of that consul. They need him on all occasions to receive his assistance and support in their dealings with the Turks; he in turn uses his influence to convince the Turks to maintain the capitulations and to conduct themselves according to the agreements. Nevertheless, the Turks do not refrain from continuing their oppressive acts against both the monks and the Catholic Christians who are not monks.

These acts would have been a thousandfold more difficult to bear if they were not kept in check by the French consul whom the king has appointed for this purpose. . . . The reason that the attitude of the Turkish authorities toward the monks and the Christian Catholics in Jerusalem is more overbearing than in any other part of the sultan's realms is that there is no [longer a] consul there. For the Turks, realizing that it was M. Jean Lempereur, whom the king sent as consul, who prevented their carrying out their customary tyranny toward the monks, made false accusations against him to the pasha in Damascus, and he was conducted there by a troop of Turks. Once there, however, he demonstrated his innocence and went on to Constantinople. The pashas and the qadis who have since been in Jerusalem do everything in their power to prevent his return, since he would prevent their filling their pockets in the same manner as when there is no consul. Daily they invent, under the pretext of administrative action, new means of little by little destroying us. And when we have managed to escape from one snare, they come up with another worse than the first. They do this to us not only during our lifetime, but even after our death. For it is forbidden to conduct burial services for a monk or a Catholic Christian unless the father guardian has first obtained permission from the qadi. This latter demands twelve dinars for the permit, although the terms of the permit, which I wish to cite here in order to show the contempt in which they hold us, reads as follows: "I, Abu Sulayman, chief qadi of Jerusalem, permit the guardian of the Franks to bury the accursed monk so-and-so. . . ." (Roger 1664: 461-464)

Jerusalem remained without a French consul until 1669, and on this occasion the newly appointed official lasted only a few months in the city. There was another abortive attempt by the French in 1713 to establish a representative in the city, but it was not until 1843 that a permanent French consul, eventually followed by representatives of most of the other European powers, was resident in the Holy City. In the interval the best that could be done, as we saw in the case of Henry Maundrell in Chapter Twelve, was for the French consul posted in Sidon or Acre to come to Jerusalem during Easter to insure that the Latin clergy could perform the rites and the European pilgrims attend them without molestation.

On the longer view, this Christian intervention in the affairs of Muslim Jerusalem had been going on since the time of Charlemagne in the late eighth century and that of the Byzantine emperors of the eleventh century who negotiated with the Fatimid rulers of Jerusalem on behalf of the Christians who lived in the city, whether it was for the rebuilding of the city walls or the Church of the Holy Sepulcher, or indeed the Christians' right to have their own quarter and whatever autonomy that implied. On those occasions, however, the negotiations were between equals and may even have displayed a rather generous Muslim concession that foreign rulers might speak for their own Christian subjects. By the seventeenth century there was generosity on neither side. The Ottomans were in full military and political decline everywhere in their still immense empire, and the now overwhelming commercial and military supremacy of Europe enabled the powers there to dictate terms. [5] Those inevitably included a clause on Jerusalem.

Austria in 1642, France at the Treaty of Adrianople in 1673 won special privileges for Latin clerics inside the sultan's domains, and Poland in a treaty in 1676 forced the sultan to accept a clause whereby "the Turks promise by the letter of the present agreement to restore the Franciscans to the Holy Sepulcher and to put an end to the presence there of all the schismatics." [6] At Karlowitz in 1699 Austria demanded and won the right for its ambassador to speak at the court of the sultan on behalf of Christian interests "concerning the Faith and the places of Christian pilgrimage in the Holy City of Jerusalem and to bring his demands before the Imperial Throne." [7] The climax of European pressure regarding Jerusalem came in the same treaty of Belgrade that made the capitulation agreements concluded with France binding upon the sultans in perpetuity. Article 33 of that treaty reads:

The Franciscans, who according to ancient custom are established in and around the city of Jerusalem, in the Church of the Holy Sepulcher called Qumama, shall not be molested regarding the places which they inhabit and which are in their hands and which shall remain in their hands further on as before. [8]

The treaty was not long honored. During Holy Week of 1757 there were anti-Latin riots in Jerusalem. The Greeks burst into the Church of the Holy Sepulcher where they tore down the Franciscans' lamps and decorations and then marched against St. Savior's and held the Friars there in a state of siege. Since France had its own troubles in Europe and was no longer in a position to intervene, Sultan Uthman III issued his famous decree reestablishing the Greeks to all the places taken from them in 1690, a position in which all parties in the Holy Sepulcher more or less rest to this day. [9] When the French ambassador at the Porte lodged the expected protest and cited the usual precedents, he received from the Ottoman grand vizier a remarkable candid response: "These places belong, Sir, to the sultan, and he gives them to whom he pleases; it may well be possible that they were always in the hands of the Franks, but today His Highness wishes they belong to the Greeks." [10]

An Ironic Turn in Fortune

These were all matters of high diplomacy, settled more often than not in the chanceries of Istanbul, but the turn in the fortunes of both East and West can be illustrated in a minor but graphic vein by simply comparing the reflections of two Jews in Jerusalem, first the Polish immigrant Gedaliah, writing at the very beginning of the eighteenth century, when a "foreign" or European look was a considerable disadvantage, and second from Joseph Schwarz of Bavaria, when the situation was dramatically different:

A few Jews have grocery shops here. Some of them have a Turk as a partner in order to protect themselves from unfair treatment. There are also a couple of Jewish spice dealers in the non-Jewish markets. There are Jews here who are called Maghrebis [Moroccans] or "Moriscos" in their own language. They have a language of their own, but also understand Aramaic [Arabic]. They go dressed like the Arabs and it is scarcely possible to distinguish them, as the Arabs likewise follow the custom of leaving the beard uncut. These Maghrebis travel on their asses from place to place

*with spices and other things, and in return bring wheat and barley to
Jerusalem. From this they make a meager living. If they, who know the
languages of the country, live in poverty, what shall we poor Ashkenazis
do here when we have to pass to and fro among the non-Jews as though
we were dumb? If we buy something from an Arab, he shows us the price
on his fingers and we have to answer on our fingers; so we become a
laughing stock in their sight and cannot make a living. (Wilhelm 1946:
79)*

But in 1834:

*Both we Germans and all other immigrants from Europe who are not
subject to the Turkish sultan—we are known in the language of the country as Franks—are entirely exempt from the above-mentioned taxes as well
as, in general, from all the oppressive burdens which the pasha imposes
on his subjects. We, thank God, enjoy the special protection of our respective European consuls, and the oppressive laws of the land do not
affect us in the least; whereas only a few years ago Jews dressed after the
Western fashion were liable to public insult and physical manhandling by
the mob. For which reason I found it necessary, immediately upon my
arrival in Palestine, to change my German clothing for Turkish. European
Jews are now met agreeably and respectfully. I always appear before the
courts in German clothes and am then treated as a European, with special
consideration. (Wilhelm 1946: 103-104)*

Joseph Schwarz was the beneficiary of a general change in Ottoman attitudes toward the Western powers, from scorn to a kind of wary respect,
and the gains that were achieved on the battlefield and around the bargaining tables of European diplomacy were eventually reflected in a
change in the climate in Jerusalem itself. No one of those powers was as
yet bargaining on behalf of the Jews of Jerusalem, but they too had ave-
nues through which requests, not yet demands, might be put forth in
respect to the Holy City.

When Gedaliah was describing Jewish services at the Western Wall of
the Temple shortly after 1700, he expressed a grateful satisfaction, as we
have seen, that the Muslim authorities did not interfere, even though some
of the Jews made noise there. By 1840, however, the situation was substantially different. The Egyptian ruler Muhammad Ali had temporarily
taken Palestine from the Turks in 1831, and in this newly benign atmosphere the British consul approached the Egyptian ruler with a tender from
a Jew who wished, as an act of piety, to repave part of the area before the
Wall. The request was referred to the Consultative Council of Jerusalem,
which recommended that permission not be granted, a suggestion ratified

by the governor of Syria in the following communication back to his deputy in Jerusalem:

It is evident from the copy of the deliberations of the Consultative Council in Jerusalem that the place the Jews asked for permission to pave adjoins the wall of the Haram al-Sharif and also the spot where al-Buraq was tethered and is included in the endowment charter of Abu Maydan, may God bless his memory; that the Jews never carried out any repairs in that place in the past. It has also been established that paving it by the Jews would be inadmissible under the Islamic Law. Therefore the Jews must not be enabled to pave the place. They must be warned against raising their voices and forbidden to proclaim their doctrines. They are permitted only their visits according to the ancient custom. [May 28, 1840] [11] *(Tibawi 1978: 20)*

The Holy Sepulcher: Destruction and Repair

The Jewish proposal of 1840 regarding the Western Wall seems modest enough, a simple repaving of a few yards of ground in front of the platform. But in the climate that by then surrounded the holy places in Jerusalem, any alteration, however slight, was tantamount to exercise of sovereignty, as is clear from what was occurring in the Church of the Holy Sepulcher at about the same time. The church had been repaired and restored a number of times, as we have seen in Chapter Twelve, but by all accounts the Crusader church was still essentially intact when on October 12, 1808, a fire of unknown origins broke out in the Armenian chapel and quickly spread up to the wooden dome, which soon came crashing down in flames. The damage caused by the fire was not irreparable perhaps, but it triggered a far more extensive piece of mischief. Both Latins and Greeks realized that the church would have to be repaired, and each made immediate resort to their patrons, the Franciscans to the European powers, and the Greeks through their patriarch to the sultan in Constantinople. The Europeans were far more concerned with Napoleon than with distant Jerusalem at that particular moment, so it was the Greeks—who by the sultan's decree of 1757 had the principal position in the church—whose petition was promptly granted by the sultan and who won the race to rebuild the church. [12] The reconstructed Church of the Holy Sepulcher belongs to the history of modern Jerusalem, but it is not, to put the kindest regard upon it, a very accurate representation of what stood there before. [13]

Ottoman Rule in Jerusalem

The larger affairs of the Ottoman Empire do not concern us here, except as they affect the neglected and misgoverned Sanjak of Jerusalem, the least of the districts in the entire province of Damascus, embracing only itself and the villages of Bethlehem and Hebron. In Mamluk days Jerusalem had been subject to Cairo by way of Damascus; now the central authority resided in Istanbul, but the marching orders still came from the governor of Damascus whose delegate, or *mütesellim*, was sent out to manage Jerusalem. [14] We are well instructed not merely on the system but how it worked in practice, since Westerners coming to Jerusalem from the late eighteenth century onward were less interested in the holy places than they were in social and political issues. This is the way the government of Jerusalem appeared in 1784, for example, to one of the very first of these visitors with new questions to put to the Holy City, Constantin Volney:

After Sultan Selim I took Syria from the Mamluks [in A.D. 1516], he established there, as elsewhere in the empire, viceroys, or pashas, who were vested with unlimited and absolute power. To assure himself of their obedience and to expedite their rule, he divided the country into five governorships, or pashaliks, which are still in place there. These pashaliks are those of Aleppo, of Tripoli, of Sidon, recently transferred to Acre, of Damascus, and finally of Palestine, whose capital has been at times at Gaza and at times at Jerusalem. Since Selim's time the boundaries of these pashaliks have often varied, but their substance has remained generally the same overall. It is appropriate to get some more detailed notion of the most interesting aspects of their present state, such as revenues, production, the prevailing powers, and their most remarkable places. (Volney 1959: 267)

The pasha [of Damascus] enjoys all the rights of his position, which are more considerable than in any other since, in addition to controlling the general revenue and absolute command, he is also in charge of the sacred caravan to Mecca under the highly respected title of "Amir al-Hajj." The Muslims think this responsibility so important that the person of pasha who performs it well becomes inviolable even for the sultan; it is no longer permitted to spill his blood. But the Ottoman diwan can handle anything, and when such a person is disgraced, it satisfies both the letter of the law and its own vengeance by having him crushed to death in a mortar and stuffed into a bag. (Volney 1959: 314)

From time to time Jerusalem has had its own governors with the rank of pasha, but it is more commonly a dependence of Damascus, as it is pres-

ently, from whom it received its mütesellim or deputy governor who gets his income from the general tax revenues, from customs dues, and above all from the stupidities of the Christian residents. (Volney 1959: 334)

The Holy City was not an attractive post, even for the deputy governor of the all-powerful pasha of Damascus. It was small and poor, which had a far more direct effect on the income of the mütesellim than did the economic well-being of the Ottoman Empire at large. There can be no doubt how the system worked. The Jewish immigrant Gedaliah understood as well in 1700 as the German visitor Ulrich Seetzen did in 1806:

The Jews pay taxes annually to the sultan, two red [gold] gulden for every male person over the age of fifteen years. A poor man must pay at least one gulden. Every year a pasha [mütesellim] from the sultan appears in Jerusalem at the Passover season in order to collect the taxes. Anybody who does not pay is put in prison, and the community chest must redeem him. The pasha usually remains in Jerusalem until the Feast of Weeks. Hence the poor people hide in their houses as best they can; but if the pasha catches them, the community head must pay for them. . . . Anybody who had paid is given a receipt. If an official meets a man who has no receipt with him, he drags him off to the office of the pasha, where he must pay. That applies to the Ashkenazis as well as the Sephardis.

There are many Christians dwelling in Jerusalem, almost more than Turks and Arabs. They also suffer greatly and must pay taxes. Only the poor, the blind, and the lame are exempt. Nevertheless, the Turks demand it from them as well, and nothing much can be done about it, for it is a harsh exile. . . . When the pasha arrives in Jerusalem, the Jews bring him presents and bribes, but he receives even more than he would ordinarily; and next year another pasha arrives. In the Turkish empire the officials change from year to year, and the same tax collector is never sent to the same district for two consecutive years. (Wilhelm 1946: 79-80)

Ulrich Jasper Seetzen adds, somewhat more cooly, since he was only an observer and not, like Gedaliah, a participant in the system:

The local government lacks any power or influence because the pasha of Damascus has appointed a native of Jerusalem as his mütesellim, or deputy, and for this man the inhabitants have no respect and consequently they do not fear him. Thus the Muslim population is unconstrained by any legal bonds. Many of the Muslims receive a certain yearly allotment of fabric from the three great local convents, which costs the Frankish convent a considerable sum. Recently these latter had given them their cloth according to the stipulated regulations, but some of the Muslims were not satisfied with the color and others were unhappy with the quality and demanded something different, which demand was refused. The Muslims believed that this was the fault of the three dragomans of the convent, one of whom they attacked on the street recently, beat him up and threatened him with more. So he took the opportunity of travelling to the Convent of St. John [in Ayn Karim] together with the Procurator General, and thus to leave town until tempers had calmed down. If the monastery should complain of this to the mütesellim, there would be no action taken because he has no authority. (Seetzen 1854-1859: 199-200, trans. E. Koehldorfer)

Portrait of a City Besieged, A Land Destroyed

It remained for another visitor, François-René de Chateaubriand, the already celebrated author of *The Genius of Christianity*, who was in the city for only four days in 1806, to catch with perfect clarity and yet with scarcely suppressed rage the unspeakable condition of Jerusalem and its neighborhood, not at the end of the Ottoman regime—the Turks would continue to rule the city for more than a century after Chateaubriand left—but at surely its darkest moment:

Jerusalem is attached to the pashalik of Damascus, for reasons unknown, except perhaps that it flows from the destructive system that the Turks follow naturally and as a matter of instinct. Separated from Damascus by mountains and even more so by the Arabs who infest the deserts, Jerusalem cannot always carry its complaints to the pasha when its governors oppress it. It would be a simpler matter if it depended from the nearby pashalik of Acre, and the Franks and the Latin Fathers could put themselves under the protection of the foreign consuls who reside in the ports of Syria, and the Greeks and the Turks would have to pay heed. But this is precisely what is being avoided; they wish a slavery without tongue, not that of oppressed bold spirits who might dare to say that they are being tormented.

Jerusalem is, then, in the hands of an almost independent governor; he can do with impunity the evil that he wishes, safe from a later accounting to the pasha. It is well known that every superior in Turkey has the right of delegating his powers to an inferior, and those always extend over both property and life. For a trifling sum a janissary becomes a minor agha, and this agha can put you to death or allow you to buy back your life. Thus executioners multiply throughout the villages of Judea. The only thing you hear in this country, the only justice in question is "He will pay ten, twenty, thirty purses. He will be given five hundred lashes. He will

545

be beheaded." An act of injustice leads to an even greater one. If a peasant is robbed, he must needs rob his neighbor, since, to escape the hypocritical integrity of the pasha, one must procure by a second crime the means to buy oneself out of the first.

One might think that the pasha, in superintending his government, would provide a remedy for these ills and vindicate the people. But the pasha is himself the greatest scourge of the people of Jerusalem. His arrival is anticipated like that of a principal enemy of the city. The shops are closed; people conceal themselves in cellars; they play dead on their mats or they flee to the mountains.

I can bear witness to the truth of this matter since I was in Jerusalem at the moment of the arrival of the pasha. Abdullah is possessed by a base greed, as are almost all Muslims. In his function as chief of the caravan to Mecca and under the pretext of requiring money to better protect the pilgrims, he believes himself justified in multiplying his demands. There is no method to which he will not stoop. One of the most commonly resorted to is fix the price of food at an extremely low figure. The people are excited but the merchants then close their shops. The game then begins. The pasha deals in secret with the merchants; for a certain number of purses he gives them permission to sell at whatever price they wish. The merchants then attempt to recoup what they paid to the pasha: they raise their prices to an extraordinary level, and the people, now dying of hunger a second time, are obliged, if they are to stay alive, to sell the shirts off their backs.

After having exhausted Jerusalem, the pasha left. But to avoid paying the guard garrison and to add to the escort of the caravan to Mecca, he took the city's soldiers off with him. The local governor was left with some dozen guards who scarcely sufficed to police the city, to say nothing of the countryside. The year before my trip he was himself obliged to hide in his own home to escape the bands of brigands who swarmed over the walls and set to pillaging the city.

Scarcely was the pasha out of sight when another evil, a consequence of the first, began. The devastated villages rose up and attacked their neighbors in pursuit of hereditary feuds. All communications were broken; agriculture was destroyed as peasants went out during the night to destroy the vineyards and cut down the olive trees of their enemies. The pasha returns the following year and demands the same tribute of a country where the population has been decimated. He must redouble the oppression; he must destroy entire peoples. Little by little the desert grows larger; the ruins of settlements extend further and further, and at the entries of these settlements ever growing cemeteries. Each year another hut collapses and another family dies off so that soon there remains only a cemetery to mark the place where there was once a village. (Chateau-briand 1969: 1119-1121)

A Harsh Exile

It was indeed a harsh exile, as Gedaliah had put it, and as much perhaps for the governors as for the governed. Gedaliah's complaint in the passage cited above had been about the head or poll-tax that had been imposed on the "Peoples of the Book" from the beginning of the Islamic conquest of the Near East; [15] but there were, as Volney and others remarked, far, far more, the innumerable charges, tolls, and fees, most of them illegal in the eyes of the Islamic law, which were exacted at every turn on the non-Muslim residents for the privilege of living in or visiting what was for them, as for the Muslims, a holy place. [16] Gedaliah's assessment was correct: one of the roots of the problem was the Ottomans' penchant for changing governors, who by the eighteenth century held office in any given place for a term of a single year, with quite predictable results. [17]

In the closing years of the eighteenth century the French traveller Constantin Volney visited the once prosperous Ramle and found it in ruins, even the governor's residence:

This city [of Ramle] is almost as ruined as Lud itself and you can walk inside its circuit only by traversing ruins. The agha of Gaza makes his residence there in a serai whose walls are falling down. "Why doesn't he at least repair his own lodgings?" I one day asked one of the lesser officials. "And if he is replaced the next year," was the answer, "who is going to reimburse him for the expense?"

Volney doubtless thought the answer somewhat mean-spirited; with some European industry and energy the place might have been fixed up. But when he put the same kind of question to a governor in Alexandria, the answer was somewhat more to the point:

"Yesterday I was in Marash," the governor replied, "tomorrow maybe I shall be in Jedda. Why should I deprive myself of a present that is certain for a future that is without hope?" (Volney 1959: 345, 278)

Constantin Volney in Jerusalem, 1784

The questions that Constantin Volney asked were neither accidental nor random. Volney went to Jerusalem in 1784 with a *research program*, not in the sense that earlier pilgrims had gone to the Holy Land to search out sites and the traditions connected with them, but to investigate the place called Palestine, and much in the same manner that we should do so, to collect facts and figures and then subject them to close analysis. In 1795 he published a tract entitled *Statistical Questions for the Use of Travellers*, in which he set forth his method, the one actually followed in his *Journey in Egypt and in Syria* of 1784, and one that we can immediately recognize as the product of a modern, scientific sensibility:

Being persuaded that all truth, particularly as it has to do with govern-ment, is the result only of long experience, that is to say, of many facts carefully regarded and judiciously compared . . . the Ministry [of Foreign Affairs] has decided to collect, on the important science of the public economy, as large a number of facts as possible to draw from a carefully considered comparison of them either new truths or the confirmation of known truths or finally the refutation of errors that have been accepted as truths. These facts will be all the more instructive if they present compar-isons, or even contrasts, in climate, soil, natural produce, and all circum-stances both physical and moral.[18]

With these thoughts in his mind and this program in his notebooks, Vol-ney approached Jerusalem:

A two days' journey south of Nablus, passing along the mountains which at each step become more rocky and arid, you arrive at a city which, like so many others we have gone through, offers a striking example of the fragility of human affairs. To see its destroyed walls, its debris-filled moat, its city circuit choked with ruins, you would scarcely recognize this famous metropolis which once fought against the most powerful empires in the world; which for a moment held even Rome at bay; and which, by a bizarre twist of fate, gains honor and respect in its disgrace. In short, you would scarcely recognize Jerusalem. (Volney 1959: 333)

Some years earlier the English historian Edward Gibbon had had a similar impression in looking upon the ruins of the Roman forum, and his search backward into the past for the causes of such a mighty fall led to the publication in 1776 of his *Decline and Fall of the Roman Empire*. Volney's analytical capacities worked in a somewhat different fashion, however; they were at the same time more political and, if possible, more cynical:

You are even more deeply struck by its fortune when you see its location. It is situated on difficult and waterless terrain, surrounded by ravines and steep heights, removed from all major access, and so hardly suited to be-come either a transit center or a commercial terminus. But it has defeated all these obstacles to demonstrate beyond any doubt the power of public opinion manipulated by a skillful legislator or favored by circumstances. It is this same public opinion that continues to insure its survival: the renown of its marvels, kept alive among the Easterners, always invokes and guarantees the survival of a certain number of them within its walls. Muslims, Christians, and Jews, all without distinction of sect, consider themselves honored to see or have seen the noble and holy city, as they call it. To judge from the respect which they have for these holy places, one would think there was no more pious people in the world; but that did not prevent them from acquiring, and meriting, the reputation of being the most wicked people in Syria, not even excepting Damascus. An estimate would put the population at 12,000 or 14,000 souls. (Volney 1959: 333-334)

From the outset Volney was struck by the corruption of what might be called the political economy of Jerusalem. The Turkish government lived off what he called "the stupidities of the Christian residents." He explains:

To understand the latter, one must understand that the various communions of Greeks, both schismatics and catholics, Armenians, Copts, Abyssinians, and Franks compete among themselves for the possession of the holy places and endlessly fight over them to the financial profit of the Turkish governors. It is from him that privilege is acquired; it is by him that it is denied to one's rivals; it is to him that runs the reporter of violations they may have committed. Has someone made a clandestine repair on a church? Has someone extended a procession beyond its customary limits? Has a pilgrim come in by some door other than that assigned him? It is reported to the government which does not hesitate to intervene to establish the harm and the reparation. Whence hostility and eternal warfare among the various convents and among the members of each communion. The Turks, to whom each dispute brings additional money, are not, as one might well imagine, about to let the source dry up. Great and small, all take part: some sell their protection, some their intervention, with the consequence that there is a spirit of intrigue and cabal that has spread corruption among all classes.

For the mütesellim it means a cash payment that amounts to more than 100,000 piasters a year. Every pilgrim must pay him an entry fee of ten piasters. More, he has the right to provide the escort to the Jordan, to say nothing of the windfall fines he collects by reason of whatever imprudent behavior these visitors from abroad might commit during their stay. Each convent pays him so much for the right to a procession, so much for each repair to be made. More, there are gifts, for him, alone, at the installation of each superior. More, the under the table "considerations" for every little secret favor asked of him. [19] *The entire process has reached an advanced stage with the Turks who, when it comes to squeezing, are as accomplished as the most skillful lawyers in Europe. (Volney 1959: 333-334)*

A Jerusalem Industry

The Turks had little reason to cultivate the economic development of Jerusalem so long as they could exact their painful harvest of exactions from the Christians and Jews living and visiting there, but those same communities had to somehow provide themselves with funds to meet those payments. One resort was to turn to their coreligionists in Europe, but that source of support was growing increasingly thin. As Seetzen remarked in 1806, "it appears that the pious attachment of the European Catholics diminishes from one year to the next. France and Germany have ceased sending their contributions, and if Spain, Portugal, and Italy follow their example, which seems likely in the near future, these institutions will be entirely on their own." [20]

Failing this and in the absence of anything save a subsistence agriculture, the Christians at least of Jerusalem were dependent on the one thing they could manufacture and sell, the religious articles and souvenirs commemorating the holy places:

Apart from this, the mütesellim has imposed a tax on the export of certain goods peculiar to Jerusalem. I refer to the rosaries, reliquaries, shrines, crosses, crucifixes, Agnus Dei's, scapulars, etc., about three hundred boxes of which leave the city every year. The manufacture of these articles of piety is the branch of industry that supports most of the Christian and Muslim families of Jerusalem and its environs, men, women, and children, all busy sculpting and carving the wood and coral, working in silk and mother-of-pearl and gold and silver thread. The convent of the Santa Terra alone annually earns 50,000 piasters from the business, and those of the Greeks, Armenians, and Copts taken together earn even more. This type of enterprise is all the more vital to the workers since it is the only type of manufacture by which they can earn income; and all the more lucrative to the tax gatherer since the value is enhanced by public esteem. These objects, exported to Turkey, Italy, Portugal, to Spain and its colonies, bring back considerable sums in the form of alms and payments. (Volney 1959: 335)

Ulrich Seetzen, who visited the place in 1806, gives an even more detailed analysis of this Holy Land cottage industry that supported most of the residents of Jerusalem:

The small square in front of the entrance to the Church of the Holy

Sepulcher is continuously used as a small market for a variety of souvenirs which the pilgrims take back with them to their homeland. There they give them to their families and friends who regard them as valuable and cherished presents, since everything that comes from Jerusalem is believed to be holy and that possession of them confers a blessing. . . . Apart from a few merchants, there are also many individuals, men and women, who sell all kinds of religious articles, especially rosaries of all kinds, some of which are made even of the bones of camels and water buffalo; there are crosses and such, crucifixes made of wood, mother of pearl, etc.; models of the Holy Sepulcher made of wood and inlaid with mother of pearl; images of saints incised into mother of pearl; glass articles from Hebron like rosaries, bead necklaces, bracelets, rings, mouthpieces of pipes, cups of faience and porcelain. Among the more rare religious articles are images of the saints, the Madonna, etc. carved on sheets of horn called "Hantit Horn," and which I make out to be rhinoceros horn. I was assured that it was brought from Ethiopia to Cairo whence it was then carried here and worked up mainly in Bethlehem. The price for a small piece some two inches in diameter and badly engraved with a saint's image is seventeen piasters. . . .

Curious and almost unique of its kind is the warehouse [inside the Franciscan compound of St. Savior's] for religious articles such as rosaries, crucifixes, Madonna's Milk, models of the Holy Sepulcher, etc., things which are made here, and particularly in Bethlehem. These are sent through agents to Italy, Spain, and Portugal, and on their sale in those parts depends the well-being of all the presently existing Latin convents of the Holy Land. Perhaps there are no articles in the world traded so profitably as these and one has to concede that this convent carries on the world's most lucrative trade. The Christian inhabitants of Bethlehem are the only ones who make them . . . and so it can be said that it is the industry of the people of Bethlehem that supports all the convents from the Holy Land throughout the Levant. (Seetzen 1854-1859: 15, 17, trans. E. Koehldorfer)

There was some other very modest manufacturing, but it, like almost everything else in the Holy City, led to sectarian controversy:

Beside the Church of the Holy Sepulcher there is a large factory for leather manufacture. The leather here is prepared in all kinds of colors and so is an export article. There are about twenty master craftsmen and as many apprentices working there, all of them Muslims. This factory is the cause of the most terrible smells in the neighborhood because it lacks water to wash away all the refuse that remains, the rotting blood, etc., in the narrow alleys, which are truly hideous.

The Christians are convinced that the Muslims built this factory next to the aforesaid church, the most important [Christian] holy place in the city, out of contempt, and even if there is no justification in this accusation, one must concede there is nothing better suited to exactly that purpose.

In the Jewish quarter there is a slaughterhouse which produces the same ugly odors and for the same reasons, and the Jews too are convinced that their fellow inhabitants have chosen this place for the establishment out of hatred for them.

Jerusalem has five horse-driven mills, five public baths, twenty to twenty-five coffeehouses, thirty barbers, and twenty-five baking ovens. (Seetzen 1854-1859: 22-23, trans. E. Koehldorfer)

The Pilgrim Trade

Originally the manufacture and sale of religious articles and mementos had depended upon the presence of Christian pilgrims in Jerusalem, but by the end of the eighteenth century there were few such and the manufactured souvenirs had to be sent abroad and sold through agents, as Seetzen noted. Volney had a clear appreciation of how this aspect of the economy of the Holy City had changed:

Connected with this type of manufacture is another type of business no less important for the convents, the visitation of pilgrims. It is well known that in all eras a pious curiosity to visit the holy places has brought Christians from every quarter to Jerusalem. There was even a time when the ministers of religion made it an act necessary for salvation, and one recalls that it was exactly this fervor which once stirred all of Europe and produced the Crusades. Since their unhappy conclusion the zeal of Europeans has cooled more and more from one day to the next, and the number of pilgrims is much diminished. By now it has reduced itself to a few monks from Italy, Spain, and Germany.

But it is not so with the Easterners. Faithful to the spirit of the past, they continue to regard a journey to Jerusalem as an act of the greatest merit. They are even scandalized at the Frankish falling-off in this regard and they say that they have all become heretics or infidels. Their priests and monks, who find this fervor useful, never leave off encouraging it. The Greeks in particular stress that pilgrimage merits plenary indulgences, and not only for the past; they are also applicable for the future; and that it brings absolution not only from murder, incest, and pederasty but even from the violation of a fast or a holy day, which they regard as far more serious cases.

Such encouragement has not been without effect, and each year there leaves the Morea, the Archipelago, Constantinople, Anatolia, Armenia,

Egypt, and Syria a great crowd of pilgrims of every age and both sexes. Their number in 1784 was 2,000. The monks, who discovered in their records that in the past the number was 10,000 or 12,000, insist that religion is dying and that the zeal of the faithful is somewhat expensive. A simple pilgrimage costs at least 4,000 pounds and that can often add up, with all the offerings, to as much as 50,000 or 60,000 pounds. (Volney 1959: 335-336)

We have already seen some of the causes of the decline in pilgrimage from the sixteenth century onward: increased dangers, increased skepticism, and according to the practical minded Volney, increased costs:

Jaffa is the place where the pilgrims disembark. They arrive in November and go immediately to Jerusalem where they stay until just after the feast of Easter. They are lodged arbitrarily with local families and in the cells of convents of the communions to which they belong. The religious take great pains to point out that the lodging is free, but it would be neither courteous nor a good idea to leave without making an offering which far exceeds the commercial price of such lodging. In addition, one cannot escape paying for masses, services, exorcisms, etc., which amounts to another considerable tax. Then again one must buy crucifixes, rosaries, Agnus Dei's, and so forth. On Palm Sunday the pilgrims go to purify themselves in the Jordan, and this trip requires still another contribution. In a typical year it brings to the governor 15,000 Turkish sequins or 112,500 pounds, about half of which he spends to defray the expense of the escort and the passage rights demanded by the Arabs.

One must consider, in the various accounts, the details of this pilgrimage: the tumultuous march of this devoted crowd down to the plain of Jericho; their indecent zeal to throw themselves, men, women, and children, naked into the Jordan; their weariness in getting to the shore of the Dead Sea; their discouragement at the sight of this stony country, the most savage that nature has devised; and finally, their return and visit to the holy places and the ceremony of the new fire that descends from heaven on Holy Saturday, brought down by an angel. The Easterners still believe in this miracle, although the Franks have recognized that it is the priests, concealed in the sacristy, who bring it about by the most natural of means. Easter over, each returns to his country, proud to emulate the Muslims with the title of "pilgrim." . . . There are even some who, in order to be everywhere identified as such, have tattooed on their hand or wrist or arm representations of the cross, the sacred lance or the abbreviation "Jesus" or "Mary." This painful and sometimes dangerous engraving—I have seen one pilgrim who lost an arm because his cubital nerve was severed in the process—is accomplished with a needle whose point has been covered with gunpowder or antimony. The Muslims have the same practice, and so too the Indians, the savages, and ancient peoples, always with a religious significance. But such devotion does not prevent the pilgrims from sharing in that proverb about *hajjis*, which the Christians also cite: "Watch out for the Jerusalem pilgrim."

One can understand that the stay of this crowd of pilgrims in Jerusalem for five or six months leaves behind a large sum of money. Counting only 1,500 people at a hundred pistoles a head, it comes to a million and a half. A part of this money goes as payment for goods to the people and the merchants, who hold the pilgrims for ransom, as far as they can. Water, for example, cost in 1784 fifteen sous the trip. Another part goes to the governor and his employees. Finally, the third part stays in the convent. There are complaints of how these schismatics use it, scandalized talk of their luxury, their carpets, and even of swords, kandahars, and clubs that are the furnishings of their cells. The Armenians and Franks are more modest. It is the virtue of necessity for the first group, who really are poor; but it is the virtue of prudence for the second, who are not. (Volney 1959: 336-337)

Another somewhat more pious Frenchman, François-René de Chateaubriand, in Jerusalem in 1806, the same year as Seetzen, also reflected on the costs and profits of pilgrimage and thought both were exaggerated, perhaps with Volney's estimates in mind and with enough facts and figures to satisfy his statistically minded predecessor:

Let us turn to pilgrims' finances. Modern accounts have somewhat exaggerated the wealth that pilgrims must expend in the Holy Land. First of all, what pilgrims are we speaking of? Certainly not Latin pilgrims since there no longer are any such, as is generally agreed. Over the past century the Fathers of St. Savior's have seen perhaps two hundred Catholic visitors, including religious of their own orders and missionaries to the East. That Latin pilgrims never have been very numerous can be proved by a thousand examples. Thévenot tells us that in 1656 he found himself the twenty-second pilgrim to the Holy Sepulcher. Often the pilgrims were fewer than twelve since the religious had to fill in to complete that number in the ceremony of the washing of feet on Holy Thursday. Thus in 1589, sixty-seven years before Thévenot, Villamont encountered only six Frankish pilgrims in Jerusalem. If in 1589, when religion was in such a flourishing state, there were only seven pilgrims in Palestine, what is one to think of 1806? My arrival at the Convent of St. Savior's was truly an event. M. Seetzen, who was there at Easter in the same year, says that he was the only Catholic present.

The money that the Holy Sepulcher is supposed to gush forth is cer-

tainly not brought to Jerusalem by Catholic pilgrims, and so it must come from Jewish, Greek, and Armenian pilgrims, and in those cases too I think the totals are inflated.

The greatest expense of the pilgrims are the dues which they are expected to pay to the Turks and Arabs, whether as entry fees to the holy places or as kaffaras, or tolls, upon the roads. But the total amounts to no more than sixty-five piasters, twenty-nine paras. If you take the piaster at its maximum value of fifty French sous . . . that will give you [about] sixty-four livres; and if you take it at its minimum of thirty-three French sous, the sum is [about] 108 livres. . . . Here is the account that I got from the father procurator at the Convent of St. Savior's. I have left it in Italian, which everyone understands these days, with the Turkish names, etc., to attest to its authenticity:

Kaffara: In Jaffa after embarkation:	*5 piasters 20*
Before reembarking:	*5,20*
A mount to Ramle, and for the Arab as a guide to Jerusalem:	*1,20*
Payment for the Arab:	*10,30*
To the local who will accompany to Jerusalem:	*10,30*
Mount from Ramle to Jerusalem:	*10*
Kaffara along the road:	*1,16*
Entry to the Holy Sepulcher:	*26,38*
Entry to the city:	*15*
A first and second dragoman:	*3,30*
For a total of:	*65,29*

If the pilgrim should make the trip to the Jordan, twelve piasters should be added to the total expenses. (Chateaubriand 1964: 1092-1094)

Nor did Seetzen think the Fathers were getting rich on the pilgrimage trade:

The principal purpose for the establishment of such institutions [as St. Savior's Convent] was, as far as I know, to give foreigners a hospitable reception during their visit to the holy places. One would assume, therefore, that the annual support of those foreigners would require large sums of money. This purpose remains unfulfilled, however. First of all, the number of European pilgrims is so low that only one a year is expected on average. Second, it is customary for such pilgrims to leave a gift for the monastery at their departure in return for their stay and sustenance, and this gift generally exceeds the expenses incurred by the convent. Such a donation is not actually requested, but were it omitted, one would be looked upon much as a traveller who has skipped without settling his account. . . . (Seetzen 1854-1859: 208, trans. E. Koehldorfer)

The Franciscans in Jerusalem

Volney had made the comment: "The Armenians and Franks are more modest. It is the virtue of necessity for the first group, who really are poor; but it is the virtue of prudence for the second, who are not." The phrase is well turned, doubtless, but he may not have got it quite right. Seetzen too had taken note of the Jerusalem Armenians:

The Armenian clergy appear to possess enormous riches, and since these are given only by laymen, it demonstrates that their merchants have acquired great wealth by their energy, versatility, and extensive commercial activity. Monks are held in high respect by the Armenian nation, and so one finds among their number members of the richest and most prestigious families. It is said that the Greek monks have pawned their chief valuables to this Armenian convent since they are always lacking for funds, which never befalls the Armenians.

And on the Armenian convent of St. James:

This convent lies near the Citadel and is favorably situated in a more spacious area than the churches and convents of the other religious groups. It is of considerable size and has a remarkable number of rooms designated for the reception of Armenian pilgrims. It has, however, a very irregular shape. In addition to one large courtyard it includes several other smaller courtyards as well. This building is the most attractive and beautiful in Jerusalem. It forms a long quadrangle, and at its center there is a cupola supported by four stout pillars. The church pavement has a very beautiful mosaic, most of which is, however, covered with carpets to preserve it. The walls as well as the pillars are ornamented with gilded decorations and paintings, and the altar is gilded in an exceptionally generous fashion. In addition to the cupola, the church is most tastefully illuminated and the lamps, many of which are made of silver, form garlands about it. The church is chiefly illuminated, by an opening at the top of the cupola, like the one above the Holy Sepulcher. . . . (Seetzen 1854-1859: 14, 13, trans. E. Koehldorfer)

While the Armenians might provoke some passing and perhaps grudging admiration for their prudent management, it was naturally the European Christian establishment that provoked the interest, though only rarely the admiration, of these visitors who had come to inspect Jerusalem in one of her darker hours. And that establishment was, as it had been for many centuries, the Franciscan community lodged in the Convent of St. Savior's. Volney begins by explaining how the financial administration of the *Custodia* worked:

The convent of the Franks, which is called St. Savior's, is the headquarters of all the missions to the Holy Land located in the Turkish empire. There are seventeen of them, which are staffed by Franciscans of all nations, but mostly French, Italians, and Germans. The general administration is in the hands of three individuals of these nations in such a manner that the superior should always be a born subject of the pope, the procurator of His Catholic Majesty, and the vicar of His Most Christian Majesty. Each one of these administrators has a key to the general cash-box so that the management of the funds can only be done by common consent. Each of them is assisted by a second person called a discret. *The board of these six people plus a Portugese discret makes up the* Discretoire, *or sovereign chapter, which governs the convent and the entire Order. Thus a balance, struck by the first legislators, has so distributed the powers of these administrators that the will of one of them cannot determine the will of all. (Volney 1959: 337)*

But just as all governments are subject to revolution, there occurred something a few years ago that undermined the arrangement. And this is its history in one or two words. About twenty years ago, by the kind of mismanagement familiar enough to large corporations, the Terra Santa Convent found itself burdened by a debt of six hundred purses, about 750,000 pounds. It grew day by day since expenses continued to outrun receipts. They could have freed themselves from it at a single stroke since the treasure of the Holy Sepulcher possessed diamonds and all sorts of precious stones, chalices, crosses, golden ciboria, and other gifts of Christian princes to a sum in excess of a million pounds. But in addition to the usual aversion that ministers of temples have always had to touching sacred objects, it was important in this particular case not to display to the Turks, nor even to the Christians, an abundance of resources. The situation became embarrassing, the more so by the mutterings of the Spanish procurator who loudly complained that he had to bear the debt alone because it was he in effect who supplied most of the funds. In these circumstances J. Ribeira, who held this post, died, and circumstances put in his place a man who was even more impatient to resolve the problem, whatever the cost. He drew up his plan and then addressed himself directly to the king of Spain through the latter's confessor:

Since the zeal of the Christian princes has much cooled in recent years their former largesse to the convent of the Terra Santa has diminished considerably. . . . The expenses of the establishment have not diminished accordingly, however, and the result is a deficit which each year forces us to borrow money. In this way an ever increasing debt has accrued, and it is threatening to lead us to final ruin. Among the causes of this debt one should certainly account the pilgrimages of monks who come to visit the holy places; one must pay for their trip and other expenses for two or three years. And the greater part of these monks come from countries which have cut back on their offerings, namely, Portugal, Germany, and Italy. Thus it seems strange that the king of Spain is paying the expenses of people who are not at all his subjects, and it is an abuse that the management of these funds rests with a chapter composed almost entirely of strangers. (Volney 1959: 338-339)

The result was that a Spaniard became the Franciscan procurator general in Jerusalem and each nation had to pay for its own nationals. The Spanish contribution, by then the largest by far, came by sea via Cyprus and Jaffa to Jerusalem, with the result, Volney ends, "The inhabitants there await its arrival like the Spaniards await the Galleys of the Main."

Seetzen was less interested in Franciscan finances than in the facilities within what was in effect a small city at St. Savior's. We have a detailed description of the compound by Elzear Horn in the middle of the eighteenth century, [21] from church down through the library, school, and pharmacy to the wine cellar. Horn, who was of course a member of that congregation, was particularly proud of the school:

The superiors of the Holy Land . . . right from the beginning of the regime of the Custody up to the present time have given great attention to this matter [of education] so that the tender youth of the Eastern Roman Catholics in almost all the convents, and especially in St. Savior's, Jerusalem, are well and diligently instructed both in good habits and in the holy mysteries of the faith. And this they reckon to be all the more necessary in these parts where they are exposed to many dangers of perversion amid the most depraved infidels and heretics. . . .

When they have completed twelve years they are dismissed from school and by their parents are handed over to artisans, Christians or Turks, that they may be instructed in that trade in which they seem more apt, that they may thereafter provide a living for themselves. The mechanical trades to which they apply themselves are the ordinary and more common, like that of cobbler, weaver, tailor, mason, smith, soapmaker, silversmith. Meanwhile they are pledged in marriage for a definite time in the future, and when they grow up to manhood in the said trades, they do not take monastic vows but are married off for the propagation of the true faith.

Girls must remain at home; it is unbecoming to mix boys and girls in the same school, and it is entirely unnecessary. The girls are initiated into the mysteries of the faith on Sundays after Vespers for about one hour under the special care of the parish priest of Jerusalem. The older ones spend their time plying the needle or in some other female work until they are sufficiently instructed, and when they reach the age of puberty, they are given in marriage. . . .

From the above it will be understood how much the parents of children are beholden to the Friars. Ordinarily it is for the mothers to rear the children until the end of the third year; from the end of the third year until their emancipation it pertains to the fathers, who, however, for at least six years have no need of attending to providing food and other necessities of life [for their children] since they are not only educated and fed by the Friars but even clothed with some worn-out clothes of the Friars and often also with new clothes, if the European pilgrims who visit come to their aid by their generosity. (Horn 1962: 181-183)

Seetzen looked upon almost exactly the same arrangement half a century later, but through different eyes and with a very different judgment as to its usefulness:

The Franciscan convent contains a school for native Catholic boys. There is a Levantine there who teaches reading and writing in Arabic and a monk who teaches the Italian and Latin necessary for the divine service. The school pays no attention to practical knowledge and does not even offer instruction in mathematics. The boys senselessly rattle off in parrot-like fashion Latin prayers and hymns. They stay in school until they are twelve years of age and then their parents urge them to learn a trade. The boys assist the monks during the service and sing in the choir, and for this they are given a new red cap and a pair of shoes at Christmas and Easter, and the poorer ones receive in addition a cloth outer garment. At noon all the boys eat in the monastery and for supper they are given a piece of bread. At present there are thirty students in the school. There is no girls' school. For the young men of the other religious sects there are similar schools in other monasteries, in the synagogues, and mosques. (Seetzen 1854-1859: 12, trans. E. Koehldorfer)

Where Horn and Seetzen did agree, however, was on the quality of the Franciscan pharmacy in St. Savior's. Seetzen comments:

The pharmacy of the convent [of St. Savior's] is by far the most sizeable one I have seen in the Levant. The present physician of the monastery, Brother Francisco, is a very busy man and has held this position for many years. Most of the medicines come from Europe as gifts, but others are procured locally and medicinal plants are grown in a special garden. The famous Jerusalem balsam is made of five different balms, a variety of the most pleasant flavorings, and alcohol which can ignite powder. The monastery keeps the recipe a secret, but it is claimed that it can produce the most pleasant effects, both internally and externally. And since the balsam is in such great demands, two less expensive ersatz versions are produced.

All medicines and medical advice are free of charge, but anyone who can afford a gift for the convent or the physician is expected to do so. I received two bottles of the genuine balsam with a printed text advising about its use. (Seetzen 1854-1859: 205, trans. E. Koehldorfer)

The Franciscan Archives

The historian Chateaubriand found something quite different to interest him in the same convent, and in that same year, 1806:

I could compose entire volumes on similar testimonies [to the persecutions suffered by the Latin clergy in Jerusalem] from the various Voyages en Palestine. I shall reproduce only one, which does not require a reply. I found it, this testimony to which I refer, in a monument to iniquity and oppression which is perhaps unique in the world and which was made to rest in eternal forgetfulness. The Fathers permitted me to examine the library and archives of their convent. Unfortunately the contents of these archives and this library were scattered a century ago when the pasha put the Fathers in irons and carried them captive to Damascus. A few documents escaped the destruction, in particular the firmans which the Fathers obtained, either from the Porte or the rulers of Egypt, to protect themselves against the oppression of the people or the governors. This curious archive is entitled Registro delli Capitolazioni, Baratti, Comandamenti, Oggeti, Attestazioni, Sentenze, Ordini dei Baschia, Giudici e Polizze, che se trovano nell'archivo di questa procura generale di Terra Santa. [22]

He then quotes from a number of them, all leading to the same rueful conclusion:

Thus one sees that these unfortunate Fathers, guardians of the Tomb of Jesus Christ, were solely occupied over several centuries in defending themselves, day by day, against all types of insults and tyranny. They had to obtain permission to feed themselves, to bury their dead, etc. . . . Sometimes they were forced to mount horses for no other reason than to pay the dues for such; sometimes a Turk announced himself as their dragoman against their wishes and demanded a salary from the community. The most bizarre inventions of oriental despotism—they once wanted to murder two religious at Jerusalem because a cat had fallen into the well of the convent—were exhausted against these unfortunate monks. In vain did they buy orders which seemed to protect the convent from such imposi- tions; these orders were never executed, and each year saw new oppres- sions and required a new firman. The lying commandant and the prince, in appearance their protector, are the two tyrants who busied themselves with the religious, one to commit an injustice before a law forbade it, and the other to sell them a law against the crime after it was committed. (Chateaubriand 1969: 1099-1101)

The Honor of France

The Fathers' register of firmans is a very precious document [Chateau- briand continues], worthy of the utmost care in this library of these apostles who, in the midst of trials, guard with an invincible constancy the Tomb of Jesus Christ. The Fathers do not recognize the value of this evangelical catalogue; they did not believe it could interest me since they saw nothing remarkable in it: for them suffering was natural and they were astonished at my astonishment. I avow that my admiration for so many misfortunes so courageously borne was great and sincere; but how often was I likewise moved to find again and again the following formula: "Copy of a firman obtained through the intercession of M. l'Ambassadeur de France." An honor to a nation which, from the bosom of Europe, watches even into the depths of Asia over the protection of the wretched and protects the weak against the strong! Never did my country seem to me more beautiful and glorious than when I found those deeds of its good will hidden in Jerusalem in a register where there were written down the unremarked sufferings and the unknown iniquities of the oppressed and the oppressor. (Chateaubriand 1969: 1101)

An Artist's Panorama of Jerusalem, 1806

Chateaubriand was somewhat less the historian than a penetrating ob- server of man and nature as well as an artist and stylist of a high order. [23] Though he spent only two weeks in Palestine and four days in Jerusalem, October 12 to 16, 1806, his portrait of the Holy City at the turn into the nineteenth century is vivid, deeply experienced, and in the end, profoundly sad:

The land which to that point had preserved some greenery grew naked, the slopes of the mountains grew steeper and took on an appearance that was at the same time more grand and more barren. Soon all vegetation ceased and even the moss disappeared. The mountains all round took on a burning red color. We climbed for an hour in this desolate landscape to reach a high pass that we spied before us. Once come to this pass, we journeyed for another hour across a naked plain strewn with boulders. Suddenly, at the end of this plain I saw a line of gothic walls flanked with square towers and behind them rose the peaks of buildings. At the foot of this wall appeared a camp of Turkish cavalry, in all its oriental splendor. The guide cried out: "Al-Quds! The Holy City," and went off at a great gallop.

Then I understood what the historians and travellers reported of the surprise of the Crusaders and pilgrims at their first sight of Jerusalem. I am certain that whoever has had the patience, as I did, to read nearly two hundred modern accounts of the Holy Land, the rabbinic collections, and the passages of the ancients on Judea, would still understand nothing. I stood there, my eyes fixed on Jerusalem, measuring the height of its walls, recalling all the memories of history from Abraham to Godfrey of Bouillon, reflecting how the entire world was changed by the mission of the Son of Man, and seeking in vain the Temple, on which "not a stone rests upon a stone." If I were to live a thousand years, never would I forget this wilderness which still seems to breathe with the grandeur of Jehovah and the terrors of death. (Chateaubriand 1969: 980-981)

The Silence of Death

From without there was a certain grandeur to Jerusalem, enhanced by the author's own historical imagination. But within all the grandeur took flight, and the romance as well, yielding to something different and darker, the smell of death and the dark silence of the tomb:

Seen from the Mount of Olives on the other side of the Valley of Jehoshaphat, Jerusalem is laid out on a terrain that descends from west to east. A crenellated wall fortified with towers and a gothic castle encloses the city in its entirety, presently leaving outside only part of Mount Sion, which it once enclosed.

Toward the west and center of the city, in the vicinity of Calvary, the houses are in close rows, but toward the east, all along the Kedron Valley, there appear open spaces, among others the zone around the mosque built on the ruins of the Temple and the almost deserted terrain where once rose the castle Antonia and the second palace of Herod.

The houses of Jerusalem are heavy square masses, quite low, without passages and without windows. They are finished on top with either flat terraces or domes, and they resemble prisons or sepulchers. The city

562

Looking eastward into the Kedron Valley, with tombs dating from the Hellenistic or Herodian-Roman period below and modern Jewish burials on the slope rising up on the Mount of Olives behind them.

Overleaf. Mount Sion. On the lowest level, the Tomb of David, and above, the Christians' Upper Room, or Cenacle. The Muslims, too, regard David as a prophet, hence the minaret signalling a Muslim oratory crowded into the same space.

Above, Jewish graves on the western slope of the Mount of Olives. *Below*, the tomb of Mary as it appeared in 1843; note its relation to ground level.

Above, the edicule and rotunda of the Church of the Holy Sepulcher as they appeared in 1738. *Below*, inside the edicule; on the left, the marble-encased tomb of Jesus.

A modern-day version of the "Descent of the Holy Fire."

Left, an early engraving of the Via Dolorosa looking eastward. The arch, identified as the part of the Pretorium from which Pilate displayed Jesus to the crowds below, is actually the center section of the entry to Hadrian's eastern forum. *Below*, the beginning of the via Dolorosa, or Way of the Cross. Running at a diagonal across the photograph is Lady Mary Street. The dome to the north of it marks the Convent of the Sisters of Sion; the minaret to the south is at the northwest corner of the Haram.

At top, the Western Wall today; and *below*, the Western Wall looking north-ward to the arches that mark the entry to Wilson's Arch under the Gate of the Chain Street and the Tankiziyya above. Since this area of the wall is in effect a synagogue, the sexes are separated by the metal barrier seen at the center of the photograph.

Above, the minaret marking David's oratory in the Citadel complex at the western side of the city. It was there, tradition maintained, that he composed the Psalms. *Below*, the southern end of the Temple platform. At the lower left, just within the city wall, are the yeshivas of the newly rebuilt Jewish quarter.

would present itself to the eye on a single level if the church towers, the minarets of mosques, and the tops of some cypresses did not break the uniformity. At the sight of these stone houses enclosed in a landscape of stone, one asks oneself if these are not the scattered monuments of a cemetery in the midst of a desert.

When you enter the city you find no consolation for the sadness of its exterior. You wander in the tiny unpaved streets which rise and descend over the uneven terrain and you walk amidst clouds of dust and over slippery gravel. The cloths thrown between one house and the other add to the darkness of this labyrinth; vaulted and filthy bazaars succeed in banning the light from the desolate city. Some wretched shops summon only misery to the eyes, and often these shops are closed in fear of the passing by of a qadi. There is no one on the streets, no one at the gates of the city; only here and there a peasant slips through the shadows, hiding beneath his clothes the fruits of his labors lest it be stripped from him by a soldier. In a remote corner an Arab butcher disembowels some beast suspended by his hoofs from a ruined wall, and the worn and ferocious look of the man, his bloody arms, make you think he is about to slay another like himself rather than to slaughter a lamb. The only noise in this city of deicide is the occasional clatter of the hooves of the desert cavalry: it is a janissary carrying the head of a bedouin or riding off to pillage the fellahin. (Chateaubriand 1969: 1124)

A Tour of the City

Earlier, when Chateaubriand had first entered the city he was in a more hopeful mood, curious and interested. It was soon dashed, however, when he discovered that his visit coincided with one of the governor's tax-gathering descents upon the Holy City:

We entered Jerusalem by the Pilgrims' [Jaffa] Gate. Behind this gate rises the Tower of David, more generally known as the Tower of the Pisans. We paid the tribute and followed the road that opened before us. Then, turning off to the left, between a type of plastered prison which they call houses, we arrived, at twenty-two minutes after noon, at the monastery of the Latin Fathers. It was taken over by the soldiers of [the pasha] Abdullah who helped themselves at their convenience to whatever they found there.

One must be in the place of the Fathers of the Holy Land to understand the pleasure caused by our arrival. They thought themselves saved by the presence of a single Frenchman. I gave to Father Bonaventure of Nola, the guardian of the convent, a letter from General Sebastiani. "Sir," the *guardian said to me, "it is Providence that has led you here. Do you have travel permits? Allow us to send them to the pasha so that he will know there is a Frenchman staying at the convent, and he will think we are under the special protection of the emperor. Last year they forced us to pay 60,000 piasters; according to custom we owed him only 4,000, even under the rubric of a simple present. This year he wants the same sum, and he has threatened to take extreme measures if we refuse. We will be obliged to sell the sacred vessels since for four years now we have received no alms from Europe. If that continues, we shall be constrained to abandon the Holy Land and to hand the Tomb of Christ over to the Muslims." (Chateaubriand 1969: 982)*

We left the castle [of the Tower of David] after having examined it for an hour. We took a street which leads toward the east and is called the Street of the Bazaar. It is the chief street and best quarter of Jerusalem. But what desolation and misery! . . . We met no one since most of the inhabitants had retired to the mountains at the arrival of the pasha. The doors of some of the abandoned shops were open and one could see inside small rooms of seven or eight square feet where the proprietor, now fled, ate, sat, and slept on the mat which was his only furniture.

To the right of the bazaar, between the Temple and the foot of Mount Sion, we entered the Jewish Quarter. The Jews, strengthened by their miseries, had braved the assault of the pasha; they were there all of them in rags, seated in the dust of Sion and searching out the insects that were devouring them, all the while with their eyes fastened upon the Temple. The dragoman had me enter a kind of school. I wished to buy the Hebrew Pentateuch out of which a rabbi was teaching a child to read, but the rabbi was in no wise willing to sell it to me. One notes that the foreign Jews who take up residence in Jerusalem do not live very long. But for those native to Palestine, they are so poor that every year they send out appeals to their brethren in Egypt and Barbary. (Chateaubriand 1969: 1061-1062)

Let us take leave of Chateaubriand at this point and continue the tour with another visitor with somewhat wider perspectives who was walking the same streets and at precisely the same time, Ulrich Seetzen. First, his assessment of the population in 1806:

The following are the figures for the population according to what I was told, though I doubt if they are correct since they not only seem too low but there were other informants who told me that the total population was 12,000. Thus Jerusalem was the only place in the Levant where I was given a population figure that was considerably lower than what seemed likely.

Muslims	4,000
Jews	2,000
Greek Christians	1,400
Catholics	800
Armenians	500
Copts	50
Abyssinians	13
Syrians	11
Total:	8,774

(Seetzen 1854-1859: 18, trans. E. Koehldorfer)

If Seetzen's estimates are accurate, he saw Jerusalem at one of its low population ebbs. It had been lower at the end of the Mamluk period—perhaps fewer than 6,000 people lived in the city in 1525—but the figure had climbed steadily in the first half of the century until it was near 16,000 in 1553. [24] Then another decline set in, not merely in Jerusalem but in all the settlements in Palestine. [25] Once the nineteenth century had begun, however, the trend was once again reversed, and one recent estimate puts the population of Jerusalem at nearly 15,000 by 1840 and perhaps 20,000 in 1860. [26]

Seetzen next turned to the city at large, more soberly and matter-of-factly than Chateaubriand, but much to the same point:

Jerusalem has no suburbs, that is, all the houses and buildings are located inside the city walls. Some few of the main streets are more or less straight and are tolerably paved. Most of the side-streets, however, are unpaved, narrow, winding, crooked, and dirty. Already the chief side-streets have several neglected, partially ruined living quarters. In other parts of the city there is much more debris and rubble on top of which are wretchedly built houses, much like houses one finds in villages, and neglected gardens.

If all the space in Jerusalem were covered with buildings, then the number of the population would be considerable, since it took me eight minutes short of an hour to walk around the city.

There are no significant public squares in Jerusalem. The open places in front of the Citadel and the entrance to the Holy Sepulcher are insignificant because they are so small, and the beautiful wide platform of the Haram, which is one of the most beautiful places in the Ottoman Empire, does not merit being called a public place since Jews and Christians may not enter it without risking their lives. Next to the Haram there is a lofty date-palm and one may find other such here and there, but there are at most only half a dozen date-palms in Jerusalem. (Seetzen 1854-1859: 24, trans. E. Koehldorfer)

The Quarters of Ottoman Jerusalem

As we have already seen in Chapter Seven, organization of the quarters of Jerusalem began as early as in eleventh century when the Christians were granted the right, and perhaps a certain degree of autonomy along with it, to reside in the northwest quadrant of the city under the jurisdiction of their patriarch. The area around the Church of the Holy Sepulcher continued from that day to this to constitute the "Christian quarter" of Jerusalem. But it was not the only such; immediately south of it, across David Street and stretching southward to Mount Sion, lay the Armenian enclave, with its center at the church and convent of St. James. The Armenians may have lived there from very early in the city's history, but what constituted it a "quarter" was more likely the Armenians' ability to buy up parcels of land—they were, as Seetzen noted, the wealthiest of the Christians communities in the city—and so enclose themselves in a secure place.

We are here using "quarter" in its broadest sense, as an area in the city characterized by some kind of spatial, religious, or ethnic unity; the first two in the case of the "Christian quarter," all three in the "Armenian quarter." The same considerations enable us to locate the Jews in the southeastern part of Jerusalem, between the Armenians on the west and the Moroccan Muslims packed in tightly against the Haram wall on their east. As for the Muslims, they lived where they always had, around the northern and western sides of the Haram. In Mamluk times most of the streets in the immediate vicinity of the Haram were filled with public buildings, law schools, convents, and the like, and the general residential areas for Muslims were somewhat further out to the west and north. By the eighteenth century, however, many of those public endowments appear to have lapsed into private ownership and been converted into multiple dwellings or even to have become the preserve of squatters.

The Muslims themselves viewed the quarters somewhat differently. We have already noted in Mujir al-Din's itinerary through Jerusalem that his "quarters" were somewhat closer to what we would consider neighborhoods, and the same impression emerges from the Ottoman tax registers from the sixteenth century, where the quarters and their residents are inventoried. [27] What is perhaps the most notable feature of these records, and of the Muslim court records that supplement them, [28] is that there was, at least in the sixteenth century, no such thing as a "Christian quarter" or a "Jewish quarter" in Ottoman Jerusalem. Jews and Christians were treated as units for tax purposes, the former as a single collective, the latter according to sectarian and ethnic differences, and they may even have lived on streets inhabited only by their own coreligionists; but there is no evidence to indicate that they constituted a single and exclusive quarter. Or, to put it another way, the Jews, Christians, and Muslims tended to intermingle in the quarters, though not certainly in the same proportions. [29]

But sixteenth-century Jerusalem was a relatively secure place compared with what we find at the beginning of the nineteenth century, and the deterioration of municipal order and the growing government fiscal oppression must have hastened the segregation of the population into quarters where the population was overwhelmingly Jewish, Christian, or Muslim and so could provide some safety and support by its homogeneity. [30] Thus on a map of Jerusalem prepared by the British Admiralty in 1841, the city shows six quarters, the Christian, Muslim, Hitta Gate (north of the Haram, also Muslim), the Maghrebi (the Muslims at the southwest corner of the Haram), the Jewish, and Armenian quarters. [31]

But the segregation was not complete. Whereas other Muslim cities developed quarter bazaars, Jerusalem did not. The central market area of the city, where all it residents had perforce to mingle with each other, remained where it had been since the time of Hadrian, in the triple bazaars along the old Roman cardo near where it crossed David Street. There were some specialized markets, of course, like that which specialized in Christian religious articles in the streets immediately adjoining the Holy Sepulcher. But for their daily staples the inhabitants of the Old City went where they still go today, to the shops under the Crusader arches of the triple bazaar.

Muslims and Jews

Most European visitors to Jerusalem did not concern themselves with the Muslim localities in Jerusalem, but Seetzen, like Felix Fabri more than three centuries earlier, made some effort to see and report on those quarters as well as on the Christian condition in Jerusalem:

Jerusalem has fifteen mosques within its walls. The main mosque, the Haram, is situated where the former Jewish Temple stood. There are two buildings associated with it, the [Dome of the] Rock and the Aqsa. They are very remarkable buildings and it is deplorable that only Muslims are permitted to enter the Haram. . . . Apart from these mosques there are also five private oratories for Muslims, and outside the city there are three additional mosques of which that of Nabi Da'ud [the Prophet David] is by far the most splendid. I assume that many of the above-mentioned mosques are not in use.

The Haram contains a convent for Indian monks who come from the most distant regions and find free accommodation here. One of the Muslim charitable institutions is a hospice located at the Lady Mary Gate, where hot food is distributed daily to the poor. (Seetzen 1854-1859: 18-19)

At the side of the Haram is a building which is very interesting to pious Christian pilgrims, although it might arouse great anger in many of them. This is the so-called Palace of Pilate. The former entrance is walled up, but the marble doorframe still receives many a pious kiss in passing. Though it seems to be very old, it is difficult to prove that this building is the former palace of that ill-famed Roman governor, since there can be no doubt that even this palace was not spared during the later destruction of the city. Meanwhile, since the pilgrims are shown all the places and objects mentioned by the biographers of the man of Nazareth, this place may not be omitted.

This building is a part of the residence of each of the successive governors of the city. Even if there was no religious interest to prompt travellers to visit this building, it still deserves note, since from the upper room, which is believed to be the place where Pilate decided by a predetermined judgment the fate of Jesus, there is a panorama over the whole wide beautiful platform of the Haram with its fine looking buildings, one of the most impressive places of the Ottoman Empire, as I have already remarked.

To one side stands the spacious residence of the governor, together with some other buildings. There are some trees which beautifully adorn this place. I feel inclined to go there and also visit the Haram, but a non-Muslim would risk great danger in so doing: either a Muslim or death! At that moment I cursed the religious hatred and the sectarian spirit which embitters and deprives us of so many pleasures.

... I was taken to a house in the vicinity of the Haram devoted to the reception of Indian dervishes who come here on pilgrimage from distant places. Since there was not a single one staying there at that moment, the place was deserted. Further, I was shown a beautiful building whose outside walls were covered with polished marble but which is presently in a very bad state of decay. It is called the "Dervish Convent" and is a charitable institution where in former times pilgrims and poor travellers received food free of charge. (Seetzen 1854-1859: 35-36)

It may have been his contemplation of the Haram from an upper room of a building outside its northern side that prompted Seetzen's reflection on the predicament of the Jews:

The [Rabbanite] Jews have five synagogues, and the Karaites, who num-

*ber only about twelve souls, have one. All of them, so I hear, are unim-
portant, and this at a place where they once, during the flourishing time
of their nation, owned one of the most important temples in the world,
whose holy site they can still look upon every day, though they dare not
even look through the gates which lead to it. This luckless people, which here
as elsewhere is among the most despised, is much like Tantalus, who is always so
close to what he so deeply yearns for and yet will never be able to attain it. . . .
(Seetzen 1854-1859: 19, trans. E. Koehldorfer)*

Three decades after Seetzen, another visitor, an American archeologist
went up into that same building and enjoyed the same view of the Haram,
still the only one possible for the non-Muslim:

*We found no difficulty at any time in approaching the entrances [of the
Haram] and looking upon the area as long as we pleased. Wishing however to obtain a better view of the Haram and also to visit the Citadel
near the Jaffa Gate, Mr. Smith with our friends waited on the Kaim
Makâm, the military commander of the city, to obtain an order for this
purpose. This officer received them with great courtesy, immediately
granted their request, and even sent his secretary to accompany them and
introduce them at each place. They now came back for me, and we went
first to the building on the northwest corner of the Haram. This was
formerly the residence of the governor and stands near the site of the
ancient fortress Antonia. Now it is used as barracks. [32] From the flat roof
there is a full view of the mosque and its court, a large and beautiful area,
with trees scattered over it and several fountains, the whole forming a fine
promenade. We saw there quite a number of females and many children
playing. (Robinson 1841: I, 360)*

The Eastern Christian Communities

*The buildings of the Christians are more respectable and worth seeing
[Seetzen continues]. They, however, have always had to sacrifice large
sums of money to gain this advantage. The Greeks own nine convents for
monks and these are devoted chiefly to accommodating pilgrims of this
religious group. Most of the convents have only a few monks, who have
been transferred here from the mother house, the actual seat of the Greek
patriarch of Jerusalem. Apart from these monasteries there are five nunneries, two of them set aside for widows who want to spend the remaining
years of their lives in pious peace.*

*Each of the nunneries has a procurator who takes care of money matters
and a priest who conducts the daily service. For many years now the*

569

[Greek] patriarch has resided in Constantinople. The present patriarch is named Antimus. He is one of the very few learned men among the Greek clergy, and he became famous for the printing of two large theological volumes in Vienna for which he provided the funds but which do not appear to be very important for scientific research.

Judging from the number of ecclesiastical buildings, one would expect to encounter many truly pious people. What I found is exactly the opposite. All the Christian inhabitants have their children educated in the convents, but all they learn is the repetition of empty prayers where both soul and heart are neglected. Failing to go to church and breaking their fast is reckoned by them a great sin, yet to me they seemed to have no character and appeared mean, insincere, and liars, people one can never rely upon. The mindless charity of the monasteries makes them idle, and by taking the pilgrims as their example, they thoroughly indulge themselves in inactivity. This is why a wealthy man is so rarely found among the Christians. The Armenians, so it is said, are the most prosperous among them. (Seetzen 1854-1859: 19-21, trans. E. Koehldorfer)

In 1831 Ibrahim Pasha, son of Muhammad Ali, the newly independent ruler of Egypt, invaded and occupied Syria, and thus Jerusalem was temporarily relieved of the Ottoman rulers who had become its oppressors. It was a brief respite—the Egyptians were forced out by the European powers in 1840—but for as long as it lasted, a new energy began to flow through the Christian communities in the Holy City, as is reflected in this official Greek Orthodox account of the building activity during those years of Ibrahim Pasha's rule in Palestine:

As I have often spoken about what we [the Greek Orthodox] have constructed and repaired during these years, it would be unfair to omit mention of the work done by others, for such fall within the scope of this history. We have already told you that the monasteries of the Franks, Greeks, and Armenians had been damaged by the earthquake of May 23, 1834. The monastery of the Franks was greatly damaged; when Ibrahim Pasha came to Jerusalem for the third time, they received a permit to carry out repairs, and they began work on September 5, 1834. They finished only in July 1836, having built the greater part of the monastery from the foundation. The Franks also in the convent of St. Savior's in Jerusalem raised many new buildings. But the Armenians surpassed them and us in the question of building. They built on very solid foundations a new narthex to the Church of St. James and joined it to the Church; by other additions they made an enclosure for women. . . . They erected a printing press and a big hospice for pilgrims. . . .

Meanwhile the pasha's secretaries, being Arab Greek-Catholics, bought some houses near the Coptic monastery of St. George, on the way to David's Gate, and built there a residence where they planted their Catholic monks with their Kalamakions. A scandal was thereby added to a scandal, for they formed a new religious branch, one day to join in the fight against us, demanding a place in the Holy Sepulcher for their prayers. Two years before we had explained to Mehmet Ali Pasha that the Greek-Catholic monks should not wander about the streets of Jerusalem and that his decree to this effect was dormant, because his Catholic secretaries did as they wished. . . .

As we are on the subject of repairs, we must say something of the Jewish synagogue. One year ago only, seeing the liberal dispositions of Muhammad Ali Pasha and Ibrahim Pasha, they [the Jews] dared to speak about their synagogue. They asked that their House of Prayer, being in a ruinous condition and in danger of falling in, must be repaired. So those who did not even dare change a tile on the roof of the synagogue at one time, now received a permit and a decree to build. They finished at the end of August. They built the synagogue all of stone, and in place of the wooden roof they erected a cupola. The building was large and spacious and could contain about 1,000 persons. It was long but only ten pics in height. The cupola was also very low for they feared the stability and certainty of the government. Rather careless in expending on such an affair, it cost them over one million piasters. (Spyridon 1938: 123-125)

The Easterners and the Holy Fire

For the Eastern Christians the central liturgical event of the year in Jerusalem was, as it had been for many centuries, the annual Descent of the Holy Fire. The Latin Christians in Jerusalem had long since withdrawn themselves from the ceremony out of either disdain or disbelief, [33] and most Western visitors attended the event much as Seetzen did, out of curiosity and lingered on to mock:

From the gallery [inside the Church of the Holy Sepulcher], I had the pleasure of watching the congregation for some time without being disturbed. The Greeks took their place on one side of the Sepulcher, which is also the center part of the church, where they conduct their service, while the Armenians gathered on the other side of the Tomb. These latter were composed, while the Greeks behaved in a most indecent manner and were so noisy that my ears rang. The constantly growing crowd consisted of men of all ages. The younger ones pushed, shoved, and scuffled. Three or four fell upon another and carried him around the Sepulcher whether he wished it or not, while a mob followed after them screaming and shout-

ing wildly. They had barely completed one round when they did it again with someone else. It was a carnival, and instead of a Christian celebration one seemed to be attending a Bacchanalian feast.

Young Muslims mingled with the frolicsome crowd and added to the tumult so that it became complete chaos. It seems that the Greeks are incapable of making a pilgrimage without such wild outbursts of joy. From the gallery I also noticed some women pilgrims.

The Descent of the Holy Fire is a triumph for the Greeks, by which the Armenians, Copts, etc., should also be convinced. They pride themselves a great deal on this, and in order to humiliate their chief enemy, the Armenians, they tell the following story. Once, it seems, the Armenian clergy paid a large sum of money to the governor of the city in order to obtain permission to be the recipients of the Holy Fire. The Armenian bishop had already entered the Tomb and everyone was in a ferment of expectation. Then, after a long period of waiting, the Armenian clergy came out again, ashamed and afraid, and explained that they could not obtain the Holy Fire through their prayers. Then the Greek bishop entered the Tomb and in a few minutes the Holy Fire appeared. Angry with the audacity of the Armenians, the governor had them seized and forced them to eat something which politeness does not permit me to name. This is the reason for the abusive name of "Sh-teaters" given to the Armenians by the Greek rabble. It is amazing what religious fanaticism can do to men! (Seetzen 1854-1859: 5-7, trans. E. Koehldorfer)

Disaster at the Holy Sepulcher, 1834

Seetzen's final comments were a moral judgment, a deep European sigh at the debasement of a religious ceremony which had passed from an act of piety into something that a Westerner could no longer commend nor even comprehend. But there were physical dangers as well in that ceremony of the Holy Fire. Many earlier visitors noted the frightening effect of so many people brought to a state of near religious hysteria in so confined a space. Finally, in 1834, the inevitable occurred. It is graphically described by one who was there, the English traveller Robert Curzon, in the midst of his tour of the monasteries of the Levant:

It was on Friday, the third of May [1834] (Good Friday, according to the calendar of the Greeks) that my companions and myself went, about five o'clock in the evening, to the Church of the Holy Sepulcher, where we had places assigned to us in the gallery of the Latin monks, as well as a good bedroom in their convent. The church was very full, and the numbers kept increasing every moment. We first saw a small procession of

Copts go round the sepulcher, and after them one of the Syrian Maronites. I then went to bed, and at midnight was awakened to see the procession of the Greeks, which was rather grand. By the rules of their church they are not permitted to carry any images, and therefore to make up for this they bore aloft a piece of brocade, upon which was embroidered a representation of the body of our Saviour. This was placed in the tomb, and, after some short time, brought out again and carried into the chapel of the Greeks, when the ceremonies of the night ended; for there was no procession of the Armenians, as the Armenian patriarch had made an address to his congregation, and had, it was said, explained the falsity of the miracle of the holy fire, to the excessive astonishment of his hearers, who for centuries have considered an unshakeable belief in this yearly wonder as one of the leading articles of their faith. After the Greek procession I went quietly to bed again and slept soundly till next morning.

The behaviour of the pilgrims was riotous in the extreme; the crowd was so great that many persons actually crawled over the heads of others, and some made pyramids of men by standing on one another's shoulders. . . . At one time, before the church was full, they made a racecourse round the sepulcher; and some, almost in a state of nudity, danced about with frantic gestures, yelling and screaming as if they were possessed. Altogether it was a scene of disorder and profanation, which it is impossible to describe. In consequence of the number of people and the quantities of lamps, the heat was excessive, and steam arose which prevented your seeing clearly across the church. But every window and cornice, and every place where a man's foot could rest, excepting the gallery—which was reserved for Ibrahim Pasha and ourselves—appeared to be crammed with people; for 17,000 pilgrims were said to be in Jerusalem, almost the whole of whom had come to the Holy City for no other reason than to see the sacred fire. . . .

The next morning a way was made through the crowd for Ibrahim Pasha, by the soldiers with the butt-ends of their muskets and by the kawasses with their kour-batches and whips made by a quantity of small rope. The pasha sat in the gallery, on a divan which the monks had made for him between the two columns nearest the Greek chapel. They had got up a sort of procession to do him honor, the appearance of which did not add to the solemnity of the scene: three monks playing crazy fiddles led the way; then came the choristers with lighted candles; next two Nizam soldiers with muskets and fixed bayonets; a number of doctors, instructors, and officers, tumbling over each other's heels, brought up the rear. He was received by the women, of whom there were thousands in the church, with a very peculiar shrill cry, which had a strange unearthly effect. It was the monosyllable "la, la, la," uttered in a shrill trembling tone, which I thought much more like pain than rejoicing. The pasha was dressed in full trousers of dark cloth, a light lilac-colored jacket, and a red cap without a turban. When he was seated, the monks brought us some sherbet, which was excellently made; and as our seats were very near the great man, we saw everything in an easy and luxurious way; and it being announced that the Muhammadan pasha was ready, the Christian miracle, which had been waiting for some time, was now at the point of being displayed.

The people were by this time become furious; they were worn out with standing in such a crowd all night, and as the time approached for the exhibition of the holy fire, they could not contain themselves for joy. Their excitement increased as the time for the miracle in which they all believed drew near. At about one o'clock a magnificent procession moved out of the Greek chapel. It conducted the patriarch three times around the tomb, after which he took off his outer robes of cloth and silver, and went into the sepulcher, the door of which was then closed. The agitation of the pilgrims was now extreme: they screamed aloud; and the dense mass of the people shook to and fro, like a field of corn in the wind.

There is a round hole in one part of the chapel over the sepulcher, out of which the holy fire is given, and up to this the man who had agreed to pay the highest sum for this honor was then conducted by a strong guard of soldiers. There was silence for a minute; and then a light appeared out the tomb and the happy pilgrim received the holy fire from the patriarch within. It consisted of a bundle of thin wax candles, lit, and enclosed in an iron frame, to prevent their being torn asunder and put out by the crowd; for a furious battle commenced immediately; everyone being so eager to obtain the holy light, that one man put out the candle of his neighbor in trying to light his own. . . .

This was the whole of the ceremony; there was no sermon or prayers, except a little chanting during the processions, and nothing that could tend to remind you of the awful event which this feast was designed to commemorate.

Soon you saw the light increasing in all directions, everyone having lit his candle from the holy flame: the chapels, the galleries, and every corner where a candle could possibly be displayed immediately appeared to be in a blaze. The people in their frenzy put the bunches of lighted tapers to their faces, hands, and breasts to purify themselves from their sins. The patriarch was carried out of the sepulcher in triumph, on the shoulders of the people he had deceived, amid the cries and exclamations of joy which resounded from every nook of the immense pile of buildings. As he appeared in a fainting state, I supposed that he was ill; but I found that it is the uniform custom on these occasions to feign insensibility, that the pilgrim may imagine that he is overcome with the glory of the Almighty, from whose immediate presence they believe him to have returned.

In a short time the smoke of the candles obscured everything in the place, and I could see it rolling in great volumes out of the aperture at the top of the dome. The smell was terrible; and three unhappy people, overcome by heat and bad air, fell from the upper range of galleries and were dashed to pieces on the heads of the people below. One poor Armenian lady, seventy years of age, died where she sat, of heat, thirst, and fatigue.

After a while, when he had seen all that was to be seen, Ibrahim Pasha got up and went away, his numerous guards making a line for him by main force through the dense mass of people which filled the body of the church. As the crowd was so immense, we waited for a little while, and then set out all together to return to our convent. I went first and my friends followed me, the soldiers making way for us across the church. I got as far as the place where the Virgin is said to have stood during the Crucifixion, when I saw a number of people lying one on another all about this part of the church, and as far as I could see towards the door. I made my way between them as well as I could, till they were so thick that there were actually a great heap of bodies on which I trod. It then suddenly struck me that they were all dead! I had not perceived this at first, for I thought that they were only very much fatigued with the ceremonies and had lain down to rest there; but when I came to so great a heap of bodies, I looked down at them and saw that sharp, hard appearance of the face which is never to be mistaken. Many of them were quite black with suffocation, and further on were others all bloody and covered with the brains and entrails of those who had been trodden to pieces by the crowd.

At this time there was no crowd in this part of the church; but a little farther on, round the corner toward the great door, the people, who were quite panic-struck, continued to press forward, and everyone was doing his utmost to escape. The guards outside, frightened by the rush from within, thought that the Christians wished to attack them, and the confusion soon grew into a battle. The soldiers with their bayonets killed a number of fainting wretches, and the walls were splattered with the blood and brains of men who had been felled, like oxen, with the butt-ends of the soldiers' muskets. Everyone struggled to defend himself or to get away, and in the mêlée all who fell were immediately trampled to death by the rest. So desperate and savage did the fight become, that even the panic-struck and frightened pilgrims appeared at last to have been more intent upon the destruction of each other than desirous to save themselves.

For my part, as soon as I perceived the danger, I cried out to my companions to turn back, which they had done; but I myself was carried on by the press till I came near the door, where all were fighting for their lives. Here, seeing certain destruction before me, I made every endeavor to get back. An officer of the pasha's, who by his star was a colonel, or bin bashee, equally alarmed with myself, was also trying to return: he caught hold of my cloak, or burnouse, and pulled me down on the body of an old man who was breathing out his last sigh. As the officer was pressing me to the ground, we wrestled together among the dying and the dead with the energy of despair. I struggled with this man till I pulled him down, and happily got again upon my legs—I afterward found that he never rose again. I stood up for a minute in the press of the people, held up on the uncomfortable footing of dead bodies, by the dense crowd who were squeezed together in this narrow part of the church. We all stood still for a short time, when of a sudden the crowd swayed, a cry arose, the crowd opened, and I found myself standing in the center of a line of men, with another line opposite to me, all pale and ghastly with torn and bloody clothes, and there we stood glaring at each other; but in a moment a sudden impulse seized upon us, with a shriek that echoed in the long aisles of the Church of the Holy Sepulcher (how terribly dese-crated at this moment!), the two adverse lines soon dashed at each other, and I was soon engaged tearing and wrestling with a thin half-naked man whose legs were smeared with blood. The crowd fell back again, and by desperate fighting and hard struggles I made my way back into the body of the church, where I found my friends, and we succeeded in reaching the sacristy of the Catholics, and thence the room which had been assigned to us by the monks. . . .

I thanked God for my escape—I had a narrow chance. The dead were lying in heaps, even upon the stone of unction; and I saw full four hundred unhappy people, dead and living, heaped promiscuously one upon the other, in some places about five feet high. Ibrahim Pasha had left the church only a few minutes before me, and very narrowly escaped with his life; he was so pressed upon by the crowd on all sides, and it was said, attacked by several of them, that it was only by the greatest exertion of his suite, several of whom were killed, that he gained the outer court. He fainted more than once in the struggle, and I was told that some of his attendants had at last to cut a way for him with their swords through the dense ranks of the frantic pilgrims. He remained outside, giving orders for the removal of the corpses, and making his men drag out the bodies of those who appeared to be still alive from the heaps of the dead. . . .

We stayed in our room for two hours before we ventured to make another attempt to escape from this scene of horror; and then walking close together, with all our servants around us, we made a bold rush and got out the door of the church. By this time most of the bodies had been removed; but twenty or thirty were still lying in distorted attitudes at the foot of Mount Calvary; and fragments of clothes, turbans, shoes, and handkerchiefs, clotted with blood and dirt, were strewed all over the pavement.

In the court in the front of the church the sight was pitiable: mothers weeping over their children; sons bending over the dead bodies of their fathers; and one poor woman was clinging to the hand of her husband, whose body was fearfully mangled. Most of the sufferers were pilgrims and strangers. . . . When the bodies were removed, many were discovered standing upright, quite dead; and near the church door one soldier was found thus standing, with his musket shouldered, among bodies that reached nearly as high as his head; this was in a corner near the great door on the right side as you come in. It seems that this door had been shut so that many who stood near it were suffocated in the crowd; and when it was opened, the rush was so great that numbers were thrown down and never rose again, being trampled to death by the press behind them. The whole court before the entrance to the church was covered with bodies laid in rows, by the pasha's orders, so that their friends might find them and carry them away. As we walked home, we saw numbers of people carried out, some dead, some horribly wounded and in a dying state, for they had fought with their heavy silver inkstands and daggers.

In the morning I awoke at a late hour and looked out into the court. . . . People were going about their business as if nothing had occurred, excepting that now and then I heard the wail of the women lamenting for the dead. Three hundred was the number reported to have been carried out of the gates to their burial place that morning; two hundred more were badly wounded, many of whom probably died, for there were no physicians or surgeons to attend them, and it was supposed that others were buried in the courts and gardens of the city by their surviving friends; so that the precise number of those who perished was not known. . . .

The day following the occurrences which have been related, I had a long interview with Ibrahim Pasha, and the conversation turned naturally to the blasphemous imputations of the Greek and Armenian patriarchs, who for the purposes of worldly gain, had deluded their ignorant followers with the performance of a trick in relighting the candles which had been extinguished on Good Friday with fire which they affirmed had been sent down from heaven in answer to their prayers. The pasha was quite aware of the evident absurdity which I brought to his notice, of the performance of a Christian miracle being put off for some time, and being kept waiting, for the convenience of a Muhammadan prince.

It was debated what punishment was to be awarded to the Greek patriarch for the misfortunes which had been the consequence of his jugglery, *and a number of the purses which he had received from the unlucky pilgrims passed into the coffers of the pasha's treasury. I was sorry that the falsity of this imposture was not publicly exposed, as it was a good opportunity of so doing.*

It seems wonderful that so barefaced a trick should continue to be practiced every year in these enlightened times. . . . If Ibrahim Pasha had been a Christian, probably this would have been the last Easter of the lighting of the holy fire; but from the fact of his religion being opposed to that of the monks, he could not follow the example of Louis XIV, who having put a stop to some clumsy imposition which was at that time bringing scandal on the Church, a paper was found nailed upon the door of the sacred edifice the days afterwards, on which the words were read:

> *Du part du roi, défense à Dieu*
> *De faire miracle en ce lieu.*

The interference of a Muhammadan in such a case as this would only have been held as another persecution of the Christians; and the miracle of the holy fire has continued to be exhibited every year with great applause, and luckily without the unfortunate results which accompanied it on this occasion. (Curzon 1849: 192-204)

Philosophe or Christian?

Chateaubriand too made his visit to the Church of the Holy Sepulcher in 1806, happily not in season to witness the Holy Fire, else it might have distracted him from other, more interesting reflections. What had once been a simple act of piety and might later in that century be an equally uncomplicated visit to a famous church prompted by nothing more than a scholarly or touristic curiosity, as it likely already was for Ulrich Seetzen, posed for Chateaubriand, a man caught between two eras and two faiths, a peculiar dilemma:

I left the convent on the same at nine in the morning, accompanied by two religious, a dragoman, my servant, and a janissary. I went on foot to the church which encloses the tomb of Jesus Christ. All travellers have described the most venerable one on earth, whether one is taking the point of view of a philosophe or a Christian. Here I found myself in an awkward position. Should I present an exact portrait of the holy places? In that event I should only be repeating what others have said before me: never was any subject less understood by modern readers and at the same time so thoroughly treated. Should I then omit the holy places from my account? That would be to leave out the most essential part of my trip and to make disappear its very point. After weighing it for a long time, I decided to describe the principal Stations of Jerusalem for the following reasons: 1) Today the old pilgrimages to Jerusalem are no longer read, and what is commonplace will likely seem entirely new to most readers. 2) The Church of the Holy Sepulcher no longer exists; it was entirely burned down since my return from Judea [in A.D. 1808]. I am, so to speak, the last traveller to have seen it, and I shall be, for this same reason, its last historian.

But since I do not pretend to redo a portrait already well drawn, I shall take advantage of the works of my predecessors, taking care only to clarify them by my own observations. Among those works, I have deliberately preferred those of Protestant travellers because of the spirit of the present age: today we are always ready to reject what we think comes from an overly religious source. (Chateaubriand 1969: 1017-1018)

Chateaubriand summarizes his readings on the Sepulcher, and then returns to the point about religious faith:

The first travellers [to Jerusalem] were fortunate; they had no need to go into all these controversial matters: first, because they found in their readers a religious conviction which was never at odds with truth; secondly, because everyone was convinced that the only way to see a country as it truly is was to see it with all its traditions and memories. In effect it is with the Bible and the Gospels in hand that one should travel around the Holy Land. If one brings a contentious spirit to it, Judea is hardly worth the trouble of coming so far to visit. What, for example, would one say of someone who visited Greece and Italy for the sole purpose of refuting Homer and Vergil? But that is exactly how one travels today, the victims of our own self-love which in seeking to make us appear facile renders us contemptuous.

Christian readers will perhaps wish to know what I did feel on entering that awesome place. Actually, I cannot say. So many impressions came upon me that I could not pause on any one of them. I remained for about a half hour on my knees in the small chamber of the Holy Sepulcher, my gaze so firmly attached to that stone that I could not tear it away. One of the two religious who were my guides lay prostrate before me, his forehead on the marble of the tomb; the other, Gospel in hand read to me by the light of the lamps there the passages relevant to the Holy Sepulcher. . . . All I am certain of is that at the sight of this triumphant tomb I was aware only of my own weakness, and when my guide cried out with St. Paul, "Death, where is thy victory? Death, where is thy sting?" I listened attentively, as if death were about to respond that it was conquered and chained in that monument. (Chateaubriand 1969: 1030-1031)

A Knight of the Holy Sepulcher

This is the voice of a genuine Christian piety, but it has other accents as well, those of a nationalism, for instance, long-armed enough to reach back to the Crusades:

The writers of the eighteenth century were pleased to present the Crusades in an odious light. . . . The Crusades were not folly, as some affect to call them, neither in their principle nor in their results. The Christians were not at all the aggressors. If the subjects of [Caliph] Umar could start from Jerusalem, make a turn around Africa and throw themselves on Sicily, on Spain, and even on France, where Charles Martel exterminated them, why could not the subjects of Phillip I, starting from France, make a tour of Asia to work vengeance on the descendents of Umar, even unto Jerusalem? . . . To see in the Crusades only armed pilgrims who went out to deliver a tomb in Palestine, is to take a very narrow view of history. It was not merely a question of liberating this Holy Sepulcher but even more of knowing who should have the upper hand in this world, a cult which is the enemy of civilization, systematically supporting ignorance, despotism, and slavery or a cult which revived in modern times the genius of a learned antiquity and abolished slavery. . . .

If the cries of so many suffering victims in the East, if the forward march of the barbarians even to the gates of Constantinople, reawakened Christianity and made it rush to its own defense, who would dare to say that the cause of the Holy Wars was unjust? (Chateaubriand 1969: 1052-1053)

There is little wonder, then, that on his last visit to the church Chateaubriand underwent a ceremony that went back seven centuries to the Latin Kingdom, induction as a Knight of the Holy Sepulcher:

I had seen everything at Jerusalem; I knew the city inside and out and much better than the inside and outside of Paris. So I began to take thought of my departure. The Fathers of the Holy Land wished to grant me an honor which I had neither requested nor earned. In consideration of the modest services which, according to them, I had rendered to the cause of religion, they begged me accept the Order of the Holy Sepulcher. This Order, which, without tracing it back to St. Helena, is a very old one in Christianity, was once widespread in Europe, but today is rarely encountered outside of Spain and Poland. The guardian of the Holy Sepulcher alone has the right to confer it.

At one o'clock we left the convent and went to the Church of the Holy Sepulcher. We went into the chapel that belongs to the Latin Fathers.

*They carefully closed the doors for fear that the Turks might take notice
of the arms, which would cost the religious their lives. The guardian put
on his pontifical vestments. The lamps were lit and all the Friars present
formed a circle around me, their arms crossed upon their breasts. While
they chanted in a low voice the Veni Creator, the guardian went up to the
altar and I knelt. They took out from the treasury of the Holy Sepulcher
the spurs and the sword of Godfrey of Bouillon. Two religious knelt on
either side of me holding these venerable relics. The officiating officer
recited the customary prayers and then catechized me on certain customary practices. Then he fitted me with the spurs, struck me three times upon
the shoulder with the sword while giving me the formal address. The
religious chanted the Te Deum as the guardian said this prayer over me:
"Lord, God Almighty, shower Thy Grace and Blessings over this Thy
servant, etc."*

The ceremony over, the struggle between the somewhat hard-headed real-
ist and historian and the romantic Frenchmen began within the head and
heart of the new knight:

*All of it was merely the remembrance of a way of life that no longer exists.
But when you consider that I was in Jerusalem, in the church of Calvary,
a dozen paces from the Tomb of Jesus Christ and no more than thirty
from the tomb of Godfrey of Bouillon, that I had been vested with the
spurs of the liberator of the Holy Sepulcher and touched with that long,
wide sword of iron once wielded by a hand so noble and so loyal; when
you recall the circumstances, my life filled with adventure, my travels on
land and sea, you will understand that I could not but be moved. This
ceremony was not, in the end, a completely empty one. I am French, as
was Godfrey of Bouillon, and the touch of his ancient arms communicated
to me a new love for the glory and the honor of my country. I did not
share, I dare say, the sans reproche of Godfrey's motto; but I could at least
declare, like every Frenchman, that I was sans peur.*

*They gave me my patent, signed with the signature of the guardian and
the seal of the convent. Together with this distinguished diploma of
knighthood, I was given my humble certificate of pilgrimage. I am saving
them as a memorial of my voyage into the land of the old traveller Jacob.
(Chateaubriand 1969: 1122-1123)*

Mr. Seetzen on Mr. Chateaubriand

Such an important act as the knighting of the French literary luminary
Chateaubriand did not escape the notice of the tiny world of Latins in
Jerusalem, and the news inevitably came to Ulrich Seetzen's ears:

Mr. Chateaubriand comes from an important French family and is the author of a new work [Genius of Christianity] which tries to demonstrate the excellence of the Christian religion. While travelling through Barbary and the Levant, he also visited Jerusalem, where among other things he had himself ceremoniously dubbed a Knight of the Holy Sepulcher. In return for this honor he presented the convent [of St. Savior's] with an important donation. He also travelled to the convent of Mar Saba, to the west coast of the Dead Sea and to the Jordan River, whence he took back with him a bottle of its waters. The appearance here of such a person in our times, especially a Frenchman, is indeed very rare. Later in Egypt I was told that Mr. Chateaubriand had mentioned that he deeply wished that one religion, and that the Christian, would become the universal religion of mankind. (Seetzen 1854-1859: 205, trans. E. Koehldorfer)

The Next Crusade

As noted by the pragmatic Seetzen, Chateaubriand's dream of a universal Kingdom of Christ seemed to be just that, a romantic fantasy. But there was far more to it than that, and if Chateaubriand preferred to envision it as the the triumph of Christianity, he was well enough aware of other. more secular possibilities. In 1799 Napoleon had coasted the shores of Palestine with an army and a fleet, an easy day's march from Jerusalem. And though the French emperor was checked before the walls of Acre, his presence was still hovering over a conversation which Chateaubriand had with Arsenios, the Armenian patriarch of Jerusalem:

I found nothing about him [Chateaubriand relates], similar to that air of suffering and oppression that I had found among the wretched Greeks, who are everywhere slaves. The Armenian convent is pleasant, the church charming and very decorous. The patriarch, who resembled a rich Turk, sat upon cushions wrapped in a silk robe. I drank some excellent mocha coffee, and they brought me refreshments, water, and white napkins. Aloe wood was burned, and I was perfumed with attar of roses to the point where it became uncomfortable.

Arsenios spoke scornfully of the Turks. He assured me that all of Asia was awaiting the arrival of the French, and that if a single soldier of my country were to appear in his country, there would be a general uprising. No one can believe the degree of agitation in the East. I saw Ali Agha become angry with an Arab at Jericho who mocked him by saying that if the emperor had wished to take Jerusalem, he could have entered it as easily as a camel into a pasture.

The peoples of the East are far more familiar than we with the notion

582

of invasion. They have witnessed the passage of all the men who have changed the face of the earth: Sesostris, Cyrus, Alexander, Muhammad, and the last conqueror of Europe. Accustomed to follow the destiny of a master, they have no concept of a law which would attach them to ideas of order and political restraint: to kill, when they are the stronger, seems to them like a legitimate right; they rule and submit with the same indifference. They belong in principle to the sword, and they love all the wonders that it can effect. . . . Liberty they know nothing of; of property they have none: power is their God. When they go for long periods without seeing conquerors who do heaven's justice, they seem like soldiers without a leader, citizens without a lawgiver, and a family without a father. (Chateaubriand 1969: 1068-1069)

Seetzen, who was also aware of the political ferment in the East, [34] appears to have regarded his own presence in Jerusalem as somewhat more serious than that of Chateaubriand, with his somewhat frivolous indulgence in a knighthood. What he had no way of knowing, of course, was that Chateaubriand, whose work was far more widely read than Seetzen's more scholarly treatment of the East, was a powerful force fanning the enlarging European interest in the Holy Land, [35] and that before the end of the century his own kaiser would be walking the same Jerusalem streets as he and Chateaubriand.

Well before the kaiser paid his visit, however, the first archeologists and European missionaries had begun to arrive in Jerusalem, the latter not for the conversion of Muslims, assuredly, since that activity was strictly forbidden by Islamic law, but for the salvation of the Jews. A British consul was not established in Jerusalem until 1839, but the Society for Promoting Christianity among the Jews sent its first mission to Jerusalem in 1820, and the first Anglican bishop there was a converted Jew, Michael Alexander. The attempt to save Jewish souls for Christ was not a notable success, and some of the preachers were driven out of the Jewish quarter under a hail of stones and dead cats. [36]

Edward Robinson's Easter Sunday
in Jerusalem

The story of both enterprises, the missionaries' invasion of Jerusalem and the archeologists attempts to rediscover the city's past lie beyond the scope of the present work and have been been thoroughly and vividly told elsewhere. [37] But we may cite one of the earliest of the archeologists, Edward Robinson, who took up work in Jerusalem in 1838, in contrast to Chateaubriand's rationalist but still essentially Catholic piety. Chateaubriand could go through the ceremony of investiture as Knight of Holy Sepulcher with a kind of touching sincerity, could read the painful annals of the Franciscans and feel sympathy and admiration for the Friars. Not so Edward Robinson, who was fascinated by the past of the Jerusalem but for whom the religious life of the contemporary city was alien and even repulsive:

Sunday, April 15 [1838]. This was the Christian Sabbath, and it was also Easter Sunday. It was in a special manner a "great day" in Jerusalem inasmuch as the Easter of the Romish and that of the Oriental churches, which usually occur on different days, fell together for the present year. During Easter week the city had been thronged, though not very fully, with pilgrims. These were mostly Greeks and Armenians; very few Latins were seen, and only now and then a straggling Copt. The whole number had been less than usual. The annual excursion to the Jordan had been made, in which some of our friends had joined, and the annual mockery of the Greek Holy Fire had taken place just before we entered the city. The Latins too had enacted their mummery, representing the scenes of the crucifixion. In consequence of our late arrival, we thus missed all the incidents of the Holy Week. This however we counted as no loss, but rather a gain; for the object of our visit was the city itself, in relation to its ancient renown and religious associations, not as seen in its present state of decay and superstitious and fraudful degradation. The Jews also were celebrating their Passover. . . . Thus to all the inhabitants, except to the Muhammadans; and to all the strangers who were present, save the few Protestants, this was the greatest festival of the year.

"Latin mummery" was a debased form of worship in Robinson's Protestant eyes, but his deepest scorn was reserved for the Franciscan friars who performed those ceremonies:

The different sects of Christians who have possession of the Church of the Holy Sepulcher had of course been compelled to alternate in their occupancy of it and in the performance of their religious ceremonies. . . . I was struck with the splendor of [the Latin clerics'] robes, stiff with embroidery of silver and gold, the well-meant offerings probably of Catholics of every country of Europe; but I was not less struck with the vulgar and unmeaning visages that peered out from those costly vestments. The wearers looked more like ordinary ruffians than like ministers of the cross of Christ. Indeed there is reason to believe that the Latin monks in Palestine are actually for the most part ignorant and often illiterate men, chiefly from Spain, the refuse of her monks and clergy, who come or are sent hither as into a sort of exile, where they serve to excite the sympathies and the misplaced charities of the Catholics of Europe. There was hardly a face among all those before us that could be called intelligent. A few fine-looking French naval officers and one or two Irish Catholics had joined the procession but seemed quite out of place, and as if ashamed of their companions.

It may have been somewhat too strong a judgment, as even Robinson himself seems to have realized:

I make these remarks merely as relating to a matter of fact, and not, I trust, out of any spirit of prejudice against the Romish church and her clergy. I had once spent the Holy Week in Rome itself, and there admired the intelligent and noble countenances of many of the clergy and monks congregated in that city. For this very reason the present contrast struck me the more forcibly and disagreeably. The whole scene indeed was to a Protestant painful and revolting. It might perhaps have been less so had there been manifested the slightest degree of faith in the genuineness of the surrounding objects. But even the monks themselves do not pretend that the present sepulcher is anything more than an imitation of the original. But to be in the ancient city of the Most High and to see these venerated places and the very name of our holy religion profaned by idle and lying mummeries, while the proud Mussulman looks on with haughty scorn, all this excited in my mind a feeling too painful to be borne, and I never visited the place again.

Robinson and his companions soon found a more congenial place of worship, however:

We now repaired to the house of Mr. Whiting, where in a large upper room our friends had long established regular divine service in English every Sunday, in which they were assisted by Mr. Nicolayson, the able missionary of the English Church, sent out hither by the London Missionary Society for the Jews. We found a very respectable congregation, composed of all the missionary families, besides several European travellers of rank and name. It was, I presume, the largest Protestant congregation ever collected within the walls of the Holy City. And it was gratifying to see Protestants of various names here laying aside all distinctions and uniting with one heart to declare by their example in Jerusalem itself that "God is a Spirit, and they that worship him must worship him in spirit and truth." The simplicity and spirituality of the Protestant worship was to me affecting and doubly pleasing, in contrast with the pageant of which we had just been spectators. (Robinson 1841: I, 329-332)

Neither Seetzen nor Robinson was a pilgrim in anything remotely resembling the sense that many of their predecessors had been, nor even curious travellers on the order of the earlier reporters cited in this book. They were scholars and explorers in the by then well-articulated positivist tradition of Europe, and their expeditions—visits is no longer an adequate word—were followed upon their return home by the founding of new scientific and research associations, soon with branches in Jerusalem itself; in 1838 Edward Robinson conducted the first professed excursion into biblical archeology in Jerusalem. Behind them came, as we have seen, the missionaries: Christian Zionists, many of them from America; English Protestants in search of a minority to protect or convert; and a new wave of Catholic religious from the Continent poised somewhere between verifying the past and saving souls.

The Muslims of Jerusalem were chiefly passive spectators to this new colonialism. The local authorities had to be petitioned and paid and there was doubtless employment to be had in working for the new consulates and the rapidly expanding colonies of foreigners, as everything from cooks and translators to movers of stone and earth. The crumbling medieval fabric of the city was not repaired but dug into in search for an even more ancient past—the new explorers did not much fancy Islamic antiquities—but in the old Christian quarter, where most of the newcomers lived and worked, there was new construction, as there was in the northern and western suburbs of what could already be discerned as the "Old City."

Turkish sovereignty over Jerusalem remained firmly established—the city would not pass into other hands until the peace settlements after the First World War—but by the early nineteenth century Jerusalem had become in effect the world's possession, not in the sense that it had always been, what Mark Twain called in 1867 "a dream world . . . sacred to poetry and tradition," or even in that way that Twain was no longer capable of appreciating, as the land rendered holy by the acts of God, but now as a kind of freehold to be measured, sounded, dug, rebuilt, restored, and recolonized under appeals to science, theology, or tradition that barely masked the political, military, and financial *force majeure* that lay beneath.

Notes

1. These and all the following citations from the Hebrew Bible are from *A New Translation of the Holy Scriptures according to the Masoretic Text*, published by the Jewish Publication Society of America. First section: *The Torah. The Five Books of Moses*, 2d ed. (Philadelphia, 1982); second section: *The Prophets. Nevi'im* (Philadelphia, 1978); third section: *The Writings. Kethubim* (Philadelphia, 1982).

2. Peters 1983.

3. See Chapter Five. The Christians, who also traced their spiritual descent from Abraham, preferred to read the Sarah-Hagar story allegorically (see Chapter Three). And for a later, tenth-century exegesis of this story, when the Arab descendants of Ishmael actually possessed the Land of the Promise, see Chapter Six.

4. Kenyon 1974: 100.

5. It is the seizure of the Gihon spring that figures prominently in the account of the capture (Mazar 1975: 168).

6. Kenyon 1974: 104. We know nothing beyond the mere fact of the existence of David's palace; it has left no archeological trace.

7. Mazar 1975: 171.

8. See Mazar 1975: 96.

9. Cf. Ex. 20:25.

10. Some archeologists are made of adventurous stuff. Kathleen Kenyon (Kenyon 1974: 111-112) provides an elegant example of the deductive method as applied to the Temple of Solomon:

> There have been many arguments as to whether the base of the walls of the Herodian Temple platform were those of Solomon's platform. The foundations of Herod's walls were revealed in the incredible excavations of Warren. . . . The crucial point is that 37.72 meters north of the southeast corner of the Herodian platform there is a very clear straight joint between the earlier structure to the north and the Herodian addition to the south. . . . This was revealed by a clearance carried out by the Jordanian Department of Antiquities in 1966. It had in fact been observed by Warren in 1867, but the implications had not been noted. The implications are in fact clear. At the time at which Herod built his platform, he added an extension to the south against an earlier structure. There were certainly a number of vicissitudes in the history of the immediately pre-Herodian Temple, but basically it was the Temple restored by Zerubbabel after the return from the Babylonian exile. It is inconceivable that Zerubbabel, with his exiguous resources, would have increased the size of the Solomonian platform. It is reasonably certain that he built upon the basis of surviving foundations, and restored the platform as best he could.
>
> This supposition is supported by the structural evidence. The contrast seen in Plates 35-36 between the Herodian masonry to the south [of the "seam"] and the much heavier bossed masonry to the north makes it quite clear that two separate building periods are represented. [The earlier was dated by Maurice Dunand to the Persian period, and Kenyon accepts his identification.] Here therefore we have at Jerusalem a rebuilding of the Temple platform in the masonry of the Persian style. What we can see above ground at the moment is not necessarily the work of Ze-

rubbabel, for it looks as if there were several rebuilding periods, but *I believe that it represents the restoration, and probably several restorations, of the southeast corner of the platform within the Persian period (sixth, fifth, and early fourth centuries B.C.) and that this is evidence for the southeast corner of the Solomonic platform.*

Given that the southeast corner establishes the line of the southern limit of the Temple platform [under Solomon], one must then consider the position of the southwest corner. There is no corresponding straight joint in the present western wall. Herodian masonry is visible (northward) up to the position of Wilson's Arch, a distance of 180 meters. . . . The presumption is that the original south wall did not extend as far west as the Herodian one. . . . Fig. 20 shows that the south elevation of Herod's Temple platform spans the central [Tyropean] valley, with the west wall some 30 meters up the slope of the western ridge. This is improbable for the Solomonic Temple, since we know that the contemporary city was confined to the eastern ridge. . . . The resultant conjectural elevation of the south (Solomonic) wall is shown in Fig. 21. A plan developed from this south wall (Fig. 22) would enable the rock summit [the present Sakhra] to be enclosed, as surely it must have been, and would allow ample space for the Temple, whose dimensions were relatively small. The plan would also agree with the statement of Josephus (*War* I, xxi, 1) that Herod doubled the size of the earlier platform.

11. Generally on the design of Solomon's Temple, see Busink 1970; and Rosenau 1979: 12-16.

12. On the layout and components of Solomon's palace complex, see Kenyon 1974: 123-124.

13. Cf. 2 Chron. 8:11: "Solomon brought up Pharaoh's daughter from the City of David to the palace which he had built for her, for he said, 'No wife of mine shall live in the palace of King David of Israel, for the [area] is sacred since the Ark of the Lord has entered it.' "

14. Kenyon 1974: 127-128:

In Solomon's building operations there emerges the concept of a Royal Quarter. This concept finds its clearest exposition in the lay-out of the new city of Samaria, established by Omri (880 or 872 B.C.). The whole summit of the hill was occupied by palaces and official buildings, and this same process is seen in Solomon's foundations at Megiddo and Hazor, where he had a clean slate to work with. There is no suggestion in the Biblical record that he annexed areas within the ancient Jebusite-Davidic city. It is clear, however, that he set up an efficient administration for his kingdom (1 Kgs. 4:17-19). It seems to me that it is reasonable to suggest that in the newly enclosed area within the north wall of the Davidic town and the platform of Solomon's Temple was a Royal Quarter, in which were to be found the administrative buildings required by the vastly increasing elaboration of Solomon's kingdom, the palace of the king and perhaps also accommodations for his 700 wives and 300 concubines (1 Kgs. 11:3), though this is a detail upon which I would not insist.

15. See Avi-Yonah 1973: 13.

16. Broshi 1974: 21-25.

17. Simons 1952: 175-188.

18. A section of that "other wall" was unearthed high up on the western hill by Nahum Avigad during his excavations in the Jewish quarter of the Old City (Avigad 1983: 46-54).

19. The high places of pagan gods adorned, if not originally built, by Solomon re-

mained on the "mountain east of Jerusalem" for two and a half centuries (2 Kgs. 23:13-14).

20. Manasseh may possibly have placed the idol he made in the Holy of Holies. Haran (1963: 50-51) thinks that it was on this occasion that the Ark of the Covenant was removed from the Temple, never to be seen again. Most connect this disappearance with the Babylonian plundering of the Temple, but there is no specific mention of it in that connection. Nor is there here, however, and if Manasseh had in fact removed the Ark of the Covenant, it would be even more likely mentioned as a single but malicious act rather than as a consequence of a general destruction of the Temple.

21. On this newly discovered Book of the Law as Deuteronomy, see Haran 1978: 137 and n. 7. Where the Mishneh or "second" quarter of Jerusalem lay cannot be determined for certain since we know so little of the urban topography of Israelite Jerusalem, but it was likely one of the new quarters, that is, outside the old David-Solomon city complex on the eastern hill. According to Avigad 1983: 54: "Our excavations now point to the Mishneh as having been situated on the Western Hill; this hill, set off from the City of David by a deep valley, naturally developed into the second quarter of the city, alongside the parent 'downtown.' "

22. On the Temple reforms of Josiah, as well as those of Hezekiah that preceded them, see Haran 1978: 132-148.

23. The later Jewish tradition sometimes identified this "Stone of Foundation" with that under the Muslim Dome of the Rock atop Mount Moriah; see Vilnay 1973: 17-36 and Chapter Five.

24. Kenyon 1974: 170-171.

25. For the condition of Jerusalem after the Exile, see Avi-Yonah 1973: 14; Kenyon 1974: 179-180; Mazar 1975: 193-194, 200.

26. Mazar 1975: 200, relying in part on Neh. 11.

27. See in particular Mazar 1975: 193 for his reading of Neh. 3:8, often translated as "they reconstructed Jerusalem as far as the wide wall." If this latter is, as it seems to be, the wall discovered by Avigad in the Jewish quarter, it would mean that Nehemiah's city still extended to the western hill. Mazar, however, questions "reconstructed" and argues that the word means "abandoned," which fits in better with the archeological evidence, or rather its absence, on the western hill. As Avigad himself concedes (1983: 62): "From all of this above [the absence of archeological remains on the western hill dating from Nehemiah's day] we can conclude that the minimalist view of the settlement in Jerusalem in the period of the Return to Sion is correct—that is, that it was limited to the narrow confines of the City of David, and that the Mishneh (quarter) on the Western Hill remained desolate and uninhabited."

28. See Simons 1952: 429. This conjecture is doubtless influenced by the fact that it was in this place that the Hasmoneans built their citadel called Baris or the Birah and Herod his Fortress Antonia.

29. For a hypothesis on the site and extent of the platform for Zerubbabel's Temple, see Kenyon 1974 cited in my n. 10 above.

NOTES TO CHAPTER 2

1. Tcherikover 1959: 41-47.

2. See Kenyon 1974: 188.

3. For the use of this passage from Aristeas' account of Jerusalem in attempting to date the *Letter of Aristeas*, see Moses Hadas in Aristeas 1951: 139n.

4. Here, as in all that follows, the citations of Josephus, whether from the *Jewish*

Antiquities or the *Jewish War*, are drawn from the Loeb Classical Library edition of his works: *The Jewish War*, trans. H. St. J. Thackeray; *Antiquities of the Jews*, trans. H. St. J. Thackeray (bks. I-VII), R. Marcus (bks. VIII-XIV), A. Wikgren (bks. XV-XVII), and L. Feldman (bks. XVIII-XX) (Cambridge, Mass.: Harvard University Press, 1926-1965).

5. On the precise meaning of the terms in Antiochus' decree of 200 B.C., see Bickerman 1935.

6. In his treatise *Against Apion* Josephus quotes Hecateus to the effect that "the total number of Jewish priests who receive a tithe of the revenue and administer public affairs is about fifteen hundred." The Jewish law granted these tithes to the Levites (Num. 18:21,24), but it is not unlikely that the priests had appropriated that privileged income for themselves, as was certainly the case later; see Stern 1974: 141-142, commenting on the Hecateus passage.

7. As in the preceding and the following chapters, all citations from the Hebrew Bible are taken from *A New Translation of the Holy Scriptures according to the Masoretic Text*; see Chapter One, n. 1 above. Those from the Biblical Apocrypha and the New Testament are according to *The New English Bible with the Apocrypha* (New York: Oxford University Press, 1976).

8. On the use of the text in Exodus to justify a second-century B.C. tax, see Bickerman 1935: 78.

9. On the Roman subvention for the sacrifice until its discontinuance in A.D. 66, the first year of the Jewish revolt, see Bickerman 1935: 80, with an assessment of the cost of the sacrifices at that time.

10. In the sequel Heliodorus has a terrifying vision in which he is beaten by supernatural beings. As a result of this, he thinks better of confiscating the treasury. He recovered sufficiently to assassinate Seleucus IV in 175 B.C. For a detailed commentary on this passage and what it reveals of Temple finances, see Tcherikover 1959: 157 and nn. 10, 12.

11. There is a commentary on this text forbidding the entry of aliens into the Temple in Bickerman 1946-1948; and cf. Tcherikover 1959: 84-87.

12. See note 54 for the preserved Herodian era inscription, when the penalty for Gentile intrusion into the Temple was execution on the spot.

13. On Antiochus IV, see in summary Tcherikover 1959: 175-178 and Schürer 1973: 146-148; and in considerable detail, Morkholm 1966.

14. For a summary description of Hellenism in the Near East, see Peters 1983; and on the economic conditions of Hellenism and the upper priestly classes in Jerusalem, Tcherikover 1959: 119-120.

15. See Tcherikover 1959: 162, and in general, idem 161-169, for a description of the polis-izing of Jerusalem.

16. It was not Herod's citadel at the western gate of the city but an old Israelite tower called Hananel, refortified by Nehemiah (2:8), then used by the Ptolemies and fortified once again by the Hasmoneans, who called it "Baris." The same place is referred to in Ecclesiasticus or Bar Sirah 50:1-3: "It was the high priest Simon son of Onias [ca. 225-200 B.C.] in whose lifetime the House [of the Lord] was repaired, in whose days the Temple was fortified. He laid the foundation of the high double wall, and the high retaining [fortress?] wall of the Temple precinct. In his day they dug the reservoir, a cistern broad as the sea" (see Finegan 1969: 118).

17. Cf. Schürer 1973: 152n.37: "In fact, there is no reliable account of the actual series of events leading to the persecution proper, and the student is reduced to hypotheses based on his knowledge of the general situation. At this level there is of course

abundant evidence that the imposition of Gentile cults was welcomed or accepted by a substantial section of the Jewish population; cf. Hengel 1974: I, 287f. The possibility of an actual initiative on their part is suggested by the parallel case of the Samaritan request (made, however, after the inception of the persecution) to have their temple dedicated to Zeus Xenios." See also Bickerman 1937, 1979.

18. See Bickerman 1979: 62-71 for an exegesis of these texts of Maccabees; and for the sacred stones, the passage of 1 Macc. 4:43 describing the restoration in 164 B.C.: ". . . and they purified the Temple, removing to an unclean place the stones which defiled it."

19. The problem of the location of the Akra is described in detail in Schürer 1973: 154n.39.

20. The Akra would not, of course, have been directly south of the Herodian Temple, which did not then exist and which extended its platform southward over the presumed site of the Akra (see Tsafrir 1976: 86). The hill of the Akra, which once loomed higher than the Temple mount, was substantially levelled in the mid-second century B.C.

21. This last paragraph in Maccabees marks the origin of the "Feast of the Dedication of the Temple," called in Greek the Encaenia (*enkainia*), whose celebration in Jerusalem in Jesus' day is noted in John 10:22. Josephus (*Ant.* XII, 7, 7) calls it "Lights," and in Hebrew it was Hanukka and celebrated for eight days (see Stein 1954). The Christians later celebrated it in Jerusalem as the feast of the dedication of the Church of the Holy Sepulcher.

22. In 1 Macc. 14:37 it is said, however, that "he [Simon] settled Jews in it [the Akra] and fortified it for the security of the Jews and of the city" (see Schürer 1973: 192).

23. On the "ancient wall" of Jerusalem, see the texts of Josephus cited below and Avi-Yonah 1975: 221-224; on the remains of the Hasmonean fortifications of Jerusalem, see Johns 1950; Amiran/Eitan 1970; Bliss/Dickie 1898.

24. See Avi-Yonah 1975: 251-253.

25. Josephus probably refers here to the outworks of the Hasmonean fortress called Baris at the northwest corner of the Temple precinct.

26. The actual spoliation of the Temple treasury took place about ten years later. In 54 B.C. M. Licinius Crassus became proconsul of Judea—he died in a campaign against the Parthians the next year—and immediately confiscated the Temple treasures, 2,000 talents in gold alone and 8,000 talents worth of precious objects (Josephus, *Ant.* XIV, 7, 1 [105-109]; *War* I, 8, 8 [179]).

27. See Schürer 1973: 503.

28. Cf. the name Ophel ("the hump") frequently given to this portion of the city. Mazar 1975: 213 notes: "It should be noted that the ancient name 'Ophel' (in Aramaic *Ophla*, in Greek *Ophlas* in Josephus) was preserved through the centuries right up to the end of the Second Temple. Whereas it had been originally the citadel of the City of David, which protected the king's palace and the Temple, it became the quarters of the *nethinim*, servants of the Temple, from the time of the return from exile. In Josephus' day it served as a residential quarter lying close to the Temple. From [Josephus' description] it is clear that the Ophel extended as far as the southeastern corner of the Temple Mount walls."

29. Hippicus was one of the three massive towers built by Herod in a cluster around the present Jaffa Gate. Titus left all three of them standing after the siege of A.D 70, and one of them, probably the one named Phasael, still forms the foundations of the "Tower of David" of the Citadel of Jerusalem.

30. See Middoth 5:4.

31. See Kenyon 1974: 232.

32. For two surmises that put the Gate of the Essenes at the southwest corner of the city, opening onto Mount Sion, see Pixner 1976 and Yadin 1976/b; on Bethso, see Avi-Yonah 1975: 222-223.

33. The three most likely placements of the "second wall" are drawn onto Figure 38 in Kenyon 1974.

34. See Simons 1952. On this entire controversy, see Kenyon 1974: 232.

35. Josephus makes a slip here. Bezetha is almost certainly Beth Zayth, or "House of Olives," while "New Town" was *another* name for the district.

36. See Kenyon 1974: 237, 251-252; Mazar 1975: 83-84; Ben-Arieh/Netzer 1974; and the exchange in Kenyon/Ben-Arieh 1975.

37. See Schürer 1973: 304n.56: "An interesting report concerning a theater near Jerusalem which he discovered is given by C. Schick in PEFQS (1887), 161-166 (with plans). It lies south of the city (south-southwest of Bir Eiyub, north of Wadi Yasul). The semicircular auditorium can still be clearly recognized; it is cut from the natural rock on the north side of a hill so that the spectators had a glimpse of the city. The diameter below the seats amounts to 132 feet and the seats rise at a regular angle of 37 degrees. . . . The identification of Schick's theater with that of Herod is therefore quite possible and even probable. Even in Hadrian's restoration of the city, the site prepared by Herod will not have been abandoned." On the theater and amphitheater, see Smith 1907: 492-494; and Schalit 1969: 370-371. On the hippodrome, see Vincent/Abel 1914-1926: 34.

38. Josephus, *War* V, 8, 1; see Avi-Yonah 1975: 236-237, 240-241; Mazar 1975: 212-215.

39. See n. 30 in Chapter Three.

40. According to its excavators (Bahat/Broshi 1976: 55): "In building this palace Herod resorted to the same methods employed in the construction of the Temple enclosure: raising the area and leveling it off by means of a huge podium. The platform thus created *spread from the citadel on the north, along the Turkish wall on the west and to the south.* The eastern limits of the platform are as yet unknown, for the area to the east [in the present compound of the Armenian patriarchate and to its east] is densely built up and cannot be investigated. The platform extended over an area of about 300-350 meters from north to south and some 60 meters, at least, from west to east. The enormous quantities of earth fill were stabilized by a network of supporting walls, four of which were revealed in our excavations [in the Armenian gardens, 1970-1971]. Of the superstructure of the palace nothing has been found, neither in our excavations nor in those in the Citadel to the north, nor in Kathleen Kenyon's area L south of the platform." Cf. the earlier reports in Johns 1950 and Amiran/Eitan 1970.

41. The evidence on the structure of the Fortress Antonia is collected and discussed in Benoit 1971, 1976.

42. On the extension of the Antonia, see Benoit 1976; and on the question of its southern side, Benoit 1971: 139, 161.

43. The very large bibliography on the subject of Herod's Temple has been conveniently collected in Goldschmidt-Lehmann 1981.

44. See Netzer 1981 and the discussion following his article in the text.

45. In *War* V, 1, 5, Josephus describes Agrippa II's attempt to underpin the sanctuary, which was interrupted by the outbreak of the war with Rome. This must have been at the southern end of the platform, which is built over fill and vaults. It is in this same area that Palestine's frequent earthquakes did their damage to the al-Aqsa Mosque, which perches on this southern end.

46. Josephus *seems* to be saying that at least part of the eastern side of the enclosure was already in place from an earlier era and that Herod simply incorporated it into his own work. This may, then, be the origin of the "seam" on the eastern side: the pre-Herodian eastern portico north of it and Herod's extension to the south.

47. The doubts about the identity of the Herodian and the Muslim platforms and some possible solutions are put forward in Benoit 1971: 139, 161; Jacobson 1980: 33-36; and particularly Bagatti 1979: 11-13.

48. Mazar 1975: 28-29.

49. See Avi-Yonah 1975: 241.

50. On the evidence for the Sheep Pool and sanctuary associated with it in Herod's time, see Duprez 1970; cf. Wilkinson 1977: 170; and Wilkinson 1978: 95-105. By at least the fifth century A.D. there was a Christian church there, and at the time of the Crusades it was the site of St. Anne's.

51. Finegan 1969: 129-130; and for the Herodian construction of the Golden Gate, Corbett 1952: 7-8.

52. Finegan 1969: 130; on Wilson's Arch, see idem, 132; Stinespring 1966, 1967; and Mazar 1975: 217-219. Stinespring found that Wilson's Arch was an integral part of the Herodian Temple platform wall, and so even if the bridge did exist earlier—it figures in Pompey's siege of the city in 63 B.C.—it was rebuilt when Herod constructed the Temple platform.

53. The southernmost entry to the Temple enclosure has been plausibly reconstructed by its excavator Benjamin Mazar; see Mazar 1976: 26-27.

54. Two copies of the Greek version of the inscription on the courts of the Temple have been found; see Finegan 1969: 119-120. They read: "No alien may enter within the balustrade around the sanctuary and the enclosure. Whoever is caught, on himself shall be put the blame for the death which will ensue." There is a detailed commentary on this text in Bickerman 1946-1947.

55. On the question of who first noticed the rock and when, see Jacobson 1980: 39.

56. See Avi-Yonah 1976: 13; Jacobson 1980: 33-37.

57. Pro: Renov 1970 (though with Avi-Yonah's extraordinary "Editor's Note," pp. 73-74); Avi-Yonah 1975: 255; and Rosenau 1979. Contra: Gutmann 1973: 42; and Schaefer 1981: 98-101.

58. On the number of visitors to the Temple, see Jermeias 1969; and for a discussion of the population of Jerusalem before A.D 70, see Bayatt 1973; and Wilkinson 1974.

NOTES TO CHAPTER 3

1. On the accession and administration of Roman Judea, see Schürer 1973: 357-398.

2. Schürer 1973: 361-362. The only reason that the place of the governor's residence has been called into question is the later traditional identification of the Antonia as the place of Jesus' trial before the Roman prefect Pilate; for the far more convincing case that Jesus was tried in Herod's former palace, see Benoit 1952, 1971, 1976.

3. Schürer 1973: 366.

4. There are some slight differences between the accounts of Josephus and Philo (see Kraeling 1942; and Schwartz 1983).

5. See Mazar 1976.

6. This and all the following citations from the New Testament are from *The New English Bible, with the Apocrypha* (New York: Oxford University Press, 1976).

7. On the Gospels as sources for the life and topography of first-century Jerusalem, see Jeremias 1969; Wilkinson 1978.

8. The upper room mentioned in Mark 14 is the *coenaculum*, or dining room, located by the later Christian tradition on Mount Sion (see Wilkinson 1977: 173).

9. Later Christian tradition located the house of Caiaphas on Mount Sion, near the room identified as that where Jesus held his Passover supper (see Baldi 1955: 561f.; and Wilkinson 1977: 153).

10. Jesus was likely brought before Pilate in the former palace of Herod (see n.2 above and cf. Wilkinson 1978: 137-142). The earliest Christian pilgrims had "Pilate's house" pointed out to them in the Tyropean Valley, not far from the western wall of the Temple, and it was only later that it was relocated on the former site of the Antonia (see the texts in Baldi 1955: 581f.; and Wilkinson 1977: 168).

11. It is not implausible that Herod Antipas, tetrarch of Galilee from 4 B.C. to A.D. 39 (cf. Schürer 1973: 340-353), was in Jerusalem for Passover. A much later Christian tradition put his "house" on Lady Mary Street across from the site of "Pilate's Pretorium," that is, the former Antonia. We do not know where Herod Antipas resided during his visits to Jerusalem, but we do know that a later member of the family, Agrippa II, stayed at the former Hasmonean Palace at the ridge of the western hill overlooking the Temple, and it is not unlikely that Antipas would have done likewise (see Wilkinson 1978: 142).

12. In the version in Jn. 19:5 Jesus is taken out still arrayed in these garments of mock royalty and displayed by Pilate to the crowd with the words "Behold the man," in the Vulgate version, *"Ecce homo."* The Ecce Homo Arch was later shown to Christian pilgrims spanning Lady Mary Street, as it still does today. The arch is in fact Roman, but from the time of Hadrian; it constituted part of his eastern forum. The north pedestrian walkway of the same arch may still be seen in the basement of the Convent of the Sisters of Sion.

13. See the late texts in Baldi 1955: 593-616.

14. See Wilkinson 1978: 144-151.

15. For the excavations behind and beneath the traditional Golgotha, see Bagatti/Testa 1978.

16. Matthew, Mark, and John, if they were all whom the tradition says they were, may well have been eyewitnesses to the place. But what of Luke? Coüasnon 1974: 7: "He arrived in Jerusalem around the year 58, accompanying St. Paul. He was aware of the ancient text of the story of the visit of the holy women to the Tomb, since he used it himself in his own writings. Thus, the knowledge of this tradition is inseparable from a knowledge of the site to which it is attached. It appears difficult to admit, therefore, that Luke never saw the tomb. In short, Jesus really was placed in the tomb and the holy women saw where he was placed. Through them, the Christian community of Jerusalem knew where the tomb was located and the authors of the Gospels speak of it as a well-known place. Thus one can say that the tradition was already established when St. Luke came to Jerusalem in A.D. 58 and that he became familiar with this tradition."

17. See Wilkinson 1978: 164-171.

18. For the visitors to early Christian Jerusalem, see Jeremias 1969: 62-72; and for their number, idem, 77-86.

19. Jeremias 1969: 60-62.

20. The site of the stoning of St. Stephen was likewise shown by the Christian tradition to be on Mount Sion, though in the fifth century his burial place was miraculously shown outside the northern gate of the city.

21. A letter in support of admitting Gentiles into the Church without the restriction that they become Jews first was sent in the name of the Apostles and elders to the Gentile members of the Church in "Antioch, Syria, and Cilicia" (see Paul's version in Gal. 2:6, 9-10, and 1 Cor. 8:8 and 10:27).

22. On Paul's seizure by the Roman garrison of Jerusalem, see Schürer 1973: 366.

23. On the troubled rule of Felix in Judea, see Schürer 1973: 460-466.

24. That is, he was authorized to wear priestly robes.

25. This "parapet," from where James was to preach to the people of Jerusalem, was later identified by the Christians with the same "pinnacle of the Temple" upon which Jesus was tempted and was shown to pilgrims at the southeast corner of the Temple platform, where the Herodian masonry still stands higher than at any other point (see Finegan 1969: 125-126).

26. If James was buried on the spot, it was certainly not in the city but likely at the southeast corner of the Haram or somewhere along the eastern side that this occurred. Fullers would need water for their work, and that too suggests Kedron or Siloam.

27. See Schürer 1979: 231-232.

28. See Jeremias 1969: 12-13, 22.

29. The Hasmonean Palace, unused by Herod, who built his own further west by the Citadel, was located at the old Xystus on the ridge of the Upper City. It must be recalled that at that time the Tyropean Valley between the Temple and this western hill was considerably deeper than it is today, and so both the position and the prospect of buildings on the western ridge line was far more commanding vis-à-vis the Temple.

30. We know of no such tradition that prohibited one from watching proceedings in the Temple, and moreover, it is difficult to understand how he could have seen *anything*. The Temple building was very high and he was looking at it from *behind*.

31. "Upper Market" refers to the Upper City on the western hill; the richest part of Jerusalem, between the Citadel and the old Hasmonean Palace.

32. This is the viaduct that leads out from the Temple over Wilson's Arch and generally followed the line of the present Gate of the Chain Street.

33. On the custom of the rulers of Jerusalem providing the sacrifices for the Temple, see Schürer 1979: 311-312; and Chapter Two.

34. See Neusner 1970; and for the escape of Rabbi Yohanan ben Zakkai in particular, pp. 157-166. He dates it to the spring or summer of A.D. 68.

35. That is, the unidentified place where Sennecharib army had camped.

36. The site of King Alexander's tomb is unidentified.

37. Josephus probably refers here to the "Pool of the Patriarch's Baths" near the Jaffa Gate.

38. On the ceasing of the daily offering, see Num. 28:6; and Schürer 1979: 299-301. And cf. Mishna Taanith 4:6: "On 17 Tammuz the daily offering (*tamid*) ceased."

39. Schürer 1973: 506n.115, citing Montefiore 1962, notes there is good reason to think that Josephus in *War* VI, 4, 3, was attempting to whitewash Titus.

40. Both Jer. 52:12f. and the rabbinical tradition put the burning of the Temple on the ninth of Macedonian Lous, or the Hebrew Ab, while Josephus here says the tenth. What happened on the previous day was, however, ritually more significant, the burning down of the gates, those barriers against impurity, and so the desacralization of the Temple (cf. Schürer 1973: 506n.115).

41. Asochaeus is the biblical Shishak, in 992 B.C. (1 Kgs. 14:25f.).

42. "Melchizedek," in the Canaanite tongue, means "Righteous King." The same etymology is given in Heb. 7:2. In Gen. 14:18 Melchizedek is called "king of Salem," probably an archaic name for Jerusalem.

43. For the later Jewish retelling of this story of the sparing of parts of Jerusalem, but to a very different end, see Chapter Six.

44. Davies 1982: 42-43 notes:

Other elements in the Jewish liturgy also commemorate the destruction. For three weeks of sorrow, ending on the ninth day of Ab, the fifth month of the Jewish calendar, which is entirely given over to fasting, Jews annually recall the devastation of their Land and of Jerusalem. So much has that event become the quintessence of the suffering of Jewry that the Ninth of Ab is recognized as a day on which disasters again and again struck the Jewish people. The essential feature of the liturgy for the Ninth of Ab (which is the only twenty-four hour fast, apart from the Day of Atonement) was the reading of lamentations and dirges. Later, on the fast of the Ninth of Ab, an addition which concentrates on Jerusalem still further was made to the service. The prayer, as used today, begins with the words:

> "O Lord God, comfort the mourners of Zion;
> Comfort those who grieve for Jerusalem."

It ends with:

> "Praised are You, O Lord, who comforts Zion.
> Praised are you, who rebuilds Jerusalem."

45. The arguments pro and con for a Jewish settlement in Jerusalem between the wars are rehearsed in Lifshitz 1977: 471-472.

46. *Travels* 43 in Wilkinson 1891: 141.

47. Pinkerfeld 1960; and cf. Hirschberg 1976: 116-117. Some doubt has been cast on the identification of this structure as a late Roman synagogue, however, by Mackowski (1980: 145), who denies the crucial point of the orientation of the niche toward the Temple mount.

48. See Stinespring 1939; Smallwood 1976: 431-432.

49. There are two other alleged causes of the Jewish revolt of A.D. 132: 1) a purported ban by Hadrian upon circumcision (see Smallwood 1976: 429-431); and 2) a promise made and then unkept to rebuild the Temple (idem, 434-436; Lifshitz 1977: 473). Generally on the causes of the revolt, see Schaefer 1981: 29-50.

50. Smallwood 1976: 444; and cf. Schaefer 1981: 82, who is not entirely convinced that the Jewish rebels drove the Romans out of Jerusalem. Two of the chief texts are Appian, *Syriaca* 50: "Jerusalem, which Ptolemy of Egypt had overthrown, was repopulated; Vespasian destroyed it and in my own time Hadrian did the same"; and Jerome, *In Jer.* 31:15: "At its final capture under Hadrian, when the very city of Jerusalem was destroyed, an uncountable number of people of different ages and sexes were sold at the 'market of the Terebinth,' a reference to the famous fair organized at Mamre near Hebron during the festival of the Terebinth."

51. See Lifshitz 1977: 476-478; and for a more skeptical analysis, Schaefer 1981: 85-88.

52. See Smallwood 1976: 445; Lifshitz 1977: 480; and Schaefer 1981: 98-100.

53. On this passage in the *Paschal Chronicle*, see Schürer 1973: 554-555.

54. It was the Hadrianic forum north of the Temple mount to which the so-called Ecce Homo Arch and its continuation under the convent of the Sisters of Sion formed the entry (see Benoit 1971).

55. Part of the entry to the forum south of the Church of the Holy Sepulcher is still visible in the basement of the Alexander Hospice there (see Finegan 1969: 137-138; Lux 1972).

56. See Hennesey 1970.

57. Avigad 1983: 205-207, 226.

58. See Wilkinson 1981: 157 and n. 4, with additions on p. 321.

59. For the archeological evidence on Hadrian's Capitolium, see Corbo 1982: I, 34-37.

1. On these earliest Christian pilgrims to Jerusalem, see Wilkinson 1981: 10-11.

2. Wilkinson 1981: 12.

3. The "common enemy" in Eusebius' *Life of Constantine* was probably a reference to Constantine's imperial rival Licinius, who was killed in A.D. 326.

4. For the most recent archeological exploration of the Holy Sepulcher complex, always rendered difficult by the delicate political situation within the church, see Corbo 1982: 1, 39-138; and in summary in Coüasnon 1974.

5. Constantine's choice of the basilica, a building type in the Roman secular and imperial tradition, for his Christian buildings at Jerusalem and elsewhere was already significant (see Krautheimer 1967).

6. It may not have been mere carelessness on Eusebius' part not to mention St. Helena's discovery of the Cross; Rubin (1982: 86-87) sees in it an echo of the rivalry between the Sees of Jerusalem and Caesarea.

7. 2 Chr. 7:5, 9; Jn. 10:22; cf. Black 1954.

8. Wilkinson (1981: 35) comments: "Another local word equally meaning 'monks and nuns' is 'apotactites' (literally 'people set apart'), and there is no reason to suppose that these had a rule of life distinct from the *monachi*."

9. The text in Genesis suggests that of the three people who conversed with Abraham, two were angels and the third was God himself, the latter identified by the early Christian tradition as Jesus, "the Son of God."

10. On the Constantinian construction at Hebron, see Armstrong 1967: 95.

11. See Wilkinson 1981: 157n.4, and p. 321.

12. The belief that some stones on the Temple platform were stained with the blood of Zacharias grew out of the normal and long-prevailing confusion between John the Baptist's father, who served in the Temple, and the Zacharias of 2 Chron. 24:20-22, who was murdered in the courtyard of the Temple. (See Wilkinson 1981: 183n.9).

13. See Wilkinson 1981: 158nn.8, 9.

14. On the policy of Julian toward the Jews, see Lewy 1941/1983; Avi-Yonah 1976: 191-204; Meeks/Wilkin 1978: 28-32.

15. According to Socrates (*Church History* III, 20), "fire came down from heaven and consumed all the builders' tools."

16. Wilkinson 1981: 35: "It is noticeable that Egeria normally uses the word *monachi* (monks) to describe the religious outside Jerusalem, and *monazontes* for those who attend the services in the city, a word often used by Cyril of the same group. But the words are not mutually exclusive, and Egeria explains that *monazontes* meant monks and *parthenae* (virgins) nuns according to the local usage of Jerusalem."

17. As we saw, in the Bordeaux pilgrim's time, the tomb of Jesus was simply a small shrine standing in the open air. By 380 it was inside a larger building, which Egeria also calls a "basilica," and which is certainly the circular domed structure remarked upon by later visitors.

18. Wilkinson 1981: 156n.4: "According to the graphic account in bGittin 7:68a, Solomon tied a male and a female demon together to make them tell him where to find Ashmedai, the prince of the demons. When he was found, he came to stay with Solomon and helped him build the Temple. . . . There is no other reference to the Horn as a relic."

19. There were two churches on the Mount of Olives, the earlier and larger, built by Constantine and his mother, was called the "Eleona" or "Olivet" and marked the place

where Jesus had taught His disciples the secrets of the Kingdom. The other, marking the place of Jesus Ascension into heaven, was at the very summit and was called the "Imbomon." In this and the following passages, Egeria also uses "Eleona" as a name of the mount itself. On these two churches, see Wilkinson 1977: 166-167. A detailed description of the Imbomon by the pilgrim Arculf ca. A.D. 680 is cited in Chapter Five.

20. Letter 58, cited in Wilkinson 1981: 21.

21. The history of the early movement of monks to Palestine is given in Chitty 1966, esp. chap. 5.

22. See Wilkinson 1977: 4-5.

23. Tsafrir 1979.

24. Mazar 1975: 254: "The impressive building we discovered in the area south of the Triple Eastern Huldah Gate and the Single Gate turned out to be the cloister described by the historian Theodosius in A.D. 530. He located it below the corner of the Temple Mount. . . . During the second phase of its existence in the sixth century A.D., the building was a three-storied structure surrounded by walls, with only one gate on the west side. We found two cisterns and a number of tombs in the basement from which bones had been removed long since. We deduce, therefore, that the building served a different purpose in the initial phase of its existence, i.e., the fifth century, and that it may originally have been Eudocia's palace which was turned into a convent in the days of Emperor Justinian." See photos, Mazar 1975: 250-253.

25. Juvenal's opportunism on behalf of himself and his see are described in detail by Honigmann 1950, and the earlier stages of Jerusalem's rivalry with Caesarea by Rubin 1982.

26. Barsauma's *Life*, ed. François Nau, is the basis of Nau 1927, from which the following citations are taken.

27. See Peeters 1950: 53-58; and for the constructions in Kafr Gamla, Vincent/Abel 1914-1926: 766-804.

28. See Abel 1952: II, 335-336.

29. Abel 1952: II, 336.

30. On the archeological and literary evidence for Mount Sion and Siloam in the mid-fifth century, see Tsafrir 1977: 155-160. Another sure sign of the urban development toward the south was the extension of the Roman north-south cardo—which in Hadrian's time apparently reached only as far as David Street—southward toward Mount Sion. As Professor Nahum Avigad, who discovered the remains of this major Byzantine artery in the Jewish quarter, writes (1983: 226): "The *cardo* of Jerusalem, in the section which we uncovered in the southern part of the Old City, was not a component of Roman Aelia Capitolina, but belonged exclusively to the Byzantine city. This fits in well with our previous conclusion that the built up parts of the Roman city did not extend into the southern part of the Old City." For the cardo generally, see Avigad 1983: 213-228. Avigad (226-228) now inclines to the view that this southern extension of the cardo was the work of Justinian, who thereby intended to link the older street system to his "New Church."

31. See Armstrong 1979: 28-30; and for a list of foundations and donors, see Ovadiah 1970.

32. On Sabas and his monastic and theological environment, see Chitty 1966: 101-122.

33. Sometime before A.D. 400 Roman Palestine was subdivided into three distinct provinces, with First Palestine corresponding to Judea, Second to Galilee and the Golan, and Third to Idumea and the Negev.

34. An indiction was a tax cycle of fifteen years used in this period as a chronological era.

35. Justinian's hospital is a prototype institution. The hostel or hospice for the reception of travellers was a commonplace in the Greco-Roman world, but a building and staff dedicated to the care and *boarding* of the ill was an innovation of the sixth century and appears closely connected with the growth of Christian pilgrimage (see Philipsborn 1961).

36. The enormity of Justinian's church complex is confirmed by a pilgrim from Piacenza who was in Jerusalem in A.D. 570: "From Sion we went to the basilica of St. Mary, with its great congregation of monks, and its guest houses for men and women. In catering for travellers they have a vast number of tables and more than three thousand beds for the sick."

37. See Avigad 1977 and now Avigad 1983: 229-246 for both the excavation and the dedication inscription of Justinian's church.

38. "The Church of St. Mary which was cast down by an earthquake and was swallowed up by the earth . . . " (*Commemoratorium*).

39. These "measures" are measured replicas. Similar replicas were taken for shrouds at the tomb of Jesus in the Church of the Holy Sepulcher.

40. The transfer of this tradition of David's tomb from Bethlehem to Mount Sion, where it was confidently located at the time of the Crusades, had obviously not yet taken place.

41. The Christian and Jewish "competition" for the same holy places, here apparently quite peaceful, despite the implication of events that led to the construction of a "screen," reaches back to the earliest days of Christian pilgrimage (Wilkinson 1981: 19, 296-297).

42. Paulinus of Nola, Letter 49, cited in Wilkinson 1977: 40.

43. On the early relics, see Wilkinson 1977: 41-42; and for their political implication for other churches in other cities, Dagron 1977: 23.

44. The complex evidence on the complex problem of the Golden Gate is reviewed in Bagatti 1979: 13-19.

45. See Corbett 1952.

46. On the Madaba map, see Avi-Yonah 1954; and for its schematic reproduction, see the endpapers of Wilkinson 1977.

47. The most coherent account of the Jews' reclaiming the Temple mount in A.D. 614, based on the Jewish *Book of Zerubbabel*, is given in Avi-Yonah 1976: 266-267.

48. Avi-Yonah 1976: 269.

49. On the name "Saracen," see Chapter Eleven n. 24.

NOTES TO CHAPTER 5

1. For an analysis of these Muslim traditions on the destruction of the Temple, see Soucek 1976: 77-78.

2. Soucek 1976: 81.

3. See Goitein 1982: 186.

4. 1 Kgs. 8:44, 48; Berakot 4: 5, 6 in Danby 1933: 5. In Muhammad's day, and long before and after, Christians prayed, and built their churches, facing the east.

5. On the so-called Sufi commentaries, see Ayoub 1984: 33-34.

6. On the origin and possible motives for the association of Jerusalem with Muhammad's Night Journey, see Goldziher 1969-1971: II, 45-46; cf. Grabar 1973: 50-52.

7. See Busse 1968: 443-448.

8. See Fattal 1958: 45-46; and for more abbreviated forms of the capitulation terms offered to Jerusalem, Hill 1971: 59-60.

9. What the Western tradition from the Crusaders onward called the "Church on the Holy Sepulcher" was known in Greek as the Church of the Anastasis or "Resurrection," and in Arabic as *Kanîsat al-Qiyâma*. No Muslim author early or late seemed to be able to resist punning on the word *Qiyâma* and calling it, disparagingly, the *Kanîsat al-Qumâma*, or "Church of the Dungheap." The Muslims in fact recognized neither Jesus' death on the cross nor his subsequent resurrection from the dead (Quran 4:157-158). According to the Muslim tradition, Jesus ascended to heaven from the Mount of Olives while still alive and he will return again to earth to suffer death, as every man must, before the Last Day (see Parrinder 1957).

10. As implied by Sophronius' earlier Christmas Eve sermon and his reference here to the "Abomination of Desolation," there was considerable Byzantine soul-searching on the theological implications of the fall of Jerusalem to infidels (see Kaegi 1969).

11. A reference to the Jewish legend that the western wall *of the Temple* will never be destroyed; from the context it is clear that Jewish prayer in Jerusalem took place on the *eastern* side of the Temple mount, at the Gate of Mercy or the Golden Gate.

12. Petachia of Ratisbon, a Jewish visitor to Jerusalem during the Crusader occupation, had heard or copied a similar story about the rediscovery of the Temple site (Adler 1966: 88). In Petachia's version, however, the unnamed caliph, called simply "a friend of the Jews," promises that only the Jews will pray in his building. "Then the Gentiles came and put up images, that fell down."

13. "Gate of Mercy" is the name commonly given to one of the two entries to the so-called Golden Gate on the eastern side of the Haram precinct.

14. The text of Benjamin of Tudela referred to here is cited in Chapter Eight.

15. See Mann 1920-1922: I, 46; and Chapter Six.

16. See Mann 1920-1922: I, 45-46; and Mann 1935: 19.

17. The medieval Muslim descriptions of the Aqsa Mosque are collected and translated in Le Strange 1890: 89-113 and its complex history of destruction and rebuilding traced in Hamilton 1947.

18. Today only part of the rock is visible through the opening in the pavement that surrounds it under the shrine of the Dome of the Rock. It was, however, briefly exposed in 1959 for repair work in the Dome and this is the way it appeared to someone who was there on that occasion:

> The actual state of its preservation testifies to the fact that the rock actually was covered. Let us leave aside the gouges worked on the visible part of it, probably to fix a grill on it before the Crusades and a cloister and pavement during the Crusader period. The part of the rock which is under the pavement of the mosque appears generally untouched, with its natural slopes and furrows. During the work of restoration we also noticed in its cracks traces of yellow earth, which likewise appeared natural. Once the surface of the rock was stripped completely bare, a drawing made on 27 January 1959 permits us to get some idea of its general appearance. The area under the cupola and so immediately around the (normally exposed) "rock" is generally flat; the part under the outer corridor (ambulatory), particularly near the walls, slopes downward. There is in one place some marks and cuttings, but we were able to see only two deeper cavities, one near the eastern and one near the western wall, like two tombs cut out under the pavement, and the one on the east extends slightly under the (mosque) wall. On the southeast side three stones give the appearance of part of a wall, with its western face polished. Two of them are laid on their long side; the third, in the middle, is in the opposite direction. Thus the rock gives no sign of levelling done for the purpose of putting down the foun-

dations of walls and even less for the installation of any kind of cultic apparatus, nor any trace of wear from the passing of the faithful. . . . (Bagatti 1979: 28-299)

19. How quickly the Muslims were drawn to the rock atop the Temple mount is still a somewhat open question since Arculf, who saw fit to note the Muslim al-Aqsa Mosque in 580, says nothing about the Rock.

20. The legends concerning the Rock, both Jewish and Muslim, though without much regard for chronology, are conveniently collected in Vilnay 1973: 5-36.

21. The principal Muslim descriptions of the Dome of the Rock throughout the course of the Middle Ages, many of which will be cited in the following chapters, have been collected and translated in Le Strange 1890: 114-137.

22. The modern Western canonization begins with Goldziher 1969-1971: II, 46-48, and is often repeated thereafter. For its convincing refutation, see Goitein 1966: 135-138; and Grabar 1973: 49-50.

23. See Grabar 1973: 65-67 for the confirmatory evidence provided by the Dome of the Rock itself.

24. The benign reading of the historical role of the "Ishmaelite" Arabs should be compared with the tenth-century Karaite exegesis cited in Chapter Six.

25. For the evidence for the identifications suggested for these anonymous apocalyptic figures in the text, see Lewis 1950: 327-328.

26. See Goitein 1982: 176.

27. See Jacobson 1980: 33-34; and Chapter Three.

28. The original reports of the Umayyad Palace excavation are in Mazar 1969 and 1971; and the summing up in Mazar 1975: 264-266; and Ben-Dov 1982: 293-322.

29. The expression "Navel of the Earth" was already used by Jerome in his commentary on Ezek. 5:5.

30. Arculf's sketches of the Holy Sepulcher in A.D. 680 are reproduced in Wilkinson 1977: plates 1-6.

31. Early there had been a golden cross at the Church of Golgotha, the gift of the Emperor Theodosius. Wilkinson 1977: 97n.15 suggests that Theodosius' cross disappeared in the Persian looting of 614 and that this was a replacement.

32. Goitein 1982: 180.

33. The original measurements of the Haram are given in "ells," a unit which Le Strange 1890: 121 calculates at eighteen inches in length. The figures in the text cited have been converted into feet.

34. Le Strange 1890: 121 comments: "With this description of the year 903 the Dome of the Rock as it now stands tallies to a remarkable degree. . . . The perimeter of the the octagonal walls stated at 360 ells [540 feet], gives 45 ells, or 67½ feet for the length of each face of the octagon; the measurement today is 66 feet."

35. Al-Khidr or al-Khadr, the "green man," is mentioned in Quran 18:59-81 and thereafter found a widespread cult in Islam, where he was sometimes identified with Elias and sometimes with St. George (see Kriss/Kriss-Heinrich 1960: 154 f.).

NOTES TO CHAPTER 6

1. Goitein 1982: 180-181.

2. Le Strange 1890: 118-119.

3. Goitein 1982: 182.

4. On the connection of Charlemagne's alleged pilgrimage with the sense of the approach of the millennium, see Cohn 1970: 32.

5. See in particular Bréhier 1928.

6. The argument against a "protectorate" is taken up in detail in Joranson 1927 who concludes (p. 254): "Summed up, the admissible testimony signifies: 1) that Charles dispatched alms to Palestine, and that some part of these alms may have been expended on the repair of churches; 2) that he may have been the founder of a hospice which ca. 870 bore his name; and 3) that he may have equipped the library which elicited the admiration of the monk Bernard. But to concede thus much is not to arrive at a protectorate. For the benefactions were neither necessarily nor demonstrably dependent upon a protectorate."

7. See Goitein 1982: 181-182, who is willing to go further than Joranson, if not on the question of the "protectorate," then certainly on Charlemagne's donations and endowments.

8. Wilkinson 1977: 12.

9. On the poll-tax, a duty imposed on Christians and Jews from the beginning of Islam, and here levied collectively, see Gil 1980: 24-26, where the documents in evidence are from the eleventh century and pertain to the Jewish community. But as Gil notes, "they clearly reflect a situation four centuries old."

10. As we have seen in Chapter Four, the burial place of Stephen was, however, on the northern side of the city, outside the Damascus Gate.

11. This Muslim landscape in Jerusalem was all new to Bernard, as it was to most Christians. The "Temple of Solomon" may here be the entire Muslim Haram and the "Saracen synagogue" is surely the Aqsa Mosque.

12. The name "Adelacham" may represent "Abd al-Hakam" or "Abd al-Hakim" (Wilkinson 1977), but the governor of Egypt, possibly the "sultan" mentioned later in this same passage, at the time was Ahmad ibn Tulun.

13. See Mann 1920-1922: I, 45.

14. See Mann 1935: I, 313-315.

15. The arguments for this identification of both the "inner altar at the western wall" and the "cave" of the the Muslim and Jewish sources with the chamber behind Barclay's Gate are laid out in detail in Gil 1982: 270-272; for the Muslim traditions connected with the place, see Matthews 1932.

16. Auerbach 1971: 468:

> Sources about the Jews in Jerusalem up to the sixteenth century note their attachment to the site of the Holy Place but the Western Wall is not referred to specifically. In the geonic [the Fatimid] period the place of assembly and prayer of Jews was on the Mount of Olives. . . . Benjamin of Tudela (twelfth century) mentions the Western Wall together with the "Mercy Gate," which is in the eastern wall of the Temple Mount. The Western Wall is not mentioned by Nachmanides (thirteenth century) in his detailed report of the Temple site in 1267, nor in the fourteenth-century account of Estori ha-Parhi. Finally, it does not figure even in descriptions of Jerusalem in Jewish sources of the fifteenth century (e.g., Meshullam of Volterra, Obadiah of Bertinoro, etc.) [Chapter Eleven]. The name "Western Wall" used by Obadiah refers, as can be inferred from the context, to the southwestern corner of the [platform] wall, and there is no hint that there was a place of Jewish worship there.

17. For the date and the identification of the author of the *Pesikta Rabbati*, see Mann 1920-1922: I, 47-49.

18. The evidence for the earliest Karaite presence in Jerusalem is collected in Mann 1920-1922: I, 59-60.

19. Hebrew *passul*, a play on the Arabic *rasul*, "The Messenger" (of God), that is, Muhammad.

20. This and the following prophecies in Daniel's vision are generally understood to apply to Alexander the Great's successors, with the "little horn" identified as Antiochus IV Epiphanes.

21. The argument for Egyptian support of the Karaites is made by Mann 1920-1922: I, 62-63.

22. Mann 1935: 49-56.

23. See Neusner 1970: 157-165, 203-214.

24. On the Mishna, see most recently Neusner 1981; and on the Jerusalem Talmud, Neusner 1983.

25. See Goitein in his preface (xix) to the 1970 reprint of Mann 1920-1922. Goitein continues: "Because of the paucity of sources, the Jewish historian was inclined to dismiss pre-Crusader Palestine as a backwater, as irrelevant for contemporary Jewish history. All this changed with the appearance of Jacob Mann's *The Jews in Egypt and Palestine under the Fatimid Caliphs*. It was a revelation. It reclaimed pre-Crusader Palestine for Jewish history."

26. See Goitein 1971: 201.

27. See, for example, Mann 1920-1922: I, 251-280; and Goitein 1971: 40-90, 211-227.

28. On the Geniza evidence for the financial support of the Jerusalem community, see Goitein 1971: 112-121; and on the Muslim form of endowment, see Chapter Ten. For the various uses of Jewish public or "sacred" funds, the *qôdesh*, during the eleventh and twelfth centuries, see Gil 1976: 103-112.

29. See documents 11a-c and 13 in Goitein 1971: 414-415. The designation "for the poor" does not mean that they were necessarily the primary beneficiaries of the endowment; they may have been residual beneficiaries (idem, 118-119).

30. See Mann 1920-1922: I, 160.

31. It is somewhat difficult reconciling this text, which seems to emphasize the chief place of Jewish worship in Jerusalem atop the Mount of Olives, with the other references to a synagogue apparently *within* the wall of the Haram.

32. Cf. *Encyclopaedia Judaica*, s.v. "Mount of Olives": "The site of the prayers and gatherings was, according to the documents of the Genizah, above 'Absalom's monument' which was situated across from the southern third of the eastern wall of the Temple mount. This corresponds to the open space . . . which is today covered with Jewish graves, to the south of Mount's summit. Here, according to the medieval tradition, was the site 'on which the priest who burnt the red heifer stood, sought out and saw the Temple when he sprinkled the blood' (Midd. 2:6; Yoma 16a)."

33. The precise cause of the Rabbanites' excommunication of the Karaites was the latter's view of the dietary laws. See Mann 1935: 54, 65: "As regards the dietary laws, the Karaites on the one hand permitted the eating of fowl together with milk but prohibited on the other the tail-fat of animals, the slaughtering of a pregnant animal, the kidneys and the use of the large lobe of the liver. . . . Since the Karaites prohibited the eating of meat [altogether] in Jerusalem, it is rather strange that it should have at all concerned them whether the animal slaughtered underwent [ritual] examination or whether it was pregnant. . . . The evident solution to this difficulty is that the issue applied only to Ramle where the Karaites would eat meat. . . . However, the case of 'meat and milk' applied to Jerusalem proper, for though the local Karaites refrained from animal meat [in Jerusalem], they would eat fowl [with milk there] . . . and it was against this Karaite practice that the excommunication was issued."

34. The reference is to the Encaenia, or the Dedication of the Church of the Holy Sepulcher, an almost certain sign that Muqaddasi is talking about a feast cycle in *Jerusalem*.

35. One early and engaging symbol of this enjoyment of both worlds in Jerusalem is that cited by Goitein 1982: 190 from Ibn Asakir 2: 217, namely, "eating a banana in the shade of the Dome of the Rock."

36. Muqaddasi is here speaking of the celebrated Pool of Solomon to which Pilate built his troublesome aqueduct in the first century.

37. The text here has *Bâb at-Tîh*, which is rendered as the incomprehensible "Gate of the Desert of Wanderings." We accept here the emendation of *Bab al-Nia*; cf. Tsafrir 1977: 152.

38. The text has *Bab al-Balât*. *Balat* is a likely corruption of *palatium* or palace.

39. The western gate, here the "Gate of the Prayer Niche of David," was about ten meters east of the present Jaffa Gate, however, since it was the Crusaders who moved the western wall to its present line at the Jaffa Gate (see Tsafrir 1977: 154, citing Johns 1950).

40. Tsafrir 1977: 154; and cf. Broshi/Tsafrir 1977.

41. See Chapter Five, n. 35.

42. Le Strange 1890: "Roughly taken, the dimensions of the Haram area are 1,500 feet by 900 feet."

43. The Hebron sanctuary, which still survives, is actually the work of Herod.

44. The Fatimids, so called because they claimed descent from Ali and his wife Fatima, the daughter of the Prophet, were a radical and revolutionary branch of the general movement called Shi'ism which was making serious inroads in the caliph's domains in the ninth and tenth centuries. The Shi'ites denied the "traditional" (*sunni*) and consensus-affirmed succession of leadership in the Muslim community down through the line of the caliphs; they maintained instead that it was according to God's will and the specific instruction of the Prophet that both the political and spiritual leadership of the Muslim community should descend through Ali and his family, in this instance the branch derived from the union of Ali and Fatima.

45. Runciman 1954: I, 32-33.

46. On this era of bedouin anarchy in Palestine, see Gil 1981 and his English summary: page v. Goitein 1982: 184 thinks that the first major deterioration of Christian-Muslim relations in Jerusalem took place during this period, in part as a result of stronger Muslim religious ties to the city, but also, it would seem, because of the partisanship introduced by the breakdown of the normal political order.

47. The letter of Tzimisces is preserved in an Armenian version in the *Chronicle* of Matthew of Edessa, trans. A. Destourian (in Matthew of Edessa 1972) and cited here according to Walker 1977.

48. Honigmann 1961: 98-103.

49. Walker 1977: 320-321.

50. The figure 20,000 appears to be Nasir's standard one for a large number, and need not be taken literally (see Goitein 1982: 189-190).

51. Le Strange 1890: "This I understand to refer to a building occupying the position of what is now known as the Throne of Solomon."

52. See Le Strange 1890: 102-103.

NOTES TO CHAPTER 7

1. The best introduction to the debate on the causes and origins of the Crusades are Erdmann's text and Marshall Baldwin's notes in Erdmann 1977. On the Crusade as an enduring phenomenon, see Atiya 1938.

2. Cahen 1954 was among the first to draw attention to the Near Eastern milieu.

3. The same protection was later extended to the persons and property of the Crusaders; see Brundage 1969: 12-13.

4. See on this pilgrim massacre Joranson 1928.

5. On his work, now lost, on the Islamic history of the Near East, see William of Tyre 1943: introduction I, 29-30, and text I, 3: "If the reader desires to know how often and how intensely Jerusalem, worshipper of God, and the surrounding country as well, suffered under the frequent changes of conditions, circumstances and rulers, which she experienced during this time of transition, let him read the *History of the Deeds of the Princes of the East*. In that work I have compiled with much labor the chronological record of the events of five hundred and seventy years, from the time of the false prophet Muhammad to the present, which is for us the year 1182 of the Incarnation of the Lord." For the cited characterization of William, see Prawer 1972: 523.

6. That is, according to William, in 1011 and not 1009.

7. Cahen 1954: 12: "In all the lands incorporated into the Seljuq Empire, including . . . Palestine, the situation of the Christians was perfectly normal. There was perhaps a greater reluctance than under previous regimes to employ non-Muslims as high officials, but that did not affect the ordinary people and there was nothing systematic about it."

8. See Erdmann 1977: 355-371.

9. The *dhimmis* are literally "Covenanters," the protected Christian and Jewish communities in Islam.

10. The "missionary" Qutekin was one of the propaganda agents for the Isma'ili cause that al-Hakim headed.

11. Runciman 1954: I, 35; Canard 1965: 26; and for the consequences for the Jews, see Mann 1920-1922: I, 71, who thinks that the head of the Jerusalem Yeshiva had to emigrate to Ramle at this point.

12. For the demise of this "miracle," see Chapter Thirteen.

13. Canard 1965: 34-35.

14. Coüasnon 1974: 54-56.

15. The author may be referring to the churches earlier torn down by order of al-Hakim, whose stones would not unnaturally provide material for rebuilding the walls.

16. This Aqsa inscription, copied by al-Harawi in 1070 but no longer in existence, is discussed at length in van Berchem 1927: 381-392.

17. See Runciman 1948.

18. The word here, as in the text of Muqaddasi cited in Chapter Six, is *ribat*, and in the two texts we can see the evolution of the term from its original meaning of a coastal guard-post to a convent for Muslim religious, of the type that later filled Jerusalem.

19. The seventh-century patriarch of Alexandria, though the Jerusalem Hospital eventually became identified with the better-known John the Baptist.

20. On the archaeological evidence for the Hospital, see Schick 1901, 1902; and Lux 1972. On the growth of the complex, see Riley-Smith 1967: 34-35.

21. Heyd 1885: I, 104-106.

22. Mann 1920-1922: I, 71-72, and text in II, 66-68.

23. Ibid.: I, 162-163.

24. Ibid.: I, 158-161.

25. On the historical circumstances, including the Messianic expectations, that surrounded the composition of the *Mishneh Torah* see Ashtor 1956: 317-323.

NOTES TO CHAPTER 8

1. See Gabrieli 1962: 98-99; Cahen 1965b: 64; Lewis 1975: 82.

2. Goitein 1952: 163.

3. Generally on the Latin Church in Jerusalem, see Hamilton 1980.

4. Daimbert's claim had temporal as well as spiritual substance behind it: he had at his disposal a Pisan fleet anchored at Jaffa.

5. John's anonymous authority is either Bede or Arculf.

6. See Chapter Ten; on the markets of Crusader Jerusalem, see Richard 1965; Benvenisti 1970: 55-56; and Prawer 1966: 184-188.

7. They are preserved in the census of the properties of the Holy Sepulcher made in 1165 and published in Röhricht 1893-1904: #421. In A.D. 1114 Patriarch Arnulf replaced the secular canons at Holy Sepulcher with Augustinians and granted the latter various forms of income, among others "the [ecclesiastical] tithe income from the city of Jerusalem and adjacent localities, excepting only the tithes from the market, which [will continue to] belong to the Patriarch" (#75).

8. The local Syrian Christian population eventually had a court of their own, the Court of the Syrians, which judged on the basis of local customary, not statute, law and whose competence also extended to religious matters since the eastern Christians did not fall under the jurisdiction of the Latin Patriarch (Riley-Smith 1973: 87-89).

9. Cahen 1957: 186-187; Riley-Smith 1973: 86. Oddly, the Islamic *muhtasib* was itself an adaptation, again one of the very few such, of a Greco-Roman municipal office in the Near East, that of the *agoronomos* or market inspector (Foster 1970).

10. This "bridge" was likely the then-surviving elements of what has been called since the nineteenth century Wilson's Arch.

11. See the careful study of the question of *la Juiverie* in Gil 1982: 263-265.

12. This was the same convent of St. Sabas where Daniel the Abbot took up his residence while visiting the Holy City.

13. There was a variety of taxes in Jerusalem, but two of the chief were the gate duties levied on goods being brought into the city and the "sales tax" collected in the markets (Riley-Smith 1973: 94-95). It was the former that Baldwin was abolishing.

14. Benvenisti 1970: 26 continues: "The population of Crusader Jerusalem was more or less identical with its population at the end of the nineteenth century and not far from the number living within the walls [of the Old City] today." How serious the manpower problem was thought to be is reflected in the proposals for a projected Crusade put forward by Pierre Dubois (see Chapter Nine).

15. Coüasnon 1974: 57-61.

16. The Holy Fire appeared almost, but not quite, every year. According to Fulcher (1969: II, viii, 2): "On Easter Sabbath [21 April 1101] everyone was much disturbed because the Holy Fire failed to appear at the Sepulcher of the Lord."

17. This casual remark has been taken to mean that Fulcher was the chaplain of King Baldwin I for fifteen years and had entrée to the *Templum Domini* during that time (Fulcher 1913: 287).

18. See Chapter One on the fate of the Ark.

19. An earlier recension of Fulcher's work, cited by Hagenmeyer in Fulcher 1913: 291, reads "after it fell into Baldwin's and our hands, but he himself sold to merchants the lead that had fallen or come down from the roof."

20. The reference here to the "Gate of the Apostles" seems to be to the Golden Gate. Perhaps it is an echoing memory of when *it* was the Gate Beautiful associated with Peter and John?

21. On the archeological evidence for the reconstruction of some of the features of the Crusader church, see Clermont-Ganneau 1899: 153-162.

22. William of Tyre 1943: XV, 18; and de Vogüé 1881: 563.

23. This "Chapel of St. James" is the Muslim "Dome of the Chain" or *Qubbat al-Silsila*.

24. The canons' cloisters were on the north side of the *platform*; the Abbey of the canons occupied the north side of the *Haram*.

25. Cf. Theoderich 1896: 35: "The [Golden] Gate itself is never opened except on Palm Sunday and on the day of the Exaltation of the Cross, because Emperor Heraclius passed through it with a large piece of the wood of the Cross which he had brought from Persia."

26. For the Crusaders fallen in the conquest of the city, see ibid.: 40.

27. Herod, it will be noted, has fallen out of the account, as frequently happens in Christian, Muslim, and Jewish versions of Temple history.

28. The "ammiraldo" is very likely *Amir al-Mu'minîn*, or possibly *Ma'mûn*, if somebody read off the inscription for this anonymous pilgrim, since Ma'mun's name had been substituted for Abd al-Malik's in the original dedication.

29. On the archeological evidence for the more permanent, and more traditional, residence of the king at the Citadel complex, see Bahat/Broshi 1976: 56.

30. See Benvenisti 1970: 64-68.

31. Riley-Smith 1967: 376-377.

32. On the early archeological exploration of the Muristan complex, see Schick 1901; and more recently, Lux 1972.

33. Cf. Riley-Smith 1967: 331-334.

34. Another manuscript reads "four" in place of "200" Jews in Jerusalem, and that seems more likely since Rabbi Petachia of Ratisbon, who passed through Jerusalem not more than a few years after Benjamin, notes a single Jewish family in the city and they were dyers (Adler 1966: 88).

35. Adler 1966: 90; and for a similar text of Isaac ben Joseph, already cited in Chapter Five, see idem, 131.

36. See Broshi 1976: 60.

37. Benjamin bought his way into the shrine; Petachia of Ratisbon, another Jewish visitor who was there at the same time, posed as a Gentile when he went to Hebron. Here too, as in Benjamin's account, the custodian of the shrine appears to be a Muslim, and Petachia also managed, one assumes likewise by paying the custodian for the privilege, to get past the "tourist" graves and into the inner sanctuary where the authentic tombs were (Adler 1966: 89).

NOTES TO CHAPTER 9

1. Damascus received its first law school sometime after 1103. By 1217 there were twenty in the city; and in 1233, ninety-three (Ahmad 1962: 80).

2. See Cahen 1965: 64; Sivan 1968: 12.

3. Sivan 1968: 30-35.

4. The evidence for Nur al-Din's intentions regarding Jerusalem is collected and analyzed in Sivan 1968: 59-87.

5. Sivan 1968: 63.

6. See Sivan 1967, 1971; and Hasson 1981: 172.

7. On the tradition types in such "Merits of Jerusalem," see Hasson 1981: 174-175.

8. See, for example, the Rock anthology in Ludolph von Suchem 1895: 99 (written about 1350) and the Jewish traditions collected in Vilnay 1972: 17-27.

9. Cautions concerning religious cult at the Rock will be echoed by other authors concerned with exaggerating the importance of Jerusalem (see Ibn Taymiyya).

10. Hasson in Wasiti 1979: 14, the last definition of the Holy Land comes from Tabari.

11. Sivan 1968: 64, citing a tradition from Ibn al-Athir. For Mujir al-Din's definition of Palestine, see Mujir 1876: 203.

12. See Sivan 1968: 112-124, and generally, pp. 93-124.

13. The "Table" is that of the Eucharist in Quran 5, and the Christ Child speaking is influenced by Quran 19:31.

14. See Busee 1968: 461-462.

15. See Tamari 1968 for the archeological and literary history of the site of St. Anne's.

16. Clermont-Ganneau 1899: 121-123. The market referred to by Ludolph is in fact the center of the three parallel bazaars. Cf. Chapter Eight.

17. See Tibawi 1978: 13; and on this court and its records, Mandaville 1975.

18. The truce specifically stipulated that "commercial relations should be freely exercised." Lewis 1982: 26 cites a letter written as early as 1174 in which Saladin, in making his case for a Counter-Crusade to the caliph in Baghdad, remarks:

> ... the Venetians, the Pisans, and the Genoese all used to come, sometimes as raiders, the voracity of whose harm could not be contained and the fire of whose evil could not be quenched, sometimes as travellers trying to prevail over Islam with the goods they bring, and our fearsome decrees could not cope with them ... and now there is not one of them but brings to our land his weapons of war and battle and bestows upon us the choicest of what he makes and inherits. ...

One way of controlling this commercial imperialism on the part of the Italian maritime republics, Saladin argues, was to open formal relations with them and attempt to impose "such terms as we desire and they deplore, such as we prefer and they do not." (Lewis 1982: 25-27.)

19. See De Sandoli 1983: 152.

20. For the repopulation of the city, see Benvenisti 1970: 46.

21. On the authenticity of Harizi's testimony on Saladin's readmission of the Jews to Jerusalem, see Ashtor 1956: 324-326.

22. See Van Cleve 1969: 455.

23. Gibb 1969: 702.

24. A somewhat later report on Jerusalem, that by the Jewish scholar Nachmanides, who was there in 1267, reflects the city's still desolate condition (see Chapter Ten).

25. See Atiya 1938: 186-187.

26. Atiya 1938: 189.

27. A Church Council convoked at Vienne in 1311 abolished the Order of the Knights of the Temple, which was executed by the Bull *Vox in excelso* in 1312.

28. Uniforms for the military did not come into general use before the sixteenth and seventeenth centuries.

29. "See the bull of Innocent IV, June 22, 1248, to the Chancellor of the University of Paris: 'We have arranged that certain youths versed both in Arabic and other languages of the oriental countries be sent to Paris to study, so that after learning from the sacred page the ways of the Lord's commandments they can, when their education is completed, teach others the way of salvation in the lands beyond the sea' " (*Cartularium universitatis Parisiensis* I, 212, cited by Brandt in his footnote in Dubois 1956).

30. This construction program is described in detail in Chapter Ten.

31. Cited in Sivan 1968: 118.

32. See Busse 1968: 465.

33. The reference is probably the entry into the western wall of the platform presently known as Barclay's Gate.

34. For the terrain covered by these concentric circles, see Busse 1968: 466; and for another example of Muslim "Stations," perhaps with clear Christian antecedents, Ashtor

1981: 189, who comments: "This anonymous work provides actual guidelines for a Muslim pilgrimage to Jerusalem in imitation of a guide to the *stationes*—lacking only the antiphonies and remarks about the sins thereby cleansed. The very fact that the author specifies where one should go, points to Christian influence. Indeed, it would be truly inconceivable that, after seeing Christian pilgrims touring so often with guidebooks in their hands, the Muslims should not be influenced and not begin to compose similar works themselves."

35. See Goitein 1966: 140-142; Kister 1969: 193-194; Hasson 1981: 175.

36. On this famous tradition see Kister 1969 and Chapter Five.

37. On this allegation against Abd al-Malik, see Chapter Five.

NOTES TO CHAPTER 10

1. There is a useful survey of the slave-soldier phenomenon, from Turkish slave-soldiers to ruling Mamluks, in Ayalon 1968.

2. Ayalon 1968: 313.

3. But see the remarks of Ayalon 1968: 327 and 1958: 291.

4. Drory 1981: 192; and for the bedouin problem, see Sharon 1975: 14-16.

5. See Gaudefroy-Demombynes 1923: 176; Drory 1981: 193.

6. See Ayalon 1972: 34, and for the Mamluks' preference for Jerusalem over Mecca as their place of "retirement," idem, 37; and Drory 1981: 196-197.

7. Massignon 1951/1963: 189.

8. On the Mamluks' attempts to solve some of the problems of peculation and embezzlement in the endowment system, see Darrag 1961: 132-134, 137-138.

9. See Hopkins 1971: 68-69; and Chapters Twelve and Thirteen.

10. The phrase "the Two Sanctuaries," scil. *par excellence*, is usually reserved for Mecca and Medina, but it was also used on occasion for Jerusalem and Hebron.

11. This "Quarter of the Banu Harith" appears to be a bedouin suburb, a settlement of semisedentary Arabs outside the city perimeter. This process is better attested in the northeast corner of the city, where some of these tribal names are connected with quarters inside the obviously porous unwalled city.

12. Drory 1981: 209.

13. See in particular Massignon 1951/1963: 190-200; and Tibawi 1978.

14. On this village Ayn Karim about five miles distant from Jerusalem and the reputed birthplace of John the Baptist, see Finegan 1969: 3-5; and Wilkinson 1977: 156 under "En Kerem."

15. Mazar 1975: "Another long and interesting underground area faces the Wilson Arch due west. It lies approximately at the level of the present pavement of the arch (apparently of Arab [Umayyad] origin) and consists of a complex of vaulted chambers of all shapes and dimensions. There are storehouses, recesses, cisterns, and even stairways, all of them flanking both sides of a narrow subterranean alley which runs for a distance of some 330 feet. This alley, which may be found to extend further west should it be excavated, actually runs a few feet under the present Street of the Chain which leads to the Haram al-Sharif. More than 1,500 years ago it ran over the east to west Via Praetoria of Christian Aelia. It may even have been in use as late as Crusader times. . . ." Apparently no further excavation has been done on the underground passageway since its rediscovery in the nineteenth century.

16. There is a detailed literary and architectural analysis of the Market of the Cotton Merchants in Golvin 1967.

17. The restoration forestalled the dire prophecy made by Golvin 1967: 117: "The

architectural ensemble of the Bazaar of the Cotton Merchants, which does not lack for a certain grandeur, fell little by little into ruin. And if something is not done the vaulting will collapse and leave only the monumental gate of the Haram, which appears able to hold out for a few centuries longer." The restoration has not, however, brought commercial prosperity back to the bazaar, principally because there is no longer any access to the Haram through its monumental gate. The bazaar is now in effect a dead-end street.

18. As a matter of fact, a number of dedicatory inscriptions have been preserved, published by van Berchem 1922: 263 and Grabar 1965. Golvin 1967: 103 summarizes: "From these different testimonies it is possible to conclude that in the years A.D. 736-737/1336-1337 the governor of Damascus, Tankiz al-Nasiri, had, under the orders of Sultan al-Malik al-Nasir Muhammad ibn Qala'un, effected large works of restoration and organization around the Haram in Jerusalem. Everything points to the fact that the present day monumental gate replaced, in the fourteenth century, an older one. . . . We know nothing of the style of this older gate, nor of what kind of a street it opened, and so it is impossible to judge the exact extent of the work taken up by Tankiz. Nevertheless, if the terms used in the inscriptions of the gate have to do with a work of restoration, those generally found in the Arab authors are more appropriate to a reconstruction. . . ."

19. See the summary in Drory 1981: 198-199.

20. The fountain of Qa'it Bay is analyzed in Kessler/Burgoyne 1978.

21. The great khan of the Tartars or Mongols at that time, the beginning of the fourteenth century, was Ghazan, who was helped by the Christians who hoped thereby to recover the holy places.

22. Al-Ghazali (d. 1111) was a professor at the premier law school in Baghdad, who went into retreat first in Damascus and here in Jerusalem, where he wrote most of his "Revitalization of the Sciences of Religion," a kind of summa of Sunni Islam and probably the single most influential book of Islamic theology and religious practice.

23. The temptation to put *any* new building on the Haram platform now appears to have been checked, and the enclosure is now considerably less cluttered than it appears to have been, at least on Mujir's testimony. In his day there were, for example, two Sufi convents on the platform of the Dome of the Rock itself (Mujir 1876: 118). They are long gone, but a third building mentioned by Mujir (p. 140), the Nahwiyya School built in 1207 and noted in Chapter Nine, still sits demurely on the southwest edge of that same platform.

24. See Burgoyne 1973: 29-30, and 64: "The clustering of the majority of the Mamluk monuments round the Haram suggests that proximity to the Haram was important to their founders. Jawhar in particular seems to have been anxious to build close to important religious sites. . . . This may partly explain why Jawhar extended his law school over the Convent Ribat Kurd to abut the Haram wall. Kurd, who built one hundred and fifty years earlier than Jawhar, at a time when prime sites were more readily available, had no need to resort to such devices to build his modest convent beside the al-Hadid Gate."

25. On the Tashtimuriyya madrasa and its builder, see Kessler 1979.

26. The Ashrafiyya madrasa has been studied in detail by Tamari 1976.

27. A Turkish traveller passing through Jerusalem in 1690 noted that the Ashrafiyya was already falling into ruin at that date. As happened in many similar cases, the properties that fed the endowment had probably become illegally alienated (see Tamari 1976: 546).

28. The plan of the Ashrafiyya departs from the traditional function of the cruciform

madrasa where the four recessed and arched iwans served as classrooms. See Tamari 1976: 563: "An important and singular transformation has taken place, the conversion of the 'eastern iwan' into a lounge. The point of this conversion lies in the loss of its original functional significance as a classroom, assuming instead a new and even alien 'functional' role within the traditional cruciform arrangement. As a result of the transformation of the iwan into a loggia (bearing a similarity to contemporary elements, i.e., in Italy of the early Renaissance) with its arches resting on marble columns and framed stained glass windows, a singular perspective opens up on the Haram in general and the Dome of the Rock in particular. When seen in the overall framework of the said plan, still regarded by the chroniclers as comprising four iwans, the transformation has therefore a definite implication."

29. Arnold von Harff also noticed the Ashrafiyya in 1496 and was able to go inside since he was disguised as a Muslim Mamluk during his visit to the Haram. Arnold von Harff 1946: 210-211: "We went from this crypt [the Stables of Solomon] into a beautiful little mosque or church which is built quite close to the church of the Porch of Solomon. This was built by the old Sultan Kathubee [Qa'it Bay], who died five years ago and is honorably buried there. A hundred lamps burn there daily." Qa'it Bay was as a matter of fact buried in Cairo.

30. On the Sufi population of Mamluk Jerusalem, see Drory 1981: 202-205; and for their lodgings and institutions, Burgoyne 1973: 12-20.

31. Though the evidence on Sufi convents, and much else in Mamluk Jerusalem, may now be at hand. There was recently discovered in the Islamic Museum atop the Haram in Jerusalem a large cache of documents dating from the Mamluk era in Jerusalem, and at least some of them deal with convents in the Holy City; see Little 1980 for an account of this discovery and a survey of the contents.

32. See the summary account in Busse 1968: 462.

33. On the possible intent of the two minarets flanking the Holy Sepulcher, see Walls 1976.

34. A number of Christian visitors had experience of this police prison (see Chapter Eleven).

35. On the late medieval contest for Mount Sion, see Darrag 1961: 279-281; Hirschberg 1976: 117; and Drory 1981: 212 for two Jewish accounts; and Hoade 1981: 308f. for one Franciscan's version.

36. There was another party interested in real estate on Mount Sion, perhaps the principal one, a certain Margaret of Sicily, whose good works Ludolph mentions in connection with the Holy Sepulcher but not with Mount Sion. The Franciscans' own archives reveal, however, that it was the same Margaret who made the first purchase on Sion from Sultan al-Nasir Muhammad (A.D. 1294-1309) and then resold the property to the Franciscan Roger Garin (Baldi 1955: 506-507).

37. See Baldi 1955: 509-510 for the papal bull *Gratias agimus* issued by Clement VI in 1342 and confirming the Franciscan superior in Jerusalem as "Guardian of Mount Sion."

38. The contest for Sion was infinitely more complex than Felix allows, involving as it did economic pressures brought to bear by the pope and the Christian powers upon the European Jews for their presumption (Adler 1966: 243) and two trials in Muslim courts in Jerusalem (see Darrag 1961: 280).

NOTES TO CHAPTER 11

1. The pilgrim Ludolph von Suchem in about 1350 offered another explanation for why the pope excommunicated the land of Israel, one with slightly different nuances:

He who would go to said Holy Land must beware lest he travel there without leave from the Apostolic Father, for as soon as he touches the sultan's country he falls under the sentence of the pope, because from the time the Holy Land came [once again] into the hands of the sultan, it was, and remains, excommunicate, as are likewise all who travel there without the pope's leave, lest by receiving tribute from the Christians the Muslims should be brought to despise the Church. For this reason, when any traveller receives his license to go there from the Apostolic Father, in addition to the leave which is granted him, there is a clause in the bull to the effect that he shall not buy or sell anything in the world, save only victuals and clothes and bodily necessaries, and if he contravenes this, he is to know that he has fallen back again under sentence of excommunication. (Ludolph von Suchem 1895: 3)

2. See Daniel 1960: 114-115; Savage 1977: 39.
3. Atiya 1938: 114; Savage 1977: 66.
4. See Darrag 1961: 269-277 for a detailed breakdown on the expenses.
5. On the hostel called variously *funduq* or khan, see Gil 1976: 112-115. It is enlightening to compare Ibn Battuta's account in the text with the following reflections on accommodations on the way to Jerusalem made by the Englishman Henry Maundrell who in 1697 had European referents for his experience:

It must here be noted that in travelling the country a man does not meet with a market-town and inns every night, as in England. The best reception you can find here is either under your own tent, if the season permit, or else in certain public lodgements founded in charity for the use of travellers. These are called by the Turks *khans* and are seated sometimes in the towns and villages, sometimes at convenient distances upon the open road. They are built in the fashion of a cloister, encompassing a court of thirty or forty yards square, more of less, according to the measure of the founder's ability or charity. At these places all comers are free to take shelter, paying only small fee to the khan-keeper, and very often without that acknowledgment. But must expect nothing here generally but bare walls. As for other accommodations, of meat, drink, bed, fire, provender, with these it must be everyone's care to furnish himself. (Maundrell 1963: 2)

6. One of the most extraordinary assaults to take place on this violent road between Jaffa and Ramle, and thence to Jerusalem, was the bedouin siege of Arnold bishop of Bamberg and an immense number of pilgrims in the days before the Crusades (see Joranson 1928).
7. There appears to have been some attempt on the part of the Italian republics like Genoa and Venice, who carried the bulk of the pilgrims to Palestine, to arrange to have some kind of consular representation in Jerusalem for the protection of pilgrims and of their own considerable commercial interest in them, but if they succeeded, very few of the visitors of that era were aware of it (see Heyd 1884: 357-362).
8. The Arabic word behind "calinus" is uncertain; possibly it was a proper name like "Khalil" that had become transformed into a title.
9. On the language problems of the pilgrim and the role of the translator, see Sumption 1975: 193-194; Niccolo of Poggibonsi 1945: xv-xvii.
10. On the Franciscans as guides in Jerusalem, see Niccolo 1945: xvii-xix; and on the earliest form of the Way of the Cross, Baldi 1955: 599n.1.
11. On the touristic side of late medieval pilgrimage, and not merely in the Holy Land, see Sumption 1975: 257-259.

12. Compare Arnold von Harff's investiture with Chateaubriand's ceremony described in Chapter Twelve.

13. What was called "the odor of sanctity" was a commonplace phenomenon of holy places and holy persons. See Felix Fabri 1893: I, 558-559 on the birthplace of Jesus in Bethlehem: "Not only this place but all the places wherein we read that the Lord Jesus appeared naked enjoy this privilege of exhaling a sweet odor. Nor need anyone wonder at this since we read the same thing takes place from the tombs and sepulchers of the saints."

14. On this quality of Burchard, and the more general change of attitude it reflected, see Grabois 1982: 287-288.

15. It was much the same thought perhaps that created in the nineteenth century the newest of Jerusalem's Christian holy places, the so-called Garden Tomb in the northern outskirts of the Old City. It has little claim to authenticity, but it is indeed outside the city and it responds far more directly to some Christian sensibilities about what the tomb of Jesus should have looked like than the present Greek rococo edicule that sits inside the dark and incense-filled Church of the Holy Sepulcher (see Silberman 1982: 152-153).

16. Wilkinson 1977: 53.

17. See Le Strange 1890: 220.

18. Goitein 1982: 183.

19. Horn 1962: 70-75.

20. Felix Fabri was one who wished to be buried in the Valley of Jehoshaphat: "I very often used to come down to this place from Mount Sion and read my hours on the holy field, and I desired exceedingly that, if it were possible, I might end my days there among the brethren and be buried there" (Felix Fabri 1893: I, 536). On the earlier history of Aceldama, the "Potters' Field" of Mt. 27:7, see Wilkinson 1977: 149; and the texts collected in Baldi 1955: 575-580.

21. See Maehl 1962: 20; Sumption 1975: 130-132.

22. On the different attitudes the Muslim and Christian cultures held for each other, see Lewis 1982: 297-301.

23. On the growth, size, and contents of the body of anti-Muslim polemic in the West, see Daniel 1960, and particularly 281-282 on the conflict in Christian pilgrims' minds between what they had read about Islam in the traditional polemics and what they were experiencing through contact with Muslim society.

24. On the life and work of Ricoldo of Monte Croce, see Ricoldo 1884 (with an edition of his letters): 260-263; and Atiya 1938: 158-160.

25. On Ludolph and his work, see Atiya 1938: 170-171.

26. There is no evidence that the Muslims ever called themselves "Saracens." The word may indeed have an Arab etymology, and it was commonly used by fourth-century Western authors as a synonym for Arab. But by the next century the word had become the plaything of Christian polemicists who claimed that the Arabs had coined "Saracens," "Sarah people," to disguise the fact that they were "Hagarenes," that is, they had descended not from Isaac but from Ishmael, the son of Abraham's slave woman Hagar (see Christides 1972; and Graf/O'Connor 1977).

27. Indeed the Muslims' own tradition claimed that Muhammad was illiterate, though to a very different end, namely, to demonstrate the divine origins of such a remarkable book as the Quran.

28. See Ben-Sasson 1975: 103.

29. On the condition of the Jewish community in Jerusalem during Mamluk times, see Drory 1981: 213.

NOTES TO CHAPTER 12

1. St. H. Stephan cites in Chelebi 1980: 59n.4 a firman granted in 1517 by Selim I, "in the Desert of the Noble Sanctuary," which states after the preamble that "by the help of God . . . I came to the House of God in Jerusalem on the twenty-fifth of Safar, 923 [March 20, 1517]. . . . In accordance with the august Covenant granted [the Christian monks] by his Lordship the Caliph Umar, . . . and according to the orders [given them] since the days of Saladin . . . they are now confirmed in their rights and possessions. . . ."

2. That is, the so-called Covenant of Umar (see Chapter Five).

3. According to the firman cited in n. 1 above, this is specified as follows: "They will be entirely exempted and free from paying customs duties, tolls, and other oppressive taxes levied at the gates of Jerusalem, the escort fees for the Arabs and the harbor and inspection fees. . . ."

4. See Sharon 1975.

5. On the relative Ottoman neglect of building investment in Jerusalem, see Grabar 1980: 343; and for a comparison with their vigorous secular and religious building program in Syria, Rafeq 1977: 56-57.

6. Chelebi 1980: 63-66. On the individual gates in the Ottoman wall of Jerusalem, see also Hirschberg et al. 1973: 78-80; and Ben Dov 1983: 85-117.

7. See Clermont-Ganneau 1899: 239-246.

8. Cf. Le Strange 1890: 216n. "No native authority (as far as I am aware) exists for spelling the name of this gate *Bab al-Zahari*, the 'Flower Gate,' as Robinson (*Researches*, 2d ed., I, 262) and many others after him have done. Nor is the name ever written *Bab al-Zahriyya*, 'Gate of Splendor' as has been set down in some of the *Memoirs* of the Palestine Exploration Fund. However the present inhabitants of Jerusalem may spell and pronounce the name of this small gate, which the Franks call 'Herod's Gate,' in old times it was always written *al-Sahirah*, that is, 'of the Plain,' scilicet 'of the Assembly of the Judgment Day,' which stretches beyond the city wall north-east from this gate."

9. The "blessed night" referred to by Chelebi here is probably the twenty-seventh of Ramadan, the "night of power" (*laylat al-qadr*).

10. See Schechter 1908; Heyd 1975; Cohen/Lewis 1978: 28-30.

11. Lewis 1954: 475. On the larger significance of these figures, and of the decline that set in later in the century, see Cohen/Lewis 1978: 19-28.

12. Cohen 1976: XVII, based on the sixteenth-century records of the Islamic Court in Jerusalem: "The Jewish cemetery on the Mount of Olives was a major preoccupation of the Jewish community during the sixteenth century. Part of the waqf known as al-Jismaniyya (probably after Gethsemane, adjacent), the proceeds from which were allotted to the Salahiyya Madrasa, had been in use as a Jewish burial ground for years. After the Ottoman occupation this land was leased [by the Jews] from the waqf administrators for three and a half gold pieces per annum. . . . At a later date the executor of the waqf demanded a higher sum. Upon consultation with several *sipahis* who were well acquainted with land values in this region, the lease was fixed at five gold pieces per annum. [Document No. 19 cited in the text.] In the early fifties, this was claimed to be insufficient once again, and the executor's threats were severe: if the Jews were not to come to terms with him, he would have the graves cleared away and the land leased to some other party for cultivation. [Document No. 7.] When brought before the qadi, all the relevant documents submitted by the Jewish community were declared invalid, on various legal considerations. The qadi could not deny the existence of the cemetery in

right, but he ordered the reassessment of the lease. Various authorities were consulted from among the Muslim religious scholars, including Ahmad al-Dajjani, the highest Sufi dignitary in Jerusalem. Finally it was concluded that the Jews should pay the waqf one hundred gold pieces, for which they would be entitled to use both the cemetery and another adjacent plot. This arrangement, adding a tithe to be paid to the governor of Jerusalem, was apparently agreed upon in the late fifties and once again was recorded in the tax register [Document No. 24]."

13. See Dinur 1957; Hacker 1974.

14. On this story, see Vilnay 1973: 9.

15. David Reubeni was not the only Messianic figure to appear in Jerusalem in that era. In 1662-1663 there came to the Holy City from Gaza one Sabbatai Sevi. His conduct on that occasion may have been somewhat eccentric, no more, and he was entrusted with the important task of raising funds for the Jerusalem community in Egypt. But in May 1665, once again in Gaza, he proclaimed himself the Messiah and declared his intention of returning to Jerusalem, this time with more drastic plans. Gershom Scholem (Scholem 1973: 240) continues the story:

> In Gaza he had appointed twelve rabbis who were to accompany him to the site of the Temple (occupied by the Muslim sanctuary of the Haram al-Sharif) where he was to perform a sacrifice. This symbolic action was probably intended to mark the beginning of the rebuilding of the Temple. Preparations were apparently made with a certain amount of publicity . . . and Rabbi Najara of Gaza, who was not of priestly descent, was appointed high priest. Sabbatai later told Laniado that when the news of the preparations reached the rabbis of Jerusalem, they rent their clothes in mourning over the blasphemy and in fear of the dire consequences for the community which such an entry into a Muslim holy place would provoke. They sent a message to Sabbatai: "Why do you want to deliver Israel to death and why do you destroy the Lord's inheritance?" Sabbatai abandoned his plans but smote his hands and cried: "Woe! It was so near, and now it has been put far off" because of the interference of the rabbis.

Sabbatai did come to Jerusalem where he began to abrogate laws of ritual purity. In the end the Jerusalem rabbis were constrained to cite Sabbatai to the Muslim chief justice on charges that he "wanted to rule and that he had embezzled some of money from his (fund-raising) mission." He was acquitted and regarding this as a divine sign, "Sabbatai then demanded permission to 'ride around on horseback through the city, although (Muslim) custom strictly forbade a Jew to ride a horse,' and his request was granted. Seven times he rode round the city, showing himself to the public 'on his horse and clothed in a green mantle in accordance with his mystical intentions' " (Scholem 1973: 241).

16. On Jewish and Muslim legends connected with the cavern under the Rock, see Vilnay 1973: 23-26.

17. The mystical "Book of Splendors," in which the second-century rabbi Simon ben Yohai figures prominently, was likely the work of the Spanish kabbalist Moses de Leon (d. 1305). Another effect of the increased Jewish migration to Palestine, after the expulsion from Spain, was the widespread diffusion of interest in the Zohar. In the sixteenth century the book began to have a profound effect in kabbalistic circles in Palestine, particularly through the work of Isaac Lauria (d. 1572), the chief kabbalistic sage in Safed.

18. The holders of military fiefs in the district of Palestine had the responsibility of escorting, under the command of the pasha, Meccan pilgrims at Damascus on their "side trip" to Jerusalem.

19. St. H. Stephan (Chelebi 1980: 72-73) notes: "This was normally done only in cities taken by conquest, not by treaty, as Jerusalem was. The office of preacher is hereditary. . . ."

20. Ibid.: "*musebbihs*, or special muezzins for the Haram."

21. Ibid.: "*ma'arrif*. This is an inferior functionary in a large mosque, who acts at prayer time as a kind of chorister. During Friday prayer at noon it is the custom for the *ma'arrif* to occupy the 'summer pulpit' of Judge Burhan al-Din [out on the Haram platform]. . . . He repeats the injunction of the prayer leader in the Aqsa Mosque to the congregation in the Dome of the Rock. . . ."

22. Ibid.: "*Na'ti khan*, a reciter of the 'Beautiful Names'; *Devri khan* and *Ejza khans*, reciters of various subdivisions of the Quran."

23. Ibid. (86-87): "Possibly a confusion by Chelebi between *janne*, paradise, and *jân*, spirits. This was *bir al-janne*, the cistern of [the gate of] Paradise. The 'Well of the Spirits,' on the other hand, is *under* the Rock."

24. St. H. Stephan, writing in 1935: "Most of these madrasas have been converted into private dwelling houses. An official Turkish list of these colleges and religious buildings (dated 2 November 1907) enumerates 51, of which five only were then in a ruinous state" (pp. 88-90).

25. Ibid.: "It was known until 1927 as the Mosque of the Maghrebis, and has since been converted into a [Islamic] museum."

26. See the remarks in Benvenisti 1976: 66 on the later complaint that devotions in this mosque were made deliberately loud to annoy the Jewish worshippers at the Western Wall below.

27. Baldi 1955: 524n.1 adds that an inscription in the name of Sulieman, here called Muhammad al-Ajami, and dated 1524, is still extant in the east wall of the present Coenaculum: "In the name of God, the Merciful, the Compassionate, the Lord of Creation . . . Suleiman the Emperor, offspring of Uthman, ordered this place to be purified and purged of infidels and constructed as a mosque in which the name of God is venerated."

28. Though the tradition of plans and scientific illustrations goes back at least as far as Arculf and had notable examples in works like that of Bernhard Breydenbach in the late fifteenth century, the modern era in illustration properly begins with the perspective drawings in Bernadino Amico's *Plans of the Sacred Edifices of the Holy Land* in 1609 (see Amico 1953).

29. Baldi 1955: 613n.1: "In the year 1838, at the expense of Maximillian of Bavaria, the chapel of the Flagellation was restored, and in 1929 it was enlarged and improved by the Franciscan Custodian of the Holy Land." It now serves as the headquarters of the Franciscan Biblical Institute in Jerusalem.

30. These are described in detail by Quaresmi in 1626 in Baldi 1955: 699-703.

31. The Latin inscription makes it almost certain that what was found inside the tomb of Jesus dated from the Crusader epoch in Jerusalem.

32. For the Franciscan view, see Hoade 1981: 798-799.

33. See Wardi 1975: 389: "Between 1625 and 1637 Murad IV issued no fewer than twelve firmans, each contradicting its predecessor. Obviously he was not very concerned with historical truth or the authenticity of the documents. He considered the holy places the property of the State and felt free to assign them in temporary use to the highest bidder."

34. See Atiya 1938: 187-189; and Chapter Eleven.

35. See Searight 1970: 54-55. Piety, if not dead, might easily still prove fatal. Searight (1970: 55) cites the case of one Henry Moryson who was so moved by ecstasy at

first setting foot in the "Holy Land," actually Alexandretta, that he fell to the ground, broke his nose and began to bleed profusely. His brother Fynes tells the sequel: "Howsoever this be a superstitious sign of ill, yet the event was to us tragical by his death shortly after happening."

36. A comparison of method and conclusion of early and modern scholars is not necessarily in favor of the latter, however. Witness these reflections on a parallel phenomenon by Henry Maundrell in 1696 and Burchard of Mount Sion in 1280:

> I cannot forebear to mention in this place an observation which is very obvious to all that visit the Holy Land, viz. that almost all passages and histories related in the Gospels are represented by them that undertake to show where everything was done as having been done most of them in grottos; and that even in such cases where the conditions and circumstances of the actions themselves seem to require places of another nature.
>
> Thus, if you would see the place where St. Anne was delivered of the blessed Virgin, you are carried to a grotto. . . . And in a word, wherever you go, you find almost everything is represented as done underground. Certainly grottos were anciently held in great esteem, or else they could never have been assigned, in spite of all probability, for the places in which were done so many various actions. Perhaps it was the hermits' way of living in grottos from the fifth or sixth century downward that has brought them ever since to be in so great reputation. (Maundrell 1963: 153-154)

The same question had occurred to Burchard after he was shown the site of Cana in Galilee:

> Now these places, like almost all the other places wherein the Lord wrought any work are underground, and one goes down to them by many steps into a crypt. . . . The only reason I can find for this is that owing to the frequent destruction of the churches built over these places, the ruins raised the soil above them, and then, after they had been levelled carelessly, other buildings were built upon them. Christians therefore who were zealous to visit these places and wished to get to the very spot where the thing was done had to clear out the places and make steps leading down to them. Wherefore almost all these places seem to be in crypts. (Burchard of Mount Sion 1896: 39)

37. Cited by David Howell in Maundrell 1963: xv.

38. See ibid.: xx.

39. Ibid.: xxiv-xxv:

> The duties [of the chaplain at Aleppo] can never have been particularly onerous, and most of them, to our advantage, pursued their own scholarly studies and interests. One of the chaplains at Aleppo in the seventeenth century (Edward Pocke, chaplain 1630-1636) became the first professor of Arabic and Hebrew at Oxford; two others (Charles Robson, 1624-1630 and Robert Huntington (1637-1704) made valuable collections of Arabic manuscripts now in the Bodleian Library and at Merton College, Oxford; William Halifax, Maundrell's immediate predecessor, made a valuable survey of Palmyra; while Bishop Frampton, mentioned in the dedication to Sprat, was one of those remarkable exceptions to the community who spent a great deal of time learning Arabic and getting to know the people of Aleppo. . . .

40. Britain and France were then formally at war.

41. Britain did not adopt the Gregorian calendar until 1750.

42. Howell's note in Maundrell 1963: 127-130: "In 1834 there was a stampede in the Church in which 200-300 people lost their lives and Ibrahim Pasha only got out alive because members of his suite hacked a way for him through the living mass with their swords" (see Chapter Thirteen).

43. C. W. Wilson writes in 1880, after describing the ceremony in the 1860s: "Such is the Greek Easter—the greatest moral argument against the identity of the spot which it professes to honor—stripped, indeed, of some of its most revolting features, yet still, considering the place, the time, the intention of the professed miracle, probably the most offensive imposture to be found in the world" (p. 28).

44. Both stories are told in Vilnay 1973: 161-163; and by Dov Noy in Ben-Dov et al. 1983: 108-112.

45. The Turks had by then converted the Tankiziyya Law School into the Hall of Justice of Jerusalem.

46. Cohen 1976: XVIII, commenting on Jewish pilgrimage during the Ottoman period, notes conditions already familiar from the Christian accounts cited above:

Pilgrimage was made primarily to Jerusalem, the Holy City, and thence to the tombs of the patriarchs in Hebron and the tomb of Samuel the prophet near Jerusalem. A road-toll was levied at specified check points, and those paying it enjoyed the protection of the governor of Jerusalem while on the road. The governor, however, instead of honoring the rates as fixed by the Ottoman *qanun* [legal code], regarded pilgrims as an inexhaustible source of revenue. Upon reaching Jerusalem, pilgrims were forced to pay another toll, usually between eleven and twenty paras, but occasionally more. They were allowed neither to enter Hebron nor leave it without having paid an additional three paras.

Having submitted to this extortion, the pilgrim was sometimes beaten, fined, or even imprisoned. Instead of protecting and aiding the pilgrims, the governor of Jerusalem would attach at least one of his lackeys to those hiring out beasts to the pilgrims for transportation, thus adding a further financial burden. In the same spirit, the governor would send word to the main villages along the road, urging them to levy tolls of their own on the pilgrims. And as if this were insufficient, those pilgrims arriving from Egypt or Syria were accused of introducing diseases and, in order to avoid being shut out of the cities, were forced to pay various tolls.

47. Cohen 1976: Document No. 1.
48. Cohen 1976: XIII-XIV.

NOTES TO CHAPTER 13

1. On Jerusalem's earlier "capitulations" in favor of Genoa, Venice, and Florence, see Heyd 1884; Hurewitz 1975: 1-2.

2. See Hurewitz 1975: 71-75.

3. The text of the agreement of 1740 is in Noradounghian 1897-1903: I, 277-300.

4. On the intent and paralyzing long-term effects of the capitulations between Europe and Ottoman Jerusalem, see Naff 1977: 92-102.

5. On this imbalance between Europe and Jerusalem, see Cohen 1973: 1; Naff 1977: 91-92.

6. Texts in Treaties 1855: 31, 192-200, 384-385.

7. Treaties 1855: 54, cited by Zander 1971: 45.

8. Cited by Zander 1971: 47; cf. Wardi 1975: 390-391.

9. Wardi 1975: 391. The disposition of Christian groups within the Holy Sepulcher

was canonized in the sultan's firman of 1757. This so-called Status Quo in the Holy Places pleased almost none of the parties, but eventually the issue was judged safer dead than alive, and the arrangement of 1757 has remained essentially intact through Ottoman, British, Jordanian, and Israeli rule over Jerusalem.

10. Cited by Zander 1971: 47.

11. The Jews' request in 1831 to be allowed to repave part of the area before the Wall represents the first assertion of a public and so a political Jewish claim upon the Wall. It had no immediate sequel, but in 1875 Moses Montefiore offered to buy the area before the Wall outright, an offer that was refused, and thereafter the claims become increasingly more insistent, and the Muslim resistance more determined (see Ben-Dov et al. 1983: 121-138; and Benvenisti 1976: 64-77).

12. See Baldi 1955: 705n.1.

13. To put the unkindest regard upon the reconstructed Church of the Holy Sepulcher, one may simply quote two present-day Franciscan members of the Jerusalem community, the first, Eugene Hoade, one of its historians and the other, Virgilio Corbo, an archeologist responsible for many of the investigations carried out in the church in the 1960s.:

> The restorations carried out by the Franciscans [under the guardianship of Boniface of Ragusa in 1555 and again in 1719; see Chapter Twelve] at the price of unheard of difficulties and sacrifices, had at least the merit of preserving unchanged the original aspect of the Church of the Holy Sepulcher, and, as far as it was possible, the early decoration. The same cannot be said of the restorations carried out by the Greeks at the beginning of the last century, when a disastrous fire in 1808 almost completely destroyed the rotunda of the Holy Sepulcher. While the sons of St. Francis were raising, in vain, their voices in supplications toward the Latin West to interest princes and peoples in the cause of the Holy Land, the Greek Church obtained from Constantinople a firman which authorized them to rebuild the gutted basilica. Their work was one of destruction, having followed no other design than of erasing from the edifice of the Crusaders every vestige and record of Latin civilization and Catholicism. Thus disappeared under their "sacrilegious hammer" the beautiful edicule copied by Boniface of Ragusa from the eleventh-century model; thus disappeared the precious sarcophagi of Godfrey of Boullion and his two successors on the throne of Jerusalem; thus was deleted every Latin decoration and the celebrated monument, a record of the heroic period of the Holy wars, emerged from that unhappy restoration stripped of its former beauty and more damaged than was possible by the destructive flames. (Hoade 1981: 104-105)

> Leaving aside many other observations one might make, one of the most critical points of the restoration [undertaken in 1960] was the stylistic profanation of the monument itself. One single community [the Greeks] has at times imposed on its own authority restorations which are not only inappropriate for the part requiring restoration but have destroyed the lines of the monument. Thus the two high walls built along the two sides of the Chorus Dominorum and the gigantic iconostasis have literally defiled all the beautiful superstructure of the great Crusader transformation of the church. We shall say nothing, then, of the very bad taste in having left standing in some many places the repairs of Comnenus, whether in the Katholikon, or on Calvary, as well as the horrible Shrine of the Anastasis. (Corbo 1982: I, 24)

14. On the jurisdiction of Istanbul and Damascus over Jerusalem in Ottoman times, see Cohen 1973: 169; Hirschberg et al. 1973: 90.

15. On the *jizya*, or poll-tax, during this period of the Ottoman Empire, see Lewis 1954: 484; Cohen 1982: 13-14.

16. Cohen 1973: 256 gives a partial list of the special charges levied by the Muslims on non-Muslims:

> Whenever a new governor arrived in Jerusalem, each of the non-Muslim communities was required to pay him a special tax known as the *qudumiyya*. The Greek Orthodox had to pay the *mütesellim* 17½ kurush, his officers 3 k., the pasha 75 k., and the latter's *ketkhuda* 7½ k. [plus gifts]. . . . On religious festivals there was a special tax called *bayramlik*. . . . Once every year, when the governor set out from Jerusalem at the head of the *cerde* to meet the *hajj* caravan on its return from Mecca, the Christians were required to bear part of the cost of this in the form of a contribution known as the *imdadiyya*, or "assistance tax."

There were also burial taxes, a "search tax," a wool tax, a wood tax.

> All in all, the financial burden borne by the non-Muslim communities in eighteenth-century Palestine was by no means a light one. For the pasha these communities proved to be a lucrative source of additional income; almost everything he managed to extract from them remained in his own pocket and did not have to be remitted to the treasury in Istanbul. It is hardly surprising to find, therefore, that the Porte continued to issue firman after firman forbidding the governors to levy these taxes, which were considered illegal and contrary to the Shari'a. The recurrence of these firmans at different periods during the course of the [eighteenth] century, however, seems to indicate that for the first sixty years at least, all the above taxes continued to be levied in addition to the poll-tax.

17. On the short-term governorships in the Ottoman Empire, see Inalcik 1977: 29; and with particular reference to Palestine, Cohen 1973: 6.

18. Cited by Gaulmier in Volney 1959: 6. As Gaulmier points out, Volney's method is one of the first examples of the use of a preestablished questionnaire. According to Gaulmier, those questions included two series, "one on the physical condition of the country, the other on the political condition."

> The physical condition of the country includes four categories: geographical situation, climate, soil quality, natural produce, in all forty-four precise questions which require barometric and thermal measurements.
>   The political condition of the country has five categories: eleven questions on the population (its physical condition, how its feeds itself, habitual diseases, its most striking moral qualities, its separation into city and countryside, means of transportation); thirty-seven questions on agriculture . . . ; six questions on manufacture; eleven questions on commerce . . . , finally, twenty-six questions on "government and administration."

19. See Cohen 1973: 256-257.

20. Seetzen 1854-1856: 17, trans. E. Koehldorfer.

21. Horn 1962: 161-185.

22. Cf. the catalogue presented by Castellani 1922.

23. On this aspect of Chateaubriand's *Itineraire*, see Bassan 1959: 174-181. Not all judgments on Chateaubriand's perception of the East have been so favorable. This for example from Edward Said, who regards Chateaubriand as one of the founding fathers of nineteenth-century "Orientalism," that peculiarly European view that regarded the Near East as the natural home of despotism and its Muslim and Arab inhabitants as at

best colorful though unruly children and at worst morally and politically bankrupt. After citing Stendhal's criticism of Chateaubriand's "stinking egotism," Said continues:

He [Chateaubriand] brought a very heavy load of personal objectives and suppositions to the Orient, unloaded them there, and proceeded thereafter to push people, places, and ideas around in the Orient as if nothing could resist his imperious imagination. Chateaubriand came to the Orient as a constructed *figure*, not as a true self. For him Bonaparte was the last Crusader; he in turn was "the last Frenchman who left his country to travel in the Holy Land with the ideas, the goals, and the sentiments of a pilgrim of former times. . . ."

To so precipitously constituted a figure as Chateaubriand, the Orient was a decrepit canvas awaiting his restorative efforts. The Oriental Arab was "civilized man fallen again into a savage state": no wonder, then, that as he watched Arabs trying to speak French, Chateaubriand felt like Robinson Crusoe thrilled by hearing his parrot speak for the first time. . . . (Said 1978: 171-172)

24. Cohen/Lewis 1978: 94, based on the Ottoman tax registers.
25. See Hütteroth 1975: 6.
26. Ben-Arieh 1975b: 53.
27. See Cohen/Lewis 1978: 81-87.
28. See Mandaville 1975; Cohen 1976.
29. Cohen 1982: 9-10.
30. See Hopkins 1971, Ben-Arieh 1975b.
31. Kark 1981: 105.
32. The conversion of the building on the northern side of the Haram into a barracks took place in 1837, the year before Robinson was there. The annals of the Greek patriarchate of Jerusalem supply the details:

On the site of the Pretorium of Pilate a new barracks was built from the foundations, and it was garrisoned by 700 soldiers, Egyptians, Arabs, and Turks. Some of these thought of deserting. One night 200 of them, taking arms, murdered the captain and, escaping through a breach in the barracks wall, rushed to get out of the city by the Gethsemane Gate. Unable to open the gate, they proceeded to break it and killed one of the gate keepers who resisted. The desertion having become known, the rest of the army was sent to capture them, three were killed from both sides. Some were captured, but many, abandoning their guns, let themselves down from the walls with ropes. . . . (Spyridon 1938: 123)

And later:

During this month the Pretorium of Pilate was finished. It was formerly a *serai* or palace for the pashas and governors of Jerusalem, but is now the *qishlaq* or barracks of the regular soldiers of Ibrahim Pasha. It had, in virtue of its age, to be almost entirely rebuilt from its foundations. Dressed stones were taken from many ruins throughout the city for its rebuilding, but the greater part was taken from the monastery of the Nativity of the Mother of God [St. Anne's], which stands on the left, near to the Gate of Gethsemane. (Spyridon 1938: 125)

33. The Franciscans may have withdrawn from the Holy Fire contest, but they were not without their own, more modern weapons in the endless competition that went on within the Church of the Holy Sepulcher, a pipe organ:

In the Franciscan Oratory [in the Church of the Holy Sepulcher] there is a pneumatic organ built above the floor, to which you ascend by about ten steps. It was a gift to the friars of the Most August Emperor Leopold, of glorious memory, and one which disturbs rather than delights the Eastern monks who live with us here. They are exhilarated by its sweet tones, but because it smothers their voices when singing, they are grieved. The Armenians never dare hold their functions before us; they sing Matins and the daily Mass later or take themselves off to more distant chapels, lest we disturb each other with dissimilar chants. The Greeks, however, who strive proudly to precede all other nations, by which license I know not, anticipate both Matins and Mass by one hour. I believe that this has been introduced by them little by little, owing to the too great connivance of the friars, so that now it cannot be changed without serious trouble. . . . (Horn 1962: 78-79)

34. Chateaubriand 1969: 1068n.A.
35. Bassan 1959: 240-246.
36. Searight 1970: 160.
37. See Ben Arieh 1979; Silberman 1982.

Works Cited

Abel 1952: Abel, F.-M. *Histoire de la Palestine depuis la conquête d'Alexandre jusqu'à l'invasion arabe*. 2 vols. Paris: J. Gabalda et Cie.

Aboth Rabbi Nathan 1955: *The Fathers According to Rabbi Nathan*. Trans. Judah Goldin. New Haven: Yale University Press.

Adler 1966: Adler, E. N. *Jewish Travellers. A Treasury of Travelogues from Nine Centuries*. 2d ed. New York: Hermon Books.

Ahima'as 1924: Salzman, M., ed. and trans. *The Chronicle of Ahimaaz*. New York: Columbia University Press.

Ahmad 1962: Ahmad, M.H.M. "Some Notes on Arabic Historiography during the Zengid and Ayyubid Periods (521/1127-648/1250)." In Lewis/Holt 1962: 79-97.

Amico 1953: Amico, B. *Plans of the Sacred Edifices of the Holy Land*. Translated from the Italian by T. Bellorini and E. Hoade with preface and notes by B. Bagatti. Jerusalem: The Franciscan Printing Press.

Amiran/Eitan 1970: Amiran, R., and A. Eitan. "Excavations in the Courtyard of the Citadel, Jerusalem, 1968-1969 (Preliminary Report)." *Israel Exploration Journal* 20:9-17.

Anonymous Pilgrims 1894: *Anonymous Pilgrims, I-VIII (Eleventh and Twelfth Centuries)*. Trans. A. Stewart. Palestine Pilgrims Text Society 6. Reprint. New York: AMS Press, 1971.

Archives I 1881: *Archives de l'Orient Latin*. Published under the patronage of the Société de l'Orient Latin. Vol. I. Paris: Ernest Leroux.

Archives II 1884: *Archives de l'Orient Latin*. Published under the patronage of the Société de l'Orient Latin. Vol. II. Paris: Ernest Leroux.

Aristeas 1951: *Aristeas to Philocrates (Letter of Aristeas)*. Ed. and trans. Moses Hadas. Reprint. New York: Ktav, 1973.

Armstrong 1967: Armstrong, G. T. "Imperial Church Building and Church-State Relations." *Church History* 36:3-17.

Armstrong 1969: Armstrong, G. T. "Fifth and Sixth Century Church Building in the Holy Land." *Greek Orthodox Theological Review* 14:17-30.

Arnold von Harff 1946: *The Pilgrimage of Arnold von Harff, 1496-1499*. London: The Hakluyt Society (NS 94).

Ashtor 1956: Ashtor-Strauss, L. "Saladin and the Jews." *Hebrew Union College Annual* 27:305-326.

Ashtor 1981: Ashtor, E. "Muslim and Christian Literature in Praise of Jerusalem." In Levine 1981: 187-189.

Atiya 1938: Atiya, A. S. *The Crusade in the Later Middle Ages*. London: Methuen and Co., Ltd.

Auerbach 1971: Auerbach, J. "Western Wall," *Encyclopaedia Judaica*, 16:467-472. Jerusalem: Keter Publishing House.

Avi-Yonah 1954: Avi-Yonah, M. *The Madaba Mosaic Map*. Jerusalem: Israel Exploration Society.

Avi-Yonah 1973: Avi-Yonah, M. "Building History from the Earliest Times to the Nineteenth Century." In D. Amiran, ed. *Urban Geography of Jerusalem*, pp. 13-19. New York and Berlin: W. De Gruyter.

Avi-Yonah 1975: Avi-Yonah, M. "Jerusalem in the Hellenistic and Roman Period." In Avi-Yonah, M., ed. *The World History of the Jewish People*. Vol. VII, *The Herodian Period*, pp. 207-249. New Brunswick: Rutgers University Press.

Avi-Yonah 1976: Avi-Yonah, M. *The Jews of Palestine. A Political History from the Bar Kokhba War to the Arab Conquests*. Oxford: Basil Blackwell.

Avigad 1977: Avigad, N. "A Building Inscription of the Emperor Justinian and the Nea in Jerusalem." *Israel Exploration Journal* 27:145-151.

Avigad 1983: Avigad, N. *Discovering Jerusalem*. Hebrew original. Jerusalem, 1980. Revised English translation. New York: Thomas Nelson.

Ayalon 1958: Ayalon, D. "The System of Payment in Mamluk Military Society." *Journal of the Economic and Social History of the Orient* 1:257-296.

Ayalon 1968: Ayalon, D. "The Muslim City and the Mamluk Military Aristocracy." *Proceedings of Israel Academy of Sciences and Humanities* 2:311-329.

Ayalon 1972: Ayalon, D. "Discharges from Service, Banishment, and Imprisonments in Mamluk Society." *Israel Oriental Studies* 2:324-349.

Ayoub 1984: Ayoub, M. *The Qur'an and Its Interpreters*. Vol. I. Albany: State University of New York Press.

Bagatti 1979: Bagatti, B. *Recherches sur le site du Temple de Jérusalem (I-VII siècle)*. Jerusalem: Franciscan Printing Press.

Bagatti/Testa 1978: Bagatti, B., and E. Testa. *Il Golgota e la Croce*. Jerusalem: Franciscan Printing Press.

Bahat/Broshi 1976: Bahat, D., and M. Broshi. "Excavations in the Armenian Garden." In Yadin 1976: 55-56.

Baldi 1955: Baldi, D. *Enchiridion Locorum Sanctorum*. Rev. ed. Reprint. Jerusalem, Franciscan Printing Press, 1982.

Bassan 1959: Bassan, F. *Chateaubriand et la Terre Sainte*. Paris: Presses Universitaires de France.

Bayatt 1973: Bayatt, A. "Josephus and Population Numbers in First Century Jerusalem." *Palestine Exploration Quarterly*, pp. 51-60.

Ben-Arieh 1975a: Ben-Arieh, Y. "The Growth of Jerusalem in the Nineteenth Century." *Annals of the Association of American Geographers* 65:252-269.

Ben-Arieh 1975b: Ben-Arieh, Y. "The Population of the Large Towns in Palestine during the First Eighty Years of the Nineteenth Century according to Western Sources." In Ma'oz 1975: 49-69.

Ben-Arieh 1979: Ben-Arieh, Y. *The Rediscovery of the Holy Land in the Nineteenth Century*. Jerusalem-Detroit: Magnes Press/Wayne State University Press.

Ben-Arieh/Netzer 1974: Ben-Arieh, S., and E. Netzer. "Excavations along the 'Third Wall' of Jerusalem." *Israel Exploration Journal* 24:97-107.

Ben-Dov 1982: Ben-Dov, M. *The Dig at the Temple Mount*. Jerusalem: Keter Publishing House [Hebrew].

Ben-Dov 1983: Ben-Dov, M. *Jerusalem's Fortifications: The City Walls, the Gates, and the Temple Mount*. Jerusalem: Zmora, Bitan Publishers Ltd. [Hebrew].

Ben-Dov et al. 1983: Ben-Dov, M., et al. *The Western Wall*. Jerusalem: Ministry of Defense Publishing House.

Ben-Sasson 1975: Ben-Sasson, H. H. "The Image of Eretz Israel in the View of Jews Arriving There in the Late Middle Ages." In Ma'oz 1975: 103-110.

Benjamin of Tudela 1907: Adler, M. N. *The Itinerary of Benjamin of Tudela*. Critical text, translation, and commentary. Reprint. New York: Philipp Feldheim, 1965.

Benoit 1952: Benoit, P. "Prétoire, Lithostraton, et Gabbatha." *Revue biblique* 59:531-550.

Benoit 1971: Benoit, P. "L'Antonia d'Herode le Grand et le Forum orientale d'Aelia Capitolina." *Harvard Theological Review* 64:135-167.

Benoit 1976: Benoit, P. "The Archeological Reconstruction of the Antonia Fortress." In Yadin 1976: 87-89.

Benvenisti 1970: Benvenisti, M. *The Crusaders in the Holy Land*. Jerusalem: Israel Universities Press.

Benvenisti 1976: Benvenisti, M. *Jerusalem: The Torn City*. Jerusalem: Isratypset Ltd.

Bertrandon 1848: Bertrandon de la Brocquiére, *Le Voyage d'Outremer*. Trans. T. Wright in *Early Travels in Palestine*, pp. 283-382. London: H. G. Bohn.

Bickerman 1935: Bickerman, E. "La Charte seleucide de Jérusalem." *Revue des études juives* 100:4-35. Reprinted in Bickerman 1980: 44-85.

Bickerman 1937: Bickerman, E. "Un Document relatif á la persecution d'Antiochus IV Epiphane." *Revue de histoire des religions* 115:188-221. Reprinted in Bickerman 1980: 105-135.

Bickerman 1946-1947: Bickerman, E. "The Warning Inscription of Herod's Temple." *Jewish Quarterly Review* 37:387-405. Reprinted in Bickerman 1980: 210-224.

Bickerman 1979: Bickerman, E. *The God of the Maccabees. Studies on the Origin and Meaning of the Maccabean Revolt*. Translated from the German edition of 1937. Leiden: E. J. Brill.

Bickerman 1980: Bickerman, E. *Studies in Jewish and Christian History*. Vol. 2. Leiden: E. J. Brill.

Biruni 1879: Al-Biruni. *The Chronology of Ancient Nations*. Trans. and ed. C. E. Sachau. Reprint. Frankfurt: Minerva, 1969.

Black 1954: Black, M. "The Feast of the Encaenia Ecclesiae in the Ancient Church with Special Reference to Palestine and Syria." *Journal of Ecclesiastical History* 5:78-85.

Bliss/Dickie 1898: Bliss, F. J., and A. C. Dickie. *Excavations at Jerusalem 1894-1897*. London: Palestine Exploration Fund.

Braude/Lewis 1982: Braude, B., and B. Lewis, eds. *Christians and Jews in the Ottoman Empire*. 2 vols. New York and London: Holmes and Meir.

Brehier 1928: Brehier, L. "Charlemagne et la Palestine." *Revue historique* 157:277-291.

Broshi 1974: Broshi, M. "The Expansion of Jerusalem in the Reigns of Hezekiah and Manasseh." *Israel Exploration Journal* 24:21-26.

Broshi 1976: Broshi, M. "Excavations in the House of Caiphas, Mount Zion." In Yadin 1976: 57-60.

Broshi/Tsafrir 1977: Broshi, M., and Y. Tsafrir. "Excavations at the Zion Gate, Jerusalem." *Israel Exploration Journal* 27:28-37.

Brundage 1969: Brundage, J. A. *Medieval Canon Law and the Crusader*. Madison: University of Wisconsin Press.

Burchard 1896: *Burchard of Mount Sion*. Translated from the original Latin by A. Stewart. Palestine Pilgrims Text Society 12. Reprint. New York: AMS Press, 1971.

Burgoyne 1973: Burgoyne, M. "Tariq Bab al-Hadid. A Mamluk Street in the Old City of Jerusalem." *Levant* 5:12-35.

Busink 1970-1980: Busink, T. A. *Der Tempel von Jerusalem von Solomo bis Herodes*. 2 vols. Leiden: E. J. Brill.

Busse 1968: Busse, H. "The Sanctity of Jerusalem in Islam." *Judaism* 17:441-468.

Cahen 1954: Cahen, C. "An Introduction to the First Crusade." *Past and Present* 6:6-30.

Cahen 1957: Cahen, C. "La Féodalité et les institutions politiques de l'Orient Latin." *Accademia Nazionale dei Lincei. Atti del XII Convegno "Volta,"* pp. 167-191. Rome: Accademia Nazionale.

Cahen 1965: Cahen, C. "Crusades." *The Encyclopaedia of Islam*, pp. 63-66. New ed. Leiden: E. J. Brill.

Canard 1965: Canard, M. "Le destruction de l'église de la Résurrection par le calife Hakim." *Byzantion* 35:16-43.

Cartulaire Sepulchre 1849: Rozière, E. J., ed. *Cartulaire de l'église du Saint-Sépulcre de Jérusalem*. Paris: Imprimerie nationale.

Castellani 1922: Castellani, E. *Catalogo dei Firmani ed altri documenti legali . . . concernenti i Santuari le proprieta i diritti della Custodia di Santa Terra*. Jerusalem: Franciscan Printing Press.

Chateaubriand 1969: *Chateaubriand: Oeuvres romanesques et voyages*. Vol. 2. Ed. Maurice Regard. Paris: Editions Gallimard.

Chelebi 1980: *Evliya Tshelebi's Travels in Palestine*. Trans. St. H. Stephan. Jerusalem: Ariel Publishing House.

Chitty 1966: Chitty, D. *The Desert a City*. Oxford: Basil Blackwell.

Christides 1972: Christides, V. "The Names 'Arabes,' 'Sarakenoi,' etc., and their False Byzantine Etymologies." *Byzantinische Zeitschrift* 65:329-333.

City of Jerusalem 1896: *The City of Jerusalem*. Translated from the Old French, with notes, by C. R. Conder. Palestine Pilgrims Text Society 6. Reprint. New York: AMS Press, 1971.

Clermont-Ganneau 1899: Clermont-Ganneau, C. *Archeological Researches in Palestine during the Years 1873-1874*. Vol. I. Trans. Aubrey Stewart. Reprint. Jerusalem, 1971.

Cohen 1973: Cohen, A. *Palestine in the Eighteenth Century: Patterns of Government and Administration*. Jerusalem: The Magnes Press.

Cohen 1976: Cohen, A. *Ottoman Documents on the Jewish Community of Jerusalem in the Sixteenth Century*. Jerusalem: Yad Izhak Ben-Zvi.

Cohen 1982: Cohen, A. "On the Realities of the Millet System: Jerusalem in the Sixteenth Century." In Braude/Lewis 1982: 2, 7-18.

Cohen/Lewis 1978: Cohen, A., and B. Lewis. *Population and Revenue in the Towns of Palestine in the Sixteenth Century*. Princeton: Princeton University Press.

Cohn 1970: Cohn, N. *The Pursuit of the Millennium. Revolutionary Millenarians and Mystical Anarchists of the Middle Ages*. 2d ed. London: Oxford University Press.

Conybeare 1910: Conybeare, F. "Antiochus Strategos' Account of the Sack of Jerusalem in A.D. 614." *English Historical Review* 25:502-516.

Corbett 1952: Corbett, S. "Some Observations on the Gateways to the Herodian Temple in Jerusalem." *Palestine Exploration Quarterly* 84:7-14.

Corbo 1982: Corbo, V. *Il Santo Sepolcro di Gerusalemme. Aspetti archeologici dalle origini al periodo crociato*. 3 vols. Jerusalem: Franciscan Printing Press.

Coüasnon 1974: Coüasnon, C. *The Church of the Holy Sepulchre in Jerusalem*. London: Oxford University Press.

Curzon 1849: Curzon, R. *Visits to Monasteries in the Levant*. Reprint. London: Arthur Barker Ltd., 1955.

Dagron 1977: Dagron, G. "Le Christianisme dans la ville byzantine." *Dumbarton Oaks Papers* 31:3-25.

Danby 1933: Danby, H. *The Mishna*. Translated from the Hebrew. Oxford: Oxford University Press.

Daniel 1960: Daniel, N. *Islam and the West. The Making of an Image*. Edinburgh: The University Press.

Daniel the Abbot 1895: *The Pilgrimage of the Russian Abbot Daniel in the Holy Land*. Annotated by C. W. Wilson. Palestine Pilgrims Text Society 4. Reprint. New York: AMS Press, 1971.

Darrag 1961: Darrag, A. *L'Egypte sous le Regne de Barsbay, 825-841/1422-1438*. Damascus: Institut français de Damas.

Davies 1982: Davies, W. D. *The Territorial Dimension of Judaism*. Berkeley and Los Angeles: The University of California Press.

De Sandoli 1983: De Sandoli, S. *Itinera Hierosolymitana Crucesignatorum (saec. XII-XIII)*. Vol. III, *Tempore recuperationis Terrae Sanctae (1187-1244)*. Jerusalem: Franciscan Printing Press.

de Vogué 1881: de Vogué, M. le Comte. "Archard d'Arrouaise, Poème sur le Templum Domini." In Archives I 1881: 562-579.

Dinur 1957: Dinur, B. "The Emigration from Spain to Eretz Israel after the Disorders of 1391." *Zion* 32:161-174.

Drory 1981: Drory, J. "Jerusalem during the Mamluk Period." In Levine 1981: 190-214.

Dubois 1956: Dubois, Pierre. *The Recovery of the Holy Land*. Trans. W. I. Brandt. New York: Columbia University Press.

Duprez 1970: Duprez, A. *Jésus et les Dieux Guérisseurs*. Paris: J. Gabalda.

Durrieu 1881: Durrieu, P. "Procès-verbale du martyre de quatre frères Mineurs en 1391." In Archives I 1881: 539-546.

Erdmann 1977: Erdmann, C. *The Origin of the Idea of Crusade*. Translated from the German edition. (Stuttgart, 1935) by M. W. Baldwin. Princeton: Princeton University Press.

Fattal 1958: Fattal, A. *Le Statut légal des non-musulmans en pays d'Islam*. Beirut: Imprimerie Catholique.

Felix Fabri 1893: *The Book of the Wanderings of Felix Fabri*. Trans. A. Stewart. 2 vols. Palestine Pilgrims Text Society 7-10. Reprint. New York: AMS Press, 1971.

Finegan 1969: Finegan, J. *The Archaeology of the New Testament*. Princeton: Princeton University Press.

Foster 1970: Foster, B. R. "Agoronomos and Muhtasib." *Journal of the Economic and Social History of the Orient* 13:128-144.

Fulcher of Chartres 1913: Hagenmeyer, H. *Fulcheri Carnotensis historia Hierosolymitana (1095-1127)*. Heidelberg: C. Winters Universitätsbuchhandlung.

Fulcher of Chartres 1969: *Fulcher of Chartres. A History of the Expedition to Jerusalem, 1095-1127*. Trans. F. R. Ryan. Knoxville, University of Tennessee Press.

Gabrieli 1962: Gabrieli, F. "Historiography of the Crusades." In Lewis/Holt 1962: 98-107.

Gabrieli 1969: Gabrieli, F. *Arab Historians of the Crusades*. Berkeley and Los Angeles: University of California Press.

Gätje 1976: Gätje, H., *The Qur'an and its Exegesis*. Berkeley and Los Angeles: University of California Press.

Gaudefroy-Demombynes 1923: Gaudefroy-Demombynes, M. *La Syrie à l'époque des Mamelouks d'après les auteurs arabes*. Paris: Paul Geuthner.

Gesta Francorum 1962: *Gesta Francorum. The Deeds of the Franks and Other Pilgrims to Jerusalem*. Ed. [and trans.] by Rosalind Hill. London: Thomas Nelson and Sons Ltd.

Gibb 1969: Gibb, H.A.R. "The Aiyubids." In K. M. Setton, *A History of the Crusades*. Vol. II, *The Later Crusades (1189-1311)*, pp. 693-714. Ed. R. L. Wolff and H. W. Hazard. Madison: University of Wisconsin Press.

Gil 1976: Gil, M. *Documents of the Jewish Pious Foundations from the Cairo Geniza*. Leiden: E. J. Brill.

Gil 1980: Gil, M. "Religion and Realities in Islamic Taxation." *Israel Oriental Studies* 10:21-33.

Gil 1981: Gil, M. "The Sixty Years War (969-1029 CE)." In J. Hacker, ed. *Shalem*. Vol. 3, pp. 1-56. Jerusalem: Yad Izhak Ben Zvi [Hebrew].

Gil 1982: Gil, M. "The Jewish Quarters of Jerusalem (A.D. 638-1099) According to Cairo Geniza Documents and Other Sources." *Journal of Near Eastern Studies* 41:261-278.

Goitein 1952: Goitein, S. D. "Contemporary Letters on the Capture of Jerusalem by the Crusaders." *Journal of Jewish Studies* 3:162-177.

Goitein 1966: Goitein, S. D., "The Sanctity of Jerusalem and Palestine in Early Islam." In Goitein, S. D. *Studies in Islamic History and Institutions*. Leiden: E. J. Brill.

Goitein 1971: Goitein, S. D. *A Mediterranean Society. The Jewish Communities of the Arab World as Portrayed in the Documents of the Cairo Geniza*. Vol. 2, *The Community*. Berkeley and Los Angeles: University of California Press.

Goitein 1982: Goitein, S. D. "Jerusalem in the Arab Period (638-1099)." In Levine 1982: 168-198.

Goldin 1945: Goldin, J. "The Two Versions of Avot de Rabbi Natan." *Hebrew Union College Annual* 19:97-120.

Goldschmidt-Lehman 1981: Goldschmidt-Lehmann, R. P. "The Second (Herodian) Temple: Selected Bibliography." In Levine 1981: 336-358.

Goldziher 1969-1971: Goldziher, I. *Muslim Studies*. Ed. S. M. Stern. 2 vols. London: George Allen and Unwin.

Golvin 1967: Golvin, L. "Quelques Notes sur le suq al-Qattanin et ses annexes à Jérusalem." *Bulletin d'études orientales* 20:101-117.

Grabar 1965: Grabar, O. "A New Inscription from the Haram al-Sharif in Jerusalem." In *Studies in Islamic Art and Architecture in Honour of Professor K.A.C. Creswell*, pp. 72-83. Cairo: American University in Cairo Press.

Grabar 1973: Grabar, O. *The Formation of Islamic Art*. New Haven and London: Yale University Press.

Grabar 1980: Grabar, O. "Al-Kuds: Part B. The Monuments." In *The Encyclopaedia of Islam*. New ed. Leiden: E. J. Brill.

Grabois 1982: Grabois, A. "Christian Pilgrims in the Thirteenth Century and the Latin Kingdom of Jerusalem: Burchard of Mount Sion." In B. Z. Kedar et al., *Outremer. Studies of the Crusading Kingdom of Jerusalem. Presented to Joshua Prawer*, pp. 285-296. Jerusalem: Yad Izhak Ben Zvi Institute.

Graf/O'Connor 1977: Graf, D. F., and M. O'Connor. "The Origin of the Term Saracen and the Rawaffa Inscription.," *Byzantine Studies* 4:52-66.

Gutmann 1976: Gutmann, J. *The Temple of Solomon. Archeological Fact and Medieval Tradition in Christian, Islamic and Jewish Art*. Missoula: Scholars Press.

Hacker 1974: Hacker, J. "The Connections between Spanish Jewry with Eretz Israel between 1391 and 1492." In *Shalem*. Vol. 1, pp. 105-156. Jerusalem: Yad Itzhak Ben-Zvi [Hebrew].

Halevi 1924: *Selected Poems of Judah Halevi*. Ed. H. Brody, trans. N. Salman. Reprint. New York, 1973.

Hamilton 1980: Hamilton, B. *The Latin Church in the Crusader States*. London: Variorum.

Hamilton 1947: Hamilton, W. *The Structural History of the Aqsa Mosque*. Jerusalem.

Haran 1978: Haran, M. *Temples and Temple-Service in Ancient Israel*. Oxford: At the Clarendon Press.

Harawi 1957: Abu al-Hasan al-Harawi. *Guide des Lieux de Pèlerinage*. Trans. Janine Sourdel-Thomine. Damascus: Institute français de Damas.

Harizi 1881: Schwab, M. "Al-Harizi et ses peregrinations en Terre Sainte (vers 1217)." In Archives I 1881: 231-244.

628

Hasson 1981: Hasson, I. "Muslim Literature in praise of Jerusalem: *Fada'il Bayt al-Maqdis*." In Levine 1981: 168-184.

Hazard 1977: Hazard, H. W., ed. *The Art and Architecture of the Crusader States*. Vol. IV of K. M. Setton, ed. *A History of the Crusades*. Madison: University of Wisconsin Press.

Hengel 1974: Hengel, M. *Judaism and Hellenism. Studies in their Encounter in Palestine during the Early Hellenistic Period*. London: SCM Press.

Hennessy 1970: Hennessy, J. B. "Preliminary Report on Excavations at the Damascus Gate, Jerusalem." *Levant* 2:22-27.

Heyd 1975: Heyd, U. "Turkish Documents Concerning the Jews of Safed in the Sixteenth Century." In Ma'oz 1975: 111-118.

Heyd 1884: Heyd, W. "Les Consulats établis en Terre Sainte au Moyen-Age pour la protection des pèlerins." In Archives II 1884: 355-364.

Heyd 1885: Heyd, W. *Histoire du commerce du Levant au Moyen-Age*. 2 vols. Trans. F. Raynaud. Reprint. Amsterdam, 1967.

Hill 1971: Hill, D. R. *The Termination of Hostilities in the Early Arab Conquests, A.D. 634-656*. London: Luzac and Company Ltd.

Hirschberg 1951-1952: Hirschberg, J. W. "The Sources of Moslem Traditions Concerning Jerusalem." *Rocznik Orientalistyczny* 17:314-350.

Hirschberg 1976: Hirschberg, J. W. "The Remains of an Ancient Synagogue on Mount Zion." In Yadin 1976: 116-117.

Hirschberg et al. 1973: Hirschberg, H. Z., W. P. Pick, and J. Kaniel. "Jerusalem under Ottoman Rule (1517-1917)." Reprinted from *Encyclopaedia Judaica* in *Jerusalem*, pp. 77-142. Jerusalem: Keter Publishing House.

Hoade 1981: Hoade, E. *Guide to the Holy Land*. 11th ed. Jerusalem: Franciscan Printing Press.

Holtz 1971: Holtz, A., ed. *The Holy City. Jews on Jerusalem*. New York: W. W. Norton.

Honigmann 1950: Honigmann, E. "Juvenal of Jerusalem." *Dumbarton Oaks Papers* 5:209-279.

Honigmann 1961: Honigmann, E. *Die Ostgrenze des byzantinischen Reiches*. Brussels: Institut de philologie et d'histoire orientales.

Hopkins 1971: Hopkins, I.W.J. "The Four Quarters of Jerusalem." *Palestine Exploration Quarterly*, pp. 68-85.

Horn 1962: Horn, E. *Ichnographiae Monumentorum Terrae Sanctae (1724-1744)*. 2d ed. of the Latin text with English version by E. Hoade and preface and notes by B. Bagatti. Jerusalem: Franciscan Printing Press.

Hütteroth 1975: Hütteroth, W., "The Pattern of Settlement in Palestine in the Sixteenth Century. Geographical Research on Turkish *Defter-i Mufassal*." In Ma'oz 1975: 3-10.

Hurewitz 1975: Hurewitz, J. *The Middle East and North Africa in World Politics*. Vol. I, *European Expansion 1535-1914*. 2d ed. New Haven: Yale University Press.

Ibn al-Qalanisi 1932: Ibn al-Qalanisi. *Continuation of the Chronicle of Damascus: The Damascus Chronicle of the Crusades*. Ed. and trans. H.A.R. Gibb. London.

Ibn Battuta 1959-1962: *The Travels of Ibn Battuta, A.D. 1325-1354*. Trans. H.A.R. Gibb. 2 vols. Cambridge: At the University Press.

Ibn Ishaq 1955: *Ibn Ishaq. The Life of Muhammad*. A translation of Ishaq's *Sirat Rasul Allah*, with introduction and notes by A. Guillaume. Oxford: Oxford University Press.

Ibn Khaldun 1967: Ibn Khaldun. *The Muqaddimah: An Introduction to History*. Trans. Franz Rosenthal. 3 vols. 2d ed. Princeton: Princeton University Press.

Ibn Taymiyya 1936: Matthews, C. D. "A Muslim Iconoclast: Ibn Taymiyya on the 'Merits' of Jerusalem." *Journal of the American Oriental Society* 56:1-21.

Inalcik 1977: Inalcik, H. "Centralization and Decentralization in Ottoman Administration." In Naff/Owen 1977: 27-52.

Jacobson 1980: Jacobson, M. D. "Ideas Concerning the Plan of the Herodian Temple." *Palestine Exploration Quarterly*, pp. 33-40.

Jeremias 1969: Jeremias, J. *Jerusalem in the Time of Jesus*. Philadelphia: Fortress Press.

John of Wurzburg 1896: *John of Wurzburg. Description of the Holy Land*. Trans. A. Stewart with notes by C. W. Wilson. Palestine Pilgrims Text Society 5. Reprint. New York: AMS Press, 1971.

Johns 1950: Johns, C. N. "The Citadel, Jerusalem." *Quarterly of the Department of Antiquities in Palestine* 14:121-190.

Joranson 1927: Joranson, E. "The Alleged Frankish Protectorate in Palestine." *American Historical Review* 32:241-261.

Joranson 1928: Joranson, E. "The Great German Pilgrimage of 1064-1065." In Paetow 1928: 3-43.

Kaegi 1969: Kaegi, W. E. "Initial Byzantine Reactions to the Arab Conquest." *Church History* 38:139-149.

Kark 1981: Kark, R. "The Traditional Middle Eastern City. The Case of Jerusalem and Jaffa during the Nineteenth Century." *Zeitschrift des Deutschen Palästina-vereins* 97:93-108.

Kenyon 1974: Kenyon, K. *Digging Up Jerusalem*. New York: Praeger Publishers.

Kenyon/Ben-Arieh 1975: Kenyon, K., S. Ben-Arieh, and E. Netzer. "Letters to the Editor." *Israel Exploration Journal* 25:265-267.

Kessler 1979: Kessler, C. "The Tashtimuriyya in Jerusalem in the Light of a Recent Archeological Survey." *Levant* 11:136-161.

Kessler/Burgoyne 1978: Kessler, C., and M. Burgoyne. "The Fountain of Sultan Qaytbay in the Sacred Precinct of Jerusalem." In P. Moorey and P. Parr, eds. *Archaeology in the Levant: Essays for Kathleeen Kenyon*, pp. 250-268. London: Aris and Phillips.

Kister 1969: Kister, M. J. " 'You shall only set out for three mosques': A Study of an Early Tradition." *Le Muséon* 82:173-196.

Kobler 1978: F. Kobler, ed. *Letters of Jews through the Ages from Biblical Times to the Middle of the Eighteenth Century*. 2 vols. New York: East and West Library.

Kraeling 1942: Kraeling, C. H. "The Episode of the Roman Standards at Jerusalem." *Harvard Theological Review* 35:263-289.

Krautheimer 1967: Krautheimer, R. "The Constantinian Basilica." *Dumbarton Oaks Papers* 21:117-140.

Krey 1921: Krey, A. C., ed. *The First Crusade: The Accounts of Eye-Witnesses and Participants*. Princeton: Princeton University Press.

Kriss/Kriss-Heinrich 1960: Kriss, R., and H. Kriss-Heinrich. *Volksglauben im Bereich des Islam*. Vol. I, *Wallfahrtswesen und Heiligenverehung*. Wiesbaden: Otto Harrassowitz.

Laurent 1873: Laurent, J.C.M. *Peregrinatores Medii Aevi Quatuor*. 2d ed. Leipzig: J. C. Hinrichs.

Le Strange 1890: Le Strange, G. *Palestine under the Moslems*. Reprint. Beirut: Khayats, 1965.

Levine 1981: Levine, L., ed. *The Jerusalem Cathedra. Studies in the History, Archaeology, Geography, and Ethnography of the Land of Israel*. Vol. 1. Jerusalem: Yad Izhaq Ben-Zvi Institute.

Levine 1982: Levine, L., ed. *The Jerusalem Cathedra. Studies in the History, Archaeology,*

Geography, and Ethnography of the Land of Israel. Vol. 2. Jerusalem: Yad Izhak Ben-Zvi Institute.

Levine 1983: Levine, L., ed. *The Jerusalem Cathedra. Studies in the History, Archaeology, Geography, and Ethnography of the Land of Israel.* Vol. 3. Jerusalem: Yad Izhak Ben-Zvi Institute.

Lewis 1950: Lewis, B. "An Apocalyptic Vision of Islamic History." *Bulletin of the School of Oriental and African Studies* (London) 13:308-338.

Lewis 1954: Lewis, B. "Studies in the Ottoman Archives I." *Bulletin of the School of Oriental and African Studies* (London) 16:469-501.

Lewis 1974: Lewis, B. "On That Day. A Jewish Apocalyptic Poem on the Arab Conquests." *Mélanges d'Islamologie . . . de Armand Abel,* pp. 197-200. Leiden: E. J. Brill.

Lewis 1975: Lewis, B. *History—Remembered, Recovered, Invented.* Princeton: Princeton University Press.

Lewis 1982: Lewis, B. *The Muslim Discovery of Europe.* New York: W. W. Norton and Co.

Lewis/Holt 1962: Lewis, B., and P. M. Holt. *Historians of the Middle East.* London: London University, School of African and Oriental Studies.

Lewy 1941/1983: Lewy, J. "Emperor Julian and the Building of the Temple." *Zion* 6:1-32 [Hebrew]. English translation in Levine 1983: 70-96.

Lifshitz 1977: Lifshitz, B. "Jérusalem sous la domination romaine. Histoire de la ville depuis la conquête de Pompée jusqu'au Constantin." In ANRW II/8, pp. 444-489. New York and Berlin: Walter de Gruyter.

Little 1980: Little, D. "The Significance of the Haram Documents for the Study of Medieval Islamic History." *Der Islam* 57:189-219.

Ludolph von Suchem 1895: *Ludolph von Suchem. Description of the Holy Land and the Way Thither.* Trans. A. Stewart. Palestine Pilgrims Text Society 12. Reprint. New York: AMS Press, 1971.

Lux 1972: Lux, U. "Vorlaufiger Bericht über die Ausgrabung unter der Erlöserkirche in Muristan in der Altstadt von Jerusalem in den Jahren 1970 und 1971." *Zeitschrift des Deutschen Palästina-Vereins* 88:185-201.

Ma'oz 1975: Ma'oz, M., ed. *Studies on Palestine during the Ottoman Period.* Jerusalem: The Magnes Press.

Mackowski 1980: Mackowski, R. M. *Jerusalem, City of Jesus. An Exploration of the Traditions, Writings, and Remains of the Holy City From the Time of Christ.* Grand Rapids: Eerdmans.

Maehl 1962: Maehl, S. "Jerusalem im mittelalterlichen Sicht." *Welt als Geschichte* 22:11-26.

Maimonides 1957: *The Code of Maimonides. Book Eight. The Book of Temple Service.* Yale Judaica Series vol. XII. Translated from the Hebrew by M. Lewittes. New Haven: Yale University Press.

Mandaville 1975: Mandaville, J. "The Jerusalem Shari'a Court Records: A Supplement and Complement to the Central Ottoman Archives." In Ma'oz 1975: 517-524.

Mann 1920-1922: Mann, J. *The Jews in Egypt and in Palestine under the Fatimid Caliphs.* 2 vols. Oxford: Oxford University Press. Reprinted with reader's guide by S. D. Goitein, New York, 1969.

Mann 1922: Mann, J. "A Tract by an Early Karaite Settler in Jerusalem." *Jewish Quarterly Review* 12:257-298.

Mann 1931: Mann, J. *Texts and Studies in Jewish History and Literature.* Vol I. Reprint. New York, 1970.

Mann 1935: Mann, J. *Texts and Studies in Jewish History and Literature.* Vol. II, *Karaitica.* Reprint. New York 1970.

Marmadji 1951: Marmadji, A. S. *Textes géographiques arabes sur la Palestine*. Paris: J. Gabalda et Cie.

Massignon 1951/1963: Massignon, L. "Documents sur quelques waqfs musulmans. . . ." *Revue des études islamiques* (1951), 74-140. Reprinted in Y. Moubarac, ed. *Opera minora*. Vol. 3, pp. 181-232. Beirut: Dar al-Maaref, 1963.

Matthew of Edessa 1972: "The Chronicle of Matthew of Edessa." Trans A. E. Destourian. Ph.D. diss., Rutgers University.

Matthews 1932: Matthews, C. D. "The Wailing Wall and al-Buraq: Is the 'Wailing Wall' in Jerusalem the 'Wall of al-Buraq'?" *Moslem World* 22:331-339.

Matthews 1949: Matthews, C. D. *Palestine, Mohammedan Holy Land*. New Haven: Yale University Press.

Maundrell 1963: *Henry Maundrell. A Journey from Aleppo to Jerusalem in 1697*. New introduction by David Howell. Beirut: Khayats.

Mazar 1969: Mazar, B. *The Excavations in the Old City of Jerusalem. Preliminary Report of the First Season, 1968*. Jerusalem: Israel Exploration Society.

Mazar 1971: Mazar, B. *The Excavations in the Old City of Jerusalem. Preliminary Report on the Second and Third Season, 1969-1970*. Jerusalem: Israel Exploration Society.

Mazar 1975: Mazar, B. *The Mountain of the Lord*. New York: Doubleday and Co.

Meeks/Wilken 1978: Meeks, W. A., and R. L. Wilken. *Jews and Christians in Antioch in the First Four Centuries of the Common Era*. Missoula: Scholars Press.

Montefiore 1962: Montefiore, H. "Sulpicius Severus and Titus' Council of War." *Historia* 11:156-170.

Morkholm 1966: Morkholm, O. *Antiochus IV of Syria*. Copenhagen: Gyldendalske Boghandel.

Mujir 1876: *Histoire de Jérusalem et d'Hebron*. Fragments of the Chronicle of Mujir al-Din translated from the Arabic by Henry Sauvaire. Paris: Ernest Laroux.

Muqaddasi 1896: *Al-Muqaddasi. Description of Syria, including Palestine*. Translated from the Arabic and annotated by G. Le Strange. Palestine Pilgrims Text Society 3. Reprint. New York: AMS Press, 1971.

Naff 1977: Naff, T. "Ottoman Diplomatic Relations with Europe in the Eighteenth Century: Patterns and Trends." In Naff/Owen 1977: 88-107.

Naff/Owen 1977: Naff, T., and R. Owen, eds. *Studies in Eighteenth-Century Islamic History*. Carbondale: University of Southern Illinois Press.

Nasir-i Khusraw 1893: *Nasir-i Khusraw. Diary of a Journey Through Syria and Palestine*. Translated from the Persian and annotated by G. Le Strange. Palestine Pilgrims Text Society 4. Reprint. New York: AMS Press, 1971.

Nau 1927: Nau, F. "Deux episodes de l'histoire juive sous Théodose II (423 et 438) d'après la vie de Barsauma le Syrien." *Revue des études juives* 83:184-206.

Neusner 1970: Neusner, J. *A Life of Yohanan ben Zakkai*. 2d ed. Leiden: E. J. Brill.

Neusner 1981: Neusner, J. *Judaism. The Evidence of the Mishnah*. Chicago and London: The University of Chicago Press.

Neusner 1983: Neusner, J. *Judaism in Society. The Evidence of the Yerushalmi*. Chicago: The University of Chicago Press.

Niccolo Poggibonsi 1945: *Fra Niccolo of Poggibonsi. A Voyage Beyond the Seas (1346-1350)*. Trans. T. Bellorini and E. Hoade. Jerusalem: Franciscan Printing Press.

Noradounghian 1897-1903: Noradounghian, G. *Recueil d'actes internationaux de l'Empire ottoman*. 4 vols. Paris: F. Pichon.

Ovadiah 1970: Ovadiah, A. *Corpus of the Byzantine Churches in the Holy Land*. Bonn: Peter Hanstein Verlag.

Paetow 1928: Paetow, L. J., ed. *The Crusades and Other Historical Essays Presented to Dana C. Monro*. New York: F. S. Crofts.

Parrinder 1977: Parrinder, G. *Jesus in the Qur'an*. New York: Oxford University Press.

Peeters 1950: Peeters, P. *L'Orient et Byzance: Le Tréfonds oriental de l'hagiographie byzantine*. Brussels: Societé des Bollandistes.

Perlmann 1973: Perlmann, M. "A Seventeenth-Century Exhortation Concerning Al-Aqsa." *Israel Oriental Studies* 3:261-292.

Pesikta Rabbati 1968: *Pesikta Rabbati*. Trans. William G. Braude. 2 vols. New Haven and London: Yale University Press.

Peters 1982: Peters, F. E. *The Children of Abraham: Judaism, Christianity, and Islam*. Princeton: Princeton University Press.

Peters 1983: Peters, F. E. "Hellenism and the Near East." *Biblical Archaeologist*, pp. 33-39.

Philipsborn 1961: Philipsborn, A. "Der Fortschritt in der Entwicklung des byzantinischen Krankenhauswesens." *Byzantinische Zeitschrift* 54:338-365.

Pinkerfeld 1960: Pinkerfeld, J. "David's Tomb: Notes on the History of the Building." *Bulletin Rabinowitz* 3:41-43.

Pixner 1976: Pixner, B.-G. "An Essene Quarter on Mt. Zion?" *Studia Hierosolymitana* 1:245-284.

Prawer 1966: Prawer, J. "Crusader Cities." In H. A. Mishkimin et al., eds. *The Medieval City*, pp. 179-200. New Haven and London: Yale University Press.

Prawer 1972: Prawer, J. *The Latin Kingdom of Jerusalem. European Colonialism in the Middle Ages*. London: Weidenfeld and Nicolson.

Rafeq 1977: Rafeq, A. K. "Changes in the Relationship between the Ottoman Central Administration and the Syrian Provinces from the Sixteenth to the Nineteenth Centuries." In Naff/Owen 1977: 53-73.

Recueil Lois 1841-1843: *Recueil des Historiens des Croisades. Lois*. 2 vols. Paris: Academie des Inscriptions et Belles Lettres.

Renov 1970: Renov, I. "A View of Herod's Temple from Nicanor's Gate in a Mural Panel of the Dura Europus Synagogue." *Israel Exploration Journal* 20:67-72.

Richard 1965: Richard, J. "Sur un passage du 'Pelerinage de Charlemagne': Le Marche de Jerusalem." *Revue belge de philologie et d'histoire* 13:552-555.

Ricoldo 1884: R. Röhricht. "Lettres de Ricoldo de Monte-Croce sur la prise d'Acre." In Archives II 1884: 258-296.

Riley-Smith 1967: Riley-Smith, J. *The Knights of Saint John in Jerusalem and Cyprus, 1050-1310*. London: Macmillan.

Riley-Smith 1973: Riley-Smith, J. *The Feudal Nobility and the Kingdom of Jerusalem, 1174-1277*. London: Archon Books.

Robinson 1841: Robinson, E. *Biblical Researches in Palestine, Mount Sinai and Arabia Petrea in 1838*. 3 vols. Reprint. New York, 1977.

Roger 1664: Roger, E. *La Terre Sainte*. Paris.

Röhricht 1893-1904: Röhricht, R., ed. *Regesta Regni Hierosolymitani*. 2 vols. Innsbruck: Libraria Academica Wagneriana.

Rosenau 1979: Rosenau, H. *Vision of the Temple. The Image of the Temple of Jerusalem in Judaism and Christianity*. London: Oresko Books Ltd.

Rubin 1982: Rubin, Z. "The Church of the Holy Sepulchre and the Conflict between the Sees of Jerusalem and Caesarea." In Levine 1982: 79-105.

Runciman 1948: Runciman, S. "The Byzantine 'Protectorate' in the Holy Land." *Byzantion* 18:207-215.

Runciman 1954: Runciman, S. *A History of the Crusades*. 3 vols. Cambridge: Cambridge University Press.

Saewulf 1896: *Saewulf. Pilgrimage to Jerusalem and the Holy Land*. Trans. the Lord

Bishop of Clifton. Palestine Pilgrims Text Society 4. Reprint. New York: AMS Press, 1971.

Said 1978: Said, E. W. *Orientalism*. New York: Pantheon Books.

Sanderson 1931: Forster, W., ed. *The Travels of John Sanderson in the Levant*. London: Hakluyt Society (2d series no. 67).

Savage 1977: Savage, H. L. "Pilgrimages and Pilgrim Shrines in Palestine and Syria after 1050." In Hazard 1977: 199-220.

Schaefer 1981: Schaefer, P. *Der Bar Kokhba-Aufstand. Studien zum zweiten jüdischen Krieg gegen Rom*. Tübingen: J.C.B. Mohr.

Schalit 1969: Schalit, A. *König Herodes: Der Mann und sein Werk*. Berlin: W. De Gruyter.

Schechter 1908: Schechter, S. "Safed in the Sixteenth Century: A City of Legists and Mystics." In *Studies in Judaism*. 2d series, pp. 202-285. Phildelphia: The Jewish Publication Society.

Schick 1901: Schick, C. "The Ancient Churches in the Muristan." In *Palestine Exploration Fund Quarterly Statement*, pp. 51-53.

Schick 1902: Schick, C. "The Muristan or the Site of the Hospital of St. John in Jerusalem." In *Palestine Exploration Fund Quarterly Statement*, pp. 42-56.

Scholem 1973: Scholem, G. *Sabbatai Sevi. The Mystical Messiah, 1626-1676*. Princeton: Princeton University Press.

Schürer 1973: Schürer, E. *The History of the Jewish People in the Age of Jesus Christ*. Rev. and ed. G. Vermes and F. Millar. Vol. 1. Edinburgh: T. & T. Clark Ltd.

Schürer 1979: Schürer, E. *The History of the Jewish People in the Age of Jesus Christ*. Rev. and ed. G. Vermes and F. Millar. Vol. 2. Edinburgh: T. & T. Clark Ltd.

Schwartz 1983: Schwartz, D. R. "Josephus and Philo on Pontius Pilate." In Levine 1983: 26-45.

Searight 1970: Searight, S. *The British in the Middle East*. New York: Athenaeum.

Seetzen 1854-1859: Seetzen, U. J. *Reisen durch Syrien, Palästina, etc*. Ed. F. Krause et al. 4 vols. Berlin: G. Reimer.

Sharon 1975: Sharon, M. "The Political Role of the Bedouins in Palestine in the Sixteenth and Seventeenth Centuries." In Ma'oz 1975: 11-30.

Silberman 1982: Silberman, N. A. *Digging for God and Country. Exploration, Archaeology and the Secret Struggle for the Holy Land, 1799-1917*. New York: Alfred A. Knopf.

Simons 1952: Simons, J. *Jerusalem in the Old Testament. Researches and Theories*. Leiden: E. J. Brill.

Sivan 1967: Sivan, E., "Le Charactère sacré de Jérusalem dans l'Islam aux XIIe-XIIIe siècles." *Studia Islamica* 27:149-182.

Sivan 1968: Sivan, E. *L'Islam et la Croisade. Idéologie et propagande dans les réactions musulmans aux Croisades*. Paris: Librairie d'Amerique et d'Orient.

Sivan 1971: Sivan, E. "The Beginnings of the Fada'il al-Quds Literature." *Israel Oriental Studies* 1:263-271.

Smallwood 1976: Smallwood, R. M. *The Jews under Roman Rule. From Pompey to Diocletian*. Leiden: E. J. Brill.

Smith 1907: Smith, G. A. *Jerusalem. The Topography, Economics, and History from the Earliest Times to A.D. 70*. Reprint. 2 vols. Jerusalem: Ariel, n.d.

Sokolow 1981: Sokolow, M. "The Denial of Muslim Sovereignty over Eretz-Israel in Two Tenth Century Karaite Bible Commentaries." In J. Hacker, ed. *Shalem*. Vol. 3, pp. 309-318. Jerusalem: Yad Izhak Ben Zvi.

Soucek 1976: Soucek, P. "The Temple of Solomon in Islamic Legend and Art." In Gutmann 1976: 73-124.

Spyridon 1938: Spyridon, S. N. "Annals of Palestine, 1821-1841." *Journal of the Palestine Oriental Society*, pp. 63-132.

Stein 1954: Stein, S. "The Liturgy of Hanukkah and the First Two Books of Maccabees." *Journal of Jewish Studies* 5:100-106, 148-155.

Stinespring 1939: Stinespring, W. F. "Hadrian in Palestine." *Journal of the American Oriental Society* 59:360-365.

Stinespring 1966: Stinespring, W. F. "Wilson's Arch Revisited." *Biblical Archaeologist* 29:27-36.

Stinespring 1967: Stinespring, W. F. "Wilson's Arch and the Masonic Hall, Summer 1966." *Biblical Archaeologist* 30:27-31.

Sumption 1975: Sumption, J. *Pilgrimage: An Image of Medieval Religion*. London: Faber and Faber.

Suriano 1949: *Fra Francesco Suriano. Treatise on the Holy Land*. Trans. T. Bellorini and E. Hoade. Jerusalem: Studium Biblicum Franciscanum; reprint, 1983.

Tamari 1968: Tamari, S. "Sulla conversione della chiesa di Sant'Anna a Gerusalemme nella Madrasa as-Salahiyya." *Rivista degli Studi Orientali* 43:327-354.

Tamari 1976: Tamari, S. "Al-Ashrafiyya—An Imperial Madrasa in Jerusalem." *Memorie Accademia Nazionale dei Lincei*. Vol. 15, 5, pp. 537-568. Rome: Accademia Nazionale.

Tcherikover 1959: Tcherikover, V. *Hellenistic Civilization and the Jews*. Pb. reprint. New York: Athenaeum, 1970.

Theoderich 1896: *Theoderich. Description of the Holy Places*. Trans. A. Stewart. Palestine Pilgrims Text Society 5. Reprint. New York: AMS Press, 1971.

Tibawi 1978: Tibawi, A. L. *The Islamic Pious Foundations in Jerusalem. Origins, History, and Usurpation by Israel*. London: The Islamic Cultural Centre.

Timberlake 1616: *Henry Timberlake. A True and Strange Discourse of the Travels of Two English Pilgrims*. Reprinted in William Oldys, ed. *The Harleian Miscellany*. Vol. I, pp. 337-353. London, 1808.

Treaties 1855: Foreign Office, Librarian, and Keeper of the Records [Edward Hertslet]. *Treaties etc. between Turkey and Foreign Powers, 1535-1855*. London: Harrison.

Tsafrir 1976: Tsafrir, Y. "The Location of the Seleucid Akra in Jerusalem." In Yadin 1976: 85-86.

Tsafrir 1977: Tsafrir, Y. "Muqaddasi's Gates of Jerusalem: A New Identification Based on Byzantine Sources." *Israel Exploration Journal* 27:152-161.

Tsafrir 1979: Tsafrir, Y. "The Maps Used by Theodosius: On the Pilgrims' Maps of the Holy Land and Jerusalem in the Sixth Century C.E." *Cathedra* 11:63-85 [Hebrew].

van Berchem 1922: van Berchem, M. *Corpus inscriptionum arabicarum. Syrie du Sud*. Vol. 2, *Jerusalem, "Ville."* Cairo: Institut français d'archéologie orientale.

van Berchem 1927: van Berchem, M. *Matériaux pour un Corpus Inscriptionum Arabicarum. Syrie du Sud*. Vol. 1, *Jerusalem, "Haram."* Cairo: Institut français d'archéologie orientale.

Van Cleve 1969: Van Cleve, T. C. "The Crusade of Frederick II." In K. M. Setton, ed. *A History of the Crusades*. Vol. II, *The Later Crusades*, pp. 429-462. Ed. R. L. Wolff and H. W. Hazard. Madison: University of Wisconsin Press.

Vilnay 1973: Vilnay, Z. *The Sacred Land*. Vol. I, *Legends of Jerusalem*. Philadelphia: Jewish Publication Society of America.

Vincent/Abel 1914-1926: Vincent, L.-H., and F.-M. Abel. *Jérusalem nouvelle*. 4 vols. Paris: Librarie Lecoffre.

Volney 1959: Volney, C.F.C., Comte de. *Voyage en Syrie et en Egypte pendant les années 1783, 1784 et 1785*. 1st ed. Paris, 1787. Republished with introduction and notes by Jean Gaulmier, Paris, 1959.

Walker 1977: Walker, P. "The 'Crusade' of John Tzimisces in the Light of New Arabic Evidence." *Byzantion* 47:301-327.

Walls 1976: Walls, A. "Two Minarets Flanking the Church of the Holy Sepulchre." *Levant* 8:159-161.

Wardi 1975: Wardi, C. "The Question of the Holy Places in Ottoman Times." In Ma'oz 1975: 385-393.

Wasiti 1979: al-Wasiti, Abu Bakr Muhammad b. Ahmad. *Fadâ'il al-Bayt al-Muqaddas*. Ed. Isaac Hasson. Jerusalem: The Magnes Press.

Wilhelm 1946: Wilhelm, K. *Roads to Zion: Four Centuries of Travelers' Reports*. New York: Schocken Books.

Wilkinson 1974: Wilkinson, J. "Ancient Jerusalem: Its Water Supply and Population." *Palestine Exploration Quarterly*, pp. 33-51.

Wilkinson 1977: Wilkinson, J. *Jerusalem Pilgrims before the Crusades*. Jerusalem: Ariel.

Wilkinson 1978: Wilkinson, J. *Jerusalem as Jesus Knew It: Archeology as Evidence*. London: Thames and Hudson.

Wilkinson 1981: Wilkinson, J. *Egeria's Travels in the Holy Land*. Rev. ed. Warminster: Aris and Phillips.

William of Tyre 1943: *William of Tyre, A History of Deeds Done Beyond the Sea*. Trans. E. A. Babcock and A. C. Krey. 2 vols. New York: Columbia University Press.

Wilson 1880: Wilson, C. W. *Picturesque Palestine, Sinai, and Egypt*. London, 1880. Vol.I reprinted as *Jerusalem, The Holy City*. Jerusalem: Ariel, n.d.

Wilson/Warren 1873: Wilson, C. W., and C. Warren. *The Recovery of Jerusalem: A Narrative of Exploration and Discovery in the City and the Holy Land*. New York: D. Appleton and Co.

Ya'ari 1943: Ya'ari, A. *Igrot Eretz Israel*. Jerusalem. Reprint. Ramat Gan, 1971.

Ya'ari 1947: Ya'ari, A., ed. *Zikhranot Eretz Yisrael (1625-1938)*. 2 vols. Jerusalem: World Zionist Organization.

Ya'ari 1976: Ya'ari, A. *Mas'aot Eretz Israel*. Tel-Aviv, 1946. Reprint. Jerusalem, 1976.

Yadin 1976a: Yadin, Y., ed. *Jerusalem Revealed. Archeology in the Holy City, 1968-1974*. Jerusalem: Israel Exploration Survey.

Yadin 1976b: Yadin, Y. "The Gate of the Essenes and the Temple Scroll." In Yadin 1976a: 90-91.

Zander 1971: Zander, W. *Israel and the Holy Places of Christendom*. London: Weidenfeld and Nicolson.

Index

Unless otherwise specified, all topographical entries refer to Jerusalem.

Abbasids, Muslim dynasty, 215-217, 242, 279, 379

Abd al-Malik, Umayyad caliph, 194, 197, 197-199, 214, 216, 238, 239, 338, 377, 607n28 (Dome inscription)

Abdi-Hiba, 6, 8

Abomination of Desolation, 51-55

Aboth de Rabbi Nathan, 72-73

Abraham, 3-5, 7-8, 122, 140, 155-156, 167, 194, 230, 249, 330-331, 385, 445; in Islam, 184, 240-241, 390, 452, 490, 587n3, 597n9, 613n26

Abraham of Perugia, Jewish visitor, 491-492

Abram, *see* Abraham

Absolom, tomb of, 329, 456, 485

Abu Bakr, first Muslim caliph, 184-185, 514

Abu Maydan, Moroccan benefactor, 394, 542

Aceldama, 457, 613n20

Acre, 192, 269, 284, 341, 361, 364-365, 379-380 (fall of), 421, 435, 539, 543, 545, 582

Actium, battle of, 67, 77

Acts of the Apostles, 101-103, 150, 315

Adam, 155, 312-313

Adil, brother of Saladin, 351, 352

Adomnan, abbot of Iona, 202

Adrichomius, Christianus, Christian scholar, 501-502

Aelia Capitolina, 125, 126-130, 133, 152, 176, 186, 203, 236, 297, 299

Afdal, Fatimid caliph, 289-290

Agnes, servant of the ill, 324

Agrippa I, Jewish ruler, 70, 101-102, 107, 111

Agrippa II, Jewish ruler, 70, 73-74, 107-110, 592n45, 594n11

Ahab, king of Israel, 26

Ahaz, king of Judah, 21, 25, 455

Ahima'as, Jewish chronicler, 224-225, 227

A'isha, wife of Muhammad, 183-185

Akra, *see* citadel, Hellenistic

Albinus, Roman prefect, 107

Aleppo, 333-334, 336, 349, 474, 476, 483, 516, 519, 543, 617n39

Alexander Balas, Seleucid king, 56-57

Alexander Janneus, Hasmonean king, 59-61

Alexander the Great, 42, 45, 603n20

Alexandria, 50, 100, 189, 217, 222-223, 290, 423, 476, 484, 547; See of, 157-158

Ali, fourth Muslim caliph, 377, 385, 517, 604n44

Aliya, 229. *See also* Jews, immigrants

altar of sacrifice, 12, 21, 26, 36, 51-52, 85-86, 143, 196, 407

Amalfi / Amalfitanans, 273-274, 324

Amico, Bernadino, author and illustrator, 616n28

amphitheater, 71, 592n37

Ananias, high priest, 109

Anastasis, 139, 148-149, 154, 172, 258, 291, 311, 479, 493. *See also* Church of the Holy Sepulcher

Andalus, *see* Spain

Andrew the Apostle, 98

Angelus of Messina, Franciscan Guardian, 507

Anna (Anne), mother of Mary, 315, 354-355

Antigonus, son of Aristobulus, 66

Antioch, 45, 62, 66, 102, 176, 192, 269, 291, 306, 310; See of, 157-158, 594n21

Antioch-at-Jerusalem, 50-51

Antiochus III, Seleucid king, 45-49, 89, 193, 590n5

Antiochus IV, Seleucid king, 49-55, 120, 125, 319, 590n13, 603n20

Antiochus VII, Seleucid king, 59

Antiochus Strategos, Byzantine historian, 170-174

Antipater, Hasmonean vizier, 61, 66

Antonia, 70, 74-77, 80, 84, 89, 104-105, 110, 111, 113-114, 200, 562, 569, 589n28, 592 nn. 41 and 42, 593n2, 594 nn. 10 and 11

Antony, Roman triumvir, 66, 74-75, 77

Aphrodite, temple of, 132

Apollonius, Seleucid official, 48

Apostles, 97-99, 105, 128, 153, 157, 169

aqueducts, 87, 90, 398, 480

Aquila, Roman engineer and scholar, 125

Arabia, Arabs, 37, 61, 62, 101, 142, 175, 188, 190, 192, 193, 199, 253, 306, 314, 334, 408-409, 433 (as bedouin), 435-436, 466, 475, 490, 492, 493, 519, 522, 528-529, 532-533, 540-541, 544, 547, 553, 555, 563, 570, 587n3, 609n11, 613n26

Arabic, 219, 253, 360, 373, 442, 462, 476, 478, 532, 541, 608n29, 617n39 (manuscripts)

Aramaic (Syriac), 148, 158, 159, 219-220

Araunah the Jebusite, 12-14, 319

Archelaus, son of Herod, 88

archeologists, 583

Archives, 118 (building), 560-561 (Franciscan), 611n31 (Haram Museum)

Arculf, Christian pilgrim, 195-196, 202, 601n30 (sketches), 606n5

Ardashir, Persian shah, 173-174

Aristeas, Hellenistic author, 43-44, 589n3

Aristo of Pella, historian, 128

Aristobulus II, Hasmonean ruler, 61-64

Ark of the Covenant, 8-11, 14, 16-17, 27-30, 196, 226, 314, 407, 408, 589n20

Armenia, 62, 243-244, 552. *See also* Christians, Armenian

Arnold von Harff, Christian pilgrim, 354-355, 406-407, 410-411, 442-443, 477-478, 611n19

Arnold, bishop of Bamberg, 253, 612n6

Arnulf, Latin bishop of Jerusalem, 606n7

Arsenios, Armenian patriarch, 582

Artaxerxes, Persian shah, 40

Ascalon, 193, 286, 289, 290, 361, 363, 416

ascetics, Christian, 140, 153, 159-160, 228, 597 nn. 8 and 16, 598n21

ascetics, Muslim, *see* Sufis

Asherah, idol of, 26-27

Ashot III, king of Armenia, 243-244

Asochaeus, *see* Shishak

Asses Stables, 361-362

Assyria, Assyrians, 20-25, 28, 297 (= Syrian Christians)

Athaliah, queen of Judah, 25

Athenais, *see* Eudocia

Augustus, Roman emperor, 67, 71-72, 77

Austria, 537, 539

Ayn Jalut, battle of, 380

Ayn Karim, village of, 394, 545, 609n14

Ayyubids, Muslim dynasty, 350-351, 378, 379, 381, 388, 396, 412, 417, 431, 479

Babylonia, Babylonians, 28-32, 120, 264

Babylonian exile, 30-34, 229

Baghdad, 215, 231, 250, 280, 333-334, 466

Baldwin I, Latin king of Jerusalem, 263, 265-266, 292-293, 304, 305-306, 308

Baldwin II, Latin king of Jerusalem, 300, 306, 320

Balian of Ibelin, last Crusader defender of Jerusalem, 345

Bar Abbas, convicted criminal, 95

Bar Kokhba, Jewish insurrectionist, 87, 116, 126-128

Baris, Hasmonean fortress, 75, 83, 589n28, 590n16, 591n25

Barnabas, companion of Paul, 101

Barnabas, Letter of, 123-124

barracks, 569, 621n32

Barsauma, Syrian monk, 158-161

Barsbay, Mamluk sultan, 423

Bartholomew the Apostle, 98

Baruch, bishop of Bacatha, 163

Basil of Caprarola, Franciscan Guardian, 503

Basilica of Constantine, 135-137, 145, 149, 150-151, 154, 154-155, 170, 205, 221, 267, 597n5

Basilica of David, 167

baths, 129, 237, 552

Baybars, Ayyubid sultan, 365, 387, 420

bazaars, 400. *See also* markets

Bede, Christian historian, 221, 606n5
bedouin, 252-253, 433-434, 437, 457, 464, 466, 476, 563, 604n46, 609n4, 609n11 (bedouin suburb), 612n6
Beirut, 243
Benedict, Christian chronicler, 217
Benjamin of Tudela, Jewish traveller, 192, 307, 328-332, 363
Berenice, sister of Agrippa II, 109
Bernard, Christian pilgrim, 220-223, 224, 263, 602n11
Bernard of Clairvaux, Christian theologian, 321
Bertrandon de la Brocquière, Christian traveller, 470
Bethel, 27, 315, 319-320
Bethlehem, 90, 132, 137, 144, 153, 155, 159, 167, 175, 195, 211, 240, 256, 331, 361, 362-363, 420, 422, 425, 437, 471-472, 478, 493, 514, 543, 551, 613n13
Bethso, 69
Bethsura, 56
Betthera, 128
Bezetha, 70, 75-76, 111, 592n35
Biruni, Muslim scientist, 178, 263
Bittir, *see* Betthera
Bonaventure of Nola, Franciscan Guardian, 563
Boniface of Ragusa, Franciscan Guardian, 500, 503, 504, 619n13
Bordeaux pilgrim, 126, 143-145, 147, 151, 196
Breviarius, 154-155
Breydenbach, Bernhard, author and illustrator, 616n28
bridge, 59, 83-84, 109, 118, 119, 303, 595n32, 606n10
Buraq, marvelous beast, 182, 225, 249
Burchard of Mount Sion, Christian pilgrim, 370-371, 444-445, 450, 462-464, 515, 613n14, 617n36
Burhan al-Din, 418; pulpit of, 496, 619n21
Byzantium / Byzantines, 154, 160, 168, 170, 174, 242-244, 250, 257, 267, 271-272, 276, 281, 282, 283, 288, 311, 539

Caesarea, 88, 101, 105, 108, 131-132, 157-158, 160, 169, 243, 284, 597n6

Caiaphas, house of, 94, 145, 157, 161, 447-448, 594n9
Cairo, 233, 250, 253, 258, 260, 276-277, 279, 283, 290, 359, 380-381, 383-384, 414, 417, 435, 448, 483
Calinus, 612n8. *See also* guides
Calvary, 95, 136, 138, 149, 154, 155, 156, 166, 205, 206, 219, 221, 260, 265, 311-312, 437, 444, 447, 502, 504, 506, 562, 577, 594n15 (excavations), 601n31
Canaan / Canaanites, 5-8, 10, 120, 230
capitulations, 535, 538, 539, 618 nn. 1 and 4
cardo, *see* streets, Greco-Roman
Cave of the Spirits, 214, 239, 249, 316, 318, 338, 480, 615n16 (traditions), 616n23
cemeteries, 318, 329, 364, 404, 411, 419-420, 457, 473, 485, 546, 614n12
Cenacle, 93, 125, 155, 423, 491, 498, 506, 594n8, 616n27 (inscription)
Cephas, *see* Peter
Cestius Gallus, Roman governor, 111
Chalcedon, Council of, 158
Chapel of St. James (= Dome of the Chain), 317, 606n23
Chapel of the Apparition of Mary, 508
Chapel of Mary Magdalen, 41, 445, 507
Charlemagne, Frankish king, 217-220, 273, 539, 601 nn. 4 and 6 (protectorate)
Chateaubriand, François-René, French historian, 545-546, 554-555, 560-564, 579-583, 620n23 (assessment)
cherubim, 10, 15-17
Christians, Armenian, 219, 243-244, 276, 291, 300, 304, 307, 309, 369, 393, 420-421, 441, 447-448, 464, 508 (possessions of, in the Holy Sepulcher), 520, 523-524, 542, 549, 550, 554, 555, 556, 565 (population), 570, 571-572, 573, 584, 621n33
Christians, Coptic, 276, 291, 464, 508 (possessions of, in the Holy Sepulcher), 509, 520, 549, 550, 565 (population), 584
Christians, eastern or "oriental," 310, 332, 353, 370-371, 421, 422, 430, 437, 442, 443, 449, 462-464, 507, 549, 552, 569-570, 571, 582-583

Christians, Ethiopian and Nubian, 441, 464, 508 (possessions of, in the Holy Sepulcher), 549, 565 (population)

Christians, Georgian, 219-220, 307, 328, 440-441, 500

Christians, Greek, 219, 245, 264, 266, 276, 291, 293, 307, 328, 352, 355, 369, 393, 441, 463-464, 479, 505, 506, 508 (possessions of, in the Holy Sepulcher), 509-510, 514-515, 520, 523-524, 540, 542, 547, 549, 550, 552, 555, 556, 565 (population), 569-570, 571 (Greek-Catholics), 571-572, 573, 619n13, 621n33

Christians, Indian, 441

Christians, Jacobite, 276, 291, 308, 328, 441

Christians, Latin, 151, 219-220, 264, 265-266, 273-276, 281, 291 (replace easterners in Holy Sepulcher), 294, 306, 332, 352, 361, 369-370 (replaced by Greeks in Holy Sepulcher), 393, 421, 441, 449, 463, 479, 499, 505, 508 (possessions of, in the Holy Sepulcher), 523-524, 539-540, 542, 549, 554, 565 (population), 571, 572, 584-585

Christians, Nestorian, 308, 441, 464, 468, 507, 520

Christians, Protestant, 509-515, 520, 579, 584-586

Christians, Syrian, 219, 275, 297, 303-304, 305-306, 309, 328, 361, 369, 391, 393, 421, 441, 451, 463, 520, 565 (population), 606n8

Christians and Muslims, 208-213, 222-223, 235, 237, 255-256, 281-282, 331-332, 417-425, 427-431, 446, 458-462, 464-468, 478, 502-503, 533, 538-539, 544, 549-550, 551-552, 560-561, 582-583, 604n46, 605n7, 605n3, 611n1 (arms sales banned), 613 nn. 22 and 23

Christians of the Cincture, 441. *See also* Christians, Syrian

Chronicles, Books of, 18

churches: of Abraham (at Hebron), 141, 167-168, 331, 597n10; of the Ascension, 206-207, 210-211, 219, 222, 390 (mosque at); the Eleona, 597n19; of the Holy Sepulcher (*also* of the Resurrection), 70, 96, 133-137 (Constantine's construction), 139-140 (the dedication), 145, 155, 161, 170, 198, 203-206 (in the seventh century), 219, 221, 238, 243-244, 254-255, 258-260 (Hakim's destruction), 267-268 (Byzantine reconstruction), 286, 291-292, 297, 298, 305, 306, 311-314 (Crusader rebuilding), 325-326, 328, 344, 346, 351-352, 362, 369-370 (Franciscans in), 420, 437-442, 450, 461-462 (courtyard), 467, 471, 503-506 (restorations of 1555 and 1720), 514, 521 (restored to Latins), 539-540, 542 (burned and rebuilt: 1808-1810), 566, 567, 572-576, 578-579, 584, 597n4 (excavations), 601n31 (sketches), 618n9 (the "Status Quo"), 619n13 (rebuilding);

on Mount Sion, 150, 152, 153, 157, 161, 166, 170, 188, 219, 221, 329, 352, 355, 422, 425; New, of St. Mary, 162-166, 167, 170, 216, 219, 238, 598n30, 598 nn. 36 and 37 (excavations); below the Pinnacle, 156, 598n24 (excavations); of St. Anne (*also* St. Mary of the Probatic Pool), 144, 157, 219, 221, 300, 352-356 (conversion to madrasa), 412, 593n50, 608n15 (excavations); of St. George (at Lydda), 169, 212-213, 284, 467; of St. Giles, 302; of St. James, 304, 311, 520, 566, 570; of St. John the Apostle, 161, 222; of St. Leontius, 222; of St. Mary of the Germans, 309; of St. Mary Latina, 220, 274-275, 299, 326-327; of St. Mary Magdalen, 303; of St. Mary Major, 275, 299, 326-327; of St. Peter, 157, 161, 221; of St. Sophia, 157, 161, 167-168, 284; of St. Stephen, 161-162, 169, 221, 303, 304, 361-362; at Siloam, 168, 239. *See also* Basilica of Constantine; Olives, Mount of

Cicero, 65

cisterns and reservoirs, 44, 77, 87, 143, 154, 156, 199, 296, 527

citadel, Hellenistic, 45, 50, 51, 52-55, 57-58, 67-69, 118, 590n16, 591 nn. 19, 20, and 22

Citadel, Herodian and later, 59, 69, 89,

119, 226, 286, 352, 384, 396, 480-
483, 494 (mosque in), 556, 565, 569
City of David, 7-8, 10-11, 16-17, 23,
31, 53, 55, 67, 73, 83, 239, 329, 422,
455, 589 nn. 21 and 28
City of Jerusalem, 298-299, 311-312
Claudius, Roman emperor, 70, 77, 101
Clement, Christian Father, 105
Clement VI, pope, 370, 611n37
Cleopatra, Ptolemaic queen of Egypt, 66
Clermont-Ganneau, Charles, French ar-
cheologist, 299-300 (on the covered
market), 403-404 (on the Gate of the
Chain complex)
column of Jesus' scourging, 145, 155,
157, 167
Commemoratorium, 218-220
Commerce, international, 154, 242, 272-
273, 308, 431, 535-538, 608n18
commerce, local, *see* markets
Comnenus, Greek architect, 619n13
Constantine I, Roman emperor, 93, 131-
139, 140-141, 145, 149, 170, 190,
195, 205, 276, 291, 319-320
Constantine Porphyogenitus, Byzantine
emperor, 261
Constantine IX, Byzantine emperor, 256,
257, 311
Constantine X, Byzantine emperor, 270-
271
Constantinople, 159, 161, 168, 195,
211, 257, 281, 350, 478, 506 (fall of),
525, 532, 538, 542
construction techniques, 391-392, 403-
404, 494, 562-563
consulate / consuls, 435, 519-520, 537-
540, 583
convents, Christian, 569-571; Canons of
the Holy Sepulcher, 304-305, 311-
312, 606n7; Canons of the Temple of
the Lord, 318-319, 606n24; Flagellation, 502-503, 616n29; Mary Magdalen, 274; St. Anne, 300; St. Catherine,
168; St. George, 571; St. James, 520,
556, 566, 582; St. Sabas, 163, 264,
294-295, 304, 606n12; Sisters of
Sion, 594n12, 596n54; of the Syrians,
420
convents, Franciscan: Holy Sepulcher,
369, 420, 439-440, 506-509, 576,
580-581, 621n33 (the organ); Mount

Sion, 369-370, 420, 422, 425, 430,
436, 459, 486, 498-501; St. Savior's,
500-501, 511, 519, 550, 551, 554-
555, 557-560, 563, 570, 582
convents, Sufi Muslim, 246, 280, 335,
355, 374, 383, 411, 416-417, 566,
568, 605n18 (ribats), 611 nn. 30 and
31; Dargah, 418; Kurd, 412, 610n24;
Qalandariyya, 419; Salahiyya, 352,
418-419; Zahiriyya, 400
Coponius, Roman prefect, 83
Council Chamber, 69, 118
Council of Elders, *see* Sanhedrin
Courts of the Temple, 84-85
courts: Crusader, 301-302; Muslim, 358,
608n17, 614n12, 618n45
Covenent, 4, 26-27, 54, 93, 122
Covenant of Umar, 185-186, 479, 506,
614 nn. 1 and 2
Crassus, Roman governor, 65, 591n26
Crusade, First: defense of, 580; occupa-
tion of Jerusalem, 283-290; origins of,
251-254, 257-258, 268-269, 281-282,
604n1; prospects for another, 370-373
Curzon, Robert, English traveller, 572-
578
Custodia Sanctae Terrae, 557-558. *See
also* Guardian of the Holy Land
Cyprus, 271, 423, 432, 435, 558
Cyril of Scythopolis, hagiographer, 162-
163
Cyrus, Persian shah, 34, 319

Daimbert, Latin bishop of Jerusalem,
294, 605n4
Damascus, 21, 61, 100-101, 198, 201,
235, 238, 239, 243-244, 280, 283,
334-336, 358, 364, 368, 383-384,
410, 423, 432, 465, 470, 474, 476,
483, 492-493, 543, 547, 549, 560
Damietta, 359
Daniel the abbot, Christian pilgrim, 263-
267, 294, 296, 312, 313-314, 330-
331
Daniel al-Kumisi, Karaite author, 229
Daniel, Book of, 53-54, 190-191, 230-
231, 603n20
Dargah, building near the Holy Sepulcher, 195
Darius, Persian shah, 40, 89

David, king of Israel, 7-14, 26, 31, 67, 69, 120, 121, 126, 175, 182, 196, 316, 318-319, 399, 423; Prayer Niche of, 67, 187, 286, 352, 374, 398, 481 (converted into a mosque); tomb of, 59, 67, 72, 126, 167 (at Bethlehem), 329-330, 420, 423-424, 486, 491, 498-500, 599n40

David Reubeni, Messianic claimant, 490-492, 615n15

David dei Rossi, Jewish visitor, 484

Day of Atonement, 85

Dayr al-Sari, 260

Deeds of the Franks, 284-285

Demetrius, Seleucid king, 56-57

Deuteronomy, 26, 589n21

Dhimmis, 259, 605n9

Diaspora, 47, 99, 229, 232, 233, 488, 529-530

Dio Cassius, Roman historian, 126-127

distant shrine (*al-masjid al-aqsa*), 182-183

Dome of the Rock, 79, 86, 169, 194, 197-199, 207, 213-214, 216, 239, 248-249, 286, 314, 338, 345-346, 348-350, 365, 406-407, 412, 413, 467, 478, 479, 482-483, 488, 490-491, 495, 567, 601n21 (descriptions), 601n34 (dimensions), 610n23. *See also* Rock under the Dome

Domes of the Haram: Gabriel, 249; Ascension (of Muhammad), 214, 238, 249, 374, 495; Chain, 214, 238, 318, 495 (*see also* Chapel of St. James); Prophet, 214, 238, 249, 374, 494; Solomon, 201

dragoman, *see* guides

Dubois, Pierre, Christian propagandist, 371-373

Ecclesiastes, Midrash on, 226

Edessa, 198, 335

Edom / Edomites, 33, 192, 194, 199-200

Egeria, Christian pilgrim, 125, 140, 143, 145, 147-151, 158, 203, 597n16

Eginhard, biographer of Charlemagne, 217-218

Egypt / Egyptians, 3-6, 10, 17, 28, 45, 52, 99, 120, 126, 140, 168, 218, 222-223, 224-225, 231, 235, 242, 246, 249, 254, 258, 264, 277, 334, 339, 340, 350, 363, 381-382, 433, 476, 492, 548, 553, 564, 615n15

Eleazer, Jewish insurrectionist, 109

Eleazer, priest, 128

Elias, bishop of Jerusalem, 162, 166

Elijah, prophet, 96, 490

Elizabeth, queen of England, 510-511

Emesa, 209, 211

Encaenia, 139-140, 203-204, 591n21, 603n34

endowments: Christian, 133-137, 161-166, 218-220, 233, 293, 299-300, 323, 371-372, 606n7; Jewish, 223-225, 233-234, 603 nn. 28 and 29; Muslim, 233, 240-241, 335, 352-353, 356, 357-359, 360, 374, 381-388, 394-396, 412, 416-421, 482-483, 542, 566, 609n8

England / English / British, 305, 360-361, 363, 425, 463, 511, 512, 541, 583, 612n5, 617 nn. 40 and 41

Ephesus, Council of, 157, 161

Epiphanius, Christian writer, 125, 126

Esau, 199-200

Eucharist, 93, 391, 594n9, 608n13 (in the Quran)

Eucherius, bishop of Lyons, 153, 455

Eudocia, Byzantine empress, 158-163, 169, 170, 202, 303, 355

Euphrates, 3, 339

Eusebius, Church historian, 105, 122, 128-129, 132-137, 516

Eustochium, Christian pilgrim, 152

Euthychius, Christian historian, 189

Eutropia, mother-in-law of Constantine, 141-142

Evliye Chelebi, Muslim traveller, 479, 481, 493-496

exchanges, 299, 302-303, 304

exilarch, 231

Exodus, Midrash on, 226

Ezekiel, prophet, 33-34, 47

Ezra, priest and scribe, 36-41, 319; Book of, 34, 41

Fatima, daughter of Muhammad, 604n44

Fatimids, Muslim dynasty, 224-225,

242-244, 250, 257, 269, 276-277, 279, 290, 334, 336, 379, 539, 604n44 (origins)
Fazari, Muslim author, 336-339, 374-375, 494
Felix, Roman prefect, 105, 595n23
Felix Fabri, Christian pilgrim, 354-357, 380, 386-387, 396-397, 401, 402-403, 415-416, 421-422, 423-424, 427ff., 471-472, 444, 498, 515, 567, 613n20
Festus, Roman prefect, 105
Florence, 535
forums, 129, 133, 145, 325, 596 nn. 54 and 55 (excavations)
France / French, 218, 288, 305, 308-309, 363, 422, 423, 425, 499-500, 511, 519, 535-537, 539, 550, 561, 582, 584, 617n40
Francis I, king of France, 499, 535-536
Francis of Assisi, 369
Francis of Piacenza, Franciscan Guardian, 424-425
Franciscans, 369-370, 421-425, 437, 441, 459-462, 498-508, 511-514, 520, 522, 539-540, 545, 556-561, 580-581, 584, 612n10 (as guides)
Franks, 217, 264, 272, 283, 290, 307, 318-319, 328, 333-334, 340-341, 342-344, 361, 508, 541, 557, 571. *See also* Christians, Latin
Frederick II, Holy Roman Emperor, 364-367, 369, 370
Friars Minor, *see* Franciscans
Fulcher of Chartres, Crusade chronicler, 286, 295-296, 305, 309-310, 314-315, 606n17
Fuller's Field, 202-203
Funduq, 433, 612n5. *See also* hospices
Fustat, 222, 233, 276-277

Gabinius, Roman governor, 63, 65
Gabriel, angel of God, 182, 184
Galilee, 91, 92, 94, 99, 111, 193, 199, 243, 295, 341, 445, 447, 472-473 (Jewish Holy Land); Sea of, 132, 243, 295, 472, 492
games, 71-72
Gaon, Geonim, 224-225, 232, 277
Garden Tomb, 613n15

gates of the city: Benjamin, 202; Bethlehem, 519; the Column, 203, 237, 302, 351, 399; Damascus, 129, 202-203, 258, 284, 302, 304, 361, 393, 399, 480; David, 202, 304-305, 328, 445, 480; Dung, 37, 39, 480; Ephraim, 39; Essenes, 69, 592n32; Fish, 39, 445; Fountain, 37, 39; Friend of God (al-Khalil) (*also* Abraham), 328, 397, 400, 480; Gennath, 70; Gushpat, 328; Hadrian, 129, 168-169; Hebron, 353; Herod, 614n8; Jaffa, 69-70, 112, 202, 237, 384, 393, 480, 563; Jehoshaphat, 302, 328; Jeremiah's Pit, 237-238; Jericho, 237; Jeshanah, 39; Judgment, 502-503; Lady Mary, 568; Little (Portula), 202-203; Maghrebi, 480; Merchants', 445; Nea, 237, 604n37; Neapolis (Nablus), 145; Palace, 237-238, 604n38; Pilgrims', 563; Prayer Niche of David, 237, 353, 397; Prison Compound, 39; Sahira, 480, 614n8; St. Lazarus (Postern), 362; St. Stephen's (*also* Lion), 129, 169, 202, 237, 302, 304, 361, 480; Serbs(?), 393; Sheep, 39; Siloam, 237-238; Sion, 237, 303, 480; Tekoa, 202-203; Valley, 37; Water, 39, 41; Zahira, 480, 614n8
gates of the Haram: the Ark (Sekinah), 375, 403-404; the Chain, 83, 246, 388, 394, 397, 403-404, 414 (minaret); Dawardiayya, 201, 360, 405; Forgiveness, 375; Golden, 34, 83, 169, 203, 227, 246-247, 279, 280, 298, 302, 315, 318, 329, 409-411, 480, 491, 528, 593n51 (excavations), 599n44, 600n11, 607n25; Hitta, 400, 405, 496; Inspector, 399, 419, 496; Iron (Hadid), 399; Maghrebi, 527; Mercy, 227, 247, 280, 328, 374, 409-410, 491, 528, 600 nn. 11 and 13; Market of the Cotton Merchants, 402, 610n18 (inscriptions); Mutawadda, 496; Peace, 403; the Prophet, 188, 247-248, 375; Repentance, 247, 410, 491; Tribes, 81, 189, 352, 405, 480
gates of the Temple: 80-84, 115, 117, 193; Apostles, 316, 606n20; Barclay's, 225, 608n33; Beautiful, 82-83, 169,

gates of the Temple (*cont.*)
302, 315, 316-317; Double, 81, 248;
Huldah, 80-81, 247; Kiponus, 80, 83;
Nicanor, 84; Priests', 226; Sushan or
Susa, 82-83; Tadi, 81; Triple, 81

Gaza, 42, 193, 346, 380, 416, 543,
615n15

Gedaliah, Jewish immigrant, 526, 528-
529, 531-533, 540-541, 544, 547

Gehenna, 154, 189-190, 245, 375, 455-
457, 485

Genesis, Book of, 3, 230, 315, 597n9

Geniza, 232-233, 277, 289

Genoa, Genoese, 307, 535, 608n18,
612n7

Gerald, master of the Hospital, 324

Gerizim, Mount, 37

Germanus, Greek patriarch, 506

Germany / Germans, 292, 302, 308-309,
356, 386, 401, 430, 463, 475, 477,
525, 532, 541, 550, 552, 557

Gerousia, *see* Sanhedrin

Gessius Florus, Roman prefect, 107-109

Gethsemane, 43, 166, 168-169, 195,
219-220, 444

Ghazali, Muslim scholar, 280, 411,
610n22

Ghazan, Mongol khan, 610n21

Gihon spring, 8, 22-23, 587n5

Godfrey of Bouillon, first Latin ruler of
Jerusalem, 285, 291-293, 308, 581,
619n13

Godfrey of St. Omer, founder of Templars, 320

Golden Gate, *see* gates of the Haram

Golgotha, *see* Calvary

Gospels, 91, 95, 138, 149, 450, 579,
593n7, 594n16

governors, 65, 89, 107-108, 160, 256,
284, 384, 396-397, 620 nn. 16 and
17; Ottoman, 487-488, 493, 503,
513, 532, 538, 543-547, 547, 549,
563-564; lieutenant governors (*mütesellim*), 543, 544, 549

governors, residence of, 396-397, 405,
496, 568, 569, 593n2, 621n32. *See
also* Pretorium

Gregory X, pope, 463

Gregory of Nyssa, Christian Father, 153

Guardian of the Holy Land, 423, 427,
442, 506, 510, 513, 515, 611n37

Guibert of Nogent, Crusade chronicler,
282

guidebooks, 154-157, 450, 616n28
(illustrated)

guides and interpreters, 295, 380, 428,
434-435, 437, 448, 452, 612n9 (language problems), 612n10

Guy of Lusignan, Latin king of Jerusalem, 342

gymnasium, 51, 69

Hadrian, Roman emperor, 70, 77, 125-
127, 129-130, 131, 133, 135, 143-
144 (statues of), 145, 152, 224, 273,
296-297, 299, 325, 451, 594n12,
596n50, 598n30

Hagar, concubine of Abraham, 4-5, 122,
230, 587n3, 613n26

Hagarenes, 5, 217, 613n26

Haggai, prophet, 39-40, 485

Haifa, 284, 305

hajj, Muslim pilgrimage, 197, 244, 252.
See also pilgrimage, Muslim

Hakim, Fatimid caliph, 254-255, 258-
260, 267-268, 275, 276, 311, 605n15

Hanafite legal system, 335, 360

Hananel, rabbi, 225

Hans of Prussia, knight of the Holy Sepulcher, 442

Hanukka, Feast of, 82, 591n21

Haram al-Sharif, the Noble Sanctuary,
80, 83, 86, 169, 187, 188, 194, 196,
201 (Umayyad extension?), 207, 213-
214 (the Umayyad Haram), 225, 238-
239 (in the tenth century), 246-250
(in the eleventh century), 280, 314-
316 (under the Latin Kingdom), 358,
374-375 ("stations" on the Haram),
396, 399, 402, 405-407 (the Mamluk
Haram), 412, 482-483 (Ottoman constructions), 494-498 (holy places and
holy practices), 497-498, 542, 565,
566, 569;
   dimensions of, 213-214, 238-239,
604n42, 610 nn. 23 and 24 (construction activity), 616 nn. 19-22 (Haram
functionaries); colonnades of, 246-
247, 360, 405-406, 495-496. *See also*
Muslims on the Temple Mount

Haramayn, the Two Sanctuaries, 393, 609n10

Harawi, Muslim traveller, 313, 318, 320, 322

Harun al-Rashid, Abbasid caliph, 217-218

Hasmoneans, *see* Jerusalem under the Hasmoneans

Hattin, battle of, 341-344

Hebrew, 477-478, 564, 617n39

Hebron, 4-5, 7-8, 90, 140-143, 167-168, 240-241, 294, 330-332, 360, 377, 384, 385-387, 390, 416, 445, 452, 493, 533-534, 543, 596n50, 604n43, 607n13

Hecateus, Hellenistic author, 42-43, 590n6

Hegesippus, Church historian, 105, 128

Helena, mother of Constantine, 137-139, 168, 170, 190, 195, 319-320, 437, 446, 504-505; chapel of, 311, 508, 580, 597n5

Helena of Adiabene, 70

Heliodorus, Seleucid official, 48, 590n10

Hellenic Confraternity of the Holy Sepulcher, 506

Hellenism, Hellenization, 42, 49-51, 71-72, 590n14

Hellenists, 99-100

Heraclius, Byzantine emperor, 170, 173-174, 187, 253, 302, 315, 320, 607n25

Herod Antipas, Jewish ruler, 94-95; house of, 397, 594n11

Herod, king of Israel, 66-67, 88-89, 167, 168, 399, 480, 607n27

Herodians, 47

Hezekiah, king of Judah, 21-23, 35

high priest / priesthood, 50-51, 60, 64, 75, 85, 94, 107

Hijr, wall near Ka'ba, 184

Hilkiah, high priest, 26

Hinnom Valley, 465. *See also* Gehenna

Hiram, king of Tyre, 8, 10, 14

Hisham, Umayyad caliph, 200, 212

Holy Fire, Descent of, 259, 261-267, 523-524, 553, 571-578, 584, 606n16, 618 nn. 42 and 43

Holy House, 176-178, 181, 194, 236, 340

Holy Innocents, 167, 448 (relics of)

Holy Land, 85, 131, 152-153, 178, 182, 202, 251, 268, 279, 292, 305, 334, 338-339, 370-373, 409, 418, 421, 427, 430, 449-450, 453, 468, 470, 477, 485, 506, 510, 514, 516, 537, 547, 551, 554, 557, 563, 580, 583, 607n10, 611n1

Holy of Holies, 14-15, 17, 29-30, 55, 84-85, 121, 129, 190, 196, 315, 408, 489, 589n20

Holy War, 243-244, 333-345, 417, 580

Horn, Elzear, Franciscan historian, 369-370, 411, 461-462, 481-482, 500-501, 503-508, 558-559

Hoshana Rabba, 234

hospices, lodgings, 99 (in synagogue), 161, 165, 167, 219, 220-221, 239, 304, 324, 432-433 (at Ramle), 436-437, 519-520, 520 (Greek), 520 (eastern Christian), 553, 568, 612n5

Hospital, 162-163, 240, 273-276, 298-299, 304, 324-327, 356-357, 421, 436, 599n55 (prototypes), 605n20 (excavations)

houses, *see* construction techniques

Hugh de Payens, founder of Templars, 320

Huldah, prophetess, 26, 72, 485. *See also* gates, Huldah

Humphrey of Turon, Grand Master of the Templars, 342

Hyrcanus II, Jewish ruler, 61-66

Ibn Battuta, Muslim traveller, 383-384, 438, 452, 478

Ibn Ishaq, biographer of Muhammad, 184

Ibn Khaldun, Muslim historian, 381-383

Ibn Shaddad, Muslim memorialist, 340-341, 356

Ibn Taymiyya, Muslim lawyer, 375-378

Ibn Tulun, Muslim governor of Egypt, 231

Ibn Wasil, Muslim historian, 364-367

Ibn al-Athir, Muslim historian, 283-284, 335, 342-343

Ibn al-Faqih, Muslim geographer, 213-214

Ibn al-Qalanisi, Muslim historian, 258-261, 283, 288

Ibn al-Zubayr, pretender to caliphate, 197, 377

Ibrahim Pasha, son of Muhammad Ali, 570-571, 573-578

Ilya, 236. *See also* Aelia

Imad al-Din, Muslim historian, 341-343, 346-352

Imbomon, 151, 206, 219, 390, 597n19. *See also* Church of the Ascension

Innocent IV, Pope, 369, 608n29

Isaac, Israelite patriarch, 5, 155-156, 167, 230, 249, 331, 490

Isaac Lauria, Jewish kabbalist, 615n17

Isaac ben Joseph, Jewish visitor, 191-192, 474-475

Isabel of Brienne, Latin queen of Jerusalem, 364

Isaiah, prophet, 23-24, 126, 199; "Second" Isaiah, 35

Isbeq, Mamluk amir, 424-425

Ishmael, son of Abraham, 4-5, 230-231

Ishmaelites, 5, 192, 193, 199, 224, 229-231, 290, 363, 392, 486, 490-491, 528, 587n3, 601n24

Isma'ilis, *see* Muslims, Isma'ilis

Israel, land of, 3-4, 11-12, 33, 85, 115, 192, 484-485, 492, 525, 529, 532; under Papal ban, 429, 611n1

Israelites, 4, 7, 11, 17, 19, 26, 31-32, 177, 187, 190, 193, 194-195, 228, 281, 339

Istanbul, 479

Italy / Italians, 305, 308, 365, 401, 463, 550-551, 552, 557. *See also* Genoa; Pisa; Venice

Jacob of Verona, Jewish visitor, 436

Jacob, Israelite patriarch, 5, 167-168, 190, 238, 315, 331, 363

Jaffa / Joppa, 169, 252, 292, 305, 365-367, 431-432, 435, 470, 553, 555, 558, 612n6

Jahannam, *see* Gehenna

James the Apostle, 98, 102, 166

James, the brother of Jesus, 101, 102-103, 105-107, 128, 157, 595 nn. 25 and 26

James, son of Alpheus, 98

Jaqmaq, Mamluk sultan, 420-421, 425

Jason, high priest, 50-51

Jebusites, 7-8, 11-12

Jehoash, king of Judah, 19-20

Jehoiachin, king of Judah, 28

Jehoida, high priest, 20

Jehoram, king of Judah, 25

Jehoshaphat, king of Judah, 18-19

Jehoshaphat, Valley of, 154, 202-204, 207, 210, 219, 221-222, 293, 296, 411, 451, 455-458, 477, 485, 489, 562, 613n20

Jeremiah, prophet, 28-29, 157, 168

Jeremiah, pit of, 157, 168, 237-238

Jericho, 30, 63, 168, 416, 492

Jeroboam, king of Israel, 491

Jerome, Christian scholar, 122, 144-145, 151-152

Jerusalem: Abbasid, 215-241; under the Ayyubids, 348-378; Byzantine, 131-170; Crusader, 283-331; Fatimid, 242-282; under Greek sovereignty, 45-55; Hasmonean, 55-61; Herodian, 67-87; Israelite, 7-30, 30-31 (destruction by Babylonians), 35-41 (rebuilt under the Persians), 587n10; Mamluk, 379-478; Muslim occupation, 176-177, 185-190; Ottoman, 479-586; Persian conquest, 170-173; restored to Franks, 365-376; Roman, 89-91, 111-121 (destruction in 70), 126-128 (destruction in 135), 129-130 (rebuilt); under the Turks, 250, 257-258; Umayyad, 189-214

Jerusalem, bishops of, 128-129, 148, 157-159, 291, 597n6. *See also* patriarchs

Jerusalem, heavenly, 33-34, 123

Jesus, 81-83, 91-97, 106, 131-139, 302, 315-316, 410, 444-445, 501, 593n2, 594 nn. 10 and 11, 594n16; 597n9; in Islam, 184, 312-313, 410, 463, 568, 600n9; in Jewish eyes, 489; Ascension of, 93, 137, 151, 154, 194, 206-207, 222, 312, 456; Cradle of, 480; Cross of, 137-139, 149-150, 152, 155, 157, 168, 173-174, 195, 219, 221, 282, 302 (feast of), 315, 317, 320, 341-343, 446-447, 607n25; effigy, 522; portrait of, 166-167; Tomb of, 97, 132-135, 138, 148, 152, 155, 156, 166, 205, 206, 208-209,

218, 221, 262, 263-267, 297, 311, 313-314, 438-439, 445, 449, 453-455 (authenticity of); 504-505 (reopened), 597n17, 613n15

Jewry, the, 303-304, 606n11. *See also* quarters, Syrian Christian

Jews: Ashkenazi, 475, 486-487, 525, 526, 530-533, 544; European, 227, 425, 430, 472-473, 477, 525, 529, 541; Karaite, 193-194, 233-234, 276-277, 528, 568, 602n18, 603n21, 609n33; Moroccan / North African, 289, 363, 486, 540-541; Rabbanite, 193-194, 233-234, 276-277, 568, 603n33; Sephardic, 486-487, 525, 526, 531-533, 544

Jews: and Christians, 159-160, 172, 289, 329-330, 423-424, 430, 461, 477-478, 488-489, 513-514, 583, 585, 611n38; and Crusaders, 288-290, 327-329; and Muslims, 191-194, 198-199, 230-231, 235, 237, 276-279, 289-290, 331, 363-364, 407-409, 472-477, 526, 531-534, 541-542, 544, 567-569, 608n21, 613n29, 619n11

Jews banned from Jerusalem, 137, 144, 224; immigrants and visitors, 289-290, 524-525, 529-530, 555, 564; on the Temple Mount, 143-144, 173, 193-194

Jihad, 335. *See also* Holy War

Joachim, father of Mary, 315, 354

John the Almoner, bishop of Alexandria, 273, 275, 605n19

John the Apostle, 82, 316-317, 489, 594n16; Gospel of, 82

John the Baptist, 98, 187, 605n19, 609n14

John Hyrcanus, Hasmonean king, 59-60

John Tzimisces, Byzantine emperor, 242-244

John of Wurzburg, Christian pilgrim, 298, 317-318, 326

Jordan River, 6, 81, 168-169, 295, 522, 549, 553, 584

Joseph, Israelite patriarch, 167, 241

Joseph of Arimathea, 97, 313, 522

Joseph ha-Kohen, Jewish visitor, 480

Josephus, Jewish historian, 42-43, 45, 48, 50, 55, 62, 64, 67-72, 77-87, 89,

107, 111, 196, 226, 450, 517, 590n6, 592n45, 593n4, 595n39

Josiah, king of Judah, 26-27, 227, 314, 589n22

Judah Maccabeus, 56

Judah ha-Levi, Jewish poet, 277-278

Judah the Pious, Jewish immigrant, 530-531, 532

Judah, Judea, 7, 11, 18-23, 26-27, 47, 52, 62, 64, 88-89, 95, 98, 108, 322, 362, 369, 474, 545, 593n1

Judas Iscariot, 94

Julian, Roman emperor, 145-147

Julius III, Pope, 504

Julius Caesar, 66, 319

Julius Severus, Roman general, 127

Jupiter, temple of, 126, 129-130, 596n59 (excavations)

Justinian, Byzantine emperor, 162-166, 170, 297, 320

Juvenal, bishop of Jerusalem, 157-158, 598n25

Ka'b al-Ahbar, Jewish convert to Islam, 188, 191, 196, 338

Ka'ba at Mecca, 180, 182-184, 191, 197, 238, 338, 375

Kabbala, 475, 615n17

Kafr Gamla, village of, 161, 598n27 (excavations)

Kalisker, Abraham, Jewish visitor, 525

Karramites, 228

Kedron Valley, 8, 27, 70, 111, 204, 221, 296, 450, 455, 562, 595n26

Kelim (Mishna), 85, 122

Khadija, wife of Muhammad, 469

khafara, caphars, *see* taxes and fees

Khalil, the "Friend of God," 241. *See also* Abraham

khans: Charcoal, 397; of al-Zahir, 387-388; of the Exchange, 398

khanqas, 417. *See also* convents, Sufi

Khidr, prophet in Islam, 214, 238, 601n35

Khushqadam, Mamluk sultan, 413

Khusraw, Persian shah, 173

Khwarezmians, 368

Kings, Books of, 18, 25, 315

knights: Hospitallers, 321, 342-343, 356, 371-372; Templars, 320-324,

knights (*cont.*)
342-343, 371, 608n27 (abolished); of
the Holy Sepulcher, 442-443, 515,
580, 584; Teutonic, 356

Ladino, 532
Lamentations, Book of, 31-32
Lamentations, Midrash on, 226
lance, holy, 155
languages, 148, 158-159, 219. *See also*
Arabic; Aramaic; Hebrew; Latin
Last Judgment, 221-222, 236, 455-458,
485, 489
Latin Kingdom of Jerusalem, *see* Jerusalem, Crusader
Latin kings, tombs of, 457, 619n13
Latin, 148, 220
law schools, Muslim, 280, 335, 352-360,
374, 466 (Baghdad), 495-496, 566,
607n1 (Damascus), 616n24
(conversion);
Afdaliyya, 358; Aminiyya, 405;
As'ardiyya, Ashrafiyya, 404, 413-417,
471, 496, 610n26 (survey), 610n27
(collapse), 610n28 (plan), 611n29;
Baladiyya, 415; Dawadariyya, 416-
417; Fakhriyya, 400; Farisiyya, 405;
Ghadiriyya, 405; Ghazaliyya, 280,
411; Ghoraniyya, 496; Jawhariyya,
412, 610n24; Jawliyya, 396; Krimiyya,
405; Ma'addamiyya, 418; Malikiyya,
405, 496 (mosque of); Nasiriyya, 280,
411; Nizamiyya, 280 (Baghdad); Salahiyya, 353-357, 400; Subaybiyya, 405;
Tankiziyya, 402, 527, 618n45; Tashtimuriyya, 412-413, 610n25 (survey);
Uthmaniyya, 414
lawyers, Muslim, 335, 358, 418
Leah, wife of Jacob, 331
Leo, Pope, 158
leprosarium of St. Lazarus, 362
Levant Company, 516, 617n39 (eminent
chaplains at Aleppo)
Levites, 16, 19, 47, 590n6
Licinius, Roman emperor, 597n3
Life of the Prophet, 180
Louis XIII, king of France, 538
Louis, bishop of Toulouse, 422
Lower City, 55, 59, 69, 73, 109, 118-
119

Ludolph von Suchem, Christian pilgrim,
292, 354, 422, 440, 446, 453, 468-
470, 611n1, 613n25
Luke, Gospel of, 98, 594n16
Lydda, 169, 198, 212-213, 235, 284,
416, 466, 471
Lyons, Council of, 463

Ma'mun, Abbasid caliph, 216, 606n28
(in Dome inscription)
Macarius, bishop of Jerusalem, 133-135,
139, 142
Maccabees, 55-56, 319
Maccabees, Books of, 28, 49-52, 55, 314
Madaba map, 129-130, 170, 203, 220,
599n46
madrasa, *see* law schools, Muslim
Maghreb / Morocco / North Africa, 272,
289, 357, 395, 486. *See also* Jews, Mo-
roccan; Muslims
Mahdi, Abbasid caliph, 215-216
Maimonides, Jewish scholar, 227, 278-
279, 487
Malik al-Afdal, son of Saladin, 357-359,
419
Malik al-Aziz, son of Saladin, 350
Malik al-Kamil, Ayyubid sultan, 364-
368, 369
Malik al-Nasir, Ayyubid sultan, 368,
610n18
Malikite legal system, 358, 496
Malquisinat, *see* Street of Cooking Smells
Mamluks, Muslim dynasty, 379-382,
396, 405-406, 412, 418, 431, 474,
479, 483, 506, 543, 565, 609n1. *See
also* Jerusalem, Mamluk
Mamra, *see* Hebron
Manasseh, king of Judah, 25-26, 589n20
Manfred, son of Frederich II, 365
Mansur, Abbasid caliph, 215-216
Margaret of Sicily, Christian benefactor,
436-437, 611n36
Mark the Apostle: Gospel of, 97,
594n16; house of, 157
Mark, bishop of Jerusalem, 128
markets, 38, 73, 112, 135, 136, 220,
233, 236, 245, 288, 298 (grain), 299-
301, 302 (butchers'), 303, 353-354,
393, 397-403, 412-413, 437, 443,
483, 550-551, 564, 567, 606n6,
608n16

Market of the Cotton Merchants, 353, 399, 402-403, 609 nn. 16 (survey) and 17; triple, 299, 353-354, 400-401, 567; upper, *see* Upper City

Martina, niece of Heraclius, 174

Martyrium, *see* Basilica of Constantine

Marwan, Umayyad caliph, 200, 377

Mary, the mother of Jesus, 97, 98, 210, 221, 304, 315, 354, 361, 407, 451, 489; in Islam, 238, 375, 464, 497; shrine, 480; tomb, 195, 210, 220, 222, 422, 456

Mary of Magdala, 97

Matthew the Apostle, 98, 594n16

Maundrell, Henry, English visitor, 516-524, 539, 612n5, 617n36

Maximus, bishop of Jerusalem, 125

Mecca, 174, 179-181, 182-184, 191, 197, 215, 240, 244, 252, 337, 375-378, 384, 395, 543, 546, 609n6

Medina, 174, 177, 179-181, 197, 238, 337, 376, 395

Melchizedek, 7, 120, 595n42

Menelaus, high priest, 51-52

Merits of Jerusalem, 336-340, 374-375, 607n7

Meshullam of Volerra, Jewish visitor, 408, 473-474

Mesopotamia, 4, 20, 28, 99, 140, 147, 160, 170, 335

Messiah, 34, 94, 106, 192-193, 261, 313, 344, 350, 489-492, 529-530, 605n25, 615n15

methessep, *see* muhtasib

Middoth (Mishna), 80, 84, 122, 196

Midrash Rabbah, 226-227

Millo, 8, 23, 31

minarets, 357, 358, 418-419, 496, 611n33

Mishna, 29, 78, 81, 83, 84, 101-102, 122, 196, 232

Mishneh Torah, 278-279, 605n25

missionaries, 583

Modestus, bishop of Jerusalem, 174, 204

monasteries, *see* convents

Mongols, 380, 466, 474

Monophysitism, 158

Montefiore, Moses, Jewish benefactor, 619n11

Moriah, Mount, 8, 12, 16, 27, 76, 77, 117, 191, 199, 297, 316, 450, 589n23

Morocca, *see* Maghreb; and quarters, Moroccan

Moryson, Henry, a careless pilgrim, 616n35

Mosaic Law, 5, 6, 40-41, 46, 51, 60, 102, 103, 146, 224-225, 377, 475, 530

Moses, 5-6, 11, 17, 19, 29, 103, 168; in Islam, 184, 189

Moses de Leon, Jewish mystic, 615n17

Moses of Basola, Jewish visitor, 483

mosques, 430, 466-468, 567; Afdal, 358, 419; al-Aqsa, 187, 189, 191, 195-196, 201, 202, 213, 215-216, 221, 238, 246, 247, 270, 285-286, 314, 316, 321-324, 336, 337, 345-346, 348-350, 354, 365, 366, 375, 376, 400, 406-408, 412, 413, 417, 459, 462, 479, 494, 496 (without minaret), 497-498, 567, 600n17 (survey), 605n16 (inscription); Buraq, 225, 542; Moroccans, 528, 616 nn. 25 and 26; Solomon, 247, 410, 604n51; Umar, 356-357. *See also* David, Prayer Niche of

Mosul, 334-335, 351

Mount Sion, *see* Sion

Mourners for Sion, for the Sanctuary, 224-225, 227-228

Mu'awiyah, Umayyad caliph, 183-184, 186, 199-201, 208, 375, 377

Mu'azzam Isa, Ayyubid sultan, 359-360, 364, 411, 480, 481

Mu'izz, Fatimid caliph, 225

Mu'tasim, Abbasid caliph, 216

Muhammad Ali, ruler of Egypt, 541, 570-571

Muhammad: Ascension and Night Journey, 182-184, 188, 225, 248, 319, 346, 490, 599n6; on Jerusalem, 174, 336-339, 374-375, 419; Christian view of, 253-254, 354-355, 390, 416, 460, 464, 468-470, 517

muhtasib, Muslim municipal magistrate, 301, 606n9

Mujir al-Din, Muslim historian, 194, 261, 353-354, 359-361, 374, 385-386, 388-390, 391-393, 396-401, 402-405, 413-415, 418-420, 457

mulla, *see* qadi

Muqaddasi, Muslim geographer, 197,

Muqaddasi (*cont.*)
  235-242, 247, 276, 385, 412, 455-
  456
Murad IV, Ottoman sultan, 506, 616n33
Muristan, 129, 221, 275, 299, 325,
  607n32 (excavations)
Muslims: arrival and occupation of Jerusalem, 174-177, 185-191; eastern,
  393, 425, 495, 567-568; Isma'ilis,
  279, 335, 340; reconquest of Jerusalem, 344-348; Shi'ites / Shi'ism, 254,
  272, 279-280, 334-335, 340; Sunni /
  Sunnism, 254, 279-280, 334-336,
  380, 383; on the Temple Mount, 186-
  193, 195-204, 213-214, 316-318,
  320, 348-350, 360, 405-408, 482-
  483, 528-529. *See also* Christians and
  Muslims; Jews and Muslims
Mustafa Lale Pasha, Ottoman official,
  481-483
Mustanjid, Abbasid caliph, 385
Mustansir, Fatimid caliph, 271, 275
Muthir al-Ghiram, 187-190
Muzaffar, Ayyubid sultan, 418

Nabateans, 61, 79, 187
Nablus, 269, 366, 391, 416, 548
Nachmanides, Jewish scholar, 425-426,
  474, 531 (synagogue of), 608n24
Nagid, Jewish official, 223, 486, 492
Napoleon, 542, 582
Nasir Muhammad, Mamluk sultan, 406,
  610n18, 611n30
Nasir-i Khusraw, Muslim traveller, 238,
  241, 244-245, 267-268, 456
Nathan, prophet, 10-11
Nazareth, 92, 96, 132, 138, 243, 295,
  361, 437, 568
Nea, *see* churches, New, of St. Mary
Nebuchadnezzar, king of Babylon, 28-
  31, 115, 178, 319
Nebuzaradan, Babylonian official, 31,
  319
Nehemiah, Jewish official, 36-41, 47-48,
  319, 589n27; Book of, 34
Naro, Roman emperor, 111
Nestorius / Nestorianism, 157-158. *See
  also* Christians, Nestorian
New Testament, 82, 152
Niccolo of Poggibonsi, Christian pilgrim,

391-392, 409-410, 434-435, 440,
  441-442, 453, 517
Nicea, Council of, 131-132, 138, 157
Nicephorus Phocas, Byzantine emperor,
  242
Nicholas IV, pope, 421
Nicodemus, 97, 522
Ninth of Ab, 115-116, 178, 408, 477,
  529, 595n40, 595n44
Nisaburi, Quranic commentator, 181
Nizam al-Mulk, Muslim vizier, 279. *See
  also* law school, Nizamiyya
Nur al-Din, Muslim ruler of Syria, 334-
  336, 340, 349, 607n3

Obadiah of Bertinoro, Jewish visitor,
  401-402, 408-409, 475-476
Obadiah of Bertinoro, disciple of, 392,
  476-477
Octavian, *see* Augustus
odor of sanctity, 613n13
Olives, Mount of, 80, 85, 91, 98, 125,
  137, 140, 144, 150-151, 154, 166,
  169, 171, 195, 206-207, 210-211,
  219-220, 222, 227, 234, 276, 296,
  318, 338, 364, 390, 444, 449, 451,
  455-456, 477, 485, 491, 528, 562,
  603 nn. 31 and 32 (Jewish worship
  on)
Onias, high priest, 48, 50-51
Ophel, 8, 16, 31, 38, 67, 69, 73, 99,
  118, 591n28
Ornan, *see* Araunah
Ottomans, Muslim dynasty, 384, 479,
  481-482, 506, 527, 531, 535, 614n5
  (relative neglect of Jerusalem); Empire,
  510, 535, 537, 557, 565; governance,
  493, 543-547, 549-550

palaces: of David, 145, 587n3; Hasmonean, 59, 73-74, 107, 109, 594n11,
  595n29; of Helena of Adiabene, 118;
  of Herod, 74, 89, 110, 118, 119,
  592n40 (excavations), 593n2, 594n10;
  of Solomon, 15-16; in Latins' eyes,
  285, 314-316, 320-324, 328, 587n12
  (*see also* Mosque of al-Aqsa); of Latin
  kings, 320, 355, 607n32 (excavations);
  Umayyad, 201, 247, 601n28
  (excavations)

Palestine, 6, 20, 28, 45, 126, 131-132, 137, 141, 143, 147, 151, 152, 162, 187, 216, 218, 231, 244, 253, 277, 309-310, 321, 334, 336, 339-340, 370 (British mandate over), 380, 488, 493 (Ottoman finances and officials of), 516, 519, 530, 541, 543 (Pashalik of), 548, 564, 565, 580, 584, 598n33 (Roman provinces of), 603n25, 607n11 (Mujir's definition), 615n17 (kabbala in)

Paltiel, Egyptian rabbi, 224-225

papacy / popes, see Rome, See and Church of

Parthia / Parthians, 63, 66, 591n26

Paschal Chronicle, 129, 596n53

pashaliks, 543, 547

pashas, see governors, Ottoman

Passover, 27, 92-93, 96, 102, 106

patriarch, as metropolitan archbishop, 291

patriarchs of Jerusalem, 255, 264-265, 268, 271-272, 290-293, 304, 318, 320-321, 324-327, 329-330, 493; residence of, 161, 195, 298, 304, 312, 355, 412; Greek Orthodox, 510, 512-513, 569-570, 577. See also Jerusalem, bishops

Paul the Apostle, 1, 100-105, 122, 489, 579, 594n16, 594n21, 595n22

Paul V, pope, 507

Paula, Christian pilgrim, 152, 153

Paulinus of Nola, Christian pilgrim, 153, 168

Pella, 110, 125

Pengar, Roman general, 226

Pentecost, Feast of, 98-99, 150-151. See also Weeks, Feast of

Persia / Persians, 34, 40, 147, 170-174, 220, 272, 276, 315, 417, 480, 484, 510

Pesikta Rabbati, 227, 602n17

Petachia of Ratisbon, Jewish visitor, 329, 607n37

Peter the Apostle, 82-83, 98, 101, 102, 282, 315, 316-317, 489

Peter, bishop of Jerusalem, 162-163

Pharisees, 60-61, 106

Phasael, son of Antipater, 66

Philip the Apostle, 98

Philo, Jewish theologian, 89, 593n4

Piacenza pilgrim, 83, 166-169

pilgrimage, Christian, 132, 151-157, 221, 252-253, 257-258, 294-295, 360-363, 427-439, 442-446, 522, 524, 537, 539, 552-556 (costs), 553 (tatooing), 573, 599n35, 612n7, 612n11 (as incipient tourism)

pilgrimage, Jewish, 92 (Passover), 99 (Weeks), 618n46. See also Jews, immigrants and visitors

pilgrimage, Muslim, 197, 252, 337, 366, 374-378, 493, 497, 543, 546, 600n34, 615n18. See also hajj

Pinnacle of the Temple, 80-81, 106, 143, 154, 155, 595n25

Pisa / Pisans, 307, 605n4, 608n18

Poland, 425, 526, 529, 530, 539

police station and prison, 358, 419, 510, 611n34

polis, 51-52, 59, 590n15

poll-tax, 198, 220, 223, 484, 602n9, 620n15

Pompey, Roman imperator, 61-66, 120, 319, 593n52

Pontius Pilate, Roman prefect, 89-90, 94-95, 97, 133, 138, 145, 501, 593n2, 594n10; house of, see Pretorium

pools, 143, 237; of Amygdalon, 113; of Bethesda / Bethsaida, 82, 143, 154, 390; of the Children of Israel, 237; of Iyad, 237; of Mamila, 171, 420; Patriarch's Baths, 595n37; of the Priests, 328; Probatic / Sheep, 81-82, 143-144, 157, 171, 219, 353, 390, 593n50; of Solomon (at Hebron), 69, 90, 237, 392, 398, 604n34; Struthion, 112

population, 21-22, 37-38, 43, 51, 87, 195-196, 305-306, 372-373, 408, 476, 484, 564-565, 593n58, 604n50, 606n14, 607n34, 614n11

Portugal / Portuguese, 461, 475, 550-551, 557

Poryat, Moses ben Israel, Jewish visitor, 525-527

Potters' Field, see Aceldama

Pretorium, 95, 133, 145, 157, 161, 167-168, 236, 237-238, 261-262, 397,

Pretorium (*cont.*)
485, 502-503, 568, 594 nn. 10 and
11, 621n32
priests, 16, 19, 26-27, 36-41, 50, 78, 85,
194
Procopius, Byzantine historian, 163-166
procurators, *see* governors
proselytes, 99
Psalms, 18, 32
Ptolemies, Hellenistic dynasty, 45-46
Purchas, Samuel, English editor, 512-
513

Qa'im, Abbasid caliph, 318
Qa'it Bay, Mamluk sultan, 369, 404
(fountain), 406, 413, 424-425, 471-
472, 610n20 (survey of fountain),
611n29
qadi, Muslim judge / administrator, 229,
320, 366, 415, 434, 456, 459-462,
469, 493-494, 503, 514, 523, 528-
529, 539, 615n15
Qalawun, Mamluk sultan, 369
Qashashi, Muslim religious writer, 497-
498
qibla, direction of prayer, 18, 189, 245-
246, 248, 322-323, 465, 486; change
in, 179-181, 245-246, 377
Qoja Sinan, Ottoman architect, 482
Quaresmi, Franciscus, Franciscan Guardian, 411, 501-502
quarters, 15-16, 59, 73, 269-272, 304-
305, 392-400, 567-569, 588n14 (royal
quarter), 589n21; Christian, 271, 393,
396, 500, 539, 566, 567, 586; Jewish,
393, 396, 398, 476, 529, 531-533,
552, 564, 566, 567; Muslim, 393,
396, 494, 500, 566
quarters, individual: Alam, 392-393; Armenian, 304, 396, 420-421, 566, 567,
592n40; Banu Harith, 393, 609n11;
Dawiyya, 393; Feather, 393; Ghawanima, 399-404, 405 (minaret); Hitta
Gate, 400, 567; Mishnah, 26, 589n21;
Moroccan, 357-359, 392, 393, 394-
396, 480, 566, 567; Patriarch's, 271-
272, 275-276, 294, 299, 304-305;
People of al-Salt, 393; Sharaf, 392,
397; Sion, 393; Syrian Christian, 303-
304, 396

Quds, al-, 178, 214, 244, 477, 562. *See
also* Holy House
Qumama, al-, Holy Sepulcher called,
188, 195, 258-259, 313, 356, 358,
360, 419, 420, 478, 600n9
Qunsuh al-Ghawri, Mamluk sultan, 471
Quran, 177-178, 228, 313, 318, 331,
349, 375-376, 395, 455, 462, 464,
469, 494, 496, 608n13; Latin translation of, 429, 464
Quran House, 397
Quraysh, dominant clan at Mecca, 183,
184
Qutekin, Fatimid missionary, 259,
605n10

rabbis, 229, 231, 232-233
Rachel, tomb of (near Bethlehem), 167
Ramle, 212-213, 220, 232-233, 243,
259, 269-270, 276-277, 284, 305,
346, 427, 434, 511, 547, 555, 612n6
Rasmi Ozdan, Persian official, 171, 173-
174
Raymond du Puy, founder of Hospital-
lers, 324-325
Rebecca, wife of Isaac, 241, 331
Red Heifer, 85, 603n32
relics and souvenirs, 161, 166-168, 219,
221-222, 260, 314, 428, 446-449,
454, 550-551, 553, 599n43
Revelation, Book of, 123
Richard the Lion-Hearted, king of England, 360-361
Richard, Christian pilgrim, 360-361
Ricoldo of Monte Croce, Christian missionary, 445, 457, 465-466, 477,
613n24
Robert the monk, 281-282
Robert, king of Sicily, 369, 422
Robinson, Edward, American archeologist, 569, 583-586
Robinson's Arch, 80, 83
Rock under the Dome, 86, 187, 195,
196-198, 200, 214, 239, 245, 248-
249, 314, 315, 316-317, 338-339,
349-350, 376-377, 407, 589n23,
593n55, 600n18 (description); 600-
601 nn. 19 and 20, 607 nn. 8 and 9
(traditions)

Roger, Eugene, Franciscan author, 538-539

Romans, 47, 54 (= Kittim), 58-59, 61-67, 126-128, 144, 192, 199 (= Edomites), 291 (= Byzantines)

Romanus III, Byzantine emperor, 255

Rome, 49, 59, 65-67, 88, 99, 105, 111, 152, 195, 491

Rome, See and Church of, 131, 157-158, 292, 307, 325, 327, 365, 369, 421, 427-428, 430, 460, 463-464, 506, 507, 515, 584-585

Rum / Rumis, 190, 193, 291, 339, 353; *see also* Byzantium / Byzantines

Rupert, king of Sicily, 422

Russia / Russians, 294, 303, 537

Sabas, monk, 162-163, 166, 598n32

Sabbatai Sevi, 615n15

Sadducees, 60

Saewulf, Christian pilgrim, 294, 314-315

Safed, 472, 483, 488, 534, 615n17

Sahil, coastal Palestine, 336, 340

Sahirah, plain of, 375, 456-457, 614n8

Sahl ibn Masliah, Karaite author, 231-232

St. James, liturgy of, 170

Saladin, Ayyubid sultan, 298, 336, 340-362, 367, 379-380, 608 nn. 18 and 21, 614n1

Salah al-Din, *see* Saladin

Salem, 7, 152, 595n42

Salih Isma'il, Ayyubid sultan, 369

Salman ben Yeruham, Karaite author, 193-194, 225

Salome Alexandra, Hasmonean queen, 61

Samaria / Samaritans, 36-37, 98, 162-163, 590n17

Samuel, Egyptian rabbi, 225

Sancia, queen of Sicily, 369, 422

Sanderson, John, English visitor, 488-489, 490, 510, 512-515

Sanhedrin, 45-46, 51, 105, 234

Saracens, 162, 175, 177, 209, 218, 220, 221, 275, 284-286, 294, 298, 307, 316, 331, 354-355, 361-362, 373, 387, 401, 409-410, 423, 427-431, 433, 437-438, 441-442, 446, 452, 459-462, 464-468, 478, 481, 613n26 (etymology)

Sarah, wife of Abraham, 5, 167, 230, 331, 587n3

Saul, *see* Paul

schools: Christian, 558-559; Muslim, 357, 388, 411, 412; Nahawiyya, 360, 610n23. *See also* yeshivas

Schwarz, Joseph, Jewish visitor, 540-541

Scopas, Mount, 111

Scopas, general of Ptolemies, 45

Seetzen, Ulrich, German visitor, 544-545, 550-552, 555-556, 559-560, 564-565, 567-572, 578, 581-582

Seleucids, Hellenistic dynasty, 45-59, 62, 89

Seleucus IV, Seleucid king, 48, 590n10

Selim, Ottoman sultan, 479, 481, 528, 543, 614n1

Senate, *see* Sanhedrin

Sennacherib, Assyrian king, 21-25, 595n35

Sergius, apostate monk, 468-469

Sha'ban II, Mamluk sultan, 405

Shafi'ite legal system, 280, 335, 353, 360, 416

Shaphan, Israelite official, 26

Shapira, Moses, 529-530

Shekhinah, the presence of God, 226, 279, 527

Shemoneh Esreh, 121

Shi'ites, *see* Muslims, Shi'ites

Shishak, 120, 595n21

Sibt ibn al-Jawzi, Muslim historian, 367-368

Sicily, 224, 272, 283, 350, 364-365 (Frederich II), 369, 422, 436, 611n36

Sidon, 543

Siloam, 22-23, 68, 69, 119, 145, 154, 157, 161, 167-169, 203, 222, 238, 239-240, 284, 295-296, 358, 374, 399, 485, 595n26. *See also* Church at Siloam

Simon ben Yohai, rabbi, 199, 615n17

Simon of Cyrene, 95, 444

Simon the Zealot, 98

Simon, Hasmonean king, 55, 57-58, 591n22

Simon, high priest, 590n16

Sinai, 5, 11, 19, 122, 168, 224, 252, 339, 435-436

Sion, Mount, 4, 16, 24, 28, 35, 55, 67,

Sion, Mount (*cont*).
73, 83, 93, 121, 125, 126, 145, 150, 152, 153, 154, 157, 161, 172, 203, 204, 210, 219, 278, 284, 296-297, 329-330, 361, 364, 390-391, 393, 421-423, 449, 476, 486, 494, 498-500, 564, 566, 594 nn. 8 and 9, 594n20, 598n30 (excavations), 611n35 (summary)
Sirat, Bridge of, 238
Solomon ben Hayyim, Jewish visitor, 484
Solomon, king of Israel, 13-19, 26, 28, 67, 69, 178, 247-248, 318-319, 485, 486, 490, 588n13, 597n18; ring of, 150; stables of, 143-144, 166, 322, 328, 409, 480; tomb of, 127, 176
Solyma, 120
Song of Songs, Midrash on, 226
Songs of Sion, 18
Sophronius, bishop of Jerusalem, 175, 177, 188-190, 471, 506, 600n10
Sossius, 120
Sozomen, church historian, 137-138, 139-140, 146-147, 153
Spain / Spanish, 210, 272, 283, 289, 308, 363, 381, 395, 463, 472, 475, 486 (Christian reconquest), 550-551, 552, 557-558, 584
stadium, 50
Stephen, first Christian martyr, 100, 155, 161-162, 202, 221, 594n20
Stone of Foundation, 29-30, 196, 200, 408-409, 489, 490, 529n23
stone, pierced, 143-144, 196
Stone of Unction, 508
streets: colonnaded, 130, 170, 399, 400; covered, 299, 303; Greco-Roman, 44, 130, 135, 136, 170, 296, 299, 400, 598n30 (excavations); plan, 44, 59
Street of Cooking Smells, 299, 303, 398, 401-402; David, 69, 73, 130, 298, 302, 396, 397-399, 609n15 (underground passage along), 400, 566; Gate of the Chain, 130, 226, 357, 393, 398 (underground passage at), 400, 412, 595n32; Germans, 302, 308; Greengrocers, 299, 303; Jehoshaphat, 303; Lady Mary, 76, 594 nn. 11 and 12; Lady Tunsuq, 399; Marzuban, 399; Mount Sion, 299; Patriarch's, 298; St.

Stephen's, 303; Sepulcher, 303; Temple, 302; Valley, 130, 393, 399-400, 402. *See also* markets
Sufis, 228, 246, 343, 376, 382, 416-418, 495, 496, 568, 611n30. *See also* Convents, Sufi
Suhrawardi, Muslim mystic, 340-341
Sukkoth, *see* Tabernacles, feast of
Sulayman, Umayyad caliph, 201
Suleiman, Ottoman sultan, 479-480, 482, 498-500, 506, 528, 535-536, 616n27
Sulwan, *see* Siloam
Summus, Byzantine prefect, 162-163
Sunnis, *see* Muslims, Sunni
suqs, 400. *See also* markets
Suriano, Francesco, Franciscan author, 424-425
Symeon, bishop of Jerusalem, 128
synagogues, 99-100 (of Theodotus), 103, 126, 145, 159, 224-225, 260, 276, 419, 440, 474, 475-476, 484-487, 527, 530-533 (construction of), 568, 571, 596n47 (excavation on Mount Sion); at the Western Wall of the Sanctuary, 225, 602n15, 603n31
Syria / Syrians, 28, 55, 62, 64, 77, 88, 111, 117, 126, 140, 148, 176, 182, 184, 187, 197, 200, 211, 224, 235, 242, 258, 269, 275, 277, 283, 334-335, 338-339, 340, 341, 364, 368, 382, 433, 543, 548-549, 553
Syriac, *see* Aramaic

Tabari, Muslim historian, 180, 185
Tabernacles, feast of, 14, 36, 61, 159, 234
Tablets of the Law, 17, 115, 196
Tacitus, Roman historian, 64, 76-77
Talmud, 232
Tamim al-Dari, endowment of, 240, 385-387
Tankiz al-Nasiri, Mamluk governor of Damascus, 402, 610n18. *See also* law school, Tankiziyya
tannery, 303
Tansuq, Lady, Muslim benefactor, 399, 419 (palace of)
Tartars, 409-410, 474. *See also* Mongols
Tashtimur, Mamluk amir, 413
taxes and fees, 47, 220, 222, 234, 252,

259, 255-256, 258, 274-275, 301, 306, 347 (ransom), 363, 421, 432, 434, 437-439, 471, 488, 493, 517, 521, 528, 531-534, 537, 544, 549, 553-555, 564, 590n8, 606n13, 614n3, 620n16

Tefillah, *see* Shemoneh Esreh

Tell el-Amarneh, 6

Temple, 25-27, 33-34, 43-44, 52-54, 56, 63-65, 92, 103-104, 113-119, 123-124, 154, 233-234, 278-279, 314-315, 587n10, 590n16; attempts at rebuilding, 127-128, 146-147, 173, 596n49, 599n47; cornerstone, 143; destruction, 30-31, 116-118, 120, 177-178, 195, 319, 451, 599n1; finances, 20-21, 46-48, 590n8; porticoes, 78, 82-83, 114-115; Portico of Solomon, 82-83, 167, 407, 410; Royal Portico, 78, 80, 84, 450; sanctuary, 85-87, 105

Temple: of Herod, 14, 77-87, 169, 178, 196, 200-201, 238, 527, 528 (Muslim additions to the platform), 587n10, 592n43, 593 nn. 46 and 47; of Solomon, 13-19, 40, 78-79, 167, 178, 190, 191, 196, 221, 227, 315-316, 328, 390, 587n10, 588n11; of Zerubbabel, 14, 35-36, 39-41, 77, 319, 587n10, 589n29

Temple of the Lord, 274, 291, 297, 314-315, 316-319, 390, 409, 450-451, 606n21 (as Christian church)

Temple Mount, 22, 24, 31, 35, 84-85, 102, 126, 143, 147, 155, 159-160, 191, 194-199, 225, 239, 289, 408-409, 455, 485-486, 528-529. *See also* Moriah, Mount

Templum Domini, *see* Temple of the Lord

Templum Solomonis, *see* Palace of Solomon

Tent of the Presence, 11, 16, 29

Tenth Legion, 112, 121

Terebinthus, 141

theater, 71, 592n37

Theoderich, Christian pilgrim, 321-322

Theodosius II, Byzantine emperor, 159, 161

Theodosius, author of guidebook, 154-157

Theophanes, Byzantine chronicler, 190-191

Thietmar, Christian pilgrim, 348, 362-363, 465

Thomas the Apostle, 98

Tiberias, 192, 232, 243, 342-343, 488, 534

Tiberius, Roman emperor, 89

Tiglath-pileser, Assyrian king, 21

Timberlake, Henry, English visitor, 508-509, 510-512, 513

Titus, Roman emperor, 111-121, 194, 226, 319, 595n39

Tobiads, 51

topography, 34, 37-40, 43-44, 59, 67-69, 153, 170, 202-203, 295-303, 518-519, 561-564, 565-566

Torah scrolls, 34, 475, 486, 564

towers, 39; of David, 67, 166, 286, 296-298, 316, 328, 481, 563, 591n29; of Goliath, 480; of Hananel, 38; Herodian, 119-121, 226; of Hippicus, 69-70, 74, 112, 591n29; of the Hundred, 37, 39; of Mariamne, 75; of Phasael, 74, 591n29; of Ovens, 39; of Psephinus, 70; of Tancred, 304, 480; of Pisans, 481, 563

Trikameron, 129

Tripoli, 272, 543

Troyes, Council of, 321

Turkomans, 256, 380, 464

Turks, 250, 256-257, 277, 279-280, 334, 368, 371, 379, 382-383, 387, 411, 505-506, 510-511, 517, 519, 521, 526, 532-533, 538, 544, 547, 555, 581, 582. *See also* Khwarezmians; Mamluks; Ottomans

Twain, Mark, American innocent, 586

Tyropean Valley, 8, 22, 55, 59, 67-69, 73, 83, 238, 399, 599n10, 595n29

ulama, *see* lawyers, Muslim

Umar ibn al-Khattab, second Muslim caliph, 176-177, 185-196, 316, 319, 328, 352, 356, 375, 377, 401, 410, 517

Umari, Muslim historian, 402

Umayyads, Muslim dynasty, 197-201, 202, 213-214, 215

Upper City, 22, 59, 63, 67-69, 73, 75, 80, 83, 108-109, 112, 118, 129-130,

Upper City (*cont.*)
133, 135, 273, 589n21, 595 nn. 29 and 31
Upper Room, *see* Cenacle
Urban II, Pope, 251-252, 281-282, 288
Uriah, 21
Usama ibn Munqidh, Muslim traveller, 310-311, 319, 322-323
Uthman, third Muslim caliph, 240, 377, 385
Uziah, tomb of, 329

vandalism of the Holy Places, 428, 442, 444, 447, 449
Van Geldern, Simon, Jewish immigrant, 533-534
Venice / Venetians, 305, 307, 487, 499-500, 506, 535, 608n18, 612n7
Vespasian, Roman emperor, 110-111, 120, 226, 319
Via Dolorosa, 397. *See also* Way of the Cross
Vienne, Council of, 608n27
viscount of Jerusalem, 301
Volney, Constantin, French visitor, 543-544, 547-550, 552-554, 556, 557-558, 620n18 (his method)

Walid, Umayyad caliph, 198, 201
walls, 30, 37-39, 59, 69-71, 161, 238, 269-271, 303, 350-351, 359-360, 384, 450, 480, 539, 588n18, 589n27, 591n23, 592n33, 605n15, 614n6
waqf, 353, 382-384, 387-388, 493-494, 500, 614n12. *See also* endowments, Muslim
water supply, 7, 8, 22-23, 39 (Water and Fountain Gates), 43-44, 69, 87, 90, 99, 112, 154, 204, 237, 284, 285, 295-296, 527. *See also* aqueducts; cisterns
Way of the Cross, 95, 156, 374, 437, 501-503
Weeks, Feast of, 544
Well of the Spirits, 495
Western Wall, 225-227, 409(?), 491, 527-529, 541-542, 600n11, 602n16, 619n11

William of Tyre, Crusader historian, 217, 253-258, 267-276, 286-288, 291-292, 297, 300, 304-305, 316, 319, 320-321, 324-325, 605n5
Willibald, Christian pilgrim, 205-206, 209-212
Wilson, Charles, British engineer, 618n43
Wilson's Arch, 69, 83-84, 303, 593n52 (excavations), 595n32, 606n10
Wisdom of Solomon, Book of the, 143

Xystus, 59, 69, 73, 109, 118, 119, 595n29

Ya'qubi, Muslim historian, 197
Yabneh, 111, 121, 232
Yahya ibn Sa'id, Christian historian, 260, 269-270
Yazdgard, Persian shah, 231
Yazid, Umayyad caliph, 377
Yehuda al-Harizi, Jewish poet, 363-364, 608n21
Yerushalmi, Moses, Jewish visitor, 528
yeshivas: Babylonian, 224-225, 232-233; Jerusalem, 224-225, 232-234, 276, 487, 605n11 (at Ramle?). *See also* Yabneh
Yohanan ben Zakkai, rabbi, 110-111, 121, 232, 595n34
Yoma (Mishna), 29, 196

Zachariah, prophet, 143-144, 155, 316, 375, 407, 485, 597n12
Zachariah, bishop of Jerusalem, 171, 174
Zahir Baybars, Mamluk sultan, 369
Zahir, Fatimid caliph, 255-256, 269-271, 276-277
Zamakhshari, Quranic commentator, 182
Zamzam well at Mecca, 240, 374
zawiyas, 417, 517-518. *See also* convents, Sufi
Zechariah, prophet, 39-40
Zedekiah, king of Judah, 30, 319
Zengi, Muslim ruler of Syria, 334-335, 340
Zionism, 229, 529-530, 586
Zohar, Book of, 491, 615n17

Library of Congress Cataloging in Publication Data

Peters, F. E. (Francis E.)

Jerusalem : the holy city in the eyes of chroniclers, visitors, pilgrims, and prophets from the days of Abraham to the beginnings of modern times.

Bibliography: p.
Includes index.
1. Jerusalem—History—Sources. I. Title.

DS109.9.P373 1985 956.94′4 85-42699
ISBN 0-691-07300-7